THE INTERSECTIONS COLLECTION
PEARSON CUSTOM SOCIOLOGY

Formerly published as Intersections, Crossroads & Inequalities

EDITORS

KATHLEEN A. TIEMANN
University of North Dakota
Introduction to Sociology, Social Problems & Issues, Inequalities & Diversity

RALPH B. MCNEAL, JR.
University of Connecticut
Introduction to Sociology

BETSY LUCAL
Indiana University South Bend
Inequalities & Diversity

MORTEN G. ENDER
United States Military Academy, West Point
Inequalities & Diversity

COMPILED BY:

Sociology: A Down-to-Earth Approach Core Concepts
James M. Henslin
customized by Mary Strickland

Pearson Learning Solutions

New York   Boston   San Francisco
London   Toronto   Sydney   Tokyo   Singapore   Madrid
Mexico City   Munich   Paris   Cape Town   Hong Kong   Montreal

Senior Vice President, Editorial and Marketing: Patrick F. Boles
Editor: Ana Díaz-Caneja
Development Editor: Abbey Lee Briggs
Operations Manager: Eric M. Kenney
Production Manager: Jennifer Berry
Rights Manager: Jillian Santos
Art Director: Renée Sartell
Cover Designer: Renée Sartell

Cover Art: "Figures," courtesy of Eugenie Lewalski Berg; "Abstract Crowd," courtesy of Diana Ong/Superstock; "R&B Figures," courtesy of Diana Ong/Superstock; "Bramante's Staircase," courtesy of Veer/Photodisc Photography; "Hand Prints," courtesy of Veer/Photodisc Photography; "People Running-Falling," courtesy of Veer/Campbell Laird; "Sunbathers on Beach," courtesy of Veer/Scott Barrow; "Parada Gay, Florianapolis_25 (colorful balloons being set free)," courtesy of Paul Mansfield Photography/Getty Images; "Family Tree, Relatives," courtesy of Kudryashka/iStockphoto.com.

Please visit our website at *www.pearsoncustom.com*.

Attention bookstores: For permission to return any unsold stock, contact us at *pe-uscustomreturns@pearson.com*.

Pearson Learning Solutions, 501 Boylston Street, Suite 900, Boston, MA 02116
A Pearson Education Company
www.pearsoned.com

ISBN 10: 1-256-04444-X
ISBN 13: 978-1-256-04444-4

THE INTERSECTIONS COLLECTION

Dear Student,

On behalf of Pearson Custom Library, thank you for purchasing this book for your sociology course. You might not realize this, but your instructor made a thoughtful decision when building, reviewing, and ultimately adopting this book, choosing to bypass standard—and often more costly—textbooks and using our Pearson Custom Library program to pull together material that is customized to your course syllabus and learning objectives.

This innovative program enables instructors to create what we believe is the best possible instructional material delivered at superior value to you and your classmates.

Your instructor takes your education seriously and so do we, which is why we are interested in your feedback on this custom book. How well did it support you during the semester? Please visit us on **Facebook**, keyword search "Intersections Collection," and click on **Become a Fan** to post a comment on our wall.

Sincerely,

Pearson Custom Library

Contents

1 The Sociological Perspective
James M. Henslin 1

2 Culture
James M. Henslin 37

3 Socialization
James M. Henslin 67

4 Deviance and Social Control
James M. Henslin 101

5 Sex and Gender
James M. Henslin 135

6 Race and Ethnicity
James M. Henslin 173

7 Marriage and Family
James M. Henslin 213

8 Social Stratification
James M. Henslin 251

9 Social Structure and Social Interaction
James M. Henslin 295

10 Societies to Social Networks
James M. Henslin 327

11 How Sociologists Do Research
James M. Henslin 355

Index 379

II

The Sociological Perspective

From Chapter 1 of *Sociology: A Down-to-Earth Approach: Core Concepts*, 4/e. James M. Henslin.

The Sociological Perspective

Bangladesh

Even from the glow of the faded red-and-white exit sign, its faint light barely illuminating the upper bunk, I could see that the sheet was filthy. Resigned to another night of fitful sleep, I reluctantly crawled into bed.

I kept my clothes on.

The next morning, I joined the long line of disheveled men leaning against the chain-link fence. Their faces were as downcast as their clothes were dirty. Not a glimmer of hope among them.

I was determined. "I will experience what they experience," I kept telling myself.

No one spoke as the line slowly inched forward.

When my turn came, I was handed a cup of coffee, a white plastic spoon, and a bowl of semi-liquid that I couldn't identify. It didn't look like any food I had seen before. Nor did it taste like anything I had ever eaten.

My stomach fought the foul taste, every spoonful a battle. But I was determined. "I will experience what they experience," I kept telling myself. My stomach reluctantly gave in and accepted its morning nourishment.

The room was strangely silent. Hundreds of men were eating, each one immersed in his own private hell, his mind awash with disappointment, remorse, bitterness.

As I stared at the Styrofoam cup that held my coffee, grateful for at least this small pleasure, I noticed what looked like teeth marks. I shrugged off the thought, telling myself that my long weeks as a sociological observer of the homeless were finally getting to me. "It must be some sort of crease from handling," I concluded.

I joined the silent ranks of men turning in their bowls and cups. When I saw the man behind the counter swishing out Styrofoam cups in a washtub of murky water, I began to feel sick to my stomach. I knew then that the jagged marks on my cup really had come from another person's mouth.

How much longer did this research have to last? I felt a deep longing to return to my family—to a welcome world of clean sheets, healthy food, and "normal" conversations.

The Sociological Perspective

Why were these men so silent? Why did they receive such despicable treatment? What was I doing in that homeless shelter? After all, I hold a respectable, professional position, and I have a home and family.

Sociology offers a perspective, a view of the world. The *sociological perspective* (or imagination) opens a window onto unfamiliar worlds—and offers a fresh look at familiar ones. In this text, you will find yourself in the midst of Nazis in Germany and warriors in South America, as well as among people who live in a city dump. You will also find yourself looking at your own world in a different light. As you view other worlds—or your own—the sociological perspective enables you to gain a new perception of social life. In fact, this is what many find appealing about sociology.

The sociological perspective has been a motivating force in my own life. Ever since I took my introductory course in sociology, I have been enchanted by the perspective that sociology offers. I have enjoyed both observing other groups and questioning my own assumptions about life. I sincerely hope the same happens to you.

Seeing the Broader Social Context

The **sociological perspective** stresses the social contexts in which people live. It examines how these contexts influence people's lives. At the center of the sociological perspective is the question of how groups influence people, especially how people are influenced by their **society**—a group of people who share a culture and a territory.

To find out why people do what they do, sociologists look at **social location,** the corners in life that people occupy because of where they are located in a society. Sociologists look at how jobs, income, education, gender, age, and race–ethnicity affect people's ideas and behavior. Consider, for example, how being identified with a group called *females* or with a group called *males* when you were growing up has shaped your ideas of who you are. Growing up as a female or a male has influenced not only how you feel about yourself but also your ideas of what you should attain in life and how you relate to others.

Sociologist C. Wright Mills (1959) put it this way: "The sociological imagination [perspective] enables us to grasp the connection between history and biography." By *history,* Mills meant that each society is located in a broad stream of events. This gives each society specific characteristics—such as its ideas about the proper roles of men and women. By *biography,* Mills referred to our experiences, which give us our orientations to life. In short, people don't do what they do because they inherited some internal mechanism, such as instincts. Rather, *external* influences—our experiences—become part of our thinking and motivation. In short, the society in which we grow up, and our particular location in that society, lie at the center of what we do and how we think.

Consider a newborn baby. As you know, if we were to take the baby away from its U.S. parents and place it with the Yanomamö Indians in the jungles of South America,

---

sociological perspective understanding human behavior by placing it within its broader social context

society people who share a culture and a territory

social location the group memberships that people have because of their location in history and society

---

Examining the broad social context in which people live is essential to the *sociological perspective,* for this context shapes our beliefs and attitudes and sets guidelines for what we do. From this photo of a Yanomamö man blowing yokoana, a hallucinogenic powder, up his nose, you can see how distinctive those guidelines are for the Yanomamö Indians who live on the border of Brazil and Venezuela. How has this Yanomamö man been influenced by his group? How have groups influenced *your* views and behavior?

©Victor Englebert/Time Life Pictures/Getty Images

when the child began to speak, his or her words would not be in English. You also know that the child would not think like an American. The child would not grow up wanting credit cards, for example, or a car, a cell phone, and an iPod. He or she would take his or her place in Yanomamö society—perhaps as a food gatherer or a hunter—and would not even know about the world left behind at birth. And, whether male or female, the child would grow up assuming that it is natural to want many children, not debating whether to have one, two, or three children.

If you have been thinking along with me—and I hope you have—you should be thinking about how *your* social groups have shaped *your* ideas and desires. Over and over in this text, you will see that the way you look at the world is the result of your exposure to specific human groups. I think you will enjoy the process of self-discovery that sociology offers.

The Global Context—and the Local

How life has changed! Our predecessors lived on isolated farms and in small towns. They grew their own food and made their own clothing. They bought only sugar, coffee, and a few other items that they couldn't produce. Beyond the borders of their small communities lay a world they perceived only dimly. The labels on our clothing (from Hong Kong to Italy), in contrast, as well as the many other imported products that have become part of our daily lives shout that our world has shrunk into a global village.

Even though we can pick up a telephone or use the Internet to communicate instantly with people anywhere on the planet, we continue to occupy our own little corners of life. Like those of our predecessors, our worlds, too, are marked by differences in family background, religion, gender, race–ethnicity, and social class. In these corners, we continue to learn distinctive ways of viewing the world.

One of the beautiful—and fascinating—aspects of sociology is that it enables us to look at both parts of our current reality: the changes that incorporate us into a global network *and* our unique experiences in our smaller corners of life. This text reflects both of these worlds, each so vital in understanding who we are.

Origins of Sociology

Tradition Versus Science

Just how did sociology begin? In some ways, it is difficult to answer this question. Even ancient peoples tried to figure out social life. They, too, asked questions about why war exists, why some people become more powerful than others, and why some are rich, but others are poor. However, they often based their answers on superstition, myth, or even the position of the stars and did not *test* their assumptions.

Science, in contrast, requires theories that can be tested by research. Measured by this standard, sociology emerged about the middle of the 1800s, when social observers began to use scientific methods to test their ideas.

Sociology was born in social upheaval. The Industrial Revolution had just begun, and masses of people were moving to cities in search of work. This broke their ties to the land—and to a culture that had provided ready answers to the difficult questions of life. The cities greeted them with horrible working conditions: low pay; long hours; and dangerous work. Families lived on the edge of starvation, and children worked alongside the adults. Life no longer looked the same, and tradition, which had provided the answers to social life, no longer could be counted on.

Tradition suffered further blows. With the success of the American and French revolutions, new ideas swept out the old. As the idea that individuals possess inalienable rights caught fire, many traditional Western monarchies gave way to more democratic forms of government. This stimulated even new perspectives.

The French Revolution of 1789 not only overthrew the aristocracy but also upset the entire social order. This extensive change removed the past as a sure guide to the present. The events of this period stimulated Auguste Comte to analyze how societies change. His writings are often taken as the origin of sociology. This painting shows a crowd of women marching to Versailles to capture the royal family.

scientific method the use of objective systematic observations to test theories

positivism the application of the scientific approach to the social world

sociology the scientific study of society and human behavior

class conflict Marx's term for the struggle between capitalists and workers

bourgeoisie Marx's term for capitalists, those who own the means of production

©Roger-Viollet/The Image Works

Auguste Comte (1798–1857), who is credited as the founder of sociology, began to analyze the bases of the social order. Although he stressed that the *scientific method* should be applied to the study of society, he did not apply it himself.

About this time, the **scientific method**—using objective, systematic observations to test theories—was being tried out in chemistry and physics. This opened many secrets that had been concealed in nature. With traditional answers falling, the next step was to apply the scientific method to questions about social life. The result was the birth of sociology.

Auguste Comte and Positivism

Auguste Comte (1798–1857) suggested that we apply the scientific method to the social world, a process known as **positivism.** Reflecting on the upheavals of the French Revolution and on the changes he experienced when he moved to Paris from the small town in which he had grown up, Comte wondered what holds society together. He began to ask what creates social order, instead of anarchy or chaos, and why, once society becomes set on a particular course, what causes it to change.

Comte decided that the scientific method held the key to answering such questions. Just as the scientific method had revealed the law of gravity, so, too, it would uncover the laws that underlie society. Comte called this new science **sociology**—"the study of society" (from the Greek *logos,* "study of," and the Latin *socius,* "companion," or "being with others"). The purpose of this new science, he said, would be not only to discover social principles but also to apply them to social reform. Comte developed a grandiose view: Sociologists would reform the entire society, making it a better place to live.

Comte did not do what we today call research, and his conclusions have been abandoned. Nevertheless, his insistence that we must observe and classify human activities to uncover society's fundamental laws is well taken. Because he developed and coined the term *sociology,* Comte often is credited with being the founder of sociology.

Herbert Spencer and Social Darwinism

Herbert Spencer (1820–1903), who grew up in England, is sometimes called the second founder of sociology. Spencer's views were quite different. He said that sociology should *not* guide social reform. Societies are evolving, going from lower ("barbarian") to higher ("civilized") forms. As generations pass, a society's most capable and intelligent ("the fittest") members survive, while the less capable die out. These fittest members produce a more advanced society—unless misguided do-gooders get in the way and help the less fit (the lower classes) survive.

Spencer called this principle *the survival of the fittest.* Although Spencer coined this phrase, it usually is attributed to his contemporary, Charles Darwin, who proposed that organisms evolve over time as they adapt to their environment. Where Spencer referred to the evolution of societies, Darwin referred to the evolution of organisms. Because Darwin is better known, Spencer's idea is called *social Darwinism.* History is fickle, and if fame had gone the other way, we might be speaking of "biological Spencerism."

Like Comte, Spencer did armchair philosophy instead of conducting scientific studies, and his ideas, too, were discarded.

Karl Marx and Class Conflict

Karl Marx (1818–1883) not only influenced sociology but also left his mark on world history. Marx's influence has been so great that even the *Wall Street Journal,* that staunch advocate of capitalism, has called him one of the three greatest modern thinkers (the other two being Sigmund Freud and Albert Einstein).

Like Comte, Marx thought that people should try to change society. His proposal for change was radical: revolution. This got him thrown out of Germany, and he settled in England. Marx believed that the engine of human history is **class conflict.** Society is made up of two social classes, he said, and they are natural enemies: the **bourgeoisie** (boo-shwa-ZEE) (the *capitalists,* those who own the capital, land, factories, and machines) and the **proletariat** (the exploited workers). Eventually, the workers will unite and break their chains of bondage. The workers' revolution will be bloody, but it will usher in a classless society, one free of exploitation. People will work according to their abilities and receive goods and services according to their needs (Marx and Engels 1848/1967).

Marxism is not the same as communism. Although Marx proposed revolution as the way for workers to gain control of society, he did not develop the political system called *communism.* This is a later application of his ideas. Marx himself was disgusted when he heard debates about his analysis of social life. After listening to some of the positions attributed to him, he shook his head and said, "I am not a Marxist" (Dobriner 1969b:222; Gitlin 1997:89).

Emile Durkheim and Social Integration

The primary professional goal of Emile Durkheim (1858–1917), who grew up in France, was to get sociology recognized as a separate academic discipline (Coser 1977). Until Durkheim's time, sociology was viewed as part of history and economics. Durkheim achieved his goal in 1887 when the University of Bordeaux awarded him the world's first academic appointment in sociology.

Durkheim's second goal was to show how social forces affect people's behavior. To accomplish this, he conducted rigorous research. Comparing the suicide rates of several European countries, Durkheim (1897/1966) found that each country has a different suicide rate—and that these rates remain about the same year after year. He also found that different groups within a country have different suicide rates and that these, too, remain stable from year to year: Males are more likely than females to kill themselves, Protestants more likely than Catholics or Jews, and the unmarried more likely than the married. From these observations, Durkheim concluded that suicide is not what it appears—individuals here and there deciding to take their lives for personal reasons. Instead, *social factors underlie suicide,* which is why a group's rate remains fairly constant year after year.

Durkheim identified **social integration,** the degree to which people are tied to their social groups, as a key social factor in suicide. He concluded that people who have weaker social ties are more likely to commit suicide. This, he said, explains why Protestants, males, and the unmarried have higher suicide rates. This is how it works: Protestantism encourages greater freedom of thought and action; males are more independent than females; and the unmarried lack the ties that come with marriage. In other words, members of these groups have fewer of the social bonds that keep people from committing suicide. In Durkheim's term, they have less social integration.

Despite the many years that have passed since Durkheim did his research, the principle he uncovered still applies: People who are less socially integrated have higher rates of

Herbert Spencer (1820–1903), sometimes called the second founder of sociology, coined the term "survival of the fittest." Spencer thought that helping the poor was wrong, that this merely helped the "less fit" survive.

Karl Marx (1818–1883) believed that the roots of human misery lay in class conflict, the exploitation of workers by those who own the means of production. Social change, in the form of the overthrow of the capitalists by the workers (*proletariat*), was inevitable from Marx's perspective. Although Marx did not consider himself a sociologist, his ideas have influenced many sociologists, particularly conflict theorists.

proletariat Marx's term for the exploited class, the mass of workers who do not own the means of production

social integration the degree to which members of a group or a society feel united by shared values and other social bonds; also known as *social cohesion*

The French sociologist **Emile Durkheim** (1858–1917) contributed many important concepts to sociology. His comparison of the suicide rates of several counties revealed an underlying social factor: People are more likely to commit suicide if their ties to others in their communities are weak. Durkheim's identification of the key role of *social integration* in social life remains central to sociology today.

suicide. Even today, those same groups that Durkheim identified—Protestants, males, and the unmarried—are more likely to kill themselves.

Here is the principle that was central in Durkheim's research: *Human behavior cannot be understood only in terms of the individual; we must always examine the social forces that affect people's lives.* Suicide, for example, appears to be such an intensely individual act that psychologists should study it, not sociologists. As Durkheim stressed, however, if we look at human behavior only in reference to the individual, we miss its *social* basis. To see what Durkheim meant, look at Figure 1, which shows the methods by which African Americans and whites commit suicide. I'm sure you'll be struck by how similar their methods are. It might surprise you that the patterns are so consistent that we can predict, with high accuracy, that 29,000 whites and 2,000 African Americans will commit suicide this year. The patterns are so firm that we can also predict that of the 29,000 whites about 15,500 will use guns to kill themselves, and that of the 2,000 African Americans 60 to 70 will jump to their deaths. Since these patterns recur year after year, they indicate something far beyond individuals. They reflect conditions in society, such as the popularity and accessibility of guns. They also reflect conditions that we don't understand. Perhaps this course in sociology will pique a student's interest enough to investigate these patterns.

Max Weber and the Protestant Ethic

Max Weber (Mahx VAY-ber) (1864–1920), a German sociologist and a contemporary of Durkheim, also became a professor in the new academic discipline of sociology. With Durkheim and Marx, Weber is one of the three most influential of all sociologists, and you will come across his writings and theories. For now, let's consider an issue Weber raised that remains controversial today.

Religion and the Origin of Capitalism. Weber disagreed with Marx's claim that economics is the central force in social change. That role, he said, belongs to religion. Here's how it works. Roman Catholics were taught that because they were church members they were on the road to heaven. This encouraged them to hold on to traditional ways of life. Protestants, in contrast, those of the Calvinist tradition, were told that they wouldn't know if they were saved until Judgment Day. Understandably, this teaching made them a little uncomfortable. Looking for "signs" that they were in God's will, the Calvinists concluded that financial success was a blessing, indicating that God was on their side. This motivated them to bring about this "sign" and receive spiritual comfort. They began to live frugal

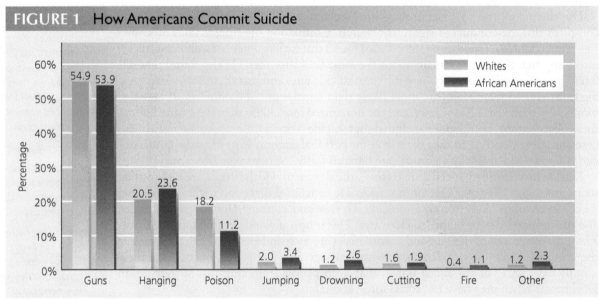

FIGURE 1   How Americans Commit Suicide

Legend: Whites, African Americans

Guns: Whites 54.9, African Americans 53.9
Hanging: Whites 20.5, African Americans 23.6
Poison: Whites 18.2, African Americans 11.2
Jumping: Whites 2.0, African Americans 3.4
Drowning: Whites 1.2, African Americans 2.6
Cutting: Whites 1.6, African Americans 1.9
Fire: Whites 0.4, African Americans 1.1
Other: Whites 1.2, African Americans 2.3

Note: These totals are the mean of years 2001–2005. ("Mean" is explained on page 23.)
Source: By the author. Based on Centers for Disease Control and Prevention 2007c, and earlier years.

lives, saving their money, and investing it in order to make even more. A surprising result of religious teaching, then, was the birth of capitalism, which transformed society.

Weber (1904/1958) called this self-denying approach to life the *Protestant ethic.* He termed the readiness to invest capital in order to make more money the *spirit of capitalism.* To test his theory, Weber compared the extent of capitalism in Roman Catholic and Protestant countries. In line with his theory, he found that capitalism was more likely to flourish in Protestant countries. Weber's conclusion that religion was the key factor in the rise of capitalism was controversial when he made it, and it continues to be debated today (Wade 2007).

Max Weber (1864–1920) was another early sociologist who left a profound impression on sociology. He used crosscultural and historical materials to trace the causes of social change and to determine how social groups affect people's orientations to life.

Sociology in North America

Sexism and Early Female Sociologists

As you may have noticed, all the sociologists we have discussed are men. In the 1800s, sex roles were rigid, with women assigned the roles of wife and mother. In the classic German phrase, women were expected to devote themselves to the four K's: *Kirche, Küchen, Kinder, und Kleider* (the four C's in English: church, cooking, children, and clothes). To try to break out of this mold meant risking severe disapproval.

Few people, male or female, attained any education beyond basic reading and writing and a little math. Higher education, for the rare few who received it, was reserved primarily for men. Of the handful of women who did pursue higher education, some became prominent in early sociology. Marion Talbot, for example, was an associate editor of the *American Journal of Sociology* for thirty years, from its founding in 1895 to 1925. The influence of some early female sociologists went far beyond sociology. Grace Abbott became the first chief of the U.S. government's Children's Bureau, and Frances Perkins was the first woman to hold a cabinet position, serving twelve years as Secretary of Labor under President Franklin Roosevelt. Jane Addams was awarded the Nobel Prize for Peace, the only sociologist to win this acclaimed honor. On the next page are photos of some of these early sociologists.

Many early female sociologists wrote extensively. Their writings—and matching social activism—were directed almost exclusively at social reform, such as ways to improve the working conditions of poorly paid workers, the need to integrate immigrants into society, and promotion of the anti-lynching movement. As sociology developed in North America, a debate arose about the proper purpose of sociology: Should it be social reform or objective analysis? At that time, the debate was won by those who held the university positions. These were men, and it was they who then wrote the history of sociology. Distancing themselves from the social reformers, they ignored the early female sociologists (Lengermann and Niebrugge 2007). Now that women have again become a voice in sociology—and have begun to rewrite its history—early female sociologists are again, as here, being acknowledged.

Harriet Martineau and Research on the United States

A good example is Harriet Martineau (1802–1876), who was born into a wealthy English family. When Martineau first began to analyze social life, she would hide her writing beneath her sewing when visitors arrived, for writing was considered "masculine" and sewing "feminine" (Gilman 1911:88). Martineau persisted in her interests, however, and she eventually studied social life in both Great Britain and the United States. In 1837, two or three decades before Durkheim and Weber were born, Martineau published *Society in America.* In this remarkable book, she analyzed this new nation's customs—family, race, gender, politics, and religion. Despite her insightful analysis of U.S. life, which is still worth reading today, Martineau's research met the same fate as that of other early female sociologists and, until recently, was ignored. Instead, she became known primarily for translating Comte's ideas into English.

Racism at the Time: W. E. B. Du Bois

Not only was sexism assumed to be normal during this early period of sociology, but so was racism, which made life difficult for African American professionals such as

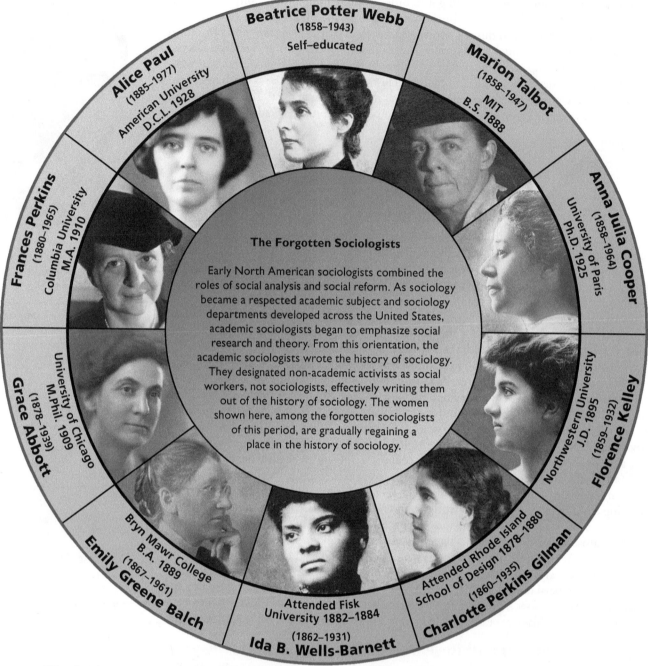

The Forgotten Sociologists

Early North American sociologists combined the roles of social analysis and social reform. As sociology became a respected academic subject and sociology departments developed across the United States, academic sociologists began to emphasize social research and theory. From this orientation, the academic sociologists wrote the history of sociology. They designated non-academic activists as social workers, not sociologists, effectively writing them out of the history of sociology. The women shown here, among the forgotten sociologists of this period, are gradually regaining a place in the history of sociology.

Beatrice Potter Webb
(1858–1943)
Self–educated

Alice Paul
(1885–1977)
American University
D.C.L. 1928

Marion Talbot
(1858–1947)
MIT
B.S. 1888

Frances Perkins
(1880–1965)
Columbia University
M.A. 1910

Anna Julia Cooper
(1858–1964)
University of Paris
Ph.D. 1925

Grace Abbott
(1878–1939)
University of Chicago
M.Phil. 1909

Florence Kelley
(1859–1932)
Northwestern University
J.D. 1895

Emily Greene Balch
(1867–1961)
Bryn Mawr College
B.A. 1889

Ida B. Wells-Barnett
(1862–1931)
Attended Fisk
University 1882–1884

Charlotte Perkins Gilman
(1860–1935)
Attended Rhode Island
School of Design 1878–1880

(Gilman): Hulton Archive/Getty Images; (Cooper): The Granger Collection, New York; (Wells-Barnett): R. Gates/Hulton Archive/Getty Images; (Kelley, Perkins & Paul): Bettmann/Corbis; (Webb): Mary Evans Picture Library/The Image Works; (Balch): Wellesley College Archives; (Abbott & Talbot): The University of Chicago Library Special Collections Research Center

W. E. B. Du Bois (1868–1963). Du Bois, who became the first African American to earn a doctorate at Harvard, also studied at the University of Berlin, where he attended lectures by Max Weber. In 1897, Du Bois went to Atlanta University, where he remained for most of his career. You can get a flavor of this period from the Down-to-Earth Sociology box on the next page.

It is difficult to grasp how racist society was at this time. As Du Bois passed a butcher shop in Georgia one day, he saw the fingers of a lynching victim displayed in the window (Aptheker 1990). When Du Bois went to national meetings of the American Sociological Society, restaurants and hotels would not allow him to eat or room with the white sociologists. How times have changed. Today, sociologists would not only boycott such establishments, but also refuse to hold meetings in that state. At that time, however, racism, like sexism, prevailed throughout society, rendering it mostly invisible to white sociologists.

Down-to-Earth Sociology
W. E. B. Du Bois: The Souls of Black Folk

Du Bois wrote more like an accomplished novelist than a sociologist. The following excerpt is from pages 66–68 of *The Souls of Black Folk* (1903). In this text, Du Bois analyzes changes that occurred in the social and economic conditions of African Americans during the thirty years following the Civil War.

For two summers, while he was a student at Fisk University, Du Bois taught in a segregated school housed in a log hut "way back in the hills" of rural Tennessee. The following excerpts help us understand conditions at that time.

In the 1800s, most people were so poor that they expended their life energies on just getting enough food, fuel, and clothing to survive. The average person died before reaching age 40. Formal education beyond the first several grades was a luxury. This photo depicts the conditions of the people Du Bois worked with.

It was a hot morning late in July when the school opened. I trembled when I heard the patter of little feet down the dusty road, and saw the growing row of dark solemn faces and bright eager eyes facing me. . . . There they sat, nearly thirty of them, on the rough benches, their faces shading from a pale cream to deep brown, the little feet bare and swinging, the eyes full of expectation, with here and there a twinkle of mischief, and the hands grasping Webster's blue-black spelling-book. I loved my school, and the fine faith the children had in the wisdom of their teacher was truly marvelous. We read and spelled together, wrote a little, picked flowers, sang, and listened to stories of the world beyond the hill. . . .

On Friday nights I often went home with some of the children—sometimes to Doc Burke's farm. He was a great, loud, thin Black, ever working, and trying to buy these seventy-five acres of hill and dale where he lived; but people said that he would surely fail and the "white folks would get it all." His wife was a magnificent Amazon, with saffron face and shiny hair, uncorseted and barefooted, and the children were strong and barefooted. They lived in a one-and-a-half-room cabin in the hollow of the farm near the spring. . . .

Often, to keep the peace, I must go where life was less lovely; for instance, 'Tildy's mother was incorrigibly dirty, Reuben's larder was limited seriously, and herds of untamed insects wandered over the Eddingses' beds. Best of all I loved to go to Josie's, and sit on the porch, eating peaches, while the mother bustled and talked: how Josie had bought the sewing-machine; how Josie worked at service in winter, but that four dollars a month was "mighty little" wages; how Josie longed to go away to school, but that it "looked liked" they never could get far

enough ahead to let her; how the crops failed and the well was yet unfinished; and, finally, how mean some of the white folks were.

For two summers I lived in this little world. . . . I have called my tiny community a world, and so its isolation made it; and yet there was among us but a half-awakened common consciousness, sprung from common joy and grief, at burial, birth, or wedding; from common hardship in poverty, poor land, and low wages, and, above all, from the sight of the Veil* that hung between us and Opportunity. All this caused us to think some thoughts together; but these, when ripe for speech, were spoken in various languages. Those whose eyes twenty-five and more years had seen "the glory of the coming of the Lord," saw in every present hindrance or help a dark fatalism bound to bring all things right in His own good time. The mass of those to whom slavery was a dim recollection of childhood found the world a puzzling thing: it asked little of them, and they answered with little, and yet it ridiculed their offering. Such a paradox they could not understand, and therefore sank into listless indifference, or shiftlessness, or reckless bravado.

*"The Veil" is shorthand for the Veil of Race, referring to how race colors all human relations. Du Bois' hope, as he put it, was that "sometime, somewhere, men will judge men by their souls and not by their skins" (p. 261).

W(illiam) **E**(dward) **B**(urghardt) **Du Bois** (1868–1963) spent his lifetime studying relations between African Americans and whites. Like many early North Americans sociologists, Du Bois combined the role of academic sociologist with that of social reformer. He was also the editor of *Crisis*, an influential journal of the time.

applied sociology the use of sociology to solve problems— from the micro level of family relationships to the macro level of global pollution

Du Bois did extensive research, for about twenty or so years publishing a book a year on black–white relations. He was also a social activist. Along with Jane Addams and others from Hull-House, Du Bois founded the National Association for the Advancement of Colored People (NAACP). Continuing to battle racism both as a sociologist and as a journalist, Du Bois eventually embraced revolutionary Marxism. He became such an outspoken critic of racism that for years the U.S. State Department, fearing he would criticize the United States, refused to issue him a passport (Du Bois 1968). At age 93, dismayed that so little improvement had been made in race relations, he moved to Ghana, where he died and is buried (Stark 1989).

Talcott Parsons and C. Wright Mills: Theory Versus Reform

Like Du Bois and Addams, many early North American sociologists worked toward the reform of society, but by the 1940s the emphasis had shifted to social theory. Talcott Parsons (1902–1979), for example, a major sociologist of this period, developed abstract models of society that influenced a generation of sociologists. Deploring Parsons' theoretical abstractions and the general dry analyses of this period, C. Wright Mills (1916–1962) urged sociologists to get back to social reform. He said that sociologists were missing the point, that our freedom was threatened by the coalescing interests of a group he called the *power elite*—the top leaders of business, politics, and the military. Shortly after Mills' death came the turbulent late 1960s and 1970s. This precedent-shaking era sparked interest in social activism, making Mills' ideas popular among a new generation of sociologists.

The Continuing Tension and Applied Sociology

As we have seen, two contradictory aims—analyzing society versus working toward its reform—have run through North American sociology since its founding. This tension is still with us. Some sociologists see their proper role as analyzing some aspect of society and publishing their findings in books and sociology journals. Others argue that sociologists have an obligation to use their expertise to try to help reform society, especially to help bring justice to the poor and oppressed.

As Figure 2 shows, somewhere between these extremes lies **applied sociology,** using sociology to solve problems. Applied sociology is not new, for as we've seen, sociologists founded the NAACP. Although today's applied sociologists lack the early sociologists' broad vision of social reform, their application of sociology is wide-ranging. Some work for business firms to solve problems in the workplace, while others investigate social problems such as pornography, rape, pollution, or the spread of AIDS. A new application of sociology is determining ways to disrupt terrorist groups (Sageman 2008).

Although applied sociology pleases many sociologists, it frustrates both those who want the emphasis to be on social reform and those who want it to be on objective analysis.

FIGURE 2 Comparing Basic and Applied Sociology

BASIC SOCIOLOGY
Audience: Fellow sociologists and anyone interested
Product: Knowledge

APPLIED SOCIOLOGY
Audience: Clients
Product: Change

- Constructing theory and testing hypotheses
- Research on basic social life, on how groups affect people
- The middle ground: criticisms of society and social policy
- Analyzing problems, evaluating programs, and suggesting solutions
- Implementing solutions (clinical sociology)

Source: By the author. Based on DeMartini 1982.

Those who favor social reform point out that the application of sociology in some specific setting is far from an attempt to rebuild society. Those who want sociology's emphasis to be the discovery of objective knowledge say that when sociology is applied, it is no longer sociology. If, for example, sociologists use sociological principles to help teenagers escape from pimps, they say, what makes it sociology?

This contemporary debate on the purpose and use of sociology, with roots that go back a century or more, is likely to continue for another generation. At this point, let's consider how theory fits into sociology.

Theoretical Perspectives in Sociology

Facts never interpret themselves. To make sense out of life, we place our experiences (our "facts") into a framework of more-or-less related ideas. Sociologists do this, too, but they place their observations into a conceptual framework called a theory. A **theory** is a general statement about how some parts of the world fit together and how they work. It is an explanation of how two or more "facts" are related to one another.

Sociologists use three major theories: symbolic interactionism, functional analysis, and conflict theory. Let's look at each theory, first examining its main elements and then applying it to the U.S. divorce rate, to see why it is so high. As we do this, you will see how each theory, or perspective, provides a distinct interpretation of social life.

Symbolic Interactionism

The central idea of **symbolic interactionism** is that *symbols*—things to which we attach meaning—are the key to understanding how we view the world and communicate with one another. This perspective was brought to sociology by Charles Horton Cooley (1864–1929), William I. Thomas (1863–1947), and George Herbert Mead (1863–1931). Let's look at the main elements of this theory.

Symbols in Everyday Life.   Without symbols, our social life would be no more sophisticated than that of animals. For example, without symbols we would have no aunts or uncles, employers or teachers—or even brothers and sisters. I know that this sounds strange, but it is symbols that define our relationships. There would still be reproduction, of course, but no symbols to tell us how we are related to whom. We would not know to whom we owe respect and obligations, or from whom we can expect privileges—the essence of human relationships.

I know it is vague to say that symbols tell you how you are related to others and how you should act toward them, so let's make this less abstract:

> Suppose that you have fallen head over heels in love. After what seems forever, it is the night before your wedding. As you are contemplating tomorrow's bliss, your mother comes to you in tears. Sobbing, she tells you that she had a child before you were born, a child that she gave up for adoption. Breaking down, she says that she has just discovered that the person you are going to marry is this child.

You can see how the symbol will change overnight—and your behavior, too!

The symbols of boyfriend and brother—or girlfriend and sister—are certainly different, and, as you know, each symbol requires rather different behavior. Not only do relationships depend on symbols, but so does society itself. Without symbols, we could not coordinate our actions with those of others. We could not make plans for a future day, time, and place. Unable to specify times, materials, sizes, or goals, we could not build bridges and highways. Without symbols, we would have no movies or musical instruments, no hospitals, no government, no religion. The class you are taking could not exist—nor could this text. On the positive side, there would be no war.

In Sum: Symbolic interactionists analyze how social life depends on the ways we define ourselves and others. They study face-to-face interaction, examining how people make sense out of life, how they determine their relationships.

theory a statement about how some parts of the world fit together and how they work; an explanation of how two or more facts are related to one another

symbolic interactionism a theoretical perspective in which society is viewed as composed of symbols that people use to establish meaning, develop their views of the world, and communicate with one another

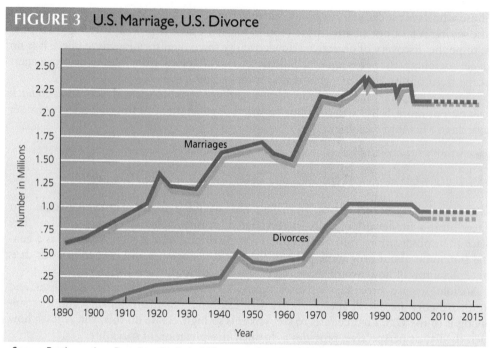

FIGURE 3 U.S. Marriage, U.S. Divorce

Source: By the author. Based on Statistical Abstract of the United States 1998: Table 92 and 2009: Tables 77, 123; earlier editions for earlier years. The broken lines indicate the author's estimates.

Applying Symbolic Interactionism. Look at Figure 3, which shows U.S. marriages and divorces over time. Let's see how symbolic interactionists would use changing symbols to explain this figure. For background, you should understand that marriage used to be a *lifelong commitment.* A hundred years ago (and less) getting divorced was viewed as immoral, a flagrant disregard for public opinion, and the abandonment of adult responsibilities. Let's see what changed.

The meaning of marriage: By the 1930s, young people were coming to view marriage in a different way, a change that was reported by sociologists of the time. In 1933, William Ogburn observed that they were placing more emphasis on the personality of their potential mates. Then in 1945, Ernest Burgess and Harvey Locke noted that couples were expecting more affection, understanding, and compatibility in marriage. In addition, less and less people saw marriage as a lifelong commitment based on duty and obligation. As they began to view marriage as an arrangement based on attraction and feelings of intimacy, it became one that could be broken when feelings changed.

The meaning of divorce: As divorce became more common, its meaning changed. Rather than being a symbol of failure, divorce came to indicate freedom and new beginnings. Removing the stigma from divorce shattered a strong barrier that had prevented husbands and wives from breaking up.

Changed guidelines: Related symbols also changed—and none of these changes strengthened marriage. For example, traditional marriage had firm guidelines, and newlyweds knew what each was supposed to do regarding work, home, and children. In contrast, today's guidelines are vague, and couples must figure out how to divide up responsibilities. This can be a struggle, even a source of conflict, and many flounder. Although couples find it a relief not to have to conform to what they consider to be burdensome notions, those traditional expectations (or symbols) did provide a structure that made marriages last. Changing symbols weakened this structure, making marriage more fragile and divorce more common.

The meaning of parenthood: Parenthood and childhood also used to be quite different. Parents had little responsibility for their children beyond providing food, clothing, shelter, and moral guidance. And they needed to do this for only a short time, because children began to contribute to the support of the family early in life. Among many people, parenthood is still like this. In Colombia, for example, children of the poor often are expected to support themselves by the age of 8 or 10. In industrial societies, however, we assume that children are vulnerable beings who must depend on their parents for financial and emotional support for many years—often until they are well into their 20s. The greater responsibilities that we assign to parenthood place heavy burdens on today's couples and, with them, more strain on marriage.

The meaning of love: And we can't overlook the love symbol. As surprising as it may sound, to have love as the main reason for marriage weakens marriage. In some depth of our being, we expect "true love" to deliver constant emotional highs. This expectation sets people up for crushed hopes, as dissatisfactions in marriage are inevitable. When they come, spouses tend to blame one another for failing to deliver the expected satisfaction.

In Sum: Symbolic interactionists look at how changing ideas (or symbols) of love, marriage, relationships, parenthood, and divorce put pressure on married couples. No single change is *the* cause of our divorce rate, but, taken together, these changes provide a strong push toward divorce.

Functional Analysis

The central idea of **functional analysis** is that society is a whole unit, made up of interrelated parts that work together. Functional analysis (also known as *functionalism* and *structural functionalism*) is rooted in the origins of sociology. Auguste Comte and Herbert Spencer viewed society as a kind of living organism. Just as a person or animal has organs that function together, they wrote, so does society. And like an organism, if society is to function smoothly, its parts must work together in harmony.

Emile Durkheim also viewed society as being composed of many parts, each with its own function. When all the parts of society fulfill their functions, society is in a "normal" state. If they do not fulfill their functions, society is in an "abnormal" or "pathological" state. To understand society, then, functionalists say that we need to look at both *structure* (how the parts of a society fit together to make the whole) and *function* (what each part does, how it contributes to society).

Robert Merton and Functionalism. Robert Merton (1910–2003) dismissed the organic analogy, but he did maintain the essence of functionalism—the image of society as a whole composed of parts that work together. Merton used the term *functions* to refer to the beneficial consequences of people's actions: Functions help keep a group (society, social system) in balance. In contrast, *dysfunctions* are consequences that harm a society: They undermine a system's equilibrium.

Functions can be either manifest or latent. If an action is *intended* to help some part of a system, it is a *manifest function*. For example, suppose that government officials become concerned about our low rate of childbirth. Congress offers a $10,000 bonus for every child born to a married couple. The intention, or manifest function, of the bonus is to increase childbearing within the family unit. Merton pointed out that people's actions can also have *latent functions;* that is, they can have *unintended* consequences that help a system adjust. Let's suppose that the bonus works. As the birth rate jumps, so does the sale of diapers and baby furniture. Because the benefits to these businesses were not the intended consequences, they are latent functions of the bonus.

Of course, human actions can also hurt a system. Because such consequences usually are unintended, Merton called them *latent dysfunctions*. Let's assume that the government has failed to specify a "stopping point" with regard to its bonus system. To collect more bonuses, some people keep on having children. The more children they have, however, the more they need the next bonus to survive. Large families become common, and poverty increases. Welfare is reinstated, taxes jump, and the nation erupts in protest. Because these results were not intended and because they harmed the social system, they would be latent dysfunctions of the bonus program.

functional analysis a theoretical framework in which society is viewed as composed of various parts, each with a function that, when fulfilled, contributes to society's equilibrium; also known as *functionalism* and *structural functionalism*

In Sum: From the perspective of functional analysis, society is a functioning unit, with each part related to the whole. Whenever we examine a smaller part, we need to look for its functions and dysfunctions to see how it is related to the larger unit. This basic approach can be applied to any social group, whether an entire society, a college, or even a group as small as a family.

Applying Functional Analysis.   Now let's apply functional analysis to the U.S. divorce rate. Functionalists stress that industrialization and urbanization undermined the traditional functions of the family. For example, before industrialization, the family formed an economic team. On the farm where most people lived, each family member had jobs or "chores" to do. The wife was in charge not only of household tasks but also of raising small animals, such as chickens. Milking cows, collecting eggs, and churning butter were also her responsibility—as were cooking, baking, canning, sewing, darning, washing, and cleaning. The daughters helped her. The husband was responsible for caring for large animals, such as horses and cattle, for planting and harvesting, and for maintaining buildings and tools. The sons helped him.

This certainly doesn't sound like life today! But what does it have to do with divorce? Simply put, the husband and wife depended on each other for survival—and there weren't many alternatives.

Other functions also bound family members to one another: educating the children, teaching them religion, providing home-based recreation, and caring for the sick and elderly. To further see how sharply family functions have changed, look at this example from the 1800s:

When Phil became sick, Ann, his wife, cooked for him, fed him, changed the bed linens, bathed him, read to him from the Bible, and gave him his medicine. (She did this in addition to doing the housework and taking care of their six children.) Phil was also surrounded by the children, who shouldered some of his chores while he was sick. When Phil died, the male relatives made the casket while Ann, her sisters, and mother washed and dressed the body. Phil was "laid out" in the front parlor (the formal living room), where friends, neighbors, and relatives paid their last respects. From there, friends moved his body to the church for the final message and then to the grave they themselves had dug.

Sociologists who use the *functionalist perspective* stress how industrialization and urbanization undermined the traditional *functions* of the family. Before industrialization, members of the family worked together as an economic unit, as in this painting of Italian farm life by Francesco Bassano (1549–1592). As production moved away from the home, it took with it first the father and, more recently, the mother. One consequence is a major dysfunction, the weakening of family ties.

©Alexander Burkatovski/Corbis

In Sum: When the family loses functions, it becomes more fragile, and an increase in divorce is inevitable. Economic production is an excellent example of how the family has lost functions. No longer is making a living a cooperative, home-based effort, where husband and wife depend on one another for their interlocking contributions to a mutual endeavor. Husbands and wives today earn individual paychecks and increasingly function as separate components in an impersonal, multinational, and even global system. The fewer functions that family members share, the fewer are their "ties that bind"—and these ties are what help husbands and wives get through the problems they inevitably experience.

conflict theory a theoretical framework in which society is viewed as composed of groups that are competing for scarce resources

Conflict Theory

Conflict theory provides a third perspective on social life. Unlike the functionalists, who view society as a harmonious whole, with its parts working together, conflict theorists stress that society is composed of groups that are competing with one another for scarce resources. Although the surface may show alliances or cooperation, scratch that surface and you will find a struggle for power.

Karl Marx and Conflict Theory. Karl Marx, the founder of conflict theory, witnessed the Industrial Revolution that transformed Europe. He saw that peasants who had left the land to seek work in cities had to work for wages that barely provided enough to eat. Things were so bad that the average worker died at age 30, the average wealthy person at age 50 (Edgerton 1992:87). Shocked by this suffering and exploitation, Marx began to analyze society and history. As he did so, he developed **conflict theory.** He concluded that the key to human history is *class conflict.* In each society, some small group controls the means of production and exploits those who are not in control. In industrialized societies, the struggle is between the *bourgeoisie,* the small group of capitalists who own the means to produce wealth, and the *proletariat,* the mass of workers who are exploited by the bourgeoisie. The capitalists also control the legal and political system: If the workers rebel, the capitalists call on the power of the state to subdue them.

When Marx made his observations, capitalism was in its infancy and workers were at the mercy of their employers. Workers had none of what we take for granted today—minimum wages, eight-hour days, coffee breaks, five-day work weeks, paid vacations and holidays, medical benefits, sick leave, unemployment compensation, Social Security, and, for union workers, the right to strike. Marx's analysis reminds us that these benefits came not from generous hearts, but by workers forcing concessions from their employers.

Conflict Theory Today. Many sociologists extend conflict theory beyond the relationship of capitalists and workers. They examine how opposing interests permeate every layer of society—whether that be a small group, an organization, a community, or the entire society. For example, when police, teachers, and parents try to enforce conformity, this creates resentment and resistance. It is the same when a teenager tries to "change the rules" to gain more independence. There is, then, a constant struggle throughout society to determine who has authority or influence and how far that dominance goes (Turner 1978; Leeson 2006; Piven 2008).

Sociologist Lewis Coser (1913–2003) pointed out that conflict is most likely to develop among people who are in close relationships. These people have worked out ways to distribute power and privilege, responsibilities and rewards. Any change in this arrangement can lead to hurt feelings, resentment, and conflict. Even in intimate relationships, then, people are in a constant balancing act, with conflict lying uneasily just beneath the surface.

Feminists and Conflict Theory. Just as Marx examined conflict between capitalists and workers, many feminists analyze conflict between men and women. A primary focus is the historical, contemporary, and global inequalities of men and women—and how the traditional dominance by men can be overcome to bring about equality of the sexes. Feminists are not united by the conflict perspective, however. They tackle a variety of topics and use whatever theory applies.

Applying Conflict Theory. To explain why the U.S. divorce rate is high, conflict theorists focus on how men's and women's relationships have changed. For millennia, men

macro level an examination of large-scale patterns of society

micro level an examination of small-scale patterns of society

social interaction what people do when they are in one another's presence

dominated women. Women had few alternatives other than to accept their exploitation. Then industrialization ushered in a new world, one in which women could meet their basic survival needs outside of marriage. Industrialization also fostered a culture in which females participate in social worlds beyond the home. With this new ability to refuse to bear burdens that earlier generations accepted as inevitable, today's women are likely to dissolve a marriage that becomes intolerable—or even unsatisfactory.

In Sum: The dominance of men over women was once considered natural and right. As women gained education and earnings, however, they first questioned and then rejected this assumption. As wives strove for more power and grew less inclined to put up with relationships that they defined as unfair, the divorce rate increased. From the conflict perspective, then, our high divorce rate does not mean that marriage has weakened, but, rather, that women are making headway in their historical struggle with men.

Putting the Theoretical Perspectives Together

Which of these theoretical perspectives is *the* right one? As you have seen, each produces a contrasting picture of divorce. The pictures that emerge are quite different from the commonsense understanding that two people are simply "incompatible." *Because each theory focuses on different features of social life, each provides a distinctive interpretation. Consequently, we need to use all three theoretical lenses to analyze human behavior. By combining the contributions of each, we gain a more comprehensive picture of social life.*

Levels of Analysis: Macro and Micro

A major difference among these three theoretical perspectives is their level of analysis. Functionalists and conflict theorists focus on the **macro level;** that is, they examine large-scale patterns of society. In contrast, symbolic interactionists usually focus on the **micro level,** on **social interaction**—what people do when they are in one another's presence. These levels are summarized in Table 1.

To make this distinction between micro and macro levels clearer, let's return to the example of the homeless, with which we opened this chapter. To study homeless people, symbolic interactionists would focus on the micro level. They would analyze what homeless people do when they are in shelters and on the streets. They would also analyze their

TABLE 1 Three Theoretical Perspectives in Sociology				
Perspective	Usual Level of Analysis	Focus of Analysis	Key Terms	Applying the Perspective to the U.S. Divorce Rate
Symbolic Interactionism	Microsociological: examines small-scale patterns of social interaction	Face-to-face interaction, how people use symbols to create social life	Symbols Interaction Meanings Definitions	Industrialization and urbanization changed marital roles and led to a redefinition of love, marriage, children, and divorce.
Functional Analysis (also called functionalism and structural functionalism)	Macrosociological: examines large-scale patterns of society	Relationships among the parts of society; how these parts are functional (have beneficial consequences) or dysfunctional (have negative consequences)	Structure Functions (manifest and latent) Dysfunctions Equilibrium	As social change erodes the traditional functions of the family, family ties weaken, and the divorce rate increases.
Conflict Theory	Macrosociological: examines large-scale patterns of society	The struggle for scarce resources by groups in a society; how the elites use their power to control the weaker groups	Inequality Power Conflict Competition Exploitation	When men control economic life, the divorce rate is low because women find few alternatives to a bad marriage. The high divorce rate reflects a shift in the balance of power between men and women.

communications, both their talk and their **nonverbal interaction** (gestures, use of space, and so on). The observations I made at the beginning of this chapter about the silence in the homeless shelter, for example, would be of interest to symbolic interactionists.

This micro level, however, would not interest functionalists and conflict theorists. They would focus instead on the macro level. Functionalists would examine how changes in the parts of society have increased homelessness. They might look at how changes in the family (fewer children, more divorce) and economic conditions (fewer unskilled jobs, loss of jobs to workers overseas) cause homelessness among people who are unable to find jobs and who have no family to fall back on. For their part, conflict theorists would stress the struggle between social classes. They would be interested in how decisions by international elites on global production and trade affect the local job market, and along with it unemployment and homelessness.

How Theory and Research Work Together

Theory cannot stand alone. As sociologist C. Wright Mills (1959) so forcefully argued, if theory isn't connected to research, it will be abstract and empty. It won't represent the way life really is. It is the same for research. Without theory, Mills said, research is also of little value; it is simply a collection of meaningless "facts."

Theory and research, then, go together like a hand and glove. Every theory must be tested, which requires research. And as sociologists do research, they often come up with surprising findings. Those findings must be explained, and for that, we need theory. As sociologists study social life, then, they combine research and theory.

Let's turn now to how sociologists do research.

Doing Sociological Research

Around the globe, people make assumptions about the way the world "is." Common sense, the things that "everyone knows are true," may or may not be true, however. It takes research to find out. Do you want to test your own common sense? Take the little quiz below.

nonverbal interaction
communication without words through gestures, use of space, silence, and so on

Down-to-Earth Sociology
Enjoying a Sociology Quiz—Sociological Findings Versus Common Sense

Some findings of sociology support commonsense understandings of social life, and others contradict them. Can you tell the difference? To enjoy this quiz, complete *all* the questions before turning the page to check your answers.

1. **True/False**   More U.S. students are killed in school shootings now than ten or fifteen years ago.
2. **True/False**   The earnings of U.S. women have just about caught up with those of U.S. men.
3. **True/False**   With life so rushed and more women working for wages, today's parents spend less time with their children than previous generations did.
4. **True/False**   It is more dangerous to walk near topless bars than fast-food restaurants.
5. **True/False**   Most rapists are mentally ill.
6. **True/False**   A large percentage of terrorists are mentally ill.
7. **True/False**   Most people on welfare are lazy and looking for a handout. They could work if they wanted to.
8. **True/False**   Compared with women, men make more eye contact in face-to-face conversations.
9. **True/False**   Couples who lived together before marriage are usually more satisfied with their marriage than couples who did not live together before marriage.
10. **True/False**   Because bicyclists are more likely to wear helmets now than a few years ago, their rate of head injuries has dropped.

Down-to-Earth Sociology
Sociological Findings Versus Common Sense—Answers to the Sociology Quiz

1. **False.** More students were shot to death at U.S. schools in the early 1990s than now (National School Safety Center 2009).
2. **False.** Over the years, the wage gap has narrowed, but only slightly. On average, full-time working women earn less than 70 percent of what full-time working men earn. This low figure is actually an improvement over earlier years.
3. **False.** Today's parents actually spend more time with their children (Bianchi et al. 2006).
4. **False.** The crime rate outside fast-food restaurants is considerably higher. The likely reason for this is that topless bars hire private security and parking lot attendants (Linz et al. 2004).
5. **False.** Sociologists compared the psychological profiles of prisoners convicted of rape and prisoners convicted of other crimes. Their profiles were

similar. Like robbery, rape is a learned behavior (Scully and Marolla 1984/2005).
6. **False.** Extensive testing of Islamic terrorists shows that they actually tend to score more "normal" on psychological tests than most "normal" people. As a group, they are in better mental health than the rest of the population (Sageman 2008b:64).
7. **False.** Most people on welfare are children, elderly, sick, mentally or physically handicapped, or young mothers with few skills. Less than 2 percent fit the stereotype of an able-bodied man.
8. **False.** Women make considerably more eye contact (Henley et al. 1985).
9. **False.** The opposite is true. Among other reasons, couples who cohabit before marriage are usually less committed to one another—and a key to marital success is a strong commitment (Dush et al. 2003; Osborne et al. 2007).
10. **False.** Bicyclists today are more likely to wear helmets, but their rate of head injuries is higher. Apparently, they take more risks because the helmets make them feel safer (Barnes 2001).

FIGURE 4 The Research Model

1. Select a topic.
2. Define the problem.
3. Review the literature.
4. Formulate a hypothesis.
5. Choose a research method.
   - Surveys
   - Participant observation
   - Case studies
   - Secondary analysis
   - Documents
   - Experiments
   - Unobtrusive measures
6. Collect the data.
7. Analyze the results.
8. Share the results.

Generates hypotheses

Stimulates more ideas for research

Source: Modification of Figure 2.2 of Schaeffer 1989.

To understand social life, we need to move beyond "common sense" and learn what is really going on. Let's look at how sociologists do their research.

A Research Model

As shown in Figure 4, scientific research follows eight basic steps. This is an ideal model, however, and in the real world of research some of these steps may run together. Some may even be omitted.

1. *Selecting a topic.* First, what do you want to know more about? Let's choose spouse abuse as our topic.
2. *Defining the problem.* The next step is to narrow the topic. Spouse abuse is too broad; we need to focus on a specific area. For example, you may want to know why men are more likely than women to be the abusers. Or perhaps you want to know what can be done to reduce domestic violence.
3. *Reviewing the literature.* You must review the literature to find out what has been published on the problem. You don't want to waste your time rediscovering what is already known.

4. *Formulating a hypothesis.* The fourth step is to formulate a **hypothesis,** a statement of what you expect to find according to predictions that are based on a theory. A hypothesis predicts a relationship between or among **variables,** factors that vary, or change, from one person or situation to another. For example, the statement "Men who are more socially isolated are more likely to abuse their wives than are men who are more socially integrated" is a hypothesis.

Your hypothesis will need **operational definitions,** that is, precise ways to measure the variables. In this example, you would need operational definitions for three variables: social isolation, social integration, and spouse abuse.

5. *Choosing a research method.* The means by which you collect your data is called a **research method** or *research design.* Sociologists use six basic research methods, which are outlined in the next section. You will want to choose the method that will best answer your particular questions.

6. *Collecting the data.* When you gather your data, you have to take care to assure their **validity;** that is, your operational definitions must measure what they are intended to measure. In this case, you must be certain that you really are measuring social isolation, social integration, and spouse abuse—and not something else. Spouse abuse, for example, seems to be obvious. Yet what some people consider to be abuse is not considered abuse by others. Which will you choose? In other words, your operational definitions must be so precise that no one has any question about what you are measuring.

You must also be sure that your data are reliable. **Reliability** means that if other researchers use your operational definitions, their findings will be consistent with yours. If your operational definitions are sloppy, husbands who have committed the same act of violence might be included in some research but excluded in other studies. You would end up with erratic results. You might show a 5 percent rate of spouse abuse, but another researcher may conclude that it is 30 percent. This would make your research unreliable.

7. *Analyzing the results.* You can choose from a variety of techniques to analyze the data you gather. If a hypothesis has been part of your research, you will test it during this step. (Some research, especially that done by participant observation, has no hypothesis. You may know so little about the setting you are going to research that you cannot even specify the variables in advance.)

8. *Sharing the results.* To wrap up your research, you will write a report to share your findings with the scientific community. You will review how you did your research, including your operational definitions. You will also show how your findings fit in with the published literature and how they support or refute the theories that apply to your topic. As Table 2 on the next page illustrates, sociologists often summarize their findings in tables.

Let's look in greater detail at the fifth step to see what research methods sociologists use.

Research Methods

As we review the seven research methods (or *research designs*) that sociologists use, we will continue our example of spouse abuse. As you will see, the method you choose will depend on the questions you want to answer. So that you can have a yardstick for comparison, you will want to know what "average" is in your study. Table 3 discusses ways to measure average.

Surveys

Let's suppose that you want to know how many wives are abused each year. Some husbands also are abused, of course, but let's assume that you are going to focus on wives.

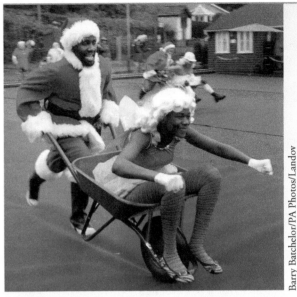

Because sociologists find all human behavior to be valid research topics, their research runs from the unusual to the routines of everyday life. Their studies range from broad scale social change, such as the globalization of capitalism, to smaller scale social interaction, such as people having fun.

Barry Batchelor/PA Photos/Landov

hypothesis a statement of how variables are expected to be related to one another, often according to predictions from a theory

variables a factor thought to be significant for human behavior, which can vary (or change) from one case to another

operational definitions the way in which a researcher measures a variable

research method one of seven procedures that sociologists use to collect data: surveys, participant observation, case studies, secondary analysis, documents, experiments, and unobtrusive measures

validity the extent to which an operational definition measures what it is intended to measure

reliability the extent to which research produces consistent or dependable results

TABLE 2 How to Read a Table

Tables summarize information. Because sociological findings are often presented in tables, it is important to understand how to read them. Tables contain six elements: title, headnote, headings, columns, rows, and source. When you understand how these elements fit together, you know how to read a table.

1 The **title** states the topic. It is located at the top of the table. What is the title of this table? Please determine your answer before looking at the correct answer at the bottom of this page.

2 The **headnote** is not always included in a table. When it is, it is located just below the title. Its purpose is to give more detailed information about how the data were collected or how data are presented in the table. What are the first eight words of the headnote of this table?

3 The **headings** tell what kind of information is contained in the table. There are three headings in this table. What are they? In the second heading, what does n = 25 mean?

Comparing Violent and Nonviolent Husbands

Based on interviews with 150 husbands and wives in a Midwestern city who were getting a divorce.

Husband's Achievement and Job Satisfaction	Violent Husbands n = 25	Nonviolent Husbands n = 125
He started but failed to complete high school or college.	44%	27%
He is very dissatisfied with his job.	44%	18%
His income is a source of constant conflict.	84%	24%
He has less education than his wife.	56%	14%
His job has less prestige than his father-in-law's.	37%	28%

Source: Modification of Table 1 in O'Brien 1975.

4 The **columns** present information arranged vertically. What is the fourth number in the second column and the second number in the third column?

5 The **rows** present information arranged horizontally. In the fourth row, which husbands are more likely to have less education than their wives?

6 The **source** of a table, usually listed at the bottom, provides information on where the data in the table originated. Often, as in this instance, the information is specific enough for you to consult the original source. What is the source for this table?

Some tables are much more complicated than this one, but all follow the same basic pattern.

ANSWERS

1. Comparing Violent and Nonviolent Husbands
2. Based on interviews with 150 husbands and wives
3. Husband's Achievement and Job Satisfaction, Violent Husbands, Nonviolent Husbands. The *n* is an abbreviation for number, and *n* = 25 means that 25 violent husbands were in the sample.
4. 56%, 18%
5. Violent Husbands
6. A 1975 article by O'Brien (listed in the References section of this text).

---

survey the collection of data by having people answer a series of questions

population a target group to be studied

An appropriate method for this purpose would be the **survey,** in which you would ask individuals a series of questions. Before you begin your research, however, you must deal with practical matters that face all researchers. Let's look at these issues.

Selecting a Sample.   Ideally, you might want to learn about all wives in the world. Obviously, your resources will not permit such research, and you will have to narrow your **population,** the target group that you are going to study.

TABLE 3 Three Ways to Measure "Average"

The Mean	The Median	The Mode
The term *average* seems clear enough. As you learned in grade school, to find the average you add a group of numbers and then divide the total by the number of cases that you added. Assume that the following numbers represent men convicted of battering their wives:	To compute the second average, the *median*, first arrange the cases in order—either from the highest to the lowest or the lowest to the highest. That arrangement will produce the following distribution.	The third measure of average, the *mode*, is simply the cases that occur the most often. In this instance the mode is 57, which is way off the mark.

The Mean	The Median		The Mode	
EXAMPLE	**EXAMPLE**		**EXAMPLE**	
321	57	1,795	57	
229	57	321	57	
57	136	289	136	
289	229 or 229		229	
136	289	136	289	
57	321	57	321	
1,795	1,795	57	1,795	

The Mean	The Median	The Mode
The total is 2,884. Divided by 7 (the number of cases), the average is 412. Sociologists call this form of average the *mean*.

The mean can be deceptive because it is strongly influenced by extreme scores, either low or high. Note that six of the seven cases are less than the mean.

Two other ways to compute averages are the median and the mode. | Then look for the middle case, the one that falls halfway between the top and the bottom. That number is 229, for three numbers are lower and three numbers are higher. When there is an even number of cases, the median is the halfway mark between the two middle cases. | Because the mode is often deceptive, and only by chance comes close to either of the other two averages, sociologists seldom use it. In addition, not every distribution of cases has a mode. And if two or more numbers appear with the same frequency, you can have more than one mode. |

Let's assume that your resources (money, assistants, time) allow you to investigate spouse abuse only on your campus. Let's also assume that your college enrollment is large, so you won't be able to survey all the married women who are enrolled. Now you must select a **sample**, individuals from among your target population. How you choose a sample is crucial, for your choice will affect the results of your research. For example, married women enrolled in introductory sociology and engineering courses might have quite different experiences. If so, surveying just one or the other would produce skewed results.

Because you want to generalize your findings to your entire campus, you need a sample that accurately represents the campus. How can you get a representative sample?

The best way is to use a **random sample.** This does *not* mean that you would stand on some campus corner and ask questions of any woman who happens to walk by. *In a random sample, everyone in your population (the target group) has the same chance of being included in the study.* In this case, because your population is every married woman enrolled in your college, all married women—whether first-year or graduate students, full- or part-time—must have the same chance of being included in your sample.

How can you get a random sample? First, you need a list of all the married women enrolled in your college. Then you assign a number to each name on the list. Using a table of random numbers, you then determine which of these women will become part of your sample. (Tables of random numbers are available in statistics books and online, or they can be generated by a computer.)

A random sample will represent your study's population fairly—in this case, married women enrolled at your college. This means that you can generalize your findings to *all* the married women students on your campus, even if they were not included in your sample.

sample the individuals intended to represent the population to be studied

random sample a sample in which everyone in the target population has the same chance of being included in the study

stratified random sample a sample from selected sub-groups of the target population in which everyone in those sub-groups has an equal chance of being included in the research

respondents people who respond to a survey, either in interviews or by self-administered questionnaires

Sociologists usually cannot interview or observe every member of a group or participant in an event that they want to study. As explained in the text, to be able to generalize their findings, they select samples. Sociologists would have several ways to study this protest in San Francisco against U.S. foreign policy.

closed-ended questions
questions that are followed by a list of possible answers to be selected by the respondent

open-ended questions
questions that respondents answer in their own words

rapport (ruh-POUR) a feeling of trust between researchers and the people they are studying

What if you want to know only about certain subgroups, such as freshmen and seniors? You could use a **stratified random sample.** You would need a list of the freshmen and senior married women. Then, using random numbers, you would select a sample from each group. This would allow you to generalize to all the freshmen and senior married women at your college, but you would not be able to draw any conclusions about the sophomores or juniors.

Asking Neutral Questions. After you have decided on your population and sample, your next task is to make certain that your questions are neutral. Your questions must allow **respondents,** the people who answer your questions, to express their own opinions. Otherwise, you will end up with biased answers—which are worthless. For example, if you were to ask, "Don't you think that men who beat their wives should go to prison?" you would be tilting the answer toward agreement with a prison sentence. The *Doonesbury* cartoon below illustrates a blatant example of biased questions. For examples of flawed research, see the Down-to-Earth Sociology box on the next page.

Types of Questions. You must also decide whether to use closed- or open-ended questions. **Closed-ended questions** are followed by a list of possible answers. This format would work for questions about someone's age (possible ages would be listed), but not for many other items. For example, how could you list all the opinions that people hold about what should be done to spouse abusers? The answers provided for closed-ended questions can miss the respondent's opinions.

As Table 4 illustrates, the alternative is **open-ended questions,** which allow people to answer in their own words. Although open-ended questions allow you to tap the full range of people's opinions, they make it difficult to compare answers. For example, how would you compare these answers to the question "Why do you think men abuse their wives?"

"They're sick."

"I think they must have had problems with their mother."

"We ought to string them up!"

Establishing Rapport. Will women who have been abused really give honest answers to strangers? If you were to walk up to women on the street and ask if their husbands have ever beaten them, there would be little reason to take your findings seriously. If, however, researchers establish **rapport** ("ruh-POUR"), a feeling of trust, with their respondents, victims will talk about sensitive matters. A good example is rape. Each year, researchers interview a random sample of 100,000 Americans. They ask them whether they have been victims of burglary, robbery, and other crimes. After establishing rapport, the researchers ask about rape. They find that rape victims will talk about their experiences. The national crime victimization survey shows that the actual incidence of rape is about 40 percent higher than the number reported to the police—and that attempted rapes are *nine* times higher than the official statistics (*Statistical Abstract* 2009:Tables 303, 304).

A new technique to gather data on sensitive areas, Computer-Assisted Self-Interviewing, overcomes lingering problems of distrust. In this technique, the interviewer gives a

Improperly worded questions can steer respondents toward answers that are not their own, which produces invalid results.

Down-to-Earth Sociology
Loading the Dice: How *Not* to Do Research

The methods of science lend themselves to distortion, misrepresentation, and downright fraud. Consider these findings from surveys:

> Americans overwhelmingly prefer Toyotas to Chryslers. Americans overwhelmingly prefer Chryslers to Toyotas.

Obviously, these opposite conclusions cannot both be true. In fact, both sets of findings are misrepresentations, even though the responses came from surveys conducted by so-called independent researchers. These researchers, however, are biased, not independent and objective.

It turns out that some consumer researchers load the dice. Hired by firms that have a vested interest in the outcome of the research, they deliver the results their clients are looking for (Armstrong 2007). Here are six ways to load the dice.

1. **Choose a biased sample.** If you want to "prove" that Americans prefer Chryslers over Toyotas, interview unemployed union workers who trace their job loss to Japanese imports. You'll get what you're looking for.

2. **Ask biased questions.** Even if you choose an unbiased sample, you can phrase questions in such a way that you direct people to the answer you're looking for. Suppose that you ask this question:

> We are losing millions of jobs to workers overseas who work for just a few dollars a day. After losing their jobs, some Americans are even homeless and hungry. Do you prefer a car that gives jobs to Americans, or one that forces our workers to lose their homes?

This question is obviously designed to channel people's thinking toward a predetermined answer—quite contrary to the standards of scientific research. Look again at the Doonesbury cartoon on the previous page.

3. **List biased choices.** Another way to load the dice is to use closed-ended questions that push people into the answers you want. Consider this finding:

> *U.S. college students overwhelmingly prefer Levis 501 to the jeans of any competitor.*

fotoshoot/Alamy Royalty Free

Sound good? Before you rush out to buy Levis, note what these researchers did: In asking students which jeans would be the most popular in the coming year, their list of choices included no other jeans but Levis 501!

4. **Discard undesirable results.** Researchers can keep silent about results they find embarrassing, or they can continue to survey samples until they find one that matches what they are looking for. As has been stressed in this chapter, research must be objective if it is to be scientific. Obviously, none of the preceding results qualifies. The underlying problem with the research cited here—and with so many surveys bandied about in the media as fact—is that survey research has become big business. Simply put, the money offered by corporations has corrupted some researchers.

The beginning of the corruption is subtle. Paul Light, dean at the University of Minnesota, put it this way: "A funder will never come to an academic and say, 'I want you to produce finding X, and here's a million dollars to do it.' Rather, the subtext is that if the researchers produce the right finding, more work—and funding—will come their way."

The first four sources of bias are inexcusable, intentional fraud. The next two sources of bias reflect sloppiness, which is also inexcusable in science.

5. **Misunderstand the subjects' world.** This route can lead to errors every bit as great as those just cited. Even researchers who use an adequate sample and word their questions properly can end up with skewed results. They may, for example, fail to anticipate that people may be embarrassed to express an opinion that isn't "politically correct." For example, surveys show that 80 percent of Americans are environmentalists. Most Americans, however, are probably embarrassed to tell a stranger otherwise. Today, that would be like going against the flag, motherhood, and apple pie.

6. **Analyze the data incorrectly.** Even when researchers strive for objectivity, the sample is good, the wording is neutral, and the respondents answer the questions honestly, the results can still be skewed. The researchers may make a mistake in their calculations, such as entering incorrect data into computers. This, too, of course, is inexcusable in science.

Sources: Based on Crossen 1991; Goleman 1993; Barnes 1995; Resnik 2000; Hotz 2007.

TABLE 4	Closed- and Open-Ended Questions
A. Closed-Ended Question	**B. Open-Ended Question**
Which of the following best fits your idea of what should be done to someone who has been convicted of spouse abuse? 1. probation 2. jail time 3. community service 4. counseling 5. divorce 6. nothing—it's a family matter	What do you think should be done to someone who has been convicted of spouse abuse?

participant observation research in which the researcher participates in a research setting while observing what is happening in that setting

case study an analysis of a single event, situation, or individual

secondary analysis the analysis of data that have been collected by other researchers

laptop computer to the respondent, then moves aside, while the individual enters his or her own answers into the computer. In some versions of this method, the respondent listens to the questions on a headphone and answers them on the computer screen. When the respondent clicks the "Submit" button, the interviewer has no idea how the respondent answered any question (Mosher et al. 2005).

Participant Observation (Fieldwork)

In **participant observation,** or **fieldwork,** the researcher *participates* in a research setting while *observing* what is happening in that setting. Obviously, this method does not mean that you would sit around and watch someone being abused. But if you wanted to learn how abuse has affected the victims' hopes and goals, their dating patterns, or their marriages, you could use participant observation.

For example, if your campus has a crisis intervention center, you might be able to observe victims of spouse abuse from the time they report the attack through their participation in counseling. With good rapport, you might even be able to spend time with them at their home or with friends. What they say and how they interact with others might help you to understand how the abuse has affected them. This, in turn, could give you insight into how to improve college counseling services.

If you were doing participant observation, you would face this dilemma: How involved should you get in the lives of the people you are observing? Consider this as you read the Down-to-Earth Sociology box on the next page.

©Dinodia/The Image Works

Case Studies

To do a **case study,** the researcher focuses on a single event, situation, or even individual. The purpose is to understand the dynamics of relationships, power, or even the thought processes that motivate people. Sociologist Ken Levi (2009), for example, wanted to study hit men. He would love to have had a large number of hit men to interview, but he had access to only one. He interviewed this man over and over, giving us an understanding of how someone can kill others for money. A case study of spouse abuse would focus on a single wife and husband, exploring the couple's history and relationship.

As you can see, case studies reveal a lot of detail about some particular situation, but the question always remains: How much of this detail applies to other situations? This problem of *generalizability,* which plagues case studies, is the primary reason that few sociologists use this method.

Secondary Analysis

If you were to analyze data that someone else has already collected, you would be doing **secondary analysis.** For example, if you were to examine the original data from a study of women who had been abused by their husbands, you would be doing secondary analysis.

Documents

Documents, or written sources, include books, newspapers, bank records, immigration records, and so on. To study spouse abuse, you might examine police reports to find out how many men in your community have been arrested for abuse. You might also use court records to find out what proportion of those men were charged, convicted, or put on probation. If you wanted to learn about the social and emotional adjustment of the

Participant observation, participating and observing in a research setting, is usually supplemented by interviewing, asking questions to better understand why people do what they do. In this instance, the sociologist would want to know what this hair removal ceremony in Gujarat, India, means to the child's family and to the community.

Down-to-Earth Sociology
Gang Leader for a Day: Adventures of a Rogue Sociologist

Next to the University of Chicago is an area of poverty so dangerous that the professors warn students to avoid it. One of the graduate students in sociology, Sudhir Venkatesh, the son of immigrants from India, who was working on a research project with William Julius Wilson, decided to ignore the warning.

With clipboard in hand, Sudhir entered "the projects." Ignoring the glares of the young men standing around, he went into the lobby of a high-rise. Seeing a gaping hole where the elevator was supposed to be, he decided to climb the stairs, where he was almost overpowered by the smell of urine. After climbing five flights, Sudhir came upon some young men shooting craps in a dark hallway. One of them jumped up, grabbed Sudhir's clipboard, and demanded to know what he was doing there.

Sudhir blurted, "I'm a student at the university, doing a survey, and I'm looking for some families to interview."

One man took out a knife and began to twirl it. Another pulled out a gun, pointed it at Sudhir's head, and said, "I'll take him."

Then came a series of rapid-fire questions that Sudhir couldn't answer. He had no idea what they meant: "You flip right or left? Five or six? You run with the Kings, right?"

Grabbing Sudhir's bag, two of the men searched it. They could find only questionnaires, pen and paper, and a few sociology books. The man with the gun then told Sudhir to go ahead and ask him a question.

Sweating despite the cold, Sudhir read the first question on his survey, "How does it feel to be black and poor?" Then he read the multiple-choice answers: "Very bad, somewhat bad, neither bad nor good, somewhat good, very good."

As you might surmise, the man's answer was too obscenity laden to be printed here.

As the men deliberated Sudhir's fate ("If he's here and he don't get back, you know they're going to come looking for him"), a powerfully built man with a few glittery gold teeth and a sizable diamond earring appeared. The man, known as J.T., who, it turned out, directed the drug trade in the building, asked what was going on. When the younger men mentioned the questionnaire, J.T. said to ask *him* a question.

Amidst an eerie silence, Sudhir asked, "How does it feel to be black and poor?"

"I'm not black," came the reply.

"Well, then, how does it feel to be African American and poor?"

"I'm not African American either. I'm a nigger."

Sudhir was left speechless. Despite his naïveté, he knew better than to ask, "How does it feel to be a nigger and poor?"

As Sudhir stood with his mouth agape, J.T. added, "Niggers are the ones who live in this building. African Americans live in the suburbs. African Americans wear ties to work. Niggers can't find no work."

Not exactly the best start to a research project.

But this weird and frightening beginning turned into several years of fascinating research. Over time, J.T. guided Sudhir into a world that few outsiders ever see. Not only did Sudhir get to know drug dealers, crackheads, squatters, prostitutes, and pimps, but he also was present at beatings by drug crews, drive-by shootings done by rival gangs, and armed robberies by the police.

How Sudhir got out of his predicament in the stairwell, his immersion into a threatening underworld—the daily life for many people in "the projects"—and his moral dilemma at witnessing so many crimes are part of his fascinating experience in doing participant observation of the Black Kings.

Sudhir, who was reared in a middle-class suburb in California, even took over this Chicago gang for a day. This is one reason that he calls himself a rogue sociologist—the decisions he made that day were serious violations of law, felonies that could bring years in prison. There are other reasons, too: During the research, he kicked a man in the stomach, and he was present as the gang planned drive-by shootings.

Sudhir eventually completed his Ph.D., and he now teaches at Columbia University.

Based on Venkatesh 2008.

Professor Sudhir Venkatesh, who now teaches at Columbia University, New York.

Paresh Gandhi Courtesy of Sudhir Venkatesh, Columbia University

---

victims, however, these documents would tell you nothing. Other documents, though, might provide those answers. For example, a crisis intervention center might have records that contain key information—but gaining access to them is almost impossible. Perhaps an unusually cooperative center might ask victims to keep diaries that you can study later.

Documents in its narrow sense, written sources that provide data; in its extended sense, archival material of any sort, including photographs, movies, CDs, DVDs, and so on

FIGURE 5 The Experiment

Source: By the author.

Experiments

A lot of people say that abusers need therapy. Yet no one knows whether therapy really works. **Experiments** are useful for determining cause and effect, whose basic requirements are outlined on Table 5 on the next page. Let's suppose that you propose an experiment to a judge and she gives you access to men who have been arrested for spouse abuse. As in Figure 5 above, you would divide the men randomly into two groups. This helps to ensure that their individual characteristics (attitudes, number of arrests, severity of crimes, education, race-ethnicity, age, and so on) are distributed between the groups. You then would arrange for the men in the **experimental group** to receive some form of therapy. The men in the **control group** would not get therapy.

Your **independent variable,** something that causes a change in another variable, would be therapy. Your **dependent variable,** the variable that might change, would be the men's behavior: whether they abuse women after they get out of jail. Unfortunately, your operational definition of the men's behavior will be sloppy: either reports from the wives or records indicating which men were rearrested for abuse. This is sloppy because some of the women will not report the abuse, and some of the men who abuse their wives will not be arrested. Yet it might be the best you can do.

Let's assume that you choose rearrest as your operational definition. If you find that the men who received therapy are *less* likely to be rearrested for abuse, you can attribute the difference to the therapy. If you find *no difference* in rearrest rates, you can conclude that the therapy was ineffective. If you find that the men who received the therapy have a *higher* rearrest rate, you can conclude that the therapy backfired.

Unobtrusive Measures

Researchers sometimes use **unobtrusive measures,** observing the behavior of people who are not aware that they are being studied. For example, social researchers studied the level of whiskey consumption in a town that was legally "dry" by counting empty bottles in trashcans. (Lee 2000). Casino operators use chips that transmit radio frequencies, allowing them to track how much their high rollers are betting at every hand of poker or blackjack (Sanders 2005; Grossman 2007). Billboards read information embedded on a chip in your car key. As you drive by, the billboard displays *your* name with a personal message (Feder 2007). The same device can *collect* information as you drive by.

It would be considered unethical to use most unobtrusive measures to research spouse abuse. You could, however, analyze 911 calls. Also, if there were a public forum held by abused or abusing spouses on the Internet, you could record and analyze the online conversations. Ethics in unobtrusive research are still a matter of dispute: To secretly record the behavior of people in public settings, such as a crowd, is generally considered acceptable, but to do so in private settings is not.

experiments the use of *control* and *experimental groups* and *dependent* and *independent variables* to test causation

experimental group the subjects in an experiment who are exposed to the independent variable

control group the subjects in an experiment who are not exposed to the independent variable

independent variable a factor that causes a change in another variable, called the dependent variable

dependent variable a factor in an experiment that is changed by an independent variable

unobtrusive measures ways of observing people so they do not know they are being studied

TABLE 5 Cause, Effect, and Spurious Correlations

Causation means that a change in one variable is caused by another variable. Three conditions are necessary for causation: correlation, temporal priority, and no spurious correlation. Let's apply each of these conditions to spouse abuse and alcohol abuse.

 The first necessary condition is *correlation*.

If two variables exist together, they are said to be correlated. If batterers get drunk, battering and alcohol abuse are correlated.

Spouse Abuse + Alcohol Abuse

People sometimes assume that correlation is causation. In this instance, they conclude that alcohol abuse causes spouse abuse.

Alcohol Abuse ⟶ Spouse Abuse

But *correlation never proves causation. Either* variable could be the cause of the other. Perhaps battering upsets men and they then get drunk.

Spouse Abuse ⟶ Alcohol Abuse

(2) The second necessary condition is *temporal priority*.

Temporal priority means that one thing happens before something else does. For a variable to be a cause (*the independent variable*), it must *precede* that which is changed (*the dependent variable*).

Alcohol Abuse — precedes ⟶ **Spouse Abuse**

If the men had not drunk alcohol until after they beat their wives, obviously alcohol abuse could not be the cause of the spouse abuse. Although the necessity of temporal priority is obvious, in many studies this is not easy to determine.

(3) The third necessary condition is *no spurious correlation*.

This is the necessary condition that really makes things difficult. Even if we identify the correlation of getting drunk and spouse abuse and can determine temporal priority, we still don't know that alcohol abuse is the cause. We could have a *spurious correlation;* that is, the cause may be some underlying third variable. These are usually not easy to identify. Some sociologists think that male culture is that underlying third variable.

Male Culture ⟶ Spouse Abuse

Socialized into dominance, some men learn to view women as objects on which to take out their frustration. In fact, this underlying third variable could be a cause of both spouse abuse and alcohol abuse.

Male Culture ⟶ **Spouse Abuse** / **Alcohol Abuse**

But since only some men beat their wives, while all males are exposed to male culture, other variables must also be involved. Perhaps specific subcultures that promote violence and denigrate women lead to both spouse abuse and alcohol abuse.

Male Subculture ⟶ **Spouse Abuse** / **Alcohol Abuse**

If so, this does *not* mean that it is the only causal variable, for spouse abuse probably has many causes. Unlike the movement of amoebas or the action of heat on some object, human behavior is infinitely complicated. Especially important are people's *definitions of the situation*, including their views of right and wrong. To explain spouse abuse, then, we need to add such variables as the ways that men view violence and their ideas about the relative rights of women and men. It is precisely to help unravel such complicating factors in human behavior that we need the experimental method.

MORE ON CORRELATIONS

Correlation simply means that two or more variables are present together. The more often that these variables are found together, the stronger their relationship. To indicate their strength, sociologists use a number called a *correlation coefficient*. If two variables are always related, that is, they are always present together, they have what is called a *perfect positive correlation*. The number 1.0 represents this correlation coefficient. Nature has some 1.0's, such as the lack of water and the death of trees. 1.0's also apply to the human physical state, such as the absence of nutrients and the absence of life. But social life is much more complicated than physical conditions, and there are no 1.0's in human behavior.

Two variables can also have a *perfect negative correlation*. This means that when one variable is present, the other is always absent. The number –1.0 represents this correlation coefficient.

Positive correlations of 0.1, 0.2, and 0.3 mean that one variable is associated with another only 1 time out of 10, 2 times out of 10, and 3 times out of 10. In other words, in most instances the first variable is *not* associated with the second, indicating a weak relationship. A strong relationship may indicate causation, but not necessarily. Testing the relationship between variables is the goal of some sociological research.

29

Gender in Sociological Research

You know how significant gender is in your own life, how it affects your orientations and your attitudes. You also may be aware that gender opens and closes doors to you. Because gender is also a factor in social research, researchers must take steps to prevent it from biasing their findings. For example, sociologists Diana Scully and Joseph Marolla (1984, 2007) interviewed convicted rapists in prison. They were concerned that their gender might lead to *interviewer bias*—that the prisoners might shift their answers, sharing certain experiences or opinions with Marolla, but saying something else to Scully. To prevent gender bias, each researcher interviewed half the sample.

Gender certainly can be an impediment in research. In our imagined research on spouse abuse, for example, could a man even do participant observation of women who have been beaten by their husbands? Technically, the answer is yes. But because the women have been victimized by men, they might be less likely to share their experiences and feelings with men. If so, women would be better suited to conduct this research, more likely to achieve valid results. The supposition that these victims will be more open with women than with men, however, is just that—a supposition. Research alone will verify or refute this assumption.

Gender issues can pop up in unexpected ways in sociological research. I vividly recall an incident in San Francisco.

The streets were getting dark, and I was still looking for homeless people. When I saw someone lying down, curled up in a doorway, I approached the individual. As I got close, I began my opening research line, "Hi, I'm Dr. Henslin from. . . . ?" The individual began to scream and started to thrash wildly. Startled by this sudden, high-pitched scream and by the rapid movements, I quickly backed away. When I later analyzed what had happened, I concluded that I had intruded into a woman's bedroom.

This incident also holds another lesson. Researchers do their best, but they make mistakes. Sometimes these mistakes are minor, and even humorous. The woman sleeping in the doorway wasn't frightened. It was only just getting dark, and there were many people on the street. She was just assertively marking her territory and letting me know in no uncertain terms that I was an intruder. If we make a mistake in research, we pick up and go on. As we do so, we take ethical considerations into account, which is the topic of our next section.

Ethics and Values in Sociological Research

In addition to choosing an appropriate research method, we must also follow the ethics of sociology (American Sociological Association 1999). Research ethics require honesty, truth, and openness (sharing findings with the scientific community). Ethics clearly forbid the falsification of results. They also condemn plagiarism—that is, stealing someone else's work. Another ethical guideline states that research subjects should generally be informed that they are being studied and never be harmed by the research. Sometimes people reveal things that are intimate, potentially embarrassing, or otherwise harmful to themselves—and their anonymity must be protected. Finally, although not all sociologists agree, it generally is considered unethical for researchers to misrepresent themselves. Sociologists take their ethical standards seriously. To illustrate the extent to which they will go to protect their respondents, consider the research conducted by Mario Brajuha.

Protecting the Subjects: The Brajuha Research

Mario Brajuha, a graduate student at the State University of New York at Stony Brook, was doing participant observation of restaurant workers. He lost his job as a waiter when the restaurant where he was working burned down—a fire of "suspicious origin," as the police said. When detectives learned that Brajuha had taken field notes (Brajuha and Hallowell 1986), they asked to see them. Because he had promised to keep the information confidential, Brajuha refused to hand them over. When the district attorney subpoenaed the notes, Brajuha still refused. The district attorney then threatened to put Brajuha in jail. By this time, Brajuha's notes had become rather famous, and unsavory characters—perhaps those who had set the fire—also wanted to know what was in them. They, too, demanded to see them, accompanying their demands with threats of a different nature. Brajuha found himself between a rock and a hard place.

For two years, Brajuha refused to hand over his notes, even though he grew anxious and had to appear at several court hearings. Finally, the district attorney dropped the subpoena. When the two men under investigation for setting the fire died, the threats to Brajuha, his wife, and their children ended.

Ethics in social research are of vital concern to sociologists. As discussed in the text, sociologists may disagree on some of the issue's finer points, but none would approve of slipping LSD to unsuspecting subjects like these Marine recruits in basic training at Parris Island, South Carolina. Researchers did this to U.S. soldiers in the 1960s just "to see what would happen."

Misleading the Subjects: The Humphreys Research

Sociologists agree on the necessity to protect respondents, and they applaud the professional manner in which Brajuha handled himself. Although it is considered acceptable for sociologists to do covert participant observation (studying some situation without announcing that they are doing research), to deliberately misrepresent oneself is considered unethical. Let's look at the case of Laud Humphreys, whose research forced sociologists to rethink and refine their ethical stance.

Laud Humphreys, a classmate of mine at Washington University in St. Louis, was an Episcopal priest who decided to become a sociologist. For his Ph.D. dissertation, Humphreys (1970, 1971, 1975) studied social interaction in "tearooms," public restrooms where some men go for quick, anonymous oral sex with other men.

Humphreys found that some restrooms in Forest Park, just across from our campus, were tearooms. He began a participant observation study by hanging around these restrooms. He found that in addition to the two men having sex, a third man—called a "watch queen"—served as a lookout for police and other unwelcome strangers. Humphreys took on the role of watch queen, not only watching for strangers but also observing what the men did. He wrote field notes after the encounters.

Humphreys decided that he wanted to learn about the regular lives of these men. For example, what about the wedding rings that many of the men wore? He came up with an ingenious technique: Many of the men parked their cars near the tearooms, and Humphreys recorded their license plate numbers. A friend in the St. Louis police department gave Humphreys each man's address. About a year later, Humphreys arranged for these men to be included in a medical survey conducted by some of the sociologists on our faculty.

Disguising himself with a different hairstyle and clothing, Humphreys visited the men's homes. As he interviewed the men, supposedly for the medical study, he found that they led conventional lives. They voted, mowed their lawns, and took their kids to Little League games. Many reported that their wives were not aroused sexually or were afraid of getting pregnant because their religion did not allow them to use birth control. Humphreys concluded that many heterosexual men were using the tearooms for a form of quick sex.

value free the view that a sociologist's personal values or biases should not influence social research

values the standards by which people define what is desirable or undesirable, good or bad, beautiful or ugly

objectivity value neutrality in research

replication the repetition of a study in order to test its findings

This study stirred controversy among sociologists and nonsociologists alike. Many sociologists criticized Humphreys, and a national columnist wrote a scathing denunciation of "sociological snoopers" (Von Hoffman 1970). One of our professors even tried to get Humphreys' Ph.D. revoked. As the controversy heated up and a court case loomed, Humphreys feared that his list of respondents might be subpoenaed. He gave me the list to take from Missouri to Illinois, where I had begun teaching. When he called and asked me to destroy it, I burned the list in my backyard.

Was this research ethical? This question is not decided easily. Although many sociologists sided with Humphreys—and his book reporting the research won a highly acclaimed award—the criticisms continued. At first, Humphreys defended his position vigorously, but five years later, in a second edition of his book (1975), he stated that he should have identified himself as a researcher.

Values in Research

Max Weber said that sociology should be **value free.** By this, he meant that a sociologist's **values**—beliefs about what is good or desirable in life and the way the world ought to be—should not affect social research. Weber wanted **objectivity,** value neutrality, to be the hallmark of social research. If values influence research, he said, sociological findings will be biased.

That bias has no place in research is not a matter of debate. All sociologists agree that no one should distort data to make them fit their values. It is equally clear that sociologists are infused with arbitrary values of all sorts, for like everyone else we are members of a particular society at a given point in history. Because values can lead to unintended distortions in how we interpret our research, sociologists stress the need of **replication,** repeating a study in order to compare the new results with the original findings. If an individual's values have distorted the research, replication by others should uncover the bias and correct it.

Despite this consensus, however, values remain a hotly debated topic in sociology (Buroway 2007; Piven 2007). As summarized in Figure 6, the disagreement centers on the proper purposes and uses of sociology. Some sociologists take the position that their goal should be to advance the understanding of social life—to gather data on any topic that interests them and to use the most appropriate theory to interpret their findings. Others are convinced that this is not enough. Sociologists, they say, should research the social arrangements that harm people—poverty, crime, racism, war, and other forms of human exploitation—with the goal of improving social life.

In the midst of this controversy, sociologists do their research: From racism and sexism to the globalization of capitalism on the macro level to the micro level of face-to-face interaction—talking, touching, and gestures. These are all topics that sociologists study and that we will explore in this text. This beautiful variety in sociology—and the contrast of going from the larger picture to the smaller picture and back again—is part of the reason that sociology holds such fascination for me. I hope that you also find this variety appealing as you read the rest of this text.

Before we close this chapter, though, I would like you to consider two trends that are shaping sociology.

FIGURE 6   The Debate over Values in Sociological Research

The Purposes of Social Research

To understand human behavior *versus* To investigate harmful social arrangements

The Uses of Social Research

Can be used by anyone for any purpose *versus* Should be used to reform society

Source: By the author.

Trends Shaping the Future of Sociology

Two major trends indicate changing directions in sociology. Let's look again at the relationship of sociology to social reform and then at globalization.

Sociology's Tension: Research Versus Reform

Public Sociology.   As we have discussed, a tension between social research and social reform runs through the history of sociology. Today, the American Sociological Association (ASA)

is promoting **public sociology,** a middle ground between research and reform. By this term, the ASA refers to the public becoming more aware of the sociological perspective, especially to politicians and policy makers using sociological data and applying the sociological understanding of how society works as they develop social policy (American Sociological Association 2004).

Public sociology is a safe way to make strides toward social reform. Few people get upset if sociologists publicize the sociological perspective by giving testimonies at hearings, serving on government committees, and submitting papers to policy makers. If those in power find the sociologists' recommendations to their liking, they can adopt them. If they don't, they can disregard them and go on their merry way. This is certainly safer than working directly with oppressed people to demand social change. The risk of government agents using what they learn from the sociological perspective to strengthen the elites in their positions of privilege, however, seems to have gone unnoticed. This is not to say that this middle ground does not hold the potential for social reform, for it does. As you can see from the Cultural Diversity box below, data from basic sociological research can become a stimulus for social policy.

With the backing of the ASA, then, the pendulum is swinging toward applying sociological knowledge. At the same time, another trend is also beginning to have a profound effect on sociology. Let's look at the implications of globalization for the future of sociology.

public sociology sociology being used for the public good; especially the sociological perspective (of how things are related to one another) guiding politicians and policy makers

Cultural Diversity in the United States

Unanticipated Public Sociology: Studying Job Discrimination

Basic sociology—research aimed at learning more about some behavior—can turn into public sociology. Here is what happened to Devah Pager, a graduate student at the University of Wisconsin in Madison, who was doing volunteer work in a homeless shelter. Some of the men told her how hard it was to find work if they had had been in prison. Were the men exaggerating she wondered? To find out what difference a prison record makes in getting a job, she sent pairs of college men to apply for 350 entry-level jobs in Milwaukee. One team was African American, and one was white. Pager prepared identical résumés for the teams, but with one difference: On each team, one of the men said he had served 18 months in prison for possession of cocaine.

Figure 7 shows the difference that the prison record made. Men without a prison record were two or three times as likely to be called back.

But Pager came up with another significant finding. Look at the difference that race–ethnicity made. White men with a prison record were more likely to be offered a job than African American men who had a clean record!

Sociological research often remains in obscure journals, read by only a few specialists. But Pager's findings got around, turning into public sociology. Someone told President George W. Bush about the research, and he announced in his State of the Union speech that he

FIGURE 7 Call-Back Rates by Race–Ethnicity and Criminal Record

Source: Courtesy of Devah Pager.

wanted Congress to fund a $300 million program to provide mentoring and other support to help former prisoners get jobs (Kroeger 2004).

As you can see, sometimes only a thin line separates basic and public sociology.

For Your Consideration

What findings would you expect if women had been included in this study?

Globalization

globalization the extensive interconnections among nations due to the expansion of capitalism

Globalization is the breaking down of national borders because of advances in communications, trade, and travel, and a resulting dispersal of products and ideas around the world. Because the United States dominates sociology and we U.S. sociologists tend to concentrate on events and relationships that occur in our own country, most of our findings are based on U.S. samples. Globalization is destined to broaden our horizons, directing us to a greater consideration of global issues. This, in turn, is likely to motivate us to try more vigorously to identify universal principles.

Application of Globalization to This Text. With each passing year, the world grows smaller as we become more connected to the global village. Increasingly, our welfare is tied to that of people in other nations. To help broaden your horizons, in this text we will visit many cultures around the world, examining what life is like for the people who live in those cultures. Seeing how *their* society affects their behavior and orientations to life helps us to understand how *our* society influences what we do and how we feel about life.

You and I are living at a great historical moment, personally experiencing one of the most significant events in all of world history. Throughout this text, I will stress the impact of globalization on your life, especially how it is likely to shape your future. From time to time, you will also confront the developing new world order, which, if it can shave off its rough edges, appears destined to play a significant role in your future.

SUMMARY *and* REVIEW

The Sociological Perspective

What is the sociological perspective?

The **sociological perspective** stresses that people's social experiences—the groups to which they belong and their experiences within these groups—underlie their behavior. C. Wright Mills referred to this as the intersection of biography (the individual) and history (social factors that influence the individual).

Origins of Sociology

When did sociology first appear as a separate discipline?

Sociology emerged in the mid-1800s in western Europe, during the onset of the Industrial Revolution. Industrialization affected all aspects of human existence—where people lived, the nature of their work, their relationships, and how they viewed life. Early sociologists who focused on these social changes include Auguste Comte, Herbert Spencer, Karl Marx, Emile Durkheim, Max Weber, Harriet Martineau, and W. E. B. Du Bois.

Sociology in North America

What was the position of women and minorities in early sociology?

The few women who received the education required to become sociologists tended to focus on social reform. The debate between social reform and social analysis was won by male university professors who ignored the contributions of the women. W. E. B. Du Bois faced deep racism in his sociological career.

Why are the positions of Parsons and Mills important?

C. Wright Mills took the position that sociology like Talcott Parsons' dispassionate analysis of the components of society does nothing for social reform, which should be the goal of sociologists. The significance of this position is that the debate about the purpose and use of sociology continues today.

Theoretical Perspectives in Sociology

What is a theory?

A **theory** is a statement about how facts are related to one another. A theory provides a conceptual framework for interpreting facts.

What are sociology's major theoretical perspectives?

Sociologists use three primary theoretical frameworks to interpret social life. **Symbolic interactionists** examine how people use symbols (meanings) to develop and share their views of the world. Symbolic interactionists usually focus on the **micro level**—on small-scale, face-to-face interaction. **Functional analysts,** in contrast, focus on the **macro level**—on large-scale patterns of society. Functional theorists stress that a social system is made up of interrelated parts. When working properly, each part contributes to the stability of the whole, fulfilling a function that contributes to the system's equilibrium. **Conflict theorists** also focus on large-scale patterns of society. They stress that society is composed of competing groups that struggle for scarce resources.

With each perspective focusing on select features of social life, and each providing a unique interpretation, no single perspective is adequate. The combined insights of all three yield a more comprehensive picture of social life.

What is the relationship between theory and research?

Theory and research depend on one another. Sociologists use theory to interpret the data they gather. Theory also generates questions that need to be answered by research, while research, in turn, helps to generate theory. Theory without research is not likely to represent real life, while research without theory is merely a collection of empty.

Doing Sociological Research

Why do we need sociological research when we have common sense?

Common sense is unreliable. Research often shows that commonsense ideas are limited or false.

What are the eight basic steps in sociological research?

1. Selecting a topic 2. Defining the problem 3. Reviewing the literature 4. Formulating a **hypothesis** 5. Choosing a **research method** 6. Collecting the data 7. Analyzing the results 8. Sharing the results

Research Methods

How do sociologists gather data?

To gather data, sociologists use seven **research methods** (or **research designs**): **surveys, participant observation,** **case studies, secondary analysis, documents, experiments,** and **unobtrusive measures.**

Ethics and Values in Sociological Research

How important are ethics in sociological research?

Ethics are of fundamental concern to sociologists, who are committed to openness, honesty, truth, and protecting their subjects from harm. The Brajuha research on restaurant workers and the Humphreys research on "tearooms" illustrate ethical issues of concern to sociologists.

What value dilemmas do sociologists face?

The first dilemma is how to make certain that research is objective, not unintentionally distorted by the researchers' values. To overcome this possible source of bias, sociologists stress **replication.** The second dilemma is whether to do research solely to analyze human behavior or with the goal of reforming harmful social arrangements.

Trends Shaping the Future of Sociology

What trends are likely to have an impact on sociology?

The first is **public sociology,** an attempt to apply sociology by publicizing sociological data and the sociological perspective. This renewed emphasis on applying sociology could take sociology closer to its roots. The second is **globalization,** which is likely to broaden sociological horizons, refocusing research and theory away from its concentration on U.S. society.

THINKING CRITICALLY

1. Do you think that sociologists should try to reform society or study it dispassionately?
2. Of the three theoretical perspectives, which one would you prefer to use if you were a sociologist? Why?
3. Considering the macro- and micro-level approaches in sociology, which one do you think better explains social life? Why?

4. In your opinion, is it right (or ethical) for sociologists to not identity themselves when they do research? To misrepresent themselves? What if identifying themselves as researchers will destroy their access to a research setting or to informants?

ADDITIONAL RESOURCES

What can you find in MySocLab? mysoclab www.mysoclab.com

- Complete Ebook
- Practice Tests and Video and Audio activities
- Mapping and Data Analysis exercises

- Sociology in the News
- Classic Readings in Sociology
- Research and Writing advice

SUGGESTED READINGS

Allan, Kenneth D. *Explorations in Classical Sociological Theory: Seeing the Social World.* Thousand Oaks, Calif.: Pine Forge Press, 2006. The author's emphasis is that sociological theory can be a guide for selecting research projects and for interpreting the results.

Berger, Peter L. *Invitation to Sociology: A Humanistic Perspective.* New York: Doubleday, 1972. This analysis of how sociology applies to everyday life has become a classic in the field.

Brooks, Arthur C. *Gross National Happiness: Why Happiness Matters for America and How We Can Get More of It.* New York: Basic Books, 2008. To see how happiness, ordinarily considered to be an intensely personal matter, can be explained by the sociological perspective, read this text.

Charon, Joel M. *Symbolic Interactionism: An Introduction, an Interpretation, an Integration,* 9th ed. Upper Saddle River, N.J.: Prentice Hall, 2008. The author lays out the main points of symbolic interactionism, providing an understanding of why this perspective is important in sociology.

Henslin, James M., ed. *Down to Earth Sociology: Introductory Readings,* 15th ed. New York: Free Press, 2010. This collection of readings about everyday life and social structure is designed to broaden the reader's understanding of society, and of the individual's place within it.

Jeffries, Vincent, ed. *Handbook of Public Sociology.* Lanham, MD: Rowman & Littlefield, 2009. The authors examine how sociology can be taken out of its academic isolation to engage wider audiences. Somewhat advanced reading.

Lengermann, Patricia Madoo, and Gillian Niebrugge. *The Women Founders: Sociology and Social Theory, 1830–1930.* Long Grove, Ill.: Waveland Press, 1998. Through their analyses and the writings they reprint, the authors/editors illuminate the struggles of female sociologists during the early period of sociology.

Mills, C. Wright. *The Sociological Imagination.* New York: Oxford University Press, 2000. First published in 1960, this classic analysis provides an overview of sociology from the framework of the conflict perspective.

Ritzer, George. *Classic Sociological Theory,* 5th ed. New York: McGraw-Hill, 2008. To help understand the personal and historical context of how theory develops, the author includes biographical sketches of the theorists.

How Sociologists Do Research
Bryman, Alan. *Social Research Methods,* 3rd ed. Oxford: Oxford University Press, 2008. An overview of the research methods used by sociologists, with an emphasis on the logic that underlies these methods.

Creswell, John W. *Research Design: Qualitative, Quantitative, and Mixed Methods Approaches,* 3rd ed. Beverly Hills, Calif.: Sage, 2008. This introduction to research methods walks you through the research experience and helps you to understand when to use a particular method.

Drew, Paul, Geoffrey Raymond, and Darin Weinberg. *Talk and Interaction in Social Research Methods.* Thousand Oaks, Calif.: Sage Publications, 2006. The authors stress the importance of talk in a variety of social research methods.

Lee, Raymond M. *Unobtrusive Methods in Social Research.* Philadelphia: Open University Press, 2000. This overview of unobtrusive ways of doing social research summarizes many interesting studies.

Neuman, W. Lawrence. *Social Research Methods: Qualitative and Quantitative Approaches,* 6th ed. Boston: Allyn and Bacon, 2006. This "how-to" book of sociological research describes how sociologists gather data and the logic that underlies each method.

Schuman, Howard. *Method and Meaning in Polls and Surveys.* Cambridge, Mass.: Harvard University Press, 2008. Examines how the wording of questions can change findings and how to understand the results of surveys.

Whyte, William Foote. *Creative Problem Solving in the Field: Reflections on a Career.* Lanham, Md.: AltaMira Press, 1997. Focusing on his extensive field experiences, the author provides insight into the researcher's role in participant observation.

Wysocki, Diane Kholos, ed. *Readings in Social Research Methods,* 3rd ed. Belmont, Calif.: Wadsworth, 2008. The authors of these articles provide an overview of research methods.

Journals
Applied Behavioral Science Review, Clinical Sociology Review, International Clinical Sociology, Journal of Applied Sociology, The Practicing Sociologist, Sociological Practice: A Journal of Clinical and Applied Sociology, and *Sociological Practice Review* report the experiences of sociologists who work in applied settings, from peer group counseling and suicide prevention to recommending changes to school boards.

Contexts: Understanding People in Their Social Worlds, published by the American Sociological Association, uses a magazine format to present sociological research in a down-to-earth fashion.

Humanity & Society, the official journal of the Association for Humanist Sociology, publishes articles intended "to advance the quality of life of the world's people."

Journal of Contemporary Ethnography, Qualitative Sociology, and *Symbolic Interaction* feature articles on symbolic interactionism and analyses of everyday life.

Electronic Journals
Electronic Journal of Sociology (http://www.sociology.org) and *Sociological Research Online* (http://www.socresonline.org.uk) publish articles on various sociological topics. Access is free.

Writing Papers for Sociology
Booth, Wayne C., Gregory G. Colomb, and Joseph M. Williams. *The Craft of Research,* 3rd ed. Chicago: University of Chicago, 2008. How to plan a paper, build an argument, anticipate and respond to the reservations of readers, and create introductions and conclusions that answer the demanding question, "So what?"

Richlin-Klonsky, Judith, William G. Roy, Ellen Strenski, and Roseann Giarusso, eds. *The Sociology Writing Group. A Guide to Writing Sociology Papers,* 6th ed. New York: Worth Publishers, 2007. The guide walks students through the steps in writing a sociology paper, from choosing the initial assignment to doing the research and turning in a finished paper. Also explains how to manage time and correctly cite sources.

About Majoring in Sociology
You like sociology and perhaps are thinking about majoring in it, but what can you do with a sociology major? Be sure to check the epilogue of this text. Also check out the resources that are available from the American Sociological Association. Go to www.asanet.org. This will bring you to the ASA's home page. Here, you can click around and get familiar with what this professional association offers students.

On the menu at the top of ASA's home page, click Students. This will bring you to a page that has links to resources for students. You may be interested in The Student Sociologist, a newsletter for students. The link, Careers, will take you to several free online publications, including those that feature information on careers in both basic and applied sociology. You will also see such links as the student forum, student involvement, and funding.

If you want to contact the ASA by snail mail or by telephone or fax, here is that information: American Sociological Association, 1430 K Street NW, Suite 600, Washington, D.C. 20005. Tel. (202) 383-9005. Fax (202) 638-0882. E-mail: Executive.Office@asanet.org

You might also be interested in *Careers in Sociology Module.* New York: Wadsworth, 2009, and Lambert, Stephen. *Great Jobs for Sociology Majors,* New York: McGraw-Hill, 2009. How can you make a living with a major in sociology? These two publications explore careers in sociology, from business and government to health care and the law.

Culture

From Chapter 2 of *Sociology: A Down-to-Earth Approach*, 10/e. James M. Henslin. Copyright © 2010 by Pearson Education. Published by Allyn & Bacon.

Culture

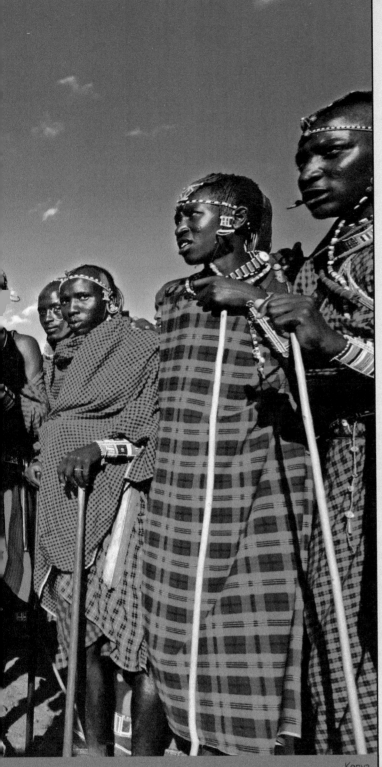

Kenya

Martin Harvey/Alamy

I had never felt heat like this before. This was northern Africa, and I wondered what it must be like closer to the equator. Sweat poured off me as the temperature climbed past 110 degrees Fahrenheit.

As we were herded into the building—which had no air conditioning—hundreds of people lunged toward the counter at the rear of the structure. With body crushed against body, we waited as the uniformed officials behind the windows leisurely examined each passport. At times like this, I wondered what I was doing in Africa.

Everyone stared. No matter where I went, they stared.

When I first arrived in Morocco, I found the sights that greeted me exotic—not unlike the scenes in *Casablanca, Raiders of the Lost Ark,* and other movies. The men, women, and even the children really did wear those white robes that reached down to their feet. What was especially striking was that the women were almost totally covered. Despite the heat, they wore not only full-length gowns but also head coverings that reached down over their foreheads and veils that covered their faces from the nose down. You could see nothing but their eyes—and every eye seemed the same shade of brown.

And how short everyone was! The Arab women looked to be, on average, 5 feet, and the men only about three or four inches taller. As the only blue-eyed, blond, 6-foot-plus person around, and the only one who was wearing jeans and a pullover shirt, in a world of white-robed short people I stood out like a creature from another planet. Everyone stared. No matter where I went, they stared. Wherever I looked, I found brown eyes watching me intently. Even staring back at those many dark brown eyes had no effect. It was so different from home, where, if you caught someone staring at you, that person would look embarrassed and immediately glance away.

And lines? The concept apparently didn't even exist. Buying a ticket for a bus or train meant pushing and shoving toward the ticket man (always a man—no women were visible in any public position), who took the money from whichever outstretched hand he decided on.

And germs? That notion didn't seem to exist here either. Flies swarmed over the food in the restaurants and the unwrapped loaves of bread in the stores. Shopkeepers would considerately shoo off the flies before handing me a loaf. They also offered home delivery. I watched a bread vendor deliver a loaf to a woman who was standing on a second-floor balcony. She first threw her money to the bread vendor, and he then threw the unwrapped bread up to her. Only, his throw was off. The bread bounced off the wrought-iron balcony railing and landed in the street, which was filled with people, wandering dogs, and the ever-present urinating and defecating donkeys. The vendor simply picked up the unwrapped loaf and threw it again. This certainly wasn't his day, for he missed again. But he made it on his third attempt. The woman smiled as she turned back into her apartment, apparently to prepare the noon meal for her family.

As I left Morocco, I entered a crowded passport-check building on the Algerian border. With no air conditioning, the oppressive heat—about 115° was made all the worse as body crushed body. As people pushed to get to the front, tempers began to flare. When a fight broke out, a little man in uniform appeared, shouting and knocking people aside as he forced his way to a little wooden box nailed to the floor. Climbing onto this makeshift platform, he shouted at the crowd, his arms flailing about him. The people fell silent. But just as soon as the man left, the shouting and shoving began again.

The situation had become unbearable. His body pressed against mine, the man behind me decided that this was a good time to take a nap. Determining that I made a good support, he placed his arm against my back and leaned his head against his arm. Sweat streamed down my back at the point where his arm and head touched me.

Finally, I realized that I had to abandon U.S. customs. So I pushed my way forward, forcing my frame into every square inch of vacant space that I could create. At the counter, I shouted in English. The official looked up at the sound of this strange tongue, and I thrust my long arms over the heads of three people, shoving my passport into his hand.

What Is Culture?

What is culture? The concept is sometimes easier to grasp by description than by definition. For example, suppose you meet a young woman from India who has just arrived in the United States. That her culture is different from yours is immediately evident. You first see it in her clothing, jewelry, makeup, and hairstyle. Next you hear it in her speech. It then becomes apparent by her gestures. Later, you might hear her express unfamiliar beliefs about relationships or what is valuable in life. All of these characteristics are indicative of **culture**—the language, beliefs, values, norms, behaviors, and even material objects that are passed from one generation to the next.

In northern Africa, I was surrounded by a culture quite different from mine. It was evident in everything I saw and heard. The **material culture**—such things as jewelry, art, buildings, weapons, machines, and even eating utensils, hairstyles, and clothing—provided a sharp contrast to what I was used to seeing. There is nothing inherently "natural" about material culture. That is, it is no more natural (or unnatural) to wear gowns on the street than it is to wear jeans.

I also found myself immersed in an unfamiliar **nonmaterial culture,** that is, a group's ways of thinking (its beliefs, values, and other assumptions about the world) and doing (its common **patterns** of behavior, including language, gestures, and other forms of interaction). North African assumptions that it is acceptable to stare at others in public and to push people aside to buy tickets are examples of nonmaterial culture. So are U.S. assumptions that it is wrong to do either of these things. Like material culture, neither custom is "right." People simply become comfortable with the customs they learn during childhood, and—as when I visited northern Africa—uncomfortable when their basic assumptions about life are challenged.

Culture and Taken-for-Granted Orientations to Life

To develop a sociological imagination, it is essential to understand how culture affects people's lives. If we meet someone from a different culture, the encounter may make us aware of culture's pervasive influence on all aspects of a person's life. Attaining the same level of

culture the language, beliefs, values, norms, behaviors, and even material objects that characterize a group and are passed from one generation to the next

material culture the material objects that distinguish a group of people, such as their art, buildings, weapons, utensils, machines, hairstyles, clothing, and jewelry

nonmaterial culture (also called symbolic culture) a group's ways of thinking (including its beliefs, values, and other assumptions about the world) and doing (its common patterns of behavior, including language and other forms of interaction)

patterns recurring characteristics or events

awareness regarding our own culture, however, is quite another matter. We usually take *our* speech, *our* gestures, *our* beliefs, and *our* customs for granted. We assume that they are "normal" or "natural," and we almost always follow them without question. As anthropologist Ralph Linton (1936) said, "The last thing a fish would ever notice would be water." So also with people: Except in unusual circumstances, most characteristics of our own culture remain imperceptible to us.

Yet culture's significance is profound; it touches almost every aspect of who and what we are. We came into this life without a language; without values and morality; with no ideas about religion, war, money, love, use of space, and so on. We possessed none of these fundamental orientations that are so essential in determining the type of people we become. Yet by this point in our lives, we all have acquired them—and take them for granted. Sociologists call this *culture within us.* These learned and shared ways of believing and of doing (another definition of culture) penetrate our beings at an early age and quickly become part of our taken-for-granted assumptions about what normal behavior is. *Culture becomes the lens through which we perceive and evaluate what is going on around us.* Seldom do we question these assumptions, for, like water to a fish, the lens through which we view life remains largely beyond our perception.

The rare instances in which these assumptions are challenged, however, can be upsetting. Although as a sociologist I should be able to look at my own culture "from the outside," my trip to Africa quickly revealed how fully I had internalized my culture. My upbringing in Western culture had given me assumptions about aspects of social life that had become rooted deeply in my being—appropriate eye contact, proper hygiene, and the use of space. But in this part of Africa these assumptions were useless in helping me navigate everyday life. No longer could I count on people to stare only surreptitiously, to take precautions against invisible microbes, or to stand in line in an orderly fashion, one behind the other.

As you can tell from the opening vignette, I found these unfamiliar behaviors upsetting, for they violated my basic expectations of "the way people *ought* to be"—and I did not even realize how firmly I held these expectations until they were challenged so abruptly. When my nonmaterial culture failed me—when it no longer enabled me to make sense out of the world—I experienced a disorientation known as **culture shock.** In the case of buying tickets, the fact that I was several inches taller than most Moroccans and thus able to outreach others helped me to adjust partially to their different ways of doing things. But I never did get used to the idea that pushing ahead of others was "right," and I always felt guilty when I used my size to receive preferential treatment.

Culture shock is a two-way street, of course. You can imagine what cultural shock people from a tribal society would experience if they were thrust into the United States. This actually happened, as the Cultural Diversity box on the next page describes.

An important consequence of culture within us is **ethnocentrism,** a tendency to use our own group's ways of doing things as a yardstick for judging others. All of us learn that the ways of our own group are good, right, and even superior to other ways of life. As sociologist William Sumner (1906), who developed this concept, said, "One's own group is the center of everything, and all others are scaled and rated with reference to it." Ethnocentrism has both positive and negative consequences. On the positive side, it creates in-group loyalties. On the negative side, ethnocentrism can lead to discrimination against people whose ways differ from ours.

The many ways in which culture affects our lives fascinate sociologists. In this chapter, we'll examine how profoundly culture influences everything we are and do. This will serve as a basis from which you can start to analyze your own assumptions of reality. I should give you a warning at this point: You might develop a changed perspective on social life and your role in it. If so, life will never look the same.

In Sum: To avoid losing track of the ideas under discussion, let's pause for a moment to summarize and, in some instances, clarify the principles we have covered.

> **1.** There is nothing "natural" about material culture. Arabs wear gowns on the street and feel that it is natural to do so. Americans do the same with jeans.

culture shock the disorientation that people experience when they come in contact with a fundamentally different culture and can no longer depend on their taken-for-granted assumptions about life

ethnocentrism the use of one's own culture as a yardstick for judging the ways of other individuals or societies, generally leading to a negative evaluation of their values, norms, and behaviors

Cultural Diversity in the United States

Culture Shock: The Arrival of the Hmong

Imagine that you were a member of a small tribal group in the mountains of Laos. Village life and the clan were all you knew. There were no schools, and you learned everything you needed to know from your relatives. U.S. agents recruited the men of your village to fight communists, and they gained a reputation as fierce fighters. When the U.S. forces were defeated in Vietnam, your people were moved to the United States so they wouldn't be killed in reprisal.

Here is what happened. Keep in mind that you had never seen a television or a newspaper and that you had never gone to school. Your entire world had been the village.

They put you in a big house with wings. It flew.

They gave you strange food on a tray. The Sani-Wipes were hard to chew.

After the trip, you were placed in a house. This was an adventure. You had never seen locks before, as no one locked up anything in the village. Most of the village homes didn't even have doors, much less locks.

You found the bathroom perplexing. At first, you tried to wash rice in the bowl of water, which seemed to be provided for this purpose. But when you pressed the handle, the water and rice disappeared. After you learned what the toilet was for, you found it difficult not to slip off the little white round thing when you stood on it. In the village, you didn't need a toilet seat when you squatted in a field to defecate.

When you threw water on the electric stove to put out the burner, it sparked and smoked. You became afraid to use the stove because it might explode.

And no one liked it when you tried to plant a vegetable garden in the park.

Your new world was so different that, to help you adjust, the settlement agency told you (Fadiman 1997):

1. To send mail, you must use stamps.
2. The door of the refrigerator must be shut.
3. Do not stand or squat on the toilet since it may break.
4. Always ask before picking your neighbor's flowers, fruit, or vegetables.
5. In colder areas you must wear shoes, socks, and appropriate outerwear. Otherwise, you may become ill.
6. Always use a handkerchief or a tissue to blow your nose in public places or inside a public building.
7. Picking your nose or ears in public is frowned upon in the United States.
8. Never urinate in the street. This creates a smell that is offensive to Americans. They also believe that it causes disease.

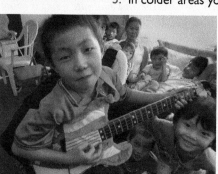

Gary Porter/Milwaukee Journal Sentinel/Newscom

Children make the fastest adjustment to a new culture, although they remain caught between the old and new ones.

To help the Hmong assimilate, U.S. officials dispersed them across the nation. This, they felt, would help them to adjust to the dominant culture and prevent a Hmong subculture from developing. The dispersal brought feelings of isolation to the clan- and village-based Hmong. As soon as they had a chance, the Hmong moved from these towns scattered across the country to the same areas, the major one being in California's Central Valley. Here they renewed village relationships and helped one another adjust to the society they had never desired to join.

For Your Consideration

Do you think you would have reacted differently if you had been a displaced Hmong? Why did the Hmong need one another more than their U.S. neighbors to adjust to their new life? What cultural shock do you think a U.S.-born 19-year-old Hmong would experience if his or her parents decided to return to Laos?

2. There is nothing "natural" about nonmaterial culture. It is just as arbitrary to stand in line as to push and shove.
3. Culture penetrates deeply into our thinking, becoming a taken-for-granted lens through which we see the world and obtain our perception of reality.
4. Culture provides implicit instructions that tell us what we ought to do and how we ought to think. It provides a fundamental basis for our decision making.

5. Culture also provides a "moral imperative"; that is, the culture that we internalize becomes the "right" way of doing things. (I, for example, believed deeply that it was wrong to push and shove to get ahead of others.)
6. Coming into contact with a radically different culture challenges our basic assumptions of life. (I experienced culture shock when I discovered that my deeply ingrained cultural ideas about hygiene and the use of personal space no longer applied.)
7. Although the particulars of culture differ from one group of people to another, culture itself is universal. That is, all people have culture, for a society cannot exist without developing shared, learned ways of dealing with the challenges of life.
8. All people are ethnocentric, which has both positive and negative consequences.

cultural relativism not judging a culture but trying to understand it on its own terms

Practicing Cultural Relativism

To counter our tendency to use our own culture as the standard by which we judge other cultures, we can practice **cultural relativism;** that is, we can try to understand a culture on its own terms. This means looking at how the elements of a culture fit together, without judging those elements as superior or inferior to our own way of life.

With our own culture embedded so deeply within us, however, practicing cultural relativism can challenge our orientations to life. For example, most U.S. citizens appear to have strong feelings against raising bulls for the purpose of stabbing them to death in front of crowds that shout "Olé!" According to cultural relativism, however, bullfighting must be viewed from the perspective of the culture in which it takes place—*its* history, *its* folklore, *its* ideas of bravery, and *its* ideas of sex roles.

You may still regard bullfighting as wrong, of course, if your culture, which is deeply ingrained in you, has no history of bullfighting. We all possess culturally specific ideas about cruelty to animals, ideas that have evolved slowly and match other elements of our culture. In the United States, for example, practices that once were common in some areas—cock fighting, dog fighting, bear–dog fighting, and so on—have been gradually eliminated.

AP Images/Daniel Ochoa de Olza

Many Americans perceive bullfighting as a cruel activity that should be illegal everywhere. To most Spaniards, bullfighting is a sport that pits matador and bull in a unifying image of power, courage, and glory. *Cultural relativism* requires that we suspend our own perspectives in order to grasp the perspectives of others, something easier described than attained.

43

None of us can be entirely successful at practicing cultural relativism. Look at the Cultural Diversity box below. My best guess is that you will evaluate these "strange" foods through the lens of your own culture. Applying cultural relativism, however, is an attempt to refocus that lens so we can appreciate other ways of life rather than simply asserting "Our way is right." Look at the photos on the next page. As you view them, try to appreciate the cultural differences in standards of beauty.

Although cultural relativism helps us to avoid cultural smugness, this view has come under attack. In a provocative book, *Sick Societies* (1992), anthropologist Robert Edgerton suggests that we develop a scale for evaluating cultures on their "quality of life," much as we do for U.S. cities. He also asks why we should consider cultures that practice female circumcision, gang rape, or wife beating, or cultures that sell little girls into prostitution, as

Cultural Diversity around the World

You Are What You Eat? An Exploration in Cultural Relativity

Here is a chance to test your ethnocentrism and ability to practice cultural relativity. You probably know that the French like to eat snails and that in some Asian cultures chubby dogs and cats are considered a delicacy ("Ah, lightly browned with a little doggy sauce!"). But did you know that cod sperm is a delicacy in Japan (Raisfeld and Patronite 2006)? That flies, scorpions, crickets, and beetles are on the menu of restaurants in parts of Thailand (Gampbell 2006)?

Marston Bates (1967), a zoologist, noted this ethnocentric reaction to food:

I remember once, in the llanos of Colombia, sharing a dish of toasted ants at a remote farmhouse. . . . My host and I fell into conversation about the general question of what people eat or do not eat, and I remarked that in my country people eat the legs of frogs.

The very thought of this filled my ant-eating friends with horror; it was as though I had mentioned some repulsive sex habit.

Then there is the experience of a friend, Dusty Friedman, who told me:

When traveling in Sudan, I ate some interesting things that I wouldn't likely eat now that I'm back in our society. Raw baby camel's liver with chopped herbs was a delicacy. So was camel's milk cheese patties that had been cured in dry camel's dung.

You might be able to see yourself eating frog legs and toasted ants, beetles, even flies. (Or maybe not.) Perhaps

B. Deconinck/The Image Works

What some consider food, even delicacies, can turn the stomachs of others. These little critters were for sale in a market in Laos.

you could even stomach cod sperm and raw camel liver, maybe even dogs and cats, but here's another test of your ethnocentrism and cultural relativity. Maxine Kingston (1975), an English professor whose parents grew up in China, wrote:

"Do you know what people in [the Nantou region of] China eat when they have the money?" my mother began. "They buy into a monkey feast. The eaters sit around a thick wood table with a hole in the middle. Boys bring in the monkey at the end of a pole. Its neck is in a collar at the end of the pole, and it is screaming. Its hands are tied behind it. They clamp the monkey into the table; the whole table fits like another collar around its neck. Using a surgeon's saw, the cooks cut a clean line in a circle at the top of its head. To loosen the bone, they tap with a tiny hammer and wedge here and there with a silver pick. Then an old woman reaches out her hand to the monkey's face and up to its scalp, where she tufts some hairs and lifts off the lid of the skull. The eaters spoon out the brains."

For Your Consideration

What is your opinion about eating toasted ants? Beetles? Flies? Fried frog legs? Cod sperm? About eating puppies and kittens? About eating brains scooped out of a living monkey?

If you were reared in U.S. society, more than likely you think that eating frog legs is okay; eating ants or beetles is disgusting; and eating flies, cod sperm, dogs, cats, and monkey brains is downright repugnant. How would you apply the concepts of ethnocentrism and cultural relativism to your perceptions of these customs?

Ecuador

John and Lisa Merrill/Corbis

New Guinea

Danita Delimont/Alamy

Thailand

Jean-Pierre Lescourret/Corbis

China

Panorama/The Image Works

Cameroon

Bill Bachmann/The Image Works

Tibet

Picture Finders Ltd./eStock Photo

Kenya

Keren Su/The Image Bank/Getty Images

United States

Helen King/Corbis

Standards of Beauty

Standards of beauty vary so greatly from one culture to another that what one group finds attractive, another may not. Yet, in its *ethnocentrism*, each group thinks that its standards are the best—that the appearance reflects what beauty "really" is.

As indicated by these photos, around the world men and women aspire to their group's norms of physical attractiveness. To make themselves appealing to others, they try to make their appearance reflect those standards.

morally equivalent to those that do not. Cultural values that result in exploitation, he says, are inferior to those that enhance people's lives.

Edgerton's sharp questions and incisive examples bring us to a topic that comes up repeatedly in this text: the disagreements that arise among scholars as they confront contrasting views of reality. It is such questioning of assumptions that keeps sociology interesting.

Components of Symbolic Culture

Sociologists sometimes refer to nonmaterial culture as **symbolic culture,** because its central component is the set of symbols that people use. A **symbol** is something to which people attach meaning and that they then use to communicate with one another. Symbols include gestures, language, values, norms, sanctions, folkways, and mores. Let's look at each of these components of symbolic culture.

Gestures

Gestures, movements of the body to communicate with others, are shorthand ways to convey messages without using words. Although people in every culture of the world use gestures, a gesture's meaning may change completely from one culture to another. North Americans, for example, communicate a succinct message by raising the middle finger in a short, upward stabbing motion. I wish to stress "North Americans," for this gesture does not convey the same message in most parts of the world.

I was surprised to find that this particular gesture was not universal, having internalized it to such an extent that I thought everyone knew what it meant. When I was comparing gestures with friends in Mexico, however, this gesture drew a blank look from them. After I explained its intended meaning, they laughed and showed me their rudest gesture—placing the hand under the armpit and moving the upper arm up and down. To me, they simply looked as if they were imitating monkeys, but to them the gesture meant "Your mother is a whore"—the worst possible insult in that culture.

With the current political, military, and cultural dominance of the United States, "giving the finger" is becoming well known in other cultures. Following the September 11, 2001, terrorist attack, the United States began to photograph and fingerprint foreign visitors. Feeling insulted, Brazil retaliated by doing the same to U.S. visitors. Angry at this, a U.S. pilot raised his middle finger while being photographed. Having become aware of the meaning of this gesture, Brazilian police arrested him. To gain his release, the pilot had to pay a fine of $13,000 ("Brazil Arrests" 2004).

Gestures not only facilitate communication but also, because they differ around the world, can lead to misunderstanding, embarrassment, or worse. One time in Mexico, for example, I raised my hand to a certain height to indicate how tall a child was. My hosts began to laugh. It turned out that Mexicans use three hand gestures to indicate height: one for people, a second for animals, and yet another for plants. They were amused because I had ignorantly used the plant gesture to indicate the child's height. (See Figure 1).

To get along in another culture, then, it is important to learn the gestures of that culture. If you don't, you will fail to achieve the simplicity of communication that gestures allow and you may overlook or misunderstand much of what is happening, run the risk of appearing foolish, and possibly offend people. In some cultures, for example, you would provoke deep offense if you were to offer food or a gift with your left hand, because the left hand is reserved for dirty tasks, such as wiping after going to the toilet. Left-handed Americans visiting Arabs, please note!

Suppose for a moment that you are visiting southern Italy. After eating one of the best meals in your life, you are so pleased that when you catch the waiter's eye, you smile broadly and use the standard U.S. "A-OK" gesture of putting your thumb and forefinger together and making a large "**O**." The

symbolic culture another term for nonmaterial culture

symbol something to which people attach meanings and then use to communicate with others

gestures the ways in which people use their bodies to communicate with one another

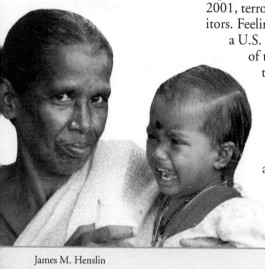

James M. Henslin

Although most *gestures* are learned, and therefore vary from culture to culture, some gestures that represent fundamental emotions such as sadness, anger, and fear appear to be inborn. This crying child whom I photographed in India differs little from a crying child in China—or the United States or anywhere else on the globe. In a few years, however, this child will demonstrate a variety of gestures highly specific to his Hindu culture.

FIGURE 1 Gestures to Indicate Height, Southern Mexico

David Young-Wolff/PhotoEdit

Steve Hamblin/Alamy Royalty Free   Tony Freeman/PhotoEdit, Inc.   Michael Newman/PhotoEdit, Inc.

waiter looks horrified, and you are struck speechless when the manager asks you to leave. What have you done? Nothing on purpose, of course, but in that culture this gesture refers to a lower part of the human body that is not mentioned in polite company (Ekman et al. 1984).

Is it really true that there are no universal gestures? There is some disagreement on this point. Some anthropologists claim that no gesture is universal. They point out that even nodding the head up and down to indicate "yes" is not universal, because in some parts of the world, such as areas of Turkey, nodding the head up and down means "no" (Ekman et al. 1984). However, ethologists, researchers who study biological bases of behavior, claim that expressions of anger, pouting, fear, and sadness are built into our biological makeup and are universal (Eibl-Eibesfeldt 1970:404; Horwitz and Wakefield 2007). They point out that even infants who are born blind and deaf, who have had no chance to *learn* these gestures, express themselves in the same way.

Although this matter is not yet settled, we can note that gestures tend to vary remarkably around the world. It is also significant that certain gestures can elicit emotions; some gestures are so closely associated with emotional messages that the gestures themselves summon up emotions. For example, my introduction to Mexican gestures took place at a dinner table. It was evident that my husband-and-wife hosts were trying to hide their embarrassment at using their culture's obscene gesture at their dinner table. And I felt the same way—not about *their* gesture, of course, which meant nothing to me—but about the one I was teaching them.

Language

The primary way in which people communicate with one another is through **language**—symbols that can be combined in an infinite number of ways for the purpose of communicating abstract thought. Each word is actually a symbol, a sound to which we have attached some particular meaning. Although all human groups have language, there is nothing universal about the meanings given to particular sounds. Like gestures, in different cultures the same sound may mean something entirely different—or may have no meaning at all. In German, for example, *gift* means "poison," so if you give a box of chocolates to a non-English-speaking German and say, "Gift, Eat" . . .

Because *language allows culture to exist,* its significance for human life is difficult to overstate. Consider the following effects of language.

Language Allows Human Experience to Be Cumulative. By means of language, we pass ideas, knowledge, and even attitudes on to the next generation. This allows others to build on experiences in which they may never directly participate. As a result, humans are able to modify their behavior in light of what earlier generations have learned. This takes us to the central sociological significance of language: *Language allows culture to develop by freeing people to move beyond their immediate experiences.*

language a system of symbols that can be combined in an infinite number of ways and can represent not only objects but also abstract thought

Without language, human culture would be little more advanced than that of the lower primates. If we communicated by grunts and gestures, we would be limited to a short time span—to events now taking place, those that have just taken place, or those that will take place immediately—a sort of slightly extended present. You can grunt and gesture, for example, that you want a drink of water, but in the absence of language how could you share ideas concerning past or future events? There would be little or no way to communicate to others what event you had in mind, much less the greater complexities that humans communicate—ideas and feelings about events.

Language Provides a Social or Shared Past. Without language, our memories would be extremely limited, for we associate experiences with words and then use words to recall the experience. Such memories as would exist in the absence of language would be highly individualized, for only rarely and incompletely could we communicate them to others, much less discuss them and agree on something. By attaching words to an event, however, and then using those words to recall it, we are able to discuss the event. As we talk about past events, we develop shared understandings about what those events mean. In short, through talk, people develop a shared past.

Language Provides a Social or Shared Future. Language also extends our time horizons forward. Because language enables us to agree on times, dates, and places, it allows us to plan activities with one another. Think about it for a moment. Without language, how could you ever plan future events? How could you possibly communicate goals, times, and plans? Whatever planning could exist would be limited to rudimentary communications, perhaps to an agreement to meet at a certain place when the sun is in a certain position. But think of the difficulty, perhaps the impossibility, of conveying just a slight change in this simple arrangement, such as "I can't make it tomorrow, but my neighbor can take my place, if that's all right with you."

Language Allows Shared Perspectives. Our ability to speak, then, provides us a social (or shared) past and future. This is vital for humanity. It is a watershed that distinguishes us from animals. But speech does much more than this. When we talk with one another, we are exchanging ideas about events; that is, we are sharing perspectives. Our words are the embodiment of our experiences, distilled into a readily exchangeable form, one that

Language is the basis of human culture around the world. The past decade has seen major developments in communication—the ease and speed with which we can "speak" to people across the globe. This development is destined to have vital effects on culture.

Richard Lord/The Image Works

is mutually understandable to people who have learned that language. *Talking about events allows us to arrive at the shared understandings that form the basis of social life.* Not sharing a language while living alongside one another, however, invites miscommunication and suspicion. This risk, which comes with a diverse society, is discussed in the Cultural Diversity box below.

Language Allows Shared, Goal-Directed Behavior.   Common understandings enable us to establish a *purpose* for getting together. Let's suppose you want to go on a picnic. You use speech not only to plan the picnic but also to decide on reasons for having the picnic—which may be anything from "because it's a nice day and it shouldn't be wasted studying" to "because it's my birthday." Language permits you to blend individual activities into an integrated sequence. In other words, through discussion you decide where you will go; who will drive; who will bring the hamburgers, the potato chips, the soda; where you will meet; and so on. Only because of language can you participate in such a common yet complex event as a picnic—or build roads and bridges or attend college classes.

In Sum: The sociological significance of language is that it takes us beyond the world of apes and allows culture to develop. Language frees us from the present, actually giving us

Cultural Diversity in the United States

Florida

Miami—Continuing Controversy over Language

Immigration from Cuba and other Spanish-speaking countries has been so vast that most residents of Miami are Latinos. Half of Miami's 385,000 residents have trouble speaking English. Only one-fourth of Miamians speak English at home. Many English-only speakers are leaving Miami, saying that not being able to speak Spanish is a handicap to getting work. "They should learn Spanish," some reply. As Pedro Falcon, an immigrant from Nicaragua, said, "Miami is the capital of Latin America. The population speaks Spanish."

As the English-speakers see it, this pinpoints the problem: Miami is in the United States, not in Latin America.

Controversy over immigrants and language isn't new. The millions of Germans who moved to the United States in the 1800s brought their language with them. Not only did they hold their religious services in German, but they also opened private schools in which the teachers taught in German, published German-language newspapers, and spoke German at home, in the stores, and in the taverns.

Jeff Greenberg/PhotoEdit, Inc.
Mural from Miami.

Some of their English-speaking neighbors didn't like this a bit. "Why don't those Germans assimilate?" they wondered. "Just whose side would they fight on if we had a war?"

This question was answered, of course, with the participation of German Americans in two world wars. It was even a general descended from German immigrants (Eisenhower) who led the armed forces that defeated Hitler.

But what happened to all this German language? The first generation of immigrants spoke German almost exclusively. The second generation assimilated, speaking English at home, but also speaking German when they visited their parents. For the most part, the third generation knew German only as "that language" that their grandparents spoke.

The same thing is happening with the Latino immigrants. Spanish is being kept alive longer, however, because Mexico borders the United States, and there is constant traffic between the countries. The continuing migration from Mexico and other Spanish-speaking countries also feeds the language.

If Germany bordered the United States, there would still be a lot of German spoken here.

Sources: Based on Sharp 1992; Usdansky 1992; Kent and Lalasz 2007; Salomon 2008.

a social past and a social future. That is, language gives us the capacity to share understandings about the past and to develop shared perceptions about the future. Language also allows us to establish underlying purposes for our activities. In short, *language is the basis of culture.*

Language and Perception: The Sapir-Whorf Hypothesis. In the 1930s, two anthropologists, Edward Sapir and Benjamin Whorf, became intrigued when they noticed that the Hopi Indians of the southwestern United States had no words to distinguish among the past, the present, and the future. English, in contrast—as well as French, Spanish, Swahili, and other languages—distinguishes carefully among these three time frames. From this observation, Sapir and Whorf began to think that words might be more than labels that people attach to things. *Eventually, they concluded that language has embedded within it ways of looking at the world.* In other words, language not only expresses our thoughts and perceptions but also shapes the way we think and perceive. When we learn a language, we learn not only words but also ways of thinking and perceiving (Sapir 1949; Whorf 1956).

The **Sapir-Whorf hypothesis** reverses common sense: It indicates that rather than objects and events forcing themselves onto our consciousness, it is our language that determines our consciousness, and hence our perception of objects and events. For English speakers, the term *nuts* combines almonds, walnuts, and pecans in such a way that we see them as belonging together. Spanish has no such overarching, combining word, so native Spanish speakers don't see such a connection. Sociologist Eviatar Zerubavel (1991) points out that his native language, Hebrew, does not have separate words for jam and jelly. Both go by the same term, and only when Zerubavel learned English could he "see" this difference, which is "obvious" to native English speakers. Similarly, if you learn to classify students as Jocks, Goths, Stoners, Skaters, Band Geeks, and Preps, you will perceive students in an entirely different way from someone who does not know these classifications.

Although Sapir and Whorf's observation that the Hopi do not have tenses was inaccurate (Edgerton 1992:27), they did stumble onto a major truth about social life. Learning a language means not only learning words but also acquiring the perceptions embedded in that language. In other words, language both reflects and shapes our cultural experiences (Drivonikou et al. 2007). The racial–ethnic terms that our culture provides, for example, influence how we see both ourselves and others, a point that is discussed in the Cultural Diversity box on the next page.

Values, Norms, and Sanctions

To learn a culture is to learn people's **values,** their ideas of what is desirable in life. When we uncover people's values, we learn a great deal about them, for values are the standards by which people define what is good and bad, beautiful and ugly. Values underlie our preferences, guide our choices, and indicate what we hold worthwhile in life.

Every group develops expectations concerning the right way to reflect its values. Sociologists use the term **norms** to describe those expectations (or rules of behavior) that develop out of a group's values. The term **sanctions** refers to the reactions people receive for following or breaking norms. A **positive sanction** expresses approval for following a norm, and a **negative sanction** reflects disapproval for breaking a norm. Positive sanctions can be material, such as a prize, a trophy, or money, but in everyday life they usually consist of hugs, smiles, a pat on the back, or even handshakes and "high fives." Negative sanctions can also be material—being fined in court is one example—but negative sanctions, too, are more likely to be symbolic: harsh words, or gestures such as frowns, stares, clenched jaws, or raised fists. Getting a raise at work is a positive sanction, indicating that you have followed the norms clustering around work values. Getting fired, however, is a negative sanction, indicating that you have violated these norms. The North American finger gesture discussed earlier is, of course, a negative sanction.

Sapir-Whorf hypothesis Edward Sapir and Benjamin Whorf's hypothesis that language creates ways of thinking and perceiving

values the standards by which people define what is desirable or undesirable, good or bad, beautiful or ugly

norms expectations, or rules of behavior, that reflect and enforce behavior

sanctions either expressions of approval given to people for upholding norms or expressions of disapproval for violating them

positive sanction a reward or positive reaction for following norms, ranging from a smile to a material reward

negative sanction an expression of disapproval for breaking a norm, ranging from a mild, informal reaction such as a frown to a formal reaction such as a prison sentence or an execution

Cultural Diversity in the United States

Race and Language: Searching for Self-Labels

The groups that dominate society often determine the names that are used to refer to racial–ethnic groups. If those names become associated with oppression, they take on negative meanings. For example, the terms *Negro* and *colored people* came to be associated with submissiveness and low status. To overcome these meanings, those referred to by these terms began to identify themselves as *black* or *African American*. They infused these new terms with respect—a basic source of self-esteem that they felt the old terms denied them.

In a twist, African Americans—and to a lesser extent Latinos, Asian Americans, and Native Americans—have changed the rejected term *colored people* to *people of color*. Those who embrace this modified term are imbuing it with meanings that offer an identity of respect. The term also has political meanings. It indicates bonds that cross racial–ethnic lines, mutual ties, and a sense of identity rooted in historical oppression.

There is *always* disagreement about racial–ethnic terms, and this one is no exception. Although most rejected the term *colored people,* some found in it a sense of respect and claimed it for themselves. The acronym

Sonda Dawes/The Image Works
The ethnic terms we choose—or which are given to us—are major self-identifiers. They indicate both membership in some group and a separation from other groups.

NAACP, for example, stands for the National Association for the Advancement of Colored People. The new term, *people of color,* arouses similar feelings. Some individuals whom this term would include claim that it is inappropriate. They point out that this new label still makes color the primary identifier of people. They stress that humans transcend race–ethnicity, that what we have in common as human beings goes much deeper than what you see on the surface. They stress that we should avoid terms that focus on differences in the pigmentation of our skin.

The language of self-reference in a society that is so conscious of skin color is an ongoing issue. As long as our society continues to emphasize such superficial differences, the search for adequate terms is not likely to ever be "finished." In this quest for terms that strike the right chord, the term *people of color* may become a historical footnote. If it does, it will be replaced by another term that indicates a changing self-identification in a changing historical context.

For Your Consideration

What terms do you use to refer to your race–ethnicity? What "bad" terms do you know that others have used to refer to your race–ethnicity? What is the difference in meaning between the terms you use and the "bad" terms? Where does that meaning come from?

Because people can find norms stifling, some cultures relieve the pressure through *moral holidays,* specified times when people are allowed to break norms. Moral holidays such as Mardi Gras often center on getting rowdy. Some activities for which people would otherwise be arrested are permitted—and expected—including public drunkenness and some nudity. The norms are never completely dropped, however—just loosened a bit. Go too far, and the police step in.

Some societies have *moral holiday places,* locations where norms are expected to be broken. Red light districts of our cities are examples. There, prostitutes are allowed to work the streets, bothered only when political pressure builds to "clean up" the area. If these same prostitutes attempt to solicit customers in adjacent areas, however, they are promptly arrested. Each year, the hometown of the team that wins the Super Bowl becomes a moral holiday place—for one night.

One of the more interesting examples is "Party Cove" at Lake of the Ozarks in Missouri, a fairly straightlaced area of the country. During the summer, hundreds of boaters—those operating cabin cruisers to jet skis—moor their vessels together in a highly publicized cove, where many get drunk, take off their clothes, and dance on the boats. In one of the more humorous incidents, boaters complained that a nude woman was riding a jet ski outside of the cove. The water patrol investigated but refused to arrest the woman because she was within the law—she had sprayed shaving cream on certain parts of her body. The Missouri Water Patrol has even given a green light to Party Cove, announcing in the local newspaper that officers will not enter this cove, supposedly because "there is so much traffic that they might not be able to get out in time to handle an emergency elsewhere."

Folkways and Mores

Norms that are not strictly enforced are called **folkways.** We expect people to comply with folkways, but we are likely to shrug our shoulders and not make a big deal about it if they don't. If someone insists on passing you on the right side of the sidewalk, for example, you are unlikely to take corrective action, although if the sidewalk is crowded and you must move out of the way, you might give the person a dirty look.

Other norms, however, are taken much more seriously. We think of them as essential to our core values, and we insist on conformity. These are called **mores** (MORE-rays). A person who steals, rapes, or kills has violated some of society's most important mores. As sociologist Ian Robertson (1987:62) put it,

A man who walks down a street wearing nothing on the upper half of his body is violating a folkway; a man who walks down the street wearing nothing on the lower half of his body is violating one of our most important mores, the requirement that people cover their genitals and buttocks in public.

It should also be noted that one group's folkways may be another group's mores. Although a man walking down the street with the upper half of his body uncovered is deviating from a folkway, a woman doing the same thing is violating the mores. In addition, the folkways and mores of a subculture (discussed in the next section) may be the opposite of mainstream culture. For example, to walk down the sidewalk in a nudist camp with the entire body uncovered would conform to that subculture's folkways.

A **taboo** refers to a norm so strongly ingrained that even the thought of its violation is greeted with revulsion. Eating human flesh and parents having sex with their children are examples of such behaviors. When someone breaks a taboo, the individual is usually

Tiffany Warmowski/ The Image Works

Many societies relax their norms during specified occasions. At these times, known as *moral holidays*, behavior that is ordinarily not permitted is allowed. Shown here at Mardi Gras in New Orleans is a woman showing her breasts to get beads dropped to her from the balcony. When a *moral holiday* is over, the usual enforcement of rules follows.

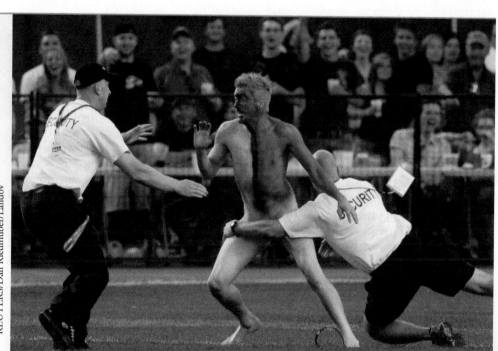

The violation of *mores* is a serious matter. In this case, it is serious enough that the security at a football match in Edmonton, Alberta (Canada) have swung into action to protect the public from seeing a "disgraceful" sight, at least one so designated by this group.

REUTERS/Dan Riedlhuber/Landov

judged unfit to live in the same society as others. The sanctions are severe and may include prison, banishment, or death.

Many Cultural Worlds

Subcultures

Groups of people who focus on some activity or who occupy some small corner in life tend to develop specialized ways to communicate with one another. To outsiders, their talk, even if it is in English, can seem like a foreign language. Here is one of my favorite quotes by a politician:

> There are things we know that we know. There are known unknowns; that is to say, there are things that we now know we don't know. But there are also unknown unknowns; there are things we do not know we don't know. (Donald Rumsfeld, quoted in Dickey and Barry 2006:38)

Whatever Rumsfeld, the former secretary of defense under George W. Bush, meant by his statement probably will remain a known unknown. (Or would it be an unknown known?)

We have a similar problem with communication in the subculture of sociology. Try to figure out what this means:

> The self-interested and self-sufficient individual remains the ideal, in which the centering of rational choice and a capacity for transcendence both occludes group-based harms of systemic oppression and conceals the complicity of individuals in the perpetuation of systemic injustices. (Reay et al. 2008:239)

People who specialize in an occupation—from cabbies to politicians—tend to develop a **subculture,** *a world within the larger world of the dominant culture.* Subcultures are not limited to occupations, for they include any corner in life in which people's experiences lead them to have distinctive ways of looking at the world. Even if we cannot understand the quotation from Donald Rumsfeld, it makes us aware that politicians don't view life in quite the same way most of us do.

U.S. society contains *thousands* of subcultures. Some are as broad as the way of life we associate with teenagers, others as narrow as those we associate with body builders—or with politicians. Some U.S. ethnic groups also form subcultures: Their values, norms, and foods set them apart. So might their religion, music, language, and clothing. Even sociologists form a subculture. As you are learning, they also use a unique language in their efforts to understand the world.

For a visual depiction of subcultures, see the photo essay on the next two pages.

Countercultures

Consider this quote from another subculture:

> If everyone applying for welfare had to supply a doctor's certificate of sterilization, if everyone who had committed a felony were sterilized, if anyone who had mental illness to any degree were sterilized—then our economy could easily take care of these people for the rest of their lives, giving them a decent living standard—but getting them out of the way. That way there would be no children abused, no surplus population, and, after a while, no pollution. . . .
>
> Now let's talk about stupidity. The level of intellect in this country is going down, generation after generation. The average IQ is always 100 because that is the accepted average. However, the kid with a 100 IQ today would have tested out at 70 when I was a lad. You get the concept . . . the marching morons. . . .
>
> When the . . . present world system collapses, it'll be good people like you who will be shooting people in the streets to feed their families. (Zellner 1995:58, 65)

Welcome to the world of the survivalists, where the message is much clearer than that of politicians—and much more disturbing.

folkways norms that are not strictly enforced

mores norms that are strictly enforced because they are thought essential to core values or to the well-being of the group

taboo a norm so strong that it brings extreme sanctions and even revulsion if someone violates it

subculture the values and related behaviors of a group that distinguish its members from the larger culture; a world within a world

Looking at Subcultures

Subcultures can form around any interest or activity. Each subculture has its own values and norms that its members share, giving them a common identity. Each also has special terms that pinpoint the group's corner of life and that its members use to communicate with one another. Some of us belong to several subcultures.

As you can see from these photos, most subcultures are compatible with the values and norms of the mainstream culture. They represent specialized interests around which its members have chosen to build tiny worlds. Some subcultures, however, conflict with the mainstream culture. Sociologists give the name *counterculture* to subcultures whose values (such as those of outlaw motorcyclists) or activities and goals (such as those of terrorists) are opposed to the mainstream culture. Countercultures, however, are exceptional, and few of us belong to them.

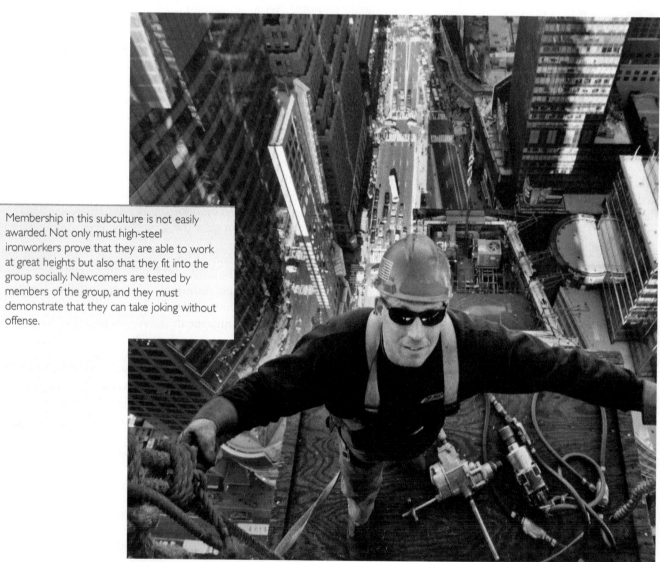

Membership in this subculture is not easily awarded. Not only must high-steel ironworkers prove that they are able to work at great heights but also that they fit into the group socially. Newcomers are tested by members of the group, and they must demonstrate that they can take joking without offense.

Peter Morgan/Reuters

David R. Frazier Photolibrary, Inc./Alamy

The cabbies' subculture, centering on their occupational activities and interests, is also broken into smaller subcultures that reflect their experiences of race-ethnicity.

Even subcultures can have subcultures. The rodeo subculture is a subculture of "western" subculture. The values that unite its members are reflected in their speech, clothing, and specialized activities, such as the one shown here.

Specialized values and interests are two of the characteristics that mark subcultures. What values and interests distinguish the modeling subculture?

Kokyat Choong/The Image Works

The subculture that centers around tattooing previously existed on the fringes of society, with seamen and circus folk its main participants. It now has entered mainstream society, but not to this extreme.

NNS/The Oregonian/Landov

Why is professional dancing a subculture and not a counterculture?

Bonnie Kamin/PhotoEdit, Inc.

Pat Thielen/Alamy

Each subculture provides its members with values and distinctive ways of viewing the world. What values and perceptions do you think are common among body builders?

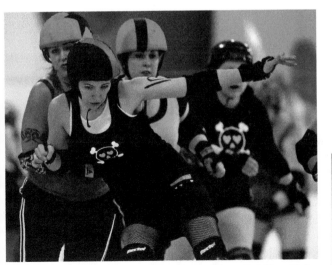

Uli Seit/The New York Times/Redux

What values, interests, language, and activities do you think characterize participants in flat-track women's roller derby leagues?

Kansas City Star/MCT/Landov

Why would someone decorate himself like this and use such an outrageous prop? Among the many reasons, one is to show solidarity with the football subculture.

The values and norms of most subcultures blend in with mainstream society. In some cases, however, as with these survivalists, some of the group's values and norms place it at odds with the dominant culture. Sociologists use the term **counterculture** to refer to such groups. To better see this distinction, consider motorcycle enthusiasts and motorcycle gangs. Motorcycle enthusiasts—who emphasize personal freedom and speed *and* affirm cultural values of success through work or education—are members of a subculture. In contrast, the Hell's Angels, Pagans, and Bandidos not only stress freedom and speed but also value dirtiness and contempt toward women, work, and education. This makes them a counterculture.

Countercultures do not have to be negative, however. Back in the 1800s, the Mormons were a counterculture that challenged the dominant culture's core value of monogamy.

An assault on core values is always met with resistance. To affirm their own values, members of the mainstream culture may ridicule, isolate, or even attack members of the counterculture. The Mormons, for example, were driven out of several states before they finally settled in Utah, which was then a wilderness. Even there, the federal government would not let them practice *polygyny* (one man having more than one wife), and Utah's statehood was made conditional on its acceptance of monogamy (Anderson 1942/1966; Williams 2007).

Values in U.S. Society

An Overview of U.S. Values

As you know, the United States is a **pluralistic society,** made up of many different groups. The United States has numerous religious and racial–ethnic groups, as well as countless interest groups that focus on activities as divergent as hunting deer and geese and collecting Barbie dolls. Within this huge diversity, sociologists have tried to identify the underlying core values that are shared by most of the groups that make up U.S. society. Here are ten that sociologist Robin Williams (1965) identified:

1. *Achievement and success.* Americans praise personal achievement, especially outdoing others. This value includes getting ahead at work and school, and attaining wealth, power, and prestige.
2. *Individualism.* Americans cherish the ideal that an individual can rise from the bottom of society to its very top. If someone fails to "get ahead," Americans generally find fault with that individual rather than with the social system for placing roadblocks in his or her path.
3. *Hard work.* Americans expect people to work hard to achieve financial success and material comfort.
4. *Efficiency and practicality.* Americans award high marks for getting things done efficiently. Even in everyday life, Americans consider it important to do things fast, and they seek ways to increase efficiency.
5. *Science and technology.* Americans have a passion for applied science, for using science to control nature—to tame rivers and harness winds—and to develop new technology, from iPods to Segways.
6. *Material comfort.* Americans expect a high level of material comfort. This includes not only good nutrition, medical care, and housing but also late-model cars and recreational playthings—from iPhones to motor homes.
7. *Freedom.* This core value pervades U.S. life. It underscored the American Revolution, and Americans pride themselves on their personal freedom. The Mass Media in Social Life box on the next page highlights an interesting study on how this core value applies to Native Americans.
8. *Democracy.* By this term, Americans refer to majority rule, to the right of everyone to express an opinion, and to representative government.
9. *Equality.* It is impossible to understand Americans without being aware of the central role that the value of equality plays in their lives. Equality of opportunity (part

counterculture a group whose values, beliefs, norms, and related behaviors place its members in opposition to the broader culture

pluralistic society a society made up of many different groups, with contrasting values and orientations to life

MASS MEDIA In SOCIAL LIFE

Why Do Native Americans Like Westerns?

Although Western movies go through a cycle of popularity, their themes are a mainstay of Hollywood. It is easy to see why Anglos might like Westerns. In the standard western format, it is they who tame the wilderness while defending themselves from the attacks of cruel, savage Indians intent on their destruction. But why would Indians like Westerns?

Sociologist JoEllen Shively, a Chippewa who grew up on Indian reservations in Montana and North Dakota, observed that Western themes are so popular that Native Americans bring bags of paperbacks into taverns to trade with one another. They even call each other "cowboy."

Intrigued, Shively decided to investigate the matter by showing a Western movie to adult Native Americans and Anglos in a reservation town. She matched the groups on education, age, income, and percentage of unemployment. To select the movie, Shively (1991, 1992) previewed more than seventy Westerns. She chose a John Wayne movie, *The Searchers,* because it not only focuses on conflict between Indians and cowboys but also shows the cowboys defeating the Indians. After the movie, the viewers filled out questionnaires, and Shively interviewed them.

She found something surprising: *All* Native Americans and Anglos identified with the cowboys; *none* identified with the Indians. Anglos and Native Americans, however, identified with the cowboys in different ways. Each

Although John Wayne often portrayed an Anglo who kills Indians, Wayne is popular among Indian men. These men tend to identify with the cowboys, who reflect their values of bravery, autonomy, and toughness.

RKO Pictures/Getty Images

projected a different fantasy onto the story. Anglos saw the movie as an accurate portrayal of the Old West and a justification of their own status in society. Native Americans, in contrast, saw it as embodying a free, natural way of life. In fact, Native Americans said that they were the "real cowboys." They said, "Westerns relate to the way I wish I could live"; "He's not tied down to an eight-to-five job, day after day"; "He's his own man."

Shively adds,

"What appears to make westerns meaningful to Indians is the fantasy of being free and independent like the cowboy. . . . Indians . . . find a fantasy in the cowboy story in which the important parts of their ways of life triumph and are morally good, validating their own cultural group in the context of a dramatically satisfying story.

To express their real identity—a combination of marginality on the one hand with a set of values which are about the land, autonomy, and being free—they [use] a cultural vehicle written for Anglos about Anglos, but it is one in which Indians invest a distinctive set of meanings that speak to their own experience, which they can read in a manner that affirms a way of life they value, or a fantasy they hold to."

In other words, it is not race–ethnicity, but values, that are the central issue in how Indians identify with Westerns. As Shively says, Native Americans make cowboys "honorary Indians," for the cowboys express their values of bravery, autonomy, and toughness.

For Your Consideration

If a Native American film industry were to produce Westerns that portrayed Native Americans with the same values that the Anglo movie industry projects onto cowboys, whom do you think that Native Americans would identify with? Why?

---

of the ideal culture discussed later) has significantly influenced U.S. history and continues to mark relations among the groups that make up U.S. society.

10. *Group superiority.* Although it contradicts the values of freedom, democracy, and equality, Americans regard some groups more highly than others and have done so throughout their history. The denial of the vote to women, the slaughter of Native Americans, and the enslavement of Africans are a few examples of how the groups considered superior have denied equality and freedom to others.

In an earlier publication, I updated Williams' analysis by adding these three values.

11. *Education.* Americans are expected to go as far in school as their abilities and finances allow. Over the years, the definition of an "adequate" education has

changed, and today a college education is considered an appropriate goal for most Americans. Those who have an opportunity for higher education and do not take it are sometimes viewed as doing something "wrong"—not merely as making a bad choice, but as somehow being involved in an immoral act.

12. *Religiosity.* There is a feeling that "every true American ought to be religious." This does not mean that everyone is expected to join a church, synagogue, or mosque, but that everyone ought to acknowledge a belief in a Supreme Being and follow some set of matching precepts. This value is so pervasive that Americans stamp "In God We Trust" on their money and declare in their national pledge of allegiance that they are "one nation under God."

13. *Romantic love.* Americans feel that the only proper basis for marriage is romantic love. Songs, literature, mass media, and "folk beliefs" all stress this value. Americans grow misty-eyed at the theme that "love conquers all."

Value Clusters

As you can see, values are not independent units; some cluster together to form a larger whole. In the **value cluster** that surrounds success, for example, we find hard work, education, material comfort, and individualism bound up together. Americans are expected to go far in school, to work hard afterward, and then to attain a high level of material comfort, which, in turn, demonstrates success. Success is attributed to the individual's efforts; lack of success is blamed on his or her faults.

Value Contradictions

You probably were surprised to see group superiority on the list of dominant American values. This is an example of how sociology upsets people and creates resistance. Few people want to bring something like this into the open. It violates today's *ideal* culture, a concept we discuss on the next page. But this is what sociologists do—they look beyond the façade to penetrate what is really going on. And when you look at our history, there is no doubt that group superiority has been a dominant value. It still is, but values change, and this one is diminishing.

Mark Peterson/Redux

The many groups that comprise the United States contribute to its culture. With their growing numbers, Latinos are making greater impact on U.S. art, entertainment, music, and literature. This is also true of other areas of everyday life, such as customized vehicles. These "tricked out" cars at a lowrider show in San Diego, California, feature bumping hydraulics and ornate paint.

Value contradictions, then, are part of culture. Not all values are wrapped in neat packages, and you can see how group superiority contradicts freedom, democracy, and equality. There simply cannot be full expression of freedom, democracy, and equality along with racism and sexism. Something has to give. One way in which Americans in the past sidestepped this contradiction was to say that freedom, democracy, and equality applied only to some groups. The contradiction was bound to surface over time, however, and so it did with the Civil War and the women's liberation movement. *It is precisely at the point of value contradictions, then, that one can see a major force for social change in a society.*

Emerging Values

A value cluster of four interrelated core values—leisure, self-fulfillment, physical fitness, and youthfulness—is emerging in the United States. So is a fifth core value—concern for the environment.

1. *Leisure.* The emergence of leisure as a value is reflected in a huge recreation industry—from computer games, boats, vacation homes, and spa retreats to sports arenas, home theaters, adventure vacations, and luxury cruises.

2. *Self-fulfillment.* This value is reflected in the "human potential" movement, which emphasizes becoming "all you can be," and in magazine articles, books, and talk shows that focus on "self-help," "relating," and "personal development."

3. *Physical fitness.* Physical fitness is not a new U.S. value, but a greater emphasis on it is moving it into this emerging cluster. You can see this trend in the publicity given to nutrition, organic foods, weight, and diet; the growing number of joggers, cyclists, and backpackers; and the countless health clubs and physical fitness centers.

4. *Youthfulness.* Valuing youth and disparaging old age are also not new, but some analysts note a sense of urgency about today's emphasis on youthfulness. They attribute this to the huge number of aging baby boomers, who, aghast at the physical changes that accompany their advancing years, attempt to deny or at least postpone their biological fate. One physician even claims that "aging is not a normal life event, but a disease" (Cowley 1996). As you age, you will be bombarded with techniques for maintaining and enhancing a youthful appearance—from cosmetic surgery to exotic creams and Botox injections.

Values don't "just happen." They are related to conditions of society, and this emerging value cluster is a response to fundamental change. Earlier generations of Americans were focused on forging a nation and fighting for economic survival. Today, millions of Americans are freed from long hours of work, and millions retire from work at an age when they anticipate decades of life ahead of them. This value cluster centers on helping people to maintain their health and vigor during their younger years and enabling them to enjoy their years of retirement.

5. *Concern for the environment.* During most of U.S. history, the environment was viewed as something to be exploited—a wilderness to be settled, forests to be cleared for farm land and lumber, rivers and lakes to be fished, and animals to be hunted. One result was the near extinction of the bison and the extinction in 1915 of the passenger pigeon, a species of bird previously so numerous that its annual migration would darken the skies for days. Today, Americans have developed a genuine and apparently long-term concern for the environment.

Again, values don't "just happen," and this emerging value of environmental concern is related to the current stage of U.S. economic development: People act on environmental concerns only after they have met their basic needs. At this point in their development, for example, the world's poor nations have a difficult time "affording" this value.

Clarke Memorial Museum, Eureka, California

Values, both those held by individuals and those that represent a nation or people, can undergo deep shifts. It is difficult for many of us to grasp the pride with which earlier Americans destroyed trees that took thousands of years to grow, are located only on one tiny speck of the globe, and that we today consider part of the nation's and world's heritage. But this is a value statement, representing current views. The pride expressed on these woodcutters' faces represents another set of values entirely.

Culture Wars: When Values Clash

Challenges in core values are met with strong resistance by the people who hold them dear. They see change as a threat to their way of life, an undermining of both their present and their future. Efforts to change gender roles, for example, arouse intense controversy, as do same-sex marriages. Alarmed at such onslaughts against their values, traditionalists fiercely defend historical family relationships and the gender roles they grew up with. *Culture wars*—a highly exaggerated term—refers to the clash in values between traditionalists and those advocating change. Compared with the violence directed against the Mormons, today's culture clashes are mild.

Values as Distorting Lenses

Values and their supporting beliefs are lenses through which we see the world. The view they produce is often of what life *ought* to be like, not what it is. For example, Americans value individualism so highly that they tend to see almost everyone as free and equal in pursuing the goal of success. This value blinds them to the significance of circumstances that keep people from achieving success. The dire consequences of family poverty, parents' low education, and dead-end jobs tend to drop from sight. Instead, Americans see the unsuccessful as not putting out enough effort. And they "know" they are right, for the mass media dangles before their eyes enticing stories of individuals who have succeeded despite the greatest of handicaps.

"Ideal" Versus "Real" Culture

Many of the norms that surround cultural values are followed only partially. Differences always exist between a group's ideals and what its members actually do. Consequently, sociologists use the term **ideal culture** to refer to the values, norms, and goals that a group considers ideal, worth aiming for. Success, for example, is part of ideal culture. Americans glorify academic progress, hard work, and the display of material goods as signs of individual achievement. What people actually do, however, usually falls short of the cultural ideal. Compared with their abilities, for example, most people don't work as hard as they could or go as far as they could in school. Sociologists call the norms and values that people actually follow **real culture.**

Cultural Universals

With the amazing variety of human cultures around the world, are there any **cultural universals**—values, norms, or other cultural traits that are found everywhere?

To answer this question, anthropologist George Murdock (1945) combed through the data that anthropologists had gathered on hundreds of groups around the world. He compared their customs concerning courtship, marriage, funerals, games, laws, music, myths, incest taboos, and even toilet training. He found that these activities are present in all cultures, but *the specific customs differ from one group to another.* There is no universal form of the family, no universal way of toilet training children, nor a universal way of disposing of the dead.

Incest is a remarkable example. Groups even differ on their view of what incest is. The Mundugumors of New Guinea extend the incest taboo so far that for each man, *seven* of every eight women are ineligible marriage partners (Mead 1935/1950). Other groups go in the opposite direction and allow some men to marry their own daughters (La Barre 1954). Some groups even *require* that brothers and sisters marry one another, although only in certain circumstances (Beals and Hoijer 1965). The Burundi of Africa even insist that a son have sex with his mother—but only to remove a certain curse (Albert 1963). Such sexual relations, so surprising to us, are limited to special people (royalty) or to extraordinary situations (such as when a lion hunter faces a dangerous hunt). No society permits generalized incest for its members.

ideal culture a people's ideal values and norms; the goals held out for them

real culture the norms and values that people actually follow

cultural universal a value, norm, or other cultural trait that is found in every group

In Sum: Although there are universal human activities (singing, playing games, story-telling, preparing food, marrying, child rearing, disposing of the dead, and so on), there is no universally accepted way of doing any of them. Humans have no biological imperative that results in one particular form of behavior throughout the world. As indicated in the following Thinking Critically section, although a few sociologists take the position that genes significantly influence human behavior, almost all sociologists reject this view.

ThinkingCRITICALLY

Are We Prisoners of Our Genes? Sociobiology and Human Behavior

A controversial view of human behavior, called **sociobiology** (also known as neo-Darwinism and evolutionary psychology), provides a sharp contrast to the perspective of this chapter, that human behavior is primarily due to culture. Sociobiologists (evolutionary psychologists, evolutionary anthropologists) believe that because of natural selection, biology is the basic cause of human behavior.

Charles Darwin (1859), who adopted Spencer's idea of natural selection, pointed out that the genes of a species—the units that contain the individual's traits—are not distributed evenly among the offspring. The characteristics that some members inherit make it easier for them to survive their environment, increasing the likelihood that they will pass their genetic traits to the next generation. Over thousands of generations, the genetic traits that aid survival become common in a species, while those that do not aid survival become less common or even disappear. Natural selection explains not only the physical characteristics of animals but also their behavior, for over countless generations, instincts emerged.

Edward Wilson (1975), an insect specialist, set off an uproar when he claimed that human behavior is also the result of natural selection. Human behavior, he said, is no different from the behavior of cats, dogs, rats, bees, or mosquitoes—it has been bred into *Homo sapiens* through evolutionary principles. Wilson went on to claim that competition and cooperation, envy and altruism—even religion, slavery, genocide, and war and peace—can be explained by sociobiology. He provocatively added that because human behavior can be explained in terms of genetic programming, sociobiology will eventually absorb sociology, as well as anthropology and psychology.

Obviously, most sociologists disagree with Wilson's position. Not only is it a direct attack on our discipline but it also bypasses the essence of what sociologists focus on: humans developing their own cultures, their own unique ways of life. Sociologists do not deny that biology underlies human behavior—at least not in the sense that it takes a highly developed brain to develop human culture and abstract thought and that there would be no speech if humans had no tongue or larynx.

But most sociologists find it difficult to believe that anyone would claim that genetic programming causes human behavior. Pigs act like pigs because they don't have a cerebral cortex, and instincts control their behavior. So it is for spiders, elephants, and so on (Howe et al. 1992). We humans, in contrast, possess a self and engage in abstract thought. We discuss the reasons that underlie what we do. We develop purposes and goals. We immerse ourselves in a world of symbols that allow us to consider, reflect, and make reasoned choices.

This controversy has turned into much more than simply an academic debate among scientists. Homosexuals, for example, have a personal interest in its outcome. If homosexuality is a lifestyle *choice*, then those who consider that lifestyle to be immoral will try to use this as a basis to exclude homosexuals from full social participation. If, however, homosexuality has a genetic base, then choice as a reason for social exclusion is eliminated. Sociologist

sociobiology a framework of thought that views human behavior as the result of natural selection and considers biological factors to be the fundamental cause of human behavior

technology in its narrow sense, tools; its broader sense includes the skills or procedures necessary to make and use those tools

new technology the emerging technologies of an era that have a significant impact on social life

Peter Conrad (1997) expressed the dominant sociological position when he pointed out that not all homosexuals have Xq28, the so-called gay gene, and that some people who have this gene are not homosexual. This gene, then, does not determine behavior. Instead, we must look for *social* causes (Bearman and Bruckner 2002). That there are social causes is not a basis for excluding anyone from anything.

In short, sociobiologists and sociologists stand on opposite sides, the one looking at human behavior as determined by genetics, the other looking at human behavior as determined by social learning, by experiences in the human group. Sociologists point out that if we humans were prisoners of our genes, we would not have developed such fascinatingly different ways of life around the world; instead, we would live in a monoculture of some sort.

Technology in the Global Village

The New Technology

The gestures, language, values, folkways, and mores that we have discussed—all are part of symbolic (nonmaterial) culture. Culture, as you recall, also has a material aspect: a group's *things,* from its houses to its toys. Central to a group's material culture is its technology. In its simplest sense, **technology** can be equated with tools. In a broader sense, technology also includes the skills or procedures necessary to make and use those tools.

We can use the term **new technology** to refer to an emerging technology that has a significant impact on social life. People develop minor technologies all the time. Most are slight modifications of existing technologies. Occasionally, however, they develop a technology that makes a major impact on human life. It is primarily to these innovations that the term *new technology* refers. Five hundred years ago, the new technology was the printing press. For us, the new technology consists of computers, satellites, and the Internet.

The sociological significance of technology goes far beyond the tool itself. *Technology sets the framework for a group's nonmaterial culture.* If a group's technology changes, so do the ways people's think and how they relate to one another. An example is gender relations. Through the centuries and throughout the world, it has been the custom (nonmaterial culture) for men to dominate women. Today's global communications (material culture) make this custom more difficult to maintain. For example, when Arab women watch Western television, they observe a freedom in gender relations that is unknown to them.

The use of new forms of communication by people who not long ago were cut off from events in the rest of the world is bound to change their *nonmaterial culture.* How do you think computers are changing this man's thinking and views of the world?

PhotoAlto/Alamy Royalty Free

As these women use e-mail and telephones to talk to one another about what they have seen, they both convey and create discontent, as well as feelings of sisterhood. These communications motivate some of them to agitate for social change.

In today's world, the long-accepted idea that it is proper to withhold rights on the basis of someone's sex can no longer be sustained. What usually lies beyond our awareness in this revolutionary change is the role of the new technology, which joins the world's nations into a global communications network.

Cultural Lag and Cultural Change

About three generations ago, sociologist William Ogburn (1922/1938) coined the term **cultural lag.** By this, Ogburn meant that not all parts of a culture change at the same pace. When one part of a culture changes, other parts lag behind.

Ogburn pointed out that *a group's material culture usually changes first, with the nonmaterial culture lagging behind.* This leaves the nonmaterial (or symbolic) culture playing a game of catch-up. For example, when we get sick, we can type our symptoms into a computer and get an immediate diagnosis and a recommended course of treatment. In some tests, computer programs outperform physicians. Yet our customs have not caught up with our technology, and we continue to visit the doctor's office.

Sometimes nonmaterial culture never does catch up. We can rigorously hold onto some outmoded form—one that once was needed, but that long ago was bypassed by technology. Have you ever wondered why our "school year" is nine months long, and why we take summers off? For most of us, this is "just the way it's always been," and we have never questioned it. But there is more to this custom than meets the eye. In the late 1800s, when universal schooling came about, the school year matched the technology of the time. Most parents were farmers, and for survival they needed their children's help at the crucial times of planting and harvesting. Today, generations later, when few people farm and there is no need for the "school year" to be so short, we still live with this cultural lag.

Technology and Cultural Leveling

For most of human history, communication was limited and travel slow. Consequently, in their relative isolation, human groups developed highly distinctive ways of life as they responded to the particular situations they faced. The unique characteristics they developed that distinguished one culture from another tended to change little over time. The Tasmanians, who live on a remote island off the coast of Australia, provide an extreme example. For thousands of years, they had no contact with other people. They were so isolated that they did not even know how to make clothing or fire (Edgerton 1992).

Except in such rare instances, humans have always had *some* contact with other groups. During these contacts, people learned from one another, adopting things they found desirable. In this process, called **cultural diffusion,** groups are most open to changes in their technology or material culture. They usually are eager, for example, to adopt superior weapons and tools. In remote jungles in South America one can find metal cooking pots, steel axes, and even bits of clothing spun in mills in South Carolina. Although the direction of cultural diffusion today is primarily from the West to other parts of the world, cultural diffusion is not a one-way street—as bagels, woks, hammocks, and sushi in the United States attest.

With today's travel and communications, cultural diffusion is occurring rapidly. Air travel has made it possible to journey around the globe in a matter of hours. In the not-so-distant past, a trip from the United States to Africa was so unusual that only a few

LITERATURE

"JUST THINK OF IT AS IF YOU'RE READING A LONG TEXT-MESSAGE."

© Dave Carpenter/www.CartoonStock.com

Technological advances are now so rapid that there can be cultural gaps between generations.

cultural lag Ogburn's term for human behavior lagging behind technological innovations

cultural diffusion the spread of cultural traits from one group to another; includes both material and nonmaterial cultural traits

This Barbie doll, sold in Japan, is dressed in a stage costume of a Japanese singer. As objects diffuse from one culture to another, they are modified to meet the tastes of the adoptive culture. In this instance, the modification has been done intentionally as part of the globalization of capitalism.

Peter Kneffel/dpa/Landov

cultural leveling the process by which cultures become similar to one another; refers especially to the process by which Western culture is being exported and diffused into other nations

adventurous people made it, and newspapers would herald their feat. Today, hundreds of thousands make the trip each year.

The changes in communication are no less vast. Communication used to be limited to face-to-face speech, written messages that were passed from hand to hand, and visual signals such as smoke or light that was reflected from mirrors. Despite newspapers and even the telegraph, people in some parts of the United States did not hear that the Civil War had ended until weeks and even months after it was over. Today's electronic communications transmit messages across the globe in a matter of seconds, and we learn almost instantaneously what is happening on the other side of the world. During the Iraq War, reporters traveled with U.S. soldiers, and for the first time in history, the public was able to view live video reports of battles as they took place and of people as they died.

Travel and communication bridge time and space to such an extent that there is almost no "other side of the world" anymore. One result is **cultural leveling,** a process in which cultures become similar to one another. The globalization of capitalism brings with it both technology and Western culture. Japan, for example, has adopted not only capitalism but also Western forms of dress and music, transforming it into a blend of Western and Eastern cultures.

Cultural leveling is apparent to any traveler. The Golden Arches of McDonald's welcome visitors to Tokyo, Paris, London, Madrid, Moscow, Hong Kong, and Beijing. When I visited a jungle village in India—no electricity, no running water, and so remote that the only entrance was by a footpath—I saw a young man sporting a cap with the Nike emblem.

Although the bridging of geography, time, and culture by electronic signals and the exportation of Western icons do not in and of themselves mark the end of traditional cultures, the inevitable result is some degree of *cultural leveling*. We are producing a blander, less distinctive way of life—U.S. culture with French, Japanese, and Brazilian accents, so to speak. Although the "cultural accent" remains, something vital is lost forever.

SUMMARY *and* REVIEW

What Is Culture?

All human groups possess **culture**—language, beliefs, values, norms, and material objects that are passed from one generation to the next. **Material culture** consists of objects (art, buildings, clothing, weapons, tools). **Nonmaterial (or symbolic) culture** is a group's ways of thinking and its patterns of behavior. **Ideal culture** is a group's ideal values, norms, and goals. **Real culture** is people's actual behavior, which often falls short of their cultural ideals.

What are cultural relativism and ethnocentrism?

People are **ethnocentric;** that is, they use their own culture as a yardstick for judging the ways of others. In contrast, those who embrace **cultural relativism** try to understand other cultures on those cultures' own terms.

Components of Symbolic Culture

What are the components of nonmaterial culture?

The central component is **symbols,** anything to which people attach meaning and that they use to communicate with others. Universally, the symbols of nonmaterial culture are **gestures, language, values, norms, sanctions, folkways,** and **mores.**

Why is language so significant to culture?

Language allows human experience to be goal-directed, cooperative, and cumulative. It also lets humans move beyond the present and share a past, future, and other common perspectives. According to the **Sapir-Whorf hypothesis,** language even shapes our thoughts and perceptions.

How do values, norms, sanctions, folkways, and mores reflect culture?

All groups have **values,** standards by which they define what is desirable or undesirable, and **norms,** rules or expectations about behavior. Groups use **positive sanctions** to show approval of those who follow their norms and **negative sanctions** to show disapproval of those who do not. Norms that are not strictly enforced are called **folkways,** while **mores** are norms to which groups demand conformity because they reflect core values.

Many Cultural Worlds

How do subcultures and countercultures differ?

A **subculture** is a group whose values and related behaviors distinguish its members from the general culture. A **counterculture** holds some values that stand in opposition to those of the dominant culture..

Values in U.S. Society

What are some core U.S. values?

Although the United States is a **pluralistic society,** made up of many groups, each with its own set of values, certain values dominate: achievement and success, individualism, hard work, efficiency and practicality, science and technology, material comfort, freedom, democracy, equality, group superiority, education, religiosity, and romantic love. Some values cluster together

(**value clusters**) to form a larger whole. **Value contradictions** (such as equality, sexism, and racism) indicate areas of tension, which are likely points of social change. Leisure, self-fulfillment, physical fitness, youthfulness, and concern for the environment are emerging core values. Core values do not change without opposition.

Cultural Universals

Do cultural universals exist?

Cultural universals are values, norms, or other cultural traits that are found in all cultures. Although all human groups have customs concerning cooking, childbirth, funerals, and so on, because these customs differ from one culture to another, there are no cultural universals.

Technology in the Global Village

How is technology changing culture?

William Ogburn coined the term **cultural lag** to describe how a group's nonmaterial culture lags behind its changing technology. With today's technological advances in travel and communications, **cultural diffusion** is occurring rapidly. This leads to **cultural leveling,** groups becoming similar as they adopt items from other cultures. Much of the richness of the world's diverse cultures is being lost in the process.

THINKING CRITICALLY

1. Do you favor ethnocentrism or cultural relativism? Explain your position.
2. Do you think that the language change in Miami, Florida, indicates the future of the United States? Why or why not?
3. Are you a member of any subcultures? Which one(s)? Why do you think that your group is a subculture? What is your group's relationship to the mainstream culture?

ADDITIONAL RESOURCES

What can you find in MySocLab? mysoclab www.mysoclab.com

- Complete Ebook
- Practice Tests and Video and Audio activities
- Mapping and Data Analysis exercises

- Sociology in the News
- Classic Readings in Sociology
- Research and Writing advice

Where Can I Read More on This Topic?

Borofsky, Robert, and Bruce Albert. *Yanomani: The Fierce Controversy and What We Can Learn from It.* Berkeley: University of California Press, 2006. The authors criticize the research on the Yanomani, including that by Chagnon in the next book, with an emphasis on anthropologists' lack of consideration for human rights.

Chagnon, Napoleon A. *Yanomamö: The Fierce People,* 5th ed. New York: Harcourt, Brace, Jovanovich, 1997. This account of a tribal people whose customs are extraordinarily different from ours will help you to see how arbitrary the choices are that underlie human culture. This research has aroused enormous controversy over human rights.

Davis, Wade, K. David Harrison, and Catherine Herbert Howell, eds. *Book of Peoples of the World: A Guide to Cultures.* New York: Random House, 2009. A panoramic view of over 200 ethnic groups across the world, from the Kallawaya of the Peruvian Andes, numbering fewer than 1,000, to the Bengalis of India, a group of 172 million.

Fulbeck, Kip. *Permanence: Tattoo Portraits.* New York: Chronicle Books, 2008. Through photographs of tattoos and the accounts of those who have those tattoos, you can gain insight and understanding of the tattoo subcultures, which are being adopted and modified by mainstreamers.

Griswold, Wendy. *Cultures and Societies in a Changing World,* 3rd ed. Thousand Oaks, Calif.: Pine Forge Press, 2008. Analyzes how culture shapes people's individual identity, including their norms, values, beliefs, and behavior; also indicates how globalization is changing cultures.

Inglis, David. *Culture and Everyday Life.* Oxford, UK: Routledge, 2006. An overview of how culture shapes, influences, and structures our everyday lives.

Jacobs, Mark D., and Nancy Weiss Hanrahan, eds. *The Blackwell Companion to the Sociology of Culture.* Malden, Mass.: Blackwell, 2005. The authors of these articles explore cultural systems, everyday life, identity, collective memory, and citizenship in a global economy.

Lenski, Gerhard, and Patrick Nolan. *Human Societies,* 10th ed. Boulder, Colo.: Paradigm, 2006. This wide-ranging examination of the fundamentals of human societies also analyzes social change, including globalization, outsourcing, the end of cheap oil, Islamic fundamentalism, and the rise of China.

Zellner, William W. *Countercultures: A Sociological Analysis.* New York: St. Martin's Press, 1995. The author's analysis of skinheads, the Ku Klux Klan, survivalists, satanists, the Church of Scientology, and the Unification Church (Moonies) helps us understand why people join countercultures.

Journals

Cultural Sociology and *Space for Difference* focus on sociological analyses of culture, with crossovers into art history, gender studies, human geography, racism, literary studies, and social activism.

Socialization

Socialization

Florida

© Jeff Greenberg/The Image Works

The old man was horrified when he found out. Life never had been good since his daughter lost her hearing when she was just 2 years old. She couldn't even talk—just fluttered her hands around trying to tell him things.

Over the years, he had gotten used to that. But now . . . he shuddered at the thought of her being pregnant. No one would be willing to marry her; he knew that. And the neighbors, their tongues would never stop wagging. Everywhere he went, he could hear people talking behind his back.

> Her behavior toward strangers, especially men, was almost that of a wild animal, manifesting much fear and hostility.

If only his wife were still alive, maybe she could come up with something. What should he do? He couldn't just kick his daughter out into the street.

After the baby was born, the old man tried to shake his feelings, but they wouldn't let loose. Isabelle was a pretty name, but every time he looked at the baby he felt sick to his stomach.

He hated doing it, but there was no way out. His daughter and her baby would have to live in the attic.

Unfortunately, this is a true story. Isabelle was discovered in Ohio in 1938 when she was about 6½ years old, living in a dark room with her deaf-mute mother. Isabelle couldn't talk, but she did use gestures to communicate with her mother. An inadequate diet and lack of sunshine had given Isabelle a disease called rickets.

> [Her legs] were so bowed that as she stood erect the soles of her shoes came nearly flat together, and she got about with a skittering gait. Her behavior toward strangers, especially men, was almost that of a wild animal, manifesting much fear and hostility. In lieu of speech she made only a strange croaking sound. (Davis 1940/2007:156–157)

When the newspapers reported this case, sociologist Kingsley Davis decided to find out what had happened to Isabelle after her discovery. We'll come back to that later, but first let's use the case of Isabelle to gain insight into human nature.

Society Makes Us Human

"What do you mean, society makes us human?" is probably what you are asking. "That sounds ridiculous. I was born a human." The meaning of this statement will become more apparent as we get into the chapter. Let's start by considering what is human about human nature. How much of a person's characteristics comes from "nature" (heredity) and how much from "nurture" (the **social environment,** contact with others)? Experts are trying to answer the nature–nurture question by studying identical twins who were separated at birth and reared in different environments, such as those discussed in the Down-to-Earth Sociology box on the next page. Another way is to examine children who have had little human contact. Let's consider such children.

Feral Children

> The naked child was found in the forest, walking on all fours, eating grass and lapping water from the river. When he saw a small animal, he pounced on it. Growling, he ripped at it with his teeth. Tearing chunks from the body, he chewed them ravenously.

This is an apt description of reports that have come in over the centuries. Supposedly, these **feral** (wild) **children** could not speak; they bit, scratched, growled, and walked on all fours. They drank by lapping water, ate grass, tore ravenously at raw meat, and showed insensitivity to pain and cold. Why am I even mentioning stories that sound so exaggerated?

It is because of what happened in 1798. In that year, such a child was found in the forests of Aveyron, France. "The wild boy of Aveyron," as he became known, would have been written off as another folk myth, except that French scientists took the child to a laboratory and studied him. Like the feral children in the earlier informal reports, this child, too, gave no indication of feeling the cold. Most startling, though, the boy would growl when he saw a small animal, pounce on it, and devour it uncooked. Even today, the scientists' detailed reports make fascinating reading (Itard 1962).

Ever since I read Itard's account of this boy, I've been fascinated by the seemingly fantastic possibility that animals could rear human children. In 2002, I received a report from a contact in Cambodia that a feral child had been found in the jungles. When I had the opportunity the following year to visit the child and interview his caregivers, I grabbed it. The boy's photo is to the left. If we were untouched by society, would we be like feral children? By nature, would our behavior be like that of wild animals? That is the sociological question. Unable to study feral children, sociologists have studied isolated children, like Isabelle in our opening vignette. Let's see what we can learn from them.

One of the reasons I went to Cambodia was to interview a feral child—the boy shown here—who supposedly had been raised by monkeys. When I arrived at the remote location where the boy was living, I was disappointed to find that the story was only partially true. During its reign of terror, the Khmer Rouge had shot and killed the boy's parents, leaving him, at about the age of two, abandoned on an island. Some months later, villagers found him in the care of monkeys. They shot the female monkey who was carrying the boy. Not quite a feral child—but the closest I'll ever come to one.

Isolated Children

What can isolated children tell us about human nature? We can first conclude that humans have no natural language, for Isabelle and others like her are unable to speak.

But maybe Isabelle was mentally impaired. Perhaps she simply was unable to progress through the usual stages of development. It certainly looked that way—she scored practically zero on her first intelligence test. But after a few months of language training, Isabelle was able to speak in short sentences. In just a year, she could write a few words, do simple addition, and retell stories after hearing them. Seven months later, she had a vocabulary of almost 2,000 words. In just two years, Isabelle reached the intellectual level that is normal for her age. She then went on to school, where she was "bright, cheerful, energetic . . . and participated in all school activities as normally as other children" (Davis 1940/2007:157–158).

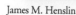

James M. Henslin

Down-to-Earth Sociology
Heredity or Environment? The Case of Jack and Oskar, Identical Twins

Identical twins are identical in their genetic heritage. They are born when one fertilized egg divides to produce two embryos. If heredity determines personality—or attitudes, temperament, skills, and intelligence—then identical twins should be identical not only in their looks but also in these characteristics.

The fascinating case of Jack and Oskar helps us unravel this mystery. From their experience, we can see the far-reaching effects of the environment—how social experiences override biology.

Jack Yufe and Oskar Stohr are identical twins. Born in 1932 to a Roman Catholic mother and a Jewish father, they were separated as babies after their parents divorced. Jack was reared in Trinidad by his father. There, he learned loyalty to Jews and hatred of Hitler and the Nazis. After the war, Jack and his father moved to Israel. When he was 17, Jack joined a kibbutz and later served in the Israeli army.

Oskar's upbringing was a mirror image of Jack's. Oskar was reared in Czechoslovakia by his mother's mother, who was a strict Catholic. When Oskar was a toddler, Hitler annexed this area of Czechoslovakia, and Oskar learned to love Hitler and to hate Jews. He joined the Hitler Youth (a sort of Boy Scout organization, except that this one was designed to instill the "virtues" of patriotism, loyalty, obedience—and hatred).

In 1954, the two brothers met. It was a short meeting, and Jack had been warned not to tell Oskar that they were Jews. Twenty-five years later, in 1979, when they were 47 years old, social scientists at the University of Minnesota brought them together again. These researchers figured that because Jack and Oskar had the same genes, any differences they showed would have to be the result of their environment—their different social experiences.

Not only did Jack and Oskar hold different attitudes toward the war, Hitler, and Jews, but their basic orientations to life were also different. In their politics, Jack was liberal, while Oskar was more conservative. Jack was a workaholic, while Oskar enjoyed leisure. And, as you can predict, Jack was proud of being a Jew. Oskar, who by this time knew that he was a Jew, wouldn't even mention it.

The question of the relative influence of heredity and the environment in human behavior has fascinated and plagued researchers. To try to answer this question, researchers have studied identical twins. In this photo, what behaviors can you see that are clearly due to the environment? Any that are due to biology?

Frank Siteman Photography

That would seem to settle the matter. But there were other things. As children, Jack and Oskar had both excelled at sports but had difficulty with math. They also had the same rate of speech, and both liked sweet liqueur and spicy foods. Strangely, both flushed the toilet both before and after using it, and they both enjoyed startling people by sneezing in crowded elevators.

For Your Consideration

Heredity or environment? How much influence does each have? The question is not yet settled, but at this point it seems fair to conclude that the *limits* of certain physical and mental abilities are established by heredity (such as ability at sports and aptitude for mathematics), while attitudes are the result of the environment. Basic temperament, though, seems to be inherited. Although the answer is still fuzzy, we can put it this way: For some parts of life, the blueprint is drawn by heredity; but even here the environment can redraw those lines. For other parts, the individual is a blank slate, and it is up to the environment to determine what is written on that slate.

Sources: Based on Begley 1979; Chen 1979; Wright 1995; Segal and Hershberger 2005; De Moor et al. 2007.

Language is the key to human development. Without language, people have no mechanism for developing thought and communicating their experiences. Unlike animals, humans have no instincts that take the place of language. If an individual lacks language, he or she lives in a world of internal silence, without shared ideas, lacking connections to others.

Without language, there can be no culture—no shared way of life—and culture is the key to what people become. Each of us possesses a biological heritage, but this heritage does not determine specific behaviors, attitudes, or values. It is our culture that superimposes the specifics of what we become onto our biological heritage.

Institutionalized Children

Other than language, what else is required for a child to develop into what we consider a healthy, balanced, intelligent human being? We find part of the answer in an intriguing experiment from the 1930s. Back then, orphanages were common because parents were more likely than now to die before their children were grown. Children reared in orphanages tended to have low IQs. "Common sense" (which is unreliable) made it obvious that their low intelligence was because of poor brains ("They're just born that way"). But two psychologists, H. M. Skeels and H. B. Dye (1939), began to suspect a social cause.

Skeels (1966) provides this account of a "good" orphanage in Iowa, one where he and Dye were consultants:

> Until about six months, they were cared for in the infant nursery. The babies were kept in standard hospital cribs that often had protective sheeting on the sides, thus effectively limiting visual stimulation; no toys or other objects were hung in the infants' line of vision. Human interactions were limited to busy nurses who, with the speed born of practice and necessity, changed diapers or bedding, bathed and medicated the infants, and fed them efficiently with propped bottles.

Perhaps, thought Skeels and Dye, the problem was the absence of stimulating social interaction, not the children's brains. To test their controversial idea, they selected thirteen infants who were so mentally slow that no one wanted to adopt them. They placed them in an institution for mentally retarded women. They assigned each infant, then about 19 months old, to a separate ward of women ranging in mental age from 5 to 12 and in chronological age from 18 to 50. The women were pleased with this. They enjoyed taking care of the infants' physical needs—diapering, feeding, and so on. And they also loved to play with the children. They cuddled them and showered them with attention. They even competed to see which ward would have "its baby" walking or talking first. In each ward, one woman became particularly attached to the child and figuratively adopted him or her:

> As a consequence, an intense one-to-one adult–child relationship developed, which was supplemented by the less intense but frequent interactions with the other adults in the environment. Each child had some one person with whom he [or she] was identified and who was particularly interested in him [or her] and his [or her] achievements. (Skeels 1966)

The researchers left a control group of twelve infants at the orphanage. These infants received the usual care. They also had low IQs, but they were considered somewhat higher in

Infants in this orphanage in Siem Reap, Cambodia, are drugged and hung in these mesh baskets for up to ten hours a day. The staff of the orphanage pockets most of the money contributed by Westerners for the children's care. The treatment of these children is likely to affect their ability to reason and to function as adults.

Zoriah/The Image Works

intelligence than the thirteen in the experimental group. Two and a half years later, Skeels and Dye tested all the children's intelligence. Their findings are startling: Those cared for by the women in the institution gained an average of 28 IQ points while those who remained in the orphanage lost 30 points.

What happened after these children were grown? Did these initial differences matter? Twenty-one years later, Skeels and Dye did a follow-up study. The twelve in the control group, those who had remained in the orphanage, averaged less than a third-grade education. Four still lived in state institutions, and the others held low-level jobs. Only two had married. The thirteen in the experimental group, those cared for by the institutionalized women, had an average education of twelve grades (about normal for that period). Five had completed one or more years of college. One had even gone to graduate school. Eleven had married. All thirteen were self-supporting or were homemakers (Skeels 1966). Apparently, "high intelligence" depends on early, close relations with other humans.

A recent experiment in India confirms this early research. Many of India's orphanages are like those that Skeels and Dye studied—dismal places where unattended children lie in bed all day. When experimenters added stimulating play and interaction to the children's activities, the children's motor skills improved and their IQs increased (Taneja et al. 2002). The longer that children lack stimulating interaction, though, the more difficulty they have intellectually (Meese 2005).

Let's consider Genie, a 13-year-old girl who had been locked in a small room and tied to a chair since she was 20 months old:

Apparently Genie's father (70 years old when Genie was discovered in 1970) hated children. He probably had caused the death of two of Genie's siblings. Her 50-year-old mother was partially blind and frightened of her husband. Genie could not speak, did not know how to chew, was unable to stand upright, and could not straighten her hands and legs. On intelligence tests, she scored at the level of a 1-year-old. After intensive training, Genie learned to walk and to say simple sentences (although they were garbled). Genie's language remained primitive as she grew up. She would take anyone's property if it appealed to her, and she went to the bathroom wherever she wanted. At the age of 21, she was sent to a home for adults who cannot live alone. (Pines 1981)

In Sum: From Genie's pathetic story and from the research on institutionalized children, we can conclude that the basic human traits of intelligence and the ability to establish close bonds with others depend on early interaction with other humans. In addition, there seems to be a period prior to age 13 in which children must learn language and experience human bonding if they are to develop normal intelligence and the ability to be sociable and follow social norms.

Deprived Animals

Finally, let's consider animals that have been deprived of normal interaction. In a series of experiments with rhesus monkeys, psychologists Harry and Margaret Harlow demonstrated the importance of early learning. The Harlows (1962) raised baby monkeys in isolation. They gave each monkey two artificial mothers. One "mother" was only a wire frame with a wooden head, but it did have a nipple from which the baby could nurse. The frame of the other "mother," which had no bottle, was covered with soft terrycloth. To obtain food, the baby monkeys nursed at the wire frame.

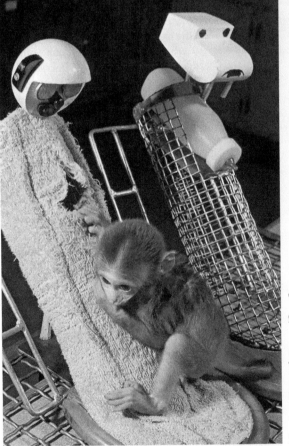

Like humans, monkeys need interaction to thrive. Those raised in isolation are unable to interact with others. In this photograph, we see one of the monkeys described in the text. Purposefully frightened by the experimenter, the monkey has taken refuge in the soft terrycloth draped over an artificial "mother."

Nina Leen/Time Life Pictures/Getty Images

When the Harlows (1965) frightened the baby monkeys with a mechanical bear or dog, the babies did not run to the wire frame "mother." Instead, as shown in the photo on the previous page, they would cling pathetically to their terrycloth "mother." The Harlows concluded that infant–mother bonding is not the result of feeding but, rather, of what they termed "intimate physical contact." To most of us, this phrase means cuddling.

The monkeys raised in isolation could not adjust to monkey life. Placed with other monkeys when they were grown, they didn't know how to participate in "monkey interaction"— to play and to engage in pretend fights—and the other monkeys rejected them. They didn't even know how to have sexual intercourse, despite futile attempts to do so. The experimenters designed a special device, which allowed some females to become pregnant. Their isolation, however, made them "ineffective, inadequate, and brutal mothers." They "struck their babies, kicked them, or crushed the babies against the cage floor."

In one of their many experiments, the Harlows isolated baby monkeys for different lengths of time and then put them in with the other monkeys. Monkeys that had been isolated for shorter periods (about three months) were able to adjust to normal monkey life. They learned to play and engage in pretend fights. Those isolated for six months or more, however, couldn't make the adjustment, and the other monkeys rejected them. In other words, the longer the period of isolation, the more difficult its effects are to overcome. In addition, there seems to be a critical learning stage: If that stage is missed, it may be impossible to compensate for what has been lost. This may have been the case with Genie.

Because humans are not monkeys, we must be careful about extrapolating from animal studies to human behavior. The Harlow experiments, however, support what we know about children who are reared in isolation.

In Sum: Babies do not develop "naturally" into social adults. If children are reared in isolation, their bodies grow, but they become little more than big animals. Without the concepts that language provides, they can't grasp relationships between people (the "connections" we call brother, sister, parent, friend, teacher, and so on). And without warm, friendly interactions, they can't bond with others. They don't become "friendly" or cooperate with others. In short, it is through human contact that people learn to be members of the human community. This process by which we learn the ways of society (or of particular groups), called **socialization,** is what sociologists have in mind when they say "Society makes us human."

Further keys to understanding how society makes us human are our self-concept, ability to "take the role of others," reasoning, morality, and emotions. Let's look at how we develop these capacities.

Socialization into the Self and Mind

When you were born, you had no ideas. You didn't know that you were a son or daughter. You didn't even know that you were a he or she. How did you develop a **self,** your image of who you are? How did you develop your ability to reason? Let's find out.

Cooley and the Looking-Glass Self

About a hundred years ago, Charles Horton Cooley (1864–1929), a symbolic interactionist who taught at the University of Michigan, concluded that the self is part of how *society* makes us human. He said that *our sense of self develops from interaction with others.* To describe the process by which this unique aspect of "humanness" develops, Cooley (1902) coined the term **looking-glass self.** He summarized this idea in the following couplet:

> **Each to each a looking-glass**
> **Reflects the other that doth pass.**

The looking-glass self contains three elements:

1. *We imagine how we appear to those around us.* For example, we may think that others perceive us as witty or dull.

---

socialization the process by which people learn the characteristics of their group—the knowledge, skills, attitudes, values, norms, and actions thought appropriate for them

self the unique human capacity of being able to see ourselves "from the outside"; the views we internalize of how others see us

looking-glass self a term coined by Charles Horton Cooley to refer to the process by which our self develops through internalizing others' reactions to us

taking the role of the other putting oneself in someone else's shoes; understanding how someone else feels and thinks and thus anticipating how that person will act

significant other an individual who significantly influences someone else's life

generalized other the norms, values, attitudes, and expectations of people "in general"; the child's ability to take the role of the generalized other is a significant step in the development of a self

2. *We interpret others' reactions.* We come to conclusions about how others evaluate us. Do they like us for being witty? Do they dislike us for being dull?

3. *We develop a self-concept.* How we interpret others' reactions to us frames our feelings and ideas about ourselves. A favorable reflection in this *social mirror* leads to a positive self-concept; a negative reflection leads to a negative self-concept.

Note that the development of the self does *not* depend on accurate evaluations. Even if we grossly misinterpret how others think about us, those misjudgments become part of our self-concept. Note also that *although the self-concept begins in childhood, its development is an ongoing, lifelong process.* During our everyday lives, we monitor how others react to us. As we do so, we continually modify the self. The self, then, is never a finished product—it is always in process, even into our old age.

Mead and Role Taking

Another symbolic interactionist, George Herbert Mead (1863–1931), who taught at the University of Chicago, pointed out how important play is as we develop a self. As we play with others, we learn to **take the role of the other.** That is, we learn to put ourselves in someone else's shoes—to understand how someone else feels and thinks and to anticipate how that person will act.

This doesn't happen overnight. We develop this ability over a period of years (Mead 1934; Denzin 2007). Psychologist John Flavel (1968) asked 8- and 14-year-olds to explain a board game to children who were blindfolded and to others who were not. The 14-year-olds gave more detailed instructions to those who were blindfolded, but the 8-year-olds gave the same instructions to everyone. The younger children could not yet take the role of the other, while the older children could.

As we develop this ability, at first we can take only the role of **significant others,** individuals who significantly influence our lives, such as parents or siblings. By assuming their roles during play, such as dressing up in our parents' clothing, we cultivate the ability to put ourselves in the place of significant others.

As our self gradually develops, we internalize the expectations of more and more people. Our ability to take the role of others eventually extends to being able to take the role of "the group as a whole." Mead used the term **generalized other** to refer to our perception of how people in general think of us.

Taking the role of others is essential if we are to become cooperative members of human groups—whether they be our family, friends, or co-workers. This ability allows us to modify our behavior by anticipating how others will react—something Genie never learned.

As Figure 1 illustrates, we go through three stages as we learn to take the role of the other:

1. *Imitation.* Under the age of 3, we can only mimic others. We do not yet have a sense of self separate from others, and we can only imitate people's gestures and words. (This stage is actually not role taking, but it prepares us for it.)

2. *Play.* During the second stage, from the ages of about 3 to 6, we pretend to take the roles of specific people. We might pretend that we are a firefighter, a wrestler, a nurse, Supergirl, Spiderman, a princess, and so on. We also like costumes at this stage and enjoy dressing up in our parents' clothing, or tying a towel around our neck to "become" Superman or Wonder Woman.

3. *Team Games.* This third stage, organized play, or team games, begins roughly when we enter school. The

FIGURE 1 How We Learn to Take the Role of the Other: Mead's Three Stages

Stage 1: Imitation
Children under age 3
No sense of self
Imitate others

Stage 2: Play
Ages 3 to 6
Play "pretend" others
(princess, Spiderman, etc.)

Stage 3: Team Games
After about age 6 or 7
Team games
("organized play")
Learn to take multiple roles

To help his students understand the term *generalized other*, Mead used baseball as an illustration. Why are team sports and organized games excellent examples to use in explaining this concept?

Ariel Skelley/Corbis

75

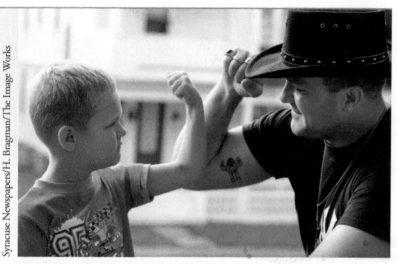

Mead analyzed *taking the role of the other* as an essential part of learning to be a full-fledged member of society. At first, we are able to take the role only of *significant others*, as this child is doing. Later we develop the capacity to take the role of the *generalized other*, which is essential not only for cooperation but also for the control of antisocial desires.

significance for the self is that to play these games we must be able to take multiple roles. One of Mead's favorite examples was that of a baseball game, in which each player must be able to take the role of all the other players. To play baseball, it isn't enough that we know our own role; we also must be able to anticipate what everyone else on the field will do when the ball is hit or thrown.

Mead also said there were two parts of the self, the "I" and the "me." The "*I*" is *the self as subject*, the active, spontaneous, creative part of the self. In contrast, the "*me*" is *the self as object*. It is made up of attitudes we internalize from our interactions with others. Mead chose these pronouns because in English "I" is the active agent, as in "I shoved him," while "me" is the object of action, as in "He shoved me." Mead stressed that we are not passive in the socialization process. We are not like robots, with programmed software shoved into us. Rather, our "I" is active. It evaluates the reactions of others and organizes them into a unified whole. Mead added that the "I" even monitors the "me," fine-tuning our ideas and attitudes to help us better meet what others expect of us.

In Sum: In studying the details, you don't want to miss the main point, which some find startling: *Both our self and our mind are social products.* Mead stressed that we cannot think without symbols. But where do these symbols come from? Only from society, which gives us our symbols by giving us language. If society did not provide the symbols, we would not be able to think and so would not possess a self-concept or that entity we call the mind. The self and mind, then, like language, are products of society.

Piaget and the Development of Reasoning

Shown here is Jean Piaget with one of the children he studied in his analysis of the development of human reasoning.

The development of the mind—specifically, how we learn to reason—was studied in detail by Jean Piaget (1896–1980). This Swiss psychologist noticed that when young children take intelligence tests, they often give similar wrong answers. This set him to thinking that the children might be using some consistent, but incorrect, reasoning. It might even indicate that children go through some natural process as they learn how to reason.

Stimulated by such an intriguing possibility, Piaget set up a laboratory where he could give children of different ages problems to solve (Piaget 1950, 1954; Flavel et al. 2002). After years of testing, Piaget concluded that children do go through a natural process as they develop their ability to reason. This process has four stages. (If you mentally substitute "reasoning skills" for the term *operational* as we review these stages, Piaget's findings will be easier to understand.)

1. **The sensorimotor stage** (from birth to about age 2) During this stage, our understanding is limited to direct contact—sucking, touching, listening, looking. We aren't able to "think." During the first part of this stage, we do not even know that our bodies are separate from the environment. Indeed, we have yet to discover that we have toes. Neither can we recognize cause and effect. That is, we do not know that our actions cause something to happen.

2. **The preoperational stage** (from about age 2 to age 7) During this stage, we *develop the ability to use symbols*. However, we do not yet understand common concepts such as size, speed, or causation. Although we are learning to count, we do not really understand what

numbers mean. Nor do we yet have the ability to take the role of the other. Piaget asked preoperational children to describe a clay model of a mountain range. They did just fine. But when he asked them to describe how the mountain range looked from where another child was sitting, they couldn't do it. They could only repeat what they saw from their view.

3. **The concrete operational stage** (from the age of about 7 to 12) Our reasoning abilities are more developed, but they remain *concrete*. We can now understand numbers, size, causation, and speed, and we are able to take the role of the other. We can even play team games. Unless we have concrete examples, however, we are unable to talk about concepts such as truth, honesty, or justice. We can explain why Jane's answer was a lie, but we cannot describe what truth itself is.

4. **The formal operational stage** (after the age of about 12) We now are capable of abstract thinking. We can talk about concepts, come to conclusions based on general principles, and use rules to solve abstract problems. During this stage, we are likely to become young philosophers (Kagan 1984). If we were shown a photo of a slave during our concrete operational stage, we might have said, "That's wrong!" Now at the formal operational stage we are likely to add, "If our county was founded on equality, how could anyone own slaves?"

Global Aspects of the Self and Reasoning

Cooley's conclusions about the looking-glass self appear to be true for everyone around the world. So do Mead's conclusions about role taking and the mind and self as social products, although researchers are finding that the self may develop earlier than Mead indicated. The stages of reasoning that Piaget identified probably also occur worldwide, although researchers have found that the stages are not as distinct as Piaget concluded and the ages at which individuals enter the stages differ from one person to another (Flavel et al. 2002). Even during the sensorimotor stage, for example, children show early signs of reasoning, which may indicate an innate ability that is wired into the brain. Although Piaget's theory is being refined, his contribution remains: *A basic structure underlies the way we develop reasoning, and children all over the world begin with the concrete and move to the abstract.* Interestingly, some people seem to get stuck in the concreteness of the third stage and never reach the fourth stage of abstract thinking (Kohlberg and Gilligan 1971; Suizzo 2000). College, for example, nurtures the fourth stage, and people with this experience apparently have more ability for abstract thought. Social experiences, then, can modify these stages.

Learning Personality, Morality, and Emotions

Our personality, morality, and emotions are vital aspects of who we are. Let's look at how we learn these essential aspects of our being.

Freud and the Development of Personality

Along with the development of the mind and the self comes the development of the personality. Sigmund Freud (1856–1939) developed a theory of the origin of personality that has had a major impact on Western thought. Freud, a physician in Vienna in the early 1900s, founded *psychoanalysis,* a technique for treating emotional problems through long-term exploration of the subconscious mind. Let's look at his theory.

Freud believed that personality consists of three elements. Each child is born with the first element, an **id,** Freud's term for inborn drives that cause us to seek self-gratification. The id of the newborn is evident in its cries of hunger or pain. The pleasure-seeking id operates throughout life. It demands the immediate fulfillment of basic needs: food, safety, attention, sex, and so on.

id Freud's term for our inborn basic drives

77

Mary Evans/The Image Works

Sigmund Freud in 1932 in Hochroterd, Austria. Although Freud was one of the most influential theorists of the 20th century, most of his ideas have been discarded.

The id's drive for immediate gratification, however, runs into a roadblock: primarily the needs of other people, especially those of the parents. To adapt to these constraints, a second component of the personality emerges, which Freud called the ego. The **ego** is the balancing force between the id and the demands of society that suppress it. The ego also serves to balance the id and the **superego,** the third component of the personality, more commonly called the *conscience.*

The superego represents *culture within us,* the norms and values we have internalized from our social groups. As the *moral* component of the personality, the superego provokes feelings of guilt or shame when we break social rules, or pride and self-satisfaction when we follow them.

According to Freud, when the id gets out of hand, we follow our desires for pleasure and break society's norms. When the superego gets out of hand, we become overly rigid in following those norms and end up wearing a straitjacket of rules that inhibit our lives. The ego, the balancing force, tries to prevent either the superego or the id from dominating. In the emotionally healthy individual, the ego succeeds in balancing these conflicting demands of the id and the superego. In the maladjusted individual, the ego fails to control the conflict between the id and the superego. Either the id or the superego dominates this person, leading to internal confusion and problem behaviors.

Sociological Evaluation. Sociologists appreciate Freud's emphasis on socialization—his assertion that the social group into which we are born transmits norms and values that restrain our biological drives. Sociologists, however, object to the view that inborn and subconscious motivations are the primary reasons for human behavior. *This denies the central principle of sociology:* that factors such as social class (income, education, and occupation) and people's roles in groups underlie their behavior (Epstein 1988; Bush and Simmons 1990).

Feminist sociologists have been especially critical of Freud. Although what I just summarized applies to both females and males, Freud assumed that what is "male" is "normal." He even referred to females as inferior, castrated males (Chodorow 1990; Gerhard 2000). It is obvious that sociologists need to continue to research how we develop personality.

Kohlberg, Gilligan, and the Development of Morality

If you have observed young children, you know that they want immediate gratification and show little or no concern for others. ("Mine!" a 2-year-old will shout, as she grabs a toy from another child.) Yet, at a later age this same child will become considerate of others and try to be fair in her play. How does this change happen?

Kohlberg's Theory. Psychologist Lawrence Kohlberg (1975, 1984, 1986; Reed 2008) concluded that we go through a sequence of stages as we develop morality. Building on Piaget's work, he found that children start in the *amoral stage* I just described. For them, there is no right or wrong, just personal needs to be satisfied. From about ages 7 to 10, children are in what Kohlberg called a *preconventional stage.* They have learned rules, and they follow them to stay out of trouble. They view right and wrong as what pleases or displeases their parents, friends, and teachers. Their concern is to avoid punishment. At

ego Freud's term for a balancing force between the id and the demands of society

superego Freud's term for the conscience; the internalized norms and values of our social groups about age 10, they enter the *conventional stage*. During this period, morality means following the norms and values they have learned. In the *postconventional stage,* which Kohlberg says most people don't reach, individuals reflect on abstract principles of right and wrong and judge people's behavior according to these principles.

Gilligan and Gender Differences in Morality.   Carol Gilligan, another psychologist, grew uncomfortable with Kohlberg's conclusions. They just didn't match her own experience. Then she noticed that Kohlberg had studied only boys. By this point, more women had become social scientists, and they had begun to question a common assumption of male researchers, that research on boys would apply to girls as well.

Gilligan (1982, 1990) decided to find out if there were differences in how men and women looked at morality. After interviewing about 200 men and women, she concluded that women are more likely to evaluate morality in terms of *personal relationships*. Women want to know how an action affects others. They are more concerned with personal loyalties and with the harm that might come to loved ones. Men, in contrast, tend to think more along the lines of *abstract principles* that define right and wrong. As they see things, an act either matches or violates a code of ethics, and personal relationships have little to do with the matter.

Researchers tested Gilligan's conclusions. They found that *both* men and women use personal relationships and abstract principles when they make moral judgments (Wark and Krebs 1996). Although Gilligan no longer supports her original position (Brannon 1999), the matter is not yet settled. Some researchers have found differences in how men and women make moral judgments (White 1999; Jaffee and Hyde 2000). Others stress that both men and women learn cultural forms of moral reasoning (Tappan 2006).

As with personality, in this vital area of human development, sociological research is also notably absent.

Socialization into Emotions

Emotions, too, are an essential aspect of who we become. Sociologists who research this area of our "humanness" find that emotions are not simply the results of biology. Like the mind, emotions depend on socialization (Hochschild 2008). This may sound strange. Don't all people get angry? Doesn't everyone cry? Don't we all feel guilt, shame, sadness, happiness, fear? What has socialization to do with emotions?

Global Emotions.   At first, it may look as though socialization is not relevant, that we simply express universal feelings. Paul Ekman (1980), a psychologist who studied emotions in several countries, concluded that everyone experiences six basic emotions: anger, disgust, fear, happiness, sadness, and surprise. He also observed that we all show the same facial expressions when we feel these emotions. A person from Peru, for example, could tell from just the look on an American's face that she is angry, disgusted, or fearful, and we could tell from the Peruvian's face that he is happy, sad, or surprised. Because we all show the same facial expressions when we experience these six emotions, Ekman concluded that they are wired into our biology.

Expressing Emotions.   If we have universal facial expressions to express basic emotions, then this is biology, something that Darwin noted back in the 1800s (Horwitz and Wakefield 2007:41). What, then, does sociology have to do with them? Facial expressions are only one way by which we show emotions. We also use our bodies, voices, and gestures.

> Jane and Sushana have been best friends since high school. They were hardly ever apart until Sushana married and moved to another state a year ago. Jane has been waiting eagerly at the arrival gate for Sushana's flight, which has been delayed. When Sushana exits, she and Jane hug one another, making "squeals of glee" and even jumping a bit.

If you couldn't tell from their names that these were women, you could tell from their behavior. To express delighted surprise, U.S. women are allowed to make "squeals of glee" in public places and to jump as they hug. In contrast, in the exact circumstances, U.S. men

James Marshall/The Image Works | Elie Bernager/Digital Vision/ Getty Images Royalty Free | AP Images/Mary Altaffer | AP Images/Laurent Rebours | Tim Graham Picture Library/ Getty Images

What emotions are these people expressing? Are these emotions global? Is their way of expressing them universal?

are expected to shake hands, and they might even give a brief hug. If they gave out "squeals of glee," they would be violating a fundamental "gender rule."

In addition to "gender rules" for expressing emotions, there also are "rules" of culture, social class, relationships, and settings. Consider *culture*. Two close Japanese friends who meet after a long separation don't shake hands or hug—they bow. Two Arab men will kiss. *Social class* is so significant that it, too, cuts across other lines, even gender. Upon seeing a friend after a long absence, upper-class women and men are likely to be more reserved in expressing their delight than are lower-class women and men. *Relationships* also make a big difference. We express our feelings more openly if we are with close friends, more guardedly if we are at a staff meeting with the corporate CEO. The *setting*, then, is also important, with each setting having its own "rules" about emotions. As you know, the emotions we can express at a rock concert differ considerably from those we can express in a classroom. A good part of our socialization during childhood centers on learning our culture's *feeling rules*.

What We Feel

> Joan, a U.S. woman who had been married for seven years, had no children. When she finally gave birth and the doctor handed her a healthy girl, she was almost overcome with happiness. Tafadzwa, in Zimbabwe, had been married for seven years and had no children. When the doctor handed her a healthy girl, she was almost overcome with sadness.

The effects of socialization on our emotions go much deeper than guiding how, where, and when we express our feelings. From this example, you can see that socialization also affects *what* we feel (Clark 1997; Shields 2002). To understand why the woman in Zimbabwe felt sadness, you need to know that in her culture to not give birth to a male child is serious. It lowers her social status and is a good reason for her husband to divorce her (Horwitz and Wakefield 2007:43).

People in one culture may even learn to experience feelings that are unknown in another culture. For example, the Ifaluk, who live on the western Caroline Islands of Micronesia, use the word *fago* to refer to the feelings they have when they see someone suffer. This comes close to what we call sympathy or compassion. But the Ifaluk also use this term to refer to what they feel when they are with someone who has high status, someone they highly respect or admire (Kagan 1984). To us, these are two distinct emotions, and they require separate words to express them.

Research Needed. Although Ekman identified six emotions as universal in feeling and facial expression, I suspect that there are more. It is likely that all people around the world have similar feelings and facial expressions when they experience helplessness, despair, confusion, and shock. We need cross-cultural research to find out whether these are universal emotions. We also need research into how culture guides us in feeling and expressing emotions.

Society Within Us: The Self and Emotions as Social Control

Much of our socialization is intended to turn us into conforming members of society. Socialization into the self and emotions is essential to this process, for both the self and our emotions mold our behavior. Although we like to think that we are "free," consider for a moment just some of the factors that influence how you act: the expectations of friends and parents, of neighbors and teachers; classroom norms and college rules; city, state, and federal laws. For example, if in a moment of intense frustration, or out of a devilish desire to shock people, you wanted to tear off your clothes and run naked down the street, what would stop you?

The answer is your socialization—*society within you.* Your experiences in society have resulted in a self that thinks along certain lines and feels particular emotions. This helps to keep you in line. Thoughts such as "Would I get kicked out of school?" and "What would my friends (parents) think if they found out?" represent an awareness of the self in relationship to others. So does the desire to avoid feelings of shame and embarrassment. Your *social mirror,* then—the result of your being socialized into a self and emotions—sets up effective controls over your behavior. In fact, socialization into self and emotions is so effective that some people feel embarrassed just thinking about running naked in public!

In Sum: Socialization is essential for our development as human beings. From interaction with others, we learn how to think, reason, and feel. The net result is the shaping of our behavior—including our thinking and emotions—according to cultural standards. This is what sociologists mean when they refer to "*society within us.*"

Socialization into Gender

Learning the Gender Map

For a child, society is uncharted territory. A major signpost on society's map is **gender,** the attitudes and behaviors that are expected of us because we are a male or a female. In learning the gender map (called **gender socialization**), we are nudged into different lanes in life—into contrasting attitudes and behaviors. We take direction so well that, as adults, most of us act, think, and even feel according to this gender map, our culture's guidelines to what is appropriate for our sex. Let's briefly consider some of the "gender messages" that we get from our family and the mass media.

Gender Messages in the Family

Our parents are the first significant others who show us how to follow the gender map. Sometimes they do so consciously, perhaps by bringing into play pink and blue, colors that have no meaning in themselves but that are now associated with gender. Our parents' own gender orientations have become embedded so firmly that they do most of this teaching without being aware of what they are doing.

This is illustrated in a classic study by psychologists Susan Goldberg and Michael Lewis (1969), whose results have been confirmed by other researchers (Fagot et al. 1985; Connors 1996; Clearfield and Nelson 2006).

> Goldberg and Lewis asked mothers to bring their 6-month-old infants into their laboratory, supposedly to observe the infants' development. Covertly, however, they also observed the mothers. They found that the mothers kept their daughters closer to them. They also touched their daughters more and spoke to them more frequently than they did to their sons.
>
> By the time the children were 13 months old, the girls stayed closer to their mothers during play, and they returned to their mothers sooner and more often than the boys did. When Goldberg and Lewis set up a barrier to separate the children from their mothers, who were holding toys, the girls were more likely to cry and motion for help; the boys, to try to climb over the barrier.

Goldberg and Lewis concluded that mothers subconsciously reward daughters for being passive and dependent, and sons for being active and independent.

gender the behaviors and attitudes that a society considers proper for its males and females; masculinity or femininity

gender socialization the ways in which society sets children on different paths in life *because* they are male or female

The *gender roles* that we learn during childhood become part of our basic orientations to life. Although we refine these roles as we grow older, they remain built around the framework established during childhood.

Frank and Ernest

Our gender lessons continue throughout childhood. On the basis of our sex, we are given different kinds of toys. Boys are more likely to get guns and "action figures" that destroy enemies. Girls are more likely to get dolls and jewelry. Some parents try to choose "gender neutral" toys, but kids know what is popular, and they feel left out if they don't have what the other kids have. The significance of toys in gender socialization can be summarized this way: Almost all parents would be upset if someone gave their son Barbie dolls.

Parents also subtly encourage boys to participate in more rough-and-tumble play. They expect their sons to get dirtier and to be more defiant, their daughters to be daintier and more compliant (Gilman 1911/1971; Henslin 2007). In large part, they get what they expect. Such experiences in socialization lie at the heart of the sociological explanation of male–female differences. For a fascinating account of how socialization trumps biology, read the Cultural Diversity box on the next page.

Gender Messages from Peers

peer group a group of individuals of roughly the same age who are linked by common interests

Sociologists stress how this sorting process that begins in the family is reinforced as the child is exposed to other aspects of society. Of those other influences, one of the most powerful is the **peer group,** individuals of roughly the same age who are linked by common interests. Examples of peer groups are friends, classmates, and "the kids in the neighborhood."

The family is one of the primary ways that we learn gender. Shown here is a woman in South Africa. What gender messages do you think her daughter is learning?

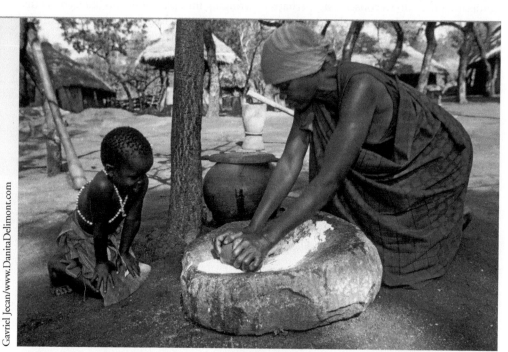

82

Cultural Diversity around the World

Women Becoming Men: The Sworn Virgins

"I will become a man," said Pashe. "I will do it."

The decision was final. Taking a pair of scissors, she soon had her long, black curls lying at her feet. She took off her dress—never to wear one again in her life—and put on her father's baggy trousers. She armed herself with her father's rifle. She would need it.

Going before the village elders, she swore to never marry, to never have children, and to never have sex.

Pashe had become a sworn virgin—and a man.

There was no turning back. The penalty for violating the oath was death.

In Albania, where Pashe Keqi lives, and in parts of Bosnia and Serbia, it is the custom for some women to become men. They are neither transsexuals nor lesbians. Nor do they have a sex-change operation, something unknown in those parts.

The custom is a practical matter, a way to support the family. In these traditional societies, women must stay home and take care of the children and household. They can go hardly anywhere except to the market and mosque. Women depend on men for survival.

And when there is no man? That is the problem.

Pashe's father was killed in a blood feud. In these traditional groups, when the family patriarch (male head) dies and there are no male heirs, how are the women to survive? In the fifteenth century, people in this area hit upon a solution: One of the women takes an oath of life-long virginity and takes over the man's role. She then becomes a social he, wears male clothing, carries a gun, owns property, and moves freely throughout the society.

She drinks in the tavern with the men. She sits with the men at weddings. She prays with the men at the mosque.

When a man wants to marry a girl of the family, she is the one who approves or disapproves of the suitor.

In short, the woman really becomes a man. Actually, a social man, sociologists would add. Her biology does not change, but her gender does. Pashe had become the

Stuart Freedman/Corbis

Pashke Ndocaj, shown here in Thethi, Albania, became a sworn virgin after the death of her father and brothers.

man of the house, a status she occupied her entire life.

Taking this position at the age of 11—she is in her 70s now—also made Pashe responsible for avenging her father's murder. But when his killer was released from prison, her 15-year-old nephew (she is his uncle) rushed in and did the deed instead.

Sworn virgins walk like men, they talk like men, they hunt with the men, and they take up manly occupations. They become shepherds, security guards, truck drivers, and political leaders. Those around them know that they are women, but in all ways they treat them as men. When they talk to women, the women recoil in shyness.

The sworn virgins of Albania are a fascinating cultural contradiction: In the midst of a highly traditional group, one built around male superiority that severely limits women, we find both the belief and practice that a biological woman can do the work of a man and function in all of a man's social roles. The sole exception is marriage.

Under a communist dictator until 1985, with travel restricted by law and custom, mountainous northern Albania had been cut off from the rest of the world. Now there is a democratic government, and the region is connected to the rest of the world by better roads, telephones, and even television. As modern life trickles into these villages, few women want to become men. "Why should we?" they ask. "Now we have freedom. We can go to the city and work and support our families."

For Your Consideration

How do the sworn virgins of Albania help to explain what gender is? Apply functionalism: How was the custom and practice of sworn virgins functional for this society? Apply symbolic interactionism: How do symbols underlie and maintain women becoming men in this society? Apply conflict theory: How do power relations between men and women underlie this practice?

Based on Zumbrun 2007; Bilefsky 2008; Smith 2008.

As you grew up, you saw girls and boys teach one another what it means to be a female or a male. You might not have recognized what was happening, however, so let's eavesdrop on a conversation between two eighth-grade girls studied by sociologist Donna Eder (2007).

CINDY: The only thing that makes her look anything is all the makeup . . .

PENNY: She had a picture, and she's standing like this. (Poses with one hand on her hip and one by her head)

CINDY: Her face is probably this skinny, but it looks that big 'cause of all the makeup she has on it.

PENNY: She's ugly, ugly, ugly.

Do you see how these girls were giving gender lessons? They were reinforcing images of appearance and behavior that they thought were appropriate for females. Boys, too, reinforce cultural expectations of gender. Sociologist Melissa Milkie (1994), who studied junior high school boys, found that much of their talk centered on movies and TV programs. Of the many images they saw, the boys would single out those associated with sex and violence. They would amuse one another by repeating lines, acting out parts, and joking and laughing at what they had seen.

If you know boys in their early teens, you've probably seen a lot of behavior like this. You may have been amused, or even have shaken your head in disapproval. But did you peer beneath the surface? Milkie did. What is really going on? The boys, she concluded, were using media images to develop their identity as males. They had gotten the message: "Real" males are obsessed with sex and violence. Not to joke and laugh about murder and promiscuous sex would have marked a boy as a "weenie," a label to be avoided at all costs.

Gender Messages in the Mass Media

As you can see with the boys Milkie studied, a major guide to the gender map is the **mass media,** forms of communication that are directed to large audiences. Let's look further at how media images reinforce **gender roles,** the behaviors and attitudes considered appropriate for our sex.

Advertising. The advertising assault of stereotypical images begins early. The average U.S. child watches about 25,000 commercials a year (Gantz et al. 2007). In these commercials, girls are more likely to be shown as cooperative and boys as aggressive (Larson 2001). Girls are also more likely to be portrayed as giggly and less capable at tasks (Browne 1998).

The gender messages continue in advertising directed at adults. I'm sure you have you noticed the many ads that portray men as dominant and rugged and women as sexy and submissive. *Your mind and internal images* are the target of this assault of stereotypical, culturally molded images—from cowboys who roam the wide-open spaces to scantily clad women, whose physical assets couldn't possibly be real. Although the purpose is to sell products—from booze and bras to cigarettes and cellphones—the ads also give lessons in gender. Through images both overt and exaggerated and subtle and below our awareness, they help teach what is expected of us as men and women in our culture.

Television. Television reinforces stereotypes of the sexes. On prime-time television, male characters outnumber female characters. Male characters are also more likely to be portrayed in higher-status positions (Glascock 2001). Sports news also maintains traditional stereotypes. Sociologists who studied the content of televised sports news in Los Angeles found that female athletes receive less coverage and are sometimes trivialized (Messner et al. 2003). Male newscasters often focus on humorous events in women's sports or turn the female athlete into a sexual object. Newscasters even manage to emphasize breasts and bras and to engage in locker-room humor.

Stereotype-breaking characters, in contrast, are a sign of changing times. In comedies, women are more verbally aggressive than men (Glascock 2001). The powers of the teenager *Buffy, The Vampire Slayer,* were remarkable. On *Alias,* Sydney Bristow exhibited extraordinary strength. In cartoons, Kim Possible divides her time between cheerleading practice and saving the world from evil, while, also with tongue in cheek, the Powerpuff

mass media forms of communication, such as radio, newspapers, television, and blogs that are directed to mass audiences

gender role the behaviors and attitudes expected of people because they are female or male

Girls are touted as "the most elite kindergarten crime-fighting force ever assembled." This new gender portrayal continues in a variety of programs, such as *Totally Spies.*

The gender messages on these programs are mixed. Girls are powerful, but they have to be skinny and gorgeous and wear the latest fashions. Such messages present a dilemma for girls, for this model continuously thrust before them is almost impossible to replicate in real life.

Video Games.   The movement, color, virtual dangers, unexpected dilemmas, and ability to control the action make video games highly appealing. High school and college students, especially men, find them a seductive way of escaping from the demands of life. The first members of the "Nintendo Generation," now in their thirties, are still playing video games—with babies on their laps.

Sociologists have begun to study how video games portray the sexes, but we still know little about their influence on the players' ideas of gender (Dietz 2000; Berger 2002). Women, often portrayed with exaggerated breasts and buttocks, are now more likely to be main characters than they were just a few years ago (Jansz and Martis 2007). Because these games are on the cutting edge of society, they sometimes also reflect cutting-edge changes in sex roles, the topic of the Mass Media in Social Life box on the next page.

Anime.   *Anime* is a Japanese cartoon form. Because anime crosses boundaries of video games, television, movies, and books (comic), we shall consider it as a separate category. As shown below, one of the most recognizable features of anime is the big-eyed little girls and the fighting little boys. Japanese parents are concerned about anime's antisocial heroes and its depiction of violence, but to keep peace they reluctantly buy anime for their children (Khattak 2007). In the United States, violence is often part of the mass media aimed at children—so with its cute characters, anime is unlikely to bother parents. Anime's depiction of active, dominant little boys and submissive little girls leads to the question, of course, of what gender lessons it is giving children.

In Sum: "Male" and "female" are such powerful symbols that learning them forces us to interpret the world in terms of gender. As children learn their society's symbols of gender, they learn that different behaviors and attitudes are expected of boys and girls. First transmitted by the family, these gender messages are reinforced by other social institutions. As they become integrated into our views of the world, gender messages form a picture of "how" males and females "are." Because gender serves as a primary basis for **social inequality**—giving privileges and obligations to one group of people while denying them to another—gender images are especially important in our socialization.

social inequality a social condition in which privileges and obligations are given to some but denied to others

Anime is increasing in popularity—cartoons and comics aimed at children and pornography targeted to adults. Its gender messages, especially those directed to children, are yet to be explored.

Courtesy Everett Collection

MASS MEDIA In SOCIAL LIFE

Lara Croft, Tomb Raider: Changing Images of Women in the Mass Media

Vince Maher/WENN/Newscom

The mass media not only reflect gender stereotypes but they also play a role in changing them. Sometimes they do both simultaneously. The images of Lara Croft not only reflect women's changing role in society, but also, by exaggerating the change, they mold new stereotypes.

SHNS photo courtesy Eido via Newscom

With digital advances, video games have crossed the line from what are usually thought of as games to something that more closely resembles interactive movies. Costing an average of $10 million to produce and another $10 million to market, some video games have intricate subplots and use celebrity voices for the characters (Nussenbaum 2004). Some introduce new songs by major rock groups (Levine 2008). Sociologically, what is significant is the *content* of video games. They expose gamers not only to action but also to ideas and images. Just as in other forms of the mass media, the gender images of video games communicate powerful messages.

Amidst the traditional portrayals of women as passive and subordinate, a new image has broken through. As exaggerated as it is, this new image reflects a fundamental change in gender relations. Lara Croft, an adventure-seeking archeologist and star of *Tomb Raider* and its many sequels, is the essence of the new gender image. Lara is smart, strong, and able to utterly vanquish foes. With both guns blazing, she is the cowboy of the twenty-first century, the term *cowboy* being purposefully chosen, as Lara breaks stereotypical gender roles and dominates what previously was the domain of men. She was the first female protagonist in a field of muscle-rippling, gun-toting macho caricatures (Taylor 1999).

Yet the old remains powerfully encapsulated in the new. As the photos on this page make evident, Lara is a fantasy girl for young men of the digital generation. No matter her foe, no matter her predicament, Lara oozes sex. Her form-fitting outfits, which flatter her voluptuous figure, reflect the mental images of the men who fashioned this digital character.

Lara has caught young men's fancy to such an extent that they have bombarded corporate headquarters with questions about her personal life. Lara is the star of two movies and a comic book. There is also a Lara Croft action figure.

For Your Consideration

A sociologist who reviewed this text said, "It seems that for women to be defined as equal, we have to become symbolic males—warriors with breasts." Why is gender change mostly one-way—females adopting traditional male characteristics? To see why men get to keep their gender roles, these two questions should help: Who is moving into the traditional territory of the other? Do people prefer to imitate power or weakness?

Finally, consider just how far stereotypes have actually been left behind. One reward for beating time trials is to be able to see Lara wearing a bikini.

Agents of Socialization

agents of socialization individuals or groups that affect our self-concept, attitudes, behaviors, or other orientations toward life

Individuals and groups that influence our orientations to life—our self-concept, emotions, attitudes, and behavior—are called **agents of socialization.** We have already considered how three of these agents—the family, our peers, and the mass media—influence our ideas of gender. Now we'll look more closely at how agents of socialization prepare us in other ways to take our place in society. We shall first consider the family, then the neighborhood, religion, day care, school and peers, and the workplace.

This photo captures an extreme form of family socialization. The father seems to be more emotionally involved in the goal—and in more pain—than his daughter, as he pushes her toward the finish line in the Teen Tours of America Kid's Triathlon.

Lannis Waters/The Palm Beach Post

The Family

The first group to have a major impact on us is our family. Our experiences in the family are so intense that their influence is lifelong. These experiences establish our initial motivations, values, and beliefs. In the family, we receive our basic sense of self, ideas about who we are and what we deserve out of life. It is here that we begin to think of ourselves as strong or weak, smart or dumb, good-looking or ugly—or somewhere in between. And as already noted, the lifelong process of defining ourselves as female or male also begins in the family.

The Family and Social Class. Social class makes a huge difference in how parents socialize their children. Sociologist Melvin Kohn (1959, 1963, 1976, 1977; Kohn et al. 1986) found that working-class parents are mainly concerned that their children stay out of trouble. For discipline, they tend to use physical punishment. Middle-class parents, in contrast, focus more on developing their children's curiosity, self-expression, and self-control. They are more likely to reason with their children than to use physical punishment.

But why such differences? As a sociologist, Kohn knew that the answer was life experiences of some sort. He found that answer in the world of work. Blue-collar workers are usually told exactly what to do. Since they expect their children's lives to be like theirs, they stress obedience. Middle-class parents, in contrast, have work that requires more initiative, and they socialize their children into the qualities they find valuable.

Kohn wanted to know why some working-class parents act more like middle-class parents, and vice versa. As he probed further, he found the key—the parents' type of job. Some middle-class workers, such as office workers, are supervised closely. It turned out that they follow the working-class pattern and emphasize conformity. And some blue-collar workers, such as those who do home repairs, have a good deal of freedom. These workers follow the middle-class model in rearing their children (Pearlin and Kohn 1966; Kohn and Schooler 1969).

Social class also makes a difference in the ideas that parents have of how children develop, ideas that have fascinating consequences for children's play (Lareau 2002).

Working-class parents think of children as similar to wild flowers—they develop naturally. Since the child's development will take care of itself, they see parenting primarily as providing food, shelter, and comfort. They set limits on their children's play ("Don't go near the railroad tracks") and let them play as they wish. Middle-class parents, in contrast, think of children as more like tender house plants—to develop correctly, they need a lot of guidance. With this orientation, they try to structure their children's play to help them develop knowledge and social skills. They may want them to play baseball, for example, not for the enjoyment of the sport, but to help them learn how to be team players.

The Neighborhood

As all parents know, some neighborhoods are better than others for their children. Parents try to move to those neighborhoods—if they can afford them. Their commonsense evaluations are borne out by sociological research. Children from poor neighborhoods are more likely to get in trouble with the law, to become pregnant, to drop out of school, and even to have worse mental health in later life (Brooks-Gunn et al. 1997; Sampson et al. 2001; Wheaton and Clarke 2003; Yonas et al. 2006).

Sociologists have also found that the residents of more affluent neighborhoods keep a closer eye on the children than do the residents of poor neighborhoods (Sampson et al. 1999). The basic reason is that the more affluent neighborhoods have fewer families in transition, so the adults are more likely to know the local children and their parents. This better equips them to help keep the children safe and out of trouble.

Religion

How important is religion in your life? You could be among the two-thirds of Americans who belong to a local congregation, but what if you are among the other third (Gallup Poll 2007b)? Why would religion be significant for you? To see the influence of religion, we can't look only at people who are religious. Even in the extreme—people who wouldn't be caught dead near a church, synagogue, or mosque—religion plays a powerful role. Perhaps this is the most significant aspect of religion: Religious ideas so pervade U.S. society that they provide the foundation of morality for both the religious and the nonreligious.

For many Americans, the influence of religion is more direct. This is especially true for the two of every five Americans who report that during a typical week they attend a religious service (Gallup Poll 2007). Through their participation in congregational life, they learn doctrine, values, and morality, but the effects on their lives are not limited to these obvious factors. For example, people who participate in religious services learn not only beliefs about the hereafter but also ideas about what kinds of clothing, speech, and manners are appropriate for formal occasions. Life in congregations also provides a sense of identity for its participants, giving them a feeling of belonging. It also helps to integrate immigrants into their new society, offers an avenue of social mobility for the poor, provides social contacts for jobs, and in the case of African American churches, has been a powerful influence in social change.

Day Care

It is rare for social science research to make national news, but occasionally it does. This is what happened when researchers published their findings on 1,200 kindergarten children they had studied since they were a month old. They observed the children multiple times both at home and at day care. They also videotaped and made detailed notes on the children's interaction with their mothers (National Institute of Child Health and Human Development 1999; Guensburg 2001). What caught the media's attention? Children who spend more time in day care have weaker bonds with their mothers and are less affectionate to them. They are also less cooperative with others and more likely to fight and to be "mean." By the time they get to kindergarten, they are more likely to talk back to teachers and to disrupt the classroom. This holds true regardless of the quality of the day care, the family's social class, or whether the child is a girl or a boy (Belsky 2006). On the positive side, the children also scored higher on language tests.

Are we producing a generation of "smart but mean" children? This is not an unreasonable question, since the study was designed well and an even larger study of children in England has come up with similar findings (Belsky 2006). Some point out that the differences between children who spend a lot of time in day care and those who spend less time are slight. Others stress that with 5 million children in day care (*Statistical Abstract* 2009:Table 559), slight differences can be significant for society. The researchers are following these children as they continue in school. The most recent report on the children, when they were in the 6th grade, indicates that these patterns are continuing (Belsky et al. 2007).

The School

Part of the **manifest function,** or *intended* purpose, of formal education is to teach knowledge and skills, such as reading, writing, and arithmetic. The teaching of such skills is certainly part of socialization, but so are the schools' **latent functions,** their *unintended* consequences that help the social system. Let's look at this less visible aspect of education.

At home, children learn attitudes and values that match their family's situation in life. At school, they learn a broader perspective that helps prepare them to take a role in the world beyond the family. At home, a child may have been the almost exclusive focus of doting parents, but in school, the child learns *universality*—that the same rules apply to everyone, regardless of who their parents are or how special they may be at home. The Cultural Diversity box on the next page explores how these new values and ways of looking at the world sometimes even replace those the child learns at home.

Sociologists have also identified a *hidden curriculum* in our schools. This term refers to values that, although not explicitly taught, are part of a school's "cultural message." For example, the stories and examples that are used to teach math and English may bring with them lessons in patriotism, democracy, justice, and honesty. There is also a *corridor curriculum,* what students teach one another outside the classroom. Unfortunately, the corridor curriculum seems to emphasize racism, sexism, illicit ways to make money, and coolness (Hemmings 1999). You can determine for yourself which of these is functional and which is dysfunctional.

Conflict theorists point out that social class separates children into different educational worlds. Children born to wealthy parents go to private schools, where they learn skills and values that match their higher position. Children born to middle- and lower-class parents go to public schools, which further refine the separate worlds of social class. Middle-class children learn that good jobs, even the professions, beckon, while children from blue-collar families learn that not many of "their kind" will become professionals or leaders. This is one of the many reasons that children from blue-collar families are less likely to take college prep courses or to go to college. In short, schools around the world reflect and reinforce their nation's social class, economic, and political systems.

Peer Groups

As a child's experiences with agents of socialization broaden, the influence of the family decreases. Entry into school marks only one of many steps in this transfer of allegiance.

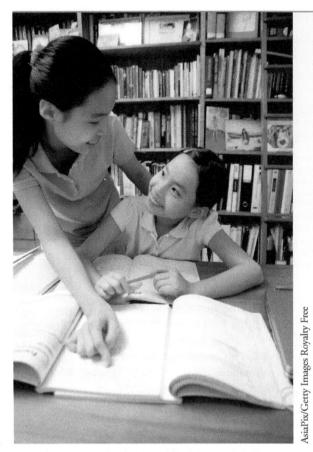

AsiaPix/Getty Images Royalty Free

Schools are one of the primary *agents of socialization.* One of their chief functions is to sort young people into the adult roles thought appropriate for them, and to teach them the attitudes and skills that match these roles. What sorts of attitudes, motivations, goals, and adult roles do you think this child is learning?

manifest functions the intended beneficial consequences of people's actions

latent functions unintended beneficial consequences of people's actions

Cultural Diversity in the United States

Immigrants and Their Children: Caught Between Two Worlds

It is a struggle to adapt to a new culture, for its behaviors and ways of thinking may be at odds with the ones already learned. This can lead to inner turmoil. One way to handle the conflict is to cut ties with your first culture. Doing so, however, can create a sense of loss, one that is perhaps recognized only later in life.

Richard Rodriguez, a literature professor and essayist, was born to working-class Mexican immigrants. Wanting their son to be successful in their adopted land, his parents named him Richard instead of Ricardo. While his English–Spanish hybrid name indicates the parents' aspirations for their son, it was also an omen of the conflict that Richard would experience.

Like other children of Mexican immigrants, Richard first spoke Spanish—a rich mother tongue that introduced him to the world. Until the age of 5, when he began school, Richard knew only fifty words in English. He describes what happened when he began school:

Bob Daemmrich/The Image Works

> The change came gradually but early. When I was beginning grade school, I noted to myself the fact that the classroom environment was so different in its styles and assumptions from my own family environment that survival would essentially entail a choice between both worlds. When I became a student, I was literally "remade"; neither I nor my teachers considered anything I had known before as relevant. I had to forget most of what my culture had provided, because to remember it was a disadvantage. The past and its cultural values became detachable, like a piece of clothing grown heavy on a warm day and finally put away.

As happened to millions of immigrants before him, whose parents spoke German, Polish, Italian, and so on, learning English eroded family and class ties and ate away at his ethnic roots. For Rodriguez, language and education were not simply devices that eased the transition to the dominant culture. They also slashed at the roots that had given him life.

To face conflicting cultures is to confront a fork in the road. Some turn one way and withdraw from the new culture—a clue that helps to explain why so many Latinos drop out of U.S. schools. Others go in the opposite direction. Cutting ties with their family and cultural roots, they wholeheartedly adopt the new culture.

Rodriguez took the second road. He excelled in his new language—so much, in fact, that he graduated from Stanford University and then became a graduate student in English at the University of California at Berkeley. He was even awarded a Fulbright fellowship to study English Renaissance literature at the University of London.

But the past shadowed Rodriguez. Prospective employers were impressed with his knowledge of Renaissance literature. At job interviews, however, they would skip over the Renaissance training and ask him if he would teach the Mexican novel and be an adviser to Latino students. Rodriguez was also haunted by the image of his grandmother, the warmth of the culture he had left behind, and the language and thought to which he had become a stranger.

Richard Rodriguez represents millions of immigrants—not just those of Latino origin but those from other cultures, too—who want to be a part of life in the United States without betraying their past. They fear that to integrate into U.S. culture is to lose their roots. They are caught between two cultures, each beckoning, each offering rich rewards.

For Your Consideration

I saw this conflict firsthand with my father, who did not learn English until after the seventh grade (his last in school). German was left behind, but broken English and awkward expressions remained for a lifetime. Then, too, there were the lingering emotional connections to old ways, as well as the suspicions, haughtiness, and slights of more assimilated Americans. He longed for security by grasping the past, but at the same time, he wanted to succeed in the everyday reality of the new culture. Have you seen similar conflicts?

Sources: Based on Richard Rodriguez 1975, 1982, 1990, 1991, 1995.

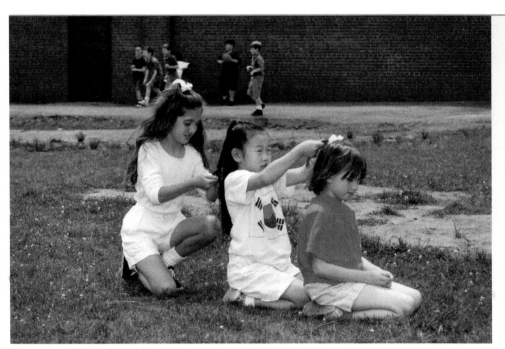

Ellen Senisi/The Image Works

Gradeschool boys and girls often separate themselves by gender, as in this playground in Schenectady, New York. The socialization that occurs during self-segregation by gender is a topic of study by sociologists.

One of the most significant aspects of education is that it exposes children to peer groups that help them resist the efforts of parents and schools to socialize them.

When sociologists Patricia and Peter Adler (1998) observed children at two elementary schools in Colorado, they saw how children separate themselves by sex and develop separate gender worlds. The norms that made boys popular were athletic ability, coolness, and toughness. For girls, popularity was based on family background, physical appearance (clothing and use of makeup), and the ability to attract popular boys. In this children's subculture, academic achievement pulled in opposite directions: For boys, high grades lowered their popularity, but for girls, good grades increased their standing among peers.

You know from your own experience how compelling peer groups are. It is almost impossible to go against a peer group, whose cardinal rule seems to be "conformity or rejection." Anyone who doesn't do what the others want becomes an "outsider," a "nonmember," an "outcast." For preteens and teens just learning their way around in the world, it is not surprising that the peer group rules.

As a result, the standards of our peer groups tend to dominate our lives. If your peers, for example, listen to rap, Nortec, death metal, rock and roll, country, or gospel, it is almost inevitable that you also prefer that kind of music. In high school, if your friends take math courses, you probably do, too (Crosnoe et al. 2008). It is the same for clothing styles and dating standards. Peer influences also extend to behaviors that violate social norms. If your peers are college-bound and upwardly striving, that is most likely what you will be; but if they use drugs, cheat, and steal, you are likely to do so, too.

The Workplace

Another agent of socialization that comes into play somewhat later in life is the workplace. Those initial jobs that we take in high school and college are much more than just a way to earn a few dollars. From the people we rub shoulders with at work, we learn not only a set of skills but also perspectives on the world.

Most of us eventually become committed to some particular line of work, often after trying out many jobs. This may involve **anticipatory socialization,** learning to play a role before entering it. Anticipatory socialization is a sort of mental rehearsal for some future activity. We may talk to people who work in a particular career, read novels about that type of work, or take a summer internship in that field. Such activities allow us to

anticipatory socialization
the process of learning in advance an anticipated future role or status

gradually identify with the role, to become aware of what would be expected of us. Sometimes this helps people avoid committing themselves to an unrewarding career, as with some of my students who tried student teaching, found that they couldn't stand it, and then moved on to other fields more to their liking.

An intriguing aspect of work as a socializing agent is that the more you participate in a line of work, the more the work becomes a part of your self-concept. Eventually you come to think of yourself so much in terms of the job that if someone asks you to describe yourself, you are likely to include the job in your self-description. You might say, "I'm a teacher," "I'm a nurse," or "I'm a sociologist."

Resocialization

What does a woman who has just become a nun have in common with a man who has just divorced? The answer is that they both are undergoing **resocialization;** that is, they are learning new norms, values, attitudes, and behaviors to match their new situation in life. In its most common form, resocialization occurs each time we learn something contrary to our previous experiences. A new boss who insists on a different way of doing things is resocializing you. Most resocialization is mild.

Resocialization can also be intense. People who join Alcoholics Anonymous (AA), for example, are surrounded by reformed drinkers who affirm the destructive effects of excessive drinking. Some students experience an intense period of resocialization when they leave high school and start college—especially during those initially scary days before they find companions, start to fit in, and feel comfortable. The experiences of people who join a cult or begin psychotherapy are even more profound, for they learn views that conflict with their earlier socialization. If these ideas "take," not only does the individual's behavior change but he or she also learns a fundamentally different way of looking at life.

Total Institutions

Relatively few of us experience the powerful agent of socialization that sociologist Erving Goffman (1961) called the **total institution.** He coined this term to refer to a place in which people are cut off from the rest of society and where they come under almost total control of the officials who are in charge. Boot camp, prisons, concentration camps, convents, some religious cults, and some military schools, such as West Point, are total institutions.

A person entering a total institution is greeted with a **degradation ceremony** (Garfinkel 1956), an attempt to remake the self by stripping away the individual's current identity and stamping a new one in its place. This unwelcome greeting may involve fingerprinting, photographing, or shaving the head. Newcomers may be ordered to strip, undergo an examination (often in a humiliating, semipublic setting), and then put on a uniform that designates their new status. Officials also take away the individual's *personal identity kit,* items such as jewelry, hairstyles, clothing, and other body decorations used to express individuality.

Total institutions are isolated from the public. The bars, walls, gates, and guards not only keep the inmates in but also keep outsiders out. Staff members supervise the day-to-day lives of the residents. Eating, sleeping, showering, recreation—all are standardized. Inmates learn that their previous statuses—student, worker, spouse, parent—mean nothing. The only thing that counts is their current status.

No one leaves a total institution unscathed, for the experience brands an indelible mark on the individual's self and colors the way he or she sees the world. Boot camp, as described in the Down-to-Earth Sociology box on the next page, is brutal but swift. Prison, in contrast, is brutal and prolonged. Neither recruit nor prisoner, however, has difficulty in knowing that the institution has had profound effects on attitudes and orientations to life.

resocialization the process of learning new norms, values, attitudes, and behaviors

total institution a place that is almost totally controlled by those who run it, in which people are cut off from the rest of society and the society is mostly cut off from them

degradation ceremony a term coined by Harold Garfinkel to refer to a ritual whose goal is to strip away someone's position (social status); in doing so, a new social and self-identity is stamped on the individual

Down-to-Earth Sociology
Boot Camp as a Total Institution

The bus arrives at Parris Island, South Carolina, at 3 A.M. The early hour is no accident. The recruits are groggy, confused. Up to a few hours ago, the young men were ordinary civilians. Now, as a sergeant sneeringly calls them "maggots," their heads are buzzed (25 seconds per recruit), and they are quickly thrust into the harsh world of Marine boot camp.

Buzzing the boys' hair is just the first step in stripping away their identity so that the Marines can stamp a new one in its place. The uniform serves the same purpose. There is a ban on using the first person "I." Even a simple request must be made in precise Marine style or it will not be acknowledged. ("Sir, Recruit Jones requests permission to make a head call, Sir.")

Every intense moment of the next eleven weeks reminds the recruits, men and women, that they are joining a subculture of self-discipline. Here pleasure is suspect and sacrifice is good. As they learn the Marine way of talking, walking, and thinking, they are denied the diversions they once took for granted: television, cigarettes, cars, candy, soft drinks, video games, music, alcohol, drugs, and sex.

Lessons are taught with fierce intensity. When Sgt. Carey checks brass belt buckles, Recruit Robert Shelton nervously blurts, "I don't have one." Sgt. Carey's face grows red as his neck cords bulge. "I?" he says, his face just inches from the recruit. With spittle flying from his mouth, he screams, " 'I' is gone!"

"Nobody's an individual" is the lesson that is driven home again and again. "You are a team, a Marine. Not a civilian. Not black or white, not Hispanic or Indian or some hyphenated American—but a Marine. You will live like a Marine, fight like a Marine, and, if necessary, die like a Marine."

Each day begins before dawn with close-order formations. The rest of the day is filled with training in hand-to-hand combat, marching, running, calisthenics, Marine history, and—always—following orders.

"An M-16 can blow someone's head off at 500 meters," Sgt. Norman says. "That's beautiful, isn't it?"

A recruit with drill sergeants

Norm Rowan/The Image Works

"Yes, sir!" shout the platoon's fifty-nine voices.

"Pick your nose!" Simultaneously fifty-nine index fingers shoot into nostrils.

The pressure to conform is intense. Those who are sent packing for insubordination or suicidal tendencies are mocked in cadence during drills. ("Hope you like the sights you see/Parris Island casualty.") As lights go out at 9 P.M., the exhausted recruits perform the day's last task: The entire platoon, in unison, chants the virtues of the Marines.

Recruits are constantly scrutinized. Subpar performance is not accepted, whether it be a dirty rifle or a loose thread on a uniform. The underperformer is shouted at, derided, humiliated. The group suffers for the individual. If one recruit is slow, the entire platoon is punished.

The system works.

One of the new Marines (until graduation, they are recruits, not Marines) says, "I feel like I've joined a new society or religion."

He has.

For Your Consideration

Of what significance is the recruits' degradation ceremony? Why are recruits not allowed video games, cigarettes, or calls home? Why are the Marines so unfair as to punish an entire platoon for the failure of an individual? Use concepts in this chapter to explain why the system works.

Sources: Based on Garfinkel 1956; Goffman 1961; Ricks 1995; Dyer 2007.

Socialization Through the Life Course

You are at a particular stage in your life now, and college is a good part of it. You know that you have more stages ahead of you as you go through life. These stages, from birth to death, are called the **life course** (Elder 1975; 1999). The sociological significance of the life course is twofold. First, as you pass through a stage, it affects your behavior and orientations. You simply don't think about life in the same way when you are 30, are

life course the stages of our life as we go from birth to death

The Gallery Collection/Corbis

In contemporary Western societies such as the United States, children are viewed as innocent and in need of protection from adult responsibilities such as work and self-support. Ideas of childhood vary historically and cross-culturally. From paintings, such as this 1559 Italian painting by Sofonisba Anguissola (1532–1625), "The Artist's Family," some historians conclude that Europeans once viewed children as miniature adults who assumed adult roles early in life.

married, and have a baby and a mortgage, as you do when you are 18 or 20, single, and in college. (Actually, you don't even see life the same way as a freshman and as a senior.) Second, your life course differs by social location. Your social class, race–ethnicity, and gender, for example, map out distinctive worlds of experience. This means that the typical life course differs for males and females, the rich and the poor, and so on. To emphasize this major sociological point, in the sketch that follows I will stress the *historical* setting of people's lives. Because of your particular social location, your own life course may differ from this sketch, which is a composite of stages that others have suggested (Levinson 1978; Carr et al. 1995; Quadagno 2007).

Childhood (from birth to about age 12)

Consider how different your childhood would have been if you had grown up in another historical era. Historian Philippe Ariès (1965) noticed that in European paintings from about A.D. 1000 to 1800 children were always dressed in adult clothing. If they were not depicted stiffly posed, as in a family portrait, they were shown doing adult activities.

From this, Ariès drew a conclusion that sparked a debate among historians: He said that during this era in Europe, childhood was not regarded as a special time of life. He said that adults viewed children as miniature adults and put them to work at an early age. At the age of 7, for example, a boy might leave home for good to learn to be a jeweler or a stonecutter. A girl, in contrast, stayed home until she married, but by the age of 7 she assumed her share of the household tasks. Historians do not deny that these were the customs of that time, but some say that Ariès' conclusion is ridiculous. They say that other evidence of that period indicates that childhood was viewed as a special time of life (Orme 2002).

Having children work like adults did not disappear with the Middle Ages. It is still common in the Least Industrialized Nations today, where children work in many occupations—from blacksmiths to waiters. They are most visible as street peddlers, hawking everything from shoelaces to chewing gum and candy.

Child rearing, too, was remarkably different. Three hundred years ago, parents and teachers considered it their moral duty to *terrorize* children to keep them in line. They would lock children in dark closets, frighten them with bedtime stories of death and hellfire, and force them to witness gruesome events. Consider this:

A common moral lesson involved taking children to visit the gibbet [an upraised post on which executed bodies were left hanging], where they were forced to inspect the rotting corpses as an example of what happens to bad children when they grow up. Whole classes were taken out of school to witness hangings, and parents would often whip their children afterwards to make them remember what they had seen. (DeMause 1975)

Industrialization transformed the way we perceive children. When children had the leisure to go to school and postponed taking on adult roles, parents and officials came to think of them as tender and innocent, as needing more care, comfort, and protection. Such attitudes of dependency grew, and today we view children as needing gentle guidance if they are to develop emotionally, intellectually, morally, even physically. We take our

transitional adulthood
a term that refers to a period following high school when young adults have not yet taken on the responsibilities ordinarily associated with adulthood; also called *adultolescence*

view for granted—after all, it is only "common sense." Yet, as you can see, our view is not "natural." It is, instead, rooted in geography, history, and economic development.

In Sum: Childhood is more than biology. Everyone's childhood occurs at some point in history and is embedded in particular social locations, especially social class and gender. *These social factors are as vital as our biology, for they determine what our childhood will be like.* Although a child's *biological* characteristics (such as being small and dependent) are universal, the child's *social* experiences (the kind of life the child lives) are not. Because of this, sociologists say that childhood varies from culture to culture.

Adolescence (ages 13–17)

It might seem strange to you, but adolescence is a *social invention,* not a "natural" age division. In earlier centuries, people simply moved from childhood to young adulthood, with no stopover in between. The Industrial Revolution allowed adolescence to be invented. It brought such an abundance of material surpluses that for the first time in history people in their teens were not needed in the labor force. At the same time, education became more important for achieving success. As these two forces in industrialized societies converged, they created a gap between childhood and adulthood. The term *adolescence* was coined to indicate this new stage in life (Hall 1904), one that has become renowned for inner turmoil.

To mark the passage of children into adulthood, tribal societies hold *initiation rites.* This grounds their self-identity. They know how they fit in the society. In the industrialized world, however, adolescents must "find" themselves, grappling with the dilemma of "I am neither a child nor an adult. Who am I?" As they attempt to carve out an identity that is distinct from both the "younger" world being left behind and the "older" world that is still out of reach, adolescents develop their own subcultures, with distinctive clothing, hairstyles, language, gestures, and music. We usually fail to realize that contemporary society, not biology, created this period of inner turmoil that we call *adolescence.*

Transitional Adulthood (ages 18–29)

If society invented adolescence, can it also invent other periods of life? As Figure 2 illustrates, this is actually happening now. Postindustrial societies are adding another period of extended youth to the life course, which sociologists call **transitional adulthood** (also known as *adultolescence*). After high school, millions of young adults postpone adult responsibilities by going to college. They are mostly freed from the control of their parents, yet they don't have to support themselves. After college, many live at home, so they can live cheaply while they establish themselves in a career—and, of course, continue to "find themselves." During this time, people are "neither psychological adolescents nor sociological adults" (Keniston 1971). At some point during this period of extended youth, young adults ease into adult responsibilities. They take a full-time job, become serious about a career, engage in courtship rituals, get married—and go into debt.

Michael MacIntyre/The Hutchison Library

In many societies, manhood is not bestowed upon males simply because they reach a certain age. Manhood, rather, signifies a standing in the community that must be achieved. Shown here is an initiation ceremony in Indonesia, where boys, to lay claim to the status of manhood, must jump over this barrier.

FIGURE 2 Transitional Adulthood: A New Stage in the Life Course

Who has completed the transition?

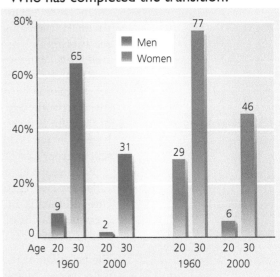

The data show the percentage who have completed the transition to adulthood, as measured by leaving home, finishing school, getting married, having a child, and being financially independent.

Source: Furstenberg, et al. 2004.

The Middle Years (ages 30–65)

The Early Middle Years (ages 30–49).   During their early middle years, most people are more sure of themselves and of their goals in life. As with any point in the life course, however, the self can receive severe jolts. Common in this period are divorce and losing jobs. It may take years for the self to stabilize after such ruptures.

The early middle years pose a special challenge for many U.S. women, who have been given the message, especially by the media, that they can "have it all." They can be super-workers, superwives, and supermoms—all rolled into one. Reality, however, hits them in the face: too little time, too many demands, even too little sleep. Something has to give, and attempts to resolve this dilemma are anything but easy.

The Later Middle Years (ages 50–65).   During the later middle years, health issues and mortality begin to loom large as people feel their bodies change, especially if they watch their parents become frail, fall ill, and die. The consequence is a fundamental reorientation in thinking—*from time since birth to time left to live* (Neugarten 1976). With this changed orientation, people attempt to evaluate the past and come to terms with what lies ahead. They compare what they have accomplished with what they had hoped to achieve. Many people also find themselves caring not only for their own children but also for their aging parents. Because of this double burden, which is often crushing, people in the later middle years sometimes are called the "sandwich generation."

Life during this stage isn't stressful for everyone. Many find late middle age to be the most comfortable period of their lives. They enjoy job security and a standard of living higher than ever before; they have a bigger house (one that may even be paid for), drive newer cars, and take longer and more exotic vacations. The children are grown, the self is firmly planted, and fewer upheavals are likely to occur.

As they anticipate the next stage of life, however, most people do not like what they see.

The Older Years (about age 65 on)

The Transitional Older Years.   In agricultural societies, when most people died early, old age was thought to begin at around age 40. As industrialization brought improved nutrition, medicine, and public health, allowing more people to live longer, the beginning of "old age" gradually stretched out. People who are in good health today are coming to experience their 60s not as old age, but as an extension of their middle years. This change is so recent that a *new stage of life* seems to be evolving, the period between retirement (averaging about 63) and old age—which people are increasingly coming to see as beginning around age 75 ("Schwab Study . . ." 2008). We can call this stage the *transitional older years.*

Researchers are focusing more on this transitional stage of life. They have found that social isolation harms both the body and brain, that people who are more integrated into social networks stay mentally sharper (Ertel et al. 2008). With improved heath, two-thirds of the men and two-fifths of the women between their late 60s and age 75 continue to be sexually active (Lindau et al. 2007). Not only are people in this stage of life having more sex, but they also are enjoying it more (Beckman et al. 2008).

Because we have a self and can reason abstractly, we can contemplate death. In our early years, we regard death as a vague notion, a remote possibility. As people see their parents and friends die and observe their own bodies no longer functioning as before, however, the thought of death becomes less abstract. Increasingly during this stage in the life course, people feel that "time is closing in" on them.

The Later Older Years.   As with the preceding periods of life, except the first one, there is no precise beginning point to this last stage. For some, the 75th birthday may mark entry into this period of life. For others, that marker may be the 80th or even the 85th birthday. For most, this stage is marked by growing frailty and illness; for all who reach this stage, it is ended by death. For some, the physical decline is slow, and a rare few manage to see their 100th birthday mentally alert and in good physical health.

The Sociological Significance of the Life Course

The sociological significance of the life course is that it does not merely represent biology, things that naturally occur to all of us as we add years to our lives. Rather, *social* factors influence our life course. As you just saw, *when* you live makes a huge difference in the course that your life takes. And with today's rapid social change, the difference in historical time does not have to be vast. Being born just ten years earlier or later may mean that you experience war or peace, an expanding economy or a depression—factors that vitally affect what happens to you not just during childhood but throughout your life.

Your *social location,* such as social class, gender, and race–ethnicity, is also highly significant. Your experience of society's events will be similar to that of people who share your social location, but different from that of people who do not. If you are poor, for example, you likely will feel older sooner than most wealthy people for whom life is less demanding. Individual factors—such as your health or marrying early or entering college late—may throw your life course "out of sequence."

For all these reasons, this sketch of the life course may not adequately reflect your own past, present, and future. As sociologist C. Wright Mills (1959) would say, because employers are beating a path to your door, or failing to do so, you are more inclined to marry, to buy a house, and to start a family—or to postpone these life course events. In short, changing times change lives, steering the life course into different directions.

This January 1937 photo from Sneedville, Tennessee, shows Eunice Johns, age 9, and her husband, Charlie Johns, age 22. The groom gave his wife a doll as a wedding gift. The new husband and wife planned to build a cabin, and, as Charlie Johns phrased it, "go to housekeepin'." This couple illustrates the cultural relativity of life stages, which we sometimes mistake as fixed. It also is interesting from a symbolic interactionist perspective—that of changing definitions.

The marriage lasted. The couple had 7 children, 5 boys and 2 girls. Charlie died in 1997 at age 83, and Eunice in 2006 at age 78. The two were buried in the Johns Family Cemetery.

Are We Prisoners of Socialization?

From our discussion of socialization, you might conclude that sociologists think of people as robots: The socialization goes in, and the behavior comes out. People cannot help what they do, think, or feel, for everything is simply a result of their exposure to socializing agents.

Sociologists do *not* think of people in this way. Although socialization is powerful, and affects all of us profoundly, we have a self. Established in childhood and continually modified by later experience, our self is dynamic. Our self is not a sponge that passively absorbs influences from the environment but, rather, a vigorous, essential part of our being that allows us to act on our environment.

It is precisely because people are not robots that their behavior is so hard to predict. The countless reactions of others merge in each of us. As the self develops, we each internalize or "put together" these innumerable reactions, producing a unique whole called the *individual.* Each of us uses our mind to reason and to make choices in life.

In this way, *each of us is actively involved in the construction of the self.* Although our experiences in the family lay down our fundamental orientations to life, we are not doomed to keep those orientations if we do not like them. We can purposely expose ourselves to other groups and ideas. Those experiences, in turn, will have their own effects on our self. In short, although socialization is powerful, we can change even the self within the limitations of the framework laid down by our social locations. And that self—along with the options available within society—is the key to our behavior.

By the Numbers: *Then and Now*

Percentage of men who complete the transition to adulthood by age 30

1960	NOW
65%	31%

Percentage of women who complete the transition to adulthood by age 30

1960	NOW
77%	46%

About when does old age begin?

40 PREINDUSTRIAL TIMES	75 NOW (IN TRANSITION)

SUMMARY *and* REVIEW

Society Makes Us Human

How much of our human characteristics come from "nature" (heredity) and how much from "nurture" (the social environment)?

Observations of isolated, institutionalized, and **feral children** help to answer the nature–nurture question, as do experiments with monkeys that were raised in isolation. Language and intimate social interaction—aspects of "nurture"—are essential to the development of what we consider to be human characteristics.

Socialization into the Self and Mind

How do we acquire a self?

Humans are born with the *capacity* to develop a **self,** but the self must be socially constructed; that is, its contents depend on social interaction. According to Charles Horton Cooley's concept of the **looking-glass self,** our self develops as we internalize others' reactions to us. George Herbert Mead identified the ability to **take the role of the other** as essential to the development of the self. Mead concluded that even the mind is a social product.

How do children develop reasoning skills?

Jean Piaget identified four stages that children go through as they develop the ability to reason: (1) *sensorimotor,* in which understanding is limited to sensory stimuli such as touch and sight; (2) *preoperational,* the ability to use symbols; (3) *concrete operational,* in which reasoning ability is more complex but not yet capable of complex abstractions; and (4) *formal operational,* or abstract thinking.

Learning Personality, Morality, and Emotions

How do sociologists evaluate Freud's psychoanalytic theory of personality development?

Sigmund Freud viewed personality development as the result of our **id** (inborn, self-centered desires) clashing with the demands of society. The **ego** develops to balance the id and the **superego,** the conscience. Sociologists, in contrast, do not examine inborn or subconscious motivations, but, instead, consider how *social* factors—social class, gender, religion, education, and so forth—underlie personality.

How do people develop morality?

Children are born without morality. Lawrence Kohlberg identified four stages children go through as they learn morality: amoral, preconventional, conventional, and postconventional. As they make moral decisions, both men and women use personal relationships and abstract principles.

How does socialization influence emotions?

Socialization influences not only *how we express our emotions* but also *what emotions we feel.* Socialization into emotions is one of the means by which society produces conformity.

Socialization into Gender

How does gender socialization affect our sense of self?

Gender socialization—sorting males and females into different roles—is a primary means of controlling human behavior. Children receive messages about gender even in infancy. A society's ideals of sex-linked behaviors are reinforced by its social institutions.

Agents of Socialization

What are the main agents of socialization?

The **agents of socialization** include the family, neighborhood, religion, day care, school, **peer groups,** the **mass media,** and the workplace. Each has its particular influences in socializing us into becoming full-fledged members of society.

Resocialization

What is resocialization?

Resocialization is the process of learning new norms, values, attitudes, and behavior. Most resocialization is voluntary, but some, as with residents of **total institutions,** is involuntary.

Socialization Through the Life Course

Does socialization end when we enter adulthood?

Socialization occurs throughout the life course. In industrialized societies, the **life course** can be divided into childhood, adolescence, young adulthood, the middle years, and the older years. The West is adding a new stage, **transitional adulthood.** Life course patterns vary by geography, history, gender, race–ethnicity, and social class, as well as by individual experiences such as health and age at marriage.

Are We Prisoners of Socialization?

Although socialization is powerful, we are not merely the sum of our socialization experiences. Just as socialization influences human behavior, so humans act on their environment and influence even their self-concept.

THINKING CRITICALLY

1. What two agents of socialization have influenced you the most? Can you pinpoint their influence on your attitudes, beliefs, values, or other orientations to life?

2. Summarize your views of the "proper" relationships of women and men. What in your socialization has led you to have these views?

3. What is your location in the life course? How does the text's summary of that location match your experiences? Explain the similarities and differences.

ADDITIONAL RESOURCES

What can you find in MySocLab? mysoclab www.mysoclab.com

- Complete Ebook
- Practice Tests and Video and Audio activities
- Mapping and Data Analysis exercises

- Sociology in the News
- Classic Readings in Sociology
- Research and Writing advice

Where Can I Read More on This Topic?

Ariès, Philippe. *Centuries of Childhood: A Social History of Family Life.* New York: Vintage Books, 1972. The author analyzes how childhood in Europe during the Middle Ages differs from childhood today.

Blumer, Herbert. *George Herbert Mead and Human Conduct.* Lanham, Md.: AltaMira Press, 2004. An overview of symbolic interactionism by a sociologist who studied under Mead.

Greco, Monica, and Paul Stenner, eds. *Emotions: A Social Science Reader.* New York: Routledge, 2008. The authors examine the increasing significance of the study of emotions in the social sciences.

Grusec, Joan E., and Paul D. Hastings, eds. *Handbook of Socialization: Theory and Research.* New York: Guilford Press, 2007. Extensive overview of socialization from earliest childhood into adulthood.

Handel, Gerald, Spencer Cahill, and Frederick Elkin. *Children and Society: The Sociology of Children and Childhood Socialization.* New York: Oxford University Press, 2007. A symbolic interactionist perspective on childhood from birth to adolescence with an emphasis on the development of the self.

Hunt, Stephen J. *The Life Course: A Sociological Introduction.* New York: Palgrave McMillan, 2006. Gives an overview of the life course while considering what is distinct about a sociological approach to this topic.

Lareau, Annette. *Unequal Childhoods: Class, Race, and Family Life.* Berkeley: University of California Press, 2003. The author documents differences in child rearing in poor, working-class, and middle-class U.S. families.

Pugh, Allison J. *Longing and Belonging: Parents, Children, and Consumer Culture.* Berkeley: University of California Press, 2009. Through participant observation and interviewing, the author analyzes why parents, even though they are financially strapped, give in to their children's material wants.

Settersten, Richard A., Jr., and Timothy J. Owens, eds. *New Frontiers in Socialization.* Greenwich, Conn.: JAI Press, 2003. The authors of these articles focus on the adult years in the life course, examining the influence of families, neighborhoods, communities, friendship, education, work, volunteer associations, medical institutions, and the media.

Sociological Studies of Child Development: A Research Annual. Greenwich, Conn.: JAI Press, published annually. Along with theoretical articles, this publication reports on sociological research on the socialization of children.

Turmel, André. *A Historical Sociology of Childhood: Developmental Thinking, Categorization and Graphic Visualization.* New York: Cambridge University Press, 2008. The author examines how the idea of what a "normal" child is has changed over time.

Deviance and Social Control

Deviance and Social Control

South Dakota

Ed Kashi/Corbis

In just a few moments I was to meet my first Yanomamö, my first primitive man. What would it be like? . . . I looked up [from my canoe] and gasped when I saw a dozen burly, naked, filthy, hideous men staring at us down the shafts of their drawn arrows. Immense wads of green tobacco were stuck between their lower teeth and lips, making them look even more hideous, and strands of dark-green slime dripped or hung from their noses. We arrived at the village while the men were blowing a hallucinogenic drug up their noses. One of the side effects of the drug is a runny nose. The mucus is always saturated with the green powder, and the Indians usually let it run freely from their nostrils. . . . I just sat there holding my notebook, helpless and pathetic . . .

> They would "clean" their hands by spitting slimy tobacco juice into them.

The whole situation was depressing, and I wondered why I ever decided to switch from civil engineering to anthropology in the first place. . . . [Soon] I was covered with red pigment, the result of a dozen or so complete examinations. . . . These examinations capped an otherwise grim day. The Indians would blow their noses into their hands, flick as much of the mucus off that would separate in a snap of the wrist, wipe the residue into their hair, and then carefully examine my face, arms, legs, hair, and the contents of my pockets. I said [in their language], "Your hands are dirty"; my comments were met by the Indians in the following way: they would "clean" their hands by spitting a quantity of slimy tobacco juice into them, rub them together, and then proceed with the examination.

This is how Napoleon Chagnon describes the culture shock he felt when he met the Yanomamö tribe of the rain forests of Brazil. His ensuing months of fieldwork continued to bring surprise after surprise, and often Chagnon (1977) could hardly believe his eyes—or his nose.

deviance the violation of norms (or rules or expectations)

crime the violation of norms written into law

stigma "blemishes" that discredit a person's claim to a "normal" identity

If you were to list the deviant behaviors of the Yanomamö, what would you include? The way they appear naked in public? Use hallucinogenic drugs? Let mucus hang from their noses? Or the way they rub hands filled with mucus, spittle, and tobacco juice over a frightened stranger who doesn't dare to protest? Perhaps. But it isn't this simple, for as we shall see, deviance is relative.

What Is Deviance?

Sociologists use the term **deviance** to refer to any violation of norms, whether the infraction is as minor as driving over the speed limit, as serious as murder, or as humorous as Chagnon's encounter with the Yanomamö. This deceptively simple definition takes us to the heart of the sociological perspective on deviance, which sociologist Howard S. Becker (1966) described this way: *It is not the act itself, but the reactions to the act, that make something deviant.* What Chagnon saw disturbed him, but to the Yanomamö those same behaviors represented normal, everyday life. What was deviant to Chagnon was *conformist* to the Yanomamö. From their viewpoint, you *should* check out strangers the way they did—and nakedness is good, as are hallucinogenic drugs and letting mucus be "natural."

Chagnon's abrupt introduction to the Yanomamö allows us to see the *relativity of deviance,* a major point made by symbolic interactionists. Because different groups have different norms, *what is deviant to some is not deviant to others.* This principle holds both *within* a society and across cultures. Thus, acts that are acceptable in one culture—or in one group within a society—may be considered deviant in another culture or by another group within the same society. This idea is explored in the photo on this page and in the Cultural Diversity box on the next page.

This principle also applies to a specific form of deviance known as **crime,** the violation of rules that have been written into law. In the extreme, an act that is applauded by one group may be so despised by another group that it is punishable by death. Making a huge profit on business deals is one example. Americans who do this are admired. Like Donald Trump, Jack Welch, and Warren Buffet, they may even write books about their exploits. In China, however, until recently this same act was considered a crime called *profiteering.* Those found guilty were hanged in a public square as a lesson to all.

Unlike the general public, sociologists use the term *deviance* nonjudgmentally, to refer to any act to which people respond negatively. When sociologists use this term, it does not mean that they agree that an act is bad, just that people judge it negatively. To sociologists, then, *all* of us are deviants of one sort or another, for we all violate norms from time to time.

To be considered deviant, a person does not even have to *do* anything. Sociologist Erving Goffman (1963) used the term **stigma** to refer to characteristics that discredit people. These include violations of norms of ability (blindness, deafness, mental handicaps) and norms of appearance (a facial birthmark, a huge nose). They also include involuntary memberships, such as being a victim of AIDS or the brother of a rapist. The stigma can become a person's master status, defining him or her as deviant. A master status cuts across all other statuses that a person occupies.

James M. Henslin

I took this photo on the outskirts of Hyderabad, India. Is this man deviant? If this were a U.S. street, he would be. But here? No houses have running water in his neighborhood, and the men, women, and children bathe at the neighborhood water pump. This man, then, would not be deviant in this culture. And yet, he is actually mugging for my camera, making the three bystanders laugh. Does this additional factor make this a scene of deviance?

How Norms Make Social Life Possible

No human group can exist without norms, for *norms make social life possible by making behavior predictable.* What would life be like if you could not predict what others would do? Imagine for a moment that you have gone to a store to purchase milk:

> Suppose the clerk says, "I won't sell you any milk. We're overstocked with soda, and I'm not going to sell anyone milk until our soda inventory is reduced."

Cultural Diversity around the World

Human Sexuality in Cross-Cultural Perspective

Human sexuality illustrates how a group's *definition* of an act, not the act itself, determines whether it will be considered deviant. Let's look at some examples reported by anthropologist Robert Edgerton (1976).

Norms of sexual behavior vary so widely around the world that what is considered normal in one society may be considered deviant in another. In Kenya, a group called the Pokot place high emphasis on sexual pleasure, and they expect that both a husband and wife will reach orgasm. If a husband does not satisfy his wife, he is in trouble—especially if she thinks that his failure is because of adultery. If this is so, the wife and her female friends will sneak up on her husband when he is asleep. The women will tie him up, shout obscenities at him, beat him, and then urinate on him. Before releasing him, as a final gesture of their contempt they will slaughter and eat his favorite ox. The husband's hours of painful humiliation are intended to make him more dutiful concerning his wife's conjugal rights.

People can also become deviants for following their group's ideal norms instead of its real norms. As with

Brian A. Vikander/Corbis
A Pokot married man
Northern Kenya

many groups, the Zapotec Indians of Mexico profess that sexual relations should take place exclusively between husband and wife. Sexual affairs among the Zapotec are common, however, as the Zapotec also have a covert norm, an unspoken understanding, that married people will have affairs, but that they should be discreet about them. In one Zapotec community, the *only* person who did not have an extramarital affair was condemned by everyone in the village. The reason was not that she did not have an affair but that she told the other wives the names of the women their husbands were sleeping with. It is an interesting case, for if this virtuous woman had had an affair—and kept her mouth shut—she would not have become a deviant. Clearly, real norms can conflict with ideal norms—another illustration of the gap between ideal and real culture.

For Your Consideration

How do the behaviors of the Pokot wives and husbands mentioned here look from the perspective of U.S. norms? What are those U.S. norms? Did the Zapotec woman break norms of sexual behavior or of gossip and privacy? How does cultural relativity apply to the Pokot and Zapotec?

You don't like it, but you decide to buy a case of soda. At the checkout, the clerk says, "I hope you don't mind, but there's a $5 service charge on every fifteenth customer." You, of course, are the fifteenth.

Just as you start to leave, another clerk stops you and says, "We're not working any more. We decided to have a party." Suddenly a CD player begins to blast, and everyone in the store begins to dance. "Oh, good, you've brought the soda," says a different clerk, who takes your package and passes sodas all around.

Life is not like this, of course. You can depend on grocery clerks to sell you milk. You can also depend on paying the same price as everyone else and not being forced to attend a party in the store. Why can you depend on this? Because we are socialized to follow norms, to play the basic roles that society assigns to us.

Without norms, we would have social chaos. Norms lay out the basic guidelines for how we should play our roles and interact with others. In short, norms bring about **social order,** a group's customary social arrangements. Our lives are based on these arrangements, which is why deviance often is perceived as threatening: *Deviance undermines predictability, the foundation of social life.* Consequently, human groups develop a system of **social control**—formal and informal means of enforcing norms.

social order a group's usual and customary social arrangements, on which its members depend and on which they base their lives

social control a group's formal and informal means of enforcing its norms

105

Violating background assumptions is a common form of deviance. Although we have no explicit rule that says, "Do not put snakes through your nose," we all know that it exists (perhaps as a subcategory of "Don't do strange things in public"). Is this act also deviant for this man in Chennai, India?

Sanctions

People do not enforce folkways strictly, but they become upset when people break mores (MO-rays). Expressions of disapproval of deviance, called **negative sanctions,** range from frowns and gossip for breaking folkways to imprisonment and capital punishment for breaking mores. In general, the more seriously the group takes a norm, the harsher the penalty for violating it. In contrast, **positive sanctions**—from smiles to formal awards—are used to reward people for conforming to norms. Getting a raise is a positive sanction; being fired is a negative sanction. Getting an *A* in intro to sociology is a positive sanction; getting an *F* is a negative one.

Most negative sanctions are informal. You might stare if you observe someone dressed in what you consider to be inappropriate clothing, or you might gossip if a married person you know spends the night with someone other than his or her spouse. Whether you consider the breaking of a norm merely an amusing matter that warrants no sanction or a serious infraction that does, however, depends on your perspective. Let's suppose that a woman appears at your college graduation in a bikini. You might stare, laugh, and nudge the person next to you, but if this is *your* mother, you are likely to feel that different sanctions are appropriate. Similarly, if it is *your* father who spends the night with an 18-year-old college freshman, you are likely to do more than gossip.

In Sum: In sociology, the term *deviance* refers to all violations of social rules, regardless of their seriousness. The term is neutral, not a judgment about the behavior. Deviance is relative, for what is deviant in one group may be conformist in another. Consequently, we must consider deviance from *within* a group's own framework, for it is their meanings that underlie their behavior.

Competing Explanations of Deviance: Sociobiology, Psychology, and Sociology

If social life is to exist, norms are essential. So why do people violate them? To better understand the reasons, it is useful to know how sociological explanations differ from biological and psychological ones.

Sociobiologists explain deviance by looking for answers *within* individuals. They assume that **genetic predispositions** lead people to such deviances as juvenile delinquency and crime (Lombroso 1911; Wilson and Herrnstein 1985; Goozen et al. 2007). Among their explanations were these three theories: (1) intelligence—low intelligence leads to crime; (2) the "XYY" theory—an extra Y chromosome in males leads to crime; and (3) body type—people with "squarish, muscular" bodies are more likely to commit **street crime**—acts such as mugging, rape, and burglary.

How have these theories held up? We should first note that most people who have these supposedly "causal" characteristics do not become criminals. Regarding intelligence, you already know that some criminals are very intelligent and that most people of low intelligence do not commit crimes. Regarding the extra Y chromosome, most men who commit crimes have the normal XY chromosome combination, and most men with the XYY combination do not become criminals. No women have this combination of genes, so this explanation can't even be applied to female criminals. Regarding body type, criminals exhibit the full range of body types, and most people with "squarish, muscular" bodies do not become street criminals.

Psychologists also focus on abnormalities *within* the individual. They examine what are called **personality disorders.** Their supposition is that deviating individuals have deviating personalities (Barnes 2001; Mayer 2007) and that subconscious motives drive people to deviance. No specific childhood experience, however, is invariably linked with deviance. For example, children who had "bad toilet training," "suffocating mothers," or

negative sanction an expression of disapproval for breaking a norm, ranging from a mild, informal reaction such as a frown to a formal reaction such as a prison sentence or an execution

positive sanction a reward or positive reaction for following norms, ranging from a smile to a material award

genetic predisposition inborn tendencies (for example, a tendency to commit deviant acts)

street crime crimes such as mugging, rape, and burglary

personality disorders the view that a personality disturbance of some sort causes an individual to violate social norms

REUTERS/Babu/Landov

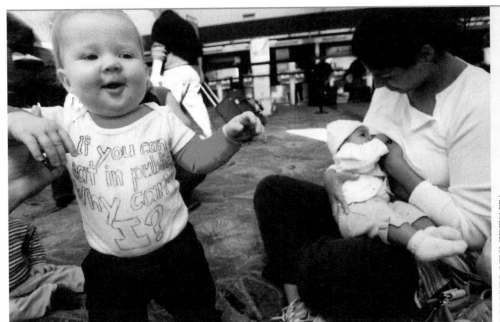

In a changing society, the boundaries of what is considered deviance are constantly changing. After a mother was kicked off a Delta flight for nursing her child, mothers protested by staging a "nurse-in" at Delta ticket counters across the country.

ROBERTO SCHMIDT/AFP/
Getty Images

"emotionally aloof fathers" may become embezzling bookkeepers—or good accountants. Just as college students, teachers, and police officers represent a variety of bad—and good—childhood experiences, so do deviants. Similarly, people with "suppressed anger" can become freeway snipers or military heroes—or anything else. In short, there is no inevitable outcome of any childhood experience. Deviance is not associated with any particular personality.

Sociologists, in contrast with both sociobiologists and psychologists, search for factors *outside* the individual. They look for social influences that "recruit" people to break norms. To account for why people commit crimes, for example, sociologists examine such external influences as socialization, membership in subcultures, and social class. *Social class* refers to people's relative standing in terms of education, occupation, and especially income and wealth.

The point stressed earlier, that deviance is relative, leads sociologists to ask a crucial question: Why should we expect to find something constant within people to account for a behavior that is conforming in one society and deviant in another? To explain deviance, sociologists apply the three sociological perspectives—symbolic interactionism, functionalism, and conflict theory.

The Symbolic Interactionist Perspective

As we examine symbolic interactionism, it will become more evident why sociologists are not satisfied with explanations that are rooted in sociobiology or psychology. A basic principle of symbolic interactionism is that we are thinking beings who act according to our interpretations of situations. Let's consider how our membership in groups influences how we view life and, from there, our behavior.

Differential Association Theory

The Theory.   Going directly against the idea that biology or personality is the source of deviance, sociologists stress our experiences in groups (Deflem 2006; Chambliss 1973/2007). Consider an extreme: boys and girls who join street gangs and those who join the Scouts. Obviously, each will learn different attitudes and behaviors concerning deviance and conformity. Edwin Sutherland coined the term **differential association** to indicate this: From the *different* groups we *associate* with, we learn to deviate from or conform to society's norms (Sutherland 1924, 1947; Sutherland et al. 1992).

differential association
Edwin Sutherland's term to indicate that people who associate with some groups learn an "excess of definitions" of deviance, increasing the likelihood that they will become deviant

To experience a sense of belonging is a basic human need. Membership in groups, especially peer groups, is a primary way that people meet this need. Regardless of the orientation of the group—whether to conformity or deviance—the process is the same. These teens belong to DEFYIT (Drug-Free Youth in Town), an organization that promotes a drug-free lifestyle.

Sutherland's theory is more complicated than this, but he basically said that the different groups with which we associate (our "*differential* association") give us messages about conformity and deviance. We may receive mixed messages, but we end up with more of one than the other (an "excess of definitions," as Sutherland put it). The end result is an imbalance—attitudes that tilt us in one direction or another. Consequently, we learn to either conform or to deviate.

Families. Since our family is so important for teaching us attitudes, it probably is obvious to you that the family makes a big difference in whether we learn deviance or conformity. Researchers have confirmed this informal observation. Of the many confirming studies, this one stands out: Of all prison inmates across the United States, about *half* have a father, mother, brother, sister, or spouse who has served time in prison (*Criminal Justice Statistics* 2003:Table 6.0011; Glaze and Maruschak 2008:Table 11). In short, families that are involved in crime tend to set their children on a lawbreaking path.

Friends, Neighborhoods, and Subcultures. Most people don't know the term *differential association,* but they do know how it works. Most parents want to move out of "bad" neighborhoods because they know that if their kids have delinquent friends, they are likely to become delinquent, too. Sociological research also supports this common observation (Miller 1958; Chung and Steinberg 2006; Yonas et al. 2006). Some neighborhoods even develop a subculture of violence. In these places, even a teasing remark can mean instant death. If the neighbors feel that a victim deserved to be killed, they refuse to testify because "he got what was coming to him" (Kubrin and Weitzer 2003).

In some neighborhoods, killing is even considered an honorable act:

Sociologist Ruth Horowitz (1983, 2005), who did participant observation in a lower-class Chicano neighborhood in Chicago, discovered how associating with people who have a certain concept of "honor" propels young men to deviance. The formula is simple. "A real man has honor. An insult is a threat to one's honor. Therefore, not to stand up to someone is to be less than a real man."

Now suppose you are a young man growing up in this neighborhood. You likely would do a fair amount of fighting, for you would interpret many things as attacks on your honor. You might even carry a knife or a gun, for words and fists wouldn't always be sufficient. Along with members of your group, you would define fighting, knifing, and shooting quite differently from the way most people do.

Members of the Mafia also intertwine ideas of manliness with violence. For them, *to kill is a measure of their manhood.* Not all killings are accorded the same respect, however, for "the more awesome and potent the victim, the more worthy and meritorious the killer" (Arlacchi 1980). Some killings are done to enforce norms. A member of the Mafia who gives information to the police, for example, has violated *omertá* (the Mafia's vow of secrecy). This offense can never be tolerated, for it threatens the very existence of the group. Mafia killings further illustrate just how relative deviance is. Although killing is deviant to mainstream society, for members of the Mafia, *not* to kill after certain rules are broken—such as when someone "squeals" to the cops—is the deviant act.

Prison or Freedom? An issue that comes up over and over again in sociology is whether we are prisoners of socialization. Symbolic interactionists stress that we are not mere pawns in the hands of others. We are not destined to think and act as our groups dictate. Rather, we *help to produce our own orientations to life.* By joining one group rather than another (differential association), for example, we help to shape the self. For instance, one college student may join a feminist group that is trying to change the treatment of women in college; another may associate with a group of women who shoplift on weekends. Their choice of groups points them in different directions. The one who joins the feminist group may develop an even greater interest in producing social change, while the one who associates with shoplifters may become even more oriented toward criminal activities.

Control Theory

Do you ever feel the urge to do something that you know you shouldn't, something that would get you in trouble if you did it? Most of us fight temptations to break society's norms. We find that we have to stifle things inside us—urges, hostilities, desires of various sorts. And most of the time, we manage to keep ourselves out of trouble. The basic question that control theory tries to answer is: With the desire to deviate so common, why don't we all just "bust loose"?

The social control of deviance takes many forms. One of its most obvious is the use of the police to enforce norms. The man in the center of this photo taken in Naples, Italy, is Edoardo Contini, a mafia boss who was considered one of Italy's 30 most dangerous fugitives.

REUTERS/Stefano Renna-AGN/Landov

The Theory. Sociologist Walter Reckless (1973), who developed **control theory,** stressed that two control systems work against our motivations to deviate. Our *inner controls* include our internalized morality—conscience, religious principles, ideas of right and wrong. Inner controls also include fears of punishment, feelings of integrity, and the desire to be a "good" person (Hirschi 1969; McShane and Williams 2007). Our *outer controls* consist of people—such as family, friends, and the police—who influence us not to deviate.

The stronger our bonds are with society, the more effective our inner controls are (Hirschi 1969). Bonds are based on *attachments* (our affection and respect for people who conform to mainstream norms), *commitments* (having a stake in society that you don't want to risk, such as a respected place in your family, a good standing at college, a good job), *involvements* (participating in approved activities), and *beliefs* (convictions that certain actions are morally wrong).

This theory can be summarized as *self*-control, says sociologist Travis Hirschi. The key to learning high self-control is socialization, especially in childhood. Parents help their children to develop self-control by supervising them and punishing their deviant acts (Gottfredson and Hirschi 1990; Hay and Forrest 2006). They sometimes use shame to keep their children in line. You probably had that forefinger shaken at you. I certainly recall it aimed at me. Do you think that more use of shaming, discussed in the Down-to-Earth Sociology box on the next page, could help increase people's internal controls?

Applying Control Theory

Suppose that some friends invite you to go to a nightclub with them. When you get there, you notice that everyone seems unusually happy—almost giddy. They seem to be euphoric in their animated conversations and dancing. Your friends tell you that almost everyone here has taken the drug Ecstasy, and they invite you to take some with them.

What do you do? Let's not explore the question of whether taking Ecstasy in this setting is a deviant or a conforming act. That is a separate issue. Instead, concentrate on the pushes and

control theory the idea that two control systems—inner controls and outer controls—work against our tendencies to deviate

Down-to-Earth Sociology
Shaming: Making a Comeback?

Shaming can be effective, especially when members of a primary group use it. In some small communities, where the individual's reputation was at stake, shaming was the centerpiece of the enforcement of norms. Violators were marked as deviant and held up for all the world to see. In Spain, where one's reputation with neighbors still matters, debt collectors, dressed in tuxedo and top hat, walk slowly to the front door. The sight shames debtors into paying (Catan 2008). In Nathaniel Hawthorne's *The Scarlet Letter*, town officials forced Hester Prynne to wear a scarlet A sewn on her dress. The A stood for *adulteress*. Wherever she went, Prynne had to wear this badge of shame, and the community expected her to wear it every day for the rest of her life.

As our society grew large and urban, its sense of community diminished, and shaming lost its effectiveness. Now shaming is starting to make a comeback. One Arizona sheriff makes the men in his jail wear striped prison uniforms—and pink underwear (Billeaud 2008). As in the photo on this page, they also wear pink while they work in chain gangs. Women prisoners, too, are put in chain gangs and forced to pick up street trash. Online shaming sites have also appeared. Captured on cell phone cameras are bad drivers, older men who leer at teenaged girls, and dog walkers who don't pick up their dog's poop (Saranow 2007). Some sites post photos of the offenders, as well as their addresses and phone numbers.

Sociologist Harold Garfinkel (1956) gave the name **degradation ceremony** to an extreme form of shaming. The individual is called to account before the group, witnesses denounce him or her, the offender is pronounced guilty, and steps are taken to strip the individual of his or her identity as a group member. In some courts martial, officers who are found guilty stand at attention before their peers while the insignia of rank are ripped from their uniforms. This procedure screams that the individual is no longer a member of the group. Although Hester Prynne was not banished from the group physically, she was banished morally; her degradation ceremony proclaimed her a *moral* outcast from the community. The scarlet A marked her as "not one" of them.

Although we don't use scarlet A's today, informal degradation ceremonies still occur. Consider what happened to this New York City police officer (Chivers 2001):

"*If you drive and drink, you'll wear pink*" is the slogan of a campaign to shame drunk drivers in Phoenix, Arizona. Shown here are convicted drunk drivers who will pick up trash while wearing pink.

Joseph Gray had been a police officer in New York City for fifteen years. As with some of his fellow officers, alcohol and sex helped relieve the pressures of police work. After spending one afternoon drinking in a topless bar, bleary-eyed, Gray plowed his car into a vehicle carrying a pregnant woman, her son, and her sister. All three died. Gray was accused of manslaughter and drunk driving.

The *New York Times* and New York television stations kept hammering this story to the public. Three weeks later, Gray resigned from the police force. As he left police headquarters after resigning, an angry crowd surrounded him. Gray hung his head in public disgrace as Victor Manuel Herrera, whose wife and son were killed in the crash, followed him, shouting, "You're a murderer!" (Gray was later convicted of drunk driving and manslaughter.)

For Your Consideration

1. How do you think law enforcement officials might use shaming to reduce law breaking?
2. How do you think school officials could use shaming?
3. Suppose that you were caught shoplifting at a store near where you live. Would you rather spend a week in jail with no one but your family knowing it (and no permanent record) or a week walking in front of the store you stole from wearing a placard that proclaims in bold red capital letters: I AM A THIEF! and in smaller letters says: "I am sorry for stealing from this store and causing you to have to pay higher prices"? Why?

pulls you would feel. The pushes toward taking the drug: your friends, the setting, and your curiosity. Then there are your inner controls—those inner voices of your conscience and your parents, perhaps of your teachers, as well as your fears of arrest and the dangers you've heard about illegal drugs. There are also the outer controls—perhaps the uniformed security guard looking in your direction.

So, what *did* you decide? Which was stronger: your inner and outer controls or the pushes and pulls toward taking the drug? It is you who can best weigh these forces, for they differ with each of us. This little example puts us at the center of what control theory is all about.

Labeling Theory

Suppose for one undesirable moment that you had the reputation as a "whore," a "pervert," or a "cheat." (Pick one.) What power such a reputation would have—both on how others would see you and on how you would see yourself. How about if you became known as "very intelligent," "truthful in everything," or "honest to the core"? (Choose one.) You can see that such a reputation would give people a different expectation of your character and behavior. This is what **labeling theory** focuses on, the significance of reputations, how they help set us on paths that propel us into deviance or that divert us away from it.

Bettmann/Corbis

Degradation ceremonies, a form of shaming, are intended to humiliate norm violators and mark them as "not members" of the group. This photo was taken by the U.S. army in 1945 after U.S. troops liberated Cherbourg, France. Members of the French resistance shaved the heads of these women, who had "collaborated" (had sex with) the occupying Nazis. They then marched the shamed women down the streets of the city, while the public shouted insults and spat on them.

Rejecting Labels: How People Neutralize Deviance. Not many of us want to be called "whores," "perverts," and so on. Most of us resist the negative labels that others try to pin on us. Some of us are so successful that even though we persist in deviance, we still consider ourselves conformists. For example, some people who beat up others and vandalize property consider themselves to be conforming members of society. How do they do it?

Sociologists Gresham Sykes and David Matza (1957/1988) studied boys like this. They found that the boys used five **techniques of neutralization** to deflect society's norms.

Denial of Responsibility Some boys said, "I'm not responsible for what happened because . . ." and then they were quite creative about the "becauses." Some said that what happened was an "accident." Other boys saw themselves as "victims" of society. What else could you expect? They were like billiard balls shot around the pool table of life.

Denial of Injury Another favorite explanation was "What I did wasn't wrong because no one got hurt." The boys would define vandalism as "mischief," gang fights as a "private quarrel," and stealing cars as "borrowing." They might acknowledge that what they did was illegal, but claim that they were "just having a little fun."

Denial of a Victim Some boys thought of themselves as avengers. Vandalizing a teacher's car was done to get revenge for an unfair grade, while shoplifting was a way to even the score with "crooked" store owners. In short, even if the boys did accept responsibility and admit that someone had gotten hurt, they protected their self-concept by claiming that the people "deserved what they got."

Condemnation of the Condemners Another technique the boys used was to deny that others had the right to judge them. They might accuse people who pointed their fingers at them of being "a bunch of hypocrites": The police were "on the take," teachers had "pets," and parents cheated on their taxes. In short, they said, "Who are *they* to accuse *me* of something?"

Appeal to Higher Loyalties A final technique the boys used to justify their activities was to consider loyalty to the gang more important than the norms of society. They might say, "I had to help my friends. That's why I got in the fight." Not incidentally, the boy may have shot two members of a rival group, as well as a bystander!

degradation ceremony a term coined by Harold Garfinkel to refer to a ritual whose goal is to reshape someone's self by stripping away that individual's self-identity and stamping a new identity in its place

labeling theory the view that the labels people are given affect their own and others' perceptions of them, thus channeling their behavior into either deviance or conformity

techniques of neutralization ways of thinking or rationalizing that help people deflect (or neutralize) society's norms

In Sum: These five techniques of neutralization have implications far beyond this group of boys, for it is not only delinquents who try to neutralize the norms of mainstream society. Look again at these five techniques—don't they sound familiar? (1) "I couldn't help myself"; (2) "Who really got hurt?"; (3) "Don't you think she deserved that, after what *she* did?"; (4) "Who are *you* to talk?"; and (5) "I had to help my friends—wouldn't you have done the same thing?" All of us attempt to neutralize the moral demands of society, for neutralization helps us to sleep at night.

Embracing Labels: The Example of Outlaw Bikers. Although most of us resist attempts to label us as deviant, some people revel in a deviant identity. Some teenagers, for example, make certain by their clothing, choice of music, hairstyles, and "body art" that no one misses their rejection of adult norms. Their status among fellow members of a subculture—within which they are almost obsessive conformists—is vastly more important than any status outside it.

One of the best examples of a group that embraces deviance is motorcycle gangs. Sociologist Mark Watson (1980/2006) did participant observation with outlaw bikers. He rebuilt Harleys with them, hung around their bars and homes, and went on "runs" (trips) with them. He concluded that outlaw bikers see the world as "hostile, weak, and effeminate." Holding this conventional world in contempt, gang members pride themselves on breaking its norms and getting in trouble, laughing at death, and treating women as lesser beings whose primary value is to provide them with services—especially sex. They pride themselves in looking "dirty, mean, and generally undesirable," taking pleasure in shocking people by their appearance and behavior. Outlaw bikers also regard themselves as losers, a factor that becomes woven into their unusual embrace of deviance.

The Power of Labels: The Saints and the Roughnecks. We can see how powerful labeling is by looking at the example of the "Saints" and the "Roughnecks." Both groups of high school boys were "constantly occupied with truancy, drinking, wild parties, petty theft, and vandalism." Yet their teachers looked on one group, the Saints, as "headed for success" and the other group, the Roughnecks, as "headed for trouble." By the time they finished high school, not one Saint had been arrested, while the Roughnecks had been in constant trouble with the police.

Why did the members of the community perceive these boys so differently? Chambliss (1973/2007) concluded that this split vision was due to *social class.* As symbolic interactionists emphasize, social class is like a lens that focuses our perceptions. The Saints came from respectable, middle-class families, while the Roughnecks were

How powerful are labels? Consider Michael Vick: Great football player or cruel dog fighter? Rich sports hero or convict? Shown here is Vick's attorney giving a press conference after Vick was sentenced to 23 months in prison. After serving 19 months in prison, he was given another NFL contract.

Jay Paul/Bloomberg News/Landov

from less respectable, working-class families. These backgrounds led teachers and the authorities to expect good behavior from the Saints but trouble from the Roughnecks. And, like the rest of us, teachers and police saw what they expected to see.

The boys' social class also affected their visibility. The Saints had automobiles, and they did their drinking and vandalism outside of town. Without cars, the Roughnecks hung around their own street corners, where their drinking and boisterous behavior drew the attention of police, confirming the negative impressions that the community already had of them.

The boys' social class also equipped them with distinct *styles of interaction*. When police or teachers questioned them, the Saints were apologetic. This show of respect for authority elicited a positive reaction from teachers and police, allowing the Saints to escape school and legal problems. The Roughnecks, said Chambliss, were "almost the polar opposite." When questioned, they were hostile. Even when they tried to assume a respectful attitude, everyone could see through it. Consequently, while teachers and police let the Saints off with warnings, they came down hard on the Roughnecks.

Certainly, what happens in life is not determined by labels alone, but the Saints and the Roughnecks did live up to the labels that the community gave them. As you may recall, all but one of the Saints went on to college. One earned a Ph.D., one became a lawyer, one a doctor, and the others business managers. In contrast, only two of the Roughnecks went to college. They earned athletic scholarships and became coaches. The other Roughnecks did not fare so well. Two of them dropped out of high school, later became involved in separate killings, and were sent to prison. One became a local bookie, and no one knows the whereabouts of the other.

How do labels work? Although the matter is complex, because it involves the self-concept and reactions that vary from one individual to another, we can note that labels open and close doors of opportunity. Unlike its meaning in sociology, the term *deviant* in everyday usage is emotionally charged with a judgment of some sort. This label can lock people out of conforming groups and push them into almost exclusive contact with people who have been similarly labeled.

In Sum: Symbolic interactionists examine how people's definitions of the situation underlie their deviating from or conforming to social norms. They focus on group membership (differential association), how people balance pressures to conform and to deviate (control theory), and the significance of people's reputations (labeling theory).

The central point of symbolic interactionism, that *deviance* involves a clash of competing definitions, is explored in the Mass Media box on the next page.

The Functionalist Perspective

When we think of deviance, its dysfunctions are likely to come to mind. Functionalists, in contrast, are as likely to stress the functions of deviance as they are to emphasize its dysfunctions.

Can Deviance Really Be Functional for Society?

Most of us are upset by deviance, especially crime, and assume that society would be better off without it. The classic functionalist theorist Emile Durkheim (1893/1933, 1895/1964), however, came to a surprising conclusion. Deviance, he said—including crime—is functional for society, for it contributes to the social order. Its three main functions are:

1. *Deviance clarifies moral boundaries and affirms norms.* A group's ideas about how people should think and act mark its *moral boundaries*. Deviant acts challenge those boundaries. To call a member into account is to say, in effect, "You broke an important rule, and we cannot tolerate that." Punishing deviants affirms the group's norms and clarifies what it means to be a member of the group.
2. *Deviance promotes social unity.* To affirm the group's moral boundaries by punishing deviants fosters a "we" feeling among the group's members. In saying, "You can't get away with that," the group affirms the rightness of its own ways.

MASS MEDIA In SOCIAL LIFE

Pornography and the Mainstream: Freedom Versus Censorship

Pornography vividly illustrates one of the sociological principles discussed in this chapter: the relativity of deviance. It is not the act, but reactions to the act, that make something deviant. Consider pornography on the Internet.

Porn surfers have a wide variety of choices. Sites are indexed by race–ethnicity, sex, hair color, age, weight, heterosexuality, homosexuality, singles, groups, and sexual activity. Sites feature teenagers, cheerleaders, sneaky shots, and "grannies who still think they have it." Some sites offer only photographs, others video and sound. There also are live sites. After agreeing to the hefty per-minute charges, you can command your "model" to do almost anything your heart desires.

What is the problem? Why can't people exchange nude photos electronically if they want to? Or watch others having sex online, if someone offers that service? Although some people object to any kind of sex site, what disturbs many are the sites that feature bondage, torture, rape, bestiality (humans having sex with animals), and sex with children.

The Internet abounds with sites where people "meet" online to discuss some topic. No one is bothered by sites that feature Roman architecture or rap music or sports, of course, but those that focus on how to torture women are another matter. So are those that offer lessons on how to seduce grade school children—or that extol the delights of having sex with three-year-olds.

The state and federal governments have passed laws against child pornography, and the police seize computers of suspects and search them for illegal pictures. The penalties can be severe. When photos of children in sex acts were found on an Arizona man's computer, he was sentenced to 200 years in prison (Greenhouse 2007). When he appealed his sentence as unconstitutional (cruel, unusual), his sentence was upheld. To exchange pictures of tortured and sexually abused women remains legal.

Roman/AgeFotoStock

The issue of censorship is front and center in the debate about pornography. While some people want to ban pornography, others, even those who find it immoral, say that we must tolerate it. No matter how much we may disagree with a point of view, or even find it repugnant, they say, we must allow communications about it. This includes photos and videos. If we let the government censor the Internet in any way, it will stretch that inch into a mile and censor the expression of other things it doesn't like—such as criticism of government officials (Foley 2008).

As this debate continues, pornography is moving into the mainstream. The online sex industry now has an annual trade show, Internext. Predictions at Internext are that hotels will soon offer not just sex videos on demand but also live images of people having sex (Johnston 2007). In its struggle for legitimacy, the sex industry is trying to get banks to invest in it—and to be listed on the stock exchanges (Richtel 2007). As social views change, this is likely to happen.

For Your Consideration

Can you disprove the central point of the symbolic interactionists—that an activity is deviant only because people decide that it is deviant? You may use any examples, but you cannot invoke God or moral absolutes in your argument, as they are outside the scope of sociology. Sociology cannot decide moral issues, even in extreme cases.

On pornography and censorship: Do you think it should be legal to exchange photos of women being sexually abused or tortured? Should it be legal to discuss ways to seduce children? If not, on what basis should these activities be banned? If we make them illegal, then what other communications should we prohibit? On what basis?

---

3. *Deviance promotes social change.* Groups do not always agree on what to do with people who push beyond their accepted ways of doing things. Some group members may even approve of the rule-breaking behavior. Boundary violations that gain enough support become new, acceptable behaviors. Deviance, then, may force a group to rethink and redefine its moral boundaries, helping groups—and whole societies—to adapt to changing circumstances.

Strain Theory: How Social Values Produce Deviance

Functionalists argue that crime is a *natural* part of society, not an aberration or some alien element in our midst. Mainstream values can even generate crime. Consider what sociologists Richard Cloward and Lloyd Ohlin (1960) identified as the crucial problem of the industrialized world: the need to locate and train its talented people—whether they were born into wealth or into poverty—so that they can take over the key technical jobs of society. When children are born, no one knows which ones will have the ability to become dentists, nuclear physicists, or engineers. To get the most talented people to compete with one another, society tries to motivate *everyone* to strive for success. It does this by arousing discontent—making people feel dissatisfied with what they have so they will try to "better" themselves.

We are quite successful in getting almost everyone to want **cultural goals,** success of some sort, such as wealth or prestige. But we aren't very successful in equalizing access to the **institutionalized means,** the legitimate ways to reach those goals. As sociologist Robert Merton (1956, 1968) analyzed socialization into success and the blocked access to it, he developed **strain theory.** *Strain* refers to the frustrations people feel when they want success but find their way to it blocked. It is easy to identify with mainstream norms (such as working hard or pursuing higher education) when they help you get ahead, but when they don't seem to be getting you anywhere, you feel frustrated. You might even feel wronged by the system. If mainstream rules seem illegitimate, you experience a gap that Merton called *anomie,* a sense of normlessness.

As part of living in society, all of us have to face these cultural goals and institutionalized means. Table 1 compares the various ways that people react to them. The first reaction, which Merton said is the most common, is *conformity,* using socially acceptable means to try to reach cultural goals. In industrialized societies most people try to get good jobs, a good education, and so on. If well-paid jobs are unavailable, they take less desirable jobs. If they are denied access to Harvard or Stanford, they go to a state university. Others take night classes and go to vocational schools. In short, most people take the socially acceptable path.

Four Deviant Paths.   The remaining four responses, which are deviant, represent reactions to the strain people feel between the goals they want and their access to the institutionalized means to reach them. Let's look at each. *Innovators* are people who accept the goals of society but use illegitimate means to try to reach them. Crack dealers, for instance, accept the goal of achieving wealth, but they reject the legitimate avenues for doing so. Other examples are embezzlers, robbers, and con artists.

The second deviant path is taken by people who become discouraged and give up on achieving cultural goals. Yet they still cling to conventional rules of conduct. Merton called this response *ritualism.* Although ritualists have given up on getting ahead at work, they survive by rigorously following the rules of their job. Teachers whose idealism is shattered (who are said to suffer from "burnout"), for example, remain in the classroom, where they teach without enthusiasm. Their response is considered deviant because they cling to the job even though they have abandoned the goal, which may have been to stimulate young minds or to make the world a better place.

People who choose the third deviant path, *retreatism,* reject both the cultural goals and the institutionalized means of achieving them. Some people stop pursuing success and retreat into alcohol or drugs. Although their path to withdrawal is considerably different, women who enter a convent or men a monastery are also retreatists.

The final type of deviant response is *rebellion.* Convinced that their society is corrupt, rebels, like retreatists, reject both society's goals and its institutionalized means. Unlike retreatists, however, rebels seek to give society new goals, as well as new means for reaching them. Revolutionaries are the most committed type of rebels.

cultural goals the objectives held out as legitimate or desirable for the members of a society to achieve

institutionalized means approved ways of reaching cultural goals

strain theory Robert Merton's term for the strain engendered when a society socializes large numbers of people to desire a cultural goal (such as success), but withholds from some the approved means of reaching that goal; one adaptation to the strain is crime, the choice of an innovative means (one outside the approved system) to attain the cultural goal

TABLE 1	How People Match Their Goals to Their Means		
Do They Feel the Strain That Leads to Anomie?	**Mode of Adaptation**	**Cultural Goals**	**Institutionalized Means**
No	Conformity	Accept	Accept
	Deviant Paths:		
	1. Innovation	Accept	Reject
Yes	2. Ritualism	Reject	Accept
	3. Retreatism	Reject	Reject
	4. Rebellion	Reject/Replace	Reject/Replace

Source: Based on Merton 1968.

illegitimate opportunity
structure opportunities for
crimes that are woven into the
texture of life

white-collar crime Edwin
Sutherland's term for crimes
committed by people of respectable and high social status
in the course of their occupations; for example, bribery of
public officials, securities violations, embezzlement, false advertising, and price fixing

corporate crime crimes
committed by executives
in order to benefit their
corporation

In Sum: Strain theory underscores the sociological principle that deviants are the product of society. Mainstream social values (cultural goals and institutionalized means to reach those goals) can produce strain (frustration, dissatisfaction). People who feel this strain are more likely than others to take the deviant (nonconforming) paths summarized in Table 1.

Illegitimate Opportunity Structures: Social Class and Crime

Let's look now at how social class produces distinct styles of crime.

Street Crime. In applying strain theory, functionalists point out that industrialized societies have no trouble socializing the poor into wanting to own things. Like others, the poor are bombarded with messages urging them to buy everything from Xboxes and iPods to designer jeans and new cars. Television and movies are filled with images of middle-class people enjoying luxurious lives. The poor get the message—all full-fledged Americans can afford society's many goods and services.

Yet, the most common route to success, the school system, presents a bewildering world. Run by the middle class, schools are at odds with the background of the poor. What the poor take for granted is unacceptable, questioned, and mocked. Their speech, for example, is built around nonstandard grammar and is often laced with what the middle class considers obscenities. Their ideas of punctuality and their poor preparation in reading and paper-and-pencil skills also make it difficult to fit in. Facing such barriers, the poor are more likely than their more privileged counterparts to drop out of school. Educational failure, of course, slams the door on most legitimate avenues to financial success.

It is not that the poor are left without opportunities for financial success. Woven into life in urban slums is what Cloward and Ohlin (1960) called an **illegitimate opportunity structure.** An alternative door to success opens: "hustles" such as robbery, burglary, drug dealing, prostitution, pimping, gambling, and other crimes (Sánchez-Jankowski 2003; Anderson 1978, 1990/2006). Pimps and drug dealers, for example, present an image of a glamorous life—people who are in control and have plenty of "easy money." For many of the poor, the "hustler" becomes a role model.

It should be easy to see, then, why street crime attracts disproportionate numbers of the poor. In the Down-to-Earth Sociology box on the next page, let's look at how gangs are part of the illegitimate opportunity structure that beckons disadvantaged youth.

White-Collar Crime. Like the poor, the *forms* of crime of the more privileged classes also match their life situation. And how different their illegitimate opportunities are! Physicians don't hold up cabbies, but they do cheat Medicare. Investment managers like Bernie Madoff run fraudulent schemes that cheat customers around the world. Mugging, pimping, and burgling are not part of this more privileged world, but evading income tax, bribing public officials, and embezzling are. Sociologist Edwin Sutherland (1949) coined the term **white-collar crime** to refer to crimes that people of respectable and high social status commit in the course of their occupations.

A special form of white-collar crime is **corporate crime,** crimes committed by executives in order to benefit their corporation. For example, to increase corporate profits, Sears executives

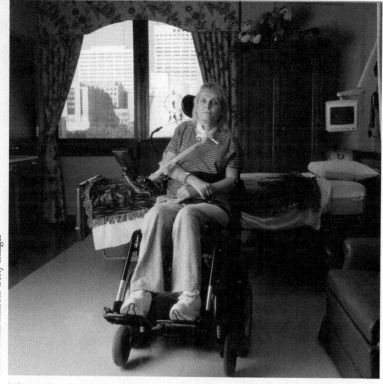

Pam Francis/Liaison/Getty Images

White collar crime usually involves only the loss of property, but not always. To save money, Ford executives kept faulty Firestone tires on their Explorers. The cost? The lives of over 200 people. Shown here in Houston is one of their victims. She survived a needless accident, but was left a quadraplegic. Not one Ford executive spent even a single day in jail.

Down-to-Earth Sociology

Islands in the Street: Urban Gangs in the United States

A. Ramey/PhotoEdit, Inc.

For more than ten years, sociologist Martín Sánchez-Jankowski (1991) did participant observation of thirty-seven African American, Chicano, Dominican, Irish, Jamaican, and Puerto Rican gangs in Boston, Los Angeles, and New York City. The gangs earned money through gambling, arson, mugging, armed robbery, and selling moonshine, drugs, guns, stolen car parts, and protection. Sánchez-Jankowski ate, slept, and fought with the gangs, but by mutual agreement he did not participate in drug dealing or other illegal activities. He was seriously injured twice during the study.

Contrary to stereotypes, Sánchez-Jankowski did not find that the motive for joining was to escape a broken home (there were as many members from intact families as from broken homes) or to seek a substitute family (the same number of boys said they were close to their families as those who said they were not). Rather, the boys joined to gain access to money, to have recreation (including girls and drugs), to maintain anonymity in committing crimes, to get protection, and to help the community. This last reason may seem surprising, but in some neighborhoods, gangs protect residents from outsiders and spearhead political change (Kontos et al. 2003). The boys also saw the gang as an alternative to the dead-end—and deadening—jobs held by their parents.

Neighborhood residents are ambivalent about gangs. On the one hand, they fear the violence. On the other hand, many of the adults once belonged to gangs, some gangs provide better protection than the police, and gang members are the children of people who live in the neighborhood.

Particular gangs will come and go, but gangs will likely always remain part of the city. As functionalists point out, gangs fulfill needs of poor youth who live on the margins of society.

For Your Consideration

What functions do gangs fulfill (what needs do they meet)? Suppose that you have been hired as an urban planner for the city of Los Angeles. How could you arrange to meet the needs that gangs fulfill in ways that minimize violence and encourage youth to follow mainstream norms?

---

defrauded $100 million from victims so poor that they had filed for bankruptcy. To avoid a criminal trial, Sears pleaded guilty. This frightened the parent companies of Macy's and Bloomingdales, which were doing similar things, and they settled out of court (McCormick 1999). Citigroup is notorious for stealing from the poor. In 2004, this firm had to pay $70 million for its crimes (O'Brien 2004). But, like a career criminal, it continued its law-breaking ways. The firm "swept" money from its customers' credit cards, even from the cards of people who had died. Caught red-handed once again—even stealing from the dead—in 2008 this company was forced to pay another $18 million (Read 2008). *Not one of the corporate thieves at Sears, Macy's, Bloomingdales, or Citigroup spent a day in jail.*

Seldom is corporate crime taken seriously, even when it results in death. One of the most notorious corporate crimes was committed by Firestone executives. They decided to recall faulty tires in Saudi Arabia and Venezuela and to allow them to remain on U.S. vehicles. This decision cost the lives of about 200 Americans (White et al. 2001). The photo on the previous page shows another human cost. Yet not a single Firestone executive went to jail.

Consider this: Under federal law, causing the death of a worker by *willfully* violating safety rules is a misdemeanor punishable by up to six months in prison. Yet to harass a wild burro on federal lands is punishable by a year in prison (Barstow and Bergman 2003).

At $400 billion a year (Reiman 2004), "crime in the suites" actually costs more than "crime in the streets." This refers only to dollar costs. No one has yet figured out a way to compare, for example, the suffering experienced by a rape victim with the pain felt by an elderly couple who have lost their life savings to white-collar fraud.

Fear, however, centers on street crime, especially the violent stranger who will change your life forever. As the Social Map on the next page shows, the chances of such an

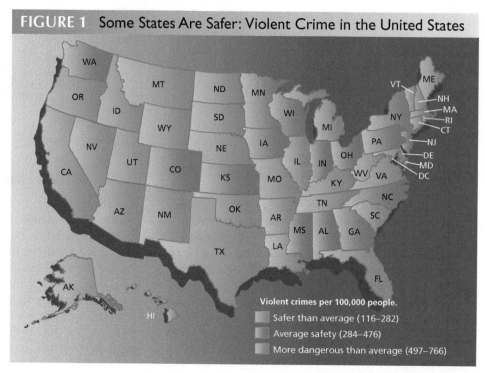

FIGURE 1 Some States Are Safer: Violent Crime in the United States

Violent crimes per 100,000 people.
Safer than average (116–282)
Average safety (284–476)
More dangerous than average (497–766)

Note: Violent crimes are murder, rape, robbery, and aggravated assault. As this figure illustrates, violent crime varies widely among the states. The chance of becoming a victim of these crimes is ten times higher in South Carolina, the most dangerous state, than in Maine, the safest state. Washington, D.C., not a state, is in a class by itself. Its rate of 1,508 is *thirteen* times higher than Maine's rate.

Source: By the author. Based on *Statistical Abstract of the United States* 2009: Table 297.

encounter depend on where you live. You can see that entire regions are safer—or more dangerous than—others. In general, the northern states are safer, and the southern states more dangerous.

Gender and Crime. Gender is not just something we are or do. It is a feature of society that surrounds us from birth. As it pushes us, as male or female, into different corners in life, gender offers and nurtures some behaviors while it withdraws and dries up others. The opportunity to commit crime is one of the many consequences of how society sets up a gender order. The social changes that opened business and the professions to women also brought new opportunities for women to commit crime. Table 2 shows some of those changes, the increase in crime by women—from car theft to possessing illegal weapons.

In Sum: Functionalists stress that just as the social classes differ in opportunities for income and education, so they differ in opportunities for crime. As a result, street crime is higher among the lower social classes and white-collar crime higher among the higher social classes. The growing crime rates of women illustrate how changing gender roles have given women more access to what sociologists call "illegitimate opportunities."

TABLE 2 Women and Crime: What a Difference a Few Years Make

Of all those arrested, what percentage are women?

Crime	1992	2006	Change
Car theft	10.8%	17.8%	+65%
Burglary	9.2%	14.4%	+57%
Stolen property	12.5%	18.8%	+50%
Aggravated assault	14.8%	20.7%	+40%
Drunken driving	13.8%	20.0%	+45%
Robbery	8.5%	11.2%	+32%
Arson	13.4%	16.7%	+25%
Larceny/theft	32.1%	37.7%	+17%
Illegal drugs	16.4%	18.9%	+15%
Forgery and counterfeiting	34.7%	39.1%	+13%
Fraud	42.1%	44.5%	+6%
Illegal Weapons	7.5%	8.0%	+7%

Source: By the author. Based on *Statistical Abstract of the United States* 2009: Table 312.

The Conflict Perspective

criminal justice system the system of police, courts, and prisons set up to deal with people who are accused of having committed a crime

Class, Crime, and the Criminal Justice System

Sioux Manufacturing in North Dakota made helmets for the U.S. ground troops in Iraq and Afghanistan. Two former managers reported that the company had set their looms to use less Kevlar—a fabric that deflects some shrapnel and bullets—than they were supposed to. The charge was serious, for doing this would endanger U.S. soldiers, perhaps causing some to die.

But would anyone actually do such a thing? Government officials investigated, and found that the accusation was true. Employees had even doctored records to show that the company had used the correct amount of Kevlar. (Lambert 2008)

What was the punishment for a crime this serious? When the executives of Sioux Manufacturing were put on trial, for how long were they sentenced to prison? Actually, those who ordered this crime weren't even put on trial, and no one spent even a night in jail. The company just paid a fine—and then the government gave them another contract to make more helmets. Of course, they had to reset their looms.

Contrast this with poor people who are caught stealing cars and sent to prison for years. How can a legal system that proudly boasts "justice for all" be so inconsistent? According to conflict theory, this question is central to the analysis of crime and the **criminal justice system**—the police, courts, and prisons that deal with people who are accused of having committed crimes. Let's see what conflict theorists have to say about this.

The Law as an Instrument of Oppression

Conflict theorists regard power and social inequality as the main characteristics of society. They stress that the power elite uses the criminal justice system to protect its position of power and privilege. The idea that the law operates impartially to bring justice, they say, is a cultural myth promoted by the capitalist class. They point out that the law is really an instrument of oppression, a tool designed by the powerful to maintain their privileged position (Chambliss 2000, 1973/2007; Spitzer 1975; Reiman 2004).

With their large numbers, the working class and those below them pose a special threat to the power elite. Receiving the least of society's material rewards, they hold

In early capitalism, children were employed alongside adults. At that time, just as today, most street criminals came from the *marginal working class*, as did the boys shown in this 1891 photo taken at a coal mine in Shenandoah, Pennsylvania.

Corbis

119

"If you want justice, it's two hundred dollars an hour. Obstruction of justice runs a bit more."

The cartoonist's hyperbole makes an excellent commentary on the social class disparity of our criminal justice system. Not only are the crimes of the wealthy not as likely to come to the attention of authorities as are the crimes of the poor, but when they do, the wealthy can afford legal expertise that the poor cannot.

the potential to rebel and overthrow the current social order. To prevent this, the law comes down hard on its members who get out of line. The working poor and the underclass are a special problem. They are the least rooted in society. They have few skills and only low-paying, part-time, or seasonal work—if they have jobs at all. Because their street crimes threaten the social order that keeps the elite in power, they are punished severely. From this class come *most* of the prison inmates in the United States.

The criminal justice system, then, does not focus on the executives of corporations and the harm they do through manufacturing unsafe products, creating pollution, and manipulating prices. Yet the violations of the capitalist class cannot be ignored totally, for if they become too outrageous or oppressive they might outrage the working class, encouraging them to rise up and revolt. To prevent this, a flagrant violation by a member of the capitalist class is occasionally prosecuted. The publicity given to the case helps to stabilize the social system by providing evidence of the "fairness" of the criminal justice system.

The powerful, however, are usually able to bypass the courts altogether, appearing instead before an agency that has no power to imprison (such as the Federal Trade Commission). These agencies are directed by people from wealthy backgrounds who sympathize with the intricacies of the corporate world. It is they who oversee most cases of manipulating the price of stocks, insider trading, violating fiduciary duty, and so on. Is it surprising, then, that the typical sanction for corporate crime is a token fine?

What do you think would happen if groups that have been denied access to power gain that access? You might surmise that one of the things they would change would be the legal system. This is precisely what is occurring now. Racial–ethnic minorities and homosexuals, for example, have more political power today than ever before in our history. In line with conflict theory, a new category called *hate crime* has been formulated. We analyze this change in a different context later in this chapter.

In Sum: Conflict theorists stress that the power elite uses the legal system to control workers and to stabilize the social order, all with the goal of keeping itself in power. The poor pose a threat, for if they rebel as a group they can dislodge members of the power elite from their place of privilege. To prevent this, the power elite makes certain that heavy penalties come down on those whose crimes could upset the social order.

Reactions to Deviance

Whether it involves cheating on a sociology quiz or holding up a liquor store, any violation of norms invites reaction. Before we examine reactions in the United States, let's take a little side trip to Greenland, an island nation three times the size of Texas located between Canada and Denmark. I think you'll enjoy this little excursion in the Cultural Diversity box, "What Kind of Prison Is This?"

Street Crime and Prisons

Let's turn back to the United States. Figure 2 shows the increase in the U.S. prison population. To get an idea of how huge this increase is, consider this: Not able to build prisons fast enough to hold all of their incoming prisoners, the states and federal government have hired private companies to operate additional prisons for them. About 120,000 prisoners are held in these "for-profit" prisons (Sabol and Couture 2008). Actually, the United States has even more prisoners than shown in Figure 2, since this total does not include jail inmates. If we add them, the total comes to 2.3 million people—about one out of every 140 citizens.

Not only does the United States have more prisoners than any other nation in the world, but it also has a larger percentage of its population in prison as well (Warren et al. 2008).

Who are these prisoners? Let's compare them with the U.S. population. As you look at Table 3, several things may strike you. Most prisoners (62 percent) are younger than 35, and almost all prisoners are men. Then there is this remarkable statistic: Although African Americans make up just 12.8 percent of the U.S. population, close to *half* of all prisoners are African Americans. On any given day, *one out of every nine* African American men ages 20 to 34 is in jail or prison. (For Latinos, the rate is one of twenty-six; for whites one of one hundred) (Warren et al. 2008.)

Finally, note how marriage and education—two of the major techniques society has of "anchoring" us—provide protection from prison. *Most* prisoners have never married. And look at the power of education, a major component of social class. As I mentioned earlier, social class funnels some people into the criminal justice system and diverts others away from it. You can see how people who drop out of high school have a high chance of ending up in prison—and how unlikely it is for a college graduate to have this unwelcome destination in life.

For about the past twenty years or so, the United States has followed a "get tough" policy. One of the most significant changes was the "three-strikes-and-you're-out" laws. When someone is convicted of a third felony, judges are required to give a mandatory sentence, sometimes life imprisonment. While few of us would feel sympathy if a man convicted of a third brutal rape or a third murder were sent to prison for life, these laws have had unanticipated consequences, as you will see in the following Thinking Critically section.

TABLE 3 Inmates in U.S. State Prisons		
Characteristics	Percentage of Prisoners with These Characteristics	Percentage of U.S. Population with These Characteristics
Age		
18–24	26.4%	9.9%
25–34	35.4%	13.5%
35–44	25.2%	14.8%
45–54	10.4%	14.3%
55 and older	1.0%	22.7%
Race–Ethnicity		
African American	47.3%	12.8%
White	36.9%	66.9%
Latino	14.2%	14.4%
Asian Americans	0.6%	4.3%
Native Americans	0.9%	1.0%
Sex		
Male	93.4%	49.3%
Female	6.3%	50.7%
Marital Status		
Never married	59.8%	28.2%
Divorced	15.5%	10.2%
Married	17.3%	58.6%
Widowed	1.1%	6.4%
Education		
Less than high school	39.7%	14.8%
High school graduate	49.0%	32.2%
Some college	9.0%	25.4%
College graduate	2.4%	27.6%

Source: By the author. Based on *Sourcebook of Criminal Justice Statistics* 2003: Tables 6.000b, 6.28; 2006: Tables 6.34, 6.45; *Statistical Abstract of the United States* 2009: Tables 8, 10, 18, 56, 223.

FIGURE 2 How Much Is Enough? The Explosion in the Number of U.S. Prisoners

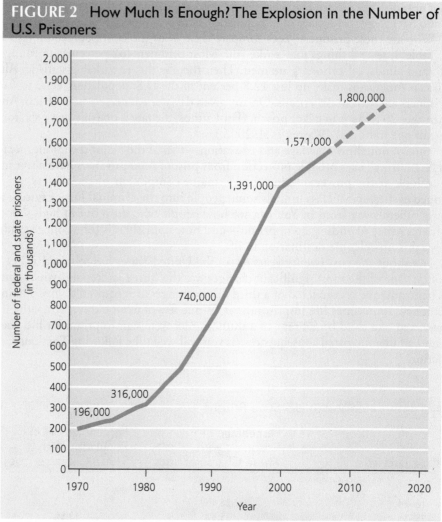

Between 1970 and 2007, the U.S. population increased 48 percent, while the number of prisoners increased 816 percent, a rate that is *17 times greater* than population growth. If the number of prisoners had grown at the same rate as the U.S. population, we would have about 286,000 prisoners, only one-eighth of today's total. Or if the U.S. population had increased at the same rate as that of U.S. prisoners, the U.S. population would be 1,673,000,000—approximately the population of China and all of Europe combined.

Sources: By the author. Based on *Statistical Abstract of the United States* 1995:Table 349; 2009:Table 333. The broken line is the author's estimate.

ThinkingCRITICALLY

"Three Strikes and You're Out!" Unintended Consequences of Well-Intended Laws

As the violent crime rate soared in the 1980s, Americans grew fearful. They demanded that their lawmakers do something. Politicians heard the message, and they responded by passing the "three-strikes" law. Anyone who is convicted of a third felony receives an automatic mandatory sentence. Judges are not allowed to consider the circumstances. Some mandatory sentences carry life imprisonment.

In their haste to appease the public, the politicians did not limit the three-strike laws to *violent* crimes. And they did not consider that some minor crimes are considered felonies. As the functionalists would say, this has led to unanticipated consequences.

Cultural Diversity around the World

"What Kind of Prison Is This?"

The prison in Nuuk, the capital of Greenland, has no wall around it. It has no fence. It doesn't even have bars.

Meeraq Lendenhann, a convicted rapist, walked out of prison. He didn't run or hide. He just walked out. Meeraq wasn't escaping. He went to a store he likes to shop at, bought a CD of his favorite group, U2, and then walked back to the prison.

If Meeraq tires of listening to music, he can send e-mail and play games on a computer. Like the other prisoners, he also has a personal TV with satellite hookup.

One woman prisoner who said she was going to a beauty salon got sidetracked and went to a bar instead. When it got late and she was quite drunk, she called the prison and asked someone to come and get her.

The prison holds 60 prisoners—the country's killers, rapists, and a few thieves. The prisoners leave the prison to work at regular jobs, where they average $28,000 or so a year. But they have to return to the prison after work. And they are locked into their rooms at 9:30 P.M.

The prisoners have to work, because the prison charges them $150 a week for room and board. The extra money goes into their savings accounts or to help support their families.

If someone from another culture asks about the prisoners running away, the head of the prison says, "Where would they run? It's warm inside, and cold outside."

And if they ran away they would miss breakfast—a buffet of five kinds of imported cheese, various breads, marmalade, honey, coffee, and tea.

And they would miss out on their free guns. A major summer sport for Greenlanders is hunting reindeer and seals. Prisoners don't want to miss out on the fun, so if they ask, they are given shotguns.

But gun use isn't as easy as it sounds. Judges have set a severe requirement: The prisoners have to be accompanied

This photo was taken inside a "cell" at Nuuk—private room, personal TV with satellite connection, VCR, adjustable reading lamp, radio-CD player, and window to the outside. The inmate's coffee maker is on the other side of the room.

by armed guards. If that isn't bad enough, the judges have added another requirement—that the prisoners not get drunk while they hunt.

For Your Consideration

Greenland's unique approach to prisons arose out of its history of hunting and fishing for a living. If men are locked up, they won't be able to hunt or fish, and their families will suffer. The main goal of Greenland's prison is to integrate offenders into society, and their treatment in prison helps them ease back into village life after they have served their sentence. The incorrigibles, those who remain dangerous—about 20 men—are sent to a prison in Copenhagen, Denmark. Meeraq, the rapist, is given injections of Androcur, a testosterone-reducing drug that lowers his sex drive. Alcoholics are given Antabuse, a drug that triggers nasty reactions if someone drinks alcohol.

How do you think we could apply Greenland's approach to the United States?

—Based on Naik 2004.

Here are some actual cases:

- In Los Angeles, a 27-year-old man who stole a pizza was sentenced to 25 years in prison (Cloud 1998).
- In Sacramento, a man passed himself off as Tiger Woods and went on a $17,000 shopping spree. He was sentenced to 200 years in prison (Reuters 2001).
- In California, Michael James passed a bad check for $94. He was sentenced to 25 years to life (Jones 2008).
- In Utah, a 25-year-old sold small bags of marijuana to a police informant. The judge who sentenced the man to 55 years in prison said the sentence was unjust, but he had no choice (Madigan 2004).

• In New York City, a man who was about to be sentenced for selling crack said to the judge, "I'm only 19. This is terrible." He then hurled himself out of a courtroom window, plunging to his death sixteen stories below (Cloud 1998).

For Your Consideration

Apply the symbolic interactionist, functionalist, and conflict perspectives to the three-strikes laws. For *symbolic interactionism,* what do these laws represent to the public? How does your answer differ depending on what part of "the public" you are referring to? For *functionalism,* who benefits from these laws? What are some of their functions? Their dysfunctions? For the *conflict perspective,* what groups are in conflict? Who has the power to enforce their will on others?

The Decline in Violent Crime

As you have seen, judges have put more and more people in prison, and legislators have passed the three-strikes laws. As these changes occurred, the crime rate dropped sharply, which has led to a controversy in sociology. Some sociologists conclude that getting tough on criminals is the main reason that violent crime dropped (Conklin 2003). Others point to higher employment, a drop in drug use, and even abortion (Rosenfeld 2002; Reiman 2004; Blumstein and Wallman 2006). This matter is not yet settled, but both tough sentencing and the economy seem to be important factors.

recidivism rate the proportion of released convicts who are rearrested

capital punishment the death penalty

Recidivism

If a goal of prisons is to teach their clients to stay away from crime, they are colossal failures. We can measure their failure by the **recidivism rate**—the percentage of former prisoners who are rearrested. For people sent to prison for crimes of violence, within just three years of their release, two out of three (62 percent) are rearrested, and half (52 percent) are back in prison (*Sourcebook of Criminal Justice Statistics* 2003:Table 6.52). Looking at Figure 3, which gives a breakdown of three-year recidivism by type of crime, it is safe to conclude that prisons do not teach people that crime doesn't pay.

The Death Penalty and Bias

As you know, **capital punishment,** the death penalty, is the most extreme measure the state takes. As you also know, the death penalty arouses impassioned opposition and support. Advances in DNA testing have given opponents of the death penalty a strong argument: Innocent people have been sent to death row, and some have been executed. Others are just as passionate about retaining the death penalty. They point to such crimes as those of the serial killers discussed in the next Down-to-Earth Sociology box.

Apart from anyone's personal position on the death penalty, it certainly is clear that the death penalty is not administered evenly. Consider geography: The

FIGURE 3 Recidivism of U.S. Prisoners

Of 272,000 prisoners released from U.S. prisons, what percentage were rearrested within three years?

The rearrest rates of those who had been convicted of:

Crime	Rate
Stealing cars	79%
Possessing or selling stolen property	77%
Larceny	75%
Burglary	74%
Robbery	70%
Illegal weapons	70%
Illegal drugs	67%
Fraud	66%
Arson	58%
Drunk driving	52%
Rape	46%
Murder	41%

Note: The individuals were not necessarily rearrested for the same crime for which they had originally been imprisoned.

Source: By the author. Based on *Sourcebook of Criminal Justice Statistics* 2003:Table 6.50.

Beneath the humor of this cartoon lies a serious point about the high *recidivism rate* of U.S. prisoners.

Social Map below shows that where people commit murder greatly affects their chances of being put to death.

The death penalty also shows social class bias. As you know from news reports, it is rare for a rich person to be sentenced to death. Although the government does not collect statistics on social class and the death penalty, this common observation is borne out by the education of the prisoners on death row. *Half* of the prisoners on death row (51 percent) have not finished high school (*Sourcebook of Criminal Justice Statistics* 2007:Table 6.81).

There is also a gender bias in the death penalty. It is so strong that it is almost unheard of for a woman to be sentenced to death, much less executed. Although women commit 9.6 percent of the murders, they make up only 1.7 percent of death row inmates (*Sourcebook of Criminal Justice Statistics* 2007:Tables 6.82, 6.83). Even on death row, the gender bias continues, for the state is more likely to execute a man than a woman. As Figure 5 shows, less than 1 percent of the 4,958 executions in the United States since 1930 have been of women. This gender bias could reflect the women's previous offenses and the relative brutality of their murders, but we need research to determine if this is so.

Bias was once so flagrant that it put a stop to the death penalty. Donald Partington (1965), a lawyer in Virginia, was shocked by the bias he saw in the courtroom, and he

FIGURE 4 Executions in the United States

Executions since 1977, when the death penalty was reinstated.

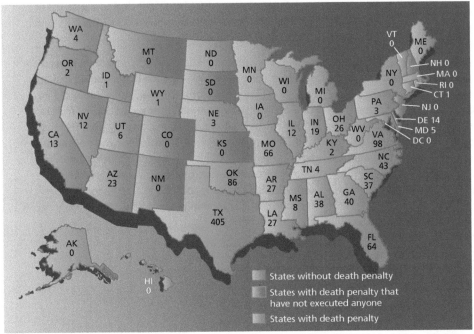

Source: By the author. Based on *Statistical Abstract of the United States* 2009:Table 340. I added the 2005 execution in Connecticut, missed by the source.

FIGURE 5 Who Gets Executed? Gender Bias in Capital Punishment

Source: By the author. Based on *Statistical Abstract of the United States* 2009:Table 339.

125

Down-to-Earth Sociology
The Killer Next Door: Serial Murderers in Our Midst

Bettmann/Corbis

One of the striking traits of most serial killers is how they blend in with the rest of society. Ted Bundy, shown here, was remarkable in this respect. Almost everyone who knew this law student liked him. Even the Florida judge who found him guilty said that he would have liked to have him practice law in his court, but, as he added, "You went the wrong way, partner." (Note the term partner—used even after Bundy was convicted of heinous crimes.)

Here is my experience with serial killers. As I was watching television one night, I was stunned by the images. Television cameras showed the Houston police digging up dozens of bodies from under a boat storage shed. Fascinated, I waited impatiently for spring break. A few days later, I drove from Illinois to Houston, where 33-year-old Dean Corll had befriended Elmer Wayne Henley and David Brooks, two teenagers from broken homes. Together, they had killed twenty-seven boys. Elmer and David would pick up young hitchhikers and deliver them to Corll to rape and kill. Sometimes they even brought him their own high school classmates.

I talked to one of Elmer's neighbors, as he was painting his front porch. His 15-year-old son had gone to get a haircut one Saturday morning. That was the last time he saw his son alive. The police refused to investigate. They insisted that his son had run away. On a city map, I plotted the locations of the homes of the local murder victims. Many clustered around the homes of the teenage killers.

I decided to spend my coming sabbatical writing a novel on this case. To get into the minds of the killers, I knew that I would have to "become" them day after day for months. Corll kept a piece of plywood in his apartment. In each of its corners, he had cut a hole. He and the boys would spread-eagle their handcuffed victims on this board, torturing them for hours. Sometimes, they would even pause to order pizza. As such details emerged, I became uncertain that I could recover psychologically from such an immersion into torture and human degradation, and I decided not to write the book.

My interviews in Houston confirmed what has since become common knowledge about serial killers: They lead double lives so successfully that their friends and family are unaware of their criminal activities. Henley's mother swore to me that her son couldn't possibly be guilty—he was a good boy. Some of Elmer's high school friends told me that that his being involved in homosexual rape and murder was ridiculous—he was interested only in girls. I was interviewing them in Henley's bedroom, and for proof they pointed to a pair of girls' panties that were draped across a lamp shade.

Serial murder is the killing of victims in three or more separate events. The murders may occur over several days, weeks, or years. The elapsed time between murders distinguishes serial killers from *mass murderers*, those who do their killing all at once. Here are some infamous examples:

- During the 1960s and 1970s, Ted Bundy raped and killed dozens of women in four states.
- Between 1979 and 1981, Wayne Williams killed 28 boys and young men in Atlanta.
- Between 1974 and 1991, Dennis Rader killed 10 people in Wichita, Kansas. Rader had written to the newspapers, proudly calling himself the BTK (Bind, Torture, and Kill) strangler.
- In the late 1980s and early 1990s, Aileen Wuornos hitchhiked along Florida's freeways. She killed 7 men after having had sex with them.
- The serial killer with the most victims appears to be Harold Shipman, a physician in Manchester, England. From 1977 to 2000, during house calls Shipman gave lethal injections to 230 to 275 of his elderly female patients.

Is serial murder more common now than it used to be? Not likely. In the past, police departments had little communication with one another, and seldom did anyone connect killings in different jurisdictions. Today's more efficient communications, investigative techniques, and DNA matching make it easier for the police to know when a serial killer is operating in an area. Part of the perception that there are more serial killers today is also due to ignorance of our history: In our frontier past, for example, serial killers went from ranch to ranch.

For Your Consideration

Do you think that serial killers should be given the death penalty? Why or why not? How do your social locations influence your opinion?

decided to document it. He found that 2,798 men had been convicted for rape and attempted rape in Virginia between 1908 and 1963—56 percent whites and 44 percent blacks. For attempted rape, 13 had been executed. For rape, 41 men had been executed. *All those executed were black.* Not one of the whites was executed.

After listening to evidence like this, in 1972 the Supreme Court ruled in *Furman v. Georgia* that the death penalty, as applied, was unconstitutional. The execution of prisoners stopped—but not for long. The states wrote new laws, and in 1977 they again began to execute prisoners. Since then, 65 percent of those put to death have been white and 35 percent African American (*Statistical Abstract* 2009:Table 339). (Latinos are evidently counted as whites in this statistic.) While living on death row is risky for anyone, the risk is higher for African Americans and Latinos who killed whites. They are more likely to be executed (Jacobs et al. 2007). The most accurate predictor of who will be put to death, though, is somewhat surprising: Those who have the least education are the most likely to be executed (Karamouzis and Harper 2007). Table 4 shows the race–ethnicity of the prisoners who are on death row.

TABLE 4	The Race–Ethnicity of the 3,316 Prisoners on Death Row	
	Percentage	
	on Death Row	in U.S. Population
Whites	45%	67%
African Americans	42%	13%
Latinos	11%	14%
Asian Americans	1%	4%
Native Americans	1%	1%

Source: By the author. Based on *Sourcebook of Criminal Justice Statistics* 2008:Table 6.80 and Figure 5 of this text.

Legal Change

Did you know that it is a crime in Saudi Arabia for a woman to drive a car (Fattah 2007)? A crime in Florida to sell alcohol before 1 P.M. on Sundays? Or illegal in Wells, Maine, to advertise on tombstones? As has been stressed in this chapter, deviance, including the form called *crime,* is so relative that it varies from one society to another, and from one group to another within the same society. Crime also varies from one time period to another, as opinions change or as different groups gain access to power. We discuss one of these changes in the following Thinking Critically section.

ThinkingCRITICALLY

Changing Views: Making Hate a Crime

Because crime consists of whatever acts authorities decide to assign that label, new crimes emerge from time to time. A prime example is juvenile delinquency, which Illinois lawmakers designated a separate type of crime in 1899. Juveniles committed crimes before 1899, of course, but youths were not considered to be a separate type of lawbreaker. They were just young people who committed crimes, and they were treated the same as adults who committed the same crime. Sometimes new technology leads to new crimes. Motor vehicle theft, a separate crime in the United States, obviously did not exist before the automobile was invented.

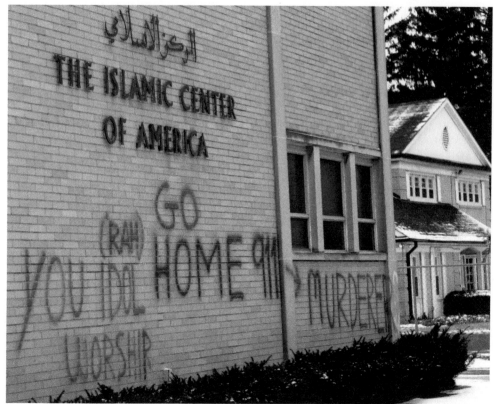

REUTERS/Rebecca Cook/Landov

Hate crimes *range from murder and injury to defacing property with symbols of hatred. This photo was taken in Detroit, Michigan.*

In the 1980s, another new crime was born when state governments developed the classification **hate crime,** crimes motivated by *bias* (dislike, hatred) against someone's race—ethnicity, religion, sexual orientation, disability, or national origin. Before this, people attacked others or destroyed their property out of these same motivations, but then the motivation was not the issue. If someone injured or killed another person because of that person's race—ethnicity, religion, sexual orientation, national origin, or disability, he or she was charged with assault or murder. Today, motivation has become a central issue, and hate crimes carry more severe sentences than do the same acts that do not have hatred as their motive. Table 5 on the next page summarizes the victims of hate crimes.

We can be certain that the "evolution" of crime is not yet complete. As society changes and as different groups gain access to power, we can expect the definitions of crime to change accordingly.

For Your Consideration

Why should we have a separate classification called hate crime? Why aren't the crimes of assault, robbery, and murder adequate? As one analyst (Sullivan 1999) said, "Was the brutal murder of gay college student Matthew Shepard in Laramie, Wyoming, in 1998 (a hate crime) worse than the abduction, rape, and murder of an eight-year-old Laramie girl by a pedophile (not a hate crime) that same year?"

How do you think your social location (race—ethnicity, gender, social class, sexual orientation, or physical ability) affects your opinion?

serial murder the killing of several victims in three or more separate events

hate crime a crime that is punished more severely because it is motivated by hatred (dislike, hostility, animosity) of someone's race—ethnicity, religion, sexual orientation, disability, or national origin

police discretion the practice of the police, in the normal course of their duties, to either arrest or ticket someone for an offense or to overlook the matter

medicalization of deviance to make deviance a medical matter, a symptom of some underlying illness that needs to be treated by physicians

The Trouble with Official Statistics

Both the findings of symbolic interactionists (that stereotypes operate when authorities deal with groups such as the Saints and the Roughnecks) and the conclusion of conflict theorists (that the criminal justice system serves the ruling elite) demonstrate the need for caution in interpreting official statistics. Crime statistics do not have an objective, independent existence. They are not like oranges that you pick out in a grocery store. Rather, crime statistics are a human creation. One major element in producing them is the particular laws that exist. Another is how those laws are enforced. Still another is how officials report their statistics. Change these factors, and the statistics also change.

Consider this: According to official statistics, working-class boys are more delinquent than middle-class boys. Yet, as we have seen, who actually gets arrested for what is influenced by social class, a point that has far-reaching implications. As symbolic interactionists point out, the police follow a symbolic system as they enforce the law. Ideas of "typical criminals" and "typical good citizens," for example, permeate their work. The more a suspect matches their stereotypes of a lawbreaker (which they call "criminal profiles"), the more likely that person is to be arrested. **Police discretion,** the decision whether to arrest someone or even to ignore a matter, is a routine part of police work. Consequently, official crime statistics reflect these and many other biases.

In Sum: Reactions to deviants vary from such mild sanctions as frowns and stares to such severe responses as imprisonment and death. Some sanctions are formal—court hearings, for example—but most are informal, as when friends refuse to talk to each other. One sanction is to label someone a deviant, which can have powerful consequences for the person's life, especially if the label closes off conforming activities and opens deviant ones. The degradation ceremony, in which someone is publicly labeled "not one of us," is a powerful sanction. So is imprisonment. Official statistics must be viewed with caution, for they reflect biases.

TABLE 5	Hate Crimes
Directed Against	Number of Victims
Race–Ethnicity	
African Americans	3,332
Whites	1,054
Latinos	819
Multiracial	320
Asian Americans	239
Native Americans	75
Religion	
Jews	1,144
Muslims	208
Catholics	86
Protestants	65
Sexual Orientation	
Homosexual	1,422
Male Homosexual	913
Female Homosexual	202
General	387
Heterosexual	29
Bisexual	21
Disabilities	
Mental	74
Physical	21

Note: A victim can be an individual, a business, or an institution. Number is the cumulative victims from year 2000.

Source: By the author. Based on *Statistical Abstract of the United States* 2009:Table 310.

The Medicalization of Deviance: Mental Illness

Another way in which society deals with deviance is to "medicalize" it. Let's look at what this entails.

Neither Mental Nor Illness? To *medicalize* something is to make it a medical matter, to classify it as a form of illness that properly belongs in the care of physicians. For the past hundred years or so, especially since the time of Sigmund Freud (1856–1939), the Viennese physician who founded psychoanalysis, there has been a growing tendency toward the **medicalization of deviance.** In this view, deviance, including crime, is a sign of mental sickness. Rape, murder, stealing, cheating, and so on are external symptoms of internal disorders, consequences of a confused or tortured mind.

Thomas Szasz (1986, 1996, 1998), a renegade in his profession of psychiatry, argues that *mental illnesses are neither mental nor illnesses. They are simply problem behaviors.* Some behaviors that are called mental illnesses have organic causes; that is, they are *physical* illnesses that result in unusual perceptions or behavior. Some depression, for example, is caused by a chemical imbalance in the brain, which can be treated by drugs. The depression, however, may appear as crying, long-term sadness, and lack of interest in family, work, school, or one's appearance. When people are disturbed by someone's deviance *and* when they cannot find a satisfying explanation for

People whose behaviors violate norms often are called mentally ill. "Why else would they do such things?" is a common response to deviant behaviors that we don't understand. Mental illness is a label that contains the assumption that there is something wrong "within" people that "causes" their disapproved behavior. The surprise with this man, who changed his legal name to "Scary Guy," is that he speaks at schools across the country, where he promotes acceptance, awareness, love, and understanding.

AP Images

why the person is "like that," they often say that a "sickness in the head" is causing the unacceptable behavior.

Attention-deficit disorder (ADD) is an excellent example. As Szasz says, "No one explains where this disease came from, why it didn't exist 50 years ago. No one is able to diagnose it with objective tests." It is diagnosed by a teacher or a parent complaining about a child misbehaving. Misbehaving children have been a problem throughout history, but now their problem behavior has become a sign of mental illness.

All of us have troubles. Some of us face a constant barrage of problems as we go through life. Most of us continue the struggle, perhaps encouraged by relatives and friends and motivated by job, family responsibilities, religious faith, and life goals. Even when the odds seem hopeless, we carry on, not perfectly, but as best we can.

Some people, however, fail to cope well with life's challenges. Overwhelmed, they become depressed, uncooperative, or hostile. Some strike out at others; and some, in Merton's terms, become retreatists and withdraw into their apartments or homes, refusing to come out. These are *behaviors, not mental illnesses,* stresses Szasz. They may be inappropriate ways of coping, but they are behaviors, not mental illnesses. Szasz concludes that "mental illness" is a myth foisted on a naive public. Our medical profession uses pseudoscientific jargon that people don't understand so it can expand its area of control and force nonconforming people to accept society's definitions of "normal."

Szasz's controversial claim forces us to look anew at the forms of deviance that we usually refer to as mental illness. To explain behavior that people find bizarre, he directs our attention not to causes hidden deep within the "subconscious," but, instead, to how people learn such behaviors. To ask, "What is the origin of someone's inappropriate or bizarre behavior?" then becomes similar to asking "Why do some women steal?" "Why do some men rape?" "Why do some teenagers cuss their parents and stalk out of the room, slamming the door?" *The answers depend on those people's particular experiences in life, not on an illness in their mind.* In short, some sociologists find Szasz's renegade analysis refreshing because it indicates that *social experiences,* not some illness of the mind, underlie bizarre behaviors—as well as deviance in general.

The Homeless Mentally III

Jamie was sitting on a low wall surrounding the landscaped courtyard of an exclusive restaurant. She appeared unaware of the stares elicited by her layers of mismatched clothing, her matted hair and dirty face, and the shopping cart that overflowed with her meager possessions.

After sitting next to Jamie for a few minutes, I saw her point to the street and concentrate, slowly moving her finger horizontally. I asked her what she was doing.

"I'm directing traffic," she replied. "I control where the cars go. Look, that one turned right there," she said, now withdrawing her finger.

"Really?" I said.

After a while she confided that her cart talked to her.

"Really?" I said again.

"Yes," she replied. "You can hear it, too." At that, she pushed the shopping cart a bit.

"Did you hear that?" she asked.

When I shook my head, she demonstrated again. Then it hit me. She was referring to the squeaking wheels!

I nodded.

Mental illness is common among the homeless. This woman is sleeping in a doorway in New York City.

When I left Jamie, she was pointing to the sky, for, as she told me, she also controlled the flight of airplanes.

To most of us, Jamie's behavior and thinking are bizarre. They simply do not match any reality we know. Could you or I become like Jamie?

Suppose for a bitter moment that you are homeless and have to live on the streets. You have no money, no place to sleep, no bathroom. You do not know *if* you are going to eat, much less where. You have no friends or anyone you can trust. You live in constant fear of rape and other violence. Do you think this might be enough to drive you over the edge?

Consider just the problems involved in not having a place to bathe. (Shelters are often so dangerous that many homeless people prefer to sleep in public settings.) At first, you try to wash in the restrooms of gas stations, bars, the bus station, or a shopping center. But you are dirty, and people stare when you enter and call the management when they see you wash your feet in the sink. You are thrown out and told in no uncertain terms never to come back. So you get dirtier and dirtier. Eventually, you come to think of being dirty as a fact of life. Soon, maybe, you don't even care. The stares no longer bother you— at least not as much.

No one will talk to you, and you withdraw more and more into yourself. You begin to build a fantasy life. You talk openly to yourself. People stare, but so what? They stare anyway. Besides, they are no longer important to you.

Jamie might be mentally ill. Some organic problem, such as a chemical imbalance in her brain, might underlie her behavior. But perhaps not. How long would it take you to exhibit bizarre behaviors if you were homeless—and hopeless? The point is that *living on the streets can cause mental illness*—or whatever we want to label socially inappropriate behaviors that we find difficult to classify. *Homelessness and mental illness are reciprocal:* Just as "mental illness" can cause homelessness, so the trials of being homeless, of living on cold, hostile streets, can lead to unusual thinking and behaviors.

The Need for a More Humane Approach

As Durkheim (1895/1964:68) pointed out, deviance is inevitable—even in a group of saints.

> Imagine a society of saints, a perfect cloister of exemplary individuals. Crimes, properly so called, will there be unknown; but faults which appear invisible to the layman will create there the same scandal that the ordinary offense does in ordinary society.

With deviance inevitable, one measure of a society is how it treats its deviants. Our prisons certainly don't say much good about U.S. society. Filled with the poor, uneducated, and unskilled, they are warehouses of the unwanted. White-collar criminals continue to get by with a slap on the wrist while street criminals are punished severely. Some deviants, who fail to meet current standards of admission to either prison or mental hospital, take refuge in shelters, as well as in cardboard boxes tucked away in urban recesses. Although no one has *the* answer, it does not take much reflection to see that there are more humane approaches than these.

Because deviance is inevitable, the larger issues are to find ways to protect people from deviant behaviors that are harmful to themselves or others, to tolerate those behaviors that are not harmful, and to develop systems of fairer treatment for deviants. In the absence of fundamental changes that would bring about an equitable social system, most efforts are, unfortunately, like putting a Band-Aid on a gunshot wound. What we need is a more humane social system, one that would prevent social inequalities.

SUMMARY *and* REVIEW

What Is Deviance?

Deviance (the violation of norms) is relative. What people consider deviant varies from one culture to another and from group to group within the same society. As symbolic interactionists stress, it is not the act, but the reactions to the act, that make something deviant. All groups develop systems of **social control** to punish **deviants**—those who violate their norms.

How do sociological and individualistic explanations of deviance differ?

To explain why people deviate, sociobiologists and psychologists look for reasons *within* the individual, such as **genetic predispositions** or **personality disorders.** Sociologists, in contrast, look for explanations *outside* the individual, in social experiences.

The Symbolic Interactionist Perspective

How do symbolic interactionists explain deviance?

Symbolic interactionists have developed several theories to explain deviance such as **crime** (the violation of norms that are written into law). According to **differential association** theory, people learn to deviate by associating with others. According to **control theory,** each of us is propelled toward deviance, but most of us conform because of an effective system of inner and outer controls. People who have less effective controls deviate.

Labeling theory focuses on how labels (names, reputations) help to funnel people into or divert them away from deviance. People who commit deviant acts often use **techniques of neutralization** to deflect social norms.

The Functionalist Perspective

How do functionalists explain deviance?

Functionalists point out that deviance, including criminal acts, is functional for society. Functions include affirming norms and promoting social unity and social change. According to **strain theory,** societies socialize their members into desiring **cultural goals.** Many people are unable to achieve these goals in socially acceptable ways—that is, by **institutionalized means.** *Deviants,* then, are people who either give up on the goals or use disapproved means to attain them. Merton identified five types of responses to cultural goals and institutionalized means: conformity, innovation, ritualism, retreatism, and rebellion. **Illegitimate opportunity theory** stresses that some people have easier access to illegal means of achieving goals.

The Conflict Perspective

How do conflict theorists explain deviance?

Conflict theorists take the position that the group in power imposes its definitions of deviance on other groups. From this perspective, the law is an instrument of oppression used by the powerful to maintain their position of privilege. The ruling class uses the **criminal justice system** to punish the crimes of the poor while diverting its own criminal activities away from this punitive system.

Reactions to Deviance

What are common reactions to deviance in the United States?

In following a "get-tough" policy, the United States has imprisoned millions of people. African Americans and Latinos make up a disproportionate percentage of U.S. prisoners. The death penalty shows biases by geography, social class, gender, and race–ethnicity. In line with conflict theory, as groups gain political power, their views are reflected in the criminal code. **Hate crime** legislation was considered in this context.

Are official statistics on crime reliable?

The conclusions of both symbolic interactionists (that the police operate with a large measure of discretion) and conflict theorists (that a power elite controls the legal system) indicate that we must be cautious when using crime statistics.

What is the medicalization of deviance?

The medical profession has attempted to **medicalize** many forms of **deviance,** claiming that they represent mental illnesses. Thomas Szasz disagrees, asserting that they are problem behaviors, not mental illnesses. The situation of homeless people indicates that problems in living can lead to bizarre behavior and thinking.

What is a more humane approach?

Deviance is inevitable, so the larger issues are to find ways to protect people from deviance that harms themselves and others, to tolerate deviance that is not harmful, and to develop systems of fairer treatment for deviants.

THINKING CRITICALLY

1. Select some deviance with which you are personally familiar. (It does not have to be your own—it can be something that someone you know did.) Choose one of the three theoretical perspectives to explain what happened.

2. As is explained in the text, deviance can be mild. Recall some instance in which you broke a social rule in dress,

etiquette, or speech. What was the reaction? Why do you think people reacted like that? What was your response to their reactions?

3. What do you think should be done about the U.S. crime problem? What sociological theories support your view?

ADDITIONAL RESOURCES

What can you find in MySocLab? mysoclab www.mysoclab.com

- Complete Ebook
- Practice Tests and Video and Audio activities
- Mapping and Data Analysis exercises

- Sociology in the News
- Classic Readings in Sociology
- Research and Writing advice

Where Can I Read More on This Topic?

Clear, Todd R. *Imprisoning Communities: How Mass Incarceration Makes Disadvantaged Neighborhoods Worse.* New York: Oxford University Press, 2009. The author's thesis is that mass incarceration breaks up family and social networks; deprives siblings, spouses, and parents of emotional and financial support; and threatens the economic and political infrastructure of struggling neighborhoods.

Cusac, Anne-Marie. *Cruel and Unusual: The Culture of Punishment in America.* New Haven, Conn.: Yale University Press, 2009. The author analyzes why the United States has become more punitive toward lawbreakers.

Deflin, Mathieu. *Surveillance and Governance: Crime Control and Beyond.* Greenwich, Conn.: JAI Press, 2008. The use of increasingly powerful surveillance techniques to monitor terrorists and other violent criminals is usually taken for granted—but what is to keep those same methods from being turned against ordinary citizens?

Domanick, Joe. *Cruel Justice: Three Strikes and the Politics of Crime in America's Golden State.* Berkeley: University of California Press, 2004. A history of California's three-strikes law and the reaction to its unintended injustice.

Goffman, Erving. *Stigma: Notes on the Management of Spoiled Identity.* New York: Simon & Schuster, 1986. First published in 1968. The author outlines the social and personal reactions to "spoiled identity," appearances that—due to disability, weight, ethnicity, birth marks, and so on—do not match dominant expectations.

Goode, Erich, and D. Angus Vail, eds. *Extreme Deviance.* Thousand Oaks, Calif.: Pine Forge Press, 2007. As the authors of these articles examine behaviors that bring extreme negative reactions, they analyze vocabularies of motive, deviance neutralization, the acquisition of a deviant identity, and the formation of deviant subcultures.

Heiner, Robert, ed. *Deviance Across Cultures.* Oxford: Oxford University Press, 2007. Cross-cultural norms and behavior are the focus of this collection of classic and contemporary articles on deviance.

Parmentier, Stephen, and Elmar Weitekamp. *Crime and Human Rights.* Greenwich, Conn.: JAI Press, 2008. The authors analyze how the emphasis on human rights is changing the ways crime and criminal justice are viewed and how this is impacting the U.S. and European justice systems.

Rathbone, Cristina. *A World Apart: Women, Prison, and Life Behind Bars.* New York: Random House, 2006. A journalist's account of the four years she spent investigating MCI Framingham, the oldest women's prison in the United States.

Reiman, Jeffrey. *The Rich Get Richer and the Poor Get Prison: Ideology, Class, and Criminal Justice,* 8th ed. Boston: Allyn and Bacon, 2007. An analysis of how social class works to produce different types of criminals and different types of justice.

Simon, David R. *Elite Deviance,* 9th ed. Boston: Allyn & Bacon, 2008. A broad overview of deviance, from scandals to organized crime syndicates.

Journals

Contemporary Justice Review, Criminology and Public Policy, Deviant Behavior, and *Journal of Law and Society* examine the social forces that shape deviance and reaction to it.

Sex and Gender

From Chapter 11 of *Sociology: A Down-to-Earth Approach*, 10/e. James M. Henslin. Copyright © 2010 by Pearson Education. Published by Allyn & Bacon. All rights reserved.

Sex and Gender

Afghanistan

Picture Contact/Alamy

In Tunis, the capital of Tunisia, on Africa's northern coast, I met some U.S. college students and spent a couple of days with them. They wanted to see the city's red light district, but I wondered whether it would be worth the trip. I already had seen other red light districts, including the unusual one in Amsterdam where a bronze statue of a female prostitute lets you know you've entered the area; the state licenses the women and men, requiring that they have medical checkups (certificates must be posted); and the prostitutes add a sales tax to the receipt they give customers. The prostitutes sit behind lighted picture windows while customers stroll along the narrow canal side streets and browse from the outside. Tucked among the brothels are day care centers, bakeries, and clothing stores. Amsterdam itself is an unusual place—you can smoke marijuana in cafes, but not tobacco.

> **In front of each open door stood a young woman. I could see . . . a well-worn bed.**

I decided to go with them. We ended up on a wharf that extended into the Mediterranean. Each side was lined with a row of one-room wooden shacks, crowded one against the next. In front of each open door stood a young woman. Peering from outside into the dark interiors, I could see that each door led to a tiny room with a well-worn bed.

The wharf was crowded with men who were eyeing the women. Many of the men wore sailor uniforms from countries that I couldn't identify.

As I looked more closely, I could see that some of the women had runny sores on their legs. Incredibly, with such visible evidence of their disease, customers still sought them out. Evidently, the $2 price was too low to resist.

With a sick feeling in my stomach and the desire to vomit, I kept a good distance between the beckoning women and myself. One tour of the two-block area was more than sufficient.

Somewhere nearby, out of sight, I knew that there were men whose wealth derived from exploiting these women who were condemned to live short lives punctuated by fear and misery.

In this chapter, we examine **gender stratification**—males' and females' unequal access to property, power, and prestige. Gender is especially significant because it is a *master status;* that is, it cuts across *all* aspects of social life. No matter what we attain in life, we carry the label *male* or *female.* These labels convey images and expectations about how we should act. They not only guide our behavior but also serve as a basis of power and privilege.

In this chapter's fascinating journey, we shall look at inequality between the sexes both around the world and in the United States. We shall explore whether it is biology or culture that makes us the way we are and review sexual harassment, unequal pay, and violence against women. This excursion will provide a good context for understanding the power differences between men and women that lead to situations such as the one described in our opening vignette. It should also give you insight into your own experiences with gender.

Issues of Sex and Gender

When we consider how females and males differ, the first thing that usually comes to mind is **sex,** the *biological characteristics* that distinguish males and females. *Primary sex characteristics* consist of a vagina or a penis and other organs related to reproduction. *Secondary sex characteristics* are the physical distinctions between males and females that are not directly connected with reproduction. These characteristics become clearly evident at puberty when males develop more muscles and a lower voice, and gain more body hair and height, while females develop breasts and form more fatty tissue and broader hips.

Gender, in contrast, is a *social,* not a biological characteristic. **Gender** consists of whatever behaviors and attitudes a group considers proper for its males and females. Consequently, gender varies from one society to another. Whereas *sex* refers to male or female, *gender* refers to masculinity or femininity. In short, you inherit your sex, but you learn your gender as you are socialized into the behaviors and attitudes your culture asserts are appropriate for your sex.

As the photo montage on the next page illustrates, the expectations associated with gender differ around the world. They vary so greatly that some sociologists suggest that we replace the terms *masculinity* and *femininity* with *masculinities* and *femininities.*

The sociological significance of gender is that it is a device by which society controls its members. Gender sorts us, on the basis of sex, into different life experiences. It opens and closes doors to property, power, and even prestige. Like social class, gender is a structural feature of society.

Before examining inequalities of gender, let's consider why the behaviors of men and women differ.

Gender Differences in Behavior: Biology or Culture?

Why are most males more aggressive than most females? Why do women enter "nurturing" occupations, such as teaching young children and nursing, in far greater numbers than men? To answer such questions, many people respond with some variation of "They're just born that way."

Is this the correct answer? Certainly biology plays a significant role in our lives. Each of us begins as a fertilized egg. The egg, or ovum, is contributed by our mother, the sperm that fertilizes the egg by our father. At the very instant the egg is fertilized, our sex is determined. Each of us receives twenty-three chromosomes from the ovum and twenty-three from the sperm. The egg has an X chromosome. If the sperm that fertilizes the egg also has an X chromosome, we become a girl (XX). If the sperm has a Y chromosome, we become a boy (XY).

That's the biology. Now, the sociological question is, Does this biological difference control our behavior? Does it, for example, make females more nurturing and submissive and males more aggressive and domineering? Almost all sociologists take the side of "nurture" in this "nature versus nurture" controversy, but a few do not, as you can see from the Thinking Critically section on the following pages.

gender stratification males' and females' unequal access to property, power, and prestige

sex biological characteristics that distinguish females and males, consisting of primary and secondary sex characteristics

gender the behaviors and attitudes that a society considers proper for its males and females; masculinity or femininity

138

Mexico

Greg Vaughn/Alamy

Jordan

Franz Lemmens/Getty Images

Kenya

Frans Lanting/Corbis

Ethiopia

Rob Howard/Corbis

Brazil

Reuters/Corbis

Chile

Art Wolfe/Getty Images

India

Jon Arnold Images Ltd/Alamy

Tibet

Jeremy Horner/Corbis

Standards of Gender

Each human group determines its ideas of "maleness" and "femaleness." As you can see from these photos of four women and four men, standards of gender are arbitrary and vary from one culture to another. Yet, in its ethnocentrism, each group thinks that its preferences reflect what gender "really" is. As indicated here, around the world men and women try to make themselves appealing by aspiring to their group's standards of gender

ThinkingCRITICALLY
Biology Versus Culture—Culture Is the Answer

Sociologist Cynthia Fuchs Epstein (1988, 1999, 2007) stresses that differences between the behavior of males and females are solely the result of social factors—specifically, socialization and social control. Her argument is as follows:

1. The anthropological record shows greater equality between the sexes in the past than we had thought. In earlier societies, women, as well as men, hunted small game, made tools, and gathered food. In hunting and gathering societies, the roles of both women and men are less rigid than those indicated by stereotypes. For example, the Agta and Mbuti are egalitarian. This proves that hunting and gathering societies exist in which women are not subordinate to men. Anthropologists claim that in these societies women have a separate but equal status.

2. The types of work that men and women do in each society are determined not by biology but by social arrangements. Few people can escape these arrangements, and almost everyone works within his or her assigned narrow range. This division of work by gender serves the interests of men, and both informal customs and formal laws enforce it. When these socially constructed barriers are removed, women's work habits are similar to those of men.

Courtesy of Cynthia Fuchs Epstein

Cynthia Fuchs Epstein, whose position in the ongoing "nature versus nurture" debate is summarized here.

3. Biology "causes" some human behaviors, but they are related to reproduction or differences in body structure. These differences are relevant for only a few activities, such as playing basketball or "crawling through a small space."

4. Female crime rates are rising in many parts of the world. This indicates that aggression, which is often considered a male behavior dictated by biology, is related instead to social factors. When social conditions permit, such as when women become lawyers, they, too, become "adversarial, assertive, and dominant."

Not incidentally, another form of this "dominant behavior" is the challenges that women make to the biased views about human nature proposed by men.

In short, rather than "women's incompetence or inability to read a legal brief, perform brain surgery, [or] to predict a bull market," social factors—socialization, gender discrimination, and other forms of social control—create gender differences in behavior. Arguments that assign "an evolutionary and genetic basis" to explain differences in the behaviors of women and men are simplistic. They "rest on a dubious structure of inappropriate, highly selective, and poor data, oversimplification in logic and in inappropriate inferences by use of analogy."

ThinkingCRITICALLY
Biology Versus Culture—Biology Is the Answer

patriarchy a society in which men as a group dominate women as a group; authority is vested in males

matriarchy a society in which women as a group dominate men as a group; authority is vested in females

Sociologist Steven Goldberg (1974, 1986, 1993, 2003) finds it astonishing that anyone should doubt "the presence of core-deep differences in males and females, differences of temperament and emotion we call masculinity and femininity." Goldberg's argument—that it is not environment but inborn differences that "give masculine and feminine direction to the emotions and behaviors of men and women"—is as follows:

1. The anthropological record shows that all societies for which evidence exists are (or were) **patriarchies** (societies in which men-as-a-group dominate women-as-a-group). Stories about long-lost **matriarchies** (societies in which women-as-a-group dominate men-as-a-group) are myths.

2. In all societies, past and present, the highest statuses are associated with men. In every society, politics is ruled by "hierarchies overwhelmingly dominated by men."

3. Men dominate societies because they "have a lower threshold for the elicitation of dominance behavior . . . a greater tendency to exhibit whatever behavior is necessary in any environment to attain dominance in hierarchies and male–female encounters and relationships." Men are more willing "to sacrifice the rewards of other motivations—the desire for affection, health, family life, safety, relaxation, vacation and the like—in order to attain dominance and status."

4. Just as a 6-foot woman does not prove the social basis of height, so exceptional individuals, such as highly achieving and dominant women, do not refute "the physiological roots of behavior."

Steven Goldberg, whose position in the ongoing "nature versus nurture" debate is summarized here.

Photo by Mitchell Meltzer, courtesy of Steven Goldberg

In short, there is only one valid interpretation of why every society from that of the Pygmy to that of the Swede associates dominance and attainment with men. Male dominance of society is "an inevitable resolution of the psychophysiological reality." Socialization and social institutions merely *reflect*—and sometimes exaggerate—inborn tendencies. Any interpretation other than inborn differences is "wrongheaded, ignorant, tendentious, internally illogical, discordant with the evidence, and implausible in the extreme." The argument that males are more aggressive because they have been socialized that way is equivalent to the claim that men can grow mustaches because boys have been socialized that way.

To acknowledge this reality is *not* to defend discrimination against women. Approval or disapproval of what societies have done with these basic biological differences is not the issue. The point is that biology leads males and females to different behaviors and attitudes—regardless of how we feel about this or whether we wish it were different.

The Dominant Position in Sociology

The dominant sociological position is that we behave the way we do because of social factors, not biology. Our visible differences of sex do not come with meanings built into them. Rather, each human group makes its own interpretation of these physical differences and assigns males and females to separate groups. In these groups, people learn what is expected of them and are given different access to property, power, prestige, and other privileges available in their society.

Most sociologists find compelling the argument that if biology were the principal factor in human behavior, all around the world we would find women behaving in one way and men in another. In fact, however, ideas of gender vary greatly from one culture to another—and, as a result, so do male–female behaviors.

Opening the Door to Biology

The matter of "nature" versus "nurture" is not so easily settled, however, and some sociologists acknowledge that biological factors are involved in some human behavior other than reproduction and childbearing (Udry 2000). Alice Rossi, a feminist sociologist and former president of the American Sociological Association, has suggested that women are better prepared biologically for "mothering" than are men. Rossi (1977, 1984) says that women are more sensitive to the infant's soft skin and to their nonverbal communications. She stresses that the issue is not either biology or society. Instead, nature provides biological predispositions, which are then overlaid with culture.

To see why the door to biology is opening just slightly in sociology, let's consider a medical accident and a study of Vietnam veterans.

A Medical Accident.   The drama began in 1963, when 7-month-old identical twin boys were taken to a doctor for a routine circumcision (Money and Ehrhardt 1972). The inept physician, who was using a heated needle, turned the electric current too high and accidentally burned off the penis of one of the boys. You can imagine the parents' disbelief—and then their horror—as the truth sank in.

What can be done in a situation like this? The damage was irreversible. The parents were told that their boy could never have sexual relations. After months of soul-searching and tearful consultations with experts, the parents decided that their son should have a sex-change operation. When he was 22 months old, surgeons castrated the boy, using the skin to construct a vagina. The parents then gave the child a new name, Brenda, dressed him in frilly clothing, let his hair grow long, and began to treat him as a girl. Later, physicians gave Brenda female steroids to promote female pubertal growth (Colapinto 2001).

At first, the results were promising. When the twins were 4 years old, the mother said (remember that the children are biologically identical):

> One thing that really amazes me is that she is so feminine. I've never seen a little girl so neat and tidy. . . . She likes for me to wipe her face. She doesn't like to be dirty, and yet my son is quite different. I can't wash his face for anything. . . . She is very proud of herself, when she puts on a new dress, or I set her hair. . . . She seems to be daintier. (Money and Ehrhardt 1972)

About a year later, the mother described how their daughter imitated her while their son copied his father:

> I found that my son, he chose very masculine things like a fireman or a policeman. . . . He wanted to do what daddy does, work where daddy does, and carry a lunch kit. . . . [My daughter] didn't want any of those things. She wants to be a doctor or a teacher. . . . But none of the things that she ever wanted to be were like a policeman or a fireman, and that sort of thing never appealed to her. (Money and Ehrhardt 1972)

If the matter were this clear-cut, we could use this case to conclude that gender is determined entirely by nurture. Seldom are things in life so simple, however, and a twist occurs in this story. Despite this promising start and her parents' coaching, Brenda did not adapt well to femininity. She preferred to mimic her father shaving, rather than her mother putting on makeup. She rejected dolls, favoring guns and her brother's

David Reimer, whose story is recounted here.

Thomas Dallal/SIPA PRESS/girlboy.

toys. She liked rough-and-tumble games and insisted on urinating standing up. Classmates teased her and called her a "cavewoman" because she walked like a boy. At age 14, she was expelled from school for beating up a girl who teased her. Despite estrogen treatment, she was not attracted to boys, and at age 14, in despair over her inner turmoil, she was thinking of suicide. In a tearful confrontation, her father told her about the accident and her sex change.

"All of a sudden everything clicked. For the first time, things made sense, and I understood who and what I was," the twin said of this revelation. David (his new name) then had testosterone shots and, later, surgery to partially reconstruct a penis. At age 25, he married a woman and adopted her children (Diamond and Sigmundson 1997; Colapinto 2001). There is an unfortunate end to this story, however. In 2004, David committed suicide.

The Vietnam Veterans Study. Time after time, researchers have found that boys and men who have higher levels of testosterone tend to be more aggressive. In one study, researchers compared the testosterone levels of college men in a "rowdy" fraternity with those of men in a fraternity that had a reputation for academic achievement and social responsibility. Men in the "rowdy" fraternity had higher levels of testosterone (Dabbs et al. 1996). In another study, researchers found that prisoners who had committed sex crimes and acts of violence against people had higher levels of testosterone than those who had committed property crimes (Dabbs et al. 1995). The samples were small, however, leaving the nagging uncertainty that these findings might be due to chance.

Then in 1985, the U.S. government began a health study of Vietnam veterans. To be certain that the study was representative, the researchers chose a random sample of 4,462 men. Among the data they collected was a measurement of testosterone. This sample supports earlier studies showing that men who have higher levels of testosterone tend to be more aggressive and to have more problems as a consequence. When the veterans with higher testosterone levels were boys, they were more likely to get in trouble with parents and teachers and to become delinquents. As adults, they were more likely to use hard drugs, to get into fights, to end up in lower-status jobs, and to have more sexual partners. Those who married were more likely to have affairs, to hit their wives, and, it follows, to get divorced (Dabbs and Morris 1990; Booth and Dabbs 1993).

This makes it sound like biology is the basis for behavior. Fortunately for us sociologists, there is another side to this research, and here is where *social class,* the topic of our previous chapter, comes into play. High-testosterone men from lower social classes are more likely to get in trouble with the law, do poorly in school, or mistreat their wives than are high-testosterone men from higher social classes (Dabbs and Morris 1990). *Social* factors such as socialization, subcultures, life goals, and self-definitions are significant in these men's behavior. Discovering how social factors work in combination with testosterone level, then, is of great interest to sociologists.

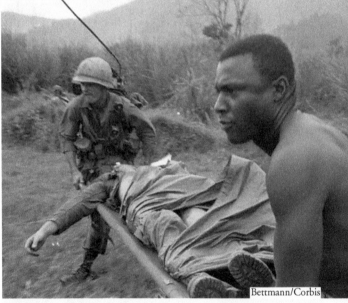

Bettmann/Corbis

Sociologists study the social factors that underlie human behavior, the experiences that mold us, funneling us into different directions in life. The research on Vietnam veterans discussed in the text indicates how the sociological door is opening slowly to also consider biological factors in human behavior. This 1966 photo shows orderlies rushing a wounded soldier to an evacuation helicopter.

In Sum: The findings are preliminary, but significant and provocative. They indicate that human behavior is not a matter of either nature or nurture, but of the two working together. Some behavior that we sociologists usually assume to be due entirely to socialization is apparently influenced by biology. In the years to come, this should prove to be an exciting—and controversial—area of sociological research. One level of research will be to determine whether any behaviors are due only to biology. The second level will be to discover the ways that social factors modify biology. The third level will be, in sociologist Janet Chafetz's (1990:30) phrase, to determine how "different" becomes translated into "unequal."

Gender Inequality in Global Perspective

Around the world, gender is *the* primary division between people. Every society sorts men and women into separate groups and gives them different access to property, power, and prestige. These divisions *always* favor men-as-a-group. After reviewing the historical record, historian and feminist Gerda Lerner (1986) concluded that "there is not a single society known where women-as-a-group have decision-making power over men (as a group)." Consequently, sociologists classify females as a *minority group*. Because females outnumber males, you may find this strange. The term *minority group* applies, however, because it refers to people who are discriminated against on the basis of physical or cultural characteristics, regardless of their numbers (Hacker 1951). For an overview of gender discrimination in Iran, see the Mass Media in Social Life box on the next page.

How Females Became a Minority Group

Have females always been a minority group? Some analysts speculate that in hunting and gathering societies, women and men were social equals (Leacock 1981; Hendrix 1994) and that horticultural societies also had less gender discrimination than is common today (Collins et al. 1993). In these societies, women may have contributed about 60 percent of the group's total food. Yet, around the world, gender is the basis for discrimination. How, then, did it happen that women became a minority group? Let's consider the primary theory that has been proposed.

The Origins of Patriarchy

The major theory of the origin of *patriarchy*—men dominating society—points to social consequences of human reproduction (Lerner 1986; Friedl 1990). In early human history, life was short. To balance the high death rate and maintain the population, women had to give birth to many children. This brought severe consequences for women. To survive, an infant needed a nursing mother. With a child at her breast or in her uterus, or one carried on her hip or on her back, women were physically encumbered. Consequently, around the world women assumed tasks that were associated with the home and child care, while men took over the hunting of large animals and other tasks that required both greater speed and longer absences from the base camp (Huber 1990).

As a result, men became dominant. It was the men who left camp to hunt animals, who made contact with other tribes, who traded with these groups, and who quarreled and waged war with them. It was also the men who made and controlled the instruments of death, the weapons that were used for hunting and warfare. It was they who accumulated possessions in trade and gained prestige by returning to the camp triumphantly, leading captured prisoners or bringing large animals they had killed to feed the tribe. In contrast, little prestige was given to the routine, taken-for-granted activities of women—who were not perceived as risking their lives for the group. Eventually, men took over society. Their sources of power were their weapons, items of trade, and knowledge gained from contact with other groups. Women became second-class citizens, subject to men's decisions.

Is this theory correct? Remember that the answer lies buried in human history, and there is no way of testing it. Male dominance may be the result of some entirely different cause. For example, anthropologist Marvin Harris (1977) proposed that because most men are stronger than most women and survival in tribal groups

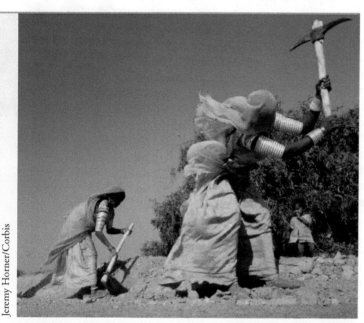

Men's work? Women's work? Customs in other societies can blow away stereotypes. As is common throughout India, these women are working on road construction.

Jeremy Horner/Corbis

required hand-to-hand combat, men became the warriors, and women became the reward that enticed men to risk their lives in battle. Frederick Engels proposed that patriarchy came with the development of private property (Lerner 1986; Jacobs 2007). He could not explain why private property should have produced male dominance, however. Gerda Lerner (1986) suggests that patriarchy may even have had different origins in different places.

Whatever its origins, a circular system of thought evolved. Men came to think of themselves as inherently superior—based on the evidence that they dominated society. They shrouded many of their activities with secrecy and constructed elaborate rules and rituals

MASS MEDIA In SOCIAL LIFE

Women in Iran: The Times Are Changing, Ever So Slowly

A woman's testimony in court is worth half that of a man's testimony.

A woman may inherit from her parents only half what her brother inherits.

A woman who has sex with a man who is not her husband can be stoned to death.

A woman who refuses to cover her hair in public can receive 80 lashes with a whip.

Not exactly equality.

As you would expect, Iranian women don't like it. Until now, though, there was little that they could do. Women are controlled by their fathers until they marry, and after marriage they come under the control of their husbands.

For the most part, they didn't know that life could be different.

Now the mass media are spearheading change in gender relations. There is a new literacy: Iranian women are logging onto the Internet, and they are reading books. Satellite television is also beaming new information across geographic lines, bringing pictures of other ways of life, of an unfamiliar equality and mutual respect between women and men.

Thanks to the mass media, their eyes are being opened to the fact that not all the women in the world live under the thumbs of men. From this awareness is coming the realization that they don't have to live like this either, that there really is a potential for new relationships.

This awareness and the glimmer of hope that another way of life can be theirs are leading to an incipient women's movement.

As in Afghanistan, the movement is still small—and protest remains dangerous. Some women have been fined, and for others it is worse. Alieh Eghamdoust, for example, is serving a three-year jail sentence for participating in a women's demonstration. Other protestors

The incipient women's movement in Iran is a sign of changing times. These students at a university in Iran indicate changing lifestyles and ideas.

Ulla Kimmig/laif/Redux

find brutality at home, from their husbands, fathers, or brothers.

Despite the danger, women are continuing to protest. They are even pressing for new rights in the Iranian courts. They are demanding divorce from abusive husbands—and some are getting it.

Not much has changed yet. A man can still divorce his wife whenever he wants, while a woman who wants to divorce a husband must go through a lengthy procedure and never can be sure she will be granted the divorce. A husband also gets automatic custody of any children over the age of seven.

But as women continue their struggle, change will come. One sign of hope: Fewer women are being stoned to death.

This, at least, is a beginning.

For Your Consideration

What do you think gender relations will be like in Iran ten years from now? Why?

If the women's movement in Iran becomes popular and effective, do you think that the relationship between men and women will be about the same as it is in the United States? Why or why not?

Based on Fathi 2009; Semple 2009.

Anthropologist George Murdock surveyed 324 traditional societies worldwide. In all of them, some work was considered "men's work," while other tasks were considered "women's work." He found that hunting is almost universally considered "men's work." These men, who live on the steppes of Mongolia, ride reindeer when they go hunting.

Hamid Sardar/Corbis

to avoid "contamination" by females, whom they openly deemed inferior by that time. Even today, patriarchy is always accompanied by cultural supports designed to justify male dominance—such as designating certain activities as "not appropriate" for women.

As tribal societies developed into larger groups, men, who enjoyed their power and privileges, maintained their dominance. Long after hunting and hand-to-hand combat ceased to be routine, and even after large numbers of children were no longer needed to maintain the population, men held on to their power. Male dominance in contemporary societies, then, is a continuation of a millennia-old pattern whose origin is lost in history.

Sex Typing of Work

Anthropologist George Murdock (1937) analyzed data that researchers had reported on 324 societies around the world. He found that in all of them, activities are *sex typed*. In other words, every society associates certain activities with one sex or the other. He also found that activities that are considered "female" in one society may be considered "male" in another. In some groups, for example, taking care of cattle is women's work, while other groups assign this task to men.

There was one exception, metalworking, which was considered men's work in all of the societies that Murdock examined. Making weapons, pursuing sea mammals, and hunting were almost universally the domain of men, but in a few societies women participated in these activities. Although Murdock found no specific work that was universally assigned only to women, he did find that making clothing, cooking, carrying water, and grinding grain were almost always female tasks. In a few societies, however, such activities were regarded as men's work.

A theory of how *patriarchy* originated centers on childbirth. Because only women give birth, they assumed tasks associated with home and child care, while men hunted and performed other survival tasks that required greater strength, speed, and absence from home. Following in the steps of her female ancestors, this woman in Yangshou, China, while she works, takes care of her grandchild.

PETER PARKS/AFP/Getty Images

From Murdock's cross-cultural survey, we can conclude that nothing about biology requires men and women to be assigned different work. Anatomy does not have to equal destiny when it comes to occupations, for as we have seen, pursuits that are considered feminine in one society may be deemed masculine in another, and vice versa. On the following pages is a photo essay on women at work in India that underscores this point.

Gender and the Prestige of Work

You might ask whether this division of labor really illustrates social inequality. Does it perhaps simply represent each group's arbitrary ways of dividing up labor, not gender discrimination?

This could be the case, except for this finding: *Universally, greater prestige is given to male activities—regardless of what those activities are* (Linton 1936; Rosaldo 1974). If taking care of goats is men's work, then the care of goats is considered important and carries high prestige, but if it is women's work, it is considered less important and is given less prestige. Let's take an example closer to home. When delivering babies was "women's work" and was done by midwives, it was given low prestige. But when men took over this task, they became "baby doctors" with high prestige (Ehrenreich and English 1973). In short, it is not the work that provides the prestige, but the sex with which the work is associated.

Other Areas of Global Discrimination

Let's briefly consider four additional aspects of global gender discrimination. Later, when we focus on the United States, we shall examine these topics in greater detail.

The Global Gap in Education. Almost 1 billion adults around the world cannot read; two-thirds are women (UNESCO 2008). Illiteracy is especially common in Africa and the Middle East, but is not limited to those areas. In North America, only about half of the women in Haiti can read and write ("Women of . . . " 2002). The United Nations has made it a priority to increase literacy and monitors each country's progress. The statistics the United Nations uses, though, underestimate the problem. Some people are counted as literate if they can write their name (Falkenberg 2008).

The Global Gap in Politics. In 2008, Rwanda became the first country in the world to elect more women (56 percent) than men to its national legislature (Pflanz 2008). It is typical for women to be highly underrepresented in politics, for on average, women make up just 18 percent of the world's national legislative bodies (UNIFEM 2008). In some countries, such as Papua New Guinea, the total is only 1 percent.

The Global Gap in Pay. In every nation, women average less pay than men. In the United States, full-time working women average only 72 percent of what men make (see Figure 8). In some countries, women make much less than this.

Global Violence Against Women. A global human rights issue is violence against women. Historical examples are foot binding in China, witch burning in Europe, and *suttee* (burning the living widow with the body of her dead husband) in India. Today we have rape, wife beating, female infanticide, and the kidnapping of women to be brides. There is also forced prostitution, which was probably the case in our opening vignette. Another notorious example is female circumcision, the topic of the Cultural Diversity box.

"Honor killings" are another form of violence against women. In some societies, such as Pakistan, Jordan, and Kurdistan, a woman who is thought to have brought disgrace on her family is killed by a male relative—usually a brother or her husband, but sometimes her father or uncles. What threat to the family's honor can be so severe that the men kill a daughter, wife, or sister? The usual reason is sex outside of marriage. Even a woman who has been raped is in danger of becoming the victim of an honor killing (Zoepf 2007; Falkenberg 2008). Killing the girl or woman removes the "stain" she has brought to the family and restores its honor in the community. Sharing this view, the police in these countries generally ignore honor killings, viewing them as private family matters.

In Sum: Inequality is not some accidental, hit-or-miss affair. Rather, each society's institutions work together to maintain the group's particular forms of inequality. Customs, often venerated throughout history, both justify and maintain these arrangements. In some cases, the prejudice and discrimination directed at females are so extreme they result in their enslavement and death.

Kazuyoshi Nomachi/Corbis

Foot binding was practiced in China until about 1900. Tiny feet were a status symbol. They made it difficult for a woman to walk, indicating that a woman's husband did not need his wife's labor. To make the feet even smaller, sometime's the baby's feet were broken and wrapped tightly. Some baby's toes were cut off. This photo was taken in Yunnan Province, China.

Work and Gender:
Women at Work in India

traveling through India was both a pleasant and an eye-opening experience. The country is incredibly diverse, the people friendly, and the land culturally rich. For this photo essay, wherever I went—whether city, village, or countryside—I took photos of women at work.

From these photos, you can see that Indian women work in a wide variety of occupations. Some of their jobs match traditional Western expectations, and some diverge sharply from our gender stereotypes. Although women in India remain subservient to men—with the women's movement hardly able to break the cultural surface—women's occupations are hardly limited to the home. I was surprised at some of the hard, heavy labor that Indian women do.

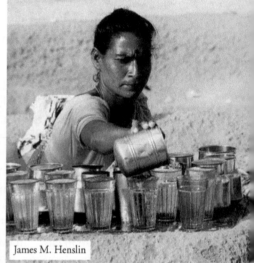

James M. Henslin

Indian women are highly visible in public places. A storekeeper is as likely to be a woman as a man. This woman is selling glasses of water at a beach on the Bay of Bengal. The structure on which her glasses rest is built of sand.

James M. Henslin

The villages of India have no indoor plumbing. Instead, each village has a well with a hand pump, and it is the women's job to fetch the water. This is backbreaking work, for, after pumping the water, the women wrestle the heavy buckets onto their heads and carry them home. This was one of the few occupations I saw that was limited to women.

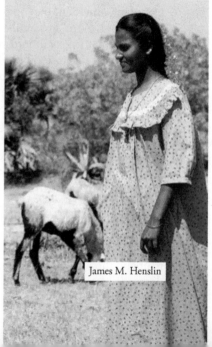

James M. Henslin

Women also take care of livestock. It looks as though this woman dressed up and posed for her photo, but this is what she was wearing and doing when I saw her in the field and stopped to talk to her. While the sheep are feeding, her job is primarily to "be" there, to make certain the sheep don't wander off or that no one steals them.

James M. Henslin

James M. Henslin

Sweeping the house is traditional work for Western women. So it is in India, but the sweeping has been extended to areas outside the home. These women are sweeping a major intersection in Chennai. When the traffic light changes here, the women will continue sweeping, with the drivers swerving around them. This was one of the few occupations that seems to be limited to women.

As in the West, food preparation in India is traditional women's work. Here, however, food preparation takes an unexpected twist. Having poured rice from the 60-pound sack onto the floor, these women in Chittoor search for pebbles or other foreign objects that might be in the rice.

James M. Henslin

I visited quarries in different parts of India, where I found men, women, and children hard at work in the tropical sun. This woman works 8 1/2 hours a day, six days a week. She earns 40 rupees a day (about ninety cents). Men make 60 rupees a day (about $1.35). Like many quarry workers, this woman is a bonded laborer. She must give half of her wages to her master.

When I saw this unusual sight, I had to stop and talk to the workers. From historical pictures, I knew that belt-driven machines were common on U.S. farms 100 years ago. This one in Tamil Nadu processes sugar cane. The woman feeds sugar cane into the machine, which disgorges the stalks on one side and sugar cane juice on the other.

James M. Henslin

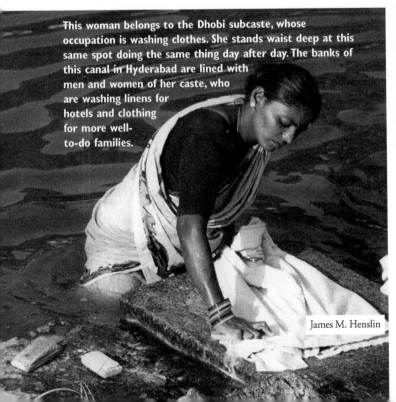

This woman belongs to the Dhobi subcaste, whose occupation is washing clothes. She stands waist deep at this same spot doing the same thing day after day. The banks of this canal in Hyderabad are lined with men and women of her caste, who are washing linens for hotels and clothing for more well-to-do families.

James M. Henslin

James M. Henslin

A common sight in India is women working on construction crews. As they work on buildings and on highways, they mix cement, unload trucks, carry rubble, and, following Indian culture, carry loads of bricks atop their heads. This photo was taken in Raipur, Chhattisgarh.

149

Cultural Diversity around the World

Female Circumcision

"Lie down there," the excisor suddenly said to me [when I was 12], pointing to a mat on the ground. No sooner had I laid down than I felt my frail, thin legs grasped by heavy hands and pulled wide apart. . . . Two women on each side of me pinned me to the ground . . . I underwent the ablation of the labia minor and then of the clitoris. The operation seemed to go on forever. I was in the throes of agony, torn apart both physically and psychologically. It was the rule that girls of my age did not weep in this situation. I broke the rule. I cried and screamed with pain . . . !

Afterwards they forced me, not only to walk back to join the other girls who had already been excised, but to dance with them. I was doing my best, but then I fainted. . . . It was a month before I was completely healed. When I was better, everyone mocked me, as I hadn't been brave, they said. (Walker and Parmar 1993:107–108)

Worldwide, between 100 million and 140 million females have been circumcised, mostly in Muslim Africa and in some parts of Malaysia and Indonesia (World Health Organization 2008). In Egypt, 97 percent of the women have been circumcised, the same as in Indonesia (Douglas 2005; Slackman 2007). In some cultures, the surgery occurs seven to ten days after birth, but in others it is not performed until girls reach adolescence. Among most groups, it takes place between the ages of 4 and 8. Because the surgery is usually done without anesthesia, the pain is so excruciating that adults hold the girl down. In urban areas, physicians sometimes perform the operation; in rural areas, a neighborhood woman usually does it.

In some cultures, only the girl's clitoris is cut off; in others, more is removed. In Sudan, the Nubia cut away most of the girl's genitalia, then sew together the remaining outer edges. They bind the girl's legs from her ankles to her waist for several weeks while scar tissue closes up the vagina. They leave a small opening the diameter of a pencil for the passage of urine and menstrual fluids. When a woman marries, the opening is cut wider to permit sexual intercourse. Before a woman gives birth, the opening is enlarged further. After birth, the vagina is again sutured shut; this cycle of surgically closing and opening begins anew with each birth.

What are the reasons for circumcising girls? Some groups believe that it reduces female sexual desire, making it more likely that a woman will be a virgin at marriage and, afterward, remain faithful to her husband. Others think that women can't bear children if they aren't circumcised.

The surgery has strong support among many women. Some mothers and grandmothers even insist that the custom continue. Their concern is that their daughters marry well, and in some of these societies uncircumcised women are considered impure and are not allowed to marry.

Feminists respond that female circumcision is a form of ritual torture to control female sexuality. They point out that men dominate the societies that practice it.

Change is on its way: A social movement to ban female circumcision has developed, and the World Health Organization has declared that female circumcision is a human rights issue. Fifteen African countries have now banned the circumcision of females. Without sanctions, though, these laws accomplish little. In Egypt, which prohibited female circumcision in 1996, almost all girls continue to be circumcised (Corbett 2008).

Louise Gubb/SABA/Corbis

Circumcision in Kapchorwa, Uganda

For Your Consideration

Do you think it is legitimate for the members of one culture to interfere with the customs of another culture? If so, under what circumstances? What makes us right and them wrong? What if some African nation said that some U.S. custom is wrong? How would you respond to this Somali woman who said, "The Somali woman doesn't need an alien woman telling her how to treat her private parts."

Sources: As cited, and Lightfoot-Klein 1989; Merwine 1993; Chalkley 1997; Collymore 2000; Tuhus-Dubrow 2007; UNIFEM 2008.

Gender Inequality in the United States

feminism the philosophy that men and women should be politically, economically, and socially equal; organized activities on behalf of this principle

As we review gender inequality in the United States, let's begin by taking a brief look at how change in this vital area of social life came about. Before we do so, though, you might enjoy the historical snapshot presented in the Down-to-Earth Sociology box on the next page.

Fighting Back: The Rise of Feminism

In the nation's early history, the second-class status of U.S. women was taken for granted. A husband and wife were legally one person—him (Chafetz and Dworkin 1986). Women could not vote, buy property in their own name, make legal contracts, or serve on juries. How could things have changed so much in the last hundred years that these examples sound like fiction?

A central lesson of conflict theory is that power yields privilege; like a magnet, power draws society's best resources to the elite. Because men tenaciously held onto their privileges and used social institutions to maintain their position, basic rights for women came only through prolonged and bitter struggle.

Feminism—the view that biology is not destiny and that stratification by gender is wrong and should be resisted—met with strong opposition, both by men who had privilege to lose and by women who accepted their status as morally correct. In 1894, for example, Jeannette Gilder said that women should not have the right to vote because "Politics is too public, too wearing, and too unfitted to the nature of women" (Crossen 2003).

Feminists, then known as suffragists, struggled against such views. In 1916, they founded the National Woman's Party, and in 1917 they began to picket the White House. After picketing for six months, the women were arrested. Hundreds were sent to prison, including Lucy Burns, a leader of the National Woman's Party. The extent to which these women had threatened male privilege is demonstrated by how they were treated in prison.

> Two men brought in Dorothy Day [the editor of a periodical that promoted women's rights], twisting her arms above her head. Suddenly they lifted her and brought her body down twice over the back of an iron bench. . . . They had been there a few minutes when Mrs. Lewis, all doubled over like a sack of flour, was thrown in. Her head struck the iron bed and she fell to the floor senseless. As for Lucy Burns, they handcuffed her wrists and fastened the handcuffs over [her] head to the cell door. (Cowley 1969)

The "first wave" of the U.S. women's movement met enormous opposition. The women in this 1920 photo had just been released after serving two months in jail for picketing the White House. Lucy Burns, mentioned on this page, is the second woman on the left. Alice Paul was placed in solitary confinement and is a subject of this 1920 protest.

Hulton-Deutsch Collection/Corbis

151

Down-to-Earth Sociology
Women and Smoking: Let's Count the Reasons

(A humorous, but serious, look at historical changes in gender)

Why Women Shouldn't Smoke

1. Smoking ruins a woman's reputation and turns her into a tramp.
   "A man may take out a woman who smokes for a good time, but he won't marry her, and if he does, he won't stay married."

   Editorial in the Washington Post, *1914*

2. Women who smoke drive young men wild, break up families, and even make men kill.
   "Young fellows go into our restaurants to find women folks sucking cigarettes. What happens? The young fellows lose all respect for the women, and the next thing you know the young fellows, vampired by these smoking women, desert their homes, their wives and children, rob their employers and even commit murder so that they can get money to lavish on these smoking women."

   A New York City alderman

3. It just doesn't look good (but it can be elegant).
   "To smoke in public is always bad taste in a woman. In private she may be pardoned if she does it with sufficient elegance."

   Alexandre Duval, a Parisian restaurateur, 1921

4. Smoking is so un-motherlike.
   It "coarsens" women and "detracts from the ideal of fine motherhood."

   The executive board of the Cleveland Boy Scouts, 1928

5. Smoking is a horrible evil that ruins women's sleep; plus it is bad for their skin.
   "The cigarette habit indulged by women tends to cause nervousness and insomnia and ruins the complexion. This is one of the most evil influences in American life today."

   Hugh S. Cumming, surgeon general of the U.S., 1920

6. Women just aren't as good as men at smoking.
   "Women really don't know how to smoke. One woman smoking one cigarette at a dinner table will stir up more smoke than a whole tableful of men smoking cigars. They don't seem to know what to do with the smoke. Neither do they know how to hold their cigarettes properly. They make a mess of the whole performance."

   The manager of a Manhattan hotel

An ad from 1929

(And with cancer, you'll lose even more weight!)

Why Women Should Smoke

1. It helps avoid those bad body parts.
   "You can't hide fat, clumsy ankles. When tempted to overindulge, reach for a Lucky."

   The American Tobacco Company, 1930s

Opposition to women's smoking was so strong that the police in New York City warned women not to light up—even in their own cars. Women's colleges also got into the act. Smith College students who were seen smoking, even off campus, were given a demerit. This was serious—three demerits and a woman would be kicked out of college.

Despite the opposition, more and more women began to smoke, evidently feeling that having "fat, clumsy ankles" was worse than risking their reputations. (In case you are wondering about those ankles, with women's clothing of the time, that's about all that men could see.)

For Your Consideration

Why do you think there was such strong opposition to women smoking in the early 1900s? What is the relationship between women smoking at this time and women's evolving political rights? Here is an historical statement that connects them: "If it were a question between their smoking and their voting, and they would promise to stay at home and smoke, I would say let them smoke."

Sen. Joseph Bailey of Texas, 1918

Source: Based on Crossen 2008.

This *first wave* of the women's movement had a radical branch that wanted to reform all the institutions of society and a conservative branch whose concern was to win the vote for women (Freedman 2001). The conservative branch dominated, and after the right to vote was won in 1920, the movement basically dissolved.

The *second wave* began in the 1960s. Sociologist Janet Chafetz (1990) points out that up to this time most women thought of work as a temporary activity intended to fill the time between completing school and getting married. To see how children's books reinforced such thinking, see Figure 1. As more women took jobs and began to regard them as careers, however, they began to compare their working conditions with those of men. This shift in their reference group changed the way women viewed their conditions at work. The result was a second wave of protest against gender inequalities. The goals of this second wave (which continues today) are broad, ranging from raising women's pay to changing policies on violence against women.

A *third wave* of feminism has emerged. Three main aspects are apparent. The first is a greater focus on the problems of women in the Least Industrialized Nations (Spivak 2000; Hamid 2006). Some are fighting battles against conditions long since overcome by women in the Most Industrialized Nations. The second is a criticism of the values that dominate work and society. Some feminists argue that competition, toughness, calloused emotions, and independence represent "male" qualities and need to be replaced with cooperation, connection, openness, and interdependence (England 2000). A third aspect is the removal of impediments to women's love and sexual pleasure (Crawford 2007). As this third wave develops, we can assume that it, too, will have its liberal and conservative branches.

Although U.S. women enjoy fundamental rights today, gender inequality continues to play a central role in social life. Let's first consider everyday life, the most pervasive form of gender inequality.

Gender Inequality in Everyday Life

One of the more common and significant aspects of gender discrimination in everyday life is the devaluation of femininity.

Devaluation of Things Feminine. In general, a higher value is placed on things considered masculine, for masculinity symbolizes strength and success while femininity is often perceived in terms of weakness and lack of accomplishment. People are often unaware that they make these relative evaluations, but if you listen carefully you can hear them pop up in their speech. Let's take a quick historical glance at one of these indicators. It might even be one that you have used:

FIGURE 1 Teaching Gender

Mother and Sally

Mother can sew.
Jane can sew.

The "Dick and Jane" readers were the top selling readers in the United States in the 1940s and 1950s. In addition to reading, they taught "gender messages." What gender message do you see here?

Housework is "women's work," a lesson girls should learn early in life.

Father

"I will help," said Dick.
"I will help you with the pigs."

What does this page teach children other than how to read the word "Father"? (Look above to see what Jane and Mother are doing.)

Besides learning words like "pigs" (relevant at that historical period), boys and girls also learned that rough outside work was for men.

Source: From *Dick and Jane: Fun with Our Family*, Illustrations © copyright 1951, 1979, and *Dick and Jane: We Play Outside*, copyright © 1965, Pearson Education, Inc., published by Scott, Foresman and Company. Used with permission.

Sociologist Samuel Stouffer headed a research team that produced *The American Soldier* (1949), a classic study of World War II combat soldiers. To motivate their men, officers used feminine terms as insults. If a man showed less-than-expected courage or endurance, an officer might say, "Whatsa matter, Bud—got lace on your drawers?" ["Drawers" was a term for shorts or underpants.] A generation later, as officers trained soldiers to fight in Vietnam, they still used accusations of femininity to motivate their men. Drill sergeants would mock their troops by saying, "Can't hack it, little girls?" (Eisenhart 1975). The practice continues. Male soldiers who show hesitation during maneuvers are mocked by others, who call them girls (Miller 1997/2007).

The same thing happens in sports. Anthropologist Douglas Foley (1990/2006), who studied high school football in Texas, reports that coaches insult boys who don't play well by shouting that they are "wearing skirts." In her research, sociologist Donna Eder (1995) heard junior high boys call one another "girl" when they didn't hit hard enough in football. When they play basketball, boys of this age also call one another a "woman" when they miss a basket (Stockard and Johnson 1980). In professional hockey, if players are not rough enough on the ice, their teammates call them "girls" (Gallmeier 1988:227).

These insults roll so easily off the tongues of men in sports and war that it is easy to lose sight of their significance, that they represent a devaluation of females. Sociologists Stockard and Johnson (1980:12) hit the nail on the head when they pointed out, "There is no comparable phenomenon among women, for young girls do not insult each other by calling each other 'man.'"

Our background assumptions focus our perception, making some things invisible. Much of our male–female interaction in everyday life is like this. Perhaps the Down-to-Earth Sociology box below will pry open those windows just a bit. That, at least, is its intention. After this excursion, we'll look at how gender shows up in health care.

Gender Inequality in Health Care

Medical researchers were perplexed. Reports were coming in from all over the country: Women were twice as likely as men to die after coronary bypass surgery. Researchers at Cedars-Sinai Medical Center in Los Angeles checked their own records. They found that of 2,300 coronary bypass patients, 4.6 percent of the women died as a result of the surgery, compared with 2.6 percent of the men.

These findings presented a sociological puzzle. To solve it, researchers first turned to biology (Bishop 1990). In coronary bypass surgery, a blood vessel is taken from one part of the body and stitched to an artery on the surface of the heart. Perhaps the surgery was more difficult to do on women because of their smaller arteries. To find out,

Down-to-Earth Sociology
Where Are the Cheerleaders? (Male, That Is)

Whenever I attend a high school or college football or basketball game, I see a group of slender young women in short, brightly colored skirts who jump into the air and cheer wildly as the boys make a basket, a touchdown, or do something exciting. At girls' games, I see no group of boys in bright colors, shaking pom-poms, and jumping into the air as they lead cheers when the girls make a score or do something exciting.

"Well, of course not," some would reply, "because . . ."

For Your Consideration
Do you think that having female cheerleaders for boys' sports and not having male cheerleaders for girls' sports is a form of gender discrimination? Why or why not?

A cheerleader in Seattle

Woods Wheatcroft/Aurora Photos

researchers measured the amount of time that surgeons kept patients on the heart-lung machine while they operated. They were surprised to learn that women spent *less* time on the machine than men. This indicated that the surgery was not more difficult to perform on women.

As the researchers probed, a surprising answer unfolded: unintended sexual discrimination. When women complained of chest pains, their doctors took them only *one tenth as seriously* as when men made the same complaints. How do we know this? Doctors were *ten* times more likely to give men exercise stress tests and radioactive heart scans. They also sent men to surgery on the basis of abnormal stress tests, but they waited until women showed clear-cut symptoms of heart disease before sending them to surgery. Patients who have surgery after heart disease is more advanced are more likely to die during and after heart surgery.

Although these findings have been publicized among physicians, the problem continues (Jneid et al. 2008). Perhaps as more women become physicians, the situation will change, since female doctors are more sensitive to women's health problems. For example, they are more likely to order Pap smears and mammograms (Lurie et al. 1993). In addition, as more women join the faculties of medical schools, we can expect that women's health problems will receive more attention in the training of physicians. Even this might not do it, however, as no one knows how stereotyping of the sexes produces this deadly discrimination, and women, too, hold our cultural stereotypes.

In contrast to unintentional sexism in heart surgery, there is a type of surgery that is a blatant form of discrimination against women. This is the focus of the Down-to-Earth Sociology box on the next page.

Gender Inequality in Education

To catch a glimpse of the past can give us a context for interpreting and appreciating the present. In many instances, change has been so extensive that the past can seem like it is from a different planet. So it is with education. Until 1832, women were not even allowed to attend college with men. When women were admitted to colleges attended by men—first at Oberlin College in Ohio—they had to wash the male students' clothing, clean their rooms, and serve them their meals (Flexner 1971/1999).

Female organs were a special focus of concern for the men who controlled education. They said that these organs dominated women's minds, making them less qualified than men for higher education. These men viewed menstruation as a special obstacle to women's success in education. It made women so feeble that they could hardly continue with their schooling, much less anything else in life. Here is how Dr. Edward Clarke, of Harvard University, put it:

> A girl upon whom Nature, for a limited period and for a definite purpose, imposes so great a physiological task, will not have as much power left for the tasks of school, as the boy of whom Nature requires less at the corresponding epoch. (Andersen 1988)

Because women are so much weaker than men, Clarke urged them to study only one-third as much as young men. And, of course, in their weakened state, they were advised to not study at all during menstruation.

REUTERS/Jeff J Mitchell/Landov

From grade school through college, male sports have been emphasized, and women's sports underfunded. Due to federal laws (*Title IX*), the funding gap has closed considerably, and there is an increasing emphasis on women's accomplishments in sports. Shown here are U. S. A.'s Mia Hamm (L) and Brazil's Elaine Moura, outstanding soccer players.

Down-to-Earth Sociology
Cold-Hearted Surgeons and Their Women Victims

Sociologist Sue Fisher (1986), who did participant observation in a hospital, was surprised to hear surgeons recommend total hysterectomy (removal of both the uterus and the ovaries) *when no cancer was present.* When she asked why, the male doctors explained that the uterus and ovaries are "potentially disease producing." They also said that these organs are unnecessary after the childbearing years, so why not remove them? Doctors who reviewed hysterectomies confirm this bias: Three out of four of these surgeries are, in their term, inappropriate (Broder et al. 2000).

Greed is a powerful motivator in many areas of social life, and it rears its ugly head in surgical sexism. Surgeons make money when they do hysterectomies, and the more of them that they do, the more money they make. Since women, to understate the matter, are reluctant to part with these organs, surgeons find that they have to "sell" this operation. As you read how one resident explained the "hard sell" to sociologist Diana Scully (1994), you might think of a used car salesperson:

> You have to look for your surgical procedures; you have to go after patients. Because no one is crazy enough to come and say, "Hey, here I am. I want you to operate on me." You have to sometimes convince the patient that she is really sick—if she is, of course [laughs], and that she is better off with a surgical procedure.

Used-car salespeople would love to have the powerful sales weapon that these surgeons have at their disposal: To "convince" a woman to have this surgery, the doctor puts on a serious face and tells her that the examination has turned up *fibroids* in her uterus—and they *might* turn into *cancer.* This statement is often sufficient to get the woman to buy the surgery. She starts to picture herself lying at death's door, her sorrowful family gathered at her death bed. Then the used car salesperson—I mean,

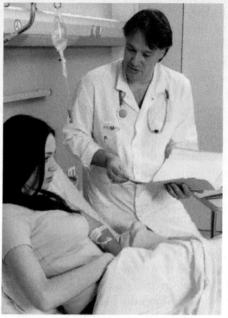

FURGOLLE/Image Point FR/Corbis

the surgeon—moves in to clinch the sale. Keeping a serious face and emitting an "I-know-how-you-feel" look, the surgeon starts to make arrangements for the surgery. What the surgeon withholds is the rest of the truth—that a lot of women have fibroids, that fibroids usually do *not* turn into cancer, and that the patient has several alternatives to surgery.

In case it is difficult for someone to see how this is sexist, let's change the context just a little. Let's suppose that there are female surgeons whose income depends on their selling a specialized operation. To sell it, they systematically suggest to older men that they get castrated—since "that organ is no longer necessary, and it might cause disease."

For Your Consideration

Hysterectomies are now so common that one of three U.S. women eventually has her uterus surgically removed (Whiteman et al. 2008). Why do you think that surgeons are so quick to operate? How can women find alternatives to surgery?

Like out-of-fashion clothing, these ideas were discarded, and women entered college in growing numbers. As Figure 2 on the next page shows, by 1900 one-third of college students were women. The change has been so extensive that 56 percent of today's college students are women. This overall average differs with racial–ethnic groups, as you can see from Figure 3 on the next page. African Americans have the fewest men relative to women, and Asian Americans the most. As another indication of how extensive the change is, women now earn 58 percent of all bachelor's degrees and 60 percent of all master's degrees (*Statistical Abstract* 2009:Table 288). As discussed in the next Down-to-Earth Sociology box, it might be time for affirmative action for men.

FIGURE 2 Changes in College Enrollment, by Sex

What percentages of U.S. college students are female and male?

*This sharp drop in female enrollment occurred when large numbers of male soldiers returned from World War II and attended college under the new GI Bill of Rights.
** Projection by U. S. Department of Education 2008.

Source: By the author. Based on *Statistical Abstract of the United States* 1938:Table 114; 1959:Table 158; 1991:Table 261; 2009:Table 272.

FIGURE 3 College Students, by Sex and Race–Ethnicity

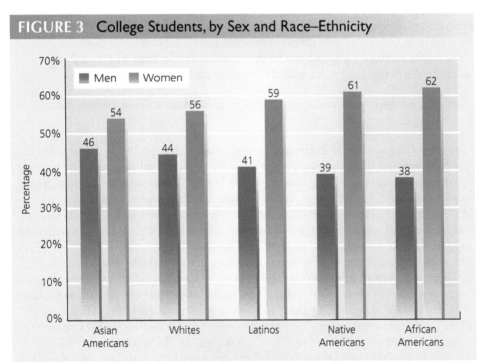

Note: This figure can be confusing. To read it, ask: What percentage of the group in college are men or women? (For example, what percentage of Asian American college students are men or women?)

Source: By the author. Based on *Statistical Abstract of the United States* 2008:Table 272; 2009:Table 272.

Down-to-Earth Sociology
Affirmative Action for Men?

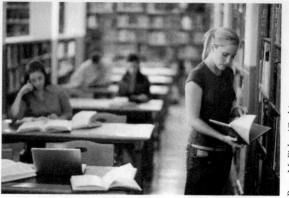

With fewer men than women in college, is it time to consider affirmative action for men?

The idea that we might need affirmative action *for men* was first proposed by psychologist Judith Kleinfeld (2002a). Many met this suggestion with laughter. After all, men dominate societies around the world, and they have done so for millennia. The discussion in this chapter has shown that as men exercised that dominance, they also suppressed and harmed women. To think that men would ever need affirmative action seems laughable at best.

In contrast to this reaction, let's pause, step back and try to see whether the idea has some merit. Look again at Figures 2 and 3. Do you see that women have not only caught up with men, but that they also have passed them up? Do you see that this applies to all racial–ethnic groups? That this is not a temporary situation, like lead cars changing place at the Indy 500, is apparent from the statistics the government publishes each year. For decades, women have steadily added to their proportion of college student enrollment and the degrees they earn.

This accomplishment is laudable, but what about the men? Why have they fallen behind? With college enrollment open equally to both men and women, why don't enrollment and degrees now match the relative proportions of women and men in the population (51 percent and 49 percent)? Although no one yet knows the reasons for this—and there are a lot of suggestions being thrown about—some have begun to consider this a problem in need of a solution. In a first,

Clark University in Massachusetts has begun a support program for men to help them adjust to their minority status (Gibbs 2008). I assume that other colleges will follow, as these totals have serious implications for the future of society—just as they did when fewer women were enrolled in college.

For Your Consideration

Do you think that women's and men's current college enrollments and degrees represent something other than an interesting historical change? Why do you think that men have fallen behind? Do you think anything should be done about this imbalance? If so, what? Behind the scenes, so as not to get anyone upset, some colleges have begun to reject more highly qualified women to get closer to a male–female balance (Kingsbury 2007). What do you think about this?

Figure 4 on the next page illustrates another major change. From this figure, you can see how women have increased their share of professional degrees. The greatest change is in dentistry: In 1970, across the entire United States, only 34 women earned degrees in dentistry. Today, about 2,000 women become dentists each year. As you can also see, almost as many women as men now graduate from U.S. medical and law schools. With the change so extensive and firm, I anticipate that women will soon outnumber men in earning these professional degrees.

With these extensive changes, it would seem that gender equality has been achieved, or at least almost so, and in some instances—as with the changed sex ratio in college—we have a new form of gender inequality. If we look closer, however, we find something beneath the surface. Underlying these degrees is *gender tracking;* that is, college degrees tend to follow gender, which reinforces male–female distinctions. Here are two extremes: Men earn 94 percent of the associate degrees in the "masculine" field of construction trades, while women are awarded 89 percent of the associate degrees in the "feminine" field of library science (*Statistical Abstract* 2009:Table 290). Because gender socialization gives men and women different orientations to life, they enter college with gender-linked aspirations. Socialization—not some presumed innate characteristic—channels men and women into different educational paths.

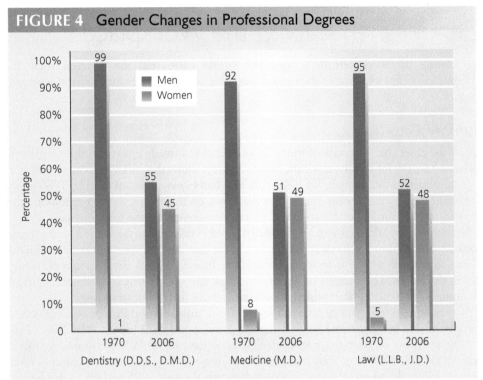

FIGURE 4   Gender Changes in Professional Degrees

Source: By the author. Based on *Digest of Education Statistics* 2007:Table 269; *Statistical Abstract of the United States* 2009:Table 293.

If we follow students into graduate school, we see that with each passing year the proportion of women drops. Table 1 below gives us a snapshot of doctoral programs in the sciences. Note how aspirations (enrollment) and accomplishments (doctorates earned) are sex linked. In five of these doctoral programs, men outnumber women, and in three, women outnumber men. In *all* of them, however, women are less likely to complete the doctorate.

If we follow those who earn doctoral degrees to their teaching careers at colleges and universities, we find gender stratification in rank and pay. Throughout the United States, women are less likely to become full professors, the highest-paying and most prestigious rank. In both private and public colleges, professors average more than twice the salary of instructors (*Statistical Abstract* 2009:Table 284). Even when women do become full professors, their average pay is less than that of men who are full professors (AAUP 2009:Table 5).

TABLE 1   Doctorates in Science, By Sex

Field	Students Enrolled		Doctorates Conferred		Completion Ratio* (Higher or Lower Than Expected)	
	Women	Men	Women	Men	Women	Men
Agriculture	48%	52%	40%	60%	−17	+15
Mathematics	36%	64%	30%	70%	−17	+ 9
Computer sciences	25%	75%	21%	79%	−16	+ 5
Social sciences	53%	47%	46%	54%	−13	+15
Biological sciences	56%	44%	49%	51%	−13	+16
Physical sciences	32%	68%	28%	72%	−13	+ 6
Engineering	23%	77%	20%	80%	−13	+ 4
Psychology	75%	25%	71%	29%	− 5	+16

*The formula for the completion ratio is X minus Y divided by Y, where X is the doctorates conferred and Y is the proportion enrolled in a program.

Source: By the author. Based on *Statistical Abstract of the United States* 2009:Tables 779, 782.

Gender Inequality in the Workplace

To examine the work setting is to make visible basic relations between men and women. Let's begin with one of the most remarkable areas of gender inequality at work, the pay gap.

The Pay Gap

One of the chief characteristics of the U.S. workforce is a steady growth in the numbers of women who work for wages outside the home. Figure 5 shows that in 1890 about one of every five paid workers was a woman. By 1940, this ratio had grown to one of four; by 1960 to one of three; and today it is almost one of two. As shown on this figure, the projections are that the ratio will remain 55 percent men and 45 percent women for the next few years.

Women who work for wages are not distributed evenly throughout the United States. From the Social Map on the next page, you can see that where a woman lives makes a difference in how likely she is to work outside the home. Why is there such a clustering among the states? The geographical patterns that you see on this map reflect regional-subcultural differences about which we currently have little understanding.

After college, you might like to take a few years off, travel around Europe, sail the oceans, or maybe sit on a beach in some South American paradise and drink piña coladas. But chances are, you are going to go to work instead. Since you have to work, how would you like to make an extra $650,000 on your job? If this sounds appealing, read on. I'm going to reveal how you can make an extra $1,356 a month between the ages of 25 and 65. Is this hard to do? Actually, it is simple for some and impossible for others. As Figure 7 on the next page shows, all you have to do is be born a male. If we compare full-time workers, based on current differences in earnings, this is how much more money the *average male* can expect to earn over the course of his career. Now if you want to boost that monthly difference to $2,482 for a whopping career total of $1,192,000, be both a male and a college graduate. Hardly any single factor pinpoints gender discrimination better than these totals. As you can see from Figure 7, the pay gap shows up at *all* levels of education.

FIGURE 5 Women's and Men's Proportion of the U.S. Labor Force

Note: Pre-1940 totals include women 14 and over: totals for 1940 and after are for women 16 and over. Broken lines are the author's projections.

Sources: By the author. Based on 1969 *Handbook on Women Workers,* 1969:10; *Manpower Report to the President,* 1971:203, 205; Mills and Palumbo, 1980:6, 45; *Statistical Abstract of the United States* 2009:Table 568.

FIGURE 6 Women in the WorkForce

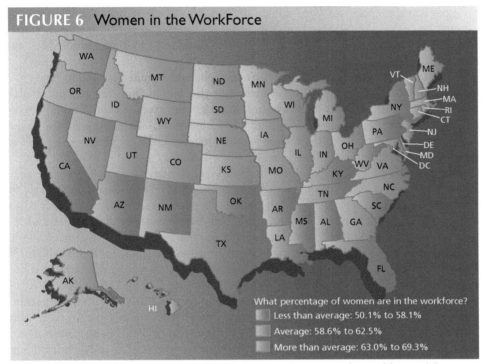

What percentage of women are in the workforce?
- Less than average: 50.1% to 58.1%
- Average: 58.6% to 62.5%
- More than average: 63.0% to 69.3%

Note: At 50.1 percent, West Virginia has the lowest rate of women in the workforce, while North Dakota, at 69.3 percent, has the highest.

Source: By the author. Based on *Statistical Abstract of the United States* 2009: Table 573.

FIGURE 7 The Gender Pay Gap, by Education[1]

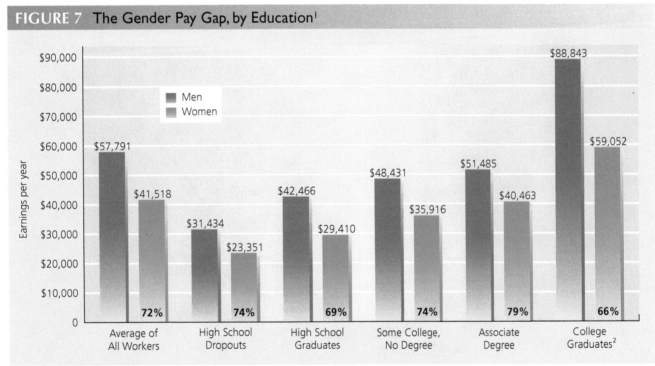

[1]Full-time workers in all fields. The percentage at the bottom of each red bar indicates the women's average percentage of the men's income.

[2]Bachelor's and all higher degrees, including professional degrees.

Source: By the author. Based on *Statistical Abstract of the United States* 2009: Table 681.

The pay gap is so great that U.S. women who work full-time average *only 72 percent* of what men are paid. As you can see from Figure 8 below, the pay gap used to be even worse. The gender gap in pay occurs not only in the United States but also in *all* industrialized nations.

If $1,192,000 in additional earnings isn't enough, how would you like to make another $166,000 extra at work? If so, just make sure that you are not only a man but also a *tall* man. Over their lifetimes, men who are over 6 feet tall average $166,000 more than men who are 5 feet 5 inches or less (Judge and Cable 2004). Taller women also make more than shorter women. But even when it comes to height, the gender pay gap persists, and tall men make more than tall women.

What logic can underlie the gender pay gap? As we just saw, college degrees are gender linked, so perhaps this gap is due to career choices. Maybe women are more likely to choose lower-paying jobs, such as teaching grade school, while men are more likely to go into better-paying fields, such as business and engineering. Actually, this is true, and researchers have found that about *half* of the gender pay gap is due to such factors. And the balance? It consists of a combination of gender discrimination (Jacobs 2003; Roth 2003) and what is called the "child penalty"—women missing out on work experience and opportunities while they care for children (Hundley 2001; Chaker and Stout 2004).

For college students, the gender gap in pay begins with the first job after graduation. You might know of a particular woman who was offered a higher salary than most men in her class, but she would be an exception. On average, men enjoy a "testosterone bonus," and employers start them out at higher salaries than women (Fuller and Schoenberger

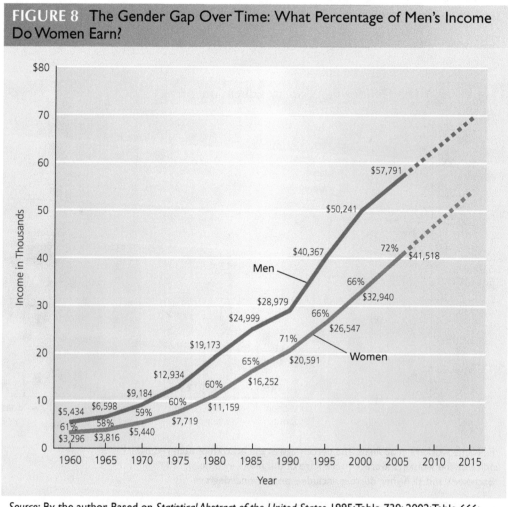

FIGURE 8 The Gender Gap Over Time: What Percentage of Men's Income Do Women Earn?

Source: By the author. Based on *Statistical Abstract of the United States* 1995:Table 739; 2002:Table 666; 2009:Table 681, and earlier years. Broken lines indicate the author's estimate.

1991; Harris et al. 2005). Depending on your sex, then, you will either benefit from the pay gap or be victimized by it.

As a final indication of the extent of the U.S. gender pay gap, consider this. Of the nation's top 500 corporations (the so-called Fortune 500), only 12 are headed by women (Kaufman and Hymowitz 2008). The highest number of these positions ever held by women is 13. I examined the names of the CEOs of the 350 largest U.S. corporations, and I found that your best chance to reach the top is to be named (in this order) John, Robert, James, William, or Charles. Edward, Lawrence, and Richard are also advantageous names. Amber, Katherine, Leticia, and Maria apparently draw a severe penalty. Naming your baby girl John or Robert might seem a little severe, but it could help her reach the top. (I say this only slightly tongue-in-cheek. One of the few women to head a Fortune 500 company—before she was fired and given $21 million severance pay—had a man's first name: Carleton Fiorina of Hewlett-Packard. Carleton's first name is actually Cara, but knowing what she was facing in the highly competitive business world, she dropped this feminine name to go by her masculine middle name.)

The Cracking Glass Ceiling

What keeps women from breaking through the **glass ceiling,** the mostly invisible barrier that prevents women from reaching the executive suite? The "pipelines" that lead to the top of a company are its marketing, sales, and production positions, those that directly affect the corporate bottom line (Hymowitz 2004; DeCrow 2005). Men, who dominate the executive suite, stereotype women as being good at "support" but less capable than men of leadership (Belkin 2007). They steer women into human resources or public relations. Successful projects in these positions are not appreciated in the same way as those that bring corporate profits—and bonuses for their managers.

As the *glass ceiling* slowly cracks, women are gradually gaining entry into the top positions in society. In 2009, Ellen Kullman, shown here, became the first female CEO of DuPont, a company founded in 1802.

Ben Baker/Redux

Another reason the glass ceiling is so powerful is that women lack mentors—successful executives who take an interest in them and teach them the ropes. Lack of a mentor is no trivial matter, for mentors can provide opportunities to develop leadership skills that open the door to the executive suite (Hymowitz 2007; Mattioli 2008).

The glass ceiling is cracking, however (Hymowitz 2004; Belkin 2007). A look at women who have broken through reveals highly motivated individuals with a fierce competitive spirit who are willing to give up sleep and recreation for the sake of career advancement.

glass ceiling the mostly invisible barrier that keeps women from advancing to the top levels at work

Dilbert

One of the frustrations felt by many women in the labor force is that no matter what they do, they hit a glass ceiling. Another is that to succeed they feel forced to abandon characteristics they feel are essential to their self.

sexual harassment the abuse of one's position of authority to force unwanted sexual demands on someone

They also learn to play by "men's rules," developing a style that makes men comfortable. In addition, women who began their careers twenty to thirty years ago are now running major divisions within the largest companies (Hymowitz 2004). With this background, some of these women have begun to emerge as the new CEOs.

When women break through the cracking glass ceiling, they still confront stereotypes of gender that portray them in less favorable light than men. The women have negotiated these stereotypes on their way to the top, so they know how to handle them. Occasionally, however, the stereotypes of male dominance lead to humorously awkward situations. When Nancy Andrews (2007), who became the first female dean of the Duke University School of Medicine, visited a school in North Carolina, she took her family with her. "As we entered," she says, "the school principal vigorously shook my husband's hand and welcomed him, saying, 'You must be the man of the moment.' Unfortunately," she adds, "it didn't cross his mind that I might be the 'woman of the moment.'"

Sexual Harassment—and Worse

Sexual harassment—unwelcome sexual attention at work or at school, which may affect a person's job or school performance or create a hostile environment—was not recognized as a problem until the 1970s. Before this, women considered unwanted sexual comments, touches, looks, and pressure to have sex to be a personal matter.

With the prodding of feminists, women began to perceive unwanted sexual advances at work and school as part of a *structural* problem. That is, they began to realize that the issue was more than a man here or there doing obnoxious things because he was attracted to a woman; rather, men were using their positions of authority to pressure women to have sex. Now that women have moved into positions of authority, they, too, have become sexual harassers (Wayne et al. 2001). With most authority still vested in men, however, most of the sexual harassers are men.

As symbolic interactionists stress, labels affect our perception. Because we have the term *sexual harassment,* we perceive actions in a different light than did our predecessors. The meaning of sexual harassment is vague and shifting, however, and court cases constantly change what this term does and does not include (Anderson 2006). Originally, sexual desire was an element of sexual harassment, but no longer. This changed when the U.S. Supreme Court considered the lawsuit of a homosexual who had been tormented by his supervisors and fellow workers. The Court ruled that sexual desire is not necessary—that sexual harassment laws also apply to homosexuals who are harassed by heterosexuals while on the job (Felsenthal 1998). By extension, the law applies to heterosexuals who are sexually harassed by homosexuals.

Central to sexual harassment is the abuse of power, a topic that is explored in the following Thinking Critically section.

ThinkingCRITICALLY
Sexual Harassment and Rape of Women in the Military

WOMEN RAPED AT WEST POINT! MORE WOMEN RAPED AT THE U.S. AIR FORCE ACADEMY!

So shrieked the headlines and the TV news teasers. For once, the facts turned out to be just as startling. Women cadets, who were studying to become officers in the U.S. military, had been sexually assaulted by their fellow cadets.

And when the women reported the attacks, *they* were the ones who were punished. The women found themselves charged with drinking alcohol and socializing with upperclassmen.

AP Images/Gautam Singh

Women in the military being sexually harassed by male soldiers knows no geographical limits. Shown here is Anjali Gupta, a Flying Officer in India's Air Force, who was court martialed for insubordination after she lodged complaints against a superior officer.

For the most part, the women's charges against the men were ignored. The one man who faced a court martial was acquitted (Schemo 2003a).

This got the attention of Congress. Hearings were held, and the commander of the Air Force Academy was replaced.

A few years earlier, several male Army sergeants at Aberdeen Proving Ground in Maryland had been accused of forcing sex on unwilling female recruits (McIntyre 1997). The drill sergeants, who claimed that the sex was consensual, were found guilty of rape. One married sergeant, who pled guilty to having consensual sex with eleven trainees (adultery is a crime in the Army), was convicted of raping another six trainees a total of eighteen times and was sentenced to twenty-five years in prison.

The Army appointed a blue-ribbon panel to investigate sexual harassment in its ranks. When Sgt. Major Gene McKinney, the highest-ranking of the Army's 410,000 noncommissioned officers, was appointed to this committee, former subordinates accused *him* of sexual harassment (Shenon 1997). McKinney was relieved of his duties and court-martialed. Found not guilty of sexual harassment, but guilty of obstruction of justice, McKinney was reprimanded and demoted. His embittered accusers claimed the Army had sacrificed them for McKinney.

Rape in the military is not an isolated event. Researchers who interviewed a random sample of women veterans found that four of five had experienced sexual harassment during their military service, and 30 percent had been victims of attempted or completed rape. Three-fourths of the women who had been raped did not report their assault (Sadler et al. 2003). A study of women graduates of the Air Force Academy showed that 12 percent had been victims of rape or attempted rape (Schemo 2003b). In light of such findings, the military appointed a coordinator of sexual assault at every military base (Stout 2005). Sexual assaults continue, however (Dreazen 2008).

After the U.S. military was sent to Iraq and Afghanistan, the headlines again screamed rape, this time in the Persian Gulf. Again, the headlines were right. And once again, Congress held hearings (Schmitt 2004). With assaults continuing and Congress still putting pressure on the military, the Army held an emergency summit attended by eighty generals (Dreazen 2008). We'll have to see how long this cycle of rape followed by hearings followed by rape repeats itself before adequate reforms are put in place.

For Your Consideration

How can we set up a structure to minimize sexual harassment and rape in the military? Can we do this and still train men and women together? Can we do this and still have men and women sleep in the same barracks and on the same ships? Be specific about the structure you would establish.

Gender and Violence

One of the consistent characteristics of violence in the United States—and the world—is its gender inequality. That is, females are more likely to be the victims of males, not the other way around. Let's briefly review this almost one-way street in gender violence as it applies to the United States.

Violence Against Women

In the Thinking Critically section on the previous page, we considered rape in the military; and earlier in the chapter, we examined violence against women in other cultures and we reviewed a form of surgical violence. Here, due to space limitations, we can review only briefly some primary features of violence.

Forcible Rape. Being raped is a common fear of U.S. women, a fear that is far from groundless. As high as the official rate of rape is, the real rate is even higher. The National Crime Victimization Survey shows that the real rate is about 40 percent higher than the number reported to the police. Since the official rate is 6.1 per 10,000 females, the actual rate would be 8.4 (*Statistical Abstract* 2009: Table 303). This would be 1 of every 1,200 U.S. females *each year*. Despite this high number, women are safer now than they were ten and twenty years ago, as the rape rate has declined.

Although any woman can be a victim of sexual assault—and victims include babies and elderly women—the typical victim is 16 to 19 years old. As you can see from Table 2, sexual assault peaks at those ages and then declines.

Women's most common fear seems to be that of strangers—who, appearing as though from nowhere, abduct and beat and rape them. Contrary to the stereotypes that underlie these fears, most victims know their attacker. As you can see from Table 3, about one of three rapes is committed by strangers.

Date (Acquaintance) Rape. What has shocked so many about date rape (also known as *acquaintance rape*) are studies showing that it is common (Littleton et al. 2008). Researchers who used a representative sample of courses to survey the students at Marietta College, a private school in Ohio, found that 2.5 percent of the women had been physically forced to have sex (Felton et al. 2001). This was just one college, but a study using a nationally representative sample of women enrolled in U.S. colleges and

TABLE 2 Rape Victims	
Age	Rate per 1,000 Females
12–15	2.3
16–19	3.9
20–24	2.5
25–34	1.4
35–49	0.7
50–64	0.3
65 and Older	0.08

Source: By the author. A ten-year average, based on *Statistical Abstract of the United States* 2000:Table 354; 2001:Table 341; 2002:Table 303; 2003:Table 295; 2004:Table 322; 2005:Table 306; 2006:Table 308; 2007:Table 311; 2008:Table 313; 2009:Table 305.

TABLE 3 Relationship of Victims and Rapists	
Relationship	Percentage
Relative	7%
Known Well	34%
Casual Acquaintance	24%
Stranger	34%
Not Reported	1%

Sources: By the author. A ten-year average, based on *Statistical Abstract of the United States* 1999:Table 355; 2000:Table 342; 2001:Table 304; 2002:Table 296; 2003:Table 323; 2004-2005:Table 307; 2006:Table 311; 2007:Table 315; 2008:Table 316; 2009:Table 306.

universities with 1,000 students or more came up with similar findings. Of these women, 1.7 percent had been raped during the preceding six months, and another 1.1 percent had been victims of attempted rape (Fisher et al. 2000).

Think about the huge numbers involved. With about 11 million women enrolled in college, 2.8 percent (1.7 plus 1.1) means that over a quarter of a million college women were victims of rape or of attempted rape *in just the past six months.* (This conclusion assumes that the rate is the same in colleges with fewer than 1,000 students, which has not been verified.) Most of the women told a friend what happened, but only *5 percent* reported the crime to the police (Fisher et al. 2003). The most common reason for not reporting was thinking that the event "was not serious enough." The next most common reason was being unsure whether a crime had been committed. Many women were embarrassed and didn't want others, especially their family, to know what happened. Others felt there was no proof ("It would be my word against his"), feared reprisal from the man, or feared the police (Fisher et al. 2000). Sometimes a rape victim feels partially responsible because she knows the person, was drinking with him, went to his place voluntarily, or invited him to her place. As a physician who treats victims of date rape said, "Would you feel responsible if someone hit you over the head with a shovel—just because you knew the person?" (Carpenito 1999).

Murder.   All over the world, men are more likely than women to be killers. Figure 9 illustrates this gender pattern in U.S. murders. Note that although females make up about 51 percent of the U.S. population, they don't even come close to making up 51 percent of the nation's killers. As you can see from this figure, when women are murdered, about 9 times out of 10 the killer is a man.

Violence in the Home.   In the family, too, women are the typical victims. Two forms of violence against women—honor killings and genital circumcision—were discussed earlier in the chapter.

Feminism and Gendered Violence.   Feminist sociologists have been especially effective in bringing violence against women to the public's attention. Some use symbolic interactionism, pointing out that to associate strength and virility with violence—as is done in many cultures—is to promote violence. Others use conflict theory. They argue that men are losing power, and that some men turn violently against women as a way to reassert their declining power and status (Reiser 1999; Meltzer 2002).

Solutions.   There is no magic bullet for this problem of gendered violence, but to be effective, any solution must break the connection between violence and masculinity. This would require an educational program that encompasses schools, churches, homes, and the media. Given the gun-slinging heroes of the Wild West and other American icons, as well as the violent messages that are so prevalent in the mass media, including video games, it is difficult to be optimistic that a change will come any time soon.

Our next topic, women in politics, however, gives us much more reason for optimism.

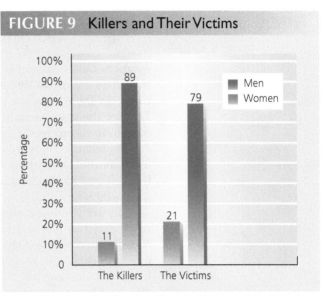

FIGURE 9   Killers and Their Victims

Source: By the author. Based on *Statistical Abstract of the United States* 2008: Table 318; 2009: Table 300.

Although women are severely underrepresented in U.S. politics, the situation is changing, at least gradually. Shown here is Nancy Pelosi, the Speaker of the U.S. House of Representatives, as she signs the financial bailout plan passed by the House.

Xinhua/Landov

167

The Changing Face of Politics

Women could take over the United States! Think about it. Eight million more women than men are of voting age, and more women than men vote in U.S. national elections. As Table 4 shows, however, men greatly outnumber women in political office. Despite the gains women have made in recent elections, since 1789 almost 2,000 men have served in the U.S. Senate, but only 38 women have served, including 17 current senators. Not until 1992 was the first African American woman (Carol Moseley-Braun) elected to the U.S. Senate. No Latina or Asian American woman has yet been elected to the Senate (National Women's Political Caucus 1998; *Statistical Abstract* 2009:Table 390).

Why are women underrepresented in U.S. politics? First, women are still underrepresented in law and business, the careers from which most politicians emerge. Most women also find that the irregular hours needed to run for office are incompatible with their role as mother. Fathers, in contrast, whose traditional roles are more likely to take them away from home, are less likely to feel this conflict. Women are also less likely to have a supportive spouse who is willing to play an unassuming background role while providing solace, encouragement, child care, and voter appeal. Finally, preferring to hold on to their positions of power, men have been reluctant to incorporate women into centers of decision making or to present them as viable candidates.

These conditions are changing. In 2002, Nancy Pelosi was the first woman to be elected by her colleagues as minority leader of the House of Representatives. Five years later, in 2007, they chose her as the first female Speaker of the House. These posts made her the most powerful woman ever in Congress. Another occurred in 2008 when Hillary Clinton came within a hair's breadth of becoming the presidential nominee of the Democratic party. That same year, Sarah Palin was chosen as the Republican vice-presidential candidate. We can also note that more women are becoming corporate executives, and, as indicated in Figure 4, more women are also becoming lawyers. In these positions, women are traveling more and making statewide and national contacts. Another change is that child care is increasingly seen as a responsibility of both mother and father. With this generation's fundamental change in women's political participation, it is only a matter of time until a woman occupies the Oval Office.

TABLE 4 U.S. Women in Political Office	Percentage of Offices Held by Women	Number of Offices Held By Women
National Office		
U.S. Senate	17%	17
U.S. House of Representatives	17%	74
State Office		
Governors	16%	8
Lt. Governors	18%	9
Attorneys General	8%	4
Secretaries of State	24%	12
Treasurers	22%	11
State Auditors	12%	6
State Legislators	24%	1,734

Source: Center for American Women and Politics 2007, 2008a, b.

Glimpsing the Future—With Hope

Women's fuller participation in the decision-making processes of our social institutions has shattered stereotypes that tended to limit females to "feminine" activities and push males into "masculine" ones. As structural barriers continue to fall and more activities are de-gendered, both males and females will have greater freedom to pursue activities that are more compatible with their abilities and desires as individuals.

As females and males develop a new consciousness both of their capacities and of their potential, relationships will change. Distinctions between the sexes will not disappear, but there is no reason for biological differences to be translated into social inequalities. If current trends continue, we may see a growing appreciation of sexual differences coupled with greater equality of opportunity—which has the potential of transforming society (Gilman 1911/1971; Offen 1990). If this happens, as sociologist Alison Jaggar (1990) observed, gender equality can become less a goal than a background condition for living in society.

By the Numbers: *Then and Now*

Percentage of college students who are women

1970	NOW
42%	57%

Percentage of dental school graduates who are women

1970	NOW
1%	45%

Percentage of medical school graduates who are women

1970	NOW
8%	49%

Women make up this percentage of the U.S. labor force

1890	1970	NOW
18%	38%	45%

Percentage of men's salary earned by women

1970	NOW
59%	72%

OTHER NUMBERS
Number of U.S. senators since 1789

MEN	WOMEN
1,800	38

SUMMARY *and* REVIEW

Issues of Sex and Gender

What is gender stratification?

The term **gender stratification** refers to unequal access to property, power, and prestige on the basis of sex. Each society establishes a structure that, on the basis of sex and gender, opens and closes doors to its privileges.

How do sex and gender differ?

Sex refers to biological distinctions between males and females. It consists of both primary and secondary sex characteristics. **Gender,** in contrast, is what a society considers proper behaviors and attitudes for its male and female members. Sex physically distinguishes males from females; gender refers to what people call "masculine" and "feminine."

Why do the behaviors of males and females differ?
The "nature versus nurture" debate refers to whether differences in the behaviors of males and females are caused by inherited (biological) or learned (cultural) characteristics. Almost all sociologists take the side of nurture. In recent years, however, sociologists have begun to cautiously open the door to biology.

Gender Inequality in Global Perspective
Is gender stratification universal?
George Murdock surveyed information on tribal societies and found that all of them have sex-linked activities and give greater prestige to male activities. **Patriarchy,** or male dominance, appears to be universal. Besides work, other areas of discrimination include education, politics, and violence.

How did females become a minority group?
The origin of discrimination against females is lost in history, but the primary theory of how females became a minority group in their own societies focuses on the physical limitations imposed by childbirth.

What forms does gender inequality take around the world?
Its many forms include inequalities in education, politics, and pay. There is also violence, including female circumcision.

Gender Inequality in the United States
Is the feminist movement new?
In what is called the "first wave," feminists made political demands for change in the early 1900s—and were met with hostility, and even violence. The "second wave" began in the 1960s and continues today. A "third wave" is emerging.

What forms does gender inequality take in everyday life, health care, and education?
In everyday life, a lower value is placed on things feminine. In health care, physicians don't take women's health complaints as seriously as those of men, and they exploit women's fears, performing unnecessary hysterectomies. In education, more women than men attend college, but many choose fields that are categorized as "feminine." More women than men also earn college degrees. Women are less likely to complete the doctoral programs in science. Fundamental change is indicated by the growing numbers of women in law and medicine.

Gender Inequality in the Workplace
How does gender inequality show up in the workplace?
All occupations show a gender gap in pay. For college graduates, the lifetime pay gap runs over a million dollars in favor of men. **Sexual harassment** also continues to be a reality of the workplace.

Gender and Violence
What is the relationship between gender and violence?
Overwhelmingly, the victims of rape and murder are females. Female circumcision and honor killing are special cases of violence against females. Conflict theorists point out that men use violence to maintain their power and privilege.

The Changing Face of Politics
What is the trend in gender inequality in politics?
A traditional division of gender roles—women as child care providers and homemakers, men as workers outside the home—used to keep women out of politics. Women continue to be underrepresented in politics, but the trend toward greater political equality is firmly in place.

Glimpsing the Future—with Hope
How might changes in gender roles and stereotypes affect our lives?
In the United States, women are more involved in the decision-making processes of our social institutions. Men, too, are reexamining their traditional roles. New gender expectations may be developing, ones that allow both males and females to pursue more individual, less stereotypical interests.

THINKING CRITICALLY

1. What is your position on the "nature versus nurture" (biology or culture) debate? What materials in this chapter support your position?

2. Why do you think that the gender gap in pay exists all over the world?

3. What do you think can be done to reduce gender inequality?

ADDITIONAL RESOURCES

What can you find in MySocLab? mysoclab www.mysoclab.com

- Complete Ebook
- Practice Tests and Video and Audio activities
- Mapping and Data Analysis exercises

- Sociology in the News
- Classic Readings in Sociology
- Research and Writing advice

Where Can I Read More on This Topic?

Andersen, Margaret L. *Thinking About Women: Sociological Perspectives on Sex and Gender,* 8th ed. New York: Allyn and Bacon, 2008. An overview of the main issues of sex and gender in contemporary society, ranging from sexism and socialization to work and health.

Brettell, Caroline B., and Carolyn F. Sargent, eds. *Gender in Cross-Cultural Perspective,* 5th ed. Upper Saddle River, N.J.: Prentice Hall, 2008. The net is spread wide as the authors examine gender and biology, in prehistory, at home, and the division of labor, and the body, property, kinship, religion, politics, and the global economy.

Casey, Emma, and Lydia Martens, eds. *Gender and Consumption: Domestic Cultures and the Commercialization of Everyday Life.* Burlington, Vt.: Ashgate, 2007. The articles in this short book focus on how gender is constructed and communicated through the purchase and use of objects.

Colapinto, John. *As Nature Made Him: The Boy Who Was Raised as a Girl, P.S.* New York: Harper Perennial, 2006. A detailed account of the event summarized in this chapter of the boy whose penis was accidentally burned off.

DeFrancisco, Victoria Priun, and Catherine Helen Palczewski. *Communicating Gender Diversity: A Critical Approach.* Los Angeles: Sage 2007. Probably the polar opposite of the Colapinto book; gender is viewed not as something that people are but as something that people do; an emphasis on how gender is constructed through communication.

Fuller, Linda K., ed. *Sport, Rhetoric, and Gender: Historical Perspectives and Media Representations.* New York: Palgrave Macmillan, 2006. The articles in this short book focus on how gender is communicated in sports; includes both historical materials and contemporary case studies.

Gilbert, Paula Ruth, and Kimberly K. Eby, eds. *Violence and Gender: An Interdisciplinary Reader.* Upper Saddle River, N.J.: Prentice Hall, 2004. The authors of these articles examine violence and youth, the human body, war, intimacy, sports, the media, and how to prevent violence.

Gilman, Charlotte Perkins. *The Man-Made World or, Our Androcentric Culture.* New York: Charlton, 1911. Reprinted in 1971 by Johnson Reprint. This early book on women's liberation provides an excellent view of gender relations at the beginning of the last century.

Gonas, Lena, and Jan Ch Karlsson, eds. *Gender Segregation: Divisions of Work in Post-Industrial Welfare States.* Burlington, Vermont: Ashgate, 2006. This short book of ten articles focuses on the gendered division of labor.

Hanson, Sandra L. *Swimming Against the Tide: African American Girls in Science Education.* Philadelphia, PA.: Temple University Press, 2009. Examines how gender and race–ethnicity coalesce to discourage African American females from becoming scientists.

Johnson, Allan G. *Privilege, Power, and Difference,* 2nd ed. New York: McGraw-Hill, 2006. The author helps us see the nature and consequences of privilege and our connection to it.

McDonagh, Eileen, and Laura Pappano. *Playing with the Boys: Why Separate Is Not Equal in Sports.* New York: Oxford University Press, 2008. A detailed history of how women have challenged men's sports; filled with anecdotes and contains fascinating historical photos.

Nelson, Robert L., and William P. Bridges. *Legalizing Gender Inequality: Courts, Markets and Unequal Pay for Women in America.* New York: Cambridge University Press, 2008. The authors analyze how organizations produce pay disparities between the sexes and how the courts legitimate them.

Siltanen, Janet, and Andrea Doucet. *Gender Relations: Intersectionality and Beyond.* New York: Oxford University Press, 2008. The authors look at how gender differences and inequalities play out in the lives of men and women throughout the life course.

Journals

These journals focus on the role of gender in social life: *Feminist Studies; Gender and Behavior; Gender and Society; Forum in Women's and Gender Studies; Gender and History; Gender, Place and Culture: A Journal of Feminist Geography; Journal of Gender, Culture, and Health; Journal of Interdisciplinary Gender Studies; Journal of Men's Health and Gender; Sex Roles;* and *Signs: Journal of Women in Culture and Society.*

Race and Ethnicity

From Chapter 12 of *Sociology: A Down-to-Earth Approach*, 10/e. James M. Henslin. Copyright © 2010 by Pearson Education. Published by Allyn & Bacon. All rights reserved.

Race and Ethnicity

Idaho

© Steve Bly/Alamy

Imagine that you are an African American man living in Macon County, Alabama, during the Great Depression of the 1930s. Your home is a little country shack with a dirt floor. You have no electricity or running water. You never finished grade school, and you make a living, such as it is, by doing odd jobs. You haven't been feeling too good lately, but you can't afford a doctor.

You have just become part of one of the most callous experiments of all time.

Then you hear incredible news. You rub your eyes in disbelief. It is just like winning the lottery! If you join *Miss Rivers' Lodge* (and it is free to join), you will get free physical examinations at Tuskegee University *for life.* You will even get free rides to and from the clinic, hot meals on examination days, and a lifetime of free treatment for minor ailments.

You eagerly join *Miss Rivers' Lodge.*

After your first physical examination, the doctor gives you the bad news. "You've got bad blood," he says. "That's why you've been feeling bad. Miss Rivers will give you some medicine and schedule you for your next exam. I've got to warn you, though. If you go to another doctor, there's no more free exams or medicine."

You can't afford another doctor anyway. You are thankful for your treatment, take your medicine, and look forward to the next trip to the university.

What has really happened? You have just become part of what is surely slated to go down in history as one of the most callous experiments of all time, outside of the infamous World War II Nazi and Japanese experiments. With heartless disregard for human life, the U.S. Public Health Service told 399 African American men that they had joined a social club and burial society called *Miss Rivers' Lodge.* What the men were *not* told was that they had syphilis, that there was no real Miss Rivers' Lodge, that the doctors were just using this term so they could study what happened when syphilis went untreated. For forty years, the "Public Health Service" allowed these men to go without treatment for their syphilis—and kept testing them each year—to study the progress of the disease. The "public health" officials even had a control group of 201 men who were free of the disease (Jones 1993).

By the way, the men did receive a benefit from "Miss Rivers Lodge," a free autopsy to determine the ravages of syphilis on their bodies.

race a group whose inherited physical characteristics distinguish it from other groups

genocide the systematic annihilation or attempted annihilation of a people because of their presumed race or ethnicity

Laying the Sociological Foundation

As unlikely as it seems, this is a true story. It really did happen. Seldom do race and ethnic relations degenerate to this point, but reports of troubled race relations surprise none of us. Today's newspapers and TV news shows regularly report on racial problems. Sociology can contribute greatly to our understanding of this aspect of social life—and this chapter may be an eye-opener for you. To begin, let's consider to what extent race itself is a myth.

Race: Myth and Reality

With its more than 6.5 billion people, the world offers a fascinating variety of human shapes and colors. People see one another as black, white, red, yellow, and brown. Eyes come in shades of blue, brown, and green. Lips are thick and thin. Hair is straight, curly, kinky, black, blonde, and red—and, of course, all shades of brown.

As humans spread throughout the world, their adaptations to diverse climates and other living conditions resulted in this profusion of complexions, hair textures and colors, eye hues, and other physical variations. Genetic mutations added distinct characteristics to the peoples of the globe. In this sense, the concept of **race**—a group of people with inherited physical characteristics that distinguish it from another group—is a reality. Humans do, indeed, come in a variety of colors and shapes.

In two senses, however, race is a myth, a fabrication of the human mind. The *first* myth is the idea that any race is superior to others. All races have their geniuses—and their idiots. As with language, no race is superior to another.

Ideas of racial superiority abound, however. They are not only false but also dangerous. Adolf Hitler, for example, believed that the Aryans were a superior race, responsible for the cultural achievements of Europe. The Aryans, he said, were destined to establish a superior culture and usher in a new world order. This destiny required them to avoid the "racial contamination" that would come from breeding with inferior races; therefore, it became a "cultural duty" to isolate or destroy races that threatened Aryan purity and culture.

Put into practice, Hitler's views left an appalling legacy—the Nazi slaughter of those they deemed inferior: Jews, Slavs, gypsies, homosexuals, and people with mental and physical disabilities. Horrific images of gas ovens and emaciated bodies stacked like cordwood haunted the world's nations. At Nuremberg, the Allies, flush with victory, put the top Nazis on trial, exposing their heinous deeds to a shocked world. Their public executions, everyone assumed, marked the end of such grisly acts.

Obviously, they didn't. In the summer of 1994 in Rwanda, Hutus slaughtered about 800,000 Tutsis—mostly with machetes (Cowell 2006). A few years later, the Serbs in Bosnia massacred Muslims, giving us the new term "ethnic cleansing." As these events sadly attest, **genocide,** the attempt to destroy a group of people because of their presumed race or ethnicity, remains alive and well. Although more recent killings are not accompanied by swastikas and gas ovens, the perpetrators' goal is the same.

The *second* myth is that "pure" races exist. Humans show such a mixture of physical characteristics—in skin color, hair texture, nose shape, head shape, eye color, and so on—that there are no "pure" races. Instead of falling into distinct types that are clearly separate from one another, human characteristics flow endlessly together. The mapping of the human genome system shows that humans are strikingly homogenous, that so-called racial groups differ from one another only once in a thousand subunits of the genome (Angler 2000; Frank 2007). As you can see from the example of Tiger Woods, discussed in the Cultural Diversity box on the next page, these minute gradations make any attempt to draw lines of race purely arbitrary.

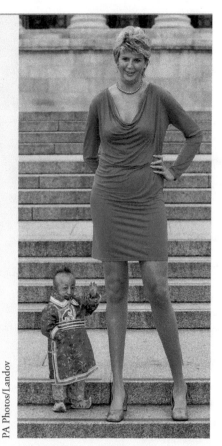

Humans show remarkable diversity. Shown here is just one example—He Pingping, from China, who at 2 feet 4 inches, is the world's shortest man, and Svetlana Pankratova, from Russia, who, according to the *Guiness Book of World Records,* is the woman with the longest legs. Race-ethnicity shows similar diversity.

PA Photos/Landov

Cultural Diversity in the United States

Tiger Woods: Mapping the Changing Ethnic Terrain

Tiger Woods, perhaps the top golfer of all time, calls himself *Cablinasian*. Woods invented this term as a boy to try to explain to himself just who he was—a combination of Caucasian, Black, Indian, and Asian (Leland and Beals 1997; Hall 2001). Woods wants to embrace all sides of his family.

Like many of us, Tiger Woods' heritage is difficult to specify. Analysts who like to quantify ethnic heritage put Woods at one-quarter Thai, one-quarter Chinese, one-quarter white, an eighth Native American, and an eighth African American. From this chapter, you know how ridiculous such computations are, but the sociological question is why many people consider Tiger Woods an African American. The U.S. racial scene is indeed complex, but a good part of the reason is simply that this is the label the media placed on him. "Everyone has to fit somewhere" seems to be our attitude. If they don't, we grow uncomfortable. And for Tiger Woods, the media chose African American.

The United States once had a firm "color line"—barriers between racial–ethnic groups that you didn't dare cross, especially in dating or marriage. This invisible barrier has broken down, and today such marriages are common (*Statistical Abstract* 2009: Table 59). Several campuses have interracial student organizations. Harvard has two, one just for students who have one African American parent (Leland and Beals 1997).

As we enter unfamiliar ethnic terrain, our classifications are bursting at the seams. Consider how Kwame Anthony Appiah, of Harvard's Philosophy and Afro-American Studies Departments, described his situation:

> "My mother is English; my father is Ghanaian. My sisters are married to a Nigerian and a Norwegian. I have nephews who range from blond-haired kids to very black kids. They are all first cousins. Now according to the American scheme of things, they're all black—even the guy with blond hair who skis in Oslo." (Wright 1994)

I marvel at what racial experts the U.S. census takers once were. When they took the census, which is done

Tiger Woods as he answers questions at a news conference.

Reuters/Mike Blake/Landov

every ten years, they looked at people and assigned them a race. At various points, the census contained these categories: mulatto, quadroon, octoroon, Negro, black, Mexican, white, Indian, Filipino, Japanese, Chinese, and Hindu. Quadroon (one-fourth black and three-fourths white) and octoroon (one-eighth black and seven-eighths white) proved too difficult to "measure," and these categories were used only in 1890. Mulatto appeared in the 1850 census, but disappeared in 1930. The Mexican government complained about Mexicans being treated as a race, and this category was used only in 1930. I don't know whose idea it was to make Hindu a race, but it lasted for three censuses, from 1920 to 1940 (Bean et al. 2004; Tafoya et al. 2005).

Continuing to reflect changing ideas about race–ethnicity, censuses have become flexible, and we now have many choices. In the 2000 census, we were first asked to declare whether we were or were not "Spanish/Hispanic/Latino." After this, we were asked to check "one or more races" that we "consider ourselves to be." We could choose from White; Black, African American, or Negro; American Indian or Alaska Native; Asian Indian, Chinese, Filipino, Japanese, Korean, Vietnamese, Native Hawaiian, Guamanian or Chamorro, Samoan, and other Pacific Islander. If these didn't do it, we could check a box called "Some Other Race" and then write whatever we wanted.

Perhaps the census should list Cablinasian, after all. We could also have ANGEL for African-Norwegian-German-English-Latino Americans, DEVIL for those of Danish-English-Vietnamese-Italian-Lebanese descent, and STUDENT for Swedish-Turkish-Uruguayan-Danish-English-Norwegian-Tibetan Americans. As you read farther in this chapter, you will see why these terms make as much sense as the categories we currently use.

For Your Consideration

Just why do we count people by "race" anyway? Why not eliminate race from the U.S. census? (Race became a factor in 1790 during the first census. To determine the number of representatives from each state, slaves were counted as three-fifths of whites!) Why is race so important to some people? Perhaps you can use the materials in this chapter to answer these questions.

The reason I selected these photos is to illustrate how seriously we must take all preaching of hatred and of racial supremacy, even though it seems to come from harmless or even humorous sources. The strange-looking person with his hands on his hips, who is wearing *lederhosen*, traditional clothing of Bavaria, Germany, is Adolf Hitler.

He caused this horrific scene at the Landsberg concentration camp, which, as shown here, the U.S. military forced German civilians to view.

Time Life Pictures/Getty Images

AP Images

Although large groupings of people can be classified by blood type and gene frequencies, even these classifications do not uncover "race." Rather, race is so arbitrary that biologists and anthropologists cannot even agree on how many "races" there are (Smedley and Smedley 2005). Ashley Montagu (1964, 1999), a physical anthropologist, pointed out that some scientists have classified humans into only two "races," while others have found as many as two thousand. Montagu (1960) himself classified humans into forty "racial" groups. As the Down-to-Earth Sociology box on the next page illustrates, even a plane ride can change someone's race!

The *idea* of race, of course, is far from a myth. Firmly embedded in our culture, it is a powerful force in our everyday lives. That no race is superior and that even biologists cannot decide how people should be classified into races is not what counts. "I know what I see, and you can't tell me any different" seems to be the common attitude. Sociologists W. I. and D. S. Thomas (1928) observed that "If people define situations as real, they are real in their consequences." In other words, people act on perceptions and beliefs, not facts. As a result, we will always have people like Hitler and, as illustrated in our opening vignette, officials like those in the U.S. Public Health Service who thought that it was fine to experiment with people whom they deemed inferior. While few people hold such extreme views, most people appear to be ethnocentric enough to believe that their own race is—at least just a little—superior to others.

Ethnic Groups

In contrast to *race*, which people use to refer to supposed biological characteristics that distinguish one group of people from another, **ethnicity** and **ethnic** refer to cultural characteristics. Derived from the word *ethnos* (a Greek word meaning "people" or "nation"), *ethnicity* and *ethnic* refer to people who identify with one another on the basis of common ancestry and cultural heritage. Their sense of belonging may center on their nation or region of origin, distinctive foods, clothing, language, music, religion, or family names and relationships.

People often confuse the terms *race* and *ethnic group*. For example, many people, including many Jews, consider Jews a race. Jews, however, are more properly considered an ethnic group, for it is their cultural characteristics, especially their religion, that bind them together. Wherever Jews have lived in the world, they have intermarried. Consequently,

ethnicity (and **ethnic**) having distinctive cultural characteristics

178

Down-to-Earth Sociology

Can a Plane Ride Change Your Race?

Common sense and sociology often differ. This is especially so when it comes to race. According to common sense, our racial classifications represent biological differences between people. Sociologists, in contrast, stress that what we call races are *social* classifications, not biological categories.

Sociologists point out that *our "race" depends more on the society in which we live than on our biological characteristics.* For example, the racial categories common in the United States are merely one of *numerous* ways by which people around the world classify physical appearances. Although various groups use different categories, each group assumes that its categories are natural, merely a response to visible biology.

To better understand this essential sociological point—that race is more social than it is biological—consider this: In the United States, children born to the same parents are all of the same race. "What could be more natural?" Americans assume. But in Brazil, children born to the same parents may be of different races—if their appearances differ. "What could be more natural?" assume Brazilians.

Consider how Americans usually classify a child born to a "black" mother and a "white" father. Why do they usually say that the child is "black"? Wouldn't it be equally as logical to classify the child as "white"? Similarly, if a child has one grandmother who is "black," but all her other ancestors are "white," the child is often considered "black." Yet she has much more "white blood" than "black blood." Why, then, is she considered "black"? Certainly not because of biology. Such thinking is a legacy of slavery. In an attempt to preserve the "purity" of their "race" in the face of the many children whose fathers were white slave masters and whose mothers were black slaves, whites classified anyone with even a "drop of black blood" as black. They actually called this the "one-drop" rule.

Even a plane trip can change a person's race. In the city of Salvador in Brazil, people classify one another by color of skin and eyes, breadth of nose and lips, and color and curliness of hair. They use at least

What "race" are these two Brazilians? Is the child's "race" different from her mother's "race"? The text explains why "race" is such an unreliable concept that it changes even with geography.

David R. Frazier/PhotoEdit, Inc.

seven terms for what we call white and black. Consider again a U.S. child who has "white" and "black" parents. If she flies to Brazil, she is no longer "black"; she now belongs to one of their several "whiter" categories (Fish 1995).

If the girl makes such a flight, would her "race" actually change? Our common sense revolts at this, I know, but it actually would. We want to argue that because her biological characteristics remain unchanged, her race remains unchanged. This is because we think of race as biological, when *race is actually a label we use to describe perceived biological characteristics.* Simply put, the race we "are" depends on our social location—on who is doing the classifying.

"Racial" classifications are also fluid, not fixed. Even now, you can see change occurring in U.S. classifications. The category "multiracial," for example, indicates changing thought and perception.

For Your Consideration

How would you explain to "Joe and Suzie Six-Pack" that race is more a social classification than a biological one? Can you come up with any arguments to refute this statement? How do you think our racial-ethnic categories will change in the future?

Jews in China may have Chinese features, while some Swedish Jews are blue-eyed blonds. The confusion of race and ethnicity is illustrated in the photo below.

Minority Groups and Dominant Groups

Sociologist Louis Wirth (1945) defined a **minority group** as people who are singled out for unequal treatment and who regard themselves as objects of collective discrimination. Worldwide, minorities share several conditions: Their physical or cultural traits are held in low esteem by the dominant group, which treats them unfairly, and they tend to marry within their own group (Wagley and Harris 1958). These conditions tend to create a sense of identity among minorities (a feeling of "we-ness"). In some instances, even a sense of common destiny emerges (Chandra 1993b).

Surprisingly, a minority group is not necessarily a *numerical* minority. For example, before India's independence in 1947, a handful of British colonial rulers dominated tens of millions of Indians. Similarly, when South Africa practiced apartheid, a smaller group of Afrikaners, primarily Dutch, discriminated against a much larger number of blacks. And all over the world, as we discussed in the previous chapter, females are a minority group. Accordingly, sociologists refer to those who do the discriminating not as the *majority,* but, rather, as the **dominant group,** for regardless of their numbers, this is the group that has the greater power and privilege.

Possessing political power and unified by shared physical and cultural traits, the dominant group uses its position to discriminate against those with different—and supposedly inferior—traits. The dominant group considers its privileged position to be the result of its own innate superiority.

Emergence of Minority Groups. A group becomes a minority in one of two ways. The *first* is through the expansion of political boundaries. With the exception of females, tribal societies contain no minority groups. Everyone shares the same culture, including the same language, and belongs to the same group. When a group expands its political boundaries, however, it produces minority groups if it incorporates people with different customs, languages, values, or physical characteristics into the same political entity and discriminates against them. For example, in 1848, after defeating Mexico in war, the United States took over the Southwest. The Mexicans living there, who had been the dominant group prior to the war, were transformed

minority group people who are singled out for unequal treatment and who regard themselves as objects of collective discrimination

dominant group the group with the most power, greatest privileges, and highest social status

Because ideas of *race* and *ethnicity* are such a significant part of society, all of us are classified according to those concepts. This photo illustrates the difficulty such assumptions posed for Israel. The Ethiopians, shown here as they arrived in Israel, although claiming to be Jews, looked so different from other Jews that it took several years for Israeli authorities to acknowledge this group's "true Jewishness."

Jim Hollander/Reuters/Landov

into a minority group, a master status that has influenced their lives ever since. Referring to his ancestors, one Latino said, "We didn't move across the border—the border moved across us."

A *second* way in which a group becomes a minority is by migration. This can be voluntary, as with the millions of people who have chosen to move from Mexico to the United States, or involuntary, as with the millions of Africans who were brought in chains to the United States. (The way females became a minority group represents a third way, but no one knows just how this occurred.)

How People Construct Their Racial–Ethnic Identity

Some of us have a greater sense of ethnicity than others. Some of us feel firm boundaries between "us" and "them." Others have assimilated so extensively into the mainstream culture that they are only vaguely aware of their ethnic origins. With interethnic marriage common, some do not even know the countries from which their families originated— nor do they care. If asked to identify themselves ethnically, they respond with something like "I'm Heinz 57—German and Irish, with a little Italian and French thrown in—and I think someone said something about being one-sixteenth Indian, too."

Why do some people feel an intense sense of ethnic identity, while others feel hardly any? Figure 1 portrays four factors, identified by sociologist Ashley Doane, that heighten or reduce our sense of ethnic identity. From this figure, you can see that the keys are relative size, power, appearance, and discrimination. If your group is relatively small, has little power, looks different from most people in society, and is an object of discrimination, you will have a heightened sense of ethnic identity. In contrast, if you belong to the dominant group that holds most of the power, look like most people in the society, and feel no discrimination, you are likely to experience a sense of "belonging"—and to wonder why ethnic identity is such a big deal.

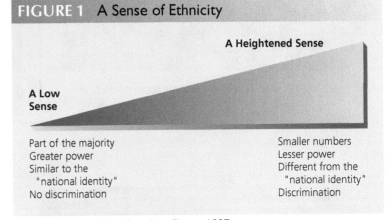

FIGURE 1 A Sense of Ethnicity

A Heightened Sense

A Low Sense

Part of the majority	Smaller numbers
Greater power	Lesser power
Similar to the "national identity"	Different from the "national identity"
No discrimination	Discrimination

Source: By the author. Based on Doane 1997.

We can use the term **ethnic work** to refer to the way people construct their ethnicity. For people who have a strong ethnic identity, this term refers to how they enhance and maintain their group's distinctions—from clothing, food, and language to religious practices and holidays. For people whose ethnic identity is not as firm, it refers to attempts to recover their ethnic heritage, such as trying to trace family lines or visiting the country or region of their family's origin. As illustrated by the photo essay on the next page many Americans are engaged in ethnic work. This has confounded the experts, who thought that the United States would be a *melting pot,* with most of its groups blending into a sort of ethnic stew. Because so many Americans have become fascinated with their "roots," some analysts have suggested that "tossed salad" is a more appropriate term than "melting pot."

Prejudice and Discrimination

With prejudice and discrimination so significant in social life, let's consider the origin of prejudice and the extent of discrimination.

Learning Prejudice

Distinguishing Between Prejudice and Discrimination. Prejudice and discrimination are common throughout the world. In Mexico, Mexicans of Hispanic descent discriminate against Mexicans of Native American descent; in Israel, Ashkenazi Jews, primarily of European descent, discriminate against Sephardi Jews from the Muslim world. In some places, the elderly discriminate against the young; in others, the young discriminate against the elderly. And all around the world, men discriminate against women.

ethnic work activities designed to discover, enhance, or maintain ethnic and racial identity

181

Ethnic Work
Explorations in Cultural Identity

Ethnic work refers to the ways that people establish, maintain, protect, and transmit their ethnic identity. As shown here, among the techniques people use to forge ties with their roots are dress, dance, and music.

AP Photo/Jesicca Griffin

Many African Americans are trying to get in closer contact with their roots. To do this, some use musical performances, as with this group in Philadelphia, Pennsylvania. Note the five-year old who is participating.

A. Ramey/PhotoEdit, Inc.

Having children participate in ethnic celebrations is a common way of passing on cultural heritage. Shown here is a Thai girl in Los Angeles getting final touches before she performs a temple dance.

AP Photo/Lincoln Journal Star, Ken Blackbird

Folk dancing (doing a traditional dance of one's cultural heritage) is often used to maintain ethnic identity Shown here is a man in Arlington, Virginia, doing a Bolivian folk dance.

Rob Crandall/The Image Works

Many European Americans are also involved in ethnic work, attempting to maintain an identity more precise than "from Europe." These women of Czech ancestry are performing for a Czech community in a small town in Nebraska.

Natalie Fobes/Corbis

Many Native Americans have maintained continuous identity with their tribal roots. This Nisqually mother is placing a traditional headdress on her daughter for a reenactment of a wedding ceremony.

Discrimination is an *action*—unfair treatment directed against someone. Discrimination can be based on many characteristics: age, sex, height, weight, skin color, clothing, speech, income, education, marital status, sexual orientation, disease, disability, religion, and politics. When the basis of discrimination is someone's perception of race, it is known as **racism.** Discrimination is often the result of an *attitude* called **prejudice**—a prejudging of some sort, usually in a negative way. There is also *positive prejudice,* which exaggerates the virtues of a group, as when people think that some group (usually their own) is more capable than others. Most prejudice, however, is negative and involves prejudging a group as inferior.

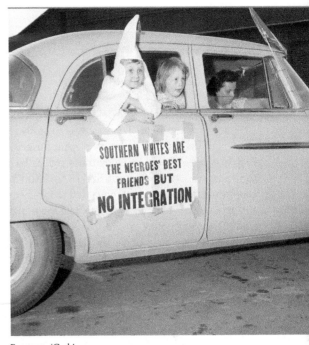

Bettmann/Corbis
This classic photo from 1956 illustrates the learning of prejudice

Learning from Association. As with our other attitudes, we are not born with prejudice. Rather, we learn prejudice from the people around us. In a fascinating study, sociologist Kathleen Blee (2005) interviewed women who were members of the KKK and Aryan Nations. Her first finding is of the "ho hum" variety: Most women were recruited by someone who already belonged to the group. Blee's second finding, however, holds a surprise: Some women learned to be racists *after* they joined the group. They were attracted to the group not because it matched their racist beliefs but because someone they liked belonged to it. Blee found that their racism was not the *cause* of their joining but, rather, the *result* of their membership.

The Far-Reaching Nature of Prejudice. It is amazing how much prejudice people can learn. In a classic article, psychologist Eugene Hartley (1946) asked people how they felt about several racial and ethnic groups. Besides Negroes, Jews, and so on, he included the Wallonians, Pireneans, and Danireans—names he had made up. Most people who expressed dislike for Jews and Negros also expressed dislike for these three fictitious groups.

Hartley's study shows that prejudice does not depend on negative experiences with others. It also reveals that people who are prejudiced against one racial or ethnic group also tend to be prejudiced against other groups. People can be, and are, prejudiced against people they have never met—and even against groups that do not exist!

The neo-Nazis and the Ku Klux Klan base their existence on prejudice. These groups believe that race is real, that white is best, and that society's surface conceals underlying conspiracies (Ezekiel 2002). What would happen if a Jew attended their meetings? Would he or she survive? In the Down-to-Earth Sociology box on the next page, sociologist Raphael Ezekiel reveals some of the insights he gained during his remarkable study of these groups.

Internalizing Dominant Norms. People can even learn to be prejudiced against their *own* group. A national survey of black Americans conducted by black interviewers found that African Americans think that lighter-skinned African American women are more attractive than those with darker skin (Hill 2002). Sociologists call this *the internalization of the norms of the dominant group.*

To study the internalization of dominant norms, psychologists Mahzarin Banaji and Anthony Greenwald created the *Implicit Association Test.* In one version of this test, good and bad words are flashed on a screen along with photos of African Americans and whites. Most subjects are quicker to associate positive words (such as "love," "peace," and "baby") with whites and negative words (such as "cancer," "bomb," and "devil") with blacks. Here's the clincher: This is true for *both* white and black subjects (Dasgupta et al. 2000; Greenwald and Krieger 2006). Apparently, we all learn the *ethnic maps* of our culture and, along with them, their route to biased perception.

Individual and Institutional Discrimination

Sociologists stress that we should move beyond thinking in terms of **individual discrimination,** the negative treatment of one person by another. Although such behavior creates problems, it is primarily an issue between individuals. With their focus on the broader

discrimination an act of unfair treatment directed against an individual or a group

prejudice an attitude or prejudging, usually in a negative way

racism prejudice and discrimination on the basis of race

individual discrimination the negative treatment of one person by another on the basis of that person's perceived characteristics

Down-to-Earth Sociology
The Racist Mind

Sociologist Raphael Ezekiel wanted to get a close look at the racist mind. The best way to study racism from the inside is to do participant observation. But Ezekiel is a Jew. Could he study these groups by participant observation? To find out, Ezekiel told Ku Klux Klan and neo-Nazi leaders that he wanted to interview them and attend their meetings. He also told them that he was a Jew. Surprisingly, they agreed. Ezekiel published his path-breaking research in a book, *The Racist Mind* (1995). Here are some of the insights he gained during his fascinating sociological adventure:

[The leader] builds on mass anxiety about economic insecurity and on popular tendencies to see an Establishment as the cause of economic threat; he hopes to teach people to identify that Establishment as the puppets of a conspiracy of Jews. [He has a] belief in exclusive categories. For the white racist leader, it is profoundly true . . . that the socially defined collections we call races represent fundamental categories. A man is black or a man is white; there are no in-betweens. Every human belongs to a racial category, and all the members of one category are radically different from all the members of other categories. Moreover, race represents the essence of the person. A truck is a truck, a car is a car, a cat is a cat, a dog is a dog, a black is a black, a white is a white. . . . These axioms have a rock-hard quality in the leaders' minds; the world is made up of racial groups. That is what exists for them.

Two further beliefs play a major role in the minds of leaders. First, life is war. The world is made of distinct racial groups; life is about the war between these groups. Second, events have secret causes, are never what they seem superficially. . . . Any myth is plausible, as long as it involves intricate plotting. . . . It does not matter to him what others say. . . . He lives in his ideas and in the little world he has created where they are taken seriously. . . . Gold can be made from the tongues of frogs; Yahweh's call can be heard in the flapping swastika banner. (pp. 66–67)

Who is attracted to the neo-Nazis and Ku Klux Klan? Here is what Ezekiel discovered:

[There is a] ready pool of whites who will respond to the racist signal. . . . This population [is] always hungry for activity—or for the talk of activity—that promises dignity and meaning to lives that are working poorly in a highly competitive world. . . . Much as I don't want to believe it, [this] movement brings a sense of meaning—at least for a while—to some of the discontented. To struggle in a cause that transcends the individual lends meaning to life, no matter how ill-founded or narrowing the cause. For the young men in the neo-Nazi group . . . membership was an alternative to atomization and drift; within the group they worked for a cause and took direct risks in the company of comrades. . . .

When interviewing the young neo-Nazis in Detroit, I often found myself driving with them past the closed factories, the idled plants of our shrinking manufacturing base. The fewer and fewer plants that remain can demand better educated and more highly skilled workers. These fatherless Nazi youths, these high-school dropouts, will find little place in the emerging economy . . . a permanently underemployed white underclass is taking its place alongside the permanent black underclass. The struggle over race merely diverts youth from confronting the real issues of their lives. Not many seats are left on the train, and the train is leaving the station. (pp. 32–33)

For Your Consideration

Use functionalism, conflict theory, and symbolic interaction to explain how the leaders and followers of these hate groups view the world. Use these same perspectives to explain why some people are attracted to the message of hate.

---

picture, sociologists encourage us to examine **institutional discrimination,** that is, to see how discrimination is woven into the fabric of society. Let's look at two examples.

Home Mortgages. Bank lending provides an excellent illustration of institutional discrimination. When a 1991 national study showed that minorities had a harder time getting mortgages, bankers said that favoring whites might *look* like discrimination, but it wasn't: Loans go to those with better credit histories, and that's what whites have. Researchers then compared the credit histories of the applicants. They found that even when applicants had identical credit, African Americans and Latinos were *60 percent* more likely to be rejected (Thomas 1991, 1992).

A new revelation surfaced with the subprime debacle that threw the stock market into a tailspin and led the U.S. Congress to put the next generation deeply in debt for the foibles of this one. Look at Figure 2 (on the next page). The first thing you will notice is that minorities are still more likely to be turned down for a loan. You can see that this happens whether their incomes are below or above the median income of their community. Beyond this hard finding lies another just as devastating. In the credit crisis that caused so many to lose their homes, African

institutional discrimination negative treatment of a minority group that is built into a society's institutions; also called *systemic discrimination*

FIGURE 2 Buying a House: Institutional Discrimination in Mortgages

This figure, based on a national sample, illustrates *institutional discrimination.* Rejecting the loan applications of minorities and gouging them with higher interest rates is a nationwide practice, not the act of a rogue banker here or there. Because the discrimination is part of the banking system, it is also called *systemic discrimination.*

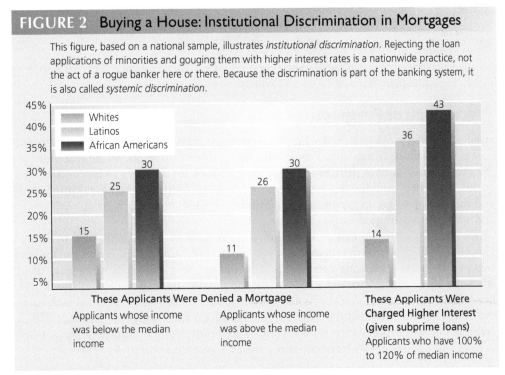

Source: By the author. Based on Kochbar and Gonzalez-Barrera 2009.

Americans and Latinos were hit harder than whites. There are many reasons for this, but the last set of bars on this figure reveals one of them: Banks purposely targeted minorities to charge higher interest rates. Over the lifetime of a loan, these higher monthly payments mean paying an extra $100,000 to $200,000 (Powell and Roberts 2009). Another consequence of the higher payments was that African Americans and Latinos were more likely to lose their homes.

Health Care. Discrimination does not have to be deliberate. It can occur even though no one is aware of it: neither those being discriminated against *nor* those doing the discriminating. White patients, for example, are more likely than either Latino or African American patients to receive knee replacements and coronary bypass surgery (Skinner et al. 2003; Popescu 2007). Treatment after a heart attack follows a similar pattern: Whites are more likely than blacks to be given cardiac catheterization, a test to detect blockage of blood vessels. This study of 40,000 patients holds a surprise: Both black *and* white doctors are more likely to give this preventive care to whites (Stolberg 2001).

Researchers do not know why race–ethnicity is a factor in medical decisions. With both white and black doctors involved, we can be certain that physicians *do not intend* to discriminate. In ways we do not yet understand—but which could be related to the implicit bias that apparently comes with the internalization of dominant norms—discrimination is built into the medical delivery system (Green et al. 2007). Race seems to work like gender: Just as women's higher death rates in coronary bypass surgery can be traced to implicit attitudes about gender, so also race–ethnicity becomes a subconscious motivation for giving or denying access to advanced medical procedures.

The stark contrasts shown in Table 1 indicate that institutional discrimination can be a life-and-death matter. In childbirth, African American mothers are *three* times as likely to die as white mothers, while their babies are more than *twice* as likely to die during their first year of life. This is not a matter of biology, as though African American mothers and children are more fragile. It is a matter of *social* conditions, primarily those of nutrition and medical care.

TABLE 1 Race–Ethnicity and Mother/Child Deaths[1]

	Infant Deaths	Maternal Deaths
White Americans	5.7	11.1
African Americans	13.7	36.5

[1]The national database used for this table does not list these totals for other racial–ethnic groups. *White* refers to non-Hispanic whites. *Infant deaths* refers to the number of deaths per year of infants under 1 year old per 1,000 live births. *Maternal deaths* refers to the number of deaths per 100,000 women who give birth in a year.

Source: Statistical Abstract of the United States 2009:Table 110.

Theories of Prejudice

Social scientists have developed several theories to explain prejudice. Let's first look at psychological explanations, then at sociological ones.

Psychological Perspectives

Frustration and Scapegoats. In 1939, psychologist John Dollard suggested that prejudice is the result of frustration. People who are unable to strike out at the real source of their frustration (such as debt and unemployment) look for someone to blame. They unfairly blame their troubles on a **scapegoat**—often a racial–ethnic or religious minority—and this person or group becomes a target on which they vent their frustrations. Gender and age are also common targets of scapegoating.

Even mild frustration can increase prejudice. A team of psychologists led by Emory Cowen (1959) measured the prejudice of a group of students. They then gave the students two puzzles to solve, making sure the students did not have enough time to solve them. After the students had worked furiously on the puzzles, the experimenters shook their heads in disgust and said that they couldn't believe the students hadn't finished such a simple task. They then retested the students and found that their scores on prejudice had increased. The students had directed their frustrations outward, transferring them to people who had nothing to do with the contempt the experimenters had shown them.

The Authoritarian Personality. Have you ever wondered whether personality is a cause of prejudice? Maybe some people are more inclined to be prejudiced, and others more fair-minded. For psychologist Theodor Adorno, who had fled from the Nazis, this was no idle speculation. With the horrors he had observed still fresh in his mind, Adorno wondered whether there might be a certain type of person who is more likely to fall for the racist spewings of people like Hitler, Mussolini, and those in the Ku Klux Klan.

To find out, Adorno (Adorno et al. 1950) tested about two thousand people, ranging from college professors to prison inmates. To measure their ethnocentrism, anti-Semitism (bias against Jews), and support for strong, authoritarian leaders, he gave them three tests. Adorno found that people who scored high on one test also scored high on the other two. For example, people who agreed with anti-Semitic statements also said that governments should be authoritarian and that foreign ways of life pose a threat to the "American" way.

Adorno concluded that highly prejudiced people are insecure conformists. They have deep respect for authority and are submissive to authority figures. He termed this the **authoritarian personality.** These people believe that things are either right or wrong. Ambiguity disturbs them, especially in matters of religion or sex. They become anxious when they confront norms and values that are different from their own. To view people who differ from themselves as inferior assures them that their own positions are right.

Adorno's research stirred the scientific community, stimulating more than a thousand research studies. In general, the researchers found that people who are older, less educated, less intelligent, and from a lower social class are more likely to be authoritarian. Critics say that this doesn't indicate a particular personality, just that the less educated are more prejudiced—which we already knew (Yinger 1965; Ray 1991). Nevertheless, researchers continue to study this concept (Nicol 2007).

Sociological Perspectives

Sociologists find psychological explanations inadequate. They stress that the key to understanding prejudice cannot be found by looking *inside* people, but, rather, by examining conditions *outside* them. For this reason, sociologists focus on how social environments influence prejudice. With this background, let's compare functionalist, conflict, and symbolic interactionist perspectives on prejudice.

Functionalism. In a telling scene from a television documentary, journalist Bill Moyers interviewed Fritz Hippler, a Nazi intellectual who at age 29 was put in charge of the entire German film industry. Hippler said that when Hitler came to power the Germans were

scapegoat an individual or group unfairly blamed for someone else's troubles

authoritarian personality Theodor Adorno's term for people who are prejudiced and rank high on scales of conformity, intolerance, insecurity, respect for authority, and submissiveness to superiors no more anti-Semitic than the French, and probably less so. He was told to increase anti-Semitism in Germany. Obediently, Hippler produced movies that contained vivid scenes comparing Jews to rats—with their breeding threatening to infest the population.

Why was Hippler told to create hatred? Prejudice and discrimination were functional for the Nazis. Germany was on its knees at this time. It had been defeated in World War I and was being devastated by fines levied by the victors. The middle class was being destroyed by runaway inflation. The Jews provided a scapegoat, a common enemy against which the Nazis could unite Germany. In addition, the Jews owned businesses, bank accounts, fine art, and other property that the Nazis could confiscate. Jews also held key positions (as university professors, reporters, judges, and so on), which the Nazis could fill with their own flunkies. In the end, hatred also showed its dysfunctional side, as the Nazi officials hanged at Nuremberg discovered.

Prejudice becomes practically irresistible when state machinery is used to advance the cause of hatred. To produce prejudice, the Nazis harnessed government agencies, the schools, police, courts, and mass media. The results were devastating. Take, for example, the case of identical twins, Jack and Oskar, separated at birth. Jack was brought up as a Jew in Trinidad, while Oskar was reared as a Catholic in Czechoslovakia. Under the Nazi regime, Oskar learned to hate Jews, unaware that he himself was a Jew.

That prejudice is functional and is shaped by the social environment was demonstrated by psychologists Muzafer and Carolyn Sherif (1953). In a boys' summer camp, they assigned friends to different cabins and then had the cabin groups compete in sports. In just a few days, strong in-groups had formed. Even lifelong friends began to taunt one another, calling each other "crybaby" and "sissy." The Sherif study teaches us several important lessons about social life. Note how it is possible to arrange the social environment to generate either positive or negative feelings about people, and how prejudice arises if we pit groups against one another in an "I win, you lose" situation. You can also see that prejudice is functional, how it creates in-group solidarity. And, of course, it is obvious how dysfunctional prejudice is, when you observe the way it destroys human relationships.

Conflict Theory.   Conflict theorists also analyze how groups are pitted against one another. Their focus, however, is on how this arrangement benefits those with power. They begin by noting that workers want better food, health care, housing, education, and leisure. To attain these goals, workers need jobs that pay well. If workers are united, they can demand higher wages and better working conditions. Divisions, in contrast, weaken them and prevent united action. To divide them and keep wages down, business owners use two main tactics.

The first tactic is to keep workers insecure. Fear of unemployment works especially well. The unemployed serve as a **reserve labor force.** Business owners draw on the unemployed to expand production during economic booms, and when the economy contracts, they release these workers to rejoin the ranks of the unemployed. The lesson is not lost on workers who have jobs. They fear eviction and worry about having their cars and furniture repossessed. Many know they are just one paycheck away from ending up "on the streets." This helps to keep workers docile.

The second tactic to weaken labor is to exploit racial–ethnic divisions (Patterson 2007). In the 1800s, when white workers in California went on strike, owners of factories replaced them with Chinese workers. When Japanese workers in Hawaii struck, owners of plantations hired Koreans (Jeong and You 2008). This division of workers along racial–ethnic and gender lines is known as a **split labor market** (Du Bois 1935/1992; Roediger 2002). Although today's exploitation is more subtle, fear and suspicion continue to split workers. Whites are aware that other racial–ethnic groups are ready to take their jobs, African Americans often perceive Latinos as competitors (Cose 2006), and men know that women are eager to get promoted. All of this helps to keep workers in line.

The consequences are devastating, say conflict theorists. Just like the boys in the Sherif experiment, African Americans, Latinos, whites, and others see themselves as able to make gains only at the expense of members of the other groups. Sometimes this rivalry shows up along very fine racial–ethnic lines, such as that in Miami between Haitians and African

reserve labor force the unemployed; unemployed workers are thought of as being "in reserve"—capitalists take them "out of reserve" (put them back to work) during times of high production and then put them back "in reserve" (lay them off) when they are no longer needed

split labor market workers split along racial, ethnic, gender, age, or any other lines; this split is exploited by owners to weaken the bargaining power of workers

selective perception seeing certain features of an object or situation, but remaining blind to others

Americans, who distrust each other as competitors. Divisions among workers deflect anger and hostility away from the power elite and direct these powerful emotions toward other racial and ethnic groups. Instead of recognizing their common class interests and working for their mutual welfare, workers learn to fear and distrust one another.

Symbolic Interactionism. While conflict theorists focus on the role of the owner (or capitalist) class in exploiting racial and ethnic divisions, symbolic interactionists examine how labels affect perception and create prejudice.

How Labels Create Prejudice: Symbolic interactionists stress that *the labels we learn affect the way we perceive people.* Labels cause **selective perception;** that is, they lead us to see certain things while they blind us to others. If we apply a label to a group, we tend to perceive its members as all alike. We shake off evidence that doesn't fit (Simpson and Yinger 1972). Racial and ethnic labels are especially powerful. They are shorthand for emotionally charged stereotypes. As you know, the term *nigger* is not neutral. Nor are *honky, cracker, spic, mick, kike, limey, kraut, dago, guinea,* or any of the other scornful words people use to belittle ethnic groups. Such words overpower us with emotions, blocking out rational thought about the people to whom they refer (Allport 1954).

Labels and the Self-Fulfilling Stereotype: Some stereotypes not only justify prejudice and discrimination but also produce the behavior depicted in the stereotype. Let's consider Group X. According to stereotypes, the members of Group X are lazy, so they don't deserve good jobs. ("They are lazy and undependable and wouldn't do the job well.") Denied the better jobs, most members of Group X are limited to doing "dirty work," the jobs few people want but that are thought appropriate for "that kind" of people. Since much "dirty work" is sporadic, members of Group X are often seen "on the streets." The sight of their idleness reinforces the original stereotype of laziness. The discrimination that created the "laziness" in the first place passes unnoticed.

To apply these three theoretical perspectives and catch a glimpse of how amazingly different things were in the past, read the Down-to-Earth Sociology box on the next page.

Global Patterns of Intergroup Relations

In their studies of racial–ethnic relations around the world, sociologists have found six basic ways that dominant groups treat minority groups. These patterns are shown in Figure 3. Let's look at each.

FIGURE 3 Global Patterns of Intergroup Relations: A Continuum

Genocide	Population Transfer	Internal Colonialism	Segregation	Assimilation	Multiculturalism (Pluralism)
The dominant group tries to destroy the minority group (e.g., Germany and Rwanda)	The dominant group expels the minority group (e.g., Native Americans forced onto reservations)	The dominant group exploits the minority group (e.g., low-paid, menial work)	The dominant group structures the social institutions to maintain minimal contact with the minority group (e.g., the U.S. South before the 1960s)	The dominant group absorbs the minority group (e.g., American Czechoslovakians)	The dominant group encourages racial and ethnic variation; when successful, there is no longer a dominant group (e.g., Switzerland)

Inhumanity / Rejection ← → Humanity / Acceptance

Down-to-Earth Sociology
The Man in the Zoo

The Bronx Zoo in New York City used to keep a 22-year-old pygmy in the Monkey House. The man—and the orangutan he lived with—became the most popular exhibit at the zoo. Thousands of visitors would arrive daily and head straight for the Monkey House. Eyewitnesses to what they thought was a lower form of human in the long chain of evolution, the visitors were fascinated by the pygmy, especially by his sharpened teeth.

To make the exhibit even more alluring, the zoo director had animal bones scattered in front of the man.

I know it sounds as though I must have made this up, but this is a true story. The World's Fair was going to be held in St. Louis in 1904, and the Department of Anthropology wanted to show villages from different cultures. They asked Samuel Verner, an explorer, if he could bring some pygmies to St. Louis to serve as live exhibits. Verner agreed, and on his next trip to Africa, in the Belgian Congo he came across Ota Benga (or Otabenga), a pygmy who had been enslaved by another tribe. Benga, then about age 20, said he was willing to go to St. Louis. After Verner bought Benga's freedom for some cloth and salt, Benga recruited another half dozen pygmies to go with them.

After the World's Fair, Verner took the pygmies back to Africa. When Benga found out that a hostile tribe had wiped out his village and killed his family, he asked Verner if he could return with him to the United States. Verner agreed.

When they returned to New York, Verner ran into financial trouble and wrote some bad checks. No longer able to care for Benga, Verner left him with friends at the American Museum of Natural History. After a few weeks, they grew tired of Benga's antics and turned him over to the Bronx Zoo. The zoo officials put Benga on display in the Monkey House, with this sign:

> The African Pygmy, 'Ota Benga.' Age 23 years. Height 4 feet 11 inches. Weight 103 pounds. Brought from the Kasai River, Congo Free State, South Central Africa by Dr. Samuel P. Verner. Exhibited each afternoon during September

Ota Benga, 1906, on exhibit in the Bronx Zoo.

© Wildlife Conservation Society

Exhibited with an orangutan, Benga became a sensation. An article in the *New York Times* said it was fortunate that Benga couldn't think very deeply, or else living with monkeys might bother him.

When the Colored Baptist Ministers' Conference protested that exhibiting Benga was degrading, zoo officials replied that they were "taking excellent care of the little fellow." They added that "he has one of the best rooms at the primate house." (I wonder what animal had the best room.)

Not surprisingly, this reply didn't satisfy the ministers. When they continued to protest, zoo officials decided to let Benga out of his cage. They put a white shirt on him and let him walk around the zoo. At night, Benga slept in the monkey house.

Benga's life became even more miserable. Zoo visitors would follow him, howling, jeering, laughing, and poking at him. One day, Benga found a knife in the feeding room of the Monkey House and flourished it at the visitors. Zoo officials took the knife away.

Benga then made a little bow and some arrows and began shooting at the obnoxious visitors. This ended the fun for the zoo officials. They decided that Benga had to leave.

After living in several orphanages for African American children, Benga ended up working as a laborer in a tobacco factory in Lynchburg, Virginia.

Always treated as a freak, Benga was desperately lonely. In 1916, at about the age of 32, in despair that he had no home or family to return to in Africa, Benga ended his misery by shooting himself in the heart.

—Based on Bradford and Blume 1992; Crossen 2006; Richman 2006.

For Your Consideration

1. See what different views emerge as you apply the three theoretical perspectives (functionalism, symbolic interactionism, and conflict theory) to exhibiting Benga at the Bronx Zoo.

2. How does the concept of ethnocentrism apply to this event?

3. Explain how the concepts of prejudice and discrimination apply to what happened to Benga.

compartmentalize to separate acts from feelings or attitudes

population transfer the forced movement of a minority group

Genocide

Last century's two most notorious examples of genocide occurred in Europe and Africa. In Germany during the 1930s and 1940s, Hitler and the Nazis attempted to destroy all Jews. In the 1990s, in Rwanda, the Hutus tried to destroy all Tutsis. One of the horrifying aspects of these slaughters was that the killers did not crawl out from under a rock someplace. Rather, they were ordinary people. In some cases, they were even the victims' neighbors and friends. Their killing was facilitated by labels that singled out the victims as enemies who deserved to die (Huttenbach 1991; Browning 1993; Gross 2001).

To better understand how ordinary people can participate in genocide, let's look at an example from the United States. To call the Native Americans "savages," as U.S. officials and white settlers did, was to label them as inferior, as somehow less than human. This identification made it easier to justify killing the Native Americans in order to take their resources.

> **When gold was discovered in northern California in 1849, the fabled "Forty-Niners" rushed in. In this region lived 150,000 Native Americans. To get rid of them, the white government put a bounty on their heads. It even reimbursed the whites for their bullets. The result was the slaughter of 120,000 Native American men, women, and children. (Schaefer 2004)**

Most Native Americans died not from bullets, however, but from the diseases the whites brought with them. Measles, smallpox, and the flu came from another continent, and the Native Americans had no immunity against them (Dobyns 1983; Schaefer 2004). The settlers also ruthlessly destroyed the Native Americans' food supply (buffalos, crops). As a result, about *95 percent* of Native Americans died (Thornton 1987; Churchill 1997).

The same thing was happening in other places. In South Africa, the Dutch settlers viewed the native Hottentots as jungle animals and totally wiped them out. In Tasmania, the British settlers stalked the local aboriginal population, hunting them for sport and sometimes even for dog food.

Labels are powerful. Those that dehumanize help people to **compartmentalize**—to separate their acts of cruelty from their sense of being good and moral people. To regard members of some group as inferior or even less than human means that it is okay to treat them inhumanely. This allows people to kill—and still retain a good self-concept (Bernard et al. 1971). In short, *labeling the targeted group as inferior or even less than fully human facilitates genocide.*

Population Transfer

There are two types of **population transfer:** indirect and direct. *Indirect transfer* is achieved by making life so miserable for members of a minority that they leave "voluntarily." Under the bitter conditions of czarist Russia, for example, millions of Jews made this "choice." *Direct transfer* occurs when a dominant group expels a minority. Examples include the U.S. government relocating Native Americans to reservations and transferring Americans of Japanese descent to internment camps during World War II.

In the 1990s, a combination of genocide and population transfer occurred in Bosnia and Kosovo, parts of the former Yugoslavia. A hatred nurtured for centuries had been kept under wraps by Tito's iron-fisted rule from 1944 to 1980. After Tito's death, these suppressed, smoldering hostilities soared to the sur-

Amid fears that Japanese Americans were "enemies within" who would sabotage industrial and military installations on the West Coast, in the early days of World War II Japanese Americans were transferred to "relocation camps." Note the identification ("baggage") tags on this woman and her child as they await relocation. The photo was taken in May 1942.

face, and Yugoslavia split into warring factions. When the Serbs gained power, Muslims rebelled and began guerilla warfare. The Serbs vented their hatred by what they termed **ethnic cleansing:** They terrorized villages with killing and rape, forcing survivors to flee in fear.

Internal Colonialism

The term *colonialism* is used to refer to one way that the Most Industrialized Nations exploit the Least Industrialized Nations. Conflict theorists use the term **internal colonialism** to describe the way in which a country's dominant group exploits minority groups for its economic advantage. The dominant group manipulates the social institutions to suppress minorities and deny them full access to their society's benefits. Slavery is an extreme example of internal colonialism, as was the South African system of *apartheid.* Although the dominant Afrikaners despised the minority, they found its presence necessary. As Simpson and Yinger (1972) put it, who else would do the hard work?

Segregation

Internal colonialism is often accompanied by **segregation**—the separation of racial or ethnic groups. Segregation allows the dominant group to maintain social distance from the minority and yet to exploit their labor as cooks, cleaners, chauffeurs, nannies, factory workers, and so on. In the U.S. South until the

As immigrants assimilate into a new culture, they learn and adapt new customs. These Muslim girls at an elementary school in Dearborn, Michigan, are in the process of assimilating into U.S. culture.

1960s, by law African Americans and whites had to use separate public facilities such as hotels, schools, swimming pools, bathrooms, and even drinking fountains. In thirty-eight states, laws prohibited marriage between blacks and whites. Violators could be sent to prison (Mahoney and Kooistra 1995; Crossen 2004b). The last law of this type was repealed in 1967 (Spickard 1989). In the villages of India, an ethnic group, the Dalits (untouchables), is forbidden to use the village pump. Dalit women must walk long distances to streams or pumps outside of the village to fetch their water (author's notes).

Assimilation

Assimilation is the process by which a minority group is absorbed into the mainstream culture. There are two types. In *forced assimilation,* the dominant group refuses to allow the minority to practice its religion, to speak its language, or to follow its customs. Before the fall of the Soviet Union, for example, the dominant group, the Russians, required that Armenian children attend schools where they were taught in Russian. Armenians could celebrate only Russian holidays, not Armenian ones. *Permissible assimilation,* in contrast, allows the minority to adopt the dominant group's patterns in its own way and at its own speed.

Multiculturalism (Pluralism)

A policy of **multiculturalism,** also called **pluralism,** permits or even encourages racial–ethnic variation. The minority groups are able to maintain their separate identities, yet participate freely in the country's social institutions, from education to politics. Switzerland provides an outstanding example of multiculturalism. The Swiss population includes four ethnic groups: French, Italians, Germans, and Romansh. These groups have kept their own languages, and they live peacefully in political and economic unity. Multiculturalism has been so successful that none of these groups can properly be called a minority.

ethnic cleansing a policy of eliminating a population; includes forcible expulsion and genocide

internal colonialism the policy of exploiting minority groups for economic gain

segregation the policy of keeping racial-ethnic groups apart

assimilation the process of being absorbed into the mainstream culture

multiculturalism (also called *pluralism*) a philosophy or political policy that permits or encourages ethnic differences

pluralism the diffusion of power among many interest groups that prevents any single group from gaining control of the government

FIGURE 4 Race–Ethnicity of the U.S. Population

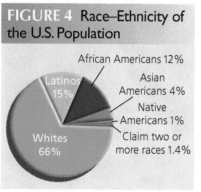

- African Americans 12%
- Asian Americans 4%
- Native Americans 1%
- Claim two or more races 1.4%
- Latinos 15%
- Whites 66%

Source: By the author. See Figure 5.

Racial–Ethnic Relations in the United States

Writing about race–ethnicity is like stepping onto a minefield: One never knows where to expect the next explosion. Even basic terms are controversial. The term *African American,* for example, is rejected by those who ask why this term doesn't include white immigrants from South Africa. Some people classified as African Americans also reject this term because they identify themselves as blacks. Similarly, some Latinos prefer the term *Hispanic American,* but others reject it, saying that it ignores the Indian side of their heritage. Some would limit the term *Chicanos*—commonly used to refer to Americans from Mexico—to those who have a sense of ethnic oppression and unity; they say that it does not apply to those who have assimilated.

No term that I use here, then, will satisfy everyone. Racial–ethnic identity is fluid, constantly changing, and all terms carry a risk as they take on politically charged meanings. Nevertheless, as part of everyday life, we classify ourselves and one another as belonging to distinct racial-ethnic groups. As Figures 4 and 5 show, on the basis of these

Notes: This figure, which follows convention and lists Latinos as a separate category, brings into focus the problem of counting "racial–ethnic" groups. Because Latinos can be of any racial–ethnic group, I have reduced the total of the groups with which they self-identify by the number of Latinos who identify with those groups.
[a]Interestingly, this total is *six times* higher than all the Irish who live in Ireland.
[b]Includes French Canadian.
[c]Includes "Scottish-Irish."
[d]Most Latinos trace at least part of their ancestry to Europe.
[e]In descending order, the largest groups of Asian Americans are from China, the Philippines, India, Korea, Vietnam, and Japan. See Figure 10. Also includes those who identify themselves as Native Hawaiian or Pacific Islander.
[f]Includes Native Alaskans
[g]Includes Native Hawaiians

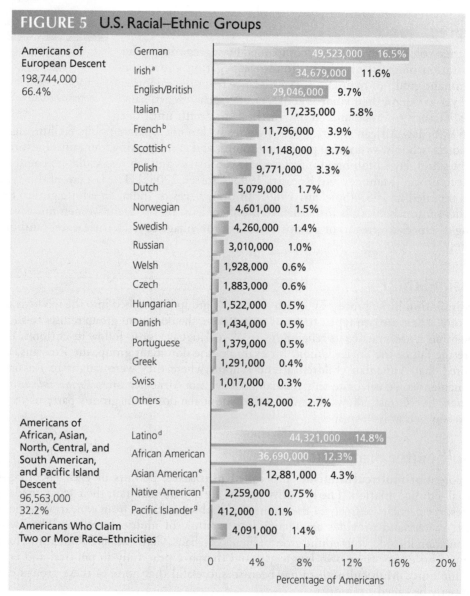

FIGURE 5 U.S. Racial–Ethnic Groups

		Percentage of Americans
Americans of European Descent 198,744,000 66.4%	German	49,523,000 16.5%
	Irish[a]	34,679,000 11.6%
	English/British	29,046,000 9.7%
	Italian	17,235,000 5.8%
	French[b]	11,796,000 3.9%
	Scottish[c]	11,148,000 3.7%
	Polish	9,771,000 3.3%
	Dutch	5,079,000 1.7%
	Norwegian	4,601,000 1.5%
	Swedish	4,260,000 1.4%
	Russian	3,010,000 1.0%
	Welsh	1,928,000 0.6%
	Czech	1,883,000 0.6%
	Hungarian	1,522,000 0.5%
	Danish	1,434,000 0.5%
	Portuguese	1,379,000 0.5%
	Greek	1,291,000 0.4%
	Swiss	1,017,000 0.3%
	Others	8,142,000 2.7%
Americans of African, Asian, North, Central, and South American, and Pacific Island Descent 96,563,000 32.2%	Latino[d]	44,321,000 14.8%
	African American	36,690,000 12.3%
	Asian American[e]	12,881,000 4.3%
	Native American[f]	2,259,000 0.75%
	Pacific Islander[g]	412,000 0.1%
Americans Who Claim Two or More Race–Ethnicities		4,091,000 1.4%

0   4%   8%   12%   16%   20%
Percentage of Americans

USA–the land of diversity

Source: By the author. Based on *Statistical Abstract of the United States* 2008:Tables 9, 51.

self-identities, whites make up 66 percent of the U.S. population, minorities (African Americans, Asian Americans, Latinos, and Native Americans) 32 percent. Between 1 and 2 percent claim membership in two or more racial–ethnic groups.

As you can see from the Social Map below, the distribution of dominant and minority groups among the states seldom comes close to the national average. This is because minority groups tend to be clustered in regions. The extreme distributions are represented by Maine and Vermont, each of which has only 5 percent minority, and by Hawaii, where minorities outnumber whites 75 percent to 25 percent. With this as background, let's review the major groups in the United States, going from the largest to the smallest.

white ethnics white immigrants to the United States whose cultures differ from WASP culture

WASP White Anglo-Saxon Protestant; narrowly, an American

European Americans

Perhaps the event that best illustrates the racial view of the nation's founders occurred at the first Continental Congress of the United States. There they passed the Naturalization Act of 1790, declaring that only white immigrants could apply for citizenship. The sense of superiority and privilege of **WASPs** (white Anglo-Saxon Protestants) was not limited to their ideas of race. They also viewed white Europeans from countries other than England as inferior. They held disdainful stereotypes of **white ethnics**—immigrants from Europe whose language and other customs differed from theirs. They despised the Irish, viewing them as dirty, lazy drunkards, but they also painted Germans, Poles, Jews, Italians, and others with similar disparaging brushstrokes.

To get an idea of how intense the feelings of the WASPs were, consider this statement by Benjamin Franklin regarding immigrants from Germany:

> Why should the Palatine boors (Germans) be suffered to swarm into our settlements and by herding together establish their language and manners to the exclusion of ours? Why should Pennsylvania, founded by the English, become a colony of aliens, who will shortly be so numerous as to germanize us instead of our anglifying them? (In Alba and Nee 2003:17)

The political and cultural dominance of the WASPs placed intense pressure on immigrants to assimilate into the mainstream culture. The children of most immigrants embraced the new way of life and quickly came to think of themselves as Americans

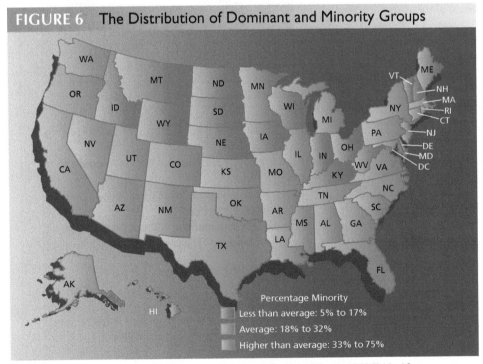

FIGURE 6   The Distribution of Dominant and Minority Groups

Percentage Minority
Less than average: 5% to 17%
Average: 18% to 32%
Higher than average: 33% to 75%

Source: By the author. Based on *Statistical Abstract of the United States* 2009:Table 18.

rather than as Germans, French, Hungarians, and so on. They dropped their distinctive customs, especially their language, often viewing them as symbols of shame. This second generation of immigrants was sandwiched between two worlds: "the old country" of their parents and their new home. Their children, the third generation, had an easier adjustment, for they had fewer customs to discard. As immigrants from other parts of Europe assimilated into this Anglo-American culture, the meaning of WASP expanded to include them.

In Sum: Because Protestant English immigrants settled the colonies, they established the culture—from the dominant language to the dominant religion. Highly ethnocentric, they regarded as inferior the customs of other groups. Because white Europeans took power, they determined the national agenda to which other ethnic groups had to react and conform. Their institutional and cultural dominance still sets the stage for current ethnic relations, a topic that is explored in the Down-to-Earth Sociology box below.

Down-to-Earth Sociology
Unpacking the Invisible Knapsack: Exploring Cultural Privilege

Overt racism in the United States has dropped sharply, but doors still open and close on the basis of the color of our skin. Whites have a difficult time grasping the idea that good things come their way because they are white. They usually fail to perceive how "whiteness" operates in their own lives.

Peggy McIntosh, of Irish descent, began to wonder why she was so seldom aware of her race–ethnicity, while her African American friends were so conscious of theirs. She realized that people are not highly aware of things that they take for granted—and that "whiteness" is a "taken-for-granted" background assumption of U.S. society. (You might want to review Figure 1.) To explore this, she drew up a list of taken-for-granted privileges that come with her "whiteness," what she calls her "invisible knapsack." Because she is white, McIntosh (1988) says:

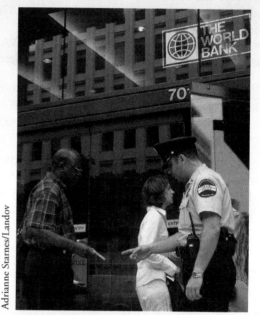

One of the cultural privileges of being white in the United States is less suspicion of wrongdoing.

1. When I go shopping, store detectives don't follow me.
2. If I don't do well as a leader, I can be sure people won't say that it is because of my race.
3. When I watch television or look at the front page of the paper, I see people of my race presented positively.
4. When I study our national heritage, I see people of my color and am taught that they made our country great.
5. To protect my children, I do not have to teach them to be aware of racism.
6. I can talk with my mouth full and not have people put this down to my color.

7. I can speak at a public meeting without putting my race on trial.
8. I can achieve something and not be "a credit to my race."
9. If a traffic cop pulls me over, I can be sure that it isn't because I'm white.
10. I can be late to a meeting without people thinking I was late because "That's how *they* are."

For Your Consideration
Can you think of other "background privileges" that come to whites because of their skin color? (McIntosh's list contains forty-six items.) Why are whites seldom aware that they carry an "invisible knapsack"?

Adrianne Starnes/Landov

Latinos (Hispanics)

A Note on Terms. Before reviewing major characteristics of Latinos, it is important to stress that *Latino* and *Hispanic* refer not to a race but to ethnic groups. Latinos may identify themselves racially as black, white, or Native American. Some Latinos who have an African heritage refer to themselves as Afro-Latinos (Navarro 2003).

Numbers, Origins, and Location. When birds still nested in the trees that would be used to build the *Mayflower,* Latinos had already established settlements in Florida and New Mexico (Bretos 1994). Today, Latinos are the largest minority group in the United States. As shown in Figure 7, about 29 million people trace their origin to Mexico, 4 million to Puerto Rico, 1 to 2 million to Cuba, and about 8 million to Central or South America.

Although Latinos are officially tallied at 44 million, another 9 million Latinos are living here illegally. About 7 million are from Mexico, and the rest from Central and South America (*Statistical Abstract* 2009:Table 46; Passel and Cohn 2009). Most Latinos are legal residents, but each year more than *1 million* Mexicans are arrested and returned to Mexico, most as they are trying to cross the border (Office of Immigration Statistics 2008). Each year, about 300,000 elude detection and make it to the United States. With this vast migration, about 20 million more Latinos live in the United States than Canadians (33 million) live in Canada. As Figure 8 shows, two-thirds live in just four states: California, Texas, Florida, and New York.

The massive unauthorized entry into the United States has aroused intense public concern. Despite protests from environmental groups and the Mexican government, U.S. officials have begun to build a 670-mile-long wall on the U.S. side of the border. A group of civilians called the Minutemen also patrols the border, but unofficially. To avoid conflict with the U.S. Border Patrol, the Minutemen do not carry guns. A second unofficial group, the Techno Patriots, also patrols the border, using computers and thermal imaging cameras. When they confirm illegal crossings, they call the Border Patrol, whose agents make the arrests (Archibold and Preston 2008; Marino 2008). Despite walls and patrols, as long as there is a need for unskilled labor and millions of Mexicans live in poverty, this flow of undocumented workers will continue. To gain insight into why, see the Cultural Diversity box on the next page.

Spanish Language. The Spanish language distinguishes most Latinos from other U.S. ethnic groups. With 34 million people speaking Spanish at home, the United States has become one of the largest Spanish-speaking nations in the world (*Statistical Abstract* 2009: Table 52). Because about half of Latinos are unable to speak English, or can do so only with difficulty, many millions face a major obstacle to getting good jobs.

The growing use of Spanish has stoked controversy (Fund 2007). Perceiving the prevalence of Spanish as a threat, Senator S. I. Hayakawa of California initiated an "English-only" movement in 1981. The constitutional amendment that he sponsored never got off the ground, but thirty states have passed laws that declare English their official language.

Diversity. For Latinos, country of origin is highly significant. Those from Puerto Rico, for example, feel that they have little in common with people from Mexico, Venezuela, or El Salvador—just as earlier immigrants from Germany, Sweden, and England felt they had little in common with one another. A sign of these divisions is that many refer to themselves in terms of their country of origin, such as *puertorriqueños* or *cubanos,* rather than as Latino or Hispanic.

As with other ethnic groups, Latinos are separated by social class. The half-million Cubans who fled Castro's rise to power in 1959, for example, were mostly well-educated, well-to-do professionals or businesspeople. In contrast, the "boat people"

FIGURE 7 Geographical Origin of U.S. Latinos

Cuba 1,661,000 3.5%
Other countries 2,358,000 5.0%
Puerto Rico 3,868,000 8.5%
Central and South America 7,882,000 18%
Mexico 29,145,000 65%

Source: By the author. Based on *Statistical Abstract* 2009:Table 38.

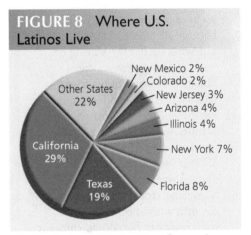

FIGURE 8 Where U.S. Latinos Live

New Mexico 2%
Colorado 2%
New Jersey 3%
Arizona 4%
Illinois 4%
New York 7%
Florida 8%
Texas 19%
California 29%
Other States 22%

Source: By the author. Based on *Statistical Abstract of the United States* 2009:Table 18.

Cultural Diversity in the United States

The Illegal Travel Guide

Manuel was a drinking buddy of Jose, a man I had met in Colima, Mexico. At 45, Manuel was friendly, outgoing, and enterprising.

Manuel, who had lived in the United States for seven years, spoke fluent English. Preferring to live in his hometown in Colima, where he palled around with his childhood friends, Manuel always seemed to have money and free time.

When Manuel invited me to go on a business trip with him, I accepted. I never could figure out what he did for a living or how he could afford a car, a luxury that none of his friends had. As we traveled from one remote village to another, Manuel would sell used clothing that he had heaped in the back of his older-model Ford station wagon.

At one stop, Manuel took me into a dirt-floored, thatched-roof hut. While chickens ran in and out, Manuel whispered to a slender man who was about 23 years old. The poverty was overwhelming. Juan, as his name turned out to be, had a partial grade school education. He also had a wife, four hungry children under the age of 5, and two pigs—his main food supply. Although eager to work, Juan had no job, for there was simply no work available in this remote village.

As we were drinking a Coke, which seems to be the national beverage of Mexico's poor, Manuel explained to me that he was not only selling clothing—he was also lining up migrants to the United States. For a fee, he would take a man to the border and introduce him to a "wolf," who would help him cross into the promised land.

A man and woman from Mexico crossing the Rio Grande on their way to Texas.

A. Ramey/PhotoEdit, Inc.

When I saw the hope in Juan's face, I knew nothing would stop him. He was borrowing every cent he could from every friend and relative to scrape the money together. Although he risked losing everything if apprehended and he would be facing unknown risks, Juan would make the trip, for wealth beckoned on the other side. He knew people who had been to the United States and spoke glowingly of its opportunities. Manuel, of course, the salesman he was, stoked the fires of hope.

Looking up from the children playing on the dirt floor with chickens pecking about them, I saw a man who loved his family. In order to make the desperate bid for a better life, he would suffer an enforced absence, as well as the uncertainties of a foreign culture whose language he did not know.

Juan opened his billfold, took something out, and slowly handed it to me. I looked at it curiously. I felt tears as I saw the tenderness with which he handled this piece of paper. It was his passport to the land of opportunity: a Social Security card made out in his name, sent by a friend who had already made the trip and who was waiting for Juan on the other side of the border.

It was then that I realized that the thousands of Manuels scurrying about Mexico and the millions of Juans they are transporting can never be stopped, for only the United States can fulfill their dreams of a better life.

For Your Consideration

The vast stream of immigrants crossing illegally across the Mexican–U.S. border has become a national issue. What do you think is the best way to deal with this issue? Why?

who fled later were mostly lower-class refugees, people with whom the earlier arrivals would not have associated in Cuba. The earlier arrivals, who are firmly established in Florida and who control many businesses and financial institutions, distance themselves from the more recent immigrants.

These divisions of national origin and social class are a major obstacle to political unity. One consequence is a severe underrepresentation in politics. Because Latinos make up 14.8 percent of the U.S. population, we might expect thirteen or fourteen U.S. Senators to be Latino. How many are there? *Three*. In addition, Latinos hold only 5 percent of the

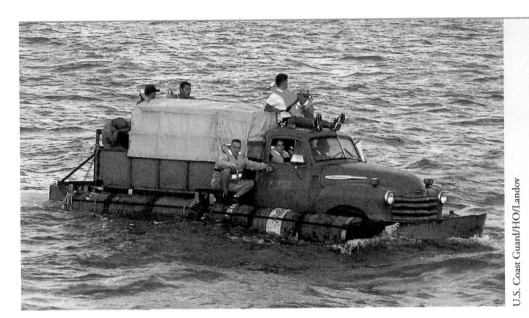

For millions of people, the United States represents a land of opportunity and freedom from oppression. Shown here are Cubans who reached the United States by transforming their 1950s truck into a boat.

U.S. Coast Guard/HO/Landov

seats in the U.S. House of Representatives (*Statistical Abstract* 2009:Table 388; 2009 election updates).

The potential political power of Latinos is remarkable, and in coming years we will see more of this potential realized. As Latinos have become more visible in U.S. society and more vocal in their demands for equality, they have come face to face with African Americans who fear that Latino gains in employment and at the ballot box will come at their expense (Hutchinson 2008). Together, Latinos and African Americans make up more than one-fourth of the U.S. population. If these two groups were to join together, their unity would produce an unstoppable political force.

Comparative Conditions.   To see how Latinos are doing on some major indicators of well-being, look at Table 2 on the next page. As you can see, compared with white Americans and Asian Americans, Latinos have less income, higher unemployment, and more poverty. They are also less likely to own their homes. Now look at how closely Latinos rank with African Americans and Native Americans. From this table, you can also see how significant country of origin is. People from Cuba score higher on all these indicators of well-being, while those from Puerto Rico score lower.

The significance of country or region of origin is also underscored by Table 3. You can see that people who trace their roots to Cuba attain more education than do those who come from other areas. You can also see that that Latinos are the most likely to drop out of high school and the least likely to graduate from college. In a postindustrial society that increasingly requires advanced skills, these totals indicate that huge numbers of Latinos will be left behind.

African Americans

After slavery was abolished, the Southern states passed legislation (*Jim Crow* laws) to segregate blacks and whites. In 1896, the U.S. Supreme Court ruled in *Plessy v. Ferguson* that it was a reasonable use of state power to require "separate but equal" accommodations for blacks. Whites used this ruling to strip blacks of the political power they had gained after the Civil War. Declaring political primaries to be "white," they prohibited blacks from voting in them. Not until 1944 did the Supreme Court rule that political primaries weren't "white" and were open to all voters. White politicians then passed laws that only people who could read could vote—and they determined that most African Americans were illiterate. Not until 1954 did African Americans gain the legal right to attend the same public schools as whites, and well into the 1960s the South was still openly—and legally—practicing segregation.

TABLE 2 Race–Ethnicity and Comparative Well-Being[1]

	Income		Unemployment		Poverty		Home Ownership	
Racial–Ethnic Group	Median Family Income	Compared to Whites	Percentage Unemployed	Compared to Whites	Percentage Below Poverty Line	Compared to Whites	Percentage Who Own Their Homes	Compared to Whites
Whites	$62,300	—	3.2%	—	9.0%	—	73.7%	—
Latinos	$37,387	39% lower	3.6%	13% higher	21.8%	142% higher	48.8%	34% lower
Country or Area of Origin								
Cuba	NA[2]	NA	2.2%	31% lower	10.7%	19% higher	62.7%	20% lower
Central and South America	NA	NA	NA	NA	16.3%	81% higher	37.3%	49% lower
Mexico	NA	NA	3.6%	13% higher	23.8%	164% higher	50.8%	31% lower
Puerto Rico	NA	NA	4.4%	38% higher	25.3%	181% higher	39.6%	46% lower
African Americans	$36,075	42% lower	6.8%	113% higher	25.6%	184% higher	45.8%	38% lower
Asian Americans[3]	$69,159	9% higher	2.5%	22% lower	11.5%	28% higher	59.1%	20% lower
Native Americans	$38,558	40% lower	NA	NA	25.4%	182% higher	56.0%	24% lower

[1]Data are from 2005 and 2006.
[2]Not Available
[3]Includes Pacific Islanders

Source: By the author. Based on *Statistical Abstract of the United States* 2008: Tables 36, 39, 609.

TABLE 3 Race–Ethnicity and Education

	Education Completed				Doctorates		
Racial–Ethnic Group	Less than High School	High School	Some College	College (BA or Higher)	Number Awarded	Percentage of all U.S. Doctorates[1]	Percentage of U.S. Population
Whites	11.0%	30.3%	28.7%	30.0%	30,261	79.0%	66.4%
Latinos	40.6%	27.0%	20.2%	12.2%	1,824	4.8%	14.8%
Country or Area of Origin							
Cuba	26.5%	30.4%	18.4%	24.7%	NA	NA	
Puerto Rico	27.8%	33.7%	24.7%	13.8%	NA	NA	
Central and South America	37.6%	25.6%	18.3%	18.5%	NA	NA	
Mexico	47.7%	26.6%	17.4%	8.3%	NA	NA	
African Americans	20.1%	32.9%	29.7%	17.3%	3,056	8.0%	12.3%
Asian Americans	14.4%	16.8%	19.7%	49.1%	2,911	7.6%	4.3%
Native Americans	23.6%	31.2%	31.5%	13.6%	237	0.6%	0.8%

[1]Percentage after the doctorates awarded to nonresidents are deducted from the total.

Source: By the author. Based on *Statistical Abstract of the United States* 2008: Tables 36, 44, 293 and Figure 5 of this text.

Until the 1960s, the South's public facilities were segregated. Some were reserved for whites, others for blacks. This *apartheid* was broken by blacks and whites who worked together and risked their lives to bring about a fairer society. Shown here is a 1963 sit-in at a Woolworth's lunch counter in Jackson, Mississippi. Sugar, ketchup, and mustard are being poured over the heads of the demonstrators.

Fred Blackwell

The Struggle for Civil Rights

It was 1955, in Montgomery, Alabama. As specified by law, whites took the front seats of the bus, and blacks went to the back. As the bus filled up, blacks had to give up their seats to whites.

When Rosa Parks, a 42-year-old African American woman and secretary of the Montgomery NAACP, was told that she would have to stand so that white folks could sit, she refused (Bray 1995). She stubbornly sat there while the bus driver raged and whites felt insulted. Her arrest touched off mass demonstrations, led 50,000 blacks to boycott the city's buses for a year, and thrust an otherwise unknown preacher into a historic role.

Reverend Martin Luther King, Jr., who had majored in sociology at Morehouse College in Atlanta, Georgia, took control. He organized car pools and preached nonviolence. Incensed at this radical organizer and at the stirrings in the normally compliant black community, segregationists also put their beliefs into practice—by bombing the homes of blacks and dynamiting their churches.

Rising Expectations and Civil Strife. The barriers came down, but they came down slowly. In 1964, Congress passed the Civil Rights Act, making it illegal to discriminate on the basis of race. African Americans were finally allowed in "white" restaurants, hotels, theaters, and other public places. Then in 1965, Congress passed the Voting Rights Act, banning the fraudulent literacy tests that the Southern states had used to keep African Americans from voting.

African Americans then experienced what sociologists call **rising expectations.** They expected that these sweeping legal changes would usher in better conditions in life. In contrast, the lives of the poor among them changed little, if at all. Frustrations built up, exploding in Watts in 1965, when people living in that ghetto of central Los Angeles took to the streets in the first of what were termed the *urban revolts*. When a white supremacist assassinated King on April 4, 1968, inner cities across the nation erupted in fiery violence. Under threat of the destruction of U.S. cities, Congress passed the sweeping Civil Rights Act of 1968.

rising expectations the sense that better conditions are soon to follow, which, if unfulfilled, increases frustration

Continued Gains. Since then, African Americans have made remarkable gains in politics, education, and jobs. At 10 percent, the number of African Americans in the U.S. House of

In 2009, Barack Obama was sworn in as the 44th president of the United States. He is the first minority to achieve this political office.

AP Images/Charles Dharapak

Representatives is almost *three times* what it was a generation ago (*Statistical Abstract* 1989: Table 423; 2009:Table 390). As college enrollments increased, the middle class expanded, and today half of all African American families make more than $40,000 a year. One in five earns more than $75,000, and one in nine over $100,000 (*Statistical Abstract* 2009:Table 672). Contrary to stereotypes, the average African American family is *not* poor.

African Americans have become prominent in politics. Jesse Jackson (another sociology major) competed for the Democratic presidential nomination in 1984 and 1988. In 1989, L. Douglas Wilder was elected governor of Virginia, and in 2006 Deval Patrick became governor of Massachusetts. These accomplishments, of course, pale in comparison to the election of Barack Obama as president of the United States in 2008.

Current Losses. Despite these remarkable gains, African Americans continue to lag behind in politics, economics, and education. Only *one* U.S. Senator is African American, but on the basis of the percentage of African Americans in the U.S. population we would expect about twelve. As Tables 2 and 3 show, African Americans average only 58 percent of white income, have much more unemployment and poverty, and are less likely to own their home or to have a college education. That half of African American families have incomes over $40,000 is only part of the story. Table 4 shows the other part—that almost one of every five African American families makes less than $15,000 a year.

The upward mobility of millions of African Americans into the middle class has created two worlds of African American experience—one educated and affluent, the other uneducated and poor. Concentrated among the poor are those with the least hope, the most despair, and the violence that so often dominates the evening news. Although homicide rates have dropped to their lowest point in thirty-five years, African Americans are *six* times as likely to be murdered as are whites (*Statistical Abstract* 2009:Table 301). Compared with whites, African Americans are about *eight* times more likely to die from AIDS (*Statistical Abstract* 2009:Table 121).

TABLE 4 Race–Ethnicity and Income Extremes		
	Less than $15,000	Over $100,000
Asian Americans	6.7%	36.2%
Whites	6.7%	25.4%
African Americans	18.7%	11.9%
Latinos	13.5%	11.4%

Note: These are family incomes. Only these groups are listed in the source.

Source: By the author: Based on *Statistical Abstract of the United States* 2009:Table 672.

Race or Social Class? A Sociological Debate.   This division of African Americans into "haves" and "have-nots" has fueled a sociological controversy. Sociologist William Julius Wilson (1978, 2000, 2007) argues that social class has become more important than race in determining the life chances of African Americans. Before civil rights legislation, he says, the African American experience was dominated by race. Throughout the United States, African Americans were excluded from avenues of economic advancement: good schools and good jobs. When civil rights laws opened new opportunities, African Americans seized them. Just as legislation began to open doors to African Americans, however, manufacturing jobs dried up, and many blue-collar jobs were moved to the suburbs. As better-educated African Americans obtained middle-class, white-collar jobs and moved out of the inner city, left behind were those with poor education and few skills.

Wilson stresses how significant these two worlds of African American experience are. The group that is stuck in the inner city lives in poverty, attends poor schools, and faces dead-end jobs or welfare. This group is filled with hopelessness and despair, combined with apathy or hostility. In contrast, those who have moved up the social class ladder live in comfortable homes in secure neighborhoods. Their jobs provide decent incomes, and they send their children to good schools. With their middle-class experiences shaping their views on life, their aspirations and values have little in common with those of African Americans who remain poor. According to Wilson, then, social class—not race—is the most significant factor in the lives of African Americans.

Some sociologists reply that this analysis overlooks the discrimination that continues to underlie the African American experience. They note that African Americans who do the same work as whites average less pay (Willie 1991; Herring 2002) and even receive fewer tips (Lynn et al. 2008). This, they argue, points to racial discrimination, not to social class.

What is the answer to this debate? Wilson would reply that it is not an either-or question. My book is titled *The **Declining** Significance of Race,* he would say, not *The **Absence** of Race.* Certainly racism is still alive, he would add, but today social class is more central to the African American experience than is racial discrimination. He stresses that we need to provide jobs for the poor in the inner city—for work provides an anchor to a responsible life (Wilson 1996, 2007).

Racism as an Everyday Burden.   Racism, though more subtle than it used to be, still walks among us (Perry 2006; Crowder and South 2008). Since racism has become more subtle, it takes more subtle methods to uncover it. In one study, researchers sent out 5,000 résumés in response to help wanted ads in the Boston and Chicago Sunday papers (Bertrand and Mullainathan 2002). The résumés were identical, except for the names of the job applicants. Some applicants had white-sounding names, such as Emily and Brandon, while others had black-sounding names, such as Lakisha and Jamal. Although the qualifications of the supposed job applicants were identical, the white-sounding names elicited *50 percent* more callbacks than the black-sounding names. The Down-to-Earth Sociology box on the next page presents another study of subtle racism.

African Americans who occupy higher statuses enjoy greater opportunities and face less discrimination. The discrimination that they encounter, however, is no less painful. Unlike whites of the same social class, they sense discrimination hovering over them. Here is how an African American professor described it:

> [One problem with] being black in America is that you have to spend so much time thinking about stuff that most white people just don't even have to think about. I worry when I get pulled over by a cop. . . . I worry what some white cop is going to think when he walks over to our car, because he's holding on to a gun. And I'm very aware of how many black folks accidentally get shot by cops. I worry when I walk into a store, that someone's going to think I'm in there shoplifting. . . . And I get resentful that I have to think about things that a lot of people, even my very close white friends whose politics are similar to mine, simply don't have to worry about. (Feagin 1999:398)

Sociologists disagree about the relative significance of race and social class in determining social and economic conditions of African Americans. William Julius Wilson, shown here, is an avid proponent of the social class side of this debate.

Ted Thai/Time Life Pictures/Getty Images

Down-to-Earth Sociology
Stealth Racism in the Rental Market: What You Reveal by Your Voice

The past often sounds unreal. Discrimination in public accommodations was once standard—and legal. With today's changed laws and the vigilance of groups such as the NAACP and the Jewish Anti-Defamation League, no hotel, restaurant, or gas station would refuse service on the basis of race–ethnicity. There was even a time when white racists could lynch African Americans and Asian Americans without fear of the law. When they could no longer do that, they could still burn crosses on their lawns. Today, such events will make the national news, and the perpetrators will be prosecuted. If local officials won't do their job, the FBI will step in.

Yesterday's overt racism has been replaced with today's stealth racism (Pager 2007; Lynn et al. 2008). There are many forms, but here's one: Sociologist Douglas Massey was talking with his undergraduate students at the University of Pennsylvania about how Americans identify one another racially by their speech. In his class were whites who spoke middle-class English, African Americans who spoke middle-class English with a black accent, and African Amer-

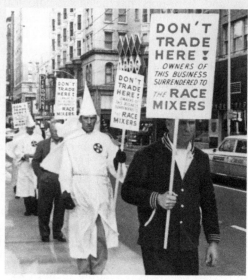

AP Images

Unlike today, racial discrimination used to be overt. These Ku Klux Klan members are protesting the 1964 integration of a restaurant in Atlanta, Georgia.

icans who spoke a dialect known as Black English Vernacular. Massey and his students decided to investigate how voice is used to discriminate in the housing market. They designed standard identities for the class members, assigning them similar incomes, jobs, and education. They also developed a standard script and translated it into Black English Vernacular. The students called on 79 apartments that were advertised for rent in newspapers. The study was done blindly, with these various English speakers not knowing how the others were being treated.

What did they find? Compared with whites, African Americans were less likely to get to talk to rental agents, who often used answering machines to screen calls. When they did get through, they were less likely to be told that an apartment was available, more likely to have to pay an application fee, and more likely to be asked about their credit history. Students who posed as lower-class blacks (speakers of Black English Vernacular) had the least access to apartments. Figure 9 summarizes the percentages of callers who were told an apartment was available.

As you can see from this figure, in all three language groups women experienced more discrimination than men, another indication of gender inequality. For African American women, sociologists use the term *double bind*, meaning that they are discriminated against both because they are African Americans and because they are women.

For Your Consideration

Missing from this study are "White English Vernacular" speakers—whites whose voice identifies them as members of the lower class. If they had been included, where do you think they would place on Figure 9?

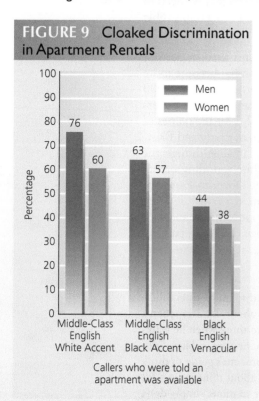

FIGURE 9 Cloaked Discrimination in Apartment Rentals

Percentage (y-axis: 0–100)

Men / Women

- Middle-Class English White Accent: 76 / 60
- Middle-Class English Black Accent: 63 / 57
- Black English Vernacular: 44 / 38

Callers who were told an apartment was available

Source: Massey and Lundy 2001.

Asian Americans

I have stressed in this chapter that our racial–ethnic categories are based more on social considerations than on biological ones. This point is again obvious when we examine the category Asian American. As Figure 10 shows, those who are called Asian Americans came to the United States from many nations. *With no unifying culture or "race," why should these people of so many backgrounds be clustered together and assigned a single label?* The reason is that others perceive them as a unit. Think about it. What culture or race–ethnicity do Samoans and Vietnamese have in common? Or Laotians and Pakistanis? Or people from Guam and those from China? Those from Japan and those from India? Yet all these groups— and more—are lumped together and called Asian Americans. Apparently, the U.S. government is not satisfied until it is able to pigeonhole everyone into some racial–ethnic category.

Since *Asian American* is a standard term, however, let's look at the characteristics of the 13 million people who are lumped together and assigned this label.

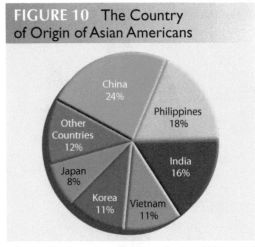

FIGURE 10 The Country of Origin of Asian Americans

Source: By the author. Based on *Statistical Abstract of the United States* 2006:Table 24.

A Background of Discrimination.   From their first arrival in the United States, Asian Americans confronted discrimination. Lured by gold strikes in the West and an urgent need for unskilled workers to build the railroads, 200,000 Chinese immigrated between 1850 and 1880. When the famous golden spike was driven at Promontory, Utah, in 1869 to mark the completion of the railroad to the West Coast, white workers prevented Chinese workers from being in the photo—even though Chinese made up 90 percent of Central Pacific Railroad's labor force (Hsu 1971).

After the railroad was complete, the Chinese took other jobs. Feeling threatened by their cheap labor, Anglos formed vigilante groups to intimidate them. They also used the law. California's 1850 Foreign Miner's Act required Chinese (and Latinos) to pay a fee of $20 a month in order to work—when wages were a dollar a day. The California Supreme Court ruled that Chinese could not testify against whites (Carlson and Colburn 1972). In 1882, Congress passed the Chinese Exclusion Act, suspending all Chinese immigration for ten years. Four years later, the Statue of Liberty was dedicated. The tired, the poor, and the huddled masses it was intended to welcome were obviously not Chinese.

When immigrants from Japan arrived, they encountered *spillover bigotry,* a stereotype that lumped Asians together, depicting them as sneaky, lazy, and untrustworthy. After Japan attacked Pearl Harbor in 1941, conditions grew worse for the 110,000 Japanese Americans who called the United States their home. U.S. authorities feared that Japan would invade the United States and that the Japanese Americans would fight on Japan's side. They also feared that Japanese Americans would sabotage military installations on the West Coast. Although no Japanese American had been involved in even a single act of sabotage, on February 19, 1942, President Franklin D. Roosevelt ordered that everyone who was *one-eighth Japanese or more* be confined in detention centers (called "internment camps"). These people were charged with no crime, and they had no trials. Japanese ancestry was sufficient cause for being imprisoned.

Diversity.   As you can see from Tables 2 and 4, the income of Asian Americans has outstripped that of all groups, including whites. This has led to the stereotype that all Asian Americans are successful. Are they? Their poverty rate is actually higher than that of whites, as you can also see from Table 2. As with Latinos, country of origin is significant: Poverty is unusual among Chinese and Japanese Americans, but it clusters among Americans from Southeast Asia. Altogether, between 1 and 2 million Asian Americans live in poverty.

Reasons for Success.   The high average income of Asian Americans can be traced to three major factors: family life, educational achievement, and assimilation into mainstream culture. Of all ethnic groups, including whites, Asian American children are the most likely to grow up with two parents and the least likely to be born to a single mother (*Statistical Abstract* 2009:Tables 68, 85). Common in these

Of the racial–ethnic groups in the United States, Asian Americans have the highest rate of inter-marriage.

Michael Newman/PhotoEdit, Inc.

families is a stress on self-discipline, thrift, and hard work (Suzuki 1985; Bell 1991). This early socialization provides strong impetus for the other two factors.

The second factor is their unprecedented rate of college graduation. As Table 3 shows, 49 percent of Asian Americans complete college. To realize how stunning this is, compare this rate with that of the other groups shown on this table. This educational achievement, in turn, opens doors to economic success.

The most striking indication of the third factor, assimilation, is a high rate of intermarriage. Of Asian Americans who graduate from college, about 40 percent of the men and 60 percent of the women marry a non-Asian American (Qian and Lichter 2007). The intermarriage of Japanese Americans is so extensive that two of every three of their children have one parent who is not of Japanese descent (Schaefer 2004). The Chinese are close behind (Alba and Nee 2003).

Asian Americans are becoming more prominent in politics. With more than half of its citizens being Asian American, Hawaii has elected Asian American governors and sent several Asian American senators to Washington, including the two now serving there (Lee 1998, *Statistical Abstract* 2009:Table 300). The first Asian American governor outside of Hawaii was Gary Locke, who served from 1997 to 2005 as governor of Washington, a state in which Asian Americans make up less than 6 percent of the population. In 2008 in Louisiana, Piyush Jindal became the first Indian American governor.

Native Americans

"I don't go so far as to think that the only good Indians are dead Indians, but I believe nine out of ten are—and I shouldn't inquire too closely in the case of the tenth. The most vicious cowboy has more moral principle than the average Indian."

—Said in 1886 by Teddy Roosevelt
(President of the United States 1901–1909)

Diversity of Groups. This quote from Teddy Roosevelt provides insight into the rampant racism of earlier generations. Yet, even today, thanks to countless grade B Westerns, some Americans view the original inhabitants of what became the United States as wild, uncivilized savages, a single group of people subdivided into separate tribes. The European immigrants to the colonies, however, encountered diverse groups of people with a variety of cultures—from nomadic hunters and gatherers to people who lived in wooden houses in settled agricultural communities. Altogether, they spoke over 700 languages (Schaefer 2004). Each group had its own norms and values—and the usual ethnocentric pride in its own culture. Consider what happened in 1744 when the colonists of Virginia offered college scholarships for "savage lads." The Iroquois replied:

"Several of our young people were formerly brought up at the colleges of Northern Provinces. They were instructed in all your sciences. But when they came back to us, they were bad runners, ignorant of every means of living in the woods, unable to bear either cold or hunger, knew neither how to build a cabin, take a deer, or kill an enemy. . . . They were totally good for nothing."

They added, "If the English gentlemen would send a dozen or two of their children to Onondaga, the great Council would take care of their education, bring them up in really what was the best manner and make men of them." (Nash 1974; in McLemore 1994)

Native Americans, who numbered about 10 million, had no immunity to the diseases the Europeans brought with them. With deaths due to disease—and warfare, a much lesser cause—their population plummeted. The low point came in 1890, when the census reported only 250,000 Native Americans. If the census and the estimate of the original population are accurate, Native Americans had been reduced to about *one-fortieth* their original size. The population has never recovered, but Native Americans now number over 2 million (see Figure 5). Native Americans, who today speak 150 different languages, do not think of themselves as a single people who fit neatly within a single label (McLemore 1994).

From Treaties to Genocide and Population Transfer. At first, the Native Americans tried to accommodate the strangers, since there was plenty of land for both the few newcomers and themselves. Soon, however, the settlers began to raid Indian villages and pillage their food supplies (Horn 2006). As wave after wave of settlers arrived, Pontiac, an Ottawa chief, saw the future—and didn't like it. He convinced several tribes to unite in an effort to push the Europeans into the sea. He almost succeeded, but failed when the English were reinforced by fresh troops (McLemore 1994).

A pattern of deception evolved. The U.S. government would make treaties to buy some of a tribe's land, with the promise to honor forever the tribe's right to what it had not sold. European immigrants, who continued to pour into the United States, would then disregard these boundaries. The tribes would resist, with death tolls on both sides. The U.S. government would then intervene—not to enforce the treaty, but to force the tribe off its lands. In its relentless drive westward, the U.S. government embarked on a policy of genocide. It assigned the U.S. cavalry the task of "pacification," which translated into slaughtering Native Americans who "stood in the way" of this territorial expansion.

The acts of cruelty perpetrated by the Europeans against Native Americans appear endless, but two are especially notable. The first is the Trail of Tears. The U.S. government adopted a policy of population transfer (see Figure 3), which it called *Indian Removal*. The goal was to confine Native Americans to specified areas called *reservations*. In the winter of 1838–1839, the U.S. Army rounded up 15,000 Cherokees and forced them to walk a thousand miles from the Carolinas and Georgia to Oklahoma. Coming from the South, many of the Cherokees wore only light clothing. Conditions were so brutal that about 4,000 of those who were forced to make this midwinter march died along the way. The second, the symbolic end to Native American resistance to the European expansion, took place in 1890 at Wounded Knee, South Dakota. There the U.S. cavalry gunned down 300 men, women, and children of the Dakota Sioux tribe. After the massacre, the soldiers threw the bodies into a mass grave (Thornton 1987; Lind 1995; DiSilvestro 2006).

The Native Americans stood in the way of the U.S. government's westward expansion. To seize their lands, the government followed a policy of *genocide*, later replaced by *population transfer*. This depiction of Apache shepherds being attacked by the U.S. Cavalry is by Rufus Zogbaum, a popular U.S. illustrator of the 1880s.

Zogbaum/North Wind Picture Archives

The Invisible Minority and Self-Determination. Native Americans can truly be called the invisible minority. Because about half live in rural areas and one-third in just three states—Oklahoma, California, and Arizona—most other Americans are hardly aware of a Native American presence in the United States. The isolation of about half of Native Americans on reservations further reduces their visibility (Schaefer 2004).

The systematic attempts of European Americans to destroy the Native Americans' way of life and their forced resettlement onto reservations continue to have deleterious effects. The rate of suicide of Native Americans is the highest of any racial–ethnic group, and their life expectancy is lower than that of the nation as a whole (Murray et al. 2006; Centers for Disease Control 2007b). Table 3 shows that their education also lags behind most groups: Only 14 percent graduate from college.

Native Americans are experiencing major changes. In the 1800s, U.S. courts ruled that Native Americans did not own the land on which they had been settled and had no right to develop its resources. They made Native Americans wards of the state, and the Bureau of Indian Affairs treated them like children (Mohawk 1991; Schaefer 2004). Then, in the 1960s, Native Americans won a series of legal victories that gave them control over reservation lands. With this legal change, many Native American tribes have opened businesses—ranging from fish canneries to industrial parks that serve metropolitan areas. The Skywalk, opened by the Hualapai, which offers breathtaking views of the Grand Canyon, gives an idea of the varieties of businesses to come.

It is the casinos, though, that have attracted the most attention. In 1988, the federal government passed a law that allowed Native Americans to operate gambling establishments on reservations. Now over 200 tribes operate casinos. *They bring in $26 billion a year, twice as much as all the casinos in Las Vegas* (Werner 2007; *Statistical Abstract* 2009: Table 1218). The Oneida tribe of New York, which has only 1,000 members, runs a casino that nets $232,000 a year for each man, woman, and child (Peterson 2003). This huge amount, however, pales in comparison with that of the Mashantucket Pequot tribe of Connecticut. With only 700 members, the tribe brings in more than $2 million a day just from slot machines (Rivlin 2007). Incredibly, one tribe has only *one* member: She has her own casino (Bartlett and Steele 2002).

A highly controversial issue is *separatism*. Because Native Americans were independent peoples when the Europeans arrived and they never willingly joined the United States, many tribes maintain the right to remain separate from the U.S. government. The chief of the Onondaga tribe in New York, a member of the Iroquois Federation, summarized the issue this way:

> For the whole history of the Iroquois, we have maintained that we are a separate nation. We have never lost a war. Our government still operates. We have refused the U.S. government's reorganization plans for us. We have kept our language and our traditions, and when we fly to Geneva to UN meetings, we carry Hau de no sau nee passports. We made some treaties that lost some land, but that also confirmed our separate-nation status. That the U.S. denies all this doesn't make it any less the case. (Mander 1992)

One of the most significant changes for Native Americans is **pan-Indianism.** This emphasis on common elements that run through their cultures is an attempt to develop an identity that goes beyond the tribe. Pan-Indianism ("We are all Indians") is a remarkable example of the plasticity of ethnicity. It embraces and substitutes for individual tribal identities the label "Indian"—originally imposed by Spanish and Italian sailors, who thought they had reached the shores of India. As sociologist Irwin Deutscher (2002:61) put it, "The peoples who have accepted the larger definition of who they are, have, in fact, little else in common with each other than the stereotypes of the dominant group which labels them."

Native Americans say that it is they who must determine whether they want to establish a common identity and work together as in pan-Indianism or to stress separatism and identify solely with their own tribe; to assimilate into the dominant culture or to remain apart from it; to move to cities or to remain on reservations; or to operate casinos or to engage only in traditional activities. "Such decisions must be ours," say the Native Americans. "We are sovereign, and we will not take orders from the victors of past wars."

Looking Toward the Future

Back in 1903, sociologist W. E. B. Du Bois said, "The problem of the twentieth century is the problem of the color line—the relation of the darker to the lighter races." Incredibly, over a hundred years later, the color line remains one of the most volatile topics facing the nation. From time to time, the color line takes on a different complexion, as with the war on terrorism and the corresponding discrimination directed against people of Middle Eastern descent.

In another hundred years, will yet another sociologist lament that the color of people's skin still affects human relationships? Given our past, it seems that although racial–ethnic walls will diminish, even crumble at some points, the color line is not likely to disappear. Let's close this chapter by looking at two issues we are currently grappling with, immigration and affirmative action.

pan-Indianism a movement that focuses on common elements in the cultures of Native Americans in order to develop a cross-tribal self-identity and to work toward the welfare of all Native Americans

The Immigration Debate

Throughout its history, the United States has both welcomed immigration and feared its consequences. The gates opened wide (numerically, if not in attitude) for waves of immigrants in the 1800s and early 1900s. During the past twenty years, a new wave of immigration has brought close to a million new residents to the United States each year. Today, more immigrants (38 million) live in the United States than at any other time in the country's history (*Statistical Abstract* 2007: Table 5; 2009:Table 39).

In contrast to earlier waves, in which immigrants came almost exclusively from western Europe, the current wave of immigrants is so diverse that it is changing the U.S. racial–ethnic mix. If current trends in immigration (and birth) persist, in about fifty years the "average" American will trace his or her ancestry to Africa, Asia, South America, the Pacific Islands, the Middle East—almost anywhere but white Europe. This change is discussed in the Cultural Diversity box on the next page.

In some states, the future is arriving much sooner than this. In California, racial–ethnic minorities have become the majority. California has 21 million minorities and 16 million whites (*Statistical Abstract* 2009:Table 18). Californians who request new telephone service from Pacific Bell can speak to customer service representatives in Spanish, Korean, Vietnamese, Mandarin, Cantonese—or English.

As in the past, there is concern that "too many" immigrants will change the character of the United States. "Throughout the history of U.S. immigration," write sociologists Alejandro Portes and Rubén Rumbaut (1990), "a consistent thread has been the fear that the 'alien element' would somehow undermine the institutions of the country and would lead it down the path of disintegration and decay." A hundred years ago, the widespread fear was that the immigrants from southern Europe would bring communism with them. Today, some fear that Spanish-speaking immigrants threaten the primacy of the English language. In addition, the age-old fear that immigrants will take jobs away from native-born Americans remains strong. Finally, minority groups that struggled for political representation fear that newer groups will gain political power at their expense.

Affirmative Action

Affirmative action in our multicultural society lies at the center of a national debate about racial–ethnic relations. In this policy, initiated by President Kennedy in 1961, goals based on race (and sex) are used in hiring, promotion, and college admission. Sociologist Barbara Reskin (1998) examined the results of affirmative action. She concluded that although it is difficult to separate the results of affirmative action from economic booms and busts and the greater numbers of women in the workforce, affirmative action has had a modest impact.

The results may have been modest, but the reactions to this program have been anything but modest. Affirmative action has been at the center of controversy for almost two generations. Liberals, both white and minority, say that this program is the most direct way to level the playing field of economic opportunity. If whites are passed over, this is an unfortunate cost that we must pay if we are to make up for past discrimination. In contrast, conservatives, both white and minority, agree that opportunity should be open to all, but claim that putting race (or sex) ahead of an individual's training and ability to perform a job is reverse discrimination. Because of their race (or sex), qualified people who had nothing to do with past inequality are discriminated against. They add that affirmative action stigmatizes the people who benefit from it, because it suggests that they hold their jobs because of race (or sex), rather than merit.

Cultural Diversity in the United States

Glimpsing the Future: The Shifting U.S. Racial–Ethnic Mix

During the next twenty-five years, the population of the United States is expected to grow by about 22 percent. To see what the U.S. population will look like at that time, can we simply add 22 percent to our current racial–ethnic mix? The answer is a resounding no. As you can see from Figure 11, some groups will grow much more than others, giving us a different-looking United States. Some of the changes in the U.S. racial–ethnic mix will be dramatic. In twenty-five years, one of every nineteen Americans is expected to have an Asian background, and in the most dramatic change, almost one of four is expected to be of Latino ancestry.

The basic causes of this fundamental shift are the racial–ethnic groups' different rates of immigration and birth. Both will change the groups' proportions of the U.S. population, but immigration is by far the more important. From Figure 11, you can see that the proportion of non-Hispanic whites is expected to shrink, that of Native Americans to remain the same, that of African Americans to increase slightly, and that of Latinos to increase sharply.

For Your Consideration

This shifting racial–ethnic mix is one of the most significant events occurring in the United States. To better understand its implications, apply the three theoretical perspectives.

Use the *conflict perspective* to identify the groups that are likely to be threatened by this change. Over what resources are struggles likely to develop? What impact do you think this changing mix might have on European Americans? On Latinos? On African Americans? On Asian Americans? On Native Americans? What changes in immigration laws (or their enforcement) can you anticipate?

To apply the *symbolic interactionist perspective*, consider how groups might perceive one another differently as their proportion of the population changes. How do you think that this changed perception will affect people's behavior?

To apply the *functionalist perspective*, try to determine how each racial-ethnic group will benefit from this changing mix. How will other parts of society (such as businesses) benefit? What functions and dysfunctions can you anticipate for politics, economics, education, or religion?

FIGURE 11 Projections of the Racial–Ethnic Makeup of the U.S. Population

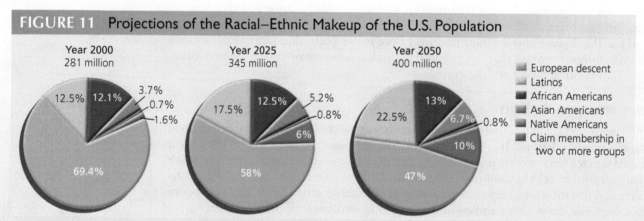

Sources: By the author. Based on Bernstein and Bergman 2003; *Statistical Abstract of the United States* 2004: Table 16; 2005: Table 1 modified the projections based on the new census category of membership in two or more groups and trends in interethnic marriage.

This national debate crystallized with a series of controversial rulings. One of the most significant was *Proposition 209*, a 1996 amendment to the California state constitution. This amendment made it illegal to give preference to minorities and women in hiring, promotion, and college admissions. Despite appeals by a coalition of civil rights groups, the U.S. Supreme Court upheld this California law.

A second significant ruling was made by the Supreme Court of Michigan in 2003. White students who had been denied admission to the University of Michigan claimed that they had been discriminated against because less qualified applicants had been admitted on the basis of their race. The Court ruled that universities can give minorities an edge in admissions, but there must be a meaningful review of individual applicants. Mechanical systems, such as giving extra points because of race, are unconstitutional. This murky message satisfied no one, as no one knew what it really meant.

To remove ambiguity, opponents of affirmative action put amendments to several state constitutions on the ballot. The amendments, which make it illegal for public institutions to even consider race or sex in hiring, in awarding contracts, or in college admissions, failed in some states, such as Colorado, but became law in Michigan and Nebraska (Lewin 2007; Kaufman and Fields 2008).

With constitutional battles continuing, the issue of affirmative action in a multicultural society is likely to remain center stage for quite some time.

Steve Chenn/Corbis

The United States is the most racially–ethnically diverse society in the world. This can be our central strength, with our many groups working together to build a harmonious society, a stellar example for the world. Or it can be our Achilles heel, with us breaking into feuding groups, a Balkanized society that marks an ill-fitting end to a grand social experiment. Our reality will probably fall somewhere between these extremes.

By the Numbers: *Then and Now*

Percentage of Americans who claim membership in these groups:

European descent

2000	NOW	2050
69%	66%	47%

Latino descent

2000	NOW	2050
13%	15%	23%

African descent

2000	NOW	2050
12%	12%	13%

Asian descent

2000	NOW	2050
3.7%	4.3%	6.7%

Native American descent

2000	NOW	2050
0.7%	0.75%	0.8%

Toward a True Multicultural Society

The United States has the potential to become a society in which racial–ethnic groups not only coexist, but also respect one another—and thrive—as they work together for mutually beneficial goals. In a true multicultural society, the minority groups that make up the United States would participate fully in the nation's social institutions while maintaining their cultural integrity. Reaching this goal will require that we understand that "the biological differences that divide one race from another add up to a drop in the genetic ocean." For a long time, we have given racial categories an importance they never merited. Now we need to figure out how to reduce them to the irrelevance they deserve. In short, we need to make real the abstraction called equality that we profess to believe (Cose 2000).

SUMMARY *and* REVIEW

Laying the Sociological Foundation

How is race both a reality and a myth?

In the sense that different groups inherit distinctive physical traits, race is a reality. There is no agreement regarding what constitutes a particular race, however, or even how many races there are. In the sense of one race being superior to another and of there being pure races, race is a myth. The *idea* of race is powerful, shaping basic relationships among people.

How do race and ethnicity differ?

Race refers to inherited biological characteristics; **ethnicity,** to cultural ones. Members of ethnic groups identify with one another on the basis of common ancestry and cultural heritage.

What are minority and dominant groups?

Minority groups are people who are singled out for unequal treatment by members of the **dominant group,** the group with more power and privilege. Minorities originate with migration or the expansion of political boundaries.

What heightens ethnic identity, and what is "ethnic work"?

A group's relative size, power, physical characteristics, and amount of discrimination heighten or reduce ethnic identity. **Ethnic work** is the process of constructing and maintaining an ethnic identity. For people without a firm ethnic identity, ethnic work is an attempt to recover one's ethnic heritage. For those with strong ties to their culture of origin, ethnic work involves enhancing group distinctions.

Prejudice and Discrimination

Why are people prejudiced?

Prejudice is an attitude, and **discrimination** is an action. Like other attitudes, prejudice is learned in association with others. Prejudice is so extensive that people can show

prejudice against groups that don't even exist. Minorities also internalize the dominant norms, and some show prejudice against their own group.

How do individual and institutional discrimination differ?

Individual discrimination is the negative treatment of one person by another, while **institutional discrimination** is negative treatment that is built into social institutions. Institutional discrimination can occur without the awareness of either the perpetrator or the object of discrimination. Discrimination in health care is one example.

Theories of Prejudice

How do psychologists explain prejudice?

Psychological theories of prejudice stress the **authoritarian personality** and frustration displaced toward **scapegoats.**

How do sociologists explain prejudice?

Sociological theories focus on how different social environments increase or decrease prejudice. *Functionalists* stress the benefits and costs that come from discrimination. *Conflict theorists* look at how the groups in power exploit racial–ethnic divisions in order to control workers and maintain power. *Symbolic interactionists* stress how labels create **selective perception** and self-fulfilling prophecies.

Global Patterns of Intergroup Relations

What are the major patterns of minority and dominant group relations?

Beginning with the least humane, they are **genocide, population transfer, internal colonialism, segregation, assimilation,** and **multiculturalism (pluralism).**

Racial–Ethnic Relations in the United States

What are the major racial–ethnic groups in the United States?

From largest to smallest, the major groups are European Americans, Latinos, African Americans, Asian Americans, and Native Americans.

What are some issues in racial–ethnic relations and characteristics of minority groups?

Latinos are divided by social class and country of origin. African Americans are increasingly divided into middle and lower classes, with two sharply contrasting worlds of experience. On many measures, Asian Americans are bet-ter off than white Americans, but their well-being varies with their country of origin. For Native Americans, the primary issues are poverty, nationhood, and settling treaty obligations. The overarching issue for minorities is over-coming discrimination.

Looking Toward the Future

What main issues dominate U.S. racial–ethnic relations?

The main issues are immigration, affirmative action, and how to develop a true multicultural society. The answers affect our future.

THINKING CRITICALLY

1. How many races do your friends or family think there are? Do they think that one race is superior to the others? What do you think their reaction would be to the sociological position that racial categories are primarily social?

2. A hundred years ago, sociologist W. E. B. Du Bois said, "The problem of the twentieth century is the problem of the color line—the relation of the darker to the lighter races."

Why do you think that the color line remains one of the most volatile topics facing the nation?

3. If you were appointed head of the U.S. Civil Service Commission, what policies would you propose to reduce racial–ethnic strife in the United States? Be ready to explain the sociological principles that might give your proposals a higher chance of success.

ADDITIONAL RESOURCES

What can you find in MySocLab? www.mysoclab.com

- Complete Ebook
- Practice Tests and Video and Audio activities
- Mapping and Data Analysis exercises

- Sociology in the News
- Classic Readings in Sociology
- Research and Writing advice

Where Can I Read More on This Topic?

Blackmon, Douglas A. *A Different Kind of Slavery, The Re-Enslavement of Black Americans from the Civil War to World War II.* New York, Doubleday, 2008. The author documents the horrible conditions African Americans suffered in Georgia during "post-slavery," especially in its criminal "justice" system.

Bullard, Robert D., and Beverly Wright, eds. *Race, Place, and Environmental Justice After Hurricane Katrina: Struggles to Reclaim, Rebuild, and Revitalize New Orleans and the Gulf Coast.* Boulder, Colo.: Westview Press, 2009. Among the other issues of race and place (geography) that the authors examine are the health and environment and what they call "the color of opportunity."

Glover, Karen S. *Racial Profiling: Research, Racism, and Resistance.* Lanham, MD: Rowman & Littlefield, 2009. The author analyzes racial profiling in traffic stops—associating criminality with race–ethnicity—in terms of the rights of citizenship.

Higginbotham, Elizabeth, and Margaret L. Andersen, eds. *Race and Ethnicity in Society: The Changing Landscape,* 2nd ed. Belmont, Calif.: Wadsworth, 2008. From race–ethnicity as a social issue to its relationship to beliefs, ideology, and personal identity, the authors provide a thorough overview of this topic.

Idler, Jose Enrique. *Officially Hispanic: Classification Policy and Identity.* Lanham, Md.: Lexington Books, 2007. How official categories are inadequate for representing the racial–ethnic experience.

Parrillo, Vincent N. *Strangers to These Shores: Race and Ethnic Relations in the United States,* 9th ed. Boston: Allyn and Bacon, 2009. This text reviews the experiences of more than 50 racial–ethnic groups.

Ross, Jeffrey Ian, and Larry Gould, eds. *Native Americans and the Criminal Justice System.* Boulder, Colo.: Paradigm, 2006. The authors of these articles address crime by Native Americans within historical, cultural, and legal contexts and the issue of criminal justices and tribal sovereignty.

Russell, James W. *Class and Race Formation in North America.* Toronto: University of Toronto Press, 2009. As the author explores how race–ethnicity and social class formed in Canada, Mexico, and the United States, he examines the effects and possible future consequences of NAFTA.

Schaefer, Richard T. *Race and Ethnicity in the United States,* 5th ed. Upper Saddle River, New Jersey: Prentice Hall, 2009. The data and analyses of this basic text can help cut through some of the emotional blinders that often accompany this topic.

Sutton, Mark Q. *An Introduction to Native North America,* 3rd ed. Boston: Allyn and Bacon, 2007. An overview of the cultures of Native Americans, with an emphasis on the effects of the European invasion.

White, Michael J., and Jennifer E. Glick. *Achieving Anew: How New Immigrants Do in American Schools, Jobs, and Neighborhoods.* New York: Russell Sage Foundation, 2009. This examination of immigrant life at school, at work, and in communities and shows that recent immigrants and their children are not forming an underclass but are making substantial progress in entering the mainstream.

Williams, Philip J., Timothy Steigenga, and Manual A. Vasquez, eds. *A Place to Be: Brazilian, Guatemalan, and Mexican Immigrants in Florida's New Destinations.* The authors analyze the challenges, resources, and strategies of immigrants as they form community and establish identity. Piscataway, New Jersey: Rutgers University Press, 2009.

Wilson, William Julius. *More Than Just Race: Being Black and Poor in the Inner City.* New York: W.W. Norton, 2009. The author analyzes both cultural and structural factors that maintain poverty in the inner city. Includes policy recommendations.

Zeitz, Joshua M. *White Ethnic New York: Jews, Catholics, and the Shaping of Postwar Politics.* Chapel Hill: University of North Carolina Press, 2007. Examines the sometimes contentious, fractious, and fragile coalition that became politically and culturally significant in this area of the United States.

Marriage and Family

From Chapter 16 of *Sociology: A Down-to-Earth Approach*, 10/e. James M. Henslin. Copyright © 2010 by Pearson Education. Published by Allyn & Bacon. All rights reserved.

Marriage and Family

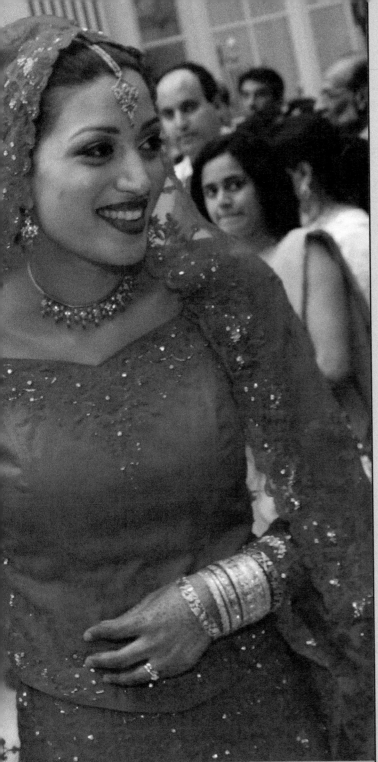

London

Gary Roebuck/Alamy

"Hold still. We're going to be late," said Sharon as she tried to put shoes on 2-year-old Michael, who kept squirming away.

Finally succeeding with the shoes, Sharon turned to 4-year-old Brittany, who was trying to pull a brush through her hair. "It's stuck, Mom," Brittany said.

"Well, no wonder. Just how did you get gum in your hair? I don't have time for this, Brittany. We've got to leave."

> "Yes, he did," Brittany said, crossing her arms defiantly as she kicked her brother's seat.

Getting to the van fifteen minutes behind schedule, Sharon strapped the kids in, and then herself. Just as she was about to pull away, she remembered that she had not checked the fridge for messages.

"Just a minute, kids. I'll be right back."

Running into the house, she frantically searched for a note from Tom. She vaguely remembered him mumbling something about being held over at work. She grabbed the Post-It and ran back to the van.

"He's picking on me," complained Brittany when her mother climbed back in.

"Oh, shut up, Brittany. He's only 2. He can't pick on you."

"Yes, he did," Brittany said, crossing her arms defiantly as she stretched out her foot to kick her brother's seat.

"Oh, no! How did Mikey get that smudge on his face? Did you do that, Brit?"

Brittany crossed her arms again, pushing out her lips in her classic pouting pose.

As Sharon drove to the day care center, she tried to calm herself. "Only two more days of work this week, and then the weekend. Then I can catch up on housework and have a little relaxed time with the kids. And Tom can finally cut the grass and buy the groceries," she thought. "And maybe we'll even have time to make love. Boy, that's been a long time."

At a traffic light, Sharon found time to read Tom's note. "Oh, no. That's what he meant. He has to work Saturday. Well, there go those plans."

What Sharon didn't know was that her boss had also made plans for Sharon's Saturday. And that their emergency Saturday babysitter wouldn't be available. And that Michael was coming down with the flu. And that Brittany would follow next. And that . . .

polygyny a form of marriage in which men have more than one wife

polyandry a form of marriage in which women have more than one husband

family two or more people who consider themselves related by blood, marriage, or adoption

household people who occupy the same housing unit

nuclear family a family consisting of a husband, wife, and child(ren)

family of orientation the family in which a person grows up

family of procreation the family formed when a couple's first child is born

"There just isn't enough time to get everything done!" Most of us have this complaint, but it is especially true for working parents of young children. Unlike parents in the past, today's young parents find themselves without the support that used to be taken for granted: stay-at-home moms who provided stability to the neighborhood, husbands whose sole income was enough to support a wife and several children, a safe neighborhood where even small children could play outside, and grandmas who could pitch in during emergencies.

Those days are gone, most likely forever. Today, more and more families are like Sharon and Tom's. They are harried, working more but haunted by debt, and seeming to have less time for one another. In this chapter, we shall try to understand what is happening to the U.S. family and to families worldwide.

Marriage and Family in Global Perspective

To better understand U.S. patterns of marriage and family, let's first look at how customs differ around the world. This will give us a context for interpreting our own experience with this vital social institution.

What Is a Family?

"What is a family, anyway?" asked William Sayres in an article on this topic. In posing this question, he (1992) meant that although the family is so significant to humanity that it is universal—every human group in the world organizes its members in families—the world's cultures display so much variety that the term *family* is difficult to define. For example, although the Western world regards a family as a husband, wife, and children, other groups have family forms in which men have more than one wife (**polygyny**) or women more than one husband (**polyandry).** How about the obvious? Can we define the family as the approved group into which children are born? Then we would be overlooking the Banaro of New Guinea. In this group, a young woman must give birth *before* she can marry—and she *cannot* marry the father of her child (Murdock 1949).

What if we were to define the family as the unit in which parents are responsible for disciplining children and providing for their material needs? This, too, is not universal. Among the Trobriand Islanders, it is not the parents but the wife's eldest brother who is responsible for providing the children's discipline and their food (Malinowski 1927).

Such remarkable variety means that we have to settle for a broad definition. A **family** consists of people who consider themselves related by blood, marriage, or adoption. A **household,** in contrast, consists of people who occupy the same housing unit—a house, apartment, or other living quarters.

We can classify families as **nuclear** (husband, wife, and children) and **extended** (including people such as grandparents, aunts, uncles, and cousins in addition to the nuclear unit). Sociologists also refer to the **family of orientation** (the family in which an individual grows up) and the **family of procreation** (the family that is formed when a couple has its first child).

What Is Marriage?

We have the same problem here. For just about every element you might regard as essential to marriage, some group has a different custom.

Consider the sex of the bride and groom. Until recently, this was taken-for-granted. Then in the 1980s and 1990s, several European

Often one of the strongest family bonds is that of mother–daughter. The young artist, an eleventh grader, wrote: "This painting expresses the way I feel about my future with my child. I want my child to be happy and I want her to love me the same way I love her. In that way we will have a good relationship so that nobody will be able to take us apart. I wanted this picture to be alive; that is why I used a lot of bright colors."

countries legalized same-sex marriages. In 2003, so did Canada, followed by several U.S. states. In 2008, California approved same-sex marriages, and a few months later banned them.

Same-sex marriages sound so new, but when Columbus landed in the Americas, some Native American tribes were already practicing same-sex marriages. Through a ceremony called the *berdache,* a man or woman who wanted to be a member of the opposite sex was officially *declared* to have his or her sex changed. The "new" man or woman put on the clothing of the opposite sex, performed the tasks associated with his or her new sex, and was allowed to marry.

Even sexual relationships don't universally characterize marriage. The Nayar of Malabar never allow a bride and groom to have sex. After a three-day celebration of the marriage, they send the groom packing—and never allow him to see his bride again (La Barre 1954). This can be a little puzzling to figure out, but it works like this: The groom is "borrowed" from another tribe for the ceremony. Although the Nayar bride can't have sex with her husband, after the marriage she can have approved lovers from her tribe. This system keeps family property intact—along matrilineal lines.

At least one thing has to be universal in marriage—that the bride and groom are alive. So you would think. But even in such a basic matter we find an exception. On the Loess Plateau in China, if a man dies without a wife, his parents look for a dead woman to be his bride. After finding one—from parents willing to sell their dead unmarried daughter— the dead man and woman are married and then buried together. Happy that their son will have intimacy in the afterlife, the parents throw a party to celebrate the marriage (Fremson 2006). This is an ancient Chinese practice, and it used to be that the couple was buried in a double coffin (Yao 2002).

With such encompassing cultural variety, we can define **marriage** this way—a group's approved mating arrangements, usually marked by a ritual of some sort (the wedding) to indicate the couple's new public status.

marriage a group's approved mating arrangements, usually marked by a ritual of some sort

Common Cultural Themes

Despite this diversity, several common themes run through marriage and family. As Table 1 illustrates, all societies use marriage and family to establish patterns of mate selection, descent, inheritance, and authority. Let's look at these patterns.

TABLE 1	Common Cultural Themes: Marriage in Traditional and Industrialized Societies	
Characteristic	Traditional Societies	Industrial (and Postindustrial) Societies
What is the structure of marriage?	*Extended* (marriage embeds spouses in a large kinship network of explicit obligations)	*Nuclear* (marriage brings fewer obligations toward the spouse's relatives)
What are the functions of marriage?	Encompassing (see the six functions listed later in this chapter)	More limited (many functions are fulfilled by other social institutions)
Who holds authority?	*Patriarchal* (authority is held by males)	Although some patriarchal features remain, authority is divided more equally
How many spouses at one time?	Most have one spouse (*monogamy*), while some have several (*polygamy*)	One spouse
Who selects the spouse?	Parents, usually the father, select the spouse	Individuals choose their own spouse
Where does the couple live?	Couples usually reside with the groom's family (*patrilocal residence*), less commonly with the bride's family (*matrilocal residence*)	Couples establish a new home (*neolocal residence*)
How is descent figured?	Usually figured from male ancestors (*patrilineal kinship*), less commonly from female ancestors (*matrilineal kinship*)	Figured from male and female ancestors equally (*bilineal kinship*)
How is inheritance figured?	Rigid system of rules; usually patrilineal, but can be matrilineal	Highly individualistic; usually bilineal

Source: By the author.

Mate Selection. Each human group establishes norms to govern who marries whom. If a group has norms of **endogamy,** it specifies that its members must marry *within* their group. For example, some groups prohibit interracial marriage. In some societies, these norms are written into law, but in most cases they are informal. In the United States, most whites marry whites, and most African Americans marry African Americans—not because of any laws but because of informal norms. In contrast, norms of **exogamy** specify that people must marry *outside* their group. The best example of exogamy is the **incest taboo,** which prohibits sex and marriage among designated relatives.

As you can see from Table 1 on the previous page, how people find mates varies around the world, from fathers selecting them, with no input from those who are to marry, to the highly individualistic, personal choices common in Western cultures. Changes in mate selection are the focus of the Sociology and the New Technology box on the next page.

Descent. How are you related to your father's father or to your mother's mother? The answer to this question is not the same all over the world. Each society has a **system of descent,** the way people trace kinship over generations. We use a **bilineal system,** for we think of ourselves as related to *both* our mother's and our father's sides of the family. "Doesn't everyone?" you might ask. Ours, however, is only one logical way to reckon descent. Some groups use a **patrilineal system,** tracing descent only on the father's side; they don't think of children as being related to their mother's relatives. Others follow a **matrilineal system,** tracing descent only on the mother's side, and not considering children to be related to their father's relatives. The Naxi of China, for example, don't even have a word for father (Hong 1999).

Inheritance. Marriage and family—in whatever form is customary in a society—are also used to determine rights of inheritance. In a bilineal system, property is passed to both males and females, in a patrilineal system only to males, and in a matrilineal system (the rarest form), only to females. No system is natural. Rather, each matches a group's ideas of justice and logic.

Authority. Historically, some form of **patriarchy,** a social system in which men dominate women, has formed a thread that runs through all societies. Contrary to what some think, there are no historical records of a true **matriarchy,** a social system in which women as a group dominate men as a group. Our marriage and family customs, then, developed within a framework of patriarchy. Although U.S. family patterns are becoming more **egalitarian,** or equal, some of today's customs still reflect their patriarchal origin. One of the most obvious examples is U.S. naming patterns. Despite some changes, the typical bride still takes the groom's last name, and children usually receive the father's last name.

Marriage and Family in Theoretical Perspective

As we have seen, human groups around the world have many forms of mate selection, ways to trace descent, and ways to view the parent's responsibility. Although these patterns are arbitrary, each group perceives its own forms of marriage and family as natural. Now let's see what pictures emerge when we view marriage and family theoretically.

The Functionalist Perspective: Functions and Dysfunctions

Functionalists stress that to survive, a society must fulfill basic functions (that is, meet its basic needs). When functionalists look at marriage and family, they examine how they are related to other parts of society, especially the ways that marriage and family contribute to the well-being of society.

endogamy the practice of marrying within one's own group

exogamy the practice of marrying outside one's own group

incest taboo the rule that prohibits sex and marriage among designated relatives

system of descent how kinship is traced over the generations

bilineal (system of descent) a system of reckoning descent that counts both the mother's and the father's side

patrilineal (system of descent) a system of reckoning descent that counts only the father's side

matrilineal (system of descent) a system of reckoning descent that counts only the mother's side

patriarchy a group in which men as a group dominate women as a group; authority is vested in males

matriarchy a society in which women as a group dominate men as a group

egalitarian authority more or less equally divided between people or groups (in marriage, for example, between husband and wife)

SOCIOLOGY and the NEW TECHNOLOGY

Finding a Mate: Not the Same as It Used to Be

Things haven't changed entirely. Boys and girls still get interested in each other at their neighborhood schools, and men and women still meet at college. Friends still serve as matchmakers and introduce friends, hoping they might click. People still meet at churches and bars, at the mall and at work.

But the Internet is bringing fundamental changes. Dating sites advertise that they offer thousands of potential companions, lovers, or spouses. For a low monthly fee, you can meet the person of your dreams.

The photos on these sites are fascinating. Some seem to be lovely people, warm, attractive, and vivacious, and one wonders why they are posting their photos and personal information online. Do they have some secret flaw that they need to do this? Others seem okay, although perhaps a bit needy. Then there are the pitiful, and one wonders whether they will ever find a mate, or even a hookup, for that matter. Some are desperate, begging for someone—anyone—to contact them: women who try for sexy poses, exposing too much flesh, suggesting the promise of at least a good time, and men who try their best to look like hulks, their muscular presence promising the same.

The Internet dating sites are not filled with losers, although there are plenty of them. Many regular, ordinary people post their profiles, too. And some do find the person of their dreams—or at least adequate

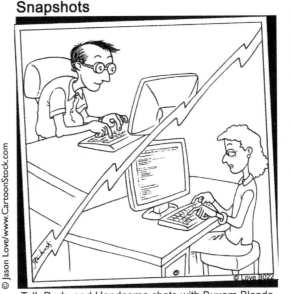

Snapshots

Tall, Dark, and Handsome chats with Buxom Blonde.

© Jason Love/www.CartoonStock.com

matches. With Internet postings losing their stigma, electronic matchmaking is becoming an acceptable way to find a mate.

Matchmaking sites tout "thousands of eligible prospects." Unfortunately, the prospects are spread over the nation, and few people want to invest in a plane ticket only to find that the "prospect" doesn't even resemble the posted photo. You can do a search for your area, but there are likely to be few candidates from it.

Not to worry. More technology to the rescue.

The ease and comfort of "dating on demand." You sit at home, turn on your TV, and use your remote to search for your partner. Your local cable company has done all the hard work—hosting singles events at bars and malls, where they tape singles talking about themselves and what they are looking for in a mate (Grant 2005).

You can view the videos free. And if you get interested in someone, for just a small fee you can contact the individual.

Now all you need to do is to hire a private detective—also available online for another fee—to see if this engaging person is already married, has a dozen kids, has been sued for paternity or child support, or is a child molester or a rapist.

For Your Consideration

What is your opinion of electronic dating sites? Have you used one? Would you consider using an electronic dating site (if you were single and unattached)? Why or why not?

Why the Family Is Universal. Although the form of marriage and family varies from one group to another, the family is universal. The reason for this, say functionalists, is that the family fulfills six needs that are basic to the survival of every society. These needs, or functions, are (1) economic production, (2) socialization of children, (3) care of the sick and aged, (4) recreation, (5) sexual control, and (6) reproduction. To make certain that these functions are performed, every human group has adopted some form of the family.

Functions of the Incest Taboo. Functionalists note that the incest taboo helps families to avoid *role confusion.* This, in turn, facilitates the socialization of children. For example, if father–daughter incest were allowed, how should a wife treat her daughter—as a daughter, as a subservient second wife, or even as a rival? Should the daughter consider her mother as a mother, as the first wife, or as a rival? Would her father be a father or a lover? And would the wife be the husband's main wife, a secondary wife—or even the "mother of the other wife" (whatever role that might be)? And if the daughter had a child by her father, what relationships would everyone have? Maternal incest would also lead to complications every bit as confusing as these.

The incest taboo also forces people to look outside the family for marriage partners. Anthropologists theorize that *exogamy* was especially functional in tribal societies, for it forged alliances between tribes that otherwise might have killed each other off. Today, exogamy still extends both the bride's and the groom's social networks by adding and building relationships with their spouse's family and friends.

Isolation and Emotional Overload. As you know, functionalists also analyze dysfunctions. One of those dysfunctions comes from the relative isolation of today's nuclear family. Because extended families are enmeshed in large kinship networks, their members can count on many people for material and emotional support. In nuclear families, in contrast, the stresses that come with crises such as the loss of a job—or even the routine pressures of a harried life, as depicted in our opening vignette—are spread among fewer people. This places greater strain on each family member, creating *emotional overload.* In addition, the relative isolation of the nuclear family makes it vulnerable to a "dark side"—incest and various other forms of abuse, matters that we examine later in this chapter.

The Conflict Perspective: Struggles Between Husbands and Wives

Anyone who has been married or who has seen a marriage from the inside knows that—despite a couple's best intentions—conflict is a part of marriage. Conflict inevitably arises between two people who live intimately and who share most everything in life—from their goals and checkbooks to their bedroom and children. At some point, their desires and approaches to life clash, sometimes mildly and sometimes quite harshly. Conflict among married people is so common that it is the grist of soap operas, movies, songs, and novels.

Throughout the generations, power has been a major source of conflict between wives and husbands: Husbands have had much more power, and wives have resented it. In the United States, as you know, the change has been far-reaching. Do your think that one day wives will have more power than their husbands? Maybe they already do. Look at Figure 1. Based on a national sample, this figure shows who makes decisions concerning the family's finances and purchases, what to do on the weekends, and even what to watch on television. As you can see, wives now have more control over the family purse and make more of these decisions than do their husbands. These findings are a surprise, and we await confirmation by future studies.

For those marriages marked by the heat of conflict or the coldness of indifference, divorce is a common solution. Divorce can mark the end of the relationship and its problems, or it can merely indicate a changed legal relationship within which the couple's problems persist as they continue to quarrel about finances and children. We will return to the topic of divorce later in this chapter.

The Symbolic Interactionist Perspective: Gender, Housework, and Child Care

Changes in Traditional Orientations. Throughout the generations, housework and child care have been regarded as "women's work," and men have resisted getting involved. As more women began to work for wages, however, men came to feel pressure to do housework and to be more involved in the care of their children. But no man wanted to be thought of as a sissy or under the control of a woman, a sharp conflict with his culturally rooted feelings of

FIGURE 1 Who Makes the Decisions at Home?

- Wife makes more — 43%
- Husband makes more — 26%
- Couples divide decisions equally — 31%

Note: Based on a nationally representative sample, with questions on who chooses weekend activities, buys things for the home, decides what to watch on television, and manages household finances.
Source: Morin and Cohn 2008.

manhood and the reputation he wanted to maintain among his friends and family.

As women put in more hours at paid work, men gradually began to do more housework and to take on more responsibility for the care of their children. When men first began to change diapers—at least openly—it was big news. Comedians even told jokes about Mr. Mom, giving expression to common concerns about a future of feminized men. (Could Mr. Mom go to war and defend the country?)

Ever so slowly, cultural ideas changed, and housework, care of children, and paid labor came to be regarded as the responsibilities of both men and women. (And ever so gradually, women have become soldiers.) Let's examine these changing responsibilities in the family.

Who Does What? Figure 2 illustrates several significant changes that have taken place in U.S. families. The first is likely to surprise you. If you look closely at this figure, you will see that not only are husbands spending more time taking care of the children but so are wives. This is fascinating: *Both* husbands and wives are spending more time in child care.

How can children be getting *more* attention from their parents than they used to? This flies in the face of our mythical past, the *Leave-It-to-Beaver* images that color our perception of the present. It also contradicts images like that in our opening vignette, of both mothers and fathers working as they struggle to support themselves and their children. We know that

In Hindu marriages, the roles of husband and wife are firmly established. Neither this woman, whom I photographed in Chittoor, India, nor her husband question whether she should carry the family wash to the village pump. Women here have done this task for millennia. As India industrializes, as happened in the West, who does the wash will be questioned—and may eventually become a source of strain in marriage.

James M. Henslin

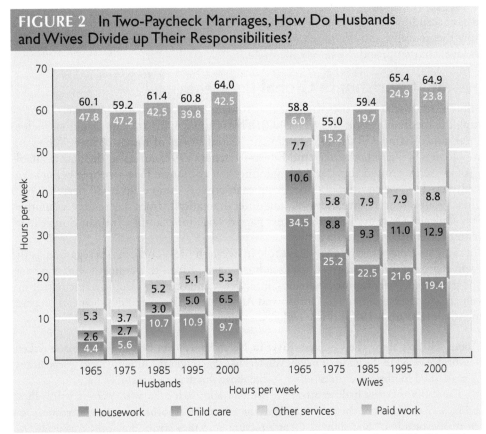

FIGURE 2 In Two-Paycheck Marriages, How Do Husbands and Wives Divide up Their Responsibilities?

Source: By the author. Based on Bianchi et al. 2006. Housework hours are from Table 5.1, child care from Table 4.1, and work hours and total hours from Table 3.4. Other services is derived by subtracting the hours for housework, child care, and paid work from the total hours.

families are not leisurely lolling through their days as huge paychecks flow in, so if parents are spending more time with their children, just where is the time coming from?

Today's parents are squeezing out more hours for their children by spending less time on social activities and by participating less in organizations. But this accounts for only some of the time. Look again at Figure 2, but this time focus on the hours that husbands and wives spend doing housework. Although men are doing more housework than they used to, women are spending so much less time on housework that the total hours that husbands and wives spend on housework have dropped from 38.9 to 29.1 hours a week. This leaves a lot more time to spend with the children.

Does this mean that today's parents aren't as fussy about housework as their parents were, and today's houses are dirtier and messier? That is one possibility. Or technology could be the explanation. Perhaps microwaves, dishwashers, more efficient washing machines and clothes dryers, and wrinkle-free clothing have saved hours of drudgery, leaving home hygiene about the same as before (Bianchi et al. 2006). The time savings from the "McDonaldization", with people eating more "fast foods," are also substantial. It is likely that both explanations are true.

Finally, from Figure 2, you can see that husbands and wives spend their time differently. In what sociologists call a *gendered division of labor,* husbands still take the primary responsibility for earning the income and wives the primary responsibility for taking care of the house and children. You can also see that a shift is taking place in this traditional gender orientation: Wives are spending more time earning the family income, while husbands are spending more time on housework and child care. In light of these trends and with changing ideas of gender—of what is considered appropriate for husbands and wives—we can anticipate greater marital equality in the future.

The Family Life Cycle

We have seen how the forms of marriage and family vary widely, looked at marriage and family theoretically, and examined major changes in family relationships. Now let's discuss love, courtship, and the family life cycle.

Love and Courtship in Global Perspective

Until recently, social scientists thought that romantic love originated in western Europe during the medieval period (Mount 1992). This is strange, for ancient accounts, such as Genesis and 1 Samuel in the Old Testament, record stories of romantic love. When anthropologists William Jankowiak and Edward Fischer (1992) surveyed the data available on 166 societies around the world, they found that **romantic love**—people being sexually attracted to one another and idealizing each other—showed up in 88 percent (147) of these groups. Ideas of love, however, can differ dramatically from one society to another. As the Cultural Diversity box on the next page details, for example, Indians don't expect love to occur until *after* marriage.

Because love plays such a significant role in Western life—and often is regarded as the *only* proper basis for marriage—social scientists have probed this concept with the tools of the trade: experiments, questionnaires, interviews, and observations. In a fascinating experiment, psychologists Donald Dutton and Arthur Aron discovered that fear can produce romantic love (Rubin 1985). Here's what they did.

About 230 feet above the Capilano River in North Vancouver, British Columbia, a rickety footbridge sways in the wind. It makes you feel like you might fall into the rocky gorge below. A more solid footbridge crosses only ten feet above the shallow stream.

The experimenters had an attractive woman approach men who were crossing these bridges. She told them she was studying "the effects of exposure to scenic attractions on creative expression." She showed them a picture, and they wrote down their associations. The sexual imagery in their stories showed that the men on the unsteady, frightening bridge were more sexually aroused than were the men on the solid bridge. More of these men also called the young woman afterward—supposedly to get information about the study.

romantic love feelings of sexual attraction accompanied by an idealization of the other

Cultural Diversity around the World

India

East Is East and West Is West: Love and Arranged Marriage in India

After Arun Bharat Ram returned to India with a degree from the University of Michigan, his mother announced that she wanted to find him a wife. Arun would be a good catch anywhere: 27 years old, educated, well-mannered, intelligent, handsome—and, not incidentally, heir to a huge fortune.

Arun's mother already had someone in mind. Manju came from a middle-class family and was a college graduate. Arun and Manju met in a coffee shop at a luxury hotel—along with both sets of parents. He found her pretty and quiet. He liked that. She was impressed that he didn't boast about his background.

After four more meetings, including one at which the two young people met by themselves, the parents asked their children whether they were willing to marry. Neither had any major objections.

The Prime Minister of India and fifteen hundred other guests came to the wedding.

"I didn't love him," Manju says. "But when we talked, we had a lot in common." She then adds, "But now I couldn't live without him. I've never thought of another man since I met him."

Despite India's many changes, parents still arrange about 90 percent of marriages. Unlike the past, however, today's couples have veto power over their parents' selection. Another innovation is that the prospective bride and groom are allowed to talk to each other before the wedding—unheard of a generation or two ago.

Why do Indians have arranged marriages? And why does this practice persist, even among the educated and upper classes? We can also ask why the United States has such an individualistic approach to marriage.

The answers to these questions take us to two sociological principles. First, *a group's marriage practices match its values.* Individual mate selection matches U.S. values of individuality and independence, while arranged marriages match the Indian value of children deferring to parental authority. To Indians, allowing unrestricted dating would mean entrusting important matters to inexperienced young people.

Second, *a group's marriage practices match its patterns of social stratification.* Arranged marriages in India affirm caste lines by channeling marriage within the same caste. Unchaperoned dating would encourage premarital sex, which, in turn, would break down family lines. Virginity at marriage, in contrast, assures the upper castes that they know who fathered the children. Consequently, Indians socialize their children to think that parents have superior wisdom in these matters. In the United States, where family lines are less important and caste is an alien concept, the practice of young people choosing their own dating partners mirrors the relative openness of our social class system.

These different backgrounds have produced contrasting ideas of love. Americans idealize love as something mysterious, a passion that suddenly seizes an individual. Indians view love as a peaceful feeling that develops when a man and a woman are united in intimacy and share life's interests and goals. For Americans, love just "happens," while for Indians the right conditions create love. Marriage is one of those right conditions.

The end result is this startling difference: *For Americans, love produces marriage—while for Indians, marriage produces love.*

James M. Henslin

This billboard in Chennai, India, caught my attention. As the text indicates, even though India is industrializing, most of its people still follow traditional customs. This billboard is a sign of changing times.

For Your Consideration

What advantages do you see to the Indian approach to love and marriage? Could the Indian system work in the United States? Why or why not? Do you think that love can be created? Or does love suddenly "seize" people? What do you think love is anyway?

Sources: Based on Gupta 1979; Bumiller 1992; Sprecher and Chandak 1992; Dugger 1998; Gautham 2002; Easley 2003, Berger 2007; Swati and Ey 2008.

homogamy the tendency of people with similar characteristics to marry one another

You may have noticed that this research was really about sexual attraction, not love. The point, however, is that romantic love usually begins with sexual attraction. Finding ourselves sexually attracted to someone, we spend time with that person. If we discover mutual interests, we may label our feelings "love." Apparently, then, *romantic love has two components*. The first is emotional, a feeling of sexual attraction. The second is cognitive, a label that we attach to our feelings. If we attach this label, we describe ourselves as being "in love."

Marriage

In the typical case, marriage in the United States is preceded by "love," but, contrary to folklore, whatever love is, it certainly is not blind. That is, love does not hit us willy-nilly, as if Cupid had shot darts blindly into a crowd. If it did, marital patterns would be unpredictable. An examination of who marries whom, however, reveals that love is socially channeled.

The Social Channels of Love and Marriage. The most highly predictable social channels are age, education, social class, and race–ethnicity. For example, a Latina with a college degree whose parents are both physicians is likely to fall in love with and marry a Latino slightly older than herself who has graduated from college. Similarly, a girl who drops out of high school and whose parents are on welfare is likely to fall in love with and marry a man who comes from a background similar to hers.

Sociologists use the term **homogamy** to refer to the tendency of people who have similar characteristics to marry one another. Homogamy occurs largely as a result of *propinquity,* or spatial nearness. That is, we tend to "fall in love" with and marry people who live near us or whom we meet at school, church, or work. The people with whom we associate are far from a random sample of the population, for social filters produce neighborhoods, schools, and places of worship that follow racial–ethnic and social class lines.

As with all social patterns, there are exceptions. Although 93 percent of Americans who marry choose someone of their same racial–ethnic background, 7 percent do not. Because there are 60 million married couples in the United States, those 7 percent add up, totaling over 4 million couples (*Statistical Abstract* 2009: Table 59).

One of the more dramatic changes in U.S. marriage patterns is the increase in marriages between African Americans and whites. Today it is difficult to realize how norm-shattering such marriages used to be, but they used to be illegal in 40 states (Staples 2008). Mississippi had the most extreme penalty for interracial marriage: *life in prison* (Crossen 2004b). Despite the risks, a few couples crossed the "color line," but it took the social upheaval of the 1960s to break this barrier permanently. In 1967, the U.S. Supreme Court struck down the state laws that prohibited such marriages.

Figure 3 illustrates this change. Look at the race–ethnicity of the husbands and wives in these marriages, and you will see that here, too, Cupid's arrows don't hit random targets. Why do you think this particular pattern exists?

Childbirth

Ideal Family Size. The number of children that Americans consider ideal has changed over the years, with preferences moving to smaller families. Figure 4 shows this change, based on questions the Gallup organization has been asking since the 1930s. Religion shows an interesting divide, not between Protestants and Roman Catholics, who give the same

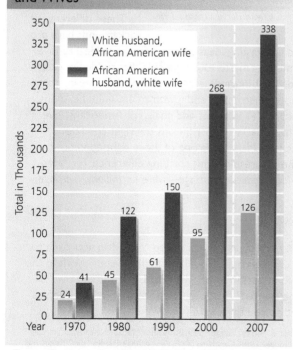

FIGURE 3 Marriages Between Whites and African Americans: The Race–Ethnicity of the Husbands and Wives

Source: By the author. *Based on Statistical Abstract of the United States* 1990: Table 53; 2009: Table 59.

FIGURE 4   The Number of Children Americans Think Are Ideal

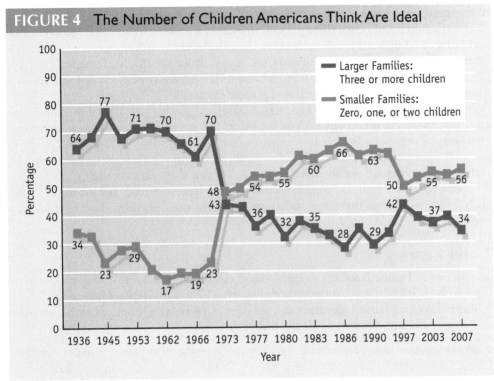

Legend:
- Larger Families: Three or more children
- Smaller Families: Zero, one, or two children

Source: Gallup Poll, June 26, 2007.

answers, but by church attendance. Those who attend services more often prefer larger families than those who attend less often. The last couple of polls have revealed a rather unexpected divide: Younger Americans (ages 18 to 34) prefer larger families than do those who are older than 34 (Gallup Poll, June 26, 2007).

Marital Satisfaction.   Sociologists have found that after the birth of a child marital satisfaction usually decreases (Claxton and Perry-Jenkins 2008; Simon 2008). To

The average woman in the United States gives birth to two children. "Average" is made up of the extremes of zero children to the 18 of Michelle Duggar and her husband Jim Bob of Rogers, Arkansas. The couple is shown here after the birth of their 18th child. One child was not present when the photo was taken.

AP Images/Beth Hal

225

understand why, keep in mind that a dyad (two persons) provides greater intimacy than a triad (after adding a third person, interaction must be shared). In addition, the birth of a child unbalances the roles that the couple have worked out (Knauth 2000). To move from the abstract to the concrete, think about the implications for marriage of coping with a fragile newborn's 24-hour-a-day needs of being fed, soothed, and diapered—while having less sleep and greater expenses.

Yet husbands and wives continue to have children, not because they don't know how to avoid conceiving them, but because having their own child brings them so much satisfaction. New parents bubble over with joy, saying things like, "There's no feeling to compare with holding your own child in your arms. Those little hands, those tiny feet, those big eyes, that little nose, that sweet face . . ." and they gush on and on.

This is why there really is no equivalent to parents. It is *their* child, and no one else takes such delight in a baby's first steps, its first word, and so on. Let's turn, then, to child rearing.

Child Rearing

As you saw in Figure 2, today's parents—both mothers and fathers—are spending more time with their children than parents did in the 1970s and 1980s. Despite this trend, with mothers and fathers spending so many hours away from home at work, we must ask: Who's minding the kids while the parents are at work?

Married Couples and Single Mothers. Figure 5 on the next page compares the child care arrangements of married couples and single mothers. As you can see, their overall arrangements are similar. A main difference is the role of the child's father while the mother is at work. For married couples, about one of five children is cared for by the father, while for single mothers, care by the father drops in half to one of ten. As you can see, grandparents and other relatives help fill the gap left by the absent father. Single mothers also rely more on organized day care.

Day Care. Figure 5 also shows that about one of four children is in day care. Apparently only a minority of U.S. day care centers offer high-quality care as measured by whether they provide safety, stimulating learning activities, and emotional warmth (Bergmann 1995; Blau 2000). A primary reason for this dismal situation is the low salaries paid to day care workers, who average only about $16,000 a year ("Child Day Care Services" 2009).

It is difficult for parents to judge the quality of day care, since they don't know what takes place when they are not there. If you ever look for day care, two factors best predict that children will receive quality care: staff who have taken courses in early childhood development and a low ratio of children per staff member (Blau 2000; Belsky et al. 2007). If you have nagging fears that your children might be neglected or even abused, choose a center that streams live Web cam images on the Internet. While at work, you can "visit" each room of the day care center via cyberspace and monitor your toddler's activities and care.

Nannies. For upper-middle-class parents, nannies have become a popular alternative to day care centers. Parents love the one-on-one care. They also like the convenience of in-home care, which eliminates the need to transport the child to an unfamiliar environment, reduces the chances that the child will catch illnesses, and eliminates the hardship of parents having to take time off from work when their child becomes ill. A recurring problem, how-

"Your attitude is sucking all the fulfillment out of motherhood."

One of the most demanding, exasperating—and also fulfilling—roles in life is that of parent. To really appreciate this cartoon, perhaps one has to have experienced this part of the life course.

ever, is tensions between the parents and the nanny: jealousy that the nanny might see the first step, hear the first word, or—worse yet—be called "mommy." There are also tensions over different discipline styles; disdain on the part of the nanny that the mother isn't staying home with her child; and feelings of guilt or envy as the child cries when the nanny leaves but not when the mother goes to work.

Social Class. Do you think that social class makes a difference in how people rear their children? If you answered "yes," you are right. But what difference? And why? Sociologists have found that working-class parents tend to think of children as wildflowers that develop naturally. Middle-class parents, in contrast, are more likely to think of children as garden flowers that need a lot of nurturing if they are to bloom (Lareau 2002). These contrasting views make a world of difference Working-class parents are more likely to set limits on their children and then let them choose their own activities, while middle-class parents are more likely to try to push their children into activities that they think will develop the children's thinking and social skills.

Sociologist Melvin Kohn (1963, 1977; Kohn and Schooler 1969) also found that the type of work that parents do has an impact on how they rear their children. Because members of the working class are closely supervised on their jobs, where they are expected to follow explicit rules, their concern is less with their children's motivation and more with their outward conformity. These parents are more apt to use physical punishment—which brings about outward conformity without regard for internal attitude. Middle-class workers, in contrast, are expected to take more initiative on the job. Consequently, middle-class parents have more concern that their children develop curiosity and self-expression. They are also more likely to withdraw privileges or affection than to use physical punishment.

FIGURE 5 Who Takes Care of Preschoolers While Their Mothers Are at Work?

MARRIED COUPLES

Mother cares for child at work 4%
Father 21%
Grandparents 17%
Other relatives 5%
Other arrangements[c] 14%
Organized child care facility[a] 23%
Other nonrelatives[b] 17%

SINGLE MOTHERS

Mother cares for child at work 3%
Father 10%
Other arrangements[c] 9%
Grandparents 23%
Other relatives 10%
Other nonrelatives[b] 18%
Organized child care facility[a] 27%

[a] Includes day care centers, nursery schools, preschools, and Head Start programs.
[b] Includes in-home babysitters and other nonrelatives providing care in either the child's or the provider's home.
[c] Includes self-care and no regular arrangements.

Source: America's Children 2005: Table POP8.B.

Family Transitions

The later stages of family life bring their own pleasures to be savored and problems to be solved. Let's look at two transitions—staying home longer and adjusting to widowhood.

"Adultolescents" and the Not-So-Empty Nest. When the last child leaves home, the husband and wife are left, as at the beginning of their marriage, "alone together." This situation, sometimes called the *empty nest*—is not as empty as it used to be. With prolonged education and the high cost of establishing a household, U.S. children are leaving home later. Many stay home during college, and others move back after college. Some (called "boomerang children") strike out on their own, but then find the cost or responsibility too great and return home. Much to their own disappointment, some even leave and return to the parents' home several times. As a result, 42 percent of all U.S. 25- to 29-year-olds are living with their parents (U.S. Census Bureau 2007a:Table A2).

Although these "adultolescents" enjoy the protection of home, they have to work out issues of remaining dependent on their parents at the same time that they are grappling with concerns and fears about establishing independent lives. For the parents, "boomerang children" mean not only a disruption of routines but also disagreements about turf, authority, and responsibilities—items they thought were long ago resolved.

Widowhood. As you know, women are more likely than men to become widowed. There are two reasons for this: On average, women live longer than men, and they usually marry men older than they are. For either women or men, the death of a spouse tears at the self, clawing at identities that had merged through the years. With the one who had become an essential part of the self gone, the survivor, as in adolescence, once again confronts the perplexing question "Who am I?"

The death of a spouse produces what is called the *widowhood effect.* The impact of the death is so strong that it increases the chances that the surviving spouse will die earlier than expected. The "widowhood effect" is not even across the board, however, and those who have gone through anticipatory grief suffer fewer health consequences (Elwert and Christakis 2008). This is apparently because they knew their spouse was going to die, and they were able to make preparations that smoothed the transition—from arranging finances to preparing themselves psychologically for being alone (Hiltz 1989). You can see how saying goodbye and cultivating treasured last memories would help people adjust to the impending death of an intimate companion. Sudden death, in contrast, rips the loved one away, offering no chance for this predeath healing.

Diversity in U.S. Families

As we review some of the vast diversity of U.S. families, it is important to note that we are not comparing any of them to *the* American family. There is no such thing. Rather, family life varies widely throughout the United States. We have already seen in several contexts how significant social class is in our lives. Its significance will continue to be evident as we examine diversity in U.S. families.

African American Families

Note that the heading reads African American *families,* not *the* African American family. There is no such thing as *the* African American family any more than there is *the* white family or *the* Latino family. The primary distinction is not between African

There is no such thing as *the* African American family, any more than there is *the* Native American, Asian American, Latino, or Irish American family. Rather, each racial–ethnic group has different types of families, with the primary determinant being social class.

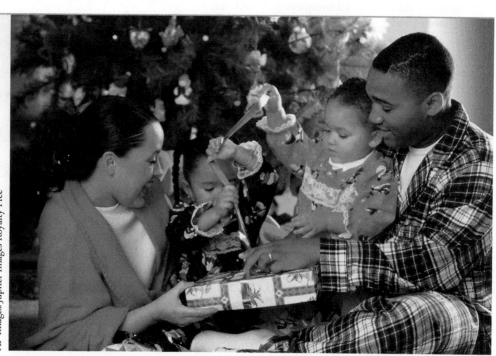

AP Images/Jupiter Images Royalty Free

Americans and other groups, but between social classes (Willie and Reddick 2003). Because African Americans who are members of the upper class follow class interests—preservation of privilege and family fortune—they are especially concerned about the family background of those whom their children marry (Gatewood 1990). To them, marriage is viewed as a merger of family lines. Children of this class marry later than children of other classes.

Middle-class African American families focus on achievement and respectability. Both husband and wife are likely to work outside the home. A central concern is that their children go to college, get good jobs, and marry well—that is, marry people like themselves, respectable and hardworking, who want to get ahead in school and pursue a successful career.

African American families in poverty face all the problems that cluster around poverty (Wilson 1987, 1996; Anderson 1990/2006; Venkatesh 2006). Because the men are likely to have few skills and to be unemployed, it is difficult for them to fulfill the cultural roles of husband and father. Consequently, these families are likely to be headed by a woman and to have a high rate of births to single women. Divorce and desertion are also more common than among other classes. Sharing scarce resources and "stretching kinship" are primary survival mechanisms. People who have helped out in hard times are considered brothers, sisters, or cousins to whom one owes obligations as though they were blood relatives; and men who are not the biological fathers of their children are given fatherhood status (Stack 1974; Hall 2008). Sociologists use the term *fictive kin* to refer to this stretching of kinship.

From Figure 6 you can see that, compared with other groups, African American families are the least likely to be headed by married couples and the most likely to be headed by women. Because African American women tend to go farther in school than African American men, they are more likely than women in other racial–ethnic groups to marry men who are less educated than themselves (Eshleman 2000; Harford 2008).

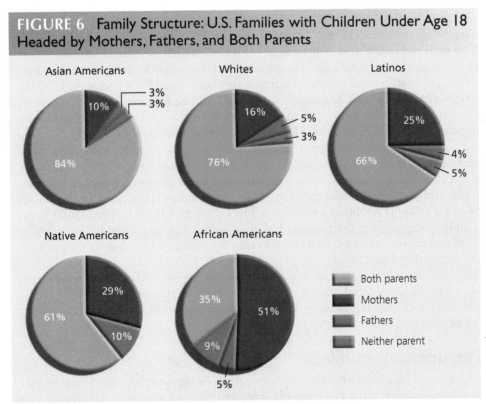

FIGURE 6 Family Structure: U.S. Families with Children Under Age 18 Headed by Mothers, Fathers, and Both Parents

Sources: By the author. For Native Americans, "American Community . . ." 2004. For other groups, *Statistical Abstract of the United States* 2009: Table 68.

229

As with other groups, there is no such thing as *the* Latino family. Some Latino families speak little or no English, while others have assimilated into U.S. culture to such an extent that they no longer speak Spanish.

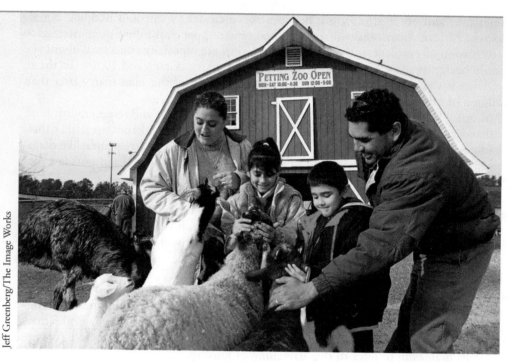

Jeff Greenberg/The Image Works

Latino Families

As Figure 6 shows, the proportion of Latino families headed by married couples and women falls in between that of whites and Native Americans. The effects of social class on families, which I just sketched, also apply to Latinos. In addition, families differ by country of origin. Families from Mexico, for example, are more likely to be headed by a married couple than are families from Puerto Rico (*Statistical Abstract* 2009:Table 38). The longer that Latinos have lived in the United States, the more their families resemble those of middle-class Americans (Saenz 2004).

With such wide variety, experts disagree on what is distinctive about Latino families. Some researchers have found that Latino husbands-fathers play a stronger role than husbands-fathers in white and African American families (Vega 1990; Torres et al. 2002). Others point to the Spanish language, the Roman Catholic religion, and a strong family orientation coupled with a disapproval of divorce, but there are Latino families who are Protestants, don't speak Spanish, and so on. Still others emphasize loyalty to the extended family, with an obligation to support the extended family in times of need (Cauce and Domenech-Rodriguez 2002), but this, too, is hardly unique to Latino families. Descriptions of Latino families used to include **machismo**—an emphasis on male strength, sexual vigor, and dominance—but *machismo* decreases with each generation in the United States and is certainly not limited to Latinos (Hurtado et al. 1992; D. Wood 2001; Torres et al. 2002). Compared to their husbands, Latina wives-mothers tend to be more family-centered and display more warmth and affection for their children, but this is probably true of all racial–ethnic groups.

With such diversity among Latino families, you can see how difficult it is to draw generalizations. The sociological point that runs through all studies of Latino families, however, is this: Social class is more important in determining family life than is either being Latino or a family's country of origin.

Asian American Families

As you can see from Figure 6 on the previous page, Asian American children are more likely than children in other racial–ethnic groups to grow up with both parents. As with the other groups, family life also reflects social class. In addition, because Asian Americans

machismo an emphasis on male strength, high sexuality, and dominance emigrated from many different countries, their family life reflects those many cultures (Jeong and You 2008). As with Latino families, the more recent their immigration, the more closely their family life reflects the patterns in their country of origin (Glenn 1994; Jeong and You 2008).

Despite such differences, sociologist Bob Suzuki (1985), who studied Chinese American and Japanese American families, identified several distinctive characteristics of Asian American families. Although Asian Americans have adopted the nuclear family structure, they tend to retain Confucian values that provide a framework for family life: humanism, collectivity, self-discipline, hierarchy, respect for the elderly, moderation, and obligation. Obligation means that each member of a family owes respect to other family members and has a responsibility never to bring shame on the family. Conversely, a child's success brings honor to the family (Zamiska 2004). To control their children, Asian American parents are more likely to use shame and guilt than physical punishment.

Seldom does the ideal translate into the real, and so it is here. The children born to Asian immigrants confront a bewildering world of incompatible expectations—those of the new culture and those of their parents. As a result, they experience more family conflict and mental problems than do children of Asian Americans who are not immigrants (Meyers 2006; Ying and Han 2008).

Native American Families

Perhaps the single most significant issue that Native American families face is whether to follow traditional values or to assimilate into the dominant culture (Frosch 2008). This primary distinction creates vast differences among families. The traditionals speak native languages and emphasize distinctive Native American values and beliefs. Those who have assimilated into the broader culture do not.

Figure 6 depicts the structure of Native American families. You can see how close it is to that of Latinos. In general, Native American parents are permissive with their children and avoid physical punishment. Elders play a much more active role in their children's families than they do in most U.S. families: Elders, especially grandparents, not only provide child care but also teach and discipline children. Like others, Native American families differ by social class.

To search for *the* Native American family would be fruitless. There are rural, urban, single-parent, extended, nuclear, rich, poor, traditional, and assimilated Native American families, to name just a few. Shown here is an Onondaga Nation family. The wife is a teacher; the husband a Webmaster.

John Berry/Syracuse Newspapers/ The Image Works

FIGURE 7 The Decline of Two-Parent Families

The percentage of children under 18 who live with both parents

*Author's estimate.
Source: By the author. Based on Statistical Abstract of the United States 1995:Table 79; 2009:Table 65.

In Sum: From this brief review, you can see that race–ethnicity signifies little for understanding family life. Rather, social class and culture hold the keys. The more resources a family has, the more it assumes the characteristics of a middle-class nuclear family. Compared with the poor, middle-class families have fewer children and fewer unmarried mothers. They also place greater emphasis on educational achievement and deferred gratification.

One-Parent Families

Another indication of how extensively U.S. families are changing is the increase in one-parent families. From Figure 7, you can see that the percentage of U.S. children who live with two parents (not necessarily their biological parents) has dropped sharply. The concerns—even alarm—that are often expressed about one-parent families may have more to do with their poverty than with children being reared by one parent. Because women head most one-parent families, these families tend to be poor. Although most divorced women earn less than their former husbands, about 85 percent of children of divorce live with their mothers (Aulette 2002).

To understand the typical one-parent family, then, we need to view it through the lens of poverty, for that is its primary source of strain. The results are serious, not just for these parents and their children but also for society. Children from one-parent families are more likely to have behavioral problems in school, to drop out of school, to get arrested, to have physical health problems, to have emotional problems, and to get divorced (McLanahan and Sandefur 1994; Menaghan et al. 1997; McLanahan and Schwartz 2002; Amato and Cheadle 2005; Wen 2008). If female, they are more likely to have sex at a younger age and to bear children while still unmarried teenagers.

Families Without Children

While most married women give birth, about one of five do not (Dye 2008). This is *double* what it was twenty years ago. As you can see from Figure 8, childlessness varies by racial–ethnic group, with whites and Latinas representing the extremes. Some couples are infertile, but most childless couples have made a *choice* to not have children—and they prefer the term *childfree* rather than *childless*. Some decide before marriage that they will never have children, often to attain a sense of freedom—to pursue a career, to be able to change jobs, to travel, and to have less stress (Letherby 2002; Koropeckyj-Cox 2007). In many cases, the couple has simply postponed the date they were going to have their first child until either it was too late to have children or it seemed too uncomfortable to add a child to their lifestyle.

With trends firmly in place—more education and careers for women, advances in contraception, legal abortion, the high cost of rearing children, and an emphasis on possessing more material things—the proportion of women who never bear children is likely to increase. Consider this statement in a newsletter:

> We are DINKS (Dual Incomes, No Kids). We are happily married. I am 43; my wife is 42. We have been married for almost twenty years. . . . Our investment strategy has a lot to do with our personal philosophy: "You can have kids—or you can have everything else!"

Many couples who are not childless by choice desperately want to have children, and they keep trying to do so. Coming to the soul-wrenching conclusion that they can never bear children, many decide to adopt. Some, in contrast, turn to solutions not available to previous generations, the topic of our Sociology and the New Technology box on the next page.

FIGURE 8 What Percentage of U.S. Married Women Never Give Birth?

Source: By the author. Based on women ages 40–44 in Dye 2008.

SOCIOLOGY and the NEW TECHNOLOGY

Rent-a-Womb: "How Much for Your Uterus?"

Let's suppose that you are a married woman—easier, of course, for some to suppose than others. Let's also suppose that you've been trying to get pregnant for several years and that nothing has worked. You and your husband have tried the usual techniques: sex at a certain time of the month, lying on your back, legs up after sex, and so on. Nothing.

You've both been examined by doctors, probed and tested. Everything is fine. You've taken some fertility drugs. Nothing. You've even taken some "just in case" pills that your doctor prescribed. Still nothing.

OK, hard to admit, but you even did some of the superstitious things that your aunt told you to try. Still nothing.

Your gynecologist has told you about surrogacy, that for a fee a woman will rent her womb to you. A fertility expert will mix your egg and your husband's sperm in a little dish and insert the fertilized egg inside a woman who will bear the child for you.

The cost? About $50,000 or so. It might as well be ten times as high. You can't afford it anyway.

Then you hear about a clinic in India. For $15,000, including your plane ticket and hotel, you can get the whole procedure: your egg fertilized and transferred to a young Indian woman, the woman's care including a balanced diet, the hospitalization, the doctor, the delivery, and the necessary papers filed. You even get to look over the young women who are offering their uteruses for rent and pick out one you like. She'll become like part of your family. Or something like that.

Outsourcing pregnancy. What a creative use of capitalism.

No matter how you try, though, you can't get the $15,000 together? Or maybe you have a fear of flying?

Or maybe you think that surrogacy in India is taking advantage of women in poverty?

So have you exhausted all alternatives? Not by a long shot. There are always friends and relatives. OK, none of them is willing. But if no one else, maybe your own old mother can revitalize her womb once more?

Sound too far-fetched to be even a possibility?

Not at all. This is just what Kim Coseno asked her 56-year old mother to do. And her mother agreed. That's their picture on this page. And, yes, Kim's mother did a great job. She delivered triplets for Kim and her husband Joe.

And she didn't charge anything either.

For Your Consideration

If you really wanted children and were not able to get pregnant (or it is your wife in this situation), would you consider surrogacy? Why or why not? Do you think that hiring a poor woman in India to be a surrogate mother for your child is exploitation? (The surrogate mothers are paid several thousand dollars, when the annual Indian wage is about $600.) What do you think about the birth of the triplets shown in the photo below?

Based on Spring 2006; Mukherjee 2007; Associated Press 2008.

An egg from the younger woman shown here in Mayfield Heights, Ohio, was fertilized by her husband and implanted in her mother, the older woman who is holding the triplets. This older woman gave birth to the triplets, making her both the triplets' surrogate mother and grandmother.

AP Images/Hillcrest Hospital

blended family a family whose members were once part of other families

Blended Families

The **blended family,** one whose members were once part of other families, is an increasingly significant type of family in the United States. Two divorced people who marry and each bring their children into a new family unit form a blended family. With divorce common, millions of children spend some of their childhood in blended families. I've never seen a better description of how blended families complicate family relationships than what one of my freshman students wrote:

I live with my dad. I should say that I live with my dad, my brother (whose mother and father are also my mother and father), my half sister (whose father is my dad, but whose mother is my father's last wife), and two stepbrothers and stepsisters (children of my father's current wife). My father's wife (my current stepmother, not to be confused with his second wife who, I guess, is no longer my stepmother) is pregnant, and soon we all will have a new brother or sister. Or will it be a half brother or half sister?

If you can't figure this out, I don't blame you. I have trouble myself. It gets very complicated around Christmas. Should we all stay together? Split up and go to several other homes? Who do we buy gifts for, anyway?

Gay and Lesbian Families

Although a handful of U.S. states allow people of the same sex to marry, 40 states have laws that do not allow same-sex marriages (McKinley and Goostein 2008). Walking a fine conceptual tightrope, some states recognize "registered domestic partnerships," giving legal status to same-sex unions but avoiding the term *marriage.* The result is that most gay and lesbian couples lack both legal marriage and the legal protection of registered "partnerships."

Gay and lesbian couples live throughout the United States, but about half live in just twenty cities, with the greatest concentrations in San Francisco, Los Angeles, Atlanta, New York City, and Washington, D.C. About one-fifth of gay and lesbian couples were previously married to heterosexuals. Twenty-two percent of female couples and 5 percent of male couples have children from their earlier heterosexual marriages (Bianchi and Casper 2000).

What are same-sex relationships like? Like everything else in life, these couples cannot be painted with a single brush stroke. Social class, as it does for opposite-sex couples, significantly shapes orientations to life. Sociologists Philip Blumstein and Pepper Schwartz (1985), who interviewed same-sex couples, found their main struggles to be housework, money, careers, problems with relatives, and sexual adjustment. If these sound familiar, they should be, as they are precisely the same problems that heterosexual couples face. Some find that their sexual orientation brings discrimination, which can add stress to their relationship (Todosijevic et al. 2005). The children they rear have about the same adjustment as children reared by heterosexual parents and are no more likely to have a gay or lesbian sexual orientation (Perrin 2002; "Lesbian and Gay Parenting" 2005). Same-sex couples are more likely to break up, and one argument for legalizing gay marriages is that this will make these relationships more stable. Where same-sex marriages are legal, like opposite-sex marriages, to break them requires negotiating around legal obstacles.

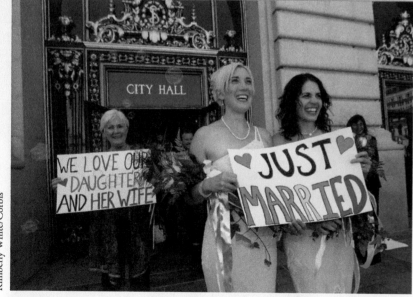

Kimberly White/Corbis

Being fought in U.S. courts is whether or not marriage should be limited to heterosexual couples. This lesbian couple was married in San Francisco, California, in 2008 but later that year California voters passed *Proposition 8,* which limits marriage to men and women.

Trends in U.S. Families

As is apparent from this discussion, marriage and family life in the United States is undergoing a fundamental shift. Let's examine other indicators of this change.

Postponing Marriage and Childbirth

Figure 9 below illustrates one of the most significant changes in U.S. marriages. As you can see, the average age of first-time brides and grooms declined from 1890 to about 1950. In 1890, the typical first-time bride was 22, but by 1950, she had just left her teens. For about twenty years, there was little change. Then in 1970, the average age started to increase sharply. *Today's average first-time bride and groom are older than at any other time in U.S. history.*

Since postponing marriage is today's norm, it may come as a surprise to many readers to learn that *most* U.S. women used to be married by the time they reached age 24. To see this remarkable change, look at Figure 10 on the next page. Postponing marriage has become so common that the percentage of women of this age who are unmarried is now more than *double* what it was in 1970. Another consequence of postponing marriage is that the average age at which U.S. women have their first child is 25.2, also the highest in U.S. history (Mathews and Hamilton 2002; Martin et al. 2007).

Why have these changes occurred? The primary reason is cohabitation. Although Americans have postponed the age at which they first marry, they have *not* postponed the age at which they first set up housekeeping with someone of the opposite sex. Let's look at this trend.

Cohabitation

Figure 11 on the next page shows the increase in **cohabitation,** adults living together in a sexual relationship without being married. This figure is one of the most remarkable in sociology. Hardly ever do we have totals that rise this steeply and consistently. Cohabitation is *ten times* more common today than it was in the 1970s. From a furtive activity, cohabitation has moved into the mainstream, and today most couples who marry have cohabited (Popenoe 2008). Cohabitation has become so common that about 40 percent of U.S. children will spend some time in a cohabiting family (Scommegna 2002).

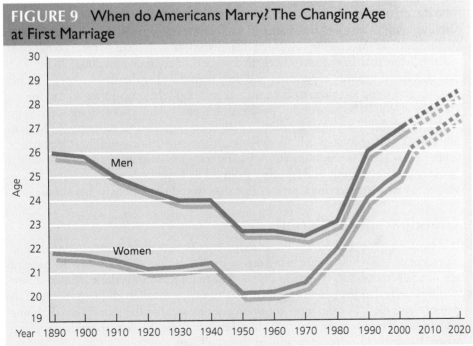

FIGURE 9   When do Americans Marry? The Changing Age at First Marriage

Note: This is the median age at first marriage. The broken lines indicate the author's estimate.

Source: By the author. Based on U.S. Census Bureau 2008.

cohabitation unmarried couples living together in a sexual relationship

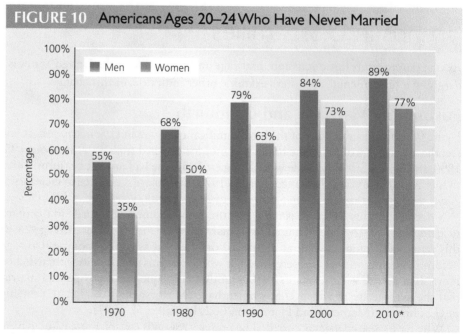

FIGURE 10 Americans Ages 20–24 Who Have Never Married

*Author's projection.

Source: By the author. Based on *Statistical Abstract of the United States* 1993: Table 60; 2002: Table 48; 2009: Table 56.

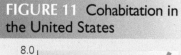

FIGURE 11 Cohabitation in the United States

Note: Broken line indicates author's estimate

Source: By the author. Based on U.S. Bureau of the Census 2007b and *Statistical Abstract of the United States* 1995: Table 60; 2009: Table 62.

Commitment is the essential difference between cohabitation and marriage. In marriage, the assumption is permanence; in cohabitation, couples agree to remain together for "as long as it works out." For marriage, individuals make public vows that legally bind them as a couple; for cohabitation, they simply move in together. Marriage requires a judge to authorize its termination; if a cohabiting relationship sours, the couple separates, telling friends and family that "it didn't work out." As you know, many cohabiting couples marry, but do you know how this is related to what cohabitation means to them? Let's explore this in our Down-to-Earth Sociology box on the next page.

Are the marriages of couples who cohabited stronger than the marriages of couples who did not live together before they married? It would seem they would be, that cohabiting couples have had the chance to work out real-life problems prior to marriage. To find out, sociologists have compared their divorce rates. It turns out that couples who cohabit before marriage are *more* likely to divorce (Lichter and Qian 2008). Why? They had that living-together experience, and only then did they decide to marry. The reason, suggest some sociologists, is because cohabiting relationships are so easy to end (Dush et al. 2003). Because of this, people are less picky about choosing someone to live with ("It's probably a temporary thing") than choosing someone to marry ("This is really serious"). After couples cohabit, however, many experience a push toward marriage. Some of this "push" comes from simply having common possessions, pets, and children. Some comes from family and friends—from subtle hints to direct statements. As a result, many end up marrying a partner that they would not otherwise have chosen.

Grandparents as Parents

It is becoming more common for grandparents to rear their grandchildren. About 6 percent of U.S. children are being reared by their grandparents, twice the percentage of a generation ago (Lagnado 2009). The main reason for these *skipped-generation families* is that the parents are incapable of caring for their children. Some of the parents have died, but the most common reasons are that the parents are ill, homeless, addicted to drugs, or in prison. In other instances, the grandparents stepped in when the parents neglected or abused their children.

Caring for grandchildren can bring great satisfaction. The grandparents know that their grandchildren are in loving hands, they build strong emotional bonds with

Down-to-Earth Sociology

"You Want Us to Live Together? What Do You Mean By That?"

What has led to the surge of cohabitation in the United States? Let's consider two fundamental changes in U.S. culture.

The first is changed ideas of sexual morality. It is difficult for today's college students to grasp the sexual morality that prevailed before the 1960s sexual revolution. Almost everyone used to consider sex before marriage to be immoral. Premarital sex existed, to be sure, but it took place furtively and often with guilt. To live together before marriage was called "shacking up," and the couple was said to be "living in sin." A double standard prevailed. It was the woman's responsibility to say no to sex before marriage. Consequently, she was considered to be the especially sinful one in cohabitation.

The second cultural change is the high U.S. divorce rate. Although the rate has declined since 1980, today's young adults have seen more divorce than any prior generation. This makes marriage seem fragile, as if it isn't going to last regardless of how much you try to make it work. This is scary. Cohabitation reduces the threat by offering a relationship of intimacy in which divorce is impossible. You can break up, but you can't get divorced.

From the outside, all cohabitation may look the same, but not to the people who are living together. As you can see from Table 2, for about 10 percent of couples, cohabitation is a substitute for marriage. These couples consider themselves married but for some reason don't want a marriage certificate. Some object to marriage on philosophical grounds ("What difference does a piece of paper make?"); others do not yet have a legal divorce from a spouse. Almost half of cohabitants (46 percent) view cohabitation as a step on the path to marriage. For them, cohabitation is more than "going steady" but less than engagement. Another 15 percent of couples are simply "giving it a try." They want to see what marriage to one another might be like. For the least committed, about 29 percent, cohabitation is a form of dating. It provides a dependable source of sex and emotional support.

If you look at these couples a half dozen years after they began to live together, you can see how important these different levels of commitment are. As you can see from Table 2, couples who view cohabitation as a substitute for marriage are the least likely to marry and the most likely to continue to cohabit. For couples who see cohabitation as a step toward marriage, the outcome is just the opposite: They are the most likely to marry and the least likely to still be cohabiting. Couples who are the most likely to break up are those who "tried" cohabitation and those for whom cohabitation was a form of dating.

For Your Consideration

Can you explain why the meaning of cohabitation makes a difference in whether couples marry? Can you classify cohabiting couples you know into these four types? Do you think there are other types? If so, what?

What Cohabitation Means	Percent of Couples	After 5 to 7 years		Of Those Still Together	
		Split Up	Still Together	Married	Cohabitating
Substitute for Marriage	10%	35%	65%	37%	63%
Step toward Marriage	46%	31%	69%	73%	27%
Trial Marriage	15%	51%	49%	66%	34%
Coresidential Dating	29%	46%	54%	61%	39%

TABLE 2 What Cohabitation Means: Does It Make a Difference?

Source: Recomputed from Bianchi and Casper 2000.

them, and they are able to transmit their family values. But taking over as parents also brings stress: the unexpected responsibilities of parenthood, the squeezed finances, the need to continue working when they were anticipating retirement, conflict with the parents of the children, and feeling trapped (Waldrop and Weber 2001; Lumpkin 2008). This added wear and tear takes its toll, and these grandparents are more likely than others to be depressed (Letiecq et al. 2008).

The "Sandwich Generation" and Elder Care

The "sandwich generation" refers to people who find themselves sandwiched between and responsible for two other generations, their children and their own aging parents. Typically between the ages of 40 and 55, these people find themselves pulled in two different directions. Many feel overwhelmed as these competing responsibilities collide. Some are plagued with guilt and anger because they can be in only one place at a time and have little time to pursue personal interests.

Concerns about elder care have gained the attention of the corporate world, and half of the 1,000 largest U.S. companies offer elder care assistance to their employees (Hewitt Associates 2004). This assistance includes seminars, referral services, and flexible work schedules to help employees meet their responsibilities without missing so much work. Why are companies responding more positively to the issue of elder care than to child care? Most CEOs are older men whose wives stayed home to take care of their children, so they don't understand the stresses of balancing work and child care. In contrast, nearly all have aging parents, and many have faced the turmoil of trying to cope with both their parents' needs and those of work and their own family.

With people living longer, this issue is likely to become increasingly urgent.

Divorce and Remarriage

The topic of family life would not be complete without considering divorce. Let's first try to determine how much divorce there really is.

Ways of Measuring Divorce

You probably have heard that the U.S. divorce rate is 50 percent, a figure that is popular with reporters. The statistic is true in the sense that each year almost half as many divorces are granted as there are marriages performed. The totals are 2.16 million marriages and about 1.04 million divorces (*Statistical Abstract* 2009:Table 123).

What is wrong, then, with saying that the divorce rate is about 50 percent? Think about it for a moment. Why should we compare the number of divorces and marriages that take place during the same year? The couples who divorced do not—with rare exceptions—come from the group that married that year. The one number has *nothing* to do with the other, so these statistics in no way establish the divorce rate.

What figures should we compare, then? Couples who divorce come from the entire group of married people in the country. Since the United States has 60,000,000 married couples, and a little over 1 million of them get divorced in a year, the divorce rate for any given year is less than 2 percent. A couple's chances of still being married at the end of a year are over 98 percent—not bad odds—and certainly much better odds than the mass media would have us believe. As the Social Map on the next page shows, the "odds"—if we want to call them that—depend on where you live.

Over time, of course, each year's small percentage adds up. A third way of measuring divorce, then, is to ask, "Of all U.S. adults, what percentage are divorced?" Figure 13 on the next page answers this question. You can see how divorce has increased over the years and how race–ethnicity makes a difference for the likelihood that couples will divorce. If you look closely, you can also see that the rate of divorce has slowed down.

Figure 13 shows us the percentage of Americans who are currently divorced, but we get yet another answer if we ask the question, "What percentage of Americans have *ever* been divorced?" This percentage increases with each age group, peaking when people reach their 50s. Forty percent of women in their 50s have been divorced at some point in their

" I NOW PRONOUNCE YOU SECOND HUSBAND AND FOURTH WIFE."

This fanciful depiction of marital trends may not be too far off the mark.

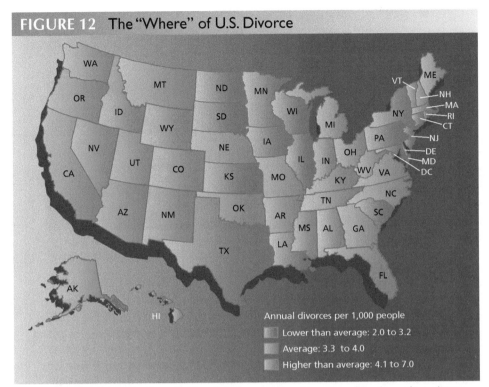

FIGURE 12 The "Where" of U.S. Divorce

Annual divorces per 1,000 people

Lower than average: 2.0 to 3.2
Average: 3.3 to 4.0
Higher than average: 4.1 to 7.0

Note: Data for California, Georgia, Hawaii, Indiana, and Louisiana, based on the earlier editions in the source, have been decreased by the average decrease in U.S. divorce.

Source: By the author. Based on *Statistical Abstract of the United States* 1995:Table 149; 2002:Table 111; 2009:Table 123.

lives; for men, the total is 43 percent ("Marital History . . ." 2004). Looked at in this way, a divorce rate of 50 percent, then, is fairly accurate.

What most of us want to know is what *our* chances of divorce are. It is one thing to know that a certain percentage of Americans are divorced, but have sociologists found out anything that will tell me about *my* chances of divorce? This is the topic of the Down-to-Earth Sociology box on the next page.

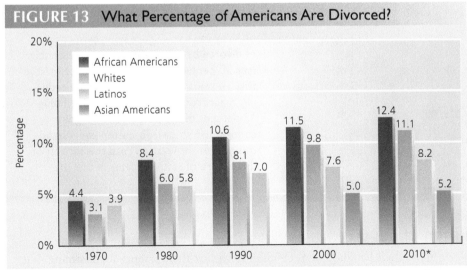

FIGURE 13 What Percentage of Americans Are Divorced?

- African Americans
- Whites
- Latinos
- Asian Americans

Note: This figure shows the percentage who are divorced and have not remarried, not the percentage who have *ever* divorced. Only these racial–ethnic groups are listed in the source. The source only recently added data on Asian Americans. *Author's estimate

Source: By the author. Based on *Statistical Abstract of the United States* 1995: Table 58; 2009: Table 56.

Down-to-Earth Sociology
"What Are Your Chances of Getting Divorced?"

Divorces are often messy. To settle the question of who gets the house, a couple in Cambodia sawed their house in half.

It is probably true that over a lifetime about half of all marriages fail (Whitehead and Popenoe 2004). If you have that 50 percent figure dancing in your head while you are getting married, you might as well make sure that you have an escape door open even while you're saying "I do."

Not every group carries the same risk of divorce. For some, the risk is much higher; for others, much lower. Let's look at some factors that reduce people's risk. As Table 3 shows, sociologists have worked out percentages that you might find useful. As you can see, people who go to college, participate in a religion, wait to get married before having children, and earn higher incomes have a much better chance that their marriage will last. You can also see that having parents who did not divorce is significant. If you reverse these factors, you will see how the likelihood of divorce increases for people who have a baby before they marry, who marry in their teens, and so on. It is important to note, however, that these factors reduce the risk of divorce for groups of people, not for any particular individual.

Three other factors increase the risk for divorce, but for these, sociologists have not computed percentages:

The first will probably strike you as strange—if a couple's firstborn child is a girl (Ananat and Michaels 2007; Dahl and Moretti 2008). Apparently, men prefer sons, and if the firstborn is a boy, the father is more likely to stick around. The second factor is more obvious: The more co-workers you have who are of the opposite sex, the more likely you are to get divorced (McKinnish 2007). (I'm sure you can figure out why.) No one knows the reason for the third factor: working with people who are recently divorced (Aberg 2003). It could be that divorced people are more likely to "hit" on their fellow workers—and human nature being what it is . . .

For Your Consideration

Why do you think that people who go to college have a lower risk of divorce? How would you explain the other factors shown in Table 3? What other factors discussed in this chapter indicate a greater or lesser risk of divorce?

Why can't you figure your own chances of divorce by starting with some percentage (say 30 percent likelihood of divorce for the first 10 years of marriage) and then reducing it according to this table (subtracting 13 percent of the 30 percent for going to college, and so on)? To better understand this, you might want to read the section on the misuse of statistics later in the chapter.

TABLE 3 What Reduces the Risk of Divorce?	
Factors that Reduce People's People's Chances of Divorce	**How Much Does This Decrease the Risk of Divorce?**
Some college (vs. high-school dropout)	−13%
Affiliated with a religion (vs. none)	−14%
Parents not divorced	−14%
Age 25 or over at marriage (vs. under 18)	−24%
Having a baby 7 months or longer after marriage (vs. before marriage)	−24%
Annual income over $25,000 (vs. under $25,000)	−30%

Note: These percentages apply to the first ten years of marriage.
Source: Whitehead and Popenoe 2004.

Children of Divorce

Each year, more than 1 million U.S. children learn that their parents are divorcing. Numbers like this are cold. They don't tell us what divorce feels like, what the children experience. In the Down-to-Earth Sociology box on the next page, we try to catch a glimpse of this.

Children whose parents divorce are more likely than children reared by both parents to experience emotional problems, both during childhood and after they grow up (Amato and

HO/AFP/Getty Images via Newscom

Down-to-Earth Sociology
Caught Between Two Worlds: The Children of Divorce

The statistics can tell you how many couples divorce, how many children these couples have, and other interesting information. But the numbers can't tell what divorce is like—how children feel their world falling apart when they learn their parents are going to get a divorce. Or how torn apart they feel when they are shuffled from one house to another.

Elizabeth Marquardt, a child of divorce herself, did a national study of children of divorce. In her book, *Between Two Worlds* (2005), she weaves her own experiences with those of the people she interviewed, taking us into the thought world of children who are being pulled apart by their parents.

It's the many little things that the statistics don't touch. The children feel like they are growing up in two families, not one. This creates painful complications that make the children feel like insiders *and* outsiders in their parents' worlds. They are outsiders when they look or act like one of the parents. This used to be a mark of an insider, a part of the family to which the child and the two parents belonged. But now it reminds one parent of the former spouse, someone they want to forget. And those children who end up with different last names than one of their parents—what a dramatic symbol of *outsider* that is. And when children learn something about one parent that they can't tell the other parent—which happens often—how uncomfortable they feel at being unable to share this information. Outsider–insider again.

What information do you share, anyway—or what do you *not* dare to share—as you travel from one world to the other? What do you say when dad asks if mom has a boyfriend? Is this supposed to be a secret? Will dad get mad if you tell him? Will he feel hurt? You don't want him to get angry or to feel hurt. Yet you don't want to keep secrets. And will mom get mad if you tell dad? It's all so complicated for a kid.

Marquardt says that as a child of divorce she tried to keep her two worlds apart, but they sometimes collided. At her mom's house, she could say that things were "screwed up." But if she used "screwed up" at her dad's

The custody and support of children are often a major source of contention in divorces. Shown here is Britney Spears, whose battle for the custody of her children and her court-ordered support of her former husband, Kevin Federline, made news around the world.

GABRIEL BOUYS/AFP/Getty Images

house, he would correct her, saying, "*Messed* up." He meant the best for her, teaching her better language, but this left her feeling silly and ashamed. Things like this, little to most people, are significant to kids who feel pinched between their parents' differing values, beliefs, and life styles.

To shuttle between two homes is to enter and leave different worlds—feeling things in common with each, but also sensing distances from each. And then come the strange relationships—their parents' girlfriends or boyfriends. Eventually come new blended families, which may not blend so easily, those that bring the new stepmom or stepdad, and perhaps their children. And then there are the new break-ups, with a recurring cycle of supposedly permanent relationships. What a complicated world for a child to traverse.

Marquardt pinpoints the dilemma for the child of divorce when she says, Being with one parent always means *not* being with the other.

For Your Consideration
If you are a child of divorce, did you have two worlds of experience? Were your experiences like those mentioned here? If you lived with both parents, how do you think your life has been different because your parents didn't divorce?

Sobolewski 2001; Weitoft et al. 2003). They are also more likely to become juvenile delinquents (Wallerstein et al. 2001) and less likely to complete high school, to attend college, and to graduate from college (McLanahan and Schwartz 2002). Finally, the children of divorce are themselves more likely to divorce (Wolfinger 2003), perpetuating a marriage–divorce cycle.

Is the greater maladjustment of the children of divorce a serious problem? This question initiated a lively debate between two researchers, both psychologists. Judith Wallerstein

serial fatherhood a pattern of parenting in which a father, after a divorce, reduces contact with his own children, serves as a father to the children of the woman he marries or lives with, then ignores these children, too, after moving in with or marrying another woman

claims that divorce scars children, making them depressed and leaving them with insecurities that follow them into adulthood (Wallerstein et al. 2001). Mavis Hetherington replies that 75 to 80 percent of children of divorce function as well as children who are reared by both of their parents (Hetherington and Kelly 2003).

Without meaning to weigh in on either side of this debate, it doesn't seem to be a simple case of the glass being half empty or half full. If 75 to 80 percent of children of divorce don't suffer long-term harm, this leaves one-fourth to one-fifth who do. Any way you look at it, one-fourth or one-fifth of a million children each year is a lot of kids who are having a lot of problems.

What helps children adjust to divorce? Children of divorce who feel close to both parents make the best adjustment, and those who don't feel close to either parent make the worst adjustment (Richardson and McCabe 2001). Other studies show that children adjust well if they experience little conflict, feel loved, live with a parent who is making a good adjustment, and have consistent routines. It also helps if their family has adequate money to meet its needs. Children also adjust better if a second adult can be counted on for support (Hayashi and Strickland 1998). Urie Bronfenbrenner (1992) says this person is like the third leg of a stool, giving stability to the smaller family unit. Any adult can be the third leg, he says—a relative, friend, or even a former mother-in-law—but the most powerful stabilizing third leg is the father, the ex-husband.

As mentioned, when the children of divorce grow up and marry, they are more likely to divorce than are adults who grew up in intact families. Have researchers found any factors that increase the chances that the children of divorce will have successful marriages? Actually, they have. They are more likely to have a lasting marriage if they marry someone whose parents did not divorce. These marriages have more trust and less conflict. If both husband and wife come from broken families, however, it is not good news. Those marriages tend to have less trust and more conflict, leading to a higher chance of divorce (Wolfinger 2003).

Grandchildren of Divorce

Paul Amato and Jacob Cheadle (2005), the first sociologists to study the grandchildren of people who had divorced, found that the effects of divorce continue across generations. Using a national sample, they compared grandchildren—those whose grandparents had divorced with those whose grandparents had not divorced. Their findings are astounding. The grandchildren of divorce have weaker ties to their parents, don't go as far in school,

It is difficult to capture the anguish of the children of divorce, but when I read these lines by the fourth-grader who drew these two pictures, my heart was touched:

Me alone in the park . . .	This is me in the picture with my son.
All alone in the park.	We are taking a walk in the park.
My Dad and Mom are divorced	I will never be like my father.
that's why I'm all alone.	I will never divorce my wife and kid.

and don't get along as well with their spouses. As these researchers put it, when parents divorce, the consequences ripple through the lives of children who are not yet born.

The Absent Father and Serial Fatherhood

With divorce common and mothers usually granted custody of the children, a new fathering pattern has emerged. In this pattern, known as **serial fatherhood,** a divorced father maintains high contact with his children during the first year or two after the divorce. As the man develops a relationship with another woman, he begins to play a fathering role with the woman's children and reduces contact with his own children. With another breakup, this pattern may repeat. Relationships are so broken that 31 percent of children who live apart from their fathers have contact with their father less than once a month—and this includes phone calls. Another 30 percent have no contact with their father (Stewart 2003). For many men, fatherhood has apparently become a short-term commitment.

The Ex-Spouses

Anger, depression, and anxiety are common feelings at divorce. But so is relief. Women are more likely than men to feel that divorce is giving them a "new chance" in life. A few couples manage to remain friends through it all—but they are the exception. The spouse who initiates the divorce usually gets over it sooner (Kelly 1992; Wang and Amato 2000) and remarries sooner (Sweeney 2002).

Divorce does not necessarily mean the end of a couple's relationship. Many divorced couples maintain contact because of their children (Fischer et al. 2005). For others, the "continuities," as sociologists call them, represent lingering attachments (Vaughan 1985; Masheter 1991; author's file 2005). The former husband may help his former wife paint a room or move furniture; she may invite him over for a meal or to watch television. They might even go to dinner or to see a movie together. Some couples even continue to make love after their divorce.

We don't yet know the financial impact of divorce. Studies used to show that divorce lowered women's income by a third (Seltzer 1994), but current research indicates that the finances of the average woman with minor children are either unchanged or actually improve after divorce (Bedard and Deschenes 2005; Ananat and Michaels 2007). There seem to be three reasons: divorced women work more hours, some move in with their parents, and others marry or cohabit with men who do better financially than their husbands did. We need more research to resolve this question.

Remarriage

Despite the number of people who emerge from divorce court swearing "Never again!" many do remarry. The rate at which they remarry, however, has slowed, and today only half of women who divorce remarry (Bramlett and Mosher 2002). Figure 14 shows how significant race–ethnicity is in determining whether women remarry. Comparable data are not available for men.

As Figure 15 shows, most divorced people marry other divorced people. You may be surprised that the women who are most likely to remarry are young mothers and those with less education (Glick and Lin 1986; Schmiege et al. 2001). Apparently women who are more educated and more independent (no children) can afford to be more selective. Men are more likely than women to remarry, perhaps because they have a larger pool of potential mates.

How do remarriages work out? The divorce rate of remarried people *without* children is the same as that of first marriages. Those who bring children into a new marriage, however, are more likely to divorce again (MacDonald and DeMaris 1995). Certainly these relationships are more complicated and stressful. A lack of clear norms to follow may also play a role (Coleman et al. 2000). As sociologist Andrew Cherlin (1989) noted, we lack satisfactory names for stepmothers, stepfathers, stepbrothers, stepsisters, stepaunts, stepuncles, stepcousins, and stepgrandparents. At the very least, these are awkward terms to use, but they also represent ill-defined relationships.

FIGURE 14 The Probability that Divorced Women Will Remarry in Five Years

White Americans 58%
Latinas 44%
African Americans 32%

Note: Only women and these groups are listed in the source. *Source:* By the author. Based on Bramlett and Mosher 2002.

FIGURE 15 The Marital History of U.S. Brides and Grooms

54
23
11   11

■ First marriage of bride and groom
■ Remarriage of bride and groom
■ First marriage of bride, remarriage of groom
■ First marriage of groom, remarriage of bride

Source: By the author. Based on *Statistical Abstract of the United States* 2000: Table 145. Table dropped in later editions.

Two Sides of Family Life

Let's first look at situations in which marriage and family have gone seriously wrong and then try to answer the question of what makes marriage work.

The Dark Side of Family Life: Battering, Child Abuse, Marital Rape, and Incest

The dark side of family life involves events that people would rather keep in the dark. We shall look at spouse battering, child abuse, rape, and incest.

Spouse Battering. To study spouse abuse, some sociologists have studied just a few victims in depth (Goetting 2001), while others have interviewed nationally representative samples of U.S. couples (Straus and Gelles 1988; Straus 1992). Although not all sociologists agree (Dobash et al. 1992, 1993; Pagelow 1992), Murray Straus concludes that husbands and wives are about equally likely to attack one another. If gender equality exists here, however, it certainly vanishes when it comes to the effects of violence— 85 percent of the injured are women (Rennison 2003). A good part of the reason, of course, is that most husbands are bigger and stronger than their wives, putting women at a physical disadvantage in this literal battle of the sexes. The Down-to-Earth Sociology box on the next page discusses why some women remain with their abusive husbands.

Violence against women is related to the sexist structure of society, and to socialization. Because they grew up with norms that encourage aggression and the use of violence, some men feel that it is their right to control women. When frustrated in a relationship—or even by events outside it—some men become violent. The basic sociological question is how to socialize males to handle frustration and disagreements without resorting to violence (Rieker et al. 1997). We do not yet have this answer.

Child Abuse.

> I answered an ad about a lakeside house in a middle-class neighborhood that was for sale by owner. As the woman showed me through her immaculate house, I was surprised to see a plywood box in the youngest child's bedroom. About 3 feet high, 3 feet wide, and 6 feet long, the box was perforated with holes and had a little door with a padlock. Curious, I asked what it was. The woman replied matter-of-factly that her son had a behavior problem, and this was where they locked him for "time out." She added that other times they would tie him to a float, attach a line to the dock, and put him in the lake.
>
> I left as soon as I could. With thoughts of a terrorized child filling my head, I called the state child abuse hotline.

As you can tell, what I saw upset me. Most of us are bothered by child abuse— helpless children being victimized by their parents and other adults who are supposed to love, protect, and nurture them. The most gruesome of these cases make the evening news: The 4-year-old girl who was beaten and raped by her mother's boyfriend, passed into a coma, and three days later passed out of this life; the 6- to 10-year-old children whose stepfather videotaped them engaging in sex acts. Unlike these cases, which made headlines in my area, most child abuse is never brought to our attention: the children who live in filth, who are neglected—left alone for hours or even days at a time—or who are beaten with extension cords—cases like the little boy I learned about when I went house hunting.

Child abuse is extensive. Each year, U.S. authorities receive about 2 million reports of children being abused or neglected. About 900,000 of these cases are substantiated (*Statistical Abstract* 2009:Table 330). The excuses that parents make are incredible. Of those I have read, the most fantastic is what a mother said to a Manhattan judge, "I slipped

Down-to-Earth Sociology
"Why Doesn't She Just Leave?" The Dilemma of Abused Women

"Why would she ever put up with violence?" is a question on everyone's mind. From the outside, it looks so easy. Just pack up and leave. "I know I wouldn't put up with anything like that."

Yet this is not what typically happens. Women tend to stay with their men after they are abused. Some stay only a short while, to be sure, but others remain in abusive situations for years. Why?

Sociologist Ann Goetting (2001) asked this question, too. To learn the answer, she interviewed women who had made the break. She wanted to find out what it was that set them apart. How were they able to leave, when so many women couldn't seem to? She found that

1. They had a positive self-image.
   Simply put, they believed that they deserved better.
2. They broke with old ideas.
   They did not believe that a wife had to stay with her husband no matter what.
3. They found adequate finances.
   For some, this was easy. But others had to save for years, putting away just a dollar or two a week.
4. They had supportive family and friends.
   A support network served as a source of encouragement to help them rescue themselves.

If you take the opposite of these four characteristics, you can understand why some women put up with abuse: They don't think they deserve anything better, they believe it is their duty to stay, they don't think they can make it financially, and they lack a supportive network. These four factors are not of equal importance to all women, of course. For some, the lack of finances is the most important, while for others, it is their low self-concept. The lack of a supportive network is also significant.

There are two additional factors: The woman must define her husband's acts as abuse that warrants her leaving, and she must decide that he is not going to change. If she defines her husband's acts as normal, or

Spouse abuse is one of the most common forms of violence. Shown here are police pulling a woman from her bathroom window, where she had fled from her husband, who was threatening to shoot her.

perhaps as deserved in some way, she does not have a motive to leave. If she defines his acts as temporary, thinking that her husband will change, she is likely to stick around to try to change her husband.

Sociologist Kathleen Ferraro (2006) reports that when she was a graduate student, her husband "monitored my movements, eating, clothing, friends, money, make-up, and language. If I challenged his commands, he slapped or kicked me or pushed me down." Ferraro was able to leave only after she defined her husband's acts as intolerable abuse—not simply that she was caught up in an unappealing situation that she had to put up with—and after she decided that her husband was not going to change. Fellow students formed the supportive network that Ferraro needed to act on her new definition. Her graduate mentor even hid her from her husband after she left him.

For Your Consideration
On the basis of these findings, what would you say to a woman whose husband is abusing her? How do you think battered women's shelters fit into this explanation? What other parts of this puzzle can you think of—such as the role of love?

in a moment of anger, and my hands accidentally wrapped around my daughter's windpipe" (LeDuff 2003).

Marital or Intimacy Rape. Sociologists have found that marital rape is more common than is usually supposed. For example, between one-third and one-half of women who seek help at shelters for battered women are victims of marital rape (Bergen 1996). Women at shelters, however, are not representative of U.S. women. To get a better answer of how common marital rape is, sociologist Diana Russell (1990) used a sampling technique that allows generalization, but only to San Francisco. She found that 14 percent of married women report that their husbands have raped them. Similarly, 10 percent of a representative sample of Boston women interviewed by sociologists David Finkelhor and Kersti Yllo (1985, 1989) reported that their husbands had used physical force to compel them to have sex. Compared with victims of rape by strangers or acquaintances, victims of marital rape are less likely to report the rape (Mahoney 1999).

With the huge numbers of couples who are cohabiting, we need a term that includes sexual assault in these relationships. Perhaps, then, we should use the term *intimacy rape.* And intimacy rape is not limited to men who sexually assault women. Sociologist Lori Girshick (2002) interviewed lesbians who had been sexually assaulted by their partners. In these cases, both the victim and the offender were women. Girshick points out that if the pronoun "he" were substituted for "she" in her interviews, a reader would believe that the events were being told by women who had been battered and raped by their husbands. Like wives who have been raped by their husbands, these victims, too, suffered from shock, depression, and self-blame.

Incest. Sexual relations between certain relatives (for example, between brothers and sisters or between parents and children) constitute **incest.** Incest is most likely to occur in families that are socially isolated (Smith 1992). Sociologist Diana Russell (n.d.) found that incest victims who experience the greatest trauma are those who were victimized the most often, whose assaults occurred over longer periods of time, and whose incest was "more intrusive"—for example, sexual intercourse as opposed to sexual touching.

Who are the offenders? The most common incest is apparently between brothers and sisters, with the sex initiated by the brother (Canavan et al. 1992; Carlson et al. 2006). With no random samples, however, we don't know for sure. Russell found that uncles are the most common offenders, followed by first cousins, stepfathers, brothers, and, finally, other relatives ranging from brothers-in-law to stepgrandfathers. All studies indicate that incest between mothers and their children is rare, more so than between fathers and their children.

The Bright Side of Family Life: Successful Marriages

Successful Marriages. After examining divorce and family abuse, one could easily conclude that marriages seldom work out. This would be far from the truth, however, for about three of every five married Americans report that they are "very happy" with their marriages (Whitehead and Popenoe 2004). (Keep in mind that each year divorce eliminates about a million unhappy marriages.) To find out what makes marriage successful, sociologists Jeanette and Robert Lauer (1992) interviewed 351 couples who had been married fifteen years or longer. Fifty-one of these marriages were unhappy, but the couples stayed together for religious reasons, because of family tradition, or "for the sake of the children."

Of the others, the 300 happy couples, all

1. Think of their spouse as their best friend
2. Like their spouse as a person
3. Think of marriage as a long-term commitment
4. Believe that marriage is sacred
5. Agree with their spouse on aims and goals
6. Believe that their spouse has grown more interesting over the years
7. Strongly want the relationship to succeed
8. Laugh together

Sociologist Nicholas Stinnett (1992) used interviews and questionnaires to study 660 families from all regions of the United States and parts of South America. He found that happy families

incest sexual relations between specified relatives, such as brothers and sisters or parents and children

1. Spend a lot of time together
2. Are quick to express appreciation
3. Are committed to promoting one another's welfare
4. Do a lot of talking and listening to one another
5. Are religious
6. Deal with crises in a positive manner

There are three more important factors: Marriages are happier when the partners get along with their in-laws (Bryant et al. 2001), find leisure activities that they both enjoy (Crawford et al. 2002), and agree on how to spend money (Bernard 2008).

Symbolic Interactionism and the Misuse of Statistics

Many students express concerns about their own marital future, a wariness born out of the divorce of their parents, friends, neighbors, relatives—even their pastors and rabbis. They wonder about their chances of having a successful marriage. Because sociology is not just about abstract ideas, but is really about our lives, it is important to stress that you are an individual, not a statistic. That is, if the divorce rate were 33 percent or 50 percent, this would *not* mean that if you marry, your chances of getting divorced are 33 percent or 50 percent. That is a misuse of statistics—and a common one at that. Divorce statistics represent all marriages and have absolutely *nothing* to do with any individual marriage. Our own chances depend on our own situations—especially the way we approach marriage.

To make this point clearer, let's apply symbolic interactionism. From a symbolic interactionist perspective, we create our own worlds. That is, because our experiences don't come with built-in meanings, we interpret our experiences and act accordingly. As we do so, we can create a self-fulfilling prophecy. For example, if we think that our marriage might fail, we are more likely to run when things become difficult. If we think that our marriage is going to work out, we are more likely to stick around and to do things to make the marriage successful. The folk saying "There are no guarantees in life" is certainly true, but it does help to have a vision that a good marriage is possible and that it is worth the effort to achieve.

The Future of Marriage and Family

What can we expect of marriage and family in the future? Despite its many problems, marriage is in no danger of becoming a relic of the past. Marriage is so functional that it exists in every society. Consequently, the vast majority of Americans will continue to find marriage vital to their welfare.

Certain trends are firmly in place. Cohabitation, births to single women, age at first marriage, and parenting by grandparents will increase. As more married women join the workforce, wives will continue to gain marital power. The number of elderly will increase, and more couples will find themselves sandwiched between caring for their parents and rearing their own children.

Our culture will continue to be haunted by distorted images of marriage and family: the bleak ones portrayed in the mass media and the rosy ones perpetuated by cultural myths. Sociological research can help to correct these distortions and allow us to see how our own family experiences fit into the patterns of our culture. Sociological research can also help to answer the big question: How do we formulate social policies that will support and enhance family life?

By the Numbers: *Then and Now*

Americans who want 3 or more children

1936	NOW
64%	**34**%

Americans who want 0, 1, or 2 children

1936	NOW
34%	**56**%

Number of marriages with a white wife and an African American husband

1970	NOW
41,000	**338,000**

Number of hours per week husbands do housework

1970	NOW
4.4	**9.7**

Percentage of children under age 18 who live with both parents

1970	NOW
85%	**66**%

Number of cohabitating couples

1970	NOW
500,000	**6,400,000**

Percentage of white Americans divorced

1970	NOW
3.1%	**11.1**%

Percentage of African Americans divorced

1970	NOW
4.4%	**12.4**%

Average age of first-time bride

1970	NOW
21	**26**

Women ages 20–24 who have never married

1970	NOW
35%	**77**%

SUMMARY *and* REVIEW

Marriage and Family in Global Perspective

What is a family—and what themes are universal?

Family is difficult to define. There are exceptions to every element that one might consider essential. Consequently, **family** is defined broadly—as people who consider themselves related by blood, marriage, or adoption. Universally, **marriage** and family are mechanisms for governing mate selection, reckoning descent, and establishing inheritance and authority.

Marriage and Family in Theoretical Perspective

What is a functionalist perspective on marriage and family?

Functionalists examine the functions and dysfunctions of family life. Examples include the **incest taboo** and how weakened family functions increase divorce.

What is a conflict perspective on marriage and family?

Conflict theorists focus on inequality in marriage, especially unequal power between husbands and wives.

What is a symbolic interactionist perspective on marriage and family?

Symbolic interactionists examine the contrasting experiences and perspectives of men and women in marriage. They stress that only by grasping the perspectives of wives and husbands can we understand their behavior.

The Family Life Cycle

What are the major elements of the family life cycle?

The major elements are love and courtship, marriage, childbirth, child rearing, and the family in later life. Most mate selection follows predictable patterns of age, social class, race–ethnicity, and religion. Child-rearing patterns vary by social class.

Diversity in U.S. Families

How significant is race–ethnicity in family life?

The primary distinction is social class, not race–ethnicity. Families of the same social class are likely to be similar, regardless of their race–ethnicity.

What other diversity do we see in U.S. families?

Also discussed are one-parent, childless, **blended,** and gay and lesbian families. Each has its unique characteristics, but social class is significant in determining their primary characteristics. Poverty is especially significant for single-parent families, most of which are headed by women.

Trends in U.S. Families

What major changes characterize U.S. families?

Three changes are postponement of first marriage, an increase in **cohabitation,** and more grandparents serving as parents to their grandchildren. With more people living longer, many middle-aged couples find themselves sandwiched between rearing their children and taking care of their aging parents.

Divorce and Remarriage

What is the current divorce rate?

Depending on what numbers you choose to compare, you can produce almost any rate you wish, from 50 percent to less than 2 percent.

How do children and their parents adjust to divorce?

Divorce is difficult for children, whose adjustment problems often continue into adulthood. Most divorced fathers do not maintain ongoing relationships with their children. Financial problems are usually greater for the former wives. The rate of remarriage has slowed.

Two Sides of Family Life

What are the two sides of family life?

The dark side is abuse—spouse battering, child abuse, marital rape, and **incest.** All these are acts that revolve around the misuse of family power. The bright side is that most people find marriage and family to be rewarding.

The Future of Marriage and Family

What is the likely future of marriage and family?

We can expect cohabitation, births to unmarried women, age at first marriage, and parenting by grandparents to increase. The growing numbers of women in the workforce are likely to continue to shift the balance of marital power.

THINKING CRITICALLY

1. Functionalists stress that the family is universal because it provides basic functions for individuals and society. What functions does your family provide? Hint: In addition to the section "The Functionalist Perspective," also consider the section "Common Cultural Themes."

2. Explain why social class is more important than race–ethnicity in determining a family's characteristics.

3. Apply this chapter's contents to your own experience with marriage and family. What social factors affect your family life? In what ways is your family life different from that of your grandparents when they were your age?

ADDITIONAL RESOURCES

What can you find in MySocLab? mysoclab www.mysoclab.com

- Complete Ebook
- Practice Tests and Video and Audio activities
- Mapping and Data Analysis exercises

- Sociology in the News
- Classic Readings in Sociology
- Research and Writing advice

Where Can I Read More on This Topic?

Agger, Ben, and Beth Anne Shelton. *Fast Families, Virtual Children: A Critical Sociology of Families and Schooling.* Boulder, Colo.: Paradigm, 2007. The authors analyze how technology has changed the way families conduct their lives, rear their children, and try to maintain a boundary between work and home.

Amato, Paul R., Alan Booth, David R. Johnson, and Stacy J. Rogers. *Alone Together: How Marriage in American Is Changing.* Cambridge, Mass.: Harvard University Press, 2007. The authors' controversial thesis is that the significance of marriage is declining, that marriage is becoming just one lifestyle choice among many.

Bianchi, Suzanne M., John P. Robinson, and Melissa A. Milkie. *Changing Rhythms of American Family Life.* New York: Russell Sage, 2007. Based on time-diaries, the authors conclude that despite their greater participation in the paid labor force U.S. mothers spend just as much time with their children as the previous generation of women did.

Conley, Dalton. *The Pecking Order: A Bold New Look at How Family and Society Determine Who We Become.* New York: Random House, 2009. Analyzes how the inequality in families—children ending up in different social classes—is related to the larger social forces that envelop the family: gender expectations, the cost of education, divorce, early loss of a parent, geographic mobility, religious and sexual orientation, trauma, and even luck and accidents.

Coontz, Stephanie. *Marriage, a History: How Love Conquered Marriage.* New York: Penguin 2006. This analysis of how the fundamental orientations to marriage have changed contains enlightening excerpts from the past.

Epstein, Cynthia Fuchs, and Arne L. Kalleberg, eds. *Fighting for Time: Shifting Boundaries of Work and Social Life.* New York: Russell Sage, 2006. Explores changes in the time people spend at work and the consequences of those changes for individuals and families.

McAdoo, Harriet Pipes, ed. *Black Families,* 4th ed. Beverly Hills, Calif.: Sage, 2007. The authors of these 23 articles analyze gender relations, family patterns, religion, social policy, and even funerary practices of African Americans.

Stone, Pamela. *Opting Out? Why Women Really Quit Careers and Head Home.* Berkeley: University of California Press, 2007. A study of high-achieving, highly educated, privileged women who quit their fast-paced professional work in order to become stay-at-home mothers—their decision, the transition, and the consequences.

Sullivan, Andrew, ed. *Same-Sex Marriage: Pro and Con.* New York: Random House, 2009. In this even-handed anthology, the editor brings together arguments and opinions concerning same-sex marriage.

Wallace, Harvey. *Family Violence: Legal, Medical, and Social Perspectives,* 5th ed. Boston: Allyn and Bacon, 2008. This overview of violence, from stalking to sexual harassment to sexual violence in the workplace, includes case studies.

Journals

Family Relations, The History of the Family, International Journal of Sociology of the Family, Journal of Comparative Family Studies, Journal of Divorce, Journal of Divorce and Remarriage, Journal of Family and Economic Issues, Journal of Family Issues, Journal of Family Violence, Journal of Marriage and Family, and *Marriage and Family Review* publish articles on almost every aspect of marriage and family life.

Social Stratification

From Chapter 7 of *Sociology: A Down-to-Earth Approach: Core Concepts*, 4/e. James M. Henslin.

Social Stratification

New York City

Ah, New Orleans, that fabled city on the Mississippi Delta. Images from its rich past floated through my head—pirates, treasure, intrigue. Memories from a pleasant vacation stirred my thoughts—the exotic French Quarter with its enticing aroma of Creole food and sounds of earthy jazz drifting through the air.

The shelter for the homeless, however, forced me back to an unwelcome reality. The shelter was like those I had visited in the North, West, and East—only dirtier. The dirt, in fact, was the worst that I had encountered during my research, and this shelter was the only one to insist on payment in exchange for sleeping in one of its filthy beds.

I was startled by a sight so out of step with the misery and despair that I stopped and stared.

The men looked the same—disheveled and haggard, wearing that unmistakable expression of despair—just like the homeless anywhere in the country. Except for the accent, you wouldn't know what region you were in. Poverty wears the same tired face wherever you are, I realized. The accent may differ, but the look remains the same.

I had grown used to the sights and smells of abject poverty. Those no longer surprised me. But after my fitful sleep with the homeless, I saw something that did. Just a block or so from the shelter, I was startled by a sight so out of step with the misery and despair I had just experienced that I stopped and stared.

Indignation swelled within me. Confronting me were life-size, full-color photos mounted on the transparent Plexiglas shelter of a bus stop. Staring back at me were images of finely dressed men and women proudly strutting about as they modeled elegant suits, dresses, diamonds, and furs.

A wave of disgust swept over me. "Something is cockeyed in this society," I thought, as my mind refused to stop juxtaposing these images of extravagance with the suffering I had just witnessed.

The disjunction that I felt in New Orleans was triggered by the ads, but it was not the first time that I had experienced this sensation. Whenever my research abruptly transported me from the world of the homeless to one of another social class, I experienced a sense of disjointed unreality. Each social class has its own way of being, and because these fundamental orientations to the world contrast so sharply, the classes do not mix well.

How extensive is the gap between the rich and the poor in the United States? What differences do wealth and poverty make for people's lives? In this chapter, we will answer such questions, but before we do, let's look at a broader context that will help us understand the situation in the United States.

An Overview of Social Stratification

Some of the world's nations are wealthy, others poor, and some in between. This layering of nations, as well as of groups of people within a nation, is called **social stratification.** This term refers to a system in which groups of people are divided into layers according to their relative property, power, and prestige. This ranking of large groups of people into a hierarchy according to their relative privileges is one of the most significant topics we discuss in this text, for it affects our life chances—from our access to material possessions to the age at which we die.

Every society stratifies its members. Some societies have greater inequality than others, but social stratification is universal. In addition, in every society of the world, *gender* is a basis for stratifying people. On the basis of their gender, people are either allowed or denied access to the good things offered by their society.

Let's consider three systems of social stratification: slavery, caste, and class.

Slavery

Slavery, whose essential characteristic is that *some individuals own other people,* has been common throughout world history. The Old Testament even lays out rules for how owners should treat their slaves. So does the Koran. The Romans also had slaves, as did the Africans and Greeks. In classical Greece and Rome, slaves did the work, freeing citizens to engage in politics and the arts. Slavery was most widespread in agricultural societies and least common among nomads, especially hunters and gatherers (Landtman 1938/1968). As we examine the major causes and conditions of slavery, you will see how remarkably slavery has varied around the world.

Causes of Slavery. Contrary to common assumption, slavery was usually based not on racism but on one of three other factors. The first was *debt.* In some societies, creditors would enslave people who could not pay their debts. The second was *crime.* Instead of being killed, a murderer or thief might be enslaved by the victim's family as compensation for their loss. The third was *war.* When one group of people conquered another, they often enslaved some of the vanquished. Historian Gerda Lerner (1986) notes that women were the first people enslaved through warfare. When tribal men raided another group, they killed the men, raped the women, and then brought the women back as slaves. The women were valued for sexual purposes, for reproduction, and for their labor.

Roughly twenty-five hundred years ago, when Greece was but a collection of city-states, slavery was common. A city that became powerful and conquered another city would enslave some of the vanquished. Both slaves and slaveholders were Greek. Similarly, when Rome became the supreme power of the Mediterranean area about two thousand years ago, following the custom of the time, the Romans enslaved some of the Greeks they had conquered.

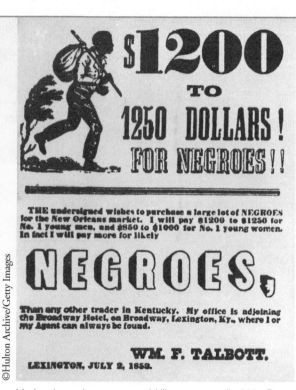

Under *slavery,* humans are sold like a commodity. Wm. F. Talbott bought slaves in Kentucky for the market in New Orleans.

More educated than their conquerors, some of these slaves served as tutors in Roman homes. Slavery, then, was a sign of debt, of crime, or of defeat in battle. It was not a sign that the slave was viewed as inherently inferior.

Conditions of Slavery. The conditions of slavery have also varied widely around the world. *In some places, slavery was temporary.* Slaves of the Israelites were set free in the year of jubilee, which occurred every fifty years. Roman slaves ordinarily had the right to buy themselves out of slavery. They knew what their purchase price was, and some were able to meet this price by striking a bargain with their owner and selling their services to others. In most instances, however, slavery was a lifelong condition. Some criminals, for example, became slaves when they were given life sentences as oarsmen on Roman war ships. There they served until death, which often came quickly to those in this exhausting service.

Slavery was not necessarily inheritable. In most places, the children of slaves were slaves themselves, but in ancient Mexico, the children of slaves were free. In some places, the child of a slave who served a rich family might even be adopted by that family, becoming an heir who bore the family name along with the other sons or daughters of the household (Landtman 1938/1968:271).

Slaves were not necessarily powerless and poor. In almost all instances, slaves owned no property and had no power. Among some groups, however, slaves could accumulate property and even rise to high positions in the community. Occasionally, a slave might even become wealthy, loan money to the master, and, while still a slave, own slaves himself or herself (Landtman 1938/1968).

Slavery in the New World. A gray area between contract labor and slavery is **bonded labor,** also called **indentured service.** Many people who wanted to start a new life in the American colonies were unable to pay their passage across the ocean. Ship captains would transport them on credit, and colonists would "buy their paper" when they arrived. This arrangement provided passage for the penniless, payment for the ship's captain, and, for wealthier colonists, servants for a set number of years. During that specified period, the servants were required by law to serve their master. If they ran away, they became outlaws who were hunted down and forcibly returned. At the end of their period of indenture, they became full citizens, able to live where they chose and free to sell their labor (Main 1965; Elkins 1968).

When there were not enough indentured servants to meet the growing need for labor, some colonists tried to enslave Native Americans. This attempt failed miserably, in part because when Indians escaped, they knew how to survive in the wilderness and were able to make their way back to their tribe. The colonists then turned to Africans, who were being brought to North and South America by the Dutch, English, Portuguese, and Spanish.

Because slavery has a broad range of causes, some analysts conclude that racism didn't lead to slavery, but, rather, that slavery led to racism. Finding it profitable to make people slaves for life, U.S. slave owners developed an **ideology,** beliefs that justify social arrangements. Ideology leads to a perception of the world that makes current social arrangements seem necessary and fair. The colonists developed the view that their slaves were inferior. Some even said that they were not fully human. In short, the colonists wove elaborate justifications for slavery, built on the presumed superiority of their own group.

To make slavery even more profitable, slave states passed laws that made slavery *inheritable;* that is, the babies born to slaves became the property of the slave owners (Stampp 1956). These children could be sold, bartered, or traded. To strengthen their control, slave states passed laws making it illegal for slaves to hold

bonded labor (indentured service) a contractual system in which someone sells his or her body (services) for a specified period of time in an arrangement very close to slavery, except that it is entered into voluntarily

ideology beliefs about the way things ought to be that justify social arrangements

James M. Henslin

During my research in India, I interviewed this 8-year-old girl. Mahashury is a *bonded laborer* who was exchanged by her parents for a 2,000 rupee loan (about $14). To repay the loan, Mahashury must do construction work for one year. She will receive one meal a day and one set of clothing for the year. Because this centuries-old practice is now illegal, the master bribes Indian officials, who inform him when they are going to inspect the construction site. He then hides his bonded laborers. I was able to interview and photograph Mahashury because her master was absent the day I visited the construction site.

meetings or to be away from the master's premises without carrying a pass (Lerner 1972). As sociologist W. E. B. Du Bois (1935/1992:12) noted, "gradually the entire white South became an armed camp to keep Negroes in slavery and to kill the black rebel."

The Civil War did not end legal discrimination. For example, until 1954 many states operated separate school systems for blacks and whites. Until the 1950s, in order to keep the races from "mixing," it was illegal in Mississippi for a white and an African American to sit together on the same seat of a car! There was no outright ban on blacks and whites being in the same car, however, so whites could employ African American chauffeurs.

Slavery Today.   Slavery has again reared its ugly head in several parts of the world. The Ivory Coast, Mauritania, Niger, and Sudan have a long history of slavery, and not until the 1980s was slavery made illegal in Mauritania and Sudan (Ayittey 1998). It took until 2003 for slavery to be banned in Niger (Polgreen 2008).

The enslavement of children for work and sex is a problem in Africa, Asia, and South America (*Trafficking in Persons Report* 2008). A unique form of child slavery occurs in Kuwait, Qatar, and Saudi Arabia. There, little boys are held in captivity because they are prized as jockeys in camel races. Facing organized opposition to this unique form of human trafficking, the United Arab Emirates is replacing boy jockeys with robots (Kahn 2007).

Caste

The second system of social stratification is caste. In a **caste system,** status is determined by birth and is lifelong. Someone who is born into a low-status group will always have low status, no matter how much that person may accomplish in life. In sociological terms, a caste system is built on ascribed status. Achieved status cannot change an individual's place in this system.

Societies with this form of stratification try to make certain that the boundaries between castes remain firm. They practice **endogamy,** marriage within their own group, and prohibit intermarriage. Elaborate rules about *ritual pollution*— touching an inferior caste contaminates the superior caste—keeps contact between castes to a minimum.

India's Religious Castes.   India provides the best example of a caste system. Based not on race but on religion, India's caste system has existed for almost three thousand years (Chandra 1993a; Jaffrelot 2006). India's four main castes are depicted in Table 1. These four castes are subdivided into about three thousand subcastes, or *jati.* Each *jati* specializes in a particular occupation. For example, one subcaste washes clothes, another sharpens knives, and yet another repairs shoes.

TABLE 1 India's Caste System	
Caste	**Occupation**
Brahman	Priests and teachers
Kshatriya	Rulers and soldiers
Vaishya	Merchants and traders
Shudra	Peasants and laborers
Dalit (untouchables)	The outcastes; degrading or polluting labor

In a *caste system*, status is determined by birth and is lifelong. At birth, these women received not only membership in a lower caste but also, because of their gender, a predetermined position in that caste. When I photographed these women, they were carrying sand to the second floor of a house being constructed in Andhra Pradesh, India.

James M. Henslin

The lowest group listed in Table 1, the Dalit, are also called India's "untouchables." If a Dalit touches someone of a higher caste, that person becomes unclean. Even the shadow of an untouchable can contaminate. Early morning and late afternoons are especially risky, for the long shadows of these periods pose a danger to everyone higher up the caste system. Consequently, Dalits are not allowed in some villages during these times. Anyone who becomes contaminated must follow *ablution,* or washing rituals, to restore purity.

Although the Indian government formally abolished the caste system in 1949, centuries-old practices cannot be eliminated so easily, and the caste system remains part of everyday life in India (Beckett 2007). The ceremonies people follow at births, marriages, and deaths, for example, are dictated by caste (Chandra 1993a). The upper castes dread the upward mobility of the untouchables, sometimes resisting it even with murder and ritual suicide (Crossette 1996; Trofimov 2007). From personal observations in India, I can add that in some villages Dalit children are not allowed in the government schools. If they try to enroll, they are beaten.

A U.S. Racial Caste System. Before leaving the subject of caste, we should note that when slavery ended in the United States, it was replaced by a *racial caste system.* From the moment of birth, everyone was marked for life (Berger 1963/2007). In this system, *all* whites, even if they were poor and uneducated, considered themselves to have a higher status than *all* African Americans. As in India and South Africa, the upper caste, fearing pollution from the lower caste, prohibited intermarriage and insisted on separate schools, hotels, restaurants, and even toilets and drinking fountains in public facilities. In the South, when any white met any African American on a sidewalk, the African American had to move aside—which the untouchables of India still must do when they meet someone of a higher caste (Deliege 2001).

Social Class

As we have seen, stratification systems based on slavery and caste are rigid. The lines drawn between people are firm, and there is little or no movement from one group to another. A **class system,** in contrast, is much more open, for it is based primarily on money or material possessions, which can be acquired. This system, too, is in place at birth, when children are ascribed the status of their parents, but, in this system, unlike the others, individuals can change their social class by what they achieve (or fail to achieve). In addition, no laws specify people's occupations on the basis of birth or prohibit marriage between the classes.

A major characteristic of the class system, then, is its relatively fluid boundaries. A class system allows **social mobility,** movement up or down the class ladder. The potential for improving one's life—or for falling down the class ladder—is a major force that drives people to go far in school and to work hard. In the extreme, the family background that a child inherits at birth may present such obstacles that he or she has little chance of climbing very far—or it may provide such privileges that it makes it almost impossible to fall down the class ladder.

Global Stratification and the Status of Females

In *every* society of the world, gender is a basis for social stratification. In no society is gender the sole basis for stratifying people, but gender cuts across *all* systems of social stratification—whether slavery, caste, or class (Huber 1990). In all these systems, on the basis of their gender, people are sorted into categories and given different access to the good things available in their society.

Apparently these distinctions always favor males. It is remarkable, for example, that in *every* society of the world men's earnings are higher than women's. Men's dominance is even more evident when we consider female circumcision. That most of the world's illiterate are females also drives home women's relative position in society. Of the several hundred million adults who cannot read, about two-thirds are women (UNESCO 2006). Because gender is such a significant factor in what happens to us in life.

class system a form of social stratification based primarily on the possession of money or material possessions

social mobility movement up or down the social class ladder

257

FIGURE 1 The Distribution of the Earth's Wealth

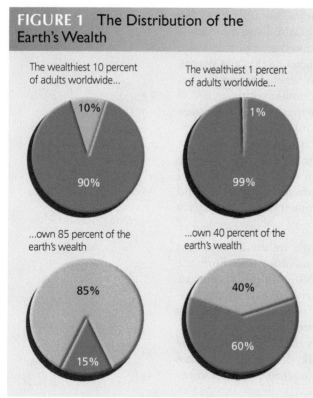

The wealthiest 10 percent of adults worldwide...

10%

90%

...own 85 percent of the earth's wealth

85%

15%

The wealthiest 1 percent of adults worldwide...

1%

99%

...own 40 percent of the earth's wealth

40%

60%

Source: Rothkopf 2008:37.

The New Global Superclass

The growing interconnections among the world's wealthiest people have produced a *global superclass,* one in which wealth and power are more concentrated than ever before in world history. There are only about 6,000 members of this superclass—*the richest 1,000 of them have more wealth than the 2½ billion poorest people on this planet* (Rothkopf 2008:37). Almost all of them are white, and except as wives and daughters, few women are an active part of the superclass. Look at Figure 1. There is nothing in history to compare with this concentration of wealth.

Global Stratification: Three Worlds

As was noted at the beginning of this chapter, just as the people within a nation are stratified by property, power, and prestige, so are the world's nations. Until recently, a simple model was used to depict global stratification: *First World* referred to the industrialized capitalist nations, *Second World* to the communist (or socialist) countries, and *Third World* to any nation that did not fit into the first two categories. The breakup of the Soviet Union in 1989 made these terms outdated. In addition, although *first, second,* and *third* did not mean "best," "better," and "worst," they implied it. An alternative classification that some now use—developed, developing, and undeveloped nations—has the same drawback. By calling ourselves "developed," it sounds as though we are mature and the "undeveloped" nations are somehow retarded.

To resolve this problem, I use more neutral, descriptive terms: *Most Industrialized, Industrializing,* and *Least Industrialized* nations. We can measure industrialization with no judgment implied as to whether a nation's industrialization represents "development," ranks it "first," or is even desirable at all. The intention is to depict on a global level the three primary dimensions of social stratification: property, power, and prestige. The Most Industrialized Nations have much greater property (wealth), power (they usually get their way in international relations), and prestige (they are looked up to as world leaders).

The Most Industrialized Nations

The Most Industrialized Nations are the United States and Canada in North America; Great Britain, France, Germany, Switzerland, and the other industrialized countries of western Europe; Japan in Asia; and Australia and New Zealand in the area of the world known as Oceania. Although there are variations in their economic systems, these nations are capitalistic. As Table 2 shows, although these nations have only 16 percent of the world's people, they possess 31 percent of the earth's land. Their wealth is so enormous that even their poor live better and longer lives than do the average citizens of the Least Industrialized Nations. The Social Map on the coming pages shows the tremendous disparities in income among the world's nations.

The Industrializing Nations

The Industrializing Nations include most of the nations of the former Soviet Union and its former satellites in eastern Europe. As Table 2 shows, these nations account for 20 percent of the earth's land and 16 percent of its people.

The dividing points between the three "worlds" are soft, making it difficult to know how to classify some nations.

TABLE 2 Distribution of the World's Land and Population

	Land	Population
Most Industrialized Nations	31%	16%
Industrializing Nations	20%	16%
Least Industrialized Nations	49%	68%

Sources: Computed from Kurian 1990, 1991, 1992.

This is especially the case with the Industrializing Nations. Exactly how much industrialization must a nation have to be in this category? Although soft, these categories do pinpoint essential differences among nations. Most people who live in the Industrializing Nations have much lower incomes and standards of living than do those who live in the Most Industrialized Nations. The majority, however, are better off than those who live in the Least Industrialized Nations. For example, on such measures as access to electricity, indoor plumbing, automobiles, telephones, and even food, most citizens of the Industrializing Nations rank lower than those in the Most Industrialized Nations, but higher than those in the Least Industrialized Nations.

The benefits of industrialization are uneven. Large numbers of people in the Industrializing Nations remain illiterate and desperately poor. Conditions can be gruesome, as we explore in the following Thinking Critically section.

ThinkingCRITICALLY
Open Season: Children as Prey

What is childhood like in the Industrializing Nations? The answer depends on who your parents are. If you are the son or daughter of rich parents, childhood can be pleasant—a world filled with luxuries and even servants. If you are born into poverty, but live in a rural area where there is plenty to eat, life can still be good—although there may be no books or television and little education. If you live in a slum, however, life can be horrible—worse even than in the slums of the Most Industrialized Nations. Let's take a glance at a notorious slum in Brazil.

Not enough food—this you can take for granted—along with wife abuse, broken homes, alcoholism, drug abuse, and a lot of crime. From your knowledge of slums in the Most Industrialized Nations, you would expect these things. What you may not expect, however, are the brutal conditions in which Brazilian slum (*favela*) children live.

Sociologist Martha Huggins (Huggins et al. 2002) reports that poverty is so deep that children and adults swarm through garbage dumps to try to find enough decaying food to keep them alive. You might also be surprised to discover that the owners of some of these dumps hire armed guards to keep the poor out—so that they can sell the garbage for pig food. And you might be shocked to learn that some shop owners have hired hit men, auctioning designated victims to the *lowest* bidder!

Life is cheap in the poor nations—but death squads for children? To understand this, we must first note that Brazil has a long history of violence. Brazil also has a high rate of poverty, has only a tiny middle class, and is controlled by a small group of families who, under a veneer of democracy, make the country's major decisions. Hordes of homeless children, with no schools or jobs, roam the streets. To survive, they wash windshields, shine shoes, beg, and steal (Huggins and Rodrigues 2004).

The "respectable" classes see these children as nothing but trouble. They hurt business, for customers feel intimidated when they see begging children—especially teenaged males—clustered in front of stores. Some shoplift; others dare to sell items that place them in competition with the stores. With no effective social institutions to care for these children, one solution is to kill them. As Huggins notes, murder sends a clear message—especially if it is accompanied by ritual torture: gouging out the eyes, ripping open the chest, cutting off the genitals, raping the girls, and burning the victim's body.

Not all life is bad in the Industrializing Nations, but this is about as bad as it gets.

For Your Consideration

Death squads for children also operate in the slums of the Philippines ("Death Squads . . ." 2008). Do you think there is anything the Most Industrialized Nations can do about this situation? Or is it, though unfortunate, just an "internal" affair that is up to the particular nation to handle as it wishes?

FIGURE 2 Global Stratification: Income[1] of the World's Nations

The Most Industrialized Nations

	Nation	Income per Person
1	Luxembourg	$79,400
2	Norway	$53,300
3	Singapore	$49,900
4	United States	$45,800
5	Hong Kong	$42,000
6	Iceland	$40,400
7	Switzerland	$40,100
8	Austria	$39,300
9	Netherlands	$39,000
10	Canada	$38,600
11	Sweden	$37,500
12	Australia	$37,300
13	Denmark	$37,200
14	Belgium	$36,200
15	Finland	$36,000
16	United Kingdom	$35,000
17	Germany	$34,100
18	Japan	$33,500
19	France	$32,600
20	Italy	$30,900
21	Taiwan	$30,100
22	Slovenia	$28,000
23	New Zealand	$27,200
24	Israel	$26,600
25	Korea, South	$25,000
26	Czech Republic	$24,500

The Industrializing Nations

	Nation	Income per Person
27	Ireland	$46,600
28	Spain	$33,600
29	Greece	$30,600
30	Estonia	$21,800
31	Portugal	$21,800
32	Slovakia	$20,200
33	Greenland	$20,000
34	Hungary	$19,300
35	Latvia	$17,700
36	Lithuania	$16,800
37	Poland	$16,200
38	Croatia	$15,500
39	Russia	$14,800
40	Malaysia	$14,500
41	Chile	$14,300
42	Gabon	$14,000
43	Argentina	$13,100
44	Venezuela	$12,800
45	Libya	$12,400
46	Mexico	$12,400
47	Turkey	$12,000
48	Bulgaria	$11,800
49	Mauritius	$11,300
50	Costa Rica	$11,100
51	Romania	$11,100
52	Cuba	$11,000
53	South Africa	$9,700
54	Brazil	$9,500

The Least Industrialized Nations

	Nation	Income per Person		Nation	Income per Person
55	Botswana[2]	$14,300	72	Algeria	$6,700
56	Kazakhstan	$11,000	73	Dominican	
57	Uruguay	$10,800		Republic	$6,600
58	Panama	$10,700	74	Bosnia	$6,100
59	Belarus	$10,600	75	El Salvador	$6,000
60	Lebanon	$10,300	76	Albania	$5,800
61	Suriname	$8,700	77	Armenia	$5,800
62	Macedonia	$8,400	78	China	$5,400
63	Azerbaijan	$8,000	79	Turkmenistan	$5,300
64	Belize	$7,900	80	Bhutan	$5,200
65	Angola	$7,800	81	Namibia	$5,200
66	Peru	$7,600	82	Guatemala	$5,100
67	Colombia	$7,400	83	Egypt	$5,000
68	Jamaica	$7,400	84	Jordan	$4,700
69	Tunisia	$7,400	85	Swaziland	$4,700
70	Ecuador	$7,200	86	Syria	$4,700
71	Ukraine	$7,000	87	Bolivia	$4,400

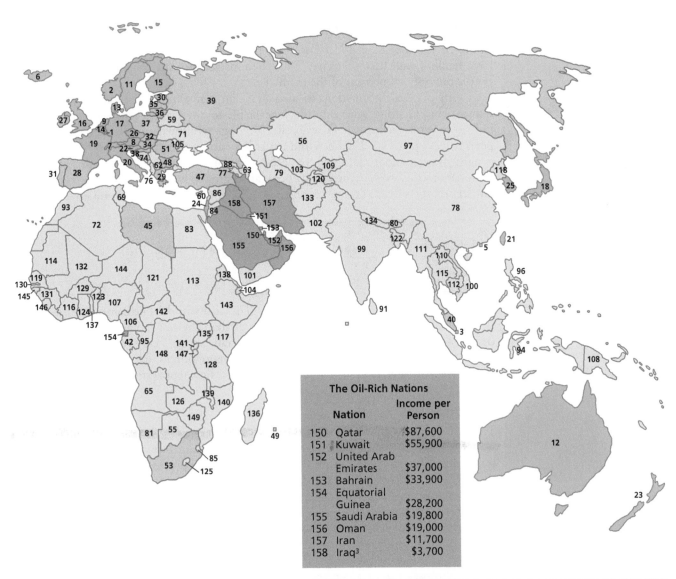

The Oil-Rich Nations	
Nation	**Income per Person**
150 Qatar	$87,600
151 Kuwait	$55,900
152 United Arab Emirates	$37,000
153 Bahrain	$33,900
154 Equatorial Guinea	$28,200
155 Saudi Arabia	$19,800
156 Oman	$19,000
157 Iran	$11,700
158 Iraq[3]	$3,700

The Least Industrialized Nations

Nation	Income per Person	Nation	Income per Person	Nation	Income per Person	Nation	Income per Person
88 Georgia	$4,400	105 Moldova	$2,300	120 Tajikistan	$1,600	137 Togo	$900
89 Honduras	$4,300	106 Cameroon	$2,200	121 Chad	$1,500	138 Eritrea	$800
90 Paraguay	$4,000	107 Nigeria	$2,100	122 Bangladesh	$1,400	139 Malawi	$800
91 Sri Lanka	$4,000	108 Papua-New Guinea	$2,100	123 Benin	$1,400	140 Mozambique	$800
92 Guyana	$3,700	109 Krygyzstan	$2,000	124 Ghana	$1,400	141 Rwanda	$800
93 Morocco	$3,700	110 Laos	$2,000	125 Lesotho	$1,400	142 Central African Republic	$700
94 Indonesia	$3,600	111 Burma (Myanmar)	$1,900	126 Zambia	$1,400	143 Ethiopia	$700
95 Congo, Rep.	$3,400	112 Cambodia	$1,900	127 Haiti	$1,300	144 Niger	$700
96 Philippines	$3,200	113 Sudan	$1,900	128 Tanzania	$1,300	145 Guinea-Bissau	$600
97 Mongolia	$2,900	114 Mauritania	$1,800	129 Burkina Faso	$1,200	146 Sierra Leone	$600
98 Nicaragua	$2,800	115 Thailand	$1,800	130 Gambia	$1,200	147 Burundi	$300
99 India	$2,600	116 Cote d'Ivoire	$1,700	131 Guinea	$1,100	148 Congo, Dem. Rep.	$300
100 Vietnam	$2,600	117 Kenya	$1,700	132 Mali	$1,100	149 Zimbabwe	$200
101 Yemen	$2,500	118 Korea, North	$1,700	133 Afghanistan	$1,000		
102 Pakistan	$2,400	119 Senegal	$1,700	134 Nepal	$1,000		
103 Uzbekistan	$2,400			135 Uganda	$1,000		
104 Djibouti	$2,300			136 Madagascar	$900		

[1]Income is a country's purchasing power parity based on a country's Gross Domestic Product, where the value of a country's goods and services are valued at prices prevailing in the United States. Totals vary from year to year and should be considered as approximations.

[2]Botswana's income is based largely on its diamond mines.

[3]Iraq's oil wealth has been disrupted by war.

Source: By the author. Based on *CIA World Factbook* 2008.

The Least Industrialized Nations

In the Least Industrialized Nations, most people live on small farms or in villages, have large families, and barely survive. These nations account for 68 percent of the world's people but only 49 percent of the earth's land.

Poverty plagues these nations to such an extent that some families actually *live* in city dumps. This is hard to believe, but look at the photos on the next few pages, which I took in Phnom Penh, the capital of Cambodia. Although wealthy nations have their pockets of poverty, *most* people in the Least Industrialized nations are poor. *Most* of them have no running water, indoor plumbing, or access to trained teachers or physicians. And it is in these nations that most of the world's population growth is occurring, placing even greater burdens on their limited resources and causing them to fall farther behind each year.

How Did the World's Nations Become Stratified?

How did the globe become stratified into such distinct worlds? The commonsense answer is that the poorer nations have fewer resources than the richer nations. As with many commonsense answers, however, this one, too, falls short. Many of the Industrializing and Least Industrialized Nations are rich in natural resources, while one Most Industrialized Nation, Japan, has few. Three theories explain how global stratification came about.

Colonialism

The first theory, **colonialism,** stresses that the countries that industrialized first got the jump on the rest of the world. Beginning in Great Britain about 1750, industrialization spread throughout western Europe. Plowing some of their profits into powerful armaments and fast ships, these countries invaded weaker nations, making colonies out of them (Harrison 1993). After subduing these weaker nations, the more powerful countries left behind a controlling force in order to exploit the nations' labor and natural resources. At one point, there was even a free-for-all among the industrialized European countries as they rushed to divide up an entire continent. As they sliced Africa into pieces, even tiny Belgium got into the act and acquired the Congo, which was *seventy-five* times larger than itself.

The purpose of colonialism was to establish *economic colonies*—to exploit the nation's people and resources for the benefit of the "mother" country. The more powerful European countries would plant their national flags in a colony and send their representatives to run the government, but the United States usually chose to plant corporate flags in a colony and let these corporations dominate the territory's government. Central and South America are prime examples. There were exceptions, such as the conquest of the Philippines, which President McKinley said was motivated by the desire "to educate the Filipinos, and uplift and civilize and Christianize them" (Krugman 2002).

Colonialism, then, shaped many of the Least Industrialized Nations. In some instances, the Most Industrialized Nations were so powerful that when dividing their spoils, they drew lines across a map, creating new states without regard for tribal or cultural considerations (Kifner 1999). Britain and France did just this as they divided up North Africa and parts of the Middle East—which is why the national boundaries of Libya, Saudi Arabia, Kuwait, and other countries are so straight. This legacy of European conquests is a background factor in much of today's racial–ethnic and tribal violence: Groups with no history of national identity were incorporated arbitrarily into the same political boundaries.

World System Theory

The second explanation of how global stratification came about was proposed by Immanuel Wallerstein (1974, 1979, 1990). According to **world system theory,** industrialization led to four groups of nations. The first group consists of the *core nations,* the countries that industrialized first (Britain, France, Holland, and later Germany), which

colonialism the process by which one nation takes over another nation, usually for the purpose of exploiting its labor and natural resources

world system theory economic and political connections that tie the world's countries together grew rich and powerful. The second group is the *semiperiphery.* The economies of these nations, located around the Mediterranean, stagnated because they grew dependent on trade with the core nations. The economies of the third group, the *periphery,* or fringe nations, developed even less. These are the eastern European countries, which sold cash crops to the core nations. The fourth group of nations includes most of Africa and Asia. Called the *external area,* these nations were left out of the development of capitalism altogether. The current expansion of capitalism has changed the relationships among these groups. Most notably, eastern Europe and Asia are no longer left out of capitalism.

The **globalization of capitalism**—the adoption of capitalism around the world—has created extensive ties among the world's nations. Production and trade are now so interconnected that events around the globe affect us all. Sometimes this is immediate, as happens when a civil war disrupts the flow of oil, or—perish the thought—as would be the case if terrorists managed to get their hands on nuclear or biological weapons. At other times, the effects are like a slow ripple, as when a government adopts some policy that gradually impedes its ability to compete in world markets. All of today's societies, then, no matter where they are located, are part of a *world system.*

The interconnections are most evident among nations that do extensive trading with one another. The following Thinking Critically section explores implications of Mexico's *maquiladoras.*

globalization of capitalism
capitalism (investing to make profits within a rational system) becoming the globe's dominant economic system

ThinkingCRITICALLY

When Globalization Comes Home:
Maquiladoras South of the Border

Two hundred thousand Mexicans rush to Juarez each year, fleeing the hopelessness of the rural areas in pursuit of a better life. They have no running water or plumbing, but they didn't have any in the country either, and here they have the possibility of a job, a weekly check to buy food for the kids.

The pay is $100 for a 48-hour work week, about $2 an hour (Harris 2008).

This may not sound like much, but it is more than twice the minimum daily wage in Mexico.

Assembly-for-export plants, known as *maquiladoras,* dot the Mexican border (Wise and Cypher 2007). The North American Free Trade Agreement (NAFTA) allows U.S. companies to export materials to Mexico without paying tax and to then import the finished products into the United States, again without tax. It's a sweet deal: few taxes and $17 a day for workers starved for jobs.

That these workers live in shacks, with no running water or sewage disposal is not the employers' concern.

Nor is the pollution. The stinking air doesn't stay on the Mexican side of the border. Neither does the garbage. Heavy rains wash torrents of untreated sewage and industrial wastes into the Rio Grande (Lacey 2007).

Where the workers live—no running water or sewage system.

The Dump People

Working and Living and Playing in the City Dump of Phnom Penh, Cambodia

went to Cambodia to inspect orphanages, to see how well the children were being cared for. While in Phnom Penh, Cambodia's capital, I was told about people who live in the city dump. *Live* there? I could hardly believe my ears. I knew that people made their living by picking scraps from the city dump, but I didn't know they actually lived among the garbage. This I had to see for myself.

I did. And there I found a highly developed social organization—an intricate support system. Because words are inadequate to depict the abject poverty of the Least Industrialized Nations, these photos can provide more insight into these people's lives than anything I could say.

This is a typical sight—family and friends working together. The trash, which is constantly burning, contains harmful chemicals. Why do people work under such conditions? Because they have few options. It is either this or starve.

The people live at the edge of the dump, in homemade huts (visible in the background). This woman, who was on her way home after a day's work, put down her sack of salvaged items to let me take her picture.

After the garbage arrives by truck, people stream around it, struggling to be the first to discover something of value. To sift through the trash, the workers use metal picks, like the one this child is holding. Note that children work alongside the adults.

The children who live in the dump also play there. These children are riding bicycles on a "road," a packed, leveled area of garbage that leads to their huts. The huge stacks in the background are piled trash. Note the ubiquitous Nike.

One of my many surprises was to find food stands in the dump. Although this one primarily offers drinks and snacks, others serve more substantial food. One even has chairs for its customers.

I was surprised to learn that ice is delivered to the dump. This woman is using a hand grinder to crush ice for drinks for her customers. The customers, of course, are other people who also live in the dump.

At the day's end, the workers wash at the community pump. This hand pump serves all their water needs—drinking, washing, and cooking. There is no indoor plumbing. The weeds in the background serve that purpose. Can you imagine drinking water that comes from below this garbage dump?

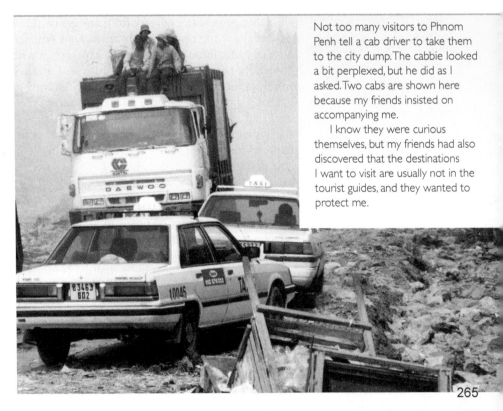

Not too many visitors to Phnom Penh tell a cab driver to take them to the city dump. The cabbie looked a bit perplexed, but he did as I asked. Two cabs are shown here because my friends insisted on accompanying me.

I know they were curious themselves, but my friends had also discovered that the destinations I want to visit are usually not in the tourist guides, and they wanted to protect me.

There is also the loss of jobs for U.S. workers. Six of the fifteen poorest cities in the United States are located along the sewage-infested Rio Grande. NAFTA didn't bring poverty to these cities. They were poor before this treaty, but residents resent the jobs they've seen move across the border (Thompson 2001).

What if the *maquiladora* workers organize and demand better pay? Farther south, even cheaper labor beckons. Guatemala and Honduras will gladly take the *maquiladoras*. Mexico has already lost many of its *maquiladora* jobs to places where people even more desperate will work for even less (Brown 2008).

Many Mexican politicians would say that this presentation is one-sided. "Sure there are problems," they would say, "but that is always how it is when a country industrializes. Don't you realize that the *maquiladoras* bring jobs to people who have no work? They also bring roads, telephone lines, and electricity to undeveloped areas." "In fact," said Vicente Fox, when he was the president of Mexico, "workers at the *maquiladoras* make more than the average salary in Mexico—and that's what we call fair wages" (Fraser 2001).

For Your Consideration

Let's apply our three theoretical perspectives. Conflict theorists say that capitalists try to weaken the bargaining power of workers by exploiting divisions among them. In what is known as the *split labor market*, capitalists pit one group of workers against another to lower the cost of labor. How do you think that *maquiladoras* fit this conflict perspective?

When functionalists analyze a situation, they identify its functions and dysfunctions. What functions and dysfunctions of *maquiladoras* do you see?

Do *maquiladoras* represent exploitation or opportunity? As symbolic interactionists point out, reality is a perspective based on our experience. What multiple realities do you see here?

Culture of Poverty

The third explanation of global stratification is quite unlike the other two. Economist John Kenneth Galbraith (1979) claimed that the cultures of the Least Industrialized Nations hold them back. Building on the ideas of anthropologist Oscar Lewis (1966a, 1966b), Galbraith argued that some nations are crippled by a **culture of poverty,** a way of life that perpetuates poverty from one generation to the next. He explained it this way: Most of the world's poor people are farmers who live on little plots of land. They barely produce enough food to survive. To experiment with new farming techniques is to court disaster, for failure would lead to hunger and death. Living close to the edge of starvation, with little room for risk, they stick closely to tried-and-true, traditional ways.

Their religion also encourages them to accept their situation, for it teaches fatalism: the belief that an individual's position in life is God's will. For example, in India, the Dalit are taught that they must have done very bad things in a previous life to suffer so. They are supposed to submit to their situation—and in the next life maybe they'll come back in a more desirable state.

Evaluating the Theories

Most sociologists prefer colonialism and world system theory. To them, an explanation based on a culture of poverty places blame on the victim—the poor nations themselves. It points to characteristics of the poor nations, rather than to international political arrangements that benefit the Most Industrialized Nations at the expense of the poor nations. But even taken together, these theories yield only part of the picture. None of these theories, for example, would have led anyone to expect that after World War II, Japan would become an economic powerhouse: Japan had a religion that stressed fatalism, two of its major cities had been destroyed by atomic bombs, and it had been stripped of its colonies.

Each theory, then, yields but a partial explanation, and the grand theorist who will put the many pieces of this puzzle together has yet to appear.

culture of poverty the assumption that the values and behaviors of the poor make them fundamentally different from other people, that these factors are largely responsible for their poverty, and that parents perpetuate poverty across generations by passing these characteristics to their children

Why Is Social Stratification Universal?

Why are all societies stratified? We shall first consider the explanation proposed by functionalists, which has aroused much controversy in sociology, and then explanations proposed by conflict theorists.

The Functionalist View: Motivating Qualified People

Functionalists take the position that the patterns of behavior that characterize a society exist because they are functional for that society. Because social inequality is universal, inequality must help societies survive. But how?

Davis and Moore's Explanation.   Two functionalists, Kingsley Davis and Wilbert Moore (1945, 1953), wrestled with this question. They concluded that stratification of society is inevitable because:

1. Some positions in a society are more important than others.
2. The more important positions must be filled by the more qualified people.
3. To motivate the more qualified people to fill these positions, they carry greater rewards.

To flesh out this functionalist argument, consider college presidents and military generals. The position of college president is more important than that of student because the president's decisions affect a large number of people, including many students. College presidents are also accountable for their performance to boards of trustees. It is the same with generals. Their decisions affect many people and sometimes even determine life and death. Generals are accountable to superior generals and to the country's leaders.

Why do people accept such high-pressure positions? Why don't they just take less demanding jobs? The answer, said Davis and Moore, is that society offers greater rewards—property, power, and prestige—for its more demanding and accountable positions. To get highly qualified people to compete with one another, some positions offer a salary of $2 million a year, country club membership, a private jet and pilot, and a chauffeured limousine. For less demanding positions, a $30,000 salary without fringe benefits is enough to get hundreds of people to compete. If a job requires rigorous training, it, too, must offer more salary and benefits. If you can get the same pay with a high school diploma, why suffer through the many tests and term papers that college requires?

Tumin's Critique of Davis and Moore.   Davis and Moore tried to explain *why* social stratification is universal; they were not attempting to justify social inequality. Nevertheless, their view makes many sociologists uncomfortable, for they see it as coming close to justifying the inequalities in society. Its bottom line seems to be: The people who contribute more to society are paid more, while those who contribute less are paid less.

Melvin Tumin (1953) was the first sociologist to point out what he saw as major flaws in the functionalist position. Here are three of his arguments.

First, how do we know that the positions that offer the higher rewards are more important? A heart surgeon, for example, saves lives and earns much more than a garbage collector, but this doesn't mean that garbage collectors are less important to society. By helping to prevent contagious diseases, garbage collectors save more lives than heart surgeons do. We need independent methods of measuring importance, and we don't have them.

Second, if stratification worked as Davis and Moore described it, society would be a **meritocracy;** that is, positions would be awarded on the basis of merit. But is this what we have? The best predictor of who goes to college, for example, is not ability but income: The more a family earns, the more likely their children are to go to college (Carnevale and Rose 2003; Belley and Lochner 2007). In this example, you see not merit, but money—a form of the inequality that is built into society. In short, people's positions in society are based on many factors other than merit.

Third, if social stratification is so functional, it ought to benefit almost everyone. Yet social stratification is *dysfunctional* for many. Think of the people who could have made valuable contributions to society had they not been born in slums, dropped out of school, and

meritocracy a form of social stratification in which all positions are awarded on the basis of merit

267

taken menial jobs to help support their families. Then there are the many who, born female, are assigned "women's work," thus ensuring that they do not maximize their mental abilities.

In Sum: Functionalists argue that some positions are more important to society than others. Offering higher rewards for these positions motivates more talented people to take them. For example, to get highly talented people to become surgeons—to undergo years of rigorous training and then cope with life-and-death situations, as well as malpractice suits—that position must provide a high payoff.

The Conflict Perspective: Class Conflict and Scarce Resources

Conflict theorists don't just criticize details of the functionalist argument. Rather, they go for the throat and attack its basic premise. Conflict, not function, they stress, is the reason that we have social stratification. Let's look at the major arguments.

Marx's Argument. If he were alive to hear the functionalist argument, Karl Marx would be enraged. From his point of view, the people in power are not there because of superior traits, as the functionalists would have us believe. This view is an ideology that members of the elite use to justify their being at the top—and to seduce the oppressed into believing that their welfare depends on keeping quiet and following authorities. What is human history, Marx asked, except the chronicle of class struggle? All of human history is an account of small groups of people in power using society's resources to benefit themselves and to oppress those beneath them—and of oppressed groups trying to overcome their oppression.

Marx predicted that the workers would revolt. Capitalist ideology blinds them, but one day class consciousness will throw off that blindfold and expose the truth. When workers realize their common oppression, they will rebel. The struggle to control the means of production may be covert at first, taking such forms as work slowdowns and industrial sabotage. Ultimately, however, resistance will break out into the open. The revolution will not be easy, for the bourgeoisie control the police, the military, and even the educational system, where they implant false class consciousness in the minds of the workers' children.

Current Applications of Conflict Theory. Just as Marx focused on overarching historic events—the accumulation of capital and power and the struggle between workers and capitalists—so do some of today's conflict sociologists. A chief focus is the current triumph of global capitalism. They analyze how the armed forces keep capitalist nations dominant and how workers are exploited as capital is moved from the Most Industrialized Nations to the Least Industrialized Nations (Sklair 2001).

Other conflict sociologists, in contrast, examine conflict wherever it is found, not just as it relates to capitalists and workers. They examine how groups *within the same class* compete with one another for a larger slice of the pie (Schellenberg 1996; Collins 1988, 1999). Even within the same industry, for example, union will fight against union for higher salaries, shorter hours, and more power. A special focus has been conflict between racial–ethnic groups as they compete for education, housing, and even prestige—whatever benefits society has to offer. Another focus has been relations between women and men, which conflict theorists say are best understood as a conflict over power—over who controls society's resources. Unlike functionalists, conflict theorists say that just beneath the surface of what may appear to be a tranquil society lies conflict that is barely held in check.

In Sum: Conflict theorists stress that in every society groups struggle with one another to gain a larger share of their society's resources. Whenever a group gains power, it uses that power to extract what it can from the groups beneath it. This elite group also uses the social institutions to keep itself in power.

Strains in the Global System

Global stratification is difficult to maintain, for every system contains unresolved issues, contradictions that can be covered up for a while, but that inevitably rear up. Some are just little dogs nipping at the heels of the world's elites. These issues can be resolved with a few tanks or bombs—or, better, with a scowl and the threat to bomb some small nation into submission.

At times, though, huge currents of history threaten to sweep a system of stratification aside—and with it, the elite who depend on that system for their positions of privilege. Such events are rare, but when they come they can bring cataclysmic disruptions. These historical shifts demand change, sometimes even the rearrangement of global power. We are now living through such a time. Russia and China's reluctant embrace of capitalism—and the more eager embrace by the eastern European nations–have been greeted with huge cracks in a creaking global banking system. Caught unaware, the global powers have desperately pumped trillions of dollars into their economic/political systems. As curious as we are about the outcome and as much as our lives are affected, we don't know the end point of this current strain in the global system. We must await the outcome of the power elites' attempts to patch up the system that supports their global domination. Inevitably, this process will lead to a realignment of power and property.

means of production the tools, factories, land, and investment capital used to produce wealth

bourgeoisie Marx's term for capitalists, those who own the means of production

proletariat Marx's term for the exploited class, the mass of workers who do not own the means of production

What Determines Social Class?

Because social class is the social stratification system of the United States, let's look at social class in greater detail. Let's begin by looking at a disagreement that arose in the early days of sociology between Marx and Weber.

Karl Marx: The Means of Production

As agricultural society gave way to an industrial one, masses of peasants were displaced from their traditional lands and occupations. Fleeing to cities, they competed for the few available jobs. Paid only a pittance for their labor, they wore rags, went hungry, and slept under bridges and in shacks. In contrast, the factory owners built mansions, hired servants, and lived in the lap of luxury. Seeing this great disparity between owners and workers, Karl Marx (1818–1883) concluded that social class depends on a single factor: people's relationship to the **means of production**—the tools, factories, land, and investment capital used to produce wealth (Marx 1844/1964; Marx and Engels 1848/1967).

To see social class, people often focus on the superficial distinctions that people make among themselves—their clothing, speech, manners, education, and income. Such things, said Marx, camouflage the only dividing line that counts. There are just two classes of people: the **bourgeoisie** (*capitalists*), those who own the means of production, and the **proletariat** (*workers*), those who work for the owners. In short, people's relationship to the means of production determines their social class.

Taken at the end of the 1800s, these photos illustrate the contrasting worlds of *social classes* produced by capitalism. The sleeping boys shown in this classic 1890 photo by Jacob Riis sold newspapers in London. They did not go to school, and they had no home. The children on the right, Cornelius and Gladys Vanderbilt, are shown in front of their parents' estate. They went to school and did not work. You can see how the social locations illustrated in these photos would have produced different orientations to life and, therefore, politics, ideas about marriage, values, and so on—the stuff of which life is made.

Jacob Riis/Bettmann/Corbis

Bettmann/Corbis

class consciousness Marx's term for awareness of a common identity based on one's position in the means of production

false class consciousness Marx's term to refer to workers identifying with the interests of capitalists

Marx did recognize other groups: farmers and peasants; a *lumpenproletariat* (people living on the margin of society, such as beggars, vagrants, and criminals); and a middle group of self-employed professionals. Marx did not consider these groups social classes, however, for they lack **class consciousness**—a shared identity based on their position in the means of production. In other words, they did not perceive themselves as exploited workers whose plight could be resolved by collective action. Marx thought of these groups as insignificant in the future he foresaw—a workers' revolution that would overthrow capitalism.

The capitalists will grow even wealthier, Marx said, and the hostilities will increase. When workers come to realize that capitalists are the source of their oppression, they will unite and throw off the chains of their oppressors. In a bloody revolution, they will seize the means of production and usher in a classless society. When this happens, no longer will the few grow rich at the expense of the many. What holds back the workers' unity and their revolution is **false class consciousness,** workers mistakenly thinking of themselves as capitalists. Workers with a few dollars in the bank often see themselves as investors, or as capitalists who are about to launch a successful business.

The only distinction worth mentioning, then, is whether a person is an owner or a worker. This decides everything else, Marx stressed, for property determines people's lifestyles, establishes their relationships with one another, and even shapes their ideas.

Max Weber: Property, Power, and Prestige

Max Weber (1864–1920) was an outspoken critic of Marx. He agreed that property is important, but said that it was only part of the picture. *Social class,* he said, has three components: property, power, and prestige (Gerth and Mills 1958; Weber 1922/1978). Some call these the three P's of social class. (Although Weber used the terms *class, power,* and *status,* some sociologists find *property, power,* and *prestige* to be clearer terms. To make them even clearer, you may wish to substitute *wealth* for *property.*)

Property (or wealth), said Weber, is certainly significant in determining a person's standing in society. On that point he agreed with Marx. But, added Weber, ownership is not the only significant aspect of property. For example, some powerful people, such as managers of corporations, *control* the means of production even though they do not *own* them. If managers can control the means of productions for their own benefit—awarding themselves huge bonuses and magnificent perks—it makes no practical difference that they do not own the property that they use so generously for their own benefit.

Power, the second element of social class, is the ability to control others, even over their objections. Weber agreed with Marx that property is a major source of power, but he added that it is not the only source. For example, prestige can be turned into power. Two well-known examples are actors Arnold Schwarzenegger, who became governor of California, and Ronald Reagan, who was elected governor of California and then president of the United States.

Prestige, the third element in Weber's analysis, is often derived from property and power, for people tend to admire the wealthy and powerful. Prestige, however, can be based on other factors. Olympic gold medalists, for example, might not own property or be powerful, yet they have high prestige. Some are even able to exchange their prestige for property—such as those who are paid a small fortune for endorsing a certain brand of sportswear or for claiming that they start their day with "the breakfast of champions." In other words, property and prestige are not one-way streets: Although property can bring prestige, prestige can also bring property. Figure 3 shows how property, power, and prestige are interrelated.

In Sum: For Marx, the only distinction that counted was property, more specifically people's relationship to the means of production. Whether we are owners or workers decides everything else, for this determines our lifestyle and shapes our orientation to life. Weber, in contrast, argued that social class has three components—a combination of property, power, and prestige.

With this background, let's turn our focus to social class in the United States.

FIGURE 3 Weber's Three Components of Social Class

Property

Power — (the wealthy men who become presidents)

Prestige — (Bill Gates; the wealthy in general)

Prestige

Power — (Ronald Reagan; Arnold Schwarzenegger)

Property — (Olympic gold medalists who endorse products)

Power

Property — (crooked politicians)

Prestige — (Abe Lincoln; Barack Obama)

Social Class in the United States

If you ask most Americans about their country's social class system, you are likely to get a blank look. If you press the matter, you are likely to get an answer like this: "There are the poor and the rich—and then there are you and I, neither poor nor rich." This is just about as far as most Americans' consciousness of social class goes. Let's try to flesh out this idea.

Sociologists have no clear-cut, agreed-on definition of social class (Lareau and Conley 2008). Few agree with Marx that there are only two social classes, those who own the means of production and those who do not. This, they feel, lumps too many people together. Teenage "order takers" at McDonald's who work for $15,000 a year are lumped together with that company's executives who make $500,000 a year—because they both are workers at McDonald's, not owners. Most sociologists use the components Weber identified and define **social class** as a large group of people who rank closely to one another in property, power, and prestige. They look at how these three elements separate people into different lifestyles, give them different chances in life, and provide them with distinct ways of looking at the self and the world.

How do sociologists measure these three components of social class?

Property

Property comes in many forms, such as animals, bank accounts, bonds, buildings, businesses, cars, furniture, jewelry, land, and machinery. When you add up the value of someone's property and subtract that person's debts, you have what sociologists call **wealth.** This term can be misleading, as some of us have little wealth—especially most college students. Nevertheless, if your net total comes to $10, then that is your wealth. (Obviously, wealth as a sociological term does not mean wealthy.)

Distinguishing Between Wealth and Income.   Wealth and income are sometimes confused, but they are not the same. Where *wealth* is a person's net worth, **income** is a flow of money. Income has many sources: The most common is a business or wages, but other sources are rent, interest, or royalties, even alimony, an allowance, or gambling. Some people have much wealth and little income. For example, a farmer may own much land (a form of wealth), but bad weather and low prices for crops can cause the income to dry up. Others have much income and little wealth. An executive with a $250,000 annual income may be debt-ridden. Below the surface prosperity—the exotic vacations, country club membership, private schools for the children, sports cars, and an elegant home—the credit cards may be maxed out, the sports cars in danger of being repossessed, and the mortgage payments "past due." Typically, however, wealth and income go together.

social class according to Marx, one of two groups: capitalists who own the means of production or workers who sell their labor; according to Weber, a large group of people who rank close to one another in wealth, power, and prestige

property material possessions: animals, bank accounts, bonds, buildings, businesses, cars, furniture, land, and stocks

wealth the total value of everything someone owns, minus the debts

Sociologists use income, education, and occupational prestige to measure social class. For most people, this works well, but not for everyone, especially entertainers. To what social class do Depp, James, Lopez, and Oh belong? Johnny Depp makes about $72 million a year, Lebron James $38 million, Jennifer Lopez $14 million, and Sandra Oh $2 million.

©Peter Andrews/Corbis; ©Nathanial S. Butler/NBAE via Getty Images; Allstar Picture Library/Alamy; Francis Specker/Landov

FIGURE 4
Distribution of the
Property of Americans

The wealthiest 10 percent
of Americans...

...own 70 percent of the
nation's wealth

The wealthiest 1 percent
of Americans...

...owns 33 percent of the
nation's wealth

Source: By the author. Based
on Beeghley 2008.

Distribution of Property. Who owns the property in the United States? One answer, of course, is "everyone." Although this statement has some merit, it overlooks how the nation's property is divided among "everyone."

Overall, Americans are worth a hefty sum, about $44 trillion (*Statistical Abstract* 2009:Table 701). This includes all real estate, stocks, bonds, and business assets in the entire country. Figure 4 shows how highly concentrated this wealth is. Most wealth, 70 percent, is owned by only *10 percent* of the nation's families. As you can also see from this figure, 1 percent of Americans own one-third of all the U.S. assets.

Distribution of Income. How is income distributed in the United States? Economist Paul Samuelson (Samuelson and Nordhaus 2005) put it this way: "If we made an income pyramid out of a child's blocks, with each layer portraying $500 of income, the peak would be far higher than Mount Everest, but most people would be within a few feet of the ground."

As Figure 5 shows, if each block were 1½ inches tall, the typical American would be just *10 feet off the ground,* for the average per capita income in the United States is about $39,000 per year. (This average income includes every American, even children.) The typical family climbs a little higher, for most families have more than one worker, and together they average about $58,000 a year. Compared with the few families who are on the mountain's peak, the average U.S. family would find itself only 15 feet off the ground (*Statistical Abstract* 2009:Tables 659, 674).

The fact that some Americans enjoy the peaks of Mount Everest while most—despite their efforts—don't even make it to a tree top at the bottom presents a striking image of income inequality in the United States. Another picture emerges if we divide the entire U.S. population into five equal groups. As Figure 6 shows, the top fifth of the population receives *half* (50.4 percent) of all the income in the entire country. In contrast, the bottom fifth receives only 3.4 percent of the nation's income.

Now look at Figure 6 on the next page. Two features of this figure are outstanding. First, notice how little change there has been in the distribution of income through the years. Second, look at how income inequality decreased from 1935 to 1970. *Since 1970, the richest 20 percent of U.S. families have grown richer, while the poorest 20 percent have grown poorer.* Despite numerous government antipoverty programs, the poorest 20 percent of Americans receive *less* of the nation's income today than they did decades ago. The richest 20 percent, in contrast, are receiving more, almost as much as they did in 1935.

The chief executive officers (CEOs) of the nation's largest corporations are especially affluent. The *Wall*

FIGURE 5
Distribution of the
Income of Americans

Some U.S. families
have incomes that
exceed the height of
Mt. Everest,
29,028 feet

Average
U.S. family
income
$58,000
or 15 feet

Average
U.S. individual
income
$39,000
or 10 feet

If a 1½-inch child's block
equals $500 of income, the
average individual's annual
income of $39,000 would
represent a height of 10 feet,
and the average family's
annual income of $58,000 would
represent a height of 15 feet.
The income of some families, in
contrast, would represent a height
greater than that of Mt. Everest.

Source: By the author.

FIGURE 6 The More Things Change, the More They Stay the Same: Dividing the Nation's Income

¹Earliest year available.
²No data for 1940.
Source: By the author. Based on *Statistical Abstract* 1960:Table 417; 1970:Table 489; 2009:Table 675.

Street Journal surveyed the 350 largest U.S. companies to find out what they paid their CEOs ("The Boss's Pay" 2008). Their median compensation (including salaries, bonuses, and stock options) came to $6,549,000 a year. (*Median* means that half received more than this amount, and half less.)

The CEOs' income—which does *not* include their income from interest, dividends, or rents, or the value of company-paid limousines and chauffeurs, airplanes and pilots, and private boxes at the symphony and sporting events—is *180 times* higher than the average pay of U.S. workers (*Statistical Abstract* 2009:Table 626). To really see the disparity, consider this: The average U.S. worker would have to work *more than 2,000 years* to earn the amount received by the highest-paid executive listed in Table 3.

Imagine how you could live with an income like this. And that is precisely the point. Beyond these cold numbers lies a dynamic reality that profoundly affects people's lives. The difference in wealth between those at the top and those at the bottom of the U.S. class structure means that people experience vastly different lifestyles. For example,

TABLE 3	The 5 Highest-Paid CEOs	
Executive	Company	Compensation
1. Sanjay Jha	Motorola	$104 million
2. Ray Irani	Occidental Petroleum	$50 million
3. Robert Iger	Disney	$50 million
4. Vikram Pandit	Citigroup	$38 million
5. Louis Camilleri	Philip Morris	$36 million

Note: Compensation includes salary, bonuses, and stock options.
Source: "The Wall Street Journal Survey..." 2009.

> a colleague of mine who was teaching at an exclusive Eastern university piqued his students' curiosity when he lectured on poverty in Latin America. That weekend, one of the students borrowed his parents' corporate jet and pilot, and in class on Monday, he and his friends related their personal observations on poverty in Latin America.

Few of us could ever say, "Mom and Dad, I've got to do a report for my soc class, so I need to borrow the jet—and the pilot—to run down to South America for the weekend." What a lifestyle! Contrast this with Americans at the low end of the income ladder who lack the funds to travel even to a neighboring town for the weekend. For parents in poverty, choices may revolve around whether to spend the little they have at the laundromat or on milk for the baby. The elderly might have to choose between purchasing the medicines they need or buying food. In short, divisions of wealth represent not "mere" numbers, but choices that make vital differences in people's lives. Let's explore this topic in the Down-to-Earth Sociology box.

Down-to-Earth Sociology
How the Super-Rich Live

It's good to see how other people live. It gives us a different perspective on life. Let's take a glimpse at the life of John Castle (his real name). After earning a degree in physics at MIT and an MBA at Harvard, John went into banking and securities, where he made more than $100 million (Lublin 1999).

Wanting to be connected to someone famous, John bought President John F. Kennedy's "Winter White House," an oceanfront estate in Palm Beach, Florida. John spent $11 million to remodel the 13,000-square-foot house so that it would be more to his liking. Among those changes: adding bathrooms number 14 and 15. He likes to show off John F. Kennedy's bed and also the dresser that has the drawer labeled "black underwear," carefully hand-lettered by Rose Kennedy.

At his beachfront estate, John gives what he calls "refined feasts" to the glitterati ("On History . . ." 1999). If he gets tired of such activities—or weary of swimming in the Olympic-size pool where JFK swam the weekend before his assassination—John entertains himself by riding one of his thoroughbred horses at his nearby 10-acre ranch. If this fails to ease his boredom, he can relax aboard his custom-built 42-foot Hinckley yacht.

The yacht is a real source of diversion. John once boarded it for an around-the-world trip. He didn't stay on board, though—just joined the cruise from time to time. A captain and crew kept the vessel on course, and whenever John felt like it he would fly in and stay a few days. Then he would fly back to the States to direct his business. He did this about a dozen times, flying perhaps 150,000 miles. An interesting way to go around the world.

How much does a custom-built Hinckley yacht cost? John can't tell you. As he says, "I don't want to know what anything costs. When you've got enough money, price doesn't make a difference. That's part of the freedom of being rich."

Right. And for John, being rich also means paying $1,000,000 to charter a private jet to fly Spot, his Appaloosa horse, back and forth to the vet. John didn't want Spot to have to endure a long trailer ride. Oh, and of course, there was the cost of Spot's medical treatment, another $500,000.

Other wealthy people spend extravagantly, too. Lee Tachman threw a four-day party for three friends. They

How do the super-rich live? This photo helps give you an idea of how different their lifestyles are from most of ours. Shown here is Wayne Huizenga, who is featured in this box, with one of his vintage automobiles.

had massages, ate well, took rides in a helicopter, a fighter jet, Ferraris, and Lamborghinis, and did a little paintballing—all for the bargain price of $50,000. At the 1 Oak Lounge in New York City, some customers pay $35,000 for a bottle of champagne (Haughney and Konigsberg 2008). Of course, it is a large bottle.

Parties are fun, but what if you want privacy? You can buy that, too. Wayne Huizenga, the founder of Blockbuster, who sold a half ownership in the Miami Dolphins for $550 million ("Builder Stephen . . ." 2008), bought a 2,000-acre country club, complete with an 18-hole golf course, a 55,000-square-foot-clubhouse, and 68 slips for visiting vessels. The club is so exclusive that its only members are Wayne and his wife (Fabrikant 2005).

Charles Simonyi has even outdone having your own country club. He bought a $25 million ticket for a rocket ride to the International Space Station. Simony liked the experience so much that he bought a second ticket (Leo 2008). No frequent flyer miles included. But at the rate prices are increasing, $50 million isn't worth what it used to be anyway.

For Your Consideration

What effects has social class had on your life? (Go beyond possessions to values, orientations, and outlooks on life.) How do you think you would see the world differently if you were John Castle, Lee Tachman, Charles Simonyi, or Mrs. Wayne Huizenga?

Power

Like many people, you may have said to yourself, "Sure, I can vote, but the big decisions are always made despite what I might think. Certainly *I* don't make the decision to send soldiers to Afghanistan or Iraq. *I* don't launch missiles into Iraq or Pakistan. *I* don't decide to raise taxes, lower interest rates, or spend billions of dollars to bail out Wall Street's fools and felons."

And then another part of you may say, "But I do participate in these decisions through my representatives in Congress, and by voting for president." True enough—as far as it goes. The trouble is, it just doesn't go far enough. Such views of being a participant in the nation's "big" decisions are a playback of the ideology we learn at an early age—an ideology that Marx said is promoted by the elites to both legitimate and perpetuate their power. Sociologists Daniel Hellinger and Dennis Judd (1991) call this the "democratic facade" that conceals the real source of power in the United States.

In the 1950s, sociologist C. Wright Mills (1956) pointed out that **power**—the ability to get your way despite resistance—was concentrated in the hands of a few. He met heavy criticism, for his analysis contradicted the dominant ideology of equality. This ideology is still dominant, and many don't like Mills' term **power elite,** which he coined to refer to those who make the big decisions in U.S. society.

Mills and others have stressed how wealth and power coalesce in a group of like-minded individuals who share ideologies, values, and world views. These individuals belong to the same private clubs and vacation at the same exclusive resorts. Their shared backgrounds and vested interests reinforce their view of both the world and their special place in it (Domhoff 1999a, 2006). This elite wields extraordinary power in the United States, so much so that *most* U.S. presidents have come from this group—millionaire white men from families with "old money" (Baltzell and Schneiderman 1988).

Continuing in the tradition of Mills, sociologist William Domhoff (1990, 2006) argues that this group is so powerful that the U.S. government makes no major decision without its approval. He analyzed how this group works behind the scenes with elected officials to determine both foreign and domestic policy—from setting Social Security taxes to imposing trade tariffs. Although Mills' and Domhoff's conclusions are controversial—and alarming—they certainly follow logically from the principle that wealth brings power, and extreme wealth brings extreme power.

Prestige

Occupations and Prestige. What are you thinking about doing after college? Chances are, you don't have the option of lolling under palm trees at the beach. Almost all of us have to choose an occupation and go to work. Look at Table 4 on the next page to see how the career you are considering stacks up in terms of **prestige** (respect or regard). Because we are moving toward a global society, this table also shows how the rankings given by Americans compare with those of the residents of sixty other countries.

Why do people give more prestige to some jobs than to others? If you look carefully at Table 4, you will notice that the jobs at the top share four features:

1. They pay more.
2. They require more education.
3. They entail more abstract thought.
4. They offer more independence (less supervision).

Look at the bottom of Table 4. You can see that people give less prestige to jobs with the opposite characteristics: These jobs are low-paying, require less preparation or education, involve more physical labor, and are closely supervised. In short, the professions and the white-collar jobs are at the top of the list, the blue-collar jobs at the bottom.

One of the more interesting aspects of these rankings is how consistent they are across countries and over time. For example, people in every country rank college professors higher than nurses, nurses higher than social workers, and social workers higher

power the ability to get your way, even over the resistance of others

power elite C. Wright Mills' term for the top people in U.S. corporations, military, and politics who make the nation's major decisions

prestige respect or regard

TABLE 4 Occupational Prestige: How the United States Compares with 60 Countries

Occupation	United States	Average of 60 Countries
Physician	86	78
Supreme Court judge	85	82
College president	81	86
Astronaut	80	80
Lawyer	75	73
College professor	74	78
Airline pilot	73	66
Architect	73	72
Biologist	73	69
Dentist	72	70
Civil engineer	69	70
Clergy	69	60
Psychologist	69	66
Pharmacist	68	64
High school teacher	66	64
Registered nurse	66	54
Professional athlete	65	48
Electrical engineer	64	65
Author	63	62
Banker	63	67
Veterinarian	62	61
Police officer	61	40
Sociologist	61	67
Journalist	60	55
Classical musician	59	56
Actor or actress	58	52
Chiropractor	57	62
Athletic coach	53	50
Social worker	52	56
Electrician	51	44
Undertaker	49	34
Jazz musician	48	38
Real estate agent	48	49
Mail carrier	47	33
Secretary	46	53
Plumber	45	34
Carpenter	43	37
Farmer	40	47
Barber	36	30
Store sales clerk	36	34
Truck driver	30	33
Cab driver	28	28
Garbage collector	28	13
Waiter or waitress	28	23
Bartender	25	23
Lives on public aid	25	16
Bill collector	24	27
Factory worker	24	29
Janitor	22	21
Shoe shiner	17	12
Street sweeper	11	13

Note. For five occupations not located in the 1994 source, the 1991 ratings were used: Supreme Court judge, astronaut, athletic coach, lives on public aid, and street sweeper.

Sources: Treiman 1977, Appendices A and D; Nakao and Treas 1991; 1994: Appendix D.

than janitors. Similarly, the occupations that were ranked high 25 years ago still rank high today—and likely will rank high in the years to come.

Status Inconsistency

Ordinarily, we have a similar rank on all three dimensions of social class—property, power, and prestige. As you know, the homeless men in our opening vignette rank very low on these three dimensions. Such people are **status consistent.** Some people, however, have a mixture of high and low ranks. This condition, called **status inconsistency,** leads to some interesting situations.

Sociologist Gerhard Lenski (1954, 1966) analyzed how people try to maximize their **status,** their position in a social group. Individuals who rank high on one dimension of social class but lower on others want people to judge them on the basis of their highest status. Those people, however, are trying to outrank others, and they may respond to status-inconsistent individuals according to their lowest ranking.

A classic study of status inconsistency was done by sociologist Ray Gold (1952). After apartment-house janitors unionized in Chicago, they made more money than some of the tenants whose garbage they carried out. Tenants became upset when they saw their janitors driving more expensive cars than they did. Some attempted to "put the janitor in his place" by making "snotty" remarks to him. For their part, the janitors took delight in knowing "dirty" secrets about the tenants, gleaned from their garbage.

Individuals with status inconsistency, then, are likely to confront one frustrating situation after another (Heames et al. 2006). They claim the higher status, but are handed the lower one. One consequence of this condition, said Lenski (1954), is that such people tend to be more politically radical. An example is college professors. Their prestige is very high, as you can see in Table 4, but their incomes are relatively low. Hardly anyone in U.S. society is more educated, and yet college professors don't even come close to the top of the income pyramid. In line with Lenski's prediction, the politics of most college professors are left of center. This hypothesis may also hold true among academic departments; that is, the higher a department's average pay, the less radical are the members' politics. Teachers in departments of business and medicine, for example, are among the most highly paid in the university—and they also are the most politically conservative.

In the Down-to-Earth Sociology box on the next page, we look at instant wealth, a fascinating case of status inconsistency.

Down-to-Earth Sociology
The Big Win: Life After the Lottery

"If I just win the lottery, life will be good. These problems I've got, they'll be gone. I can just see myself now."

So goes the dream. And many Americans shell out megabucks every week, with the glimmering hope that "Maybe this week, I'll hit it big."

Most are lucky to win $20, or maybe just another scratch-off ticket.

But there are the big hits. What happens to these winners? Are their lives all wine, roses, and chocolate afterward?

We don't have any systematic studies of the big winners, so I can't tell you what life is like for the average winner. But several themes are apparent from reporters' interviews.

The most common consequence of hitting it big is that life becomes topsy-turvy (Bernstein 2007). All of us are rooted somewhere. We have connections with others that provide the basis for our orientations to life and how we feel about the world. Sudden wealth can rip these moorings apart, and the resulting *status inconsistency* can lead to a condition sociologists call *anomie*.

First comes the shock. As Mary Sanderson, a telephone operator in Dover, New Hampshire, who won $66 million, said, "I was afraid to believe it was real, and afraid to believe it wasn't." Mary says that she never slept worse than her first night as a multimillionaire. "I spent the whole time crying—and throwing up" (Tresniowski 1999).

Reporters and TV camera operators appear on your doorstep. "What are you going to do with all that money?" they demand. You haven't the slightest idea, but in a daze you mumble something.

Then come the calls. Some are welcome. Your Mom and Dad call to congratulate you. But long-forgotten friends and distant relatives suddenly remember how close they really are to you—and strangely enough, they all have emergencies that your money can solve. You even get calls from strangers who have ailing mothers, terminally ill kids, sick dogs . . .

You have to unplug the phone and get an unlisted number.

You might be flooded with marriage proposals. You certainly didn't become more attractive or sexy overnight—or did you? Maybe money makes people sexy.

You can no longer trust people. You don't know what their real motives are. Before, no one could be after your money because you didn't have any. You may even fear kidnappers. Before, this wasn't a problem—unless some kidnapper wanted the ransom of a seven-year-old car.

The normal becomes abnormal. Even picking out a wedding gift is a problem. If you give the usual toaster, everyone will think you're stingy. But should you write a check for $25,000? If you do, you'll be invited to every wedding in town—and everyone will expect the same.

Status inconsistency *is common for lottery winners, whose new wealth is vastly greater than their education and occupational prestige. Shown here are John and Sandy Jarrell of Chicago, after they learned that they won $22 million. How do you think this will affect their lives?*

Here is what happened to some lottery winners:

When Alex Snelius of Chicago won $67 million, he lost his friends (Bernstein 2007). For some reason, they thought he should give them a large annual gift. As Alex's daughter says about Alex's (former) best friend, "He was like, 'Put me on your payroll.'"

As a tip, a customer gave a lottery ticket to Tonda Dickerson, a waitress at the Waffle House in Grand Bay, Alabama. She won $10 million. (Yes, just like the Nicholas Cage movie, *It Could Happen to You*.) Her co-workers sued her, saying that they had always agreed to split such winnings ("House Divided" 1999).

Then there is Michael Klinebiel of Rahway, New Jersey. When he won $2 million, his mother, Phyllis, said that half of it was hers, that she and her son had pooled $20 a month for years to play the lottery. He said they had done this—but he had bought the winning ticket on his own. Phyllis sued her son ("Sticky Ticket" 1998).

When Mack Metcalf, a forklift operator in Corbin, Kentucky, hit the jackpot for $34 million, he fulfilled a dream: He built and moved into a replica of George Washington's Mount Vernon home. Then his life fell apart—his former wife sued him, his current wife divorced him, and his new girlfriend got $500,000 while he was drunk. Within three years of his "good" fortune, Metcalf had drunk himself to death (Dao 2005).

Winners who avoid *anomie* seem to be people who don't make sudden changes in their lifestyle or their behavior. They hold onto their old friends and routines—the anchors in life that give them identity and a sense of belonging. Some even keep their old jobs—not for the money, of course, but because the job anchors them to an identity with which they are familiar and comfortable.

Sudden wealth, in other words, poses a threat that has to be guarded against.

And I can just hear you say, "I'll take the risk!"

For Your Consideration

How do you think your life would change if you won $10 million?

©Karim Sahib/AFP/Getty Images

How do you set yourself apart in a country so rich that of its 4.6 million people 79,000 are millionaires? Saeed Khouri (on the right) at an auction in Abu Dhabi paid $14 million for the license plate "1." His cousin was not as fortunate. His $9 million was enough to buy only "5."

Doral Chenoweth III/Columbus Dispatch/Corbis Sygma

A Model of Social Class

Sociologists Joseph Kahl and Dennis Gilbert (Gilbert and Kahl 1998; Gilbert 2003) developed a six-tier model to portray the class structure of the United States and other capitalist countries. Think of this model, illustrated in Figure 7 on the next page, as a ladder. Our discussion starts with the highest rung and moves downward. In line with Weber, on each lower rung you find less property (wealth), less power, and less prestige. Note that in this model education is also a primary measure of class.

The Capitalist Class

Sitting on the top rung of the class ladder is a powerful elite that consists of just 1 percent of the U.S. population. As you saw in Figure 4, this capitalist class is so wealthy that it owns one–third of all the nation's assets. *This tiny 1 percent is worth more than the entire bottom 90 percent of the country* (Beeghley 2008).

Power and influence cling to this small elite. They have direct access to top politicians, and their decisions open or close job opportunities for millions of people. They even help to shape the views of the nation: They own our major media and entertainment outlets—newspapers, magazines, radio and television stations, and sports franchises. They also control the boards of directors of our most influential colleges and universities. The super-rich perpetuate themselves in privilege by passing on their assets and social networks to their children.

The capitalist class can be divided into "old" and "new" money. The longer that wealth has been in a family, the more it adds to the family's prestige. The children of "old" money seldom mingle with "common" folk. Instead, they attend exclusive private schools where they learn views of life that support their privileged position. They don't work for wages; instead, many study business or become lawyers so that they can manage the family fortune. These old-money capitalists (also called "blue-bloods") wield vast power as they use their extensive political connections to protect their economic empires (Sklair 2001; Domhoff 1990, 1999b, 2006).

status consistent ranking high or low on all three dimensions of social class

status inconsistency ranking high on some dimensions of social class and low on others; also called status discrepancy

status the position that someone occupies in a social group

FIGURE 7 The U.S. Social Class Ladder

Social Class	Education	Occupation	Income	Percentage of Population
Capitalist	Prestigious university	Investors and heirs, a few top executives	$1,000,000+	1%
Upper Middle	College or university, often with postgraduate study	Professionals and upper managers	$125,000+	15%
Lower Middle	High school or college; often apprenticeship	Semiprofessionals and lower managers, craftspeople, foremen	About $60,000	34%
Working	High school	Factory workers, clerical workers, low-paid retail sales, and craftspeople	About $35,000	30%
Working Poor	Some high school	Laborers, service workers, low-paid salespeople	About $17,000	16%
Underclass	Some high school	Unemployed and part-time, on welfare	Under $10,000	4%

Source: Based on Gilbert and Kahl 1998 and Gilbert 2003; income estimates are modified from Duff 1995.

At the lower end of the capitalist class are the *nouveau riche,* those who have "new money." Although they have made fortunes in business, the stock market, inventions, entertainment, or sports, they are outsiders to the upper class. They have not attended the "right" schools, and they don't share the social networks that come with old money. Not blue-bloods, they aren't trusted to have the right orientations to life. Even their "taste" in clothing and status symbols is suspect (Fabrikant 2005). Donald Trump, whose money is "new," is not listed in the *Social Register,* the "White Pages" of the blue-bloods that lists the most prestigious and wealthy one-tenth of 1 percent of the U.S. population. Trump says he "doesn't care," but he reveals his true feelings by adding that his heirs will be in it (Kaufman 1996). He is probably right, for the children of the new-moneyed can ascend into the top part of the capitalist class—if they go to the right schools *and* marry old money.

Many in the capitalist class are philanthropic. They establish foundations and give huge sums to "causes." Their motives vary. Some feel guilty because they have so much while others have so little. Others seek prestige, acclaim, or fame. Still others feel a responsibility—even a sense of fate or purpose—to use their money for doing good. Bill Gates, who has given more money to the poor and to medical research than has anyone in history, seems to fall into this latter category.

The Upper Middle Class

Of all the classes, the upper middle class is the one most shaped by education. Almost all members of this class have at least a bachelor's degree, and many have postgraduate degrees in business, management, law, or

With a fortune of $57 billion, Bill Gates, a cofounder of Microsoft Corporation, is the second wealthiest person in the world. His 40,000-square-foot home (sometimes called a "technopalace") in Seattle, Washington, was appraised at $110 million.

©Dan Levine/ AFP/Getty Images

279

medicine. These people manage the corporations owned by the capitalist class or else operate their own business or profession. As Gilbert and Kahl (1998) say,

> [These positions] may not grant prestige equivalent to a title of nobility in the Germany of Max Weber, but they certainly represent the sign of having "made it" in contemporary America. . . . Their income is sufficient to purchase houses and cars and travel that become public symbols for all to see and for advertisers to portray with words and pictures that connote success, glamour, and high style.

Consequently, parents and teachers push children to prepare for upper-middle-class jobs. About 15 percent of the population belong to this class.

The Lower Middle Class

About 34 percent of the population belong to the lower middle class. Members of this class have jobs in which they follow orders given by members of the upper middle class. With their technical and lower-level management positions, they can afford a mainstream lifestyle, although they struggle to maintain it. Many anticipate being able to move up the social class ladder. Feelings of insecurity are common, however, with the threat of inflation, recession, and job insecurity bringing a nagging sense that they might fall down the class ladder (Kefalas 2007).

The distinctions between the lower middle class and the working class on the next rung below are more blurred than those between other classes. In general, however, members of the lower middle class work at jobs that have slightly more prestige, and their incomes are generally higher.

The Working Class

About 30 percent of the U.S. population belong to this class of relatively unskilled blue-collar and white-collar workers. Compared with the lower middle class, they have less education and lower incomes. Their jobs are also less secure, more routine, and more closely supervised. One of their greatest fears is that of being laid off during a recession. With only a high school diploma, the average member of the working class has little hope of climbing up the class ladder. Job changes usually bring "more of the same," so most concentrate on getting ahead by achieving seniority on the job rather than by changing their type of work. They tend to think of themselves as having "real jobs" and regard the "suits" above them as paper pushers who have no practical experience (Morris and Grimes 2005).

The Working Poor

Members of this class, about 16 percent of the population, work at unskilled, low-paying, temporary and seasonal jobs, such as sharecropping, migrant farm work, housecleaning, and day labor. Most are high school dropouts. Many are functionally illiterate, finding it difficult to read even the want ads. They are not likely to vote (Beeghley 2008), for they believe that no matter what party is elected to office, their situation won't change.

Although they work full time, millions of the working poor depend on food stamps and donations from local food pantries to survive on their meager incomes (O'Hare 1996b). How can they work full time and still be poor? Suppose that you are married and have a baby 3 months old and another child 4 years old. Your spouse stays home to care for them, so earning the income is up to you. But as a high-school dropout, all you can get is a minimum wage job. At $7.25 an hour, you earn $290 for 40 hours. In a year, this comes to $15,080—before deductions. You are constantly scrounging and borrowing from relatives. Your nagging fear—and recurring nightmare—is of ending up "on the streets."

underclass a group of people for whom poverty persists year after year and across generations

The Underclass

On the lowest rung, and with next to no chance of climbing anywhere, is the **underclass.** Concentrated in the inner city, this group has little or no connection with the job market. Those who are employed—and some are—do menial, low-paying, temporary work.

Welfare, if it is available, along with food stamps and food pantries, is their main support. Most members of other classes consider these people the "ne'er-do-wells" of society. Life is the toughest in this class, and it is filled with despair. About 4 percent of the population fall into this class.

The homeless men described in the opening vignette of this chapter, and the women and children like them, are part of the underclass. These are the people whom most Americans wish would just go away. Their presence on our city streets bothers passersby from the more privileged social classes—which includes just about everyone. "What are those dangerous-looking, obnoxious, dirty, foul-smelling people doing here, cluttering up my city?" appears to be a common response. Some people react with sympathy and a desire to do something. But what? Almost all of us just shrug our shoulders and look the other way, despairing of a solution and somewhat intimidated by their presence.

The homeless are the "fallout" of our postindustrial economy. In another era, they would have had plenty of work. They would have tended horses, worked on farms, dug ditches, shoveled coal, and run the factory looms. Some would have explored and settled the West. The prospect of gold would have lured others to California, Alaska, and Australia. Today, however, with no frontiers to settle, factory jobs scarce, and farms that are becoming technological marvels, we have little need for unskilled labor.

Consequences of Social Class

The man was a C student throughout school. As a businessman, he ran Arbusto, an oil company, into the ground. An alcoholic until age forty, he was arrested for drunk driving. With this background, how did he become president of the United States?

Accompanying these personal factors was the power of social class. George W. Bush was born the grandson of a wealthy senator and the son of a businessman who himself became president of the United States after serving as a member of the House of Representatives, director of the CIA, and head of the Republican party. For high school, he went to an elite private prep school, Andover; for his bachelor's degree to Yale; and for his MBA to Harvard. He was given $1 million to start his own business. When that business (Arbusto) failed, Bush fell softly, landing on the boards of several corporations. Taken care of even further, he was made the managing director of a professional baseball team, the Texas Rangers, and allowed to buy a share of the team for $600,000–which he sold for $15 million.

When it was time for him to get into politics, Bush's connections financed his run for governor of Texas and then for the presidency.

Does social class matter? And how! Think of each social class as a broad subculture with distinct approaches to life, so significant that it affects almost every aspect of our lives—our health, family life, education, and even our religion, politics, and law-breaking. Let's look at how social class affects our lives.

Physical Health

If you want to get a sense of how social class affects health, take a ride on Washington's Metro system. Start in the blighted Southeast section of downtown D.C. For every mile you travel to where the wealthy live in Montgomery County in Maryland, life expectancy rises about a year and a half. By the time you get off, you will find a twenty-year gap between the poor blacks where you started your trip and the rich whites where you ended it (Cohen 2004).

The principle is simple: As you go up the social-class ladder, health increases. As you go down the ladder, health decreases (Hout 2008). Age makes no difference. Infants born to the poor are more likely to die before their first birthday, and a larger percentage of poor people in their old age—whether 75 or 95—die each year than do the elderly who are wealthy.

How can social class have such dramatic effects on health? A fundamental reason is that health care in the United States is not a citizens' right but a commodity for sale. This gives us a two-tier system of medical care: superior care for those who can afford the cost and inferior care for those who cannot (Budrys 2003). Unlike the middle and upper classes, few poor people have a personal physician, and they often spend hours waiting in crowded public health clinics. When the poor are hospitalized, they are likely to find themselves in understaffed and underfunded public hospitals, treated by rotating interns who do not know them and cannot follow up on their progress.

A second reason is lifestyles, which are shaped by social class. People in the lower classes are more likely to smoke, eat a lot of fats, be overweight, abuse drugs and alcohol, get little or no exercise, and practice unsafe sex (Chin et al. 2000; Navarro 2002; Liu 2007). This, to understate the matter, does not improve people's health.

There is a third reason, too. Life is hard on the poor. The persistent stresses they face cause their bodies to wear out faster (Spector 2007). The rich find life better. They have fewer problems and more resources to deal with the ones they have. This gives them a sense of control over their lives, a source of both physical and mental health.

Mental Health

Sociological studies from as far back as the 1930s have found that the mental health of the lower classes is worse than that of the higher classes (Faris and Dunham 1939; Srole et al. 1978; Pratt et al. 2007). Greater mental problems are part of the higher stress that accompanies poverty. Compared with middle- and upper-class Americans, the poor have less job security and lower wages. They are more likely to divorce, to be the victims of crime, and to have more physical illnesses. Couple these conditions with bill collectors and the threat of eviction, and you can see how they can deal severe blows to people's emotional well-being.

People higher up the social class ladder experience stress in daily life, of course, but their stress is generally less, and their coping resources are greater. Not only can they afford vacations, psychiatrists, and counselors, but *their class position also gives them greater control over their lives, a key to good mental health.* Consider these factors as you read the following thinking critically section.

ThinkingCRITICALLY

Mental Illness and Inequality in Health Care

Standing among the police, I watched as the elderly nude man, looking confused, struggled to put on his clothing. The man had ripped the wires out of the homeless shelter's main electrical box and then led the police on a merry chase as he ran from room to room.

I asked the officers where they were going to take the man, and he replied, "To Malcolm Bliss" (the state mental hospital). When I commented, "I guess he'll be in there for a quite a while," they replied, "Probably just a day or two. We picked him up last week—he was crawling under cars stopped at a traffic light—and they let him out in two days."

The police explained that a person must be a danger to others or to oneself to be admitted as a long-term patient. Visualizing this old man crawling under cars in traffic and the possibility of electrocuting himself by ripping out electrical wires with his bare hands, I marveled at the definition of "danger" that the hospital psychiatrists must be using.

Stripped of its veil, the two-tier system of medical care is readily visible. The poor—such as this confused naked man—find it difficult to get into mental hospitals. If they are admitted, they are sent to the dreaded state hospitals. In contrast, private hospitals serve the wealthy and those who have good insurance. The rich are likely to be treated with "talk therapy" (forms of psychotherapy), the poor with "drug therapy" (tranquilizers to make them docile, sometimes known as "medicinal straitjackets").

Family Life

Social class also makes a significant difference in family life. Social class influences how we rear our children and influences our choice of spouse and our chances of getting divorced.

Choice of Husband or Wife. Members of the capitalist class place strong emphasis on family tradition. They stress the family's history, even a sense of purpose or destiny in life (Aldrich 1989). Children of this class learn that their choice of husband or wife affects not just them, but the entire family, that it will have an impact on the "family line." These background expectations shrink the field of "eligible" marriage partners, making it narrower than it is for the children of any other social class. As a result, parents in this class play a strong role in their children's mate selection.

Divorce. The more difficult life of the lower social classes, especially the many tensions that come from insecure jobs and inadequate incomes, leads to higher marital friction and a greater likelihood of divorce. Consequently, children of the poor are more likely to grow up in broken homes.

Education

As we saw in Figure 7, education increases as one goes up the social class ladder. It is not just the amount of education that changes, but also the type of education.

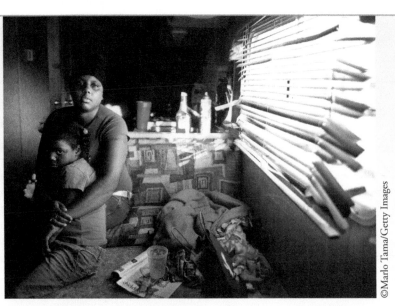

What a difference social class makes in our lives! Shown here are model Kimora Lee Simmons in her home in Saddle River, New Jersey, and Nakeva Narcisse and her daughter in their home in Port Sulphur, Louisiana. Can you see why these women see the world in highly distinctive ways? How do you think social class affects their politics and aspirations in life?

©Marko Tama/Getty Images

©Animal Fair Media/Getty Images

283

Children of the capitalist class bypass public schools. They attend exclusive private schools where they are trained to take a commanding role in society. Prep schools such as Andover, Groton, and Phillips Exeter Academy teach upper-class values and prepare their students for prestigious universities (Cookson and Persell 2005; Beeghley 2008).

Certain private preschools feed into these exclusive prep schools. To get their children into them, some upper-middle-class parents solicit letters of recommendation for their 2- and 3-year-olds. They are such a key to upward social mobility that even preschools that cost $23,000 a year have waiting lists (Rohwedder 2007). I am sure that you can see how such parental involvement and resources are major reasons why children from the more privileged classes are more likely to go to college—and to graduate.

Religion

One area of social life that we might think would not be affected by social class is religion. ("People are either religious, or they are not. What does social class have to do with it?") Social class, however, is a significant sorter of people in all areas of social life, and religion is no exception to this principle. The classes tend to cluster in different denominations. Episcopalians, for example, are more likely to attract the middle and upper classes, while Baptists and the Assemblies of God draw heavily from the lower classes (Smith and Faris 2005). Patterns of worship also follow class lines: The lower classes are attracted to more expressive worship services and louder music, while the middle and upper classes prefer more "subdued" worship.

Politics

As I have stressed throughout this text, people perceive events from their own corner in life. Political views are no exception to this principle of symbolic interaction, and the rich and the poor walk different political paths. The higher that people are on the social class ladder, the more likely they are to vote for Republicans (Hout 2008). In contrast, most members of the working class believe that the government should intervene in the economy to provide jobs and to make citizens financially secure. They are more likely to vote for Democrats. Although the working class is more liberal on *economic* issues (policies that increase government spending), its members are more conservative on *social* issues (such as opposing abortion and the Equal Rights Amendment) (Houtman 1995; Hout 2008). People toward the bottom of the class structure are also less likely to be politically active—to campaign for candidates or even to vote (Gilbert 2003; Beeghley 2008).

Crime and Criminal Justice

If justice is supposed to be blind, it certainly is not when it comes to your chances of being arrested. The social classes commit different types of crime: The white-collar crimes of the more privileged classes are more likely to be dealt with outside the criminal justice system, while the police and courts deal with the street crimes of the lower classes. One consequence of this class standard is that members of the lower classes are more likely to be in prison, on probation, or on parole. In addition, since those who commit street crimes tend to do so in or near their own neighborhoods, the lower classes are more likely to be robbed, burglarized, or murdered.

Social Mobility

No aspect of life, then—from marriage to politics—goes untouched by social class. Because life is so much more satisfying in the more privileged classes, people strive to climb the social class ladder. What affects their chances?

Three Types of Social Mobility

There are three basic types of social mobility: intergenerational, structural, and exchange. **Intergenerational mobility** refers to a change that occurs between generations—when grown-up children end up on a different rung of the social class ladder from the one occupied by their parents. If the child of someone who sells used cars graduates from college and buys a Toyota dealership, that person experiences **upward social mobility.** Conversely, if a child of the dealership's owner parties too much, drops out of college, and ends up selling cars, he or she experiences **downward social mobility.** As discussed in the Cultural Diversity box on the next page, social mobility comes at a cost.

We like to think that individual efforts are the reason people move up the class ladder—and their faults the reason they move down. In these examples, we can identify hard work, sacrifice, and ambition on the one hand, versus indolence and substance abuse on the other. Although individual factors such as these do underlie social mobility, sociologists consider **structural mobility** to be the crucial factor. This second basic type of mobility refers to changes in society that cause large numbers of people to move up or down the class ladder.

To understand *structural mobility,* think about how changes in society (its *structure*) drive some people down the social class ladder and lift others up. When computers were invented, for example, new types of jobs appeared overnight. Huge numbers of people attended workshops and took crash courses, switching from blue-collar to white-collar work. In contrast, others were thrown out of work as technology bypassed their jobs. Individual effort was certainly involved—for some seized the opportunity while others did not—but the underlying cause was a huge social change that transformed the *structure* of work. This happens during depressions, too, when opportunities disappear, forcing millions of people downward on the class ladder. In this instance, too, their changed status is due less to individual behavior than to *structural* changes in society.

The third type of social mobility, **exchange mobility,** occurs when large numbers of people move up and down the social class ladder, but, on balance, the proportions of the social classes remain about the same. Suppose that a million or so working-class people are trained in some new technology, and they move up the class ladder. Suppose also that because of a surge in imports, about a million skilled workers have to take lower-status jobs. Although millions of people change their social class, there is, in effect, an *exchange* among them. The net result more or less balances out, and the class system remains basically untouched.

Women in Studies of Social Mobility

In classic studies to determine how much social mobility there is, sociologists concluded that about half of sons passed their fathers on the social class ladder, about one-third stayed at the same level, and about one-sixth moved down (Blau and Duncan 1967; Featherman 1979). Feminists objected. They said that it wasn't good science to ignore daughters and that assigning women the class of their husbands assumed that wives had no social class positions of their own (Davis and Robinson 1988). The male sociologists of the time brushed off these objections, replying that too few women were in the labor force to make a difference.

These sociologists simply hadn't caught up with the times. The gradual but steady increase of women working for pay had caught them unprepared. Although sociologists now include women in their research on social mobility, determining how the social class of married women is related to that of their husbands is still in its infancy (McCall 2008). Sociologists Elizabeth Higginbotham and Lynn Weber (1992) studied 200 women from working-class backgrounds who had become administrators, managers, and professionals in Memphis. Almost without exception, their parents had implanted ideas of success in them while they were still little girls, encouraging them to postpone marriage and get an education. This research confirms how important the family is in the socialization process. It also supports the observation that the primary entry to the upper middle class is a college education. At the same time, if there had not been a *structural* change in society, the millions of new positions that women occupy would not exist.

intergenerational mobility the change that family members make in social class from one generation to the next

upward social mobility movement up the social class ladder

downward social mobility movement down the social class ladder

structural mobility movement up or down the social class ladder that is due to changes in the structure of society, not to individual efforts

exchange mobility about the same numbers of people moving up and down the social class ladder, such that, on balance, the social class system shows little change

Cultural Diversity in the United States

Social Class and the Upward Social Mobility of African Americans

The overview of social class presented in this chapter doesn't apply equally to all the groups that make up U.S. society. Consider geography: What constitutes the upper class of a town of 5,000 people will differ from that of a city of a million. With fewer extremes of wealth and occupation, in small towns family background and local reputation are more significant.

So it is with racial–ethnic groups. All racial–ethnic groups are marked by social class, but what constitutes a particular social class can differ from one group to another—as well as from one historical period to another. Consider social class among African Americans (Cole and Omari 2003).

The earliest class divisions can be traced to slavery—to slaves who worked in the fields and those who worked in the "big house." Those who worked in the plantation home were exposed more to the customs, manners, and forms of speech of wealthy whites. Their more privileged position—which brought with it better food and clothing, as well as lighter work—was often based on skin color. Mulattos, lighter-skinned slaves, were often chosen for this more desirable work. One result was the development of a "mulatto elite," a segment of the slave population that, proud of its distinctiveness, distanced itself from the other slaves. At this time, there also were free blacks. Not only were they able to own property but some even owned black slaves.

After the War Between the States (as the Civil War is known in the South), these two groups, the mulatto elite and the free blacks, formed an upper class. Proud of their earlier status, they distanced themselves from

© Wireimage/ Getty Images

A mere one-half percent of Americans owns over a quarter of the entire nation's wealth. Few minorities are part of this small group. An exception is Oprah Winfrey, who, at $1.3 billion, is the 215th richest person in the United States. The super-rich wield power. Oprah is shown here as she campaigned for Obama.

other blacks. From these groups came most of the black professionals.

After World War II, the black middle class expanded as African Americans entered a wider range of occupations. Today, more than half of all African American adults work at white-collar jobs, about 22 percent at the professional or managerial level (Beeghley 2008). An unwelcome cost greets many African Americans who move up the social class ladder: an uncomfortable distancing from their roots, a separation from significant others—parents, siblings, and childhood friends (Hooks 2000). The upwardly mobile enter a world unknown to those left behind, one that demands not only different appearance and speech, but also different values, aspirations, and ways of viewing the world. These severe challenges to the self often rupture relationships with those left behind.

An additional cost is a subtle racism that lurks beneath the surface of some work settings, poisoning what could be easy, mutually respectful interaction. To be aware that white co-workers perceive you as different—as a stranger, an intruder, or "the other"—engenders frustration, dissatisfaction, and cynicism. To cope, many nourish their racial identity and stress the "high value of black culture and being black" (Lacy and Harris 2008). Some move to neighborhoods of upper-middle-class African Americans, where they can live among like-minded people who have similar experiences (Lacy 2007).

For Your Consideration

In the box on upward social mobility, we discussed how Latinos face a similar situation. Why do you think this is? What connections do you see among upward mobility, frustration, and racial–ethnic identity? How do you think that the upward mobility of whites is different? Why?

Poverty

Many Americans find that the "limitless possibilities" of the American dream are quite elusive. As illustrated in Figure 7, the working poor and underclass together form about one-fifth of the U.S. population. This translates into a huge number, about 60 million people. Who are these people?

Drawing the Poverty Line

To determine who is poor, the U.S. government draws a **poverty line.** This measure was set in the 1960s, when poor people were thought to spend about one-third of their incomes on food. On the basis of this assumption, each year the government computes a low-cost food budget and multiplies it by 3. Families whose incomes are less than this amount are classified as poor; those whose incomes are higher—even by a dollar—are determined to be "not poor."

This official measure of poverty is grossly inadequate. Poor people actually spend only about 20 percent of their incomes on food, so to determine a poverty line, we ought to multiply their food budget by 5 instead of 3 (Uchitelle 2001). Another problem is that mothers who work outside the home and have to pay for child care are treated the same as mothers who don't have this expense. The poverty line is also the same for everyone across the nation, even though the cost of living is much higher in New York than in Alabama. In addition, much of the income of the poor goes uncounted: food stamps, rent assistance, subsidized child care, and the earned income tax credit (Kaufman 2007).

That a change in the poverty line would instantly make millions of people poor—or take away their poverty—would be laughable, if it weren't so serious. (The absurdity has not been lost on Parker and Hart, as you can see from their cartoon below.) Although this line is arbitrary, because it is the official measure of poverty, we'll use it to see who in the United States is poor. Before we do this, though, compare your ideas of the poor with the stereotypes explored in the Down-to-Earth Sociology box on the next page.

Race–Ethnicity.   One of the strongest factors in poverty is race–ethnicity. As Figure 8 shows, only 10 percent of Asian Americans and whites are poor. In contrast, 21 percent of Latinos live in poverty, while the total jumps even higher, to 24 percent for African Americans and 27 percent for Native Americans. Because whites are, by far, the largest group in the United States, their much lower rate of poverty still translates into larger numbers. As a result, there are more poor whites than poor people of any other racial–ethnic group.

Children of Poverty

Children are more likely to live in poverty than are adults or the elderly. This holds true regardless of race–ethnicity, but from Figure 8 on the next page, you can see how much greater poverty is among Latino, African American, and Native American children. That millions of U.S. children are reared in poverty is shocking when one considers the wealth of this country and the supposed concern for the well-being of children. This tragic aspect of poverty is the topic of the following Thinking Critically section that follows.

Library of Congress Image #USF34-T01-009095-C

High rates of rural poverty have been a part of the United States from its origin to the present. This 1937 photo shows a 32-year old woman in California who had seven children and no food.

poverty line the official measure of poverty; calculated to include incomes that are less than three times a low-cost food budget

WIZARD OF ID

This cartoon pinpoints the arbitrary nature of the poverty line. This almost makes me think that the creators of the Wizard of Id have been studying sociology.

Down-to-Earth Sociology
Taking Another Fun Quiz: Exploring Stereotypes About the Poor

Do you hold any of these stereotypes? Can you tell which are true and which are not?

Most poor people are lazy. They are poor because they do not want to work. *False.* Half of the poor are either too old or too young to work: About 40 percent are under age 18, and another 10 percent are age 65 or older. About 30 percent of the working-age poor work at least half the year.

Most of the poor are trapped in a cycle of poverty that few escape. *False.* Long-term poverty is the exception. Most poverty lasts less than a year (Lichter and Crowley 2002). Only 12 percent remain in poverty for five or more consecutive years (O'Hare 1996a). Most children who are born in poverty are *not* poor as adults (Ruggles 1989; Corcoran 2001).

There is more poverty in rural than in urban areas. *True.* We'll review this in the following section.

Most African Americans are poor. *False.* This one was easy. We just reviewed some statistics in the box on upward mobility—plus you have the bar chart below.

Most of the poor are African Americans. *False.* Look at the second part of Figure 8. *There are more poor whites than any other group.* The combined total of poor African Americans, Latinos, and Native Americans, however, is larger than the total of poor whites.

Most of the poor are single mothers and their children. *False.* About 38 percent of the poor match this stereotype, but 34 percent of the poor live in married-couple families, 22 percent live alone or with nonrelatives, and 6 percent live in other settings.

Most of the poor live in the inner city. *False.* About 42 percent of the poor do live in the inner city, but 36 percent live in the suburbs, and 22 percent live in small towns and rural areas.

Most of the poor live on welfare. *False.* Only about 25 percent of the income of poor adults comes from welfare. About half comes from wages and pensions, and about 22 percent from Social Security.

On a percentage basis, more children than adults are poor. *True.* (Okay, no one holds this stereotype. I just want to make this important point. We'll come back to it shortly.)

For Your Consideration

What stereotypes of the poor do you (or people you know) hold? How would you test these stereotypes?

Sources: O'Hare 1996a, 1996b, with other sources as indicated

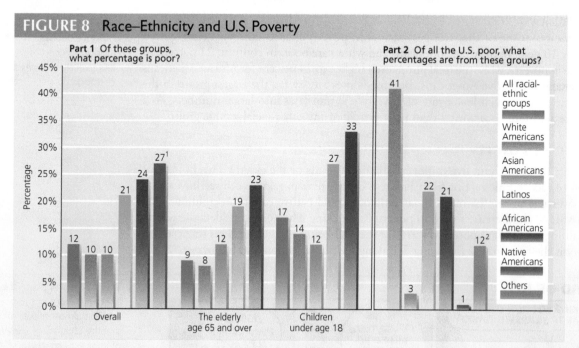

FIGURE 8 Race–Ethnicity and U.S. Poverty

Part 1 Of these groups, what percentage is poor?

Part 2 Of all the U.S. poor, what percentages are from these groups?

[1]The source does not break this total down by age. [2]Others consists of people who identify themselves as being of ancestry other than the groups listed here plus those who claim membership in two or more racial–ethnic groups.

Note: Only these groups are listed in the source. The poverty line on which this figure is based is $20,614 for a family of four.
Source: By the author. Based on *Statistical Abstract of the United States* 2009:Tables 35, 688, and 691.

ThinkingCRITICALLY

The Nation's Shame: Children in Poverty

One of the most startling statistics in sociology is shown in Figure 8. Look at the rate of childhood poverty: For Asian Americans, 1 of 8 children is poor; for whites, 1 of 7; for Latinos, 1 of 4; and for African Americans, an astounding 1 of 3. These percentages translate into incredible numbers—approximately *13 million* children.

Why do so many U.S. children live in poverty? A major reason is the large number of births to women who are not married, about 1.5 million a year. Look at how sharply this number has increased: In 1960, 1 of 20 U.S. children was born to a single woman. Today that total is about *eight times higher,* and single women now account for 2 of 5 (39 percent) of all U.S. births (*Statistical Abstract* 2009:Table 87).

But births to single women don't actually cause poverty. Consider the obvious: Children born to wealthy single women aren't reared in poverty, are they? Then consider this: Although the U.S. birth rate to single women is not the highest in the industrialized world, *our rate of child poverty is the highest in the industrialized world* (Rainwater and Smeeding 2003). In countries where the birth rate to single women is higher than ours but where child poverty is lower, the government provides extensive support for rearing these children—from day care to health check-ups and medicine. As the cause of their poverty, then, why can't we point to government support for children—or the lack of it?

Apart from the matter of government policy, births to single women follow patterns that have a negative impact on their children's welfare. The less education a single woman has, the more likely she is to bear children. As you can see from Figure 9, births to single women drop with each gain in education. As you know, people with lower education earn less, so this means that the single women who can least afford children are those most likely to give birth. Poverty brings these children huge obstacles to building a satisfying life. They are more likely to die in infancy, to go hungry, to be malnourished, to develop more slowly, and to have more health problems. They also are more likely to drop out of school, to commit street crimes, and to have children while still in their teens—thus perpetuating a cycle of poverty.

For Your Consideration

With education so important to getting high-paying jobs, in light of Figure 9 what programs would you suggest for helping women attain more education? What programs would you suggest for reducing child poverty? Be specific and practical.

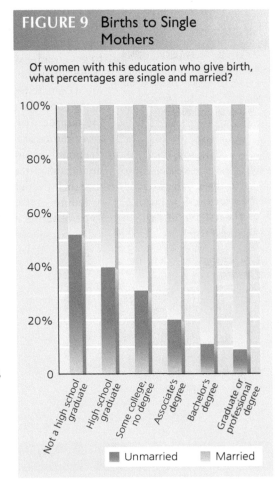

FIGURE 9 Births to Single Mothers

Of women with this education who give birth, what percentages are single and married?

■ Unmarried ■ Married

Note: Based on a national sample of all U.S. births in the preceding 12 months.
Source: Dye 2005.

Where Is Horatio Alger? The Social Functions of a Myth

In the late 1800s, Horatio Alger was one of the country's most popular authors. The rags-to-riches exploits of his fictional boy heroes and their amazing successes in overcoming severe odds motivated thousands of boys of that period. Although Alger's characters have disappeared from U.S. literature, they remain alive and well in the psyche of Americans. From real-life examples of people of humble origin who climbed the social class ladder, Americans know that anyone who really tries can get ahead. In fact, they believe that most Americans, including minorities and the working poor, have an average or better-than-average chance of getting ahead—obviously a statistical impossibility (Kluegel and Smith 1986).

The accuracy of the **Horatio Alger myth** is less important than the belief that limitless possibilities exist for everyone. Functionalists would stress that this belief is functional for society. On the one hand, it encourages people to compete for higher positions, or, as the song says, "to reach for the highest star." On the other hand, it places blame for failure squarely on the individual. If you don't make it—in the face of ample opportunities to get ahead—the fault must be your own. The Horatio Alger myth helps to stabilize society: Since the fault is viewed as the individual's, not society's, current social arrangements can be regarded as satisfactory. This reduces pressures to change the system.

As both Marx and Weber pointed out, social class penetrates our consciousness, shaping our ideas of life and our "proper" place in society. When the rich look at the world around them, they sense superiority and anticipate control over their own destiny. When the poor look around them, they are more likely to sense defeat and to anticipate that unpredictable forces will batter their lives. Both rich and poor know the dominant ideology, that their particular niche in life is due to their own efforts, that the reasons for success—or failure—lie solely with the self. Like fish that don't notice the water, people tend not to perceive the effects of social class on their own lives.

James M. Henslin

A society's dominant ideologies are reinforced throughout the society, including its literature. Horatio Alger provided inspirational heroes for thousands of boys. The central theme of these many novels, immensely popular in their time, was rags to riches. Through rugged determination and self-sacrifice, a boy could overcome seemingly insurmountable obstacles to reach the pinnacle of success. (Girls did not strive for financial success, but were dependent on fathers and husbands.)

Horatio Alger myth the belief that due to limitless possibilities anyone can get ahead if he or she tries hard enough

By the Numbers: *Then and Now*

The richest 20% of Americans receive this percentage of the nation's income

1970	NOW
41%	51%

The poorest 20% of Americans receive this percentage of the nation's income

1970	NOW
6%	3%

Frequency of births outside of marriage

1960	NOW
1 in 20	8 in 20

SUMMARY *and* REVIEW

What is social stratification?

Social stratification refers to a hierarchy of relative privilege based on property, power, and prestige. Every society stratifies its members, and in every society men as a group are placed above women as a group.

What are three major systems of social stratification?

Major systems of stratification are slavery, caste, and class. The essential characteristic of **slavery** is that some people own other people. In a **caste system,** status is determined by birth and is lifelong. A **class system** is much more open, for it is based primarily on money or material possessions. Gender cuts across all forms of social stratification.

How Did the World's Nations Become Stratified?

The main theories that account for global stratification are **colonialism, world system theory,** and the **culture of poverty.**

Why Is Social Stratification Universal?

To explain why stratification is universal, functionalists Kingsley Davis and Wilbert Moore argued that to attract the most capable people to fill its important positions, society must offer them greater rewards. Melvin Tumin said that if this view were correct, society would be a **meritocracy,** with all positions awarded on the basis of merit. Conflict theorists argue that stratification came about because resources are limited, and an elite emerges as groups struggle for them.

What Determines Social Class?

Karl Marx argued that a single factor determines **social class:** If you own the means of production, you belong to the **bourgeoisie** (capitalists); if you do not, you are one of the **proletariat** (workers). Max Weber argued that three elements determine social class: **property, power,** and **prestige.**

Social Class in the United States

Has income inequality declined in the United States? On the contrary, income inequality has increased since the Great Depression of the 1930s.

How does occupational prestige differ around the world?

How people rank occupational prestige is similar from country to country. Globally, the occupations that bring greater prestige are those that pay more, require more education and abstract thought, and offer greater independence.

What is meant by the term status inconsistency?

Status is social ranking. Most people are **status consistent;** that is, they rank high or low on all three dimensions of social class. People who rank higher on some dimensions than on others are status inconsistent. The frustrations of **status inconsistency** tend to produce political radicalism.

A Model of Social Class

What six-class model portrays the social classes?

Kahl and Gilbert developed a six-class model based on Weber. At the top is the capitalist class. In descending order are the upper middle class, the lower middle class, the working class, the working poor, and the **underclass.**

Consequences of Social Class

How does social class affect people's lives?

Social class leaves no aspect of life untouched. It affects our chances of living and dying, of getting sick, of receiving good health care, of getting divorced, and of getting an eduation. It also influences our politics, religion, and contact with the criminal justice system.

Social Mobility

What are three types of social mobility?

The term **intergenerational mobility** refers to changes in social class from one generation to the next. **Structural mobility** refers to changes in society that lead large numbers of people to change their social class. **Exchange mobility** refers to large numbers of people moving from one class to another, with the net result that the relative proportions of the population in the classes remain about the same.

Who are the poor?

The **poverty line** is arbitrary. Racial–ethnic minorities (except Asian Americans), children, and women-headed households are more likely than others to be poor. The poverty rate of the elderly is less than that of the general population.

How is the Horatio Alger myth functional for society?

The **Horatio Alger myth**—the belief that anyone can get ahead if only he or she tries hard enough—encourages people to strive to get ahead. It also deflects blame for failure from society to the individual.

THINKING CRITICALLY

1. How do slavery, caste, and class systems of social stratification differ?

2. The belief that the United States is the land of opportunity draws millions of legal and illegal immigrants to the United States. How do the materials in this chapter support or undermine this belief?

3. What social mobility has your own family experienced? In what ways has this affected your life?

ADDITIONAL RESOURCES

What can you find in MySocLab? mysoclab www.mysoclab.com

- Complete Ebook
- Practice Tests and Video and Audio activities
- Mapping and Data Analysis exercises

- Sociology in the News
- Classic Readings in Sociology
- Research and Writing advice

SUGGESTED READINGS

Global Stratification

Gu, George Zhibin, and Andre Gunder Frank. *China's Global Reach: Markets, Multinationals, and Globalization,* rev. ed. Palo Alto, Calif.: Fultus Corp., 2006. The author tries to identify the causes and consequences of global development, with a comparison of corporations in China and other nations.

Holzner, Burkart, and Leslie Holzner. *Transparency in Global Change: The Vanguard of the Open Society.* Pittsburgh: University of Pittsburgh Press, 2006. The tension between transparency and secrecy as information flows within and across international boundaries.

Lechner, Krank J., and John Boli, eds. *The Globalization Reader,* 3rd ed. Malden, Mass.: Wiley-Blackwell, 2008. A thorough introduction to globalization, including a link with environmentalism.

Ritzer, George. *The Globalization of Nothing.* 2nd ed., Thousand Oaks, Calif.: Pine Forge Press, 2007. The author expresses concerns about the short- and long-term effects of globalization.

Rothkopf, David. *Superclass: The Global Power Elite and the World They Are Making.* New York: Farrar, Straus and Giroux, 2008. The author of this overview of the world's wealthiest families has many connections with these elite, powerful people.

Sernau, Scott. *Worlds Apart: Social Inequalities in a Global Economy,* 2nd ed. Thousand Oaks, Calif.: Pine Forge Press, 2005. The author's thesis is that the market-driven global economy contributes to rather than reduces social inequality.

Wan, Ming. *The Political Economy of East Asia: Striving for Wealth and Power.* Washington, D.C.: CQ Press, 2008. The author analyzes the politics and policies that are increasing the power and wealth of east Asia.

Zakaria, Fareed. *The Post-American World.* New York: W.W. Norton, 2008. Analyzes the political and economic megatrends that are making fundamental changes in the distribution of world power.

Social Stratification in the United States

Bales, Kevin, and Ron Soodalter. *The Slave Next Door: Human Trafficking and Slavery in America Today.* Berkeley: University of California Press, 2009. The authors' thesis is that there is slavery in the United States—from prostitutes to dishwashers, people work under threat of violence and cannot walk away—and that we can put an end to it.

Beeghley, Leonard. *The Structure of Social Stratification in the United States,* 5th ed. Boston: Pearson, 2008. The author presents a concise overview of the U.S. social classes.

Engels, Friedrich. *Condition of the Working Class in England.* Sydney, Australia: Read How You Want, 2007. First published as *Die Lage der arbeitenden Klasse in England,* in 1844. One of the significant books in world history, this analysis of people who lived in poverty (the working class of the time) is based on the author's research and parliamentary reports.

Gilbert, Dennis. *The American Class Structure in an Age of Growing Inequality,* 7th ed. Thousand Oaks, Calif.: Pine Forge Press, 2008. This basic text on the U.S. social class structure, filled with facts about class, grapples with the question of why social mobility in the United States is decreasing.

Grusky, David B., ed. *Social Stratification: Class, Race, and Gender in Sociological Perspective.* Boulder, Colo.: Westview Press, 2008. This reader of over 100 articles and 1,000 pages examines almost every aspect of social stratification, from causes and consequences to likely futures.

McNamee, Stephen J., and Robert K. Miller. *The Meritocracy Myth,* 2nd ed. Lanham, MD: Rowman & Littlefield, 2009. The authors compare talent, attitude, work ethic, and character as elements of merit with social status, race, heritage, and wealth as elements of non-merit.

Newman, Katherine S., and Victor Tan Chen. *The Missing Class: Portraits of the Near Poor in America.* Boston: Beacon Press, 2007. The story of nine families who live on the edge of poverty, their experiences in education, leisure, child rearing, romance, work, the police, courts, welfare, shopping, and debt.

Sherman, Rachel. *Class Acts: Service and Inequality in Luxury Hotels.* Berkeley, Calif.: University of California Press, 2007. Based on participant observation, the author explores the relationship between workers and guests at a luxury hotel.

Sumner, William Graham. *What the Social Classes Owe to Each Other.* Charleston, South Carolina: BiblioBazaar, 2008. First published in 1883. Written when sociology had a largely conservative orientation, the author explains why the government should not redistribute wealth.

Van Galen, Jane A., and George W. Noblit, eds. *Late to Class: Social Class and Schooling in the New Economy.* Albany: State University of New York Press, 2007. The authors of these articles compare the educational experiences of poor, working-class, and middle-class students, illustrating how education reproduces social class and suggesting ways to open educational opportunity.

Journals

Journal of Children and Poverty and *Journal of Poverty* analyze issues that affect the quality of life of people who live in poverty.

Race, Gender, and Class publishes interdisciplinary articles on the topics listed in its title.

Social Structure and Social Interaction

Social Structure and
Social Interaction

Japan

M

y curiosity had gotten the better of me. When the sociology convention finished, I climbed aboard the first city bus that came along. I didn't know where the bus was going, and I didn't know where I would spend the night.

"Maybe I overdid it this time," I thought, as the bus began winding down streets I had never seen before. Actually, this was my first visit to Washington, D.C., so everything was unfamiliar to me.

Suddenly one of the men jumped up, smashed the empty bottle against the sidewalk, and . . .

I had no destination, no plans, not even a map. I carried no billfold, just a driver's license shoved into my jeans for emergency identification, some pocket change, and a $10 bill tucked into my sock. My goal was simple: If I saw something interesting, I would get off the bus and check it out.

"Nothing but the usual things," I mused, as we passed row after row of apartment buildings and stores. I could see myself riding buses the entire night. Then something caught my eye. Nothing spectacular—just groups of people clustered around a large circular area where several streets intersected.

I climbed off the bus and made my way to what turned out to be Dupont Circle. I took a seat on a sidewalk bench and began to observe what was going on around me. As the scene came into focus, I noticed several streetcorner men drinking and joking with one another. One of the men broke from his companions and sat down next to me. As we talked, I mostly listened.

As night fell, the men said that they wanted to get another bottle of wine. I contributed. They counted their money and asked if I wanted to go with them.

Although I felt my stomach churning—a combination of hesitation and fear—I heard a confident "Sure!" come out of my mouth. As we left the circle, the three men began to cut through an alley. "Oh, no," I thought. "This isn't what I had in mind."

I had but a split second to make a decision. I found myself continuing to walk with the men, but holding back half a step so that none of the three was behind me. As we walked, they passed around the remnants of their bottle. When my turn came, I didn't know what to do. I shuddered to think about the diseases lurking within that bottle. I made another quick decision. In the semidarkness I faked it, letting only my thumb and forefinger touch my lips and nothing enter my mouth.

When we returned to Dupont Circle, we sat on the benches, and the men passed around their new bottle of Thunderbird.

I couldn't fake it in the light, so I passed, pointing at my stomach to indicate that I was having digestive problems.

Suddenly one of the men jumped up, smashed the emptied bottle against the sidewalk, and thrust the jagged neck outward in a menacing gesture. He glared straight ahead at another bench, where he had spotted someone with whom he had some sort of unfinished business. As the other men told him to cool it, I moved slightly to one side of the group—ready to flee, just in case.

Levels of Sociological Analysis

On this sociological adventure, I almost got in over my head. Fortunately, it turned out all right. The man's "enemy" didn't look our way, the man put the broken bottle next to the bench "just in case he needed it," and my intriguing introduction to a life that up until then I had only read about continued until dawn.

Sociologists Elliot Liebow (1967/1999), Mitchell Duneier (2001), and Elijah Anderson (1978, 1990, 2006) have written fascinating accounts about men like my companions from that evening. Although streetcorner men may appear to be disorganized—simply coming and going as they please and doing whatever feels good at the moment—sociologists have analyzed how, like us, these men are influenced by the norms and beliefs of our society. This will become more apparent as we examine the two levels of analysis that sociologists use.

Macrosociology and Microsociology

The first level, **macrosociology,** focuses on broad features of society. Conflict theorists and functionalists use this approach to analyze such things as social class and how groups are related to one another. If they were to analyze streetcorner men, for example, they would stress that these men are located at the bottom of the U.S. social class system. Their low status means that many opportunities are closed to them: The men have few job skills, little education, hardly anything to offer an employer. As "able-bodied" men, however, they are not eligible for welfare—even for a two-year limit—so they hustle to survive. As a consequence, they spend their lives on the streets.

In the second level, **microsociology,** the focus is on **social interaction,** what people do when they come together. Sociologists who use this approach are likely to analyze the men's rules, or "codes," for getting along; their survival strategies ("hustles"); how they divide up money, wine, or whatever other resources they have; their relationships with girlfriends, family, and friends; where they spend their time and what they do there; their language; their pecking order; and so on. Microsociology is the primary focus of symbolic interactionists.

Because each approach has a different focus, macrosociology and microsociology yield distinctive perspectives, and both are needed to gain a fuller understanding of social life. We cannot adequately understand streetcorner men, for example, without using *macrosociology*. It is essential that we place the men within the broad context of how groups in U.S. society are related to one another—for, as is true for ourselves, the social class of these men helps to shape their attitudes and behavior. Nor can we adequately understand these men without *microsociology*, for their everyday situations also form a significant part of their lives—as they do for all of us.

Let's look in more detail at how these two approaches in sociology work together to help us understand social life. As we examine them more closely, you may find yourself feeling more comfortable with one approach than the other. This is what happens with sociologists. For reasons that include personal background and professional training, sociologists find themselves more comfortable with one approach and tend to use it in their research. Both approaches, however, are necessary to understand life in society.

macrosociology analysis of social life that focuses on broad features of society, such as social class and the relationships of groups to one another; usually used by functionalists and conflict theorists

microsociology analysis of social life that focuses on social interaction; typically used by symbolic interactionists

social interaction what people do when they are in one another's presence

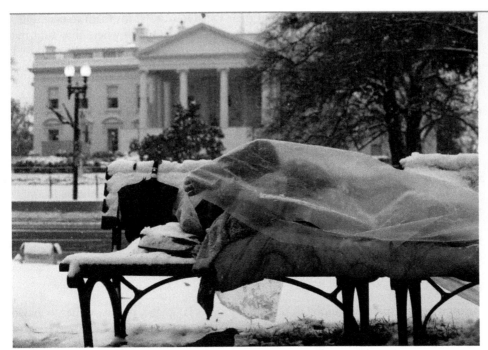

Sociologists use both macro and micro levels of analysis to study social life. Those who use *macrosociology* to analyze the homeless—or any human behavior—focus on broad aspects of society, such as the economy and social classes. Sociologists who use the *microsociological approach* analyze how people interact with one another. This photo illustrates *social structure*—the disparities between power and powerlessness are amply evident. It also illustrates the micro level—the isolation of this man.

Bettmann/Corbis

The Macrosociological Perspective: Social Structure

Why did the street people in our opening vignette act as they did, staying up all night drinking wine, prepared to use a lethal weapon? Why don't *we* act like this? Social structure helps us answer such questions.

The Sociological Significance of Social Structure

To better understand human behavior, we need to understand *social structure,* the framework of society that was already laid out before you were born. **Social structure** refers to the typical patterns of a group, such as its usual relationships between men and women or students and teachers. *The sociological significance of social structure is that it guides our behavior.*

Because this term may seem vague, let's consider how you experience social structure in your own life. As I write this, I do not know your race–ethnicity. I do not know your religion. I do not know whether you are young or old, tall or short, male or female. I do not know whether you were reared on a farm, in the suburbs, or in the inner city. I do not know whether you went to a public high school or to an exclusive prep school. But I do know that you are in college. And this, alone, tells me a great deal about you.

From this one piece of information, I can assume that the social structure of your college is now shaping what you do. For example, let's suppose that today you felt euphoric over some great news. I can be fairly certain (not absolutely, mind you, but relatively confident) that when you entered the classroom, social structure overrode your mood. That is, instead of shouting at the top of your lungs and joyously throwing this book into the air, you entered the classroom in a fairly subdued manner and took your seat.

The same social structure influences your instructor, even if he or she, on the one hand, is facing a divorce or has a child dying of cancer or, on the other, has just been awarded a promotion or a million-dollar grant. Your instructor may feel like either retreating into seclusion or celebrating wildly, but most likely he or she will conduct class in the usual manner. In short, social structure tends to override personal feelings and desires.

Just as social structure influences you and your instructor, so it also establishes limits for street people. They, too, find themselves in a specific location in the U.S. social structure— although it is quite different from yours or your instructor's. Consequently, they are

social structure the framework (or typical patterns) that surrounds us, consisting of the relationships of people and groups to one another, which gives direction to and sets limits on behavior affected in different ways. Nothing about their social location leads them to take notes or to lecture. Their behaviors, however, are as logical an outcome of where they find themselves in the social structure as are your own. In their position in the social structure, it is just as "natural" to drink wine all night as it is for you to stay up studying all night for a crucial examination. It is just as "natural" for you to nod and say, "Excuse me," when you enter a crowded classroom late and have to claim a desk on which someone has already placed books as it is for them to break off the neck of a wine bottle and glare at an enemy. To better understand social structure, read the Down-to-Earth Sociology box on the next page.

In short, people learn their behaviors and attitudes because of their location in the social structure (whether they be privileged, deprived, or in between), and they act accordingly. This is as true of street people as it is of us. *The differences in behavior and attitudes are due not to biology (race-ethnicity, sex, or any other supposed genetic factors), but to people's location in the social structure.* Switch places with street people and watch your behaviors and attitudes change!

Because social structure so crucially affects who we are and what we are like, let's look more closely at its major components: culture, social class, social status, roles, groups, and social institutions.

Culture

Sociologists use the term *culture* to refer to a group's language, beliefs, values, behaviors, and even gestures. Culture also includes the material objects that a group uses. Culture is the broadest framework that determines what kind of people we become. If we are reared in Chinese, Arab, or U.S. culture, we will grow up to be like most Chinese, Arabs, or Americans. On the outside, we will look and act like them; and on the inside, we will think and feel like them.

Social Class

To understand people, we must examine the social locations that they hold in life. Especially significant is *social class,* which is based on income, education, and occupational prestige. Large numbers of people who have similar amounts of income and education and who work at jobs that are roughly comparable in prestige make up a **social class.** It is hard to overemphasize this aspect of social structure, for our social class influences not only our behaviors but even our ideas and attitudes. We have this in common, then, with the street people described in the opening vignette: We both are influenced by our location in the social class structure. Theirs may be a considerably less privileged position, but it has no less influence on their lives.

Social Status

When you hear the word *status,* you are likely to think of prestige. These two words are welded together in people's minds. As you saw in the box on football, however, sociologists use **status** in a different way—to refer to the *position* that someone occupies. That position may carry a great deal of prestige, as in the case of a judge or an astronaut, or it may bring little prestige, as in the case of a convenience store clerk or a waitress at the local truck stop. The status may also be looked down on, as in the case of a streetcorner man, an ex-convict, or a thief.

All of us occupy several positions at the same time. You may simultaneously be a son or daughter, a worker, a date, and a student. Sociologists use the term **status set** to refer to all the statuses or positions that you occupy. Obviously your status set changes as your particular statuses change. For example, if you graduate from college and take a full-time job, get married, buy a home, have children, and so on, your status set changes to include the positions of worker, spouse, homeowner, and parent.

Picture Contact/Alamy

Social class is one of the most significant factors in social life. Fundamental to what we become, it affects our orientations to life. Can you see how this photo illustrates this point?

social class according to Weber, a large group of people who rank close to one another in property power, and prestige; according to Marx, one of two groups: capitalists who own the means of production or workers who sell their labor

status the position that someone occupies in a social group

status set all the statuses or positions that an individual occupies

Down-to-Earth Sociology
College Football as Social Structure

To gain a better idea of what *social structure* is, think of college football (Dobriner 1969a). You probably know the various positions on the team: center, guards, tackles, ends, quarterback, running backs, and the like. Each is a *status;* that is, each is a social position. For each of the statuses shown in Figure 1, there is a *role;* that is, each of these positions has certain expectations attached to it. The center is expected to snap the ball, the quarterback to pass it, the guards to block, the tackles to tackle or block, the ends to receive passes, and so on. Those role expectations guide each player's actions; that is, the players try to do what their particular role requires.

Let's suppose that football is your favorite sport and you never miss a home game at your college. Let's also suppose that you graduate, get a great job, and move across the country. Five years later, you return to your campus for a nostalgic visit. The climax of your visit is the biggest football game of the season. When you get to the game, you might be surprised to see a different coach, but you are not surprised that each playing position is occupied by people you don't know, for all the players you knew have graduated, and their places have been filled by others.

This scenario mirrors *social structure,* the framework around which a group exists. In football, that framework consists of the coaching staff and the eleven playing positions. The game does not depend on any particular individual, but, rather, on *social statuses,* the positions that the individuals occupy. When someone leaves a position, the game can go on because someone else takes over that position or status and plays the role. The game will continue even though not a single individual remains

FIGURE 1 Team Positions (Statuses) in Football

from one period of time to the next. Notre Dame's football team endures today even though Knute Rockne, the Gipper, and his teammates are long dead.

Even though you may not play football, you do live your life within a clearly established social structure. The statuses that you occupy and the roles you play were already in place before you were born. You take your particular positions in life, others do the same, and society goes about its business. Although the specifics change with time, the game—whether of life or of football—goes on.

For Your Consideration
How does social structure influence your life? To answer this question, you can begin by analyzing your social statuses.

Like other aspects of social structure, statuses are part of our basic framework of living in society. The example I gave of students and teachers who come to class and do what others expect of them despite their particular circumstances and moods illustrates how statuses affect our actions—and those of the people around us. Our statuses—whether daughter or son, teacher or student—serve as guides for our behavior.

Ascribed and Achieved Statuses. An **ascribed status** is involuntary. You do not ask for it, nor can you choose it. At birth, you inherit ascribed statuses such as your race–ethnicity, sex, and the social class of your parents, as well as your statuses as female or male, daughter or son, niece or nephew. Others, such as teenager and senior citizen, are related to the life course, and are given to you later in life.

Achieved statuses, in contrast, are voluntary. These you earn or accomplish. As a result of your efforts you become a student, a friend, a spouse, a lawyer, or a member of the

ascribed status a position an individual either inherits at birth or receives involuntarily later in life

achieved status a position that is earned, accomplished, or involves at least some effort or activity on the individual's part

status symbols items used to identify a status

master status a status that cuts across the other statuses that an individual occupies

clergy. Or, for lack of effort (or for efforts that others fail to appreciate), you become a school dropout, a former friend, an ex-spouse, a debarred lawyer, or a defrocked member of the clergy. In other words, achieved statuses can be either positive or negative; both college president and bank robber are achieved statuses.

Each status provides guidelines for how we are to act and feel. Like other aspects of social structure, statuses set limits on what we can and cannot do. Because social statuses are an essential part of the social structure, all human groups have them.

Status Symbols.   People who are pleased with their social status often want others to recognize their particular position. To elicit this recognition, they use **status symbols,** signs that identify a status. For example, people wear wedding rings to announce their marital status; uniforms, guns, and badges to proclaim that they are police officers (and not so subtly to let you know that their status gives them authority over you); and "backward" collars to declare that they are Lutheran ministers or Roman Catholic or Episcopal priests.

Some social statuses are negative and so, therefore, are their status symbols. The scarlet letter in Nathaniel Hawthorne's book by the same title is one example. Another is the CONVICTED DUI (Driving Under the Influence) bumper sticker that some U.S. courts require convicted drunk drivers to display if they wish to avoid a jail sentence.

All of us use status symbols. We use them to announce our statuses to others and to help smooth our interactions in everyday life. Can you identify your own status symbols and what they communicate? For example, how does your clothing announce your statuses of sex, age, and college student?

Master Statuses.   A **master status** cuts across your other statuses. Some master statuses are ascribed. An example is your sex. Whatever you do, people perceive you as a male or as a female. If you are working your way through college by flipping burgers, people see you not only as a burger flipper and a student but also as a *male* or *female* burger flipper and a *male* or *female* college student. Other master statuses are race–ethnicity and age.

Some master statuses are achieved. If you become very, very wealthy (and it doesn't matter whether your wealth comes from a successful invention or from winning the lottery—it is still *achieved* as far as sociologists are concerned), your wealth is likely to become a master status. For example, people might say, "She is a very rich burger flipper"—or, more likely, "She's very rich, and she used to flip burgers!"

Master Statuses are those that overshadow our other statuses. Shown here is Stephen Hawking, who is severely disabled by Lou Gehrig's disease. For some, his *master status* is that of a person with disabilities. Because Hawking is one of the greatest physicists who has ever lived, however, his outstanding achievements have given him another *master status,* that of a world-class physicist in the ranking of Einstein.

UPI Photo/Landov

Similarly, people who become disfigured find, to their dismay, that their condition becomes a master status. For example, a person whose face is scarred from severe burns will be viewed through this unwelcome master status regardless of occupation or accomplishments. In the same way, people who are confined to wheelchairs can attest to how their wheelchair overrides all their other statuses and influences others' perceptions of everything they do.

Although our statuses usually fit together fairly well, some people have a contradiction or mismatch between their statuses. This is known as **status inconsistency** (or discrepancy). A 14-year-old college student is an example. So is a 40-year-old married woman who is dating a 19-year-old college sophomore.

These examples reveal an essential aspect of social statuses: Like other components of social structure, they come with built-in *norms* (that is, expectations) that guide our behavior. When statuses mesh well, as they usually do, we know what to expect of people. This helps social interaction to unfold smoothly. Status inconsistency, however, upsets our expectations. In the preceding examples, how are you supposed to act? Are you supposed to treat the 14-year-old as you would a young teenager, or as you would your college classmate? Do you react to the married woman as you would to the mother of your friend, or as you would to a classmate's date?

Roles

All the world's a stage
And all the men and women merely players.
They have their exits and their entrances;
And one man in his time plays many parts . . .

(William Shakespeare, *As You Like It*, Act II, Scene 7)

Like Shakespeare, sociologists see roles as essential to social life. When you were born, **roles**—the behaviors, obligations, and privileges attached to a status—were already set up for you. Society was waiting with outstretched arms to teach you how it expected you to act as a boy or a girl. And whether you were born poor, rich, or somewhere in between, that, too, attached certain behaviors, obligations, and privileges to your statuses.

The difference between role and status is that you *occupy* a status, but you *play* a role (Linton 1936). For example, being a son or daughter is your status, but your expectations of receiving food and shelter from your parents—as well as their expectations that you show respect to them—are part of your role. Or, again, your status is student, but your role is to attend class, take notes, do homework, and take tests.

Roles are like a fence. They allow us a certain amount of freedom, but for most of us that freedom doesn't go very far. Suppose that a woman decides that she is not going to wear dresses—or a man that he will not wear suits and ties—regardless of what anyone says. In most situations, they'll stick to their decision. When a formal occasion comes along, however, such as a family wedding or a funeral, they are likely to cave in to norms that they find overwhelming. Almost all of us follow the guidelines for what is "appropriate" for our roles. Few of us are bothered by such constraints, for our **socialization** is thorough, and we usually *want* to do what our roles indicate is appropriate.

The sociological significance of roles is that they lay out what is expected of people. As individuals throughout society perform their roles, those many roles mesh together to form this thing called *society.* As Shakespeare put it, people's roles provide "their exits and their entrances" on the stage of life. In short, roles are remarkably effective at keeping people in line—telling them when they should "enter" and when they should "exit," as well as what to do in between.

Groups

A **group** consists of people who interact with one another and who feel that the values, interests and norms they have in common are important. The groups to which we belong—just like social class, statuses, and roles—are powerful forces in our lives. By belonging to a group, we assume an obligation to affirm the group's values, interests, and norms. To remain a member in good standing, we need to show that we share those characteristics. This means that *when we belong to a group we yield to others the right to judge our behavior*—even though we don't like it!

status inconsistency ranking high on some dimensions of social class and low on others, also called *status discrepancy*

role the behaviors, obligations, and privileges attached to a status

socialization the process by which people learn the characteristics of their group—the knowledge, skills, attitudes, values, norms, and actions thought appropriate for them

group people who have something in common and who believe that what they have in common is significant; also called a *social group*

social institution the organized, usual, or standard ways by which society meets its basic needs

Although this principle holds true for all groups, some groups wield influence over only small segments of our behavior. For example, if you belong to a stamp collector's club, the group's influence may center on your display of knowledge about stamps and perhaps your fairness in trading them. Other groups, in contrast, such as the family, control many aspects of our behavior. When parents say to their 15-year-old daughter, "As long as you are living under our roof, you had better be home by midnight," they show their expectation that their daughter, as a member of the family, will conform to their ideas about many aspects of life, including their views on curfew. They are saying that as long as the daughter wants to remain a member of the family in good standing, her behavior must conform to their expectations.

Let's look at the next component of social structure, social institutions.

Social Institutions

At first glance, the term *social institution* may seem cold and abstract—with little relevance to your life. In fact, however, **social institutions**—the standard or usual ways that a society meets its basic needs—vitally affect your life. They not only shape your behavior but even color your thoughts. How can this be?

The first step in understanding how this can be is to look at Figure 2 on the next page. Look at what social institutions are: the family, religion, education, economics, medicine, politics, law, science, the military, and the mass media. By weaving the fabric of society, the social institutions set the context for your behavior and orientations to life. Note that each institution satisfies a basic need and has its own groups, statuses, values, and norms.

The Sociological Significance of Social Institutions

To understand social institutions is to realize how profoundly social structure affects your life. Much of the influence of social institutions lies beyond your ordinary awareness. For example, because of our economic institution, it is common to work eight hours a day for five days every week. There is nothing normal or natural about this pattern, however. This rhythm is only an arbitrary arrangement for dividing work and leisure. Yet this one aspect of a single social institution has far-reaching effects. Not only does it dictate how people divide up their days, but it also lays out a structure for our interaction with family and friends and for how we meet our personal needs.

Each of the other social institutions also has far-reaching effects on our lives. Social institutions are so significant that if they were different, our orientations to the social world, even to life itself, would be different. Let's consider just the mass media.

The mass media are a major influence in contemporary life. Until 1436, when Johann Gutenberg invented movable type, printing was a slow process, and printed materials were expensive. Today, printed materials are common and often cheap. "Cheap" has a double meaning, with its second meaning illustrated in this photo.

Spencer Grant/PhotoEdit, Inc.

An Example: The Mass Media. Far beyond serving simply as sources of information, the mass media influence our attitudes toward social issues, the ways that we view other people, and even our self-concept. Because the media significantly shape public opinion, all governments attempt to influence them. Totalitarian governments try to control them.

The mass media are relatively new in human history, owing their origins to the invention of the printing press in the 1400s. This invention had profound consequences on all social institutions. The printing of the Bible altered religion, for instance, while the publication of political broadsides and newspapers altered politics. From these beginnings, a series of inventions—from radio and movies to television and the microchip—has made the media an increasingly powerful force.

One of the most significant questions we can ask about this social institution is, Who controls it? That control, which in totalitarian countries is obvious, is much less visible in democratic nations. Functionalists might conclude that the media in a democratic nation represent the varied interests of the many groups that make up that nation. Conflict theorists,

FIGURE 2 Social Institutions in Industrial and Postindustrial Societies

Social Institution	Basic Needs	Some Groups or Organizations	Some Statuses	Some Values	Some Norms
Family	Regulate reproduction, socialize and protect children	Relatives, kinship groups	Daughter, son, father, mother, brother, sister, aunt, uncle, grandparent	Sexual fidelity, providing for your family, keeping a clean house, respect for parents	Have only as many children as you can afford, be faithful to your spouse
Religion	Concerns about life after death, the meaning of suffering and loss; desire to connect with the Creator	Congregation, synagogue, mosque, denomination, charity, clergy associations	Priest, minister, rabbi, imam, worshipper, teacher, disciple, missionary, prophet, convert	Reading and adhering to holy texts such as the Bible, the Torah, and the Koran; honoring God	Attend worship services, contribute money, follow the teachings
Education	Transmit knowledge and skills across generations	School, college, student senate, sports team, PTA, teachers' union	Teacher, student, dean, principal, football player, cheerleader	Academic honesty, good grades, being "cool"	Do homework, prepare lectures, don't snitch on classmates
Economy	Produce and distribute goods and services	Credit unions, banks, credit card companies, buying clubs	Worker, boss, buyer, seller, creditor, debtor, advertiser	Making money, paying bills on time, producing efficiently	Maximize profits, "the customer is always right," work hard
Medicine	Heal the sick and injured, care for the dying	AMA, hospitals, pharmacies, HMOs, insurance companies	Doctor, nurse, patient, pharmacist, medical insurer	Hippocratic oath, staying in good health, following doctor's orders	Don't exploit patients, give best medical care available
Politics	Allocate power, determine authority, prevent chaos	Political party, congress, parliament, monarchy	President, senator, lobbyist, voter, candidate, spin doctor	Majority rule, the right to vote as a privilege and a sacred trust	One vote per person, be informed about candidates
Law	Maintain social order, enforce norms	Police, courts, prisons	Judge, police officer, lawyer, defendant, prison guard	Trial by one's peers, innocence until proven guilty	Give true testimony, follow the rules of evidence
Science	Master the environment	Local, state, regional, national, and international associations	Scientist, researcher, technician, administrator, journal editor	Unbiased research, open dissemination of research findings, originality	Follow scientific method, be objective, disclose findings, don't plagiarize
Military	Protection from enemies, enforce national interests	Army, navy, air force, marines, coast guard, national guard	Soldier, recruit, enlisted person, officer, veteran, prisoner, spy	To die for one's country is an honor, obedience unto death	Follow orders, be ready to go to war, sacrifice for your buddies
Mass Media	Disseminate information, report events, mold public opinion	TV networks, radio stations, publishers, association of bloggers	Journalist, newscaster, author, editor, publisher, blogger	Timeliness, accuracy, freedom of the press	Be accurate, fair, timely, and profitable

in contrast, see the matter quite differently: The mass media—at least a country's most influential newspapers and television stations—represent the interests of the political elite. They give coverage to mildly dissenting opinions, but they stand solidly behind the government. The most obvious example is the positive treatment that the media give to the inauguration of a president.

Since the mass media are so influential in our lives today, the answer to this question of who controls the media is of more than passing interest. This matter is vital to our understanding of contemporary society.

Comparing Functionalist and Conflict Perspectives

Just as the functionalist and conflict perspectives of the mass media differ, so do their views of the nature of social institutions. Let's compare these views.

The Functionalist Perspective. Because the first priority is to survive, all societies establish customary ways to meet their basic needs. As a result, no society is without social institutions. In tribal societies, some social institutions are less visible because the group meets its basic social needs in more informal ways. A society may be too small to have people specialize in education, for example, but it will have established ways of teaching skills and ideas to the young. It may be too small to have a military, but it will have some mechanism of self-defense.

What are society's basic needs? Functionalists identify five *functional requisites* (basic needs) that each society must meet if it is to survive (Aberle et al. 1950; Mack and Bradford 1979).

1. *Replacing members.* Obviously, if a society does not replace its members, it cannot continue to exist. With reproduction fundamental to a society's existence, and the need to protect infants and children universal, all groups have developed some version of the family. The family gives the newcomer to society a sense of belonging by providing a *lineage,* an account of how he or she is related to others. The family also functions to control people's sex drive and to maintain orderly reproduction.

2. *Socializing new members.* Each baby must be taught what it means to be a member of the group into which it is born. To accomplish this, each human group develops devices to ensure that its newcomers learn the group's basic expectations. As the primary "bearer of culture," the family is essential to this process, but other social institutions, such as religion and education, also help meet this basic need.

3. *Producing and distributing goods and services.* Every society must produce and distribute basic resources, from food and clothing to shelter and education. Consequently, every society establishes an *economic* institution, a means of producing goods and services along with routine ways of distributing them.

4. *Preserving order.* Societies face two threats of disorder: one internal, the potential for chaos, and the other external, the possibility of attack. To protect themselves from internal threat, they develop ways to police themselves, ranging from informal means such as gossip to formal means such as armed groups. To defend themselves against external conquest, they develop a means of defense, some form of the military.

5. *Providing a sense of purpose.* Every society must get people to yield self-interest in favor of the needs of the group. To convince people to sacrifice personal gains, societies instill a sense of purpose. Human groups develop many ways to implant such beliefs, but a primary one is religion, which attempts to answer questions about ultimate meaning. Actually, all of a society's institutions are involved in meeting this functional requisite; the family provides one set of answers about the sense of purpose, the school another, and so on.

The Conflict Perspective. Although conflict theorists agree that social institutions were designed originally to meet basic survival needs, they do not view social institutions as working harmoniously for the common good. On the contrary, conflict theorists stress that powerful groups control our society's institutions, manipulating them in order to maintain

Functionalist theorists have identified *functional requisites* for the survival of society. One, providing a sense of purpose, is often met through religious groups. To most people, snake handling, as in this church service in Sand Mountain, Alabama, is nonsensical. From a functional perspective, however, it makes a great deal of sense. Can you identify its sociological meanings?

Mike Maple/Woodfin Camp & Associates

their own privileged position of wealth and power (Useem 1984; Domhoff 1999a, b, 2006, 2007).

Conflict theorists point out that a fairly small group of people has garnered the lion's share of our nation's wealth. Members of this elite group sit on the boards of our major corporations and our most prestigious universities. They make strategic campaign contributions to influence (or control) our lawmakers, and it is they who are behind the nation's major decisions: to go to war or to refrain from war; to increase or to decrease taxes; to raise or to lower interest rates; and to pass laws that favor or impede moving capital, technology, and jobs out of the country.

Feminist sociologists (both women and men) have used conflict theory to gain a better understanding of how social institutions affect gender relations. Their basic insight is that gender is also an element of social structure, not simply a characteristic of individuals. In other words, throughout the world, social institutions divide males and females into separate groups, each with unequal access to society's resources.

In Sum: Functionalists view social institutions as working together to meet universal human needs, but conflict theorists regard social institutions as having a single primary purpose—to preserve the social order. For them, this means safeguarding the wealthy and powerful in their positions of privilege.

Changes in Social Structure

As you can see, this enveloping system that we call social structure powerfully affects our lives. This means that as social structure changes, so, too, do our orientations to life. Our culture is not static. It is continuously evolving as it responds to changing values, to new technology, and to contact with cultures around the world. As our culture changes, so do we. Similarly, as our economy responds to globalization, it either opens or closes opportunities, changing our lives, sometimes brutally so. New groups such as the Department of Homeland Security come into being, wielding extraordinary power over us. In short, the corner in life that we occupy, though small and seemingly private, is not closed off; rather, it is pushed and pulled and stretched in different directions as our social structure changes.

What Holds Society Together?

With its many, often conflicting, groups and its extensive social change, how can a society manage to hold together? Let's examine two answers that sociologists have proposed.

Mechanical and Organic Solidarity. Sociologist Emile Durkheim (1893/1933) was interested in how societies manage to have **social integration**—their members being united by shared values and other social bonds. For smaller groups, he found the answer in what he called **mechanical solidarity.** By this term, Durkheim meant that people who perform similar tasks develop a shared consciousness. Think of a farming community in which everyone is involved in planting, cultivating, and harvesting. Members of this group have so much in common that they know how almost everyone else in the community feels about life. Societies with mechanical solidarity tolerate little diversity in behavior, thinking, or attitudes, for their unity depends on agreement in these matters.

As societies get larger, they develop different kinds of work, a specialized **division of labor.** Some people mine gold, others sell it, while still others turn it into jewelry. Such a division of labor disperses people into different interest groups where they develop different ideas about life. No longer do they depend on one another to have similar ideas and behaviors. Rather, they depend on one another for the specific work that each person contributes to the whole group. Durkheim called this new form of solidarity based on interdependence **organic solidarity.**

To see why Durkheim used the term *organic solidarity,* think about how you depend on your teacher to guide you through this introductory course in sociology. At the same time, without students your teacher would be without a job. You and your teacher are *like two organs in the same body.* (The "body" in this case is the college or university.) Although each of you performs different tasks, you depend on one another. This creates a form of unity.

social integration the degree to which members of a group or a society feel united by shared values and other social bonds; also known as social cohesion

mechanical solidarity Durkheim's term for the unity (a shared consciousness) that people feel as a result of performing the same or similar tasks

division of labor the splitting of a group's or a society's tasks into specialties

organic solidarity Durkheim's term for the interdependence that results from the division of labor; people depending on others to fulfill their jobs

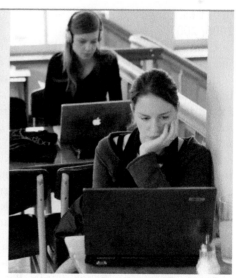

Michaela Rehlem/Reuters/Landov

The warm, more intimate relationships of *Gemeinschaft* society are apparent in the photo taken during *Oktoberfest* in Munich, Germany. The more impersonal relationships of *Gesellschaft* society are evident in this Internet cafe, where, customers are ignoring one another.

Gero Breloer/dpa/Landov

As you can see, organic solidarity produced a new basis for social integration—not a sharing of views because of planting and harvesting crops together and marrying into one another's families—but participation in separate activities that together contribute to the welfare of the group. As a result, our society can tolerate a wide diversity of orientations to life and still manage to work as a whole. Both past and present societies are based on social solidarity, but, as Durkheim pointed out, the types of solidarity differ remarkably.

Gemeinschaft* and *Gesellschaft*.** Ferdinand Tönnies (1887/1988) also analyzed this fundamental shift in relationships. He used the term ***Gemeinschaft (Guh-MINE-shoft), or "intimate community," to describe village life, the type of society in which everyone knows everyone else. He noted that in the society that was emerging, the personal ties, kinship connections, and lifelong friendships that marked village life were being crowded out by short-term relationships, individual accomplishments, and self-interest. Tönnies called this new type of society ***Gesellschaft*** (Guh-ZELL-shoft), or "impersonal association." He did not mean that we no longer have intimate ties to family and friends but, rather, that our lives no longer center on them. Few of us take jobs in a family business, for example, and contracts replace handshakes. Much of our time is spent with strangers and short-term acquaintances.

How Relevant Are These Concepts Today? I know that *Gemeinschaft, Gesellschaft,* and *mechanical* and *organic solidarity* are strange terms and that Durkheim's and Tönnies' observations must seem like a dead issue. The concern these sociologists expressed, however—that their world was changing from a community in which people were united by close ties and shared ideas and feelings to an anonymous association built around impersonal, short-term contacts—is still very real. In large part, this same concern explains the rise of Islamic fundamentalism (Volti 1995). Islamic leaders fear that Western values will uproot their traditional culture, that cold rationality will replace the warm, informal, personal relationships among families and clans. They fear, rightly so, that this will also change their views on life and morality. Although the terms may sound strange, even obscure, you can see that the ideas remain a vital part of today's world.

In Sum: Whether the terms are *Gemeinschaft* and *Gesellschaft* or *mechanical solidarity* and *organic solidarity,* they indicate that as societies change, so do people's orientations to life. *The sociological point is that social structure sets the context for what we do, feel, and think, and ultimately, then, for the kind of people we become.* As you read the Cultural Diversity box on the next page which describes one of the few remaining *Gemeinschaft* societies in the United States, think of how fundamentally different your life would be if you had been reared in an Amish family.

Gemeinschaft a type of society in which life is intimate; a community in which everyone knows everyone else and people share a sense of togetherness

Gesellschaft a type of society that is dominated by impersonal relationships, individual accomplishments, and self-interest

Cultural Diversity in the United States

The Amish: *Gemeinschaft* Community in a *Gesellschaft* Society

One of the best examples of a *Gemeinschaft* community in the United States is the Old Order Amish, followers of a sect that broke away from the Swiss-German Mennonite church in the 1600s and settled in Pennsylvania around 1727. Most of today's 225,000 Old Order Amish live in just three states—Pennsylvania, Ohio, and Indiana—but in the search for cheaper farmland, they have moved to Arkansas, Colorado, Kentucky, Maine, Mississippi, Missouri, Nebraska, and West Virginia. About 10 percent live in Lancaster County, Pennsylvania. The Amish, who believe that birth control is wrong, have doubled in population in less than two decades.

Because Amish farmers use horses instead of tractors, most of their farms are one hundred acres or less. To the five million tourists who pass through Lancaster County each year, the rolling green pastures, white farmhouses, simple barns, horse-drawn buggies, and clotheslines hung with somber-colored garments convey a sense of peace and innocence reminiscent of another era. Although just sixty-five miles from Philadelphia, "Amish country" is a world away.

Amish life is based on separation from the world—an idea taken from Christ's Sermon on the Mount—and obedience to the church's teachings and leaders. This rejection of worldly concerns, writes sociologist Donald Kraybill in *The Riddle of Amish Culture* (2002), "provides the foundation of such Amish values as humility, faithfulness, thrift, tradition, communal goals, joy of work, a slow-paced life, and trust in divine providence."

The *Gemeinschaft* of village life that has been largely lost to industrialization remains a vibrant part of Amish life. The Amish make their decisions in weekly meetings, where, by consensus, they follow a set of rules, or *Ordnung*, to guide their behavior. Religion and discipline are the glue that holds the Amish together. Brotherly love and the welfare of the community are paramount values. In times of birth, sickness, and death, neighbors pitch in with the chores. In these ways, they maintain the bonds of intimate community.

The Amish are bound by other ties, including language (a dialect of German known as Pennsylvania Dutch), plain clothing—often black, whose style has remained unchanged for almost 300 years—and church-sponsored schools. Nearly all Amish marry, and divorce is forbidden. The family is a vital ingredient in Amish life; all major events take place in the home, including weddings, births, funerals, and church services. Amish children attend church schools, but only until the age of 13. (In 1972, the Supreme Court ruled that Amish parents had the right to take their children out of school after the eighth grade.) To go to school beyond the eighth grade would expose them to values and "worldly concerns" that would drive a wedge between the children and their community. The Amish believe that violence is bad, even personal self-defense, and they register as conscientious objectors during times of war. They pay no Social Security, and they receive no government benefits.

The Amish cannot resist all change, of course. Instead, they try to adapt to change in ways that will least disrupt their core values. A special threat has come from urban sprawl, which has driven up the price of farmland. Unable to afford farms, about half of Amish men now work at jobs other than farming. Most work in farm-related businesses or in woodcrafts. They go to great lengths to avoid leaving the home. The Amish believe that when a husband works away from home, all aspects of life change—from the marital relationship to the care of the children—certainly an astute sociological insight. They also believe that if a man receives a paycheck, he will think that his work is of more value than his wife's. Because intimate, or *Gemeinschaft*, society is essential to maintain the Amish way of life, concerns are growing about the men who have begun to work for non-Amish businesses. They are being exposed to the outside world, and some are even using modern technology such as cell phones and computers at work.

Despite living in the midst of a highly materialistic and secular culture, the Amish are retaining their way of life. Perhaps the most poignant illustration of how the Amish differ from the dominant culture is this: When in 2006 a non-Amish man shot several Amish girls at a one-room school, the Amish community established charitable funds not only for the families of the dead children but also for the family of the killer.

ClassicStock/Alamy

For Your Consideration

Identify some of your *specific* ideas, attitudes, and behaviors that would be different if you had been reared in an Amish family. What do you like and dislike about Amish life? Why?

Sources: Aeppel 1996; Kephart and Zellner 2001; Kraybill 2002; Johnson-Weiner 2007; Scolforo 2008; Rifkin 2009.

The Microsociological Perspective: Social Interaction in Everyday Life

As you have seen, macrosociologists examine the broad features of society. Microsociologists, in contrast, examine narrower slices of social life. Their primary focus is *face-to-face interaction*—what people do when they are in one another's presence.

Symbolic Interaction

Symbolic interactionists are especially interested in the symbols people use. They want to know how people look at things and how this, in turn, affects their behavior and orientations to life. As you can see from the Down-to-Earth Sociology box below, jokes can be loaded with significant symbols. Of the many areas of social life symbolic interactionists study, let's look at stereotypes, personal space, eye contact, smiling, and body language.

Down-to-Earth Sociology
Looks: The Last Frontier for Socially Acceptable Discrimination?

A birthday card showing a close-up of an elderly person with sagging skin and missing teeth—asking to be kissed.

A college guy wearing a T-shirt that says, "Freshman girls. Get 'em while they're skinny."

A bumper sticker that reads: "BEER: Helping ugly people have sex since 1862."

A license plate holder that reads: "No Fat Chicks."*

Just harmless jokes, right? They show a sense of humor and might bring a few chuckles.

People used to joke openly about Jews, Poles, African Americans, the Irish, Asian Americans, people with disabilities, homosexuals, and women—among the long list of targets that used to be socially acceptable objects of public humor. We've all heard these jokes. "There was this black guy . . . this Chinese chick . . . this Jew . . . this Polish guy . . . this blonde . . . who walked into a . . ." With today's ethics, such jokes usually inhabit a subterranean area of our society.

Men still tell jokes about women—if no women are around. Whites tell jokes about blacks—if no blacks are present. Blacks tell jokes about whites—if no whites are within earshot. Except in a close circle of old friends, the jokes are told cautiously, as both the teller and the hearer know they aren't politically correct. But jokes about—and discrimination against—people who are fat, old, or ugly—these are still considered OK.

How can I say that?

©Gillian Laub

Take a look at the greeting cards in your local grocery store. You won't find cards that are anti-Semitic or that depict people of color in demeaning but humorous situations. But you will find cards about people who are considered ugly, fat, or old.

"Looksism"—the last socially acceptable area of discrimination? Probably an overstatement. Gender is still a fair target, for you will find cards about women, even some depicting men's helplessness in the kitchen.

If the incipient movement to raise our sensitivities is successful, your children won't be able to fathom how you could have lived in a society that tolerated such humor.

For Your Consideration
Why do you think the ethics of joke telling have changed? Are we getting too sensitive?

*All examples from Berry 2007.

Stereotypes in Everyday Life.   You are familiar with how first impressions set the tone for interaction. When you first meet someone, you cannot help but notice certain features, especially the person's sex, race–ethnicity, age, and clothing. Despite your best intentions, your assumptions about these characteristics shape your first impressions. They also affect how you act toward that person—and, in turn, how that person acts toward you. These fascinating aspects of our social interaction are discussed in the Down-to-Earth Sociology box on the next page.

Personal Space.   We all surround ourselves with a "personal bubble" that we go to great lengths to protect. We open the bubble to intimates—to our friends, children, and parents—but we're careful to keep most people out of this space. In a crowded hallway between classes, we might walk with our books clasped in front of us (a strategy often chosen by females). When we stand in line, we make certain there is enough space so that we don't touch the person in front of us and aren't touched by the person behind us.

At times, we extend our personal space. In the library, for example, you might place your coat on the chair next to you—claiming that space for yourself even though you aren't using it. If you want to really extend your space, you might even spread books in front of the other chairs, keeping the whole table to yourself by giving the impression that others have just stepped away.

The amount of space that people prefer varies from one culture to another. South Americans, for example, like to be closer when they speak to others than do people reared in the United States. Anthropologist Edward Hall (1959; Hall and Hall 2007) recounts a conversation with a man from South America who had attended one of his lectures.

> He came to the front of the class at the end of the lecture. . . . We started out facing each other, and as he talked I became dimly aware that he was standing a little too close and that I was beginning to back up. Fortunately I was able to suppress my first impulse and remain stationary because there was nothing to communicate aggression in his behavior except the conversational distance. . . .
>
> By experimenting I was able to observe that as I moved away slightly, there was an associated shift in the pattern of interaction. He had more trouble expressing himself. If I shifted to where I felt comfortable (about twenty-one inches), he looked somewhat puzzled and hurt, almost as though he were saying, "Why is he acting that way? Here I am doing everything I can to talk to him in a friendly manner and he suddenly withdraws. Have I done anything wrong? Said something I shouldn't?" Having ascertained that distance had a direct effect on his conversation, I stood my ground, letting him set the distance.

As you can see, despite Hall's extensive knowledge of other cultures, he still felt uncomfortable in this conversation. He first interpreted the invasion of his personal space as

AP Images

Frans Lanting/Minden Pictures

How people use space as they interact is studied by sociologists who have a microsociological focus. What do you see in common in these two photos?

Down-to-Earth Sociology
Beauty May Be Only Skin Deep, But Its Effects Go On Forever: Stereotypes in Everyday Life

Mark Snyder, a psychologist, wondered whether **stereotypes**—our assumptions of what people are like—might be self-fulfilling. He came up with an ingenious way to test this idea. He (1993) gave college men a Polaroid snapshot of a woman (supposedly taken just moments before) and told them that he would introduce them to her after they talked with her on the telephone. Actually, the photographs—showing either a pretty or a homely woman—had been prepared before the experiment began. The photo was *not* of the woman the men would talk to.

Stereotypes came into play immediately. As Snyder gave each man the photograph, he asked him what he thought the woman would be like. The men who saw the photograph of the attractive woman said that they expected to meet a poised, humorous, outgoing woman. The men who had been given a photo of the unattractive woman described her as awkward, serious, and unsociable.

The men's stereotypes influenced the way they spoke to the women on the telephone, who did *not* know about the photographs. The men who had seen the photograph of a pretty woman were warm, friendly, and humorous. This, in turn, affected the women they spoke to, for they responded in a warm, friendly, outgoing manner. And the men who had seen the photograph of a homely woman? On the phone, they were cold, reserved, and humorless, and the women they spoke to became cool, reserved, and humorless. Keep in mind that the women did not know that their looks had been evaluated—and that the photographs were not even of them. In short, stereotypes tend to produce behaviors that match the stereotype. This principle is illustrated in Figure 3.

Beauty might be only skin deep, but it has real consequences (Katz 2007). Not only do pretty people get a pass in a lot of situations, but they also are likely to make more money. For example, advertising agencies with better-looking executives have higher revenues (Bosman et al. 1997; Pfann et al. 2000). Apparently, people are more willing to hire individuals whom they perceive as good-looking.

For Your Consideration
Stereotypes have no single, inevitable effect. They are not magical. People can resist stereotypes and change outcomes. However, these studies do illustrate that stereotypes deeply influence how we react to one another.

Instead of beauty, consider gender and race–ethnicity. How do they affect those who do the stereotyping and those who are stereotyped?

Physical attractiveness underlies much of our social interaction in everyday life. The experiment reviewed in this box illustrates how college men modified their interactions on the basis of attractiveness. How do you think women would modify their interactions if they were to meet the two men in these photographs? How about men? Would they change their interactions in the same way?

FIGURE 3 How Self-Fulfilling Stereotypes Work

We see features of the person, or hear things about the person.

↓

We fit what we see or hear into stereotypes, and then expect the person to act in certain ways.

↓

How we expect the person to act shapes our attitudes and actions.

↓

From how we act, the person gets ideas of how we perceive him or her.

↓

The behaviors of the person change to match our expectations, thus confirming the stereotype.

Michael Newman/PhotoEdit, Inc.

Roy Hsu/Jupiter Images

possible aggression, for people get close (and jut out their chins and chests) when they are hostile. But when he realized that this was not the case, Hall resisted his impulse to move.

After Hall (1969; Hall and Hall 2007) analyzed situations like this, he observed that North Americans use four different "distance zones."

1. *Intimate distance.* This is the zone that the South American unwittingly invaded. It extends to about 18 inches from our bodies. We reserve this space for comforting, protecting, hugging, intimate touching, and lovemaking.

2. *Personal distance.* This zone extends from 18 inches to 4 feet. We reserve it for friends and acquaintances and ordinary conversations. This is the zone in which Hall would have preferred speaking with the South American.

3. *Social distance.* This zone, extending out from us about 4 to 12 feet, marks impersonal or formal relationships. We use this zone for such things as job interviews.

4. *Public distance.* This zone, extending beyond 12 feet, marks even more formal relationships. It is used to separate dignitaries and public speakers from the general public.

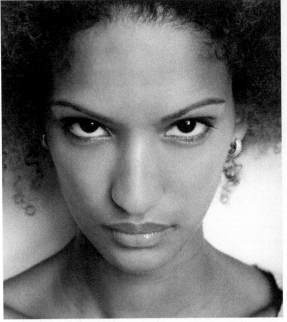

Eye contact is a fascinating aspect of everyday life. We use fleeting eye contact for most of our interactions, such as those with clerks or people we pass in the hall between classes. Just as we reserve our close personal space for intimates, so, too, we reserve soft, lingering eye contact for them.

Eye Contact. One way that we protect our personal bubble is by controlling eye contact. Letting someone gaze into our eyes—unless the person is an eye doctor—can be taken as a sign that we are attracted to that person, even as an invitation to intimacy. Wanting to become "the friendliest store in town," a chain of supermarkets in Illinois ordered its checkout clerks to make direct eye contact with each customer. Female clerks complained that male customers were taking their eye contact the wrong way, as an invitation to intimacy. Management said they were exaggerating. The clerks' reply was, "We know the kind of looks we're getting back from men," and they refused to make direct eye contact with them.

Smiling. In the United States, we take it for granted that clerks will smile as they wait on us. But it isn't this way in all cultures. Apparently, Germans aren't used to smiling clerks, and when Wal-Mart expanded into Germany, it brought its American ways with it. The company ordered its German clerks to smile at their customers. They did—and the customers complained. The German customers interpreted the smiles as flirting (Samor et al. 2006).

Applied Body Language. While we are still little children, we learn to interpret **body language,** the ways people use their bodies to give messages to others. This skill in interpreting facial expressions, posture, and gestures is essential for getting us through everyday life. Without it—as is the case for people with Asperger's syndrome—we wouldn't know how to react to others. It would even be difficult to know whether someone were serious or joking. This common and essential skill for traversing everyday life is now becoming one of the government's tools in its fight against terrorism. Because many of our body messages lie beneath our consciousness, airport personnel and interrogators are being trained to look for telltale facial signs—from a quick downturn of the mouth to rapid blinking—that might indicate nervousness or lying (Davis et al. 2002).

This is an interesting twist for an area of sociology that had been entirely theoretical. Let's now turn to dramaturgy, a special area of symbolic interactionism.

Dramaturgy: The Presentation of Self in Everyday Life

It was their big day, two years in the making. Jennifer Mackey wore a white wedding gown adorned with an 11-foot train and 24,000 seed pearls that she and her mother had sewn onto the dress. Next to her at the altar in Lexington, Kentucky, stood her intended, Jeffrey Degler, in black tie. They said their vows, then turned to gaze for a moment at the four hundred guests.

stereotype assumptions of what people are like, whether true or false

body language the ways in which people use their bodies to give messages to others

313

That's when groomsman Daniel Mackey collapsed. As the shocked organist struggled to play Mendelssohn's "Wedding March," Mr. Mackey's unconscious body was dragged away, his feet striking—loudly—every step of the altar stairs.

"I couldn't believe he would die at my wedding," the bride said. (Hughes 1990)

Sociologist Erving Goffman (1922–1982) added a new twist to microsociology when he recast the theatrical term **dramaturgy** into a sociological term. Goffman used the term to mean that social life is like a drama or a stage play: Birth ushers us onto the stage of everyday life, and our socialization consists of learning to perform on that stage. The self that we studied in the previous chapter lies at the center of our performances. We have ideas of how we want others to think of us, and we use our roles in everyday life to communicate those ideas. Goffman called these efforts to manage the impressions that others receive of us **impression management.**

Stages. Everyday life, said Goffman, involves playing our assigned roles. We have **front stages** on which to perform them, as did Jennifer and Jeffrey. (By the way, Daniel Mackey didn't really die—he had just fainted.) But we don't have to look at weddings to find front stages. Everyday life is filled with them. Where your teacher lectures is a front stage. And if you wait until your parents are in a good mood to tell them some bad news, you are using a front stage. In fact, you spend most of your time on front stages, for a front stage is wherever you deliver your lines. We also have **back stages,** places where we can retreat and let our hair down. When you close the bathroom or bedroom door for privacy, for example, you are entering a back stage.

The same setting can serve as both a back and a front stage. For example, when you get into your car and look over your hair in the mirror or check your makeup, you are using the car as a back stage. But when you wave at friends or if you give that familiar gesture to someone who has just cut in front of you in traffic, you are using your car as a front stage.

Role Performance, Conflict, and Strain. Everyday life brings with it many roles. As discussed earlier, the same person may be a student, a teenager, a shopper, a worker, and a date, as well as a daughter or a son. Although a role lays down the basic outline for a performance, it also allows a great deal of flexibility. The particular emphasis or interpretation that we give a role, our "style," is known as **role performance.** Consider your role as son or daughter. You may play the role of ideal daughter or son—being respectful, coming home at the hours your parents set, and so forth. Or this description may not even come close to your particular role performance.

---

dramaturgy an approach, pioneered by Erving Goffman, in which social life is analyzed in terms of drama or the stage; also called *dramaturgical analysis*

impression management people's efforts to control the impressions that others receive of them

front stage places where we give performances

back stage places where people rest from their performances, discuss their presentations, and plan future performances

role performance the ways in which someone performs a role within the limits that the role provides; showing a particular "style" or "personality"

In *dramaturgy,* a specialty within sociology, social life is viewed as similar to the theater. In our everyday lives, we all are actors. Like those in the cast of *Grey's Anatomy,* we, too, perform roles, use props, and deliver lines to fellow actors—who, in turn, do the same.

Scott Garfield/© ABC/Courtesy Everett Collection

Ordinarily, our statuses are separated sufficiently that we find minimal conflict between them. Occasionally, however, what is expected of us in one status (our role) is incompatible with what is expected of us in another status. This problem, known as **role conflict,** is illustrated in Figure 4, in which family, friendship, student, and work roles come crashing together. Usually, however, we manage to avoid role conflict by segregating our statuses, although doing so can require an intense juggling act.

Sometimes the *same* status contains incompatible roles, a conflict known as **role strain.** Suppose that you are exceptionally well prepared for a particular class assignment. Although the instructor asks an unusually difficult question, you find yourself knowing the answer when no one else does. If you want to raise your hand, yet don't want to make your fellow students look bad, you will experience role strain. As illustrated in Figure 4, the difference between role conflict and role strain is that role conflict is conflict *between roles,* while role strain is conflict *within* a role.

Sign-Vehicles. To communicate information about the self, we use three types of **sign-vehicles:** the social setting, our appearance, and our manner. The *social setting* is the place where the action unfolds. This is where the curtain goes up on your performance, where you find yourself on stage playing parts and delivering lines. A social setting might be an office, dorm, living room, church, gym, or bar. It is wherever you interact with others. Your social setting includes *scenery,* the furnishings you use to communicate messages, such as desks, blackboards, scoreboards, couches, and so on.

The second sign-vehicle is *appearance,* or how we look when we play our roles. Appearance includes *props,* which are like scenery except that they decorate the person rather than the setting. The teacher has books, lecture notes, and chalk, while the football player wears a costume called a uniform. Although few of us carry around a football, we all use makeup, hairstyles, and clothing to communicate messages about ourselves. Props and other aspects of appearance give us cues that help us navigate everyday life: By letting us know what to expect from others, props tell us how we should react. Think of the messages that props communicate. Some people use clothing to say they are college students, others to say they are older adults. Some use clothing to say they are clergy, others to say they are prostitutes. Similarly, people choose brands of cigarettes, liquor, and automobiles to convey messages about the self.

role conflict conflicts that someone feels *between* roles because the expectations attached to one role are incompatible with the expectations of another role

role strain conflicts that someone feels *within* a role

sign-vehicle a term used by Goffman to refer to how people use social setting, appearance, and manner to communicate information about the self

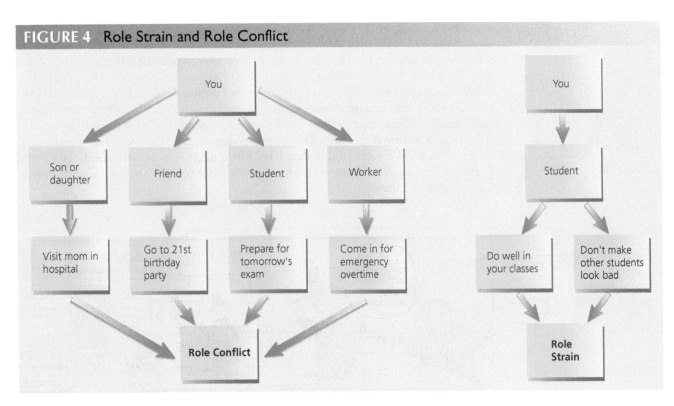

FIGURE 4 Role Strain and Role Conflict

teamwork the collaboration of two or more people to manage impressions jointly

face-saving behavior techniques used to salvage a performance (interaction) that is going sour

Our body is an especially important sign-vehicle, its shape proclaiming messages about the self. The messages that are attached to various shapes change over time, but, as explored in the Mass Media box on the next page, thinness currently screams desirability.

The third sign-vehicle is *manner,* the attitudes we show as we play our roles. We use manner to communicate information about our feelings and moods. If we show anger or indifference, sincerity or good humor, for example, we indicate to others what they can expect of us as we play our roles.

Teamwork.   Being a good role player brings positive recognition from others, something we all covet. To accomplish this, we use **teamwork**—two or more people working together to help a performance come off as planned. If you laugh at your boss's jokes, even though you don't find them funny, you are doing teamwork to help your boss give a good performance.

If a performance doesn't come off quite right, the team might try to save it by using **face-saving behavior.**

> Suppose your teacher is about to make an important point. Suppose also that her lecturing has been outstanding and the class is hanging on every word. Just as she pauses for emphasis, her stomach lets out a loud growl. She might then use a face-saving technique by remarking, "I was so busy preparing for class that I didn't get breakfast this morning."

It is more likely, however, that both the teacher and class will simply ignore the sound, giving the impression that no one heard a thing—a face-saving technique called *studied nonobservance.* This allows the teacher to make the point or, as Goffman would say, it allows the performance to go on.

Becoming the Roles We Play

Have you ever noticed how some clothing simply doesn't "feel" right for certain occasions? Have you ever changed your mind about something you were wearing and decided to change your clothing? Or maybe you just switched shirts or added a necklace?

What you were doing was fine-tuning the impressions you wanted to make. Ordinarily, we are not this aware that we're working on impressions. We become so used to the roles we play in everyday life that we tend to think we are "just doing" things, not that we are like actors on a stage who manage impressions. Yet every time we dress for school, or for any other activity, we are preparing for impression management.

Some new roles are uncomfortable at first, but after we get used to them *we tend to become the roles we play.* That is, roles become incorporated into the self-concept, especially roles for which we prepare long and hard and that become part of our everyday lives. When sociologist Helen Ebaugh (1988), who had been a nun, studied *role exit,* she interviewed people who had left marriages, police work, the military, medicine, and religious vocations. She found that the role had become so intertwined with the individual's self-concept that leaving it threatened the person's identity. The question these people struggled with was "Who am I, now that I am not a nun (or wife, police officer, colonel, physician, and so on)?" Even years after leaving these roles, many continue to perform them in their dreams.

Both individuals and organizations do *impression management,* trying to communicate messages about the self (or organization) that best meets their goals. At times, these efforts fail.

MASS MEDIA In SOCIAL LIFE

You Can't Be Thin Enough: Body Images and the Mass Media

When you stand before a mirror, do you like what you see? To make your body more attractive, do you watch your weight or work out? You have ideas about what you should look like. Where did you get them?

TV and magazine ads keep pounding home the message that our bodies aren't good enough, that we've got to improve them. The way to improve them, of course, is to buy the advertised products: hair extensions, padded bras, diet programs, anti-aging products, and exercise equipment. Muscular hulks show off machines that magically produce "six-pack abs" and incredible biceps—in just a few minutes a day. Female movie stars go through tough workouts without even breaking into a sweat. Women and men get the feeling that attractive members of the opposite sex will flock to them if they purchase that wonder-working workout machine.

Although we try to shrug off such messages, knowing that they are designed to sell products, the messages penetrate our thinking and feelings, helping to shape ideal images of how we "ought" to look. Those models so attractively clothed and coiffed as they walk down the runway, could they be any thinner? For women, the message is clear: You can't be thin enough. The men's message is also clear: You can't be muscular enough.

With impossibly shaped models at *Victoria's Secret* and skinny models showing off the latest fashions in *Vogue* and *Seventeen*, half of U.S. adolescent girls feel fat and count calories (Grabe et al. 2008). Some teens even call the plastic surgeon. Anxious lest their child violate peer ideals and trail behind in her race for popularity, parents foot the bill. Some parents pay $25,000 just to give their daughters a flatter tummy (Gross 1998).

The thinness craze has moved to the East, where glossy magazines feature skinny models. Not limited by our rules, advertisers in Japan and China push a soap that supposedly "sucks up fat through the skin's pores" (Marshall 1995). What a dream product! After all, even though our TV models smile as they go through their paces, those exercise machines do look like a lot of hard work.

And attractiveness does pay off. U.S. economists studied physical attractiveness and earnings. The result? "Good-looking" men and women earn the most, "average-looking" men and women earn more than "plain" people, and the "ugly" earn the least (Hamermesh and

Empics/Landov   Mike Blake/Reuters/Corbis

All of us contrast the reality we see when we look in the mirror with our culture's ideal body types. The thinness craze, discussed in this box, encourages some people to extremes, as with Keira Knightley. It also makes it difficult for larger people to have positive self-images. Overcoming this difficulty, Jennifer Hudson is in the forefront of promoting an alternative image.

Biddle 1994). In Europe, too, the more attractive workers earn more (Brunello and D'Hombres 2007). Then there is that potent cash advantage that "attractive" women have: They attract and marry higher-earning men (Kanazawa and Kovar 2004).

More popularity *and* more money? Maybe you can't be thin enough after all. Maybe those exercise machines are a good investment. If only we could catch up with the Japanese and develop a soap that would suck the fat right out of our pores. You can practically hear the jingle now.

For Your Consideration

What image do you have of your body? How do cultural expectations of "ideal" bodies underlie your image? Can you recall any advertisements or television programs that have affected your body image?

Most advertising and television programs that focus on weight are directed at women. Women are more likely than men to be dissatisfied with their bodies and to have eating disorders (Honeycutt 1995; Hill 2006). Do you think that the targeting of women in advertising creates these attitudes and behaviors? Or do you think that these attitudes and behaviors would exist even if there were no such ads? Why?

ethnomethodology the study of how people use background assumptions to make sense out of life

background assumption a deeply embedded common understanding of how the world operates and of how people ought to act

A statement by one of my respondents illustrates how roles become part of the person and linger even after the individual leaves them:

> After I left the ministry, I felt like a fish out of water. Wearing that backward collar had become a part of me. It was especially strange on Sunday mornings when I'd listen to someone else give the sermon. I knew that I should be up there preaching. I felt as though I had left God.

Applying Impression Management. I can just hear someone say, "Impression management is interesting, but is it really important?" In fact, it is so significant that the right impression management can make a vital difference in your career. To be promoted, you must be perceived as someone who *should* be promoted. You must appear dominant. You certainly cannot go unnoticed. But how you manage this impression is crucial. If a female executive tries to appear dominant by wearing loud clothing, using garish makeup, and cursing, this will get her noticed—but it will not put her on the path to promotion. How, then, can she exhibit dominance in the right way? To help women walk this fine line between femininity and dominance, career counselors advise women on fine details of impression management. Here are four things they recommend—clothing that doesn't wrinkle, makeup that doesn't have to be reapplied during the day, placing one's hands on the table during executive sessions, not in the lap, and carrying a purse that looks more like a briefcase (Needham 2006; Brinkley 2008).

Male or female, in your own life you will have to walk this thin line, finding the best way to manage impressions in order to further your career. Much success in the work world depends not on what you actually know but, instead, on your ability to give the impression that you know what you should know.

Ethnomethodology: Uncovering Background Assumptions

Certainly one of the strangest words in sociology is *ethnomethodology*. To better understand this term, consider the word's three basic components. *Ethno* means "folk" or "people"; *method* means how people do something; *ology* means "the study of." Putting them together, then, *ethno–method–ology* means "the study of how people do things." Specifically, **ethnomethodology** is the study of how people use commonsense understandings to make sense of life.

Let's suppose that during a routine office visit, your doctor remarks that your hair is rather long, then takes out a pair of scissors and starts to give you a haircut. You would feel strange about this, for your doctor would be violating **background assumptions**—your ideas about the way life is and the way things ought to work. These assumptions, which lie at the root of everyday life, are so deeply embedded in our consciousness that we are seldom aware of them, and most of us fulfill them unquestioningly. Thus, your doctor does not offer you a haircut, even if he or she is good at cutting hair and you need one!

The founder of ethnomethodology, sociologist Harold Garfinkel, conducted some exercises designed to reveal our background assumptions. Garfinkel (1967, 2002) asked his students to act as though they did not understand the basic rules of social life. Some tried to bargain with supermarket clerks; others would inch close to people and stare directly at them. They were met with surprise, bewilderment, even anger. In one exercise, Garfinkel asked students to act as though they were boarders in their own homes. They addressed their parents as "Mr." and "Mrs.," asked permission to use the bathroom, sat stiffly, were courteous, and spoke only when spoken to. As you can imagine, the other family members didn't know what to make of this (Garfinkel 1967):

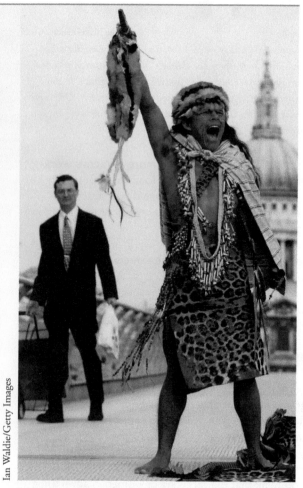

All of us have *background assumptions*, deeply ingrained assumptions of how the world operates. How do you think the background assumptions of this Londoner differ from this Ecuadoran shaman, who is performing a healing ceremony to rid London of its evil spirits?

Ian Waldie/Getty Images

They vigorously sought to make the strange actions intelligible and to restore the situation to normal appearances. Reports (by the students) were filled with accounts of astonishment, bewilderment, shock, anxiety, embarrassment, and anger, and with charges by various family members that the student was mean, inconsiderate, selfish, nasty, or impolite. Family members demanded explanations: What's the matter? What's gotten into you? . . . Are you sick? . . . Are you out of your mind or are you just stupid?

In another exercise, Garfinkel asked students to take words and phrases literally. When a student asked his girlfriend what she meant when she said that she had a flat tire, she said:

What do you mean, "What do you mean?" A flat tire is a flat tire. That is what I meant. Nothing special. What a crazy question!

Another conversation went like this:

ACQUAINTANCE: How are you?
STUDENT: How am I in regard to what? My health, my finances, my schoolwork, my peace of mind, my . . . ?
ACQUAINTANCE: (red in the face): Look! I was just trying to be polite. Frankly, I don't give a damn how you are.

Students who are asked to break background assumptions can be highly creative. The young children of one of my students were surprised one morning when they came down for breakfast to find a sheet spread across the living room floor. On it were dishes, silverware, lit candles—and bowls of ice cream. They, too, wondered what was going on, but they dug eagerly into the ice cream before their mother could change her mind.

This is a risky assignment to give students, however, for breaking some background assumptions can make people suspicious. When a colleague of mine gave this assignment, a couple of his students began to wash dollar bills in a laundromat. By the time they put the bills in the dryer, the police had arrived.

In Sum: Ethnomethodologists explore *background assumptions,* the taken-for-granted ideas about the world that underlie our behavior. Most of these assumptions, or basic rules of social life, are unstated. We learn them as we learn our culture, and we violate them only with risk. Deeply embedded in our minds, they give us basic directions for living everyday life.

The Social Construction of Reality

On a visit to Morocco, in northern Africa, I decided to buy a watermelon. When I indicated to the street vendor that the knife he was going to use to cut the watermelon was dirty (encrusted with filth would be more apt), he was very obliging. He immediately bent down and began to swish the knife in a puddle on the street. I shuddered as I looked at the passing burros that were urinating and defecating as they went by. Quickly, I indicated by gesture that I preferred my melon uncut after all.

"If people define situations as real, they are real in their consequences," said sociologists W. I. and Dorothy S. Thomas in what has become known as *the definition of the situation,* or the **Thomas theorem.** For that vendor of watermelons, germs did not exist. For me, they did. And each of us acted according to our definition of the situation. My perception and behavior did not come from the fact that germs are real but, rather, from *my having grown up in a society that teaches they are real.* Microbes, of course, *objectively* exist, and whether or not germs are part of our thought world makes no difference as to whether we are infected by them. Our behavior, however, does not depend on the *objective* existence of something but, rather, on our *subjective interpretation,* on what sociologists call our *definition of reality.* In other words, it is not the reality of microbes that impresses itself on us, but society that impresses the reality of microbes on us.

Let's consider another example, of identical twins, Oskar and Jack, who grew up so differently. Jack was reared in Trinidad and learned to hate Hitler, while Oskar was reared in Germany and learned to love Hitler. As you can see, what Hitler meant to Oskar and Jack

Thomas theorem William I. and Dorothy S. Thomas' classic formulation of the definition of the situation: "If people define situations as real, they are real in their consequences."

social construction of reality the use of background assumptions and life experiences to define what is real

(and what he means to us) depends not on Hitler's acts, but, rather, on how we view his acts—that is, on our definition of the situation.

Sociologists call this the **social construction of reality.** Our society, or the social groups to which we belong, holds particular views of life. From our groups (the *social* part of this process), we learn ways of looking at life—whether that be our view of Hitler or Osama bin Laden (they're good, they're evil), germs (they exist, they don't exist), or *anything else in life*. In short, through our interaction with others, we *construct reality;* that is, we learn ways of interpreting our experiences in life.

Gynecological Examinations. To better understand the social construction of reality, let's consider what I learned when I interviewed a gynecological nurse who had been present at about 14,000 vaginal examinations. I focused on *how doctors construct social reality in order to define this examination as nonsexual* (Henslin and Biggs 1971/2007). It became apparent that the pelvic examination unfolds much as a stage play does. I will use "he" to refer to the physician because only male physicians were part of this study. Perhaps the results would be different with women gynecologists.

Scene 1 (the patient as person) In this scene, the doctor maintains eye contact with his patient, calls her by name, and discusses her problems in a professional manner. If he decides that a vaginal examination is necessary, he tells a nurse, "Pelvic in room 1." By this statement, he is announcing that a major change will occur in the next scene.

Scene 2 (from person to pelvic) This scene is the depersonalizing stage. In line with the doctor's announcement, the patient begins the transition from a "person" to a "pelvic." The doctor leaves the room, and a female nurse enters to help the patient make the transition. The nurse prepares the "props" for the coming examination and answers any questions the woman might have.

What occurs at this point is essential for the social construction of reality, for *the doctor's absence removes even the suggestion of sexuality.* To undress in front of him could suggest either a striptease or intimacy, thus undermining the reality that the team is so carefully defining: that of nonsexuality.

The patient, too, wants to remove any hint of sexuality, and during this scene she may express concern about what to do with her panties. Some mutter to the nurse, "I don't want him to see these." Most women solve the problem by either slipping their panties under their other clothes or placing them in their purse.

Scene 3 (the person as pelvic) This scene opens when the doctor enters the room. Before him is a woman lying on a table, her feet in stirrups, her knees tightly together, and her body covered by a drape sheet. The doctor seats himself on a low stool before the woman and says, "Let your knees fall apart" (rather than the sexually loaded "Spread your legs"), and begins the examination.

The drape sheet is crucial in this process of desexualization, for it *dissociates the pelvic area from the person:* Leaning forward and with the drape sheet above his head, the physician can see only the vagina, not the patient's face. Thus dissociated from the individual, the vagina is transformed dramaturgically into an object of analysis. If the doctor examines the patient's breasts, he also dissociates them from her person by examining them one at a time, with a towel covering the unexamined breast. Like the vagina, each breast becomes an isolated item dissociated from the person.

In this third scene, the patient cooperates in being an object, becoming, for all practical purposes, a pelvis to be examined. She withdraws eye contact from the doctor, and usually from the nurse, is likely to stare at the wall or at the ceiling, and avoids initiating conversation.

Scene 4 (from pelvic to person) In this scene, the patient becomes "repersonalized." The doctor has left the examining room; the patient dresses and fixes her hair and makeup. Her reemergence as a person is indicated by such statements to the nurse as, "My dress isn't too wrinkled, is it?" showing a need for reassurance that the metamorphosis from "pelvic" back to "person" has been completed satisfactorily.

Scene 5 (the patient as person) In this final scene, the patient is once again treated as a person rather than as an object. The doctor makes eye contact with her and addresses her by name. She, too, makes eye contact with the doctor, and the usual middle-class interaction patterns are followed. She has been fully restored.

In Sum: To an outsider to our culture, the custom of women going to a male stranger for a vaginal examination might seem bizarre. But not to us. We learn that pelvic examinations are nonsexual. To sustain this definition requires teamwork—patients, doctors, and nurses working together to *socially construct reality*.

It is not just pelvic examinations or our views of microbes that make up our definitions of reality. Rather, *our behavior depends on how we define reality*. Our definitions (or constructions) provide the basis for what we do and how we feel about life. To understand human behavior, then, we must know how people define reality.

The Need for Both Macrosociology and Microsociology

Both microsociology and macrosociology make vital contributions to our understanding of human behavior. Our understanding of social life would be vastly incomplete without one or the other. The photo essay on the next two pages should help to make clear why we need *both* perspectives.

To illustrate this point, let's consider two groups of high school boys studied by sociologist William Chambliss (1973/2007). Both groups attended Hanibal High School. In one group were eight middle-class boys who came from "good" families and were perceived by the community as "going somewhere." Chambliss calls this group the "Saints." The other group consisted of six lower-class boys who were seen as headed down a dead-end road. Chambliss calls this group the "Roughnecks."

Boys in both groups skipped school, got drunk, and did a lot of fighting and vandalism. The Saints were actually somewhat more delinquent, for they were truant more often and engaged in more vandalism. Yet the Saints had a good reputation, while the Roughnecks were seen by teachers, the police, and the general community as no good and headed for trouble.

The boys' reputations set them on distinct paths. Seven of the eight Saints went on to graduate from college. Three studied for advanced degrees: One finished law school and became active in state politics, one finished medical school, and one went on to earn a Ph.D. The four other college graduates entered managerial or executive training programs with large firms. After his parents divorced, one Saint failed to graduate from high school on time and had to repeat his senior year. Although this boy tried to go to college by attending night school, he never finished. He was unemployed the last time Chambliss saw him.

In contrast, only four of the Roughnecks finished high school. Two of these boys did exceptionally well in sports and were awarded athletic scholarships to college. They both graduated from college and became high school coaches. Of the two others who graduated from high school, one became a small-time gambler and the other disappeared "up north," where he was last reported to be driving a truck. The two who did not complete high school were convicted of separate murders and sent to prison.

To understand what happened to the Saints and the Roughnecks, we need to grasp *both* social structure and social interaction. Using *macrosociology*, we can place these boys within the larger framework of the U.S. social class system. This reveals how opportunities open or close to people depending on their social class and how people learn different goals as they grow up in different groups. We can then use *microsociology* to follow their everyday lives. We can see how the Saints manipulated their "good" reputations to skip classes and how their access to automobiles allowed them to protect those reputations by spreading their troublemaking around different communities. In contrast, the Roughnecks, who did not have cars, were highly visible. Their lawbreaking, which was limited to a small area, readily came to the attention of the community. Microsociology also reveals how their reputations opened doors of opportunity to the first group of boys while closing them to the other. It is clear that we need both kinds of sociology.

When a Tornado Strikes:

Social Organization Following a Natural Disaster

as I was watching television on March 20, 2003, I heard a report that a tornado had hit Camilla, Georgia. "Like a big lawn mower," the report said, it had cut a path of destruction through this little town. In its fury, the tornado had left behind six dead and about 200 injured.

From sociological studies of natural disasters, I knew that immediately after the initial shock the survivors of natural disasters work together to try to restore order to their disrupted lives. I wanted to see this restructuring process firsthand. The next morning, I took off for Georgia.

These photos, taken the day after the tornado struck, tell the story of people in the midst of trying to put their lives back together. I was impressed at how little time people spent commiserating about their misfortune and how quickly they took practical steps to restore their lives.

As you look at these photos, try to determine why you need both microsociology and macrosociology to understand what occurs after a natural disaster.

After making sure that their loved ones are safe, one of the next steps people take is to recover their possessions. The cooperation that emerges among people, as documented in the sociological literature on natural disasters, is illustrated here.

© James M. Henslin, all photos

James M. Henslin

◀ The owners of this house invited me inside to see what the tornado had done to their home. In what had been her dining room, this woman is trying to salvage whatever she can from the rubble. She and her family survived by taking refuge in the bathroom. They had been there only five seconds, she said, when the tornado struck.

▲ In addition to the inquiring sociologist, television teams also were interviewing survivors and photographing the damage. This was the second time in just three years that a tornado had hit this neighborhood.

▲ No building or social institution escapes a tornado as it follows its path of destruction. Just the night before, members of this church had held evening worship service. After the tornado, someone mounted a U.S. flag on top of the cross, symbolic of the church members' patriotism and religiosity—and of their enduring hope.

▲ Personal relationships are essential in putting lives together. Consequently, reminders of these relationships are one of the main possessions that people attempt to salvage. This young man, having just recovered the family photo album, is eagerly reviewing the photos.

▲ Formal organizations also help the survivors of natural disasters recover. In this neighborhood, I saw representatives of insurance companies, the police, the fire department, and an electrical co-op. The Salvation Army brought meals to the neighborhood.

▲ For children, family photos are not as important as toys. This girl has managed to salvage a favorite toy, which will help anchor her to her previous life.

▲ Like electricity and gas, cable television is also restored as soon as possible.

SUMMARY *and* REVIEW

Levels of Sociological Analysis

What two levels of analysis do sociologists use?

Sociologists use macrosociological and microsociological levels of analysis. In **macrosociology,** the focus is placed on large-scale features of social life, while in **microsociology,** the focus is on **social interaction.** Functionalists and conflict theorists tend to use a macrosociological approach, while symbolic interactionists are more likely to use a microsociological approach.

The Macrosociological Perspective: Social Structure

How does social structure influence our behavior?

The term **social structure** refers to the social envelope that surrounds us and establishes limits on our behavior. Social structure consists of culture, social class, social statuses, roles, groups, and social institutions. Our location in the social structure underlies our perceptions, attitudes, and behaviors.

Culture lays the broadest framework, while **social class** divides people according to income, education, and occupational prestige. Each of us receives **ascribed statuses** at birth; later we add **achieved statuses.** Our behaviors and orientations are further influenced by the **roles** we play, the **groups** to which we belong, and our experiences with social institutions. These components of society work together to help maintain social order.

Social Institutions

What are social institutions?

Social institutions are the standard ways that a society develops to meet its basic needs. As summarized in Figure 2, industrial and postindustrial societies have ten social institutions—the family, religion, education, economy, medicine, politics, law, science, the military, and the mass media. From the functionalist perspective, social institutions meet universal group needs, or *functional requisites.* Conflict theorists stress how society's elites use social institutions to maintain their privileged positions.

What holds society together?

According to Emile Durkheim, in agricultural societies people are united by **mechanical solidarity** (having similar views and feelings). With industrialization comes **organic solidarity** (people depend on one another to do their more specialized jobs). Ferdinand Tönnies pointed out that the informal means of control in *Gemeinschaft* (small, intimate) societies are replaced by formal mechanisms in *Gesellschaft* (larger, more impersonal) societies.

The Microsociological Perspective: Social Interaction in Everyday Life

What is the focus of symbolic interactionism?

In contrast to functionalists and conflict theorists, who as macrosociologists focus on the "big picture," symbolic interactionists tend to be microsociologists who focus on face-to-face social interaction. Symbolic interactionists analyze how people define their worlds, and how their definitions, in turn, influence their behavior.

How do stereotypes affect social interaction?

Stereotypes are assumptions of what people are like. When we first meet people, we classify them according to our perceptions of their visible characteristics. Our ideas about those characteristics guide our behavior toward them. Our behavior, in turn, may influence them to behave in ways that reinforce our stereotypes.

Do all human groups share a similar sense of personal space?

In examining how people use physical space, symbolic interactionists stress that we surround ourselves with a "personal bubble" that we carefully protect. People from different cultures use "personal bubbles" of varying sizes, so the answer to the question is no. Americans typically use four different "distance zones": intimate, personal, social, and public.

What is dramaturgy?

Erving Goffman developed **dramaturgy** (or dramaturgical analysis), in which everyday life is analyzed in terms of the stage. At the core of this analysis is **impression management,** our attempts to control the impressions we make on others. For this, we use the **sign-vehicles** of setting, appearance, and manner. Our performances often call for **teamwork** and **face-saving behavior.**

What is the social construction of reality?

The phrase **the social construction of reality** refers to how we construct our views of the world, which, in turn, underlie our actions. **Ethnomethodology** is the study of how people make sense of everyday life. Ethnomethodologists try to uncover **background assumptions,** our basic ideas about the way life is.

The Need for Both Macrosociology and Microsociology

Why are both levels of analysis necessary?

Because each focuses on different aspects of the human experience, both microsociology and macrosociology are necessary for us to understand social life.

THINKING CRITICALLY

1. The major components of social structure are culture, social class, social status, roles, groups, and social institutions. Use social structure to explain why Native Americans have such a low rate of college graduation.

2. Dramaturgy is a form of microsociology. Use dramaturgy to analyze a situation with which you are intimately familiar (such as interaction with your family or friends or in one of your college classes).

3. To illustrate why we need both macrosociology and microsociology to understand social life, analyze the situation of a student getting kicked out of college.

ADDITIONAL RESOURCES

What can you find in MySocLab? mysoclab www.mysoclab.com

- Complete Ebook
- Practice Tests and Video and Audio activities
- Mapping and Data Analysis exercises

- Sociology in the News
- Classic Readings in Sociology
- Research and Writing advice

Where Can I Read More on This Topic?

Berry, Bonnie. *Beauty Bias: Discrimination and Social Power.* Westport, Conn.: Praeger, 2007. The subject is *lookism*: the many areas of discrimination, negative and positive, that are based on appearance.

Bogle, Kathleen A. *Hooking Up: Sex, Dating, and Relationships on Campus.* New York: New York University Press, 2008. An analysis of the sexual-social interaction of college students.

Cregan, Kate. *The Sociology of the Body: Mapping the Abstraction of Embodiment.* Beverly Hills, Calif.: Sage, 2006. Examines social influences on the body, the smallest unit of sociological analysis.

Day, Graham. *Community and Everyday Life.* New York: Routledge, 2006. The author reviews changing ideas and patterns of community, from urban to rural to communes and virtual communities.

Goffman, Erving. *The Presentation of Self in Everyday Life.* New York: Peter Smith, 1999. First published in 1959. This classic statement of dramaturgical analysis provides a different way of looking at everyday life. When I was a student, this was one of the most intellectually provocative books I read.

Seidman, Steven. *The Social Construction of Sexuality.* New York: W.W. Norton, 2004. The author explores how society influences our sexual choices, our beliefs about sexuality, and our sexual standards.

Tönnies, Ferdinand. *Community and Society (Gemeinschaft und Gesellschaft).* New York: Dover, 2003. Originally published in 1887, this classic work, focusing on social change, provides insight into how society influences personality. Rather challenging reading.

Waskul, Dennis, and Phillip Vannini, eds. *Body/embodiment: Symbolic Interaction and the Sociology of the Body.* London: Ashgate, 2006. Using a symbolic interactionist perspective, the authors analyze the interrelationship of the body, the self, and social interaction.

Whyte, William Foote. *Street Corner Society: The Social Structure of an Italian Slum,* 4th ed. Chicago: University of Chicago Press, 1993. Originally published in 1943. The author's analysis of interaction in a U.S Italian slum demonstrates how social structure affects personal relationships.

Journals
Qualitative Sociology, Symbolic Interaction, and *Urban Life* feature articles on symbolic interactionism and analyses of everyday life.

Societies to Social Networks

Societies to Social
Networks

Brazil

Paulo Fridman/Corbis

When Kody Scott joined the L.A. Crips, his initiation had two parts. Here's the first:

"How old is you now anyway?"

"Eleven, but I'll be twelve in November."

I never saw the blow to my head come from Huck. Bam! And I was on all fours. . . . Kicked in the stomach, I was on my back counting stars in the blackness. Grabbed by the collar, I was made to stand again. A solid blow to my chest exploded pain on the blank screen that had now become my mind. Bam! Another, then another. Blows rained on me from every direction. . . .

> "Kody, you got eight shots, you don't come back to the car unless they all are gone."

Up until this point not a word had been spoken. . . . Then I just started swinging, with no style or finesse, just anger and the instinct to survive. . . . [This] reflected my ability to represent the set [gang] in hand-to-hand combat. The blows stopped abruptly. . . . My ear was bleeding, and my neck and face were deep red. . . .

Scott's beating was followed immediately by the second part of his initiation. For this, he received the name *Monster*, which he carried proudly:

"Give Kody the pump" [12-gauge pump action shotgun] . . . Tray Ball spoke with the calm of a football coach. "Tonight we gonna rock they world." . . . Hand slaps were passed around the room. . . . "Kody, you got eight shots, you don't come back to the car unless they all are gone."

"Righteous," I said, eager to show my worth. . . .

Hanging close to buildings, houses, and bushes, we made our way, one after the other, to within spitting distance of the Bloods. . . . Huck and Fly stepped from the shadows simultaneously and were never noticed until it was too late. Boom! Boom! Heavy bodies hitting the ground, confusion, yells of dismay, running. . . . By my sixth shot I had advanced past the first fallen bodies and into the street in pursuit of those who had sought refuge behind cars and trees. . . .

Back in the shack we smoked more pot and drank more beer. I was the center of attention for my acts of aggression. . . .

Tray Ball said. "You got potential, 'cause' you eager to learn. Bangin' [being a gang member] ain't no part-time thang, it's full-time, it's a career. It's bein' down when ain't nobody else down with you. It's gettin' caught and not tellin'. Killin' and not caring, and dyin' without fear. It's love for your set and hate for the enemy. You hear what I'm sayin'?"

Kody adds this insightful remark:

Though never verbally stated, death was looked upon as a sort of reward, a badge of honor, especially if one died in some heroic capacity for the hood. . . . The supreme sacrifice was to "take a bullet for a homie" [fellow gang member]. The set functioned as a religion. Nothing held a light to the power of the set. If you died on the trigger you surely were smiled upon by the Crip God.

Excerpts from Scott 1994:8–13, 103.

group people who have something in common and who believe that what they have in common is significant; also called a *social group*

society people who share a culture and a territory

hunting and gathering society a human group that depends on hunting and gathering for its survival

shaman the healing specialist of a tribe who attempts to control the spirits thought to cause a disease or injury; commonly called a witch doctor

Could you be like Kody and shoot strangers in cold blood—just because others tell you to pull the trigger? Although none of us want to think that we could, don't bet on it. In this chapter, you are going to read some surprising things about **groups**—people who interact with one another and who think of themselves as belonging together. As we move into this topic, let's first look at the big picture, how societies have changed over time.

Societies and Their Transformation

The largest and most complex group that sociologists study is **society,** which consists of people who share a culture and a territory. Society, which surrounds us, sets the stage for our life experiences. *The sociological principle is that the type of society we live in is the fundamental reason for why we become who we are.* Not only does our society lay the broad framework for our behavior, but it also influences the ways we think and feel. Its effects are so significant that if you had grown up in a different society, you would be a different type of person.

To see how our society developed, look at Figure 1 on the next page. You can see that technology is the key to understanding the sweeping changes that produced our society. Let's review these broad changes. As we do, picture yourself as a member of each society. Consider how your life—even your thoughts and values—would be different as a member of these societies.

Hunting and Gathering Societies

The members of **hunting and gathering societies** have few social divisions and little inequality. As the name implies, in order to survive, these groups depend on hunting animals and gathering plants. In some groups, the men do the hunting, and the women the gathering. In others, both men and women (and children) gather plants, the men hunt large animals, and both men and women hunt small animals. The groups usually have a **shaman,** an individual thought to be able to influence spiritual forces, but shamans, too, must help obtain food. Although these groups give greater prestige to

As *society*—the largest and complex type of group—changes, so, too, do the groups, activities, and, ultimately, the type of people who form that society. This photo of a Norwegian competitor in the Beijing Olympics captures some of the changes occurring in Western societies. What social changes can you identify from this photo?

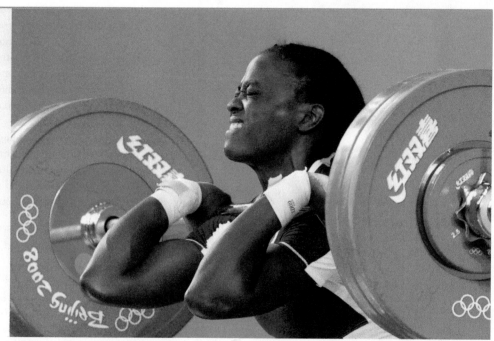

RIA Novosti/Topham/The Image Works

the men hunters, who supply most of the meat, the women gatherers contribute more food to the group, perhaps even four-fifths of their total food supply (Bernard 1992).

Because a region cannot support a large number of people who hunt animals and gather plants (group members do not plant—they only gather what is already there), hunting and gathering societies are small. They usually consist of only twenty-five to forty people. These groups are nomadic. As their food supply dwindles in one area, they move to another location. They place high value on sharing food, which is essential to their survival. Because of disease, drought, and pestilence, children have only about a fifty-fifty chance of surviving to adulthood (Lenski and Lenski 1987).

Of all societies, hunters and gatherers are the most egalitarian. Because what they hunt and gather is perishable, the people accumulate few personal possessions. Consequently, no one becomes wealthier than anyone else. There are no rulers, and most decisions are arrived at through discussion. Because their needs are basic and they do not work to store up material possessions, hunters and gatherers have the most leisure of all human groups (Sahlins 1972; Lorber 1994; Volti 1995).

As in the photo on the next page, all human groups were once hunters and gatherers. Until several hundred years ago, such societies were common, but only about 300 hunter-gatherer groups remain today (Stiles 2003). Their demise came when other groups moved into the territory on which they depended for food. The groups that remain include the pygmies of central Africa, the aborigines of Australia, and various groups in South America. As populations expand, these groups seem doomed to a similar fate, and it is likely that their way of life will soon disappear from the human scene (Lenski and Lenski 1987).

FIGURE 1 The Social Transformations of Society

The First Social Revolution: Domestication (of plants and animals)

The Second Social Revolution: Agricultural (invention of the plow)

The Third Social Revolution: Industrial (invention of the steam engine)

The Fourth Social Revolution: Information (invention of the microchip)

The Fifth Social Revolution?: Biotech (decoding of human genome system?)

Note: Not all the world's societies will go through the transformations shown in this figure. Whether any hunting and gathering societies will survive, however, remains to be seen. A few might, perhaps kept on "small reserves" that will be off limits to developers—but open to guided "ethnotours" at a hefty fee.

Source: By the author.

Pastoral and Horticultural Societies

About ten thousand years ago, some groups found that they could tame and breed some of the animals they hunted—primarily goats, sheep, cattle, and camels. Others discovered that they could cultivate plants. As a result, hunting and gathering societies branched into two directions, each with different means of acquiring food.

The key to understanding the first branching is the word *pasture;* **pastoral** (or herding) **societies** are based on the *pasturing of animals.* Pastoral societies developed in regions where low rainfall made it impractical to build life around growing crops. Groups that took this turn remained nomadic, for they followed their animals to fresh pasture. The key to understanding the second branching is the word *horticulture,* or plant cultivation. **Horticultural** (or gardening) **societies** are based on the *cultivation of plants by the use of hand tools.* Because they no longer had to abandon an area as the food supply gave out, these groups developed permanent settlements.

We can call the domestication of animals and plants the *first social revolution.* As shown in Figure 2, it transformed society. Although the **domestication revolution** was gradual, occurring over thousands of years, it represented such a fundamental

pastoral society a society based on the pasturing of animals

horticultural society a society based on cultivating plants by the use of hand tools

domestication revolution the first social revolution, based on the domestication of plants and animals, which led to pastoral and horticultural societies

John Warburton-Lee/www.DanitaDelimont.com

The simplest forms of societies are called *hunting and gathering societies.* Members of these societies have adapted well to their environments, and they have more leisure than the members of other societies. Not many hunting and gathering groups remain on earth. This man, who is spear fishing, is from the Turkana of Kenya.

break with the past that it changed human history. The more dependable food supply ushered in changes that touched almost every aspect of human life. Groups grew larger because the more dependable food supply supported more people. With more food available than was needed for survival, no longer was it necessary for everyone to work at providing food. As a result, a *division of labor* developed. Some people began to make jewelry, others tools, others weapons, and so on. This led to a surplus of objects, which, in turn, stimulated trade. As groups traded with one another, they began to accumulate objects they prized, such as gold, jewelry, and utensils.

Figure 2 illustrates how these changes led to *social inequality.* Some families (or clans) acquired more goods than others. This led to feuds and war, for groups now possessed animals, pastures, croplands, jewelry, and other material goods to fight about. War, in turn, opened the door to slavery, for people found it convenient to let captives do their drudge work. Social inequality remained limited, however, for the surplus itself was limited. As individuals passed their possessions on to their descendants, wealth grew more concentrated. So did power, and for the first time, some individuals became chiefs.

Note the pattern that runs through this transformation: the change *from fewer to more possessions and from greater to lesser equality.* Where people were located *within* the hierarchy of a society became vital for determining what happened to them in life.

Agricultural Societies

The invention of the plow about five or six thousand years ago once again changed social life forever. Compared with hoes and digging sticks, using animals to pull plows is immensely efficient. As the earth was plowed, more nutrients were returned to the soil, making the land more productive. The food surplus of the **agricultural revolution** was unlike anything ever seen in human history. It allowed even more people to engage in activities other than farming. In this new **agricultural society,** people developed cities and what is popularly known as "culture," activities such as philosophy, art, music, literature, and architecture. Accompanied by the inventions of the wheel, writing, and numbers, the changes were so profound that this period is sometimes referred to as "the dawn of civilization."

The social inequality of pastoral and horticultural societies turned out to be only a hint of what was to come. When some people managed to gain control of the growing surplus of resources in agricultural societies, *inequality became a fundamental feature of life in society.* To protect their expanding privileges and power, this elite surrounded itself with armed men. This small group even levied taxes on others, who now had become their "subjects." As conflict theorists point out, this concentration of resources and power—along with the oppression of people not in power—was the forerunner of the state.

No one knows exactly how it happened, but during this period females also became subject to males. Sociologist Elise Boulding (1976) theorizes that this change occurred because men were in charge of plowing and the cows. She suggests that when metals were

agricultural revolution the second social revolution, based on the invention of the plow, which led to agricultural societies

agricultural society a society based on large-scale agriculture

Industrial Revolution the third social revolution, occurring when machines powered by fuels replaced most animal and human power

industrial society a society based on the use of machines powered by fuels developed, men took on the new job of attaching the metal as tips to the wooden plows and doing the plowing. As a result,

> the shift of the status of the woman farmer may have happened quite rapidly, once there were two male specializations relating to agriculture: plowing and the care of cattle. This situation left women with all the subsidiary tasks, including weeding and carrying water to the fields. The new fields were larger, so women had to work just as many hours as they did before, but now they worked at more secondary tasks. . . . This would contribute further to the erosion of the status of women.

This explanation, however, creates more questions than it answers. Why, for example, did men take over metal work and plowing? Why didn't women? It also does not account for why men control societies in which women are in charge of the cattle. In short, we are left in the dark as to why and how men became dominant, a reason likely to remain lost in human history.

Industrial Societies

The *third* social invention also turned society upside down. The **Industrial Revolution** began in Great Britain in 1765 when the steam engine was first used to run machinery. Before this, a few machines (such as windmills and water wheels) had been used to harness nature, but most machines depended on human and animal power. The resulting **industrial society** is defined by sociologist Herbert Blumer (1990) as one in which goods are produced by machines powered by fuels, instead of by the brute force of humans or animals.

The steam engine ushered in even more social inequality. This new technology was far more efficient than anything that preceded it. Just as its surplus was greater, so also were its effects on social life. The cities had a massive supply of desperate labor, people who had been thrown off the lands that their ancestors had farmed as tenants for centuries. Homeless, they faced the choice of stealing, starving, or being paid the equivalent of a loaf of bread for a day's work. Some of the men who first harnessed the steam engine and employed these desperate workers accumulated such wealth that their riches outran the imagination of royalty.

Workers had no legal right to unionize, not even the right to safe working conditions. If workers banded together to protest or to ask for higher wages, they were fired. If they returned to the factory, they were arrested for trespassing on private property. Strikes were illegal, and strikers were arrested—or beaten by the employer's private security force. During the early 1900s, some U.S. strikers were shot by private police and even by the National Guard. Against these odds, workers gradually won their fight for better working conditions.

As industrialization continued, bringing an abundance of goods, and as workers won what we call basic rights, a surprising change occurred—*the pattern of growing inequality was reversed.* Home ownership became common, as did the ownership of automobiles and an incredible variety of consumer goods. Today's typical worker enjoys a high standard of living in terms of health care, food, housing, material possessions, and access to libraries and education. On an even broader scale of growing equality came the abolition of slavery, the shift from monarchies to more representative political systems, greater rights for women and minorities, and the rights to a jury trial, to cross-examine witnesses, to vote, and to travel. A recent extension of these equalities is the right to set up your own Internet blog where you can bemoan life in your school or criticize the president.

Postindustrial (Information) Societies

If you were to choose one word to characterize our society, what would it be? Of the many candidates, the word *change* would have to rank high. The primary

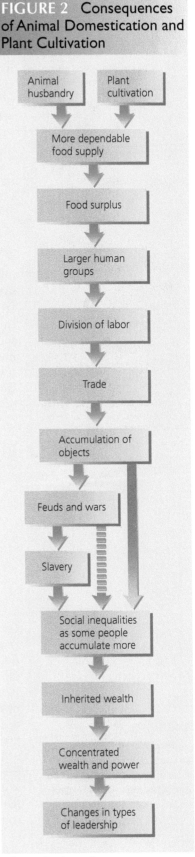

FIGURE 2 Consequences of Animal Domestication and Plant Cultivation

Source: By the author.

333

source of the sweeping changes that are transforming our lives is the technology centering on the microchip. The change is so vast that sociologists say that a new type of society has emerged. They call it the **postindustrial** (or **information**) **society.**

What are the main characteristics of this new society? Unlike the industrial society, its hallmark is not turning raw materials into products. Rather, its basic component is *information.* Teachers pass knowledge on to students, while lawyers, physicians, bankers, pilots, and interior decorators sell their specialized knowledge of law, the body, money, aerodynamics, and color schemes to clients. Unlike the factory workers of an industrial society, these individuals don't *produce* anything. Rather, they transmit or apply information to provide services that others are willing to pay for.

The United States was the first country to have more than half of its workers in service industries such as banking, counseling, education, entertainment, government, health, insurance, law, mass media, research, and sales. Australia, Japan, New Zealand, and western Europe soon followed. This trend away from manufacturing and toward selling information and services shows no sign of letting up.

The changes are so profound that they have led to a *fourth social revolution.* The surface changes of this new technology are obvious. Our purchases are scanned and billed in some remote place. While we ride in cars, trucks, boats, and airplanes, we talk to people in distant cities or even on the other side of the globe. We examine the surface of Mars and probe other remote regions of space. We spend billions of dollars on Internet purchases. And because of this tiny device, millions of children (and adults) spend countless hours battling virtual video villains. Beyond such surface changes lie much more fundamental ones: The microchip is transforming relations among people. It is also uprooting our old perspectives and replacing them with new ones. In the Sociology and the New Technology box on the next page, we explore an extreme aspect of virtual reality.

Biotech Societies: Is a New Type of Society Emerging?

- Tobacco that fights cancer. ("Yes, smoke your way to health!")
- Corn that fights herpes and is a contraceptive. ("Corn flakes in the morning—and safe sex all day!")
- Goats whose milk contains spider silk (to make fishing lines and body armor) ("Got milk? The best bulletproofing.")
- Animals that are part human so they produce medicines for humans. ("Ah, those liver secretions. Good for what ails you.")
- No-Sneeze kitties—hypoallergenic cats at $4,000 each. (You can write your own jingle for this one.)

I know that such products sound like science fiction, but we *already* have the goats that make spider silk. Human genes have been inserted into animals so that they produce medicine (Elias 2001; Kristoff 2002; Osborne 2002). The no-sneeze cats are for sale—and there is a waiting list of allergic cat lovers (Rosenthal 2006). The changes in which we are immersed are so extensive that we may be entering another new type of society. In this new **biotech society,** the economy will center on applying and altering genetic structures—both plant and animal—to produce food, medicine, and materials.

If there is a new society—and this is not certain—when did it begin? There are no firm edges to new societies, for each new one overlaps the one it is replacing. The opening to a biotech society could have been 1953, when Francis Crick and James Watson identified the double-helix structure of DNA. Or perhaps historians will trace the date to the decoding of the human genome in 2001.

Whether the changes that are swirling around us are part of a new type of society is not the main point. The larger group called society always profoundly affects people's thinking and behavior. *The sociological significance of these changes, then, is that as society is transformed, it will sweep us along with it. The transformation will be so fundamental that it will change even the ways we think about the self and life.* With cloning and bioengineering, we

postindustrial (information) society a society based on information, services, and high technology, rather than on raw materials and manufacturing

biotech society a society whose economy increasingly centers on the application of genetics to produce medicine, food, and materials

SOCIOLOGY and the NEW TECHNOLOGY

Avatar Fantasy Life: The Blurring Lines of Reality

Dissatisfied with your current life? Would you like to become someone else? Maybe someone rich? Maybe someone with no responsibilities? You can. Join a world populated with virtual people and live out your fantasy.

For some, the appeal is strong. *Second Life,* one of several Internet sites that offer an alternative virtual reality, has exploded in popularity. Of its 8 million "residents," 450,000 spend twenty to forty hours a week in their second life.

To start your second life, you select your avatar, a kind of digital hand puppet, to be your persona in this virtual world. Your avatar comes in just a basic form, although you can control its movements just fine. But that bare body certainly won't do. You will want to clothe it. For this, you have your choice of outfits for every occasion. Although you buy them from other avatars in virtual stores, you have to spend real dollars. You might want some hair, too. For that, too, you'll have your choice of designers. And again, you'll spend real dollars. And you might want to have a sex organ. There is even a specialty store for that.

All equipped the way you want to be?

Then it is time to meet other avatars, the virtual personas of real-life people. In this virtual world, they buy property, open businesses, and interact with one another. They share stories, talk about their desires in life, and have drinks in virtual bars.

Avatars flirt, too. Some even date and marry.

For most people, this second life is just an interesting game. They come and go, as if playing *Tomb Raider* or *World of Warcraft* now and then. Some people, though, get so caught up in their virtual world that their real world shrinks in appeal, and they neglect friends and family. That is, they neglect their real friends and family, but remain attentive to their virtual friends and family. As the virtual replaces the real, the virtual becomes real and the real fades into nonreality.

Ric Hoogestraat in Phoenix, Arizona, loves his virtual life. He operates his avatar, Dutch—a macho motorcycle man, who is also filthy rich—from the time he gets up to the time he goes to bed. Dutch visits his several homes, where he can lounge on specially designed furniture. He pours his favorite drink and from his penthouse watches the sun setting over the ocean.

And here he also spends time with his wife, Tenaj. Dutch met Tenaj on *Second Life.* As courtships go, theirs went well. Their wedding was announced, of course, and about

A scene from Second Life. *Each image is an avatar, a real person's fantasy self.*

Friedrich Stark/Alamy

twenty avatar friends attended. They gave the newlyweds real congratulations, in a virtual sort of way.

Dutch and Tenaj have two dogs and pay the mortgage together. They love cuddling and intimate talks. Their love life is quite good, as avatars can have virtual sex.

But then there is Sue, whose last name is Hoogestraat, and Sue is not pleased. Sue is also Ric's wife, but this one is in real life. Sue feels neglected and doesn't like Ric spending so much time in his virtual world. She also doesn't appreciate Tenaj.

The whole thing has become more than a little irritating. "I'll try to talk to him or bring him a drink, and he'll be having sex with a cartoon," she says.

Tenaj, the avatar, also has a real life counterpart, Janet, who lives in Canada. Ric and Janet have never met—nor do they plan to meet. They haven't even talked on the phone as Ric and Janet—just a lot of sweet talking in their virtual world as Dutch and Tenaj.

For gamers, the virtual always overlaps the real to some extent, but for some the virtual overwhelms the real. Their satisfactions, which are quite real, come from living a fantasy life.

This is all quite new, but quite real.

For Your Consideration

How much time do you spend on computer games? Are you involved in any virtual reality? Do you think that Ric is cheating on Sue? Is this grounds for divorce? (One wife certainly thought so. She divorced her husband when she caught a glimpse of his avatar having sex with an avatar prostitute ["Second Life Affair . . ." 2008]). Other than the sexual aspect, is having a second life really any different from people's involvement in fantasy football? (Keep in mind the term *football widows.*)

Based on Alter 2007; Corbett 2009.

could even see changes in the human species. The Sociology and the New Technology box below examines implications of cloning.

In Sum: Each society sets boundaries around its members. By laying a framework of statuses, roles, groups, and social institutions, society establishes the prevailing behaviors and beliefs. It also determines the type and extent of social inequality. These factors, in turn, set the stage for relationships between men and women, racial–ethnic groups, the young and the elderly, the rich and the poor, and so on.

Society is not stagnant, and *you* are affected directly by the sweeping historical changes that transform it. On the obvious level, if you lived in a hunting and gathering society you would not be listening to your favorite music, watching TV, playing video games—or taking this course. On a deeper level, you would not feel the same about life, have the same beliefs, or hold your particular aspirations for the future. Actually, no aspect of your life would be the same. You would be locked into the attitudes and views that come with a hunting and gathering way of life.

SOCIOLOGY and the NEW TECHNOLOGY

"So, You Want to Be Yourself?" Cloning and the Future of Society

Stockbyte/Getty Images Royalty Free

No type of society ends abruptly. The edges are fuzzy, as the old merges into the new. With time speeded up, our information society hasn't even matured, and it looks as though a biotech society is hard on its heels. Let's try to peer over the edge of today's society to glimpse the one that might be arriving. If it does, what will life be like? We could examine many issues, but since space is limited, let's consider just one: cloning. Since human embryos have been cloned, it seems inevitable that some group somewhere will complete the process. If cloning humans becomes routine—well, consider these two scenarios:

It turns out that you can't have children. You go to Cleto's Cloning Clinic, pay the standard fee, and clone either yourself or your spouse. Who is your child? Is that little boy or girl, in effect, either yourself or your spouse—as a child? Or instead of a daughter or son, even a sister or brother?

Or suppose that you love your mother dearly, and she is dying. With her permission, you decide to clone her. Who is the clone? Would you be rearing your own mother?

When we have genetic replicates, we will have to wrestle with new questions of human relationships: What is a clone's relationship to its "parents"? Indeed, what are "parents" and "children"?

Cloning also takes us to weighty ethical matters, ones that may involve the future of society. I'm sure you have heard people object that cloning is immoral.

But have you heard the opposite, that cloning should be our moral choice? Let's suppose that mass cloning becomes possible. Let's also assume that geneticists trace high creative ability, high intelligence, compassion, and a propensity for peace to specific genes—along with the ability to appreciate and create beautiful poetry, music, and architecture; to excel in mathematics, science, and other intellectual pursuits; even to be successful in love. Why, then, they argue, should we leave human reproduction to people who have inferior traits—genetic diseases, low IQs, perhaps even the propensity for crime and violence? They suggest that we select people with the finer characteristics to reproduce—and to clone.

For Your Consideration

Do you think that we have a moral obligation to try to build a society that is better for all—one without terrorism, war, violence, and greed? If so, do you think we also have the moral obligation to populate society with people who have the characteristics that would bring about such a society? Could this even be our evolutionary destiny?

Source: Based on Kaebnick 2000; McGee 2000; Bjerklie et al. 2001; Davis 2001; Weiss 2004; Regalado 2005.

Now that we have reviewed the major historical shifts in societies, let's turn to groups within society. Just how do they affect our lives?

Groups Within Society

Our society is huge, dominating, sometimes even threatening and oppressive. This can create a bewildering sense of not belonging. Sociologist Emile Durkheim (1893/1933) called this condition *anomie* (AN-uh-mee). He said that small groups help prevent anomie by standing as a buffer between the individual and the larger society. By providing intimate relationships, small groups give us a sense of belonging, something that we all need. Because smaller groups are essential for our well-being, let's look at them in detail.

Smaller groups, then, are vital for our well-being, but before we examine them in detail, we should distinguish some terms. Two terms sometimes confused with "group" are *aggregate* and *category*. An **aggregate** consists of individuals who temporarily share the same physical space but who do not see themselves as belonging together. Shoppers standing in a checkout line or drivers waiting at a red light are an aggregate. A **category** is simply a statistic. It consists of people who share similar characteristics, such as all college women who wear glasses or all men over 6 feet tall. Unlike group members, the individuals who make up a category don't think of themselves as belonging together, and they don't interact with one another. These concepts are illustrated in the photos on the next page.

Primary Groups

Our first group, the family, gives us our basic orientations to life. Later, among friends, we find more intimacy and an expanded sense of belonging. These groups are what sociologist Charles Cooley called **primary groups.** By providing intimate, face-to-face interaction, they give us an identity, a feeling of who we are. As Cooley (1909) put it,

> By primary groups I mean those characterized by intimate face-to-face association and cooperation. They are primary in several senses, but chiefly in that they are fundamental in forming the social nature and ideals of the individual.

Producing a Mirror Within. Cooley called primary groups the "springs of life." By this, he meant that primary groups, such as family and friends, are essential to our emotional well-being. As humans, we have an intense need for face-to-face interaction that generates feelings of self-esteem. By offering a sense of belonging and a feeling of being appreciated—and sometimes even loved—primary groups are uniquely equipped to meet this basic need. From our opening vignette, you can see that gangs are also primary groups.

Primary groups are also significant because their values and attitudes become fused into our identity. We internalize their views, which then become the lenses through which we view life. Even when we are adults—no matter how far we move away from our childhood roots—early primary groups remain "inside" us. There, they continue to form part of the perspective from which we look out onto the world. Ultimately, then, it is difficult, if not impossible, for us to separate the self from our primary groups, for the self and our groups merge into a "we."

Secondary Groups

Compared with primary groups, **secondary groups** are larger, more anonymous, more formal, and more impersonal. Secondary groups are based on some common interest or activity, and their members are likely to interact on the basis of specific statuses, such as president, manager, worker, or student. Examples are a college class, the American Sociological

aggregate individuals who temporarily share the same physical space but who do not see themselves as belonging together

category people who have similar characteristics

primary group a group characterized by intimate, long-term, face-to-face association and cooperation

secondary group compared with a primary group, a larger, relatively temporary, more anonymous, formal, and impersonal group based on some interest or activity

Categories, Aggregates, Primary and Secondary Groups

Groups have a deep impact on our actions, views, orientations, even what we feel and think about life. Yet, as illustrated by these photos, not everything that appears to be a group is actually a group in the sociological sense.

Ben Molyneux/Alamy

Image Source/Corbis

Matt Henry/Stone/Getty Images

Alex Segre/Alamy

▲ **Aggregates** are people who happen to be in the same place at the same time.

▲ The outstanding trait that these three people have in common does not make them a group, but a **category.**

◀ **Secondary groups** are larger and more anonymous, formal, and impersonal than primary groups. Why are the participants of a dog show an example of a secondary group?

Andrew Fox/Corbis

▶ **Primary groups** such as the family play a key role in the development of the self. As a small group, the family also serves as a buffer from the often-threatening larger group known as society. The family has been of primary significance in forming the basic orientations of this couple, as it will be for their son.

Lee Snider/The Image Works

Association, and the Democratic Party. Contemporary society could not function without secondary groups. They are part of the way we get our education, make our living, spend our money, and use our leisure time.

As necessary as secondary groups are for contemporary life, they often fail to satisfy our deep needs for intimate association. Consequently, *secondary groups tend to break down into primary groups.* At school and work, we form friendships. Our interaction with our friends is so important that we sometimes feel that if it weren't for them, school or work "would drive us crazy." The primary groups that we form within secondary groups, then, serve as a buffer between ourselves and the demands that secondary groups place on us.

In-Groups and Out-Groups

What groups do you identity with? Which groups in our society do you dislike? We all have **in-groups,** groups toward which we feel loyalty. And we all have **out-groups,** groups toward which we feel antagonism. For Monster Kody in our opening vignette, the Crips were an in-group, while the Bloods were an out-group. That the Crips— and we—make such a fundamental division of the world has far-reaching consequences for our lives.

Implications for a Socially Diverse Society: Shaping Perception and Morality. You know how vital some of your groups are to you, the sense of belonging they give you. This can bring positive consequences for others, such as our tendency to excuse the faults of people we love and to encourage them to do better. Unfortunately, dividing the world into a "we" and "them" also leads to discrimination, hatred, and, as we saw in our opening vignette, even murder.

At the center of it all is how in-group membership shapes our perception of the world. Let's look at two examples. The first you see regularly, prejudice and discrimination on the basis of sex. As sociologist Robert Merton (1968) said, our favoritism creates a fascinating double standard. We tend to view the traits of our in-group as virtues, while we perceive those *same* traits as vices in out-groups. Men may perceive an aggressive man as assertive but an aggressive woman as pushy. They may think that a male employee who doesn't speak up "knows when to keep his mouth shut," while they consider a quiet woman as too timid to make it in the business world.

The "we" and "they" division of the world can lead to such twisted perception that harming others comes to be viewed as right. The Nazis provide one of the most startling examples. For them, the Jews were an out-group who symbolized an evil that should be eliminated. Many ordinary, "good" Germans shared this view and defended the Holocaust as "dirty work" that someone had to do (Hughes 1962/2005).

An example from way back then, you might say—and the world has moved on. But our inclination to divide the world into in-groups and out-groups has not moved on— nor has the twisting of perception that accompanies it. After the terrorist attacks of September 11, 2001, top U.S. officials came to view Arabs as sinister, bloodthirsty villains. They said that it was OK for interrogators to be "cruel, inhuman, and degrading" to prisoners" (Gonzales 2002). Inflicting pain, they said, was not torture unless it caused "death, organ failure, or permanent damage" (Johnston and Shane 2008). Alan Dershowitz, a professor at Harvard Law School who usually takes very liberal views, went even further. He said that we should make torture legal so judges

"So long, Bill. This is my club. You can't come in."

How our participation in social groups shapes our self-concept is a focus of symbolic interactionists. In this process, knowing who we are *not* is as significant as knowing who we are.

in-groups groups toward which people feel loyalty

out-groups groups toward which people feel antagonism

reference group a group whose standards we refer to as we evaluate ourselves

can issue "torture warrants" (Schulz 2002). After 9/11, inflicting pain on prisoners became "dirty work" that someone had to do. Can you see the principle at work—and understand that in-group/out-group thinking can be so severe that even "good people" can torture and kill? And with a good conscience.

Economic downturns are especially perilous in this regard. The Nazis took power during a depression so severe that it was wiping out the middle classes. If such a depression were to occur in the United States, immigrants would be transformed from "nice people who for low wages will do jobs that Americans think are beneath them" to "sneaky people who steal jobs from friends and family." A national anti-immigration policy would follow, accompanied by a resurgence of hate groups such as the neo-Nazis, the Ku Klux Klan, and skinheads.

In short, to divide the world into in-groups and out-groups is a natural part of social life. But in addition to bringing functional consequences, it can also bring dysfunctional ones.

Reference Groups

Suppose you have just been offered a good job. It pays double what you hope to make even after you graduate from college. You have only two days to make up your mind. If you accept it, you will have to drop out of college. As you consider the matter, thoughts like this may go through your mind: "My friends will say I'm a fool if I don't take the job . . . but Dad and Mom will practically go crazy. They've made sacrifices for me, and they'll be crushed if I don't finish college. They've always said I've got to get my education first, that good jobs will always be there. . . . But, then, I'd like to see the look on the faces of those neighbors who said I'd never amount to much!"

Evaluating Ourselves. This is an example of how people use **reference groups,** the groups we refer to when we evaluate ourselves. Your reference groups may include your family, neighbors, teachers, classmates, co-workers, and the Scouts or the members of a church, synagogue, or mosque. If you were like Monster Kody in our opening vignette, the "set" would be your main reference group. Even a group you don't belong to can be a reference group. For example, if you are thinking about going to graduate school, graduate students or members of the profession you want to join may form a reference group. You would consider their standards as you evaluate your grades or writing skills.

Reference groups exert tremendous influence over our lives. For example, if you want to become a corporate executive, you might start to dress more formally, try to improve your vocabulary, read the *Wall Street Journal,* and change your major to business or law. In contrast, if you want to become a rock musician, you might wear jewelry in several places where you have pierced your body, get elaborate tattoos, dress in ways your parents and many of your peers consider extreme, read *Rolling Stone,* drop out of college, and hang around clubs and rock groups.

Exposure to Contradictory Standards in a Socially Diverse Society. From these examples, you can see how we use reference groups to evaluate our behavior. When we see ourselves as measuring up to a reference group's standards, we feel no conflict. If our behavior—or even aspirations—does not match the group's standards, however, the mismatch can lead to inner turmoil. For example, wanting to become a corporate executive would create no inner turmoil for most of us. It would, however, for someone who had grown up in an Amish home. The Amish strongly disapprove of such aspirations for their children. They ban high school and college education, suits and ties, and corporate employment. Similarly, if you want to join the military and your parents are dedicated pacifists, you likely would feel deep conflict, because your parents would have quite different aspirations for you.

AP Images

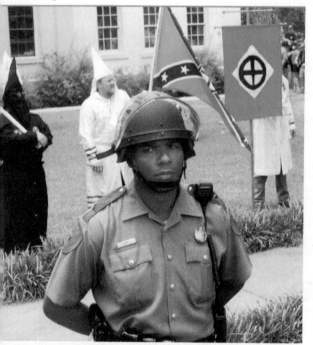

All of us have *reference groups*—the groups we use as standards to evaluate ourselves. How do you think the reference groups of these members of the KKK who are demonstrating in Jaspar, Texas, differ from those of the police officer who is protecting their right of free speech? Although the KKK and this police officer use different groups to evaluate their attitudes and behaviors, the process is the same.

Two chief characteristics of our society are social diversity and social mobility. This exposes us to standards and orientations that are inconsistent with those we learned during childhood. The "internal recordings" that play contradictory messages from different reference groups, then, are one price we pay for our social mobility.

Social Networks

Although we live in a huge and diverse society, we don't experience social life as a sea of nameless, strange faces. Instead, we interact within social networks. The term **social network** refers to people who are linked to one another. Your social network includes your family, friends, acquaintances, people at work and school, and even "friends of friends." Think of your social network as a spider's web. You are at the center, with lines extending outward, gradually encompassing more and more people.

If you are a member of a large group, you probably associate regularly with a few people within that group. In a sociology class I was teaching at a commuter campus, six women who didn't know one another ended up working together on a project. They got along well, and they began to sit together. Eventually they planned a Christmas party at one of their homes. This type of social network, the clusters within a group, or its internal factions, is called a **clique** (cleek).

The analysis of social networks has become part of applied sociology. One of its most surprising applications was the capture of Saddam Hussein.

After U.S.-led forces took over Baghdad, Hussein was nowhere to be found. Rumors placed him all over the map, from neighboring countries to safe houses in Baghdad. To find him, U.S. intelligence officers began to apply network analysis. On a color-coded "people map," they placed Hussein's photo in a yellow circle, like a bull's-eye. They then drew links to people who were connected to Hussein, placing their photos closer to or farther from Hussein's photo on the basis of how close they were to Hussein (Schmitt 2003; Hougham 2005).

The photos closest to Hussein represented an intimate and loyal group. These people were the most likely to know where Hussein was, but because of their close ties to him, they also were the least likely to reveal this information. Those who were pictured slightly farther away knew people in this more intimate group, so it was likely that some of them had information about Hussein's whereabouts. Because these people's social ties to Hussein were not as strong, they represented the weaker links that might be broken.

The approach worked. Using software programs to sift through vast amounts of information gained from informants and electronic intercepts, the analysts drew the "people map" that pictured these social relationships. Identifying the weaker links led to the capture of Saddam Hussein.

social network the social ties radiating outward from the self that link people together

clique a cluster of people within a larger group who choose to interact with one another

AP Images/www.imagesource.com

Michael Newman/PhotoEdit, Inc.

We all use *reference groups* to evaluate our accomplishments, failures, values, and attitudes. We compare what we see in ourselves with what we perceive as normative in our reference groups. From these two photos, can you see how the *reference groups* and *social networks* of these youths are not likely to lead them to the same social destination?

The Small World Phenomenon.   Social scientists have wondered just how extensive the connections are among social networks. If you list everyone you know, each of those individuals lists everyone he or she knows, and you keep doing this, would almost everyone in the United States eventually be included on those lists?

It would be too cumbersome to test this hypothesis by drawing up such lists, but psychologist Stanley Milgram (1933–1984) came up with an interesting idea. In a classic study known as "the small world phenomenon," Milgram (1967) addressed a letter to "targets": the wife of a divinity student in Cambridge and a stockbroker in Boston. He sent the letter to "starters," who did not know these people. He asked them to send the letter to someone they knew on a first-name basis, someone they thought might know the "target." The recipients, in turn, were asked to mail the letter to someone they knew who might know the "target," and so on. The question was, Would the letters ever reach the "target"? If so, how long would the chain be?

Think of yourself as part of this study. What would you do if you were a "starter," but the "target" lived in a state in which you knew no one? You would send the letter to someone you know who might know someone in that state. This, Milgram reported, is just what happened. Although none of the senders knew the targets, the letters reached the designated individual in an average of just six jumps.

Milgram's study caught the public's fancy, leading to the phrase "six degrees of separation." This expression means that, on average, everyone in the United States is separated by just six individuals. Milgram's conclusions have become so popular that a game, "Six Degrees of Kevin Bacon," was built around it.

Is the Small World Phenomenon an Academic Myth?   Unfortunately, things are not this simple. There is a problem with Milgram's research, as psychologist Judith Kleinfeld (2002a, 2002b) discovered when she decided to replicate Milgram's study. When she went to the archives at Yale University Library to get more details, she found that Milgram had stacked the deck in favor of finding a small world. The "starters" came from mailing lists of people who were likely to have higher incomes and therefore were not representative of average people. In addition, one of the "targets" was a stockbroker, and that person's "starters" were investors in blue-chip stocks. Kleinfeld also found another discrepancy: On average, only 30 percent of the letters reached their "target." In one of Milgram's studies, the success rate was just 5 percent.

Since most letters did *not* reach their targets, even with the deck stacked in favor of success, we can draw the *opposite* conclusion from the one that Milgram reported: People who don't know one another are dramatically separated by social barriers. How great the barriers are is illustrated by another attempt to replicate Milgram's study, this one using e-mail. Only 384 of 24,000 chains reached their targets (Dodds et al. 2003).

As Kleinfeld says, "Rather than living in a small world, we may live in a world that looks like a bowl of lumpy oatmeal, with many small worlds loosely connected and perhaps some small worlds not connected at all." Somehow, I don't think that the phrase, "lumpy oatmeal phenomenon," will become standard, but the criticism of Milgram's research is valid.

Kleinfeld's revelations of the flaws in Milgram's research reinforce the need for replication. For our knowledge of social life, we cannot depend on single studies—there may be problems of generalizability on the one hand, or those of negligence or even fraud on the other. Replication by objective researchers is essential to build and advance solid social knowledge.

A New Group: Electronic Communities

In the 1990s, a new type of human group, the **electronic community,** made its appearance. People "meet" online to talk about almost any conceivable topic, from donkey racing and bird watching to sociology and quantum physics. Some online encounters in chat rooms, Facebook, LinkedIn, and Twitter meet our definition of *group,* people who interact with one another and who think of themselves as belonging together. They pride themselves on the distinctive nature of their interests and knowledge—factors that give them a common identity and bind them together. Although sociologists have begun to study these groups, the results are preliminary and tentative.

electronic community individuals who regularly interact with one another on the Internet and who think of themselves as belonging together

Group Dynamics

As you know from personal experience, the lively interaction *within* groups—who does what with whom—has profound consequences for how you adjust to life. Sociologists use the term **group dynamics** to refer to how groups influence us and how we affect groups. Let's consider how the size of a group makes a difference and then examine leadership, conformity, and decision making.

Before doing so, we should see how sociologists define the term *small group*. In a **small group,** there are few enough members that each one can interact directly with all the other members. Small groups can be either primary or secondary. A wife, husband, and children make up a primary small group, as do workers who take their breaks together, while bidders at an auction and students in a small introductory sociology class are secondary small groups. You might want to look again at the photos earlier in the chapter.

Effects of Group Size on Stability and Intimacy

Writing in the early 1900s, sociologist Georg Simmel (1858–1918) noted the significance of group size. He used the term **dyad** for the smallest possible group, which consists of two people. Dyads, which include marriages, love affairs, and close friendships, show two distinct qualities. First, they are the most intense or intimate of human groups. Because only two people are involved, the interaction is focused on them. Second, dyads tend to be unstable. Because dyads require that both members participate and be committed, it takes just one member to lose interest for the dyad to collapse. In larger groups, by contrast, even if one member withdraws, the group can continue, for its existence does not depend on any single member (Simmel 1950).

A **triad** is a group of three people. As Simmel noted, the addition of a third person fundamentally changes the group. With three people, interaction between the first two decreases. This can create strain. For example, with the birth of a child, hardly any aspect of a couple's relationship goes untouched. Attention focuses on the baby, and interaction between the husband and wife diminishes. Despite this, the marriage usually becomes stronger. Although the intensity of interaction is less in triads, they are inherently stronger and give greater stability to a relationship.

Yet, as Simmel noted, triads, too, are unstable. They tend to form **coalitions**— some group members aligning themselves against others. It is not uncommon for two

group dynamics the ways in which individuals affect groups and the ways in which groups influence individuals

small group a group small enough for everyone to interact directly with all the other members

dyad the smallest possible group, consisting of two persons

triad a group of three people

coalition the alignment of some members of a group against others

Japanese companies encourage their employees to think of themselves, not as individuals, but as members of a group. Similarity of appearance and activity help to fuse group identity and company loyalty. Why do you think there are two subgroups in this photo?

AFP PHOTO/Toru YAMANAKA via Newscom

343

Christina Kennedy/Jupiter Images

Group size has a significant influence on how people interact. When a group changes from a dyad (two people) to a triad (three people), the relationships among the participants undergo a shift. How do you think the birth of this child affected the relationship between the mother and father?

members of a triad to feel stronger bonds and to prefer one another. This leaves the third person feeling hurt and excluded. Another characteristic of triads is that they often produce an arbitrator or mediator, someone who tries to settle disagreements between the other two. In one-child families, you can often observe both of these characteristics of triads—coalitions and arbitration.

The general principle is this: *As a small group grows larger, it becomes more stable, but its intensity, or intimacy, decreases.* To see why, look at Figure 3 on the next page. As each new person comes into a group, the connections among people multiply. In a dyad, there is only 1 relationship; in a triad, there are 3; in a group of four, 6; in a group of five, 10. If we expand the group to six, we have 15 relationships, while a group of seven yields 21 relationships. If we continue adding members, we soon are unable to follow the connections: A group of eight has 28 possible relationships; a group of nine, 36 relationships; a group of ten, 45; and so on.

It is not only the number of relationships that makes larger groups more stable. As groups grow, they also tend to develop a more formal structure. For example, leaders emerge and more specialized roles come into play. This often results in such familiar offices as president, secretary, and treasurer. This structure provides a framework that helps the group survive over time.

Effects of Group Size on Attitudes and Behavior

Imagine that you are taking a team-taught course in social psychology and your professors have asked you to join a few students to discuss your adjustment to college life. When you arrive, they tell you that to make the discussion anonymous they want you to sit unseen in a booth. You will participate in the discussion over an intercom, talking when your microphone comes on. The professors say that they will not listen to the conversation, and they leave.

You find the format somewhat strange, to say the least, but you go along with it. You have not seen the other students in their booths, but when they talk about their experiences, you find yourself becoming wrapped up in the problems that they begin to share. One student even mentions how frightening it is to be away from home because of his history of epileptic seizures. Later, you hear this individual breathe heavily into the microphone. Then he stammers and cries for help. A crashing noise follows, and you imagine him lying helpless on the floor.

Nothing but an eerie silence follows. What do you do?

Your professors, John Darley and Bibb Latané (1968), staged the whole thing, but you don't know this. No one had a seizure. In fact, no one was even in the other booths. Everything, except your comments, was on tape.

Some participants were told that they would be discussing the topic with just one other student, others with two, others with three, four, and five. Darley and Latané found that all students who thought they were part of a dyad rushed out to help. If they thought they were part of a triad, only 80 percent went to help—and they were slower in leaving the booth. In six-person groups, only 60 percent went to see what was wrong—and they were even slower.

This experiment demonstrates how deeply group size influences our attitudes and behavior: It even affects our willingness to help one another. Students in the dyad knew that it was up to them to help the other student. The professor was gone, and if they didn't help there was no one else. In the larger groups, including the triad, students felt *a diffusion of responsibility:* Giving help was no more their responsibility than anyone else's.

You probably have observed the second consequence of group size firsthand. When a group is small, its members act informally, but as the group grows, the members lose their sense of intimacy and become more formal with one another. No longer can the members assume that the others are "insiders" in sympathy with what they say. Now they must take a "larger audience" into consideration, and instead of merely "talking," they begin to "address" the group. As their speech becomes more formal, their body language stiffens.

You probably have observed a third aspect of group dynamics, too. In the early stages of a party, when only a few people are present, almost everyone talks with everyone else. But as others arrive, the guests break into smaller groups. Some hosts, who want their guests to mix together, make a nuisance of themselves trying to achieve *their* idea of what a group should be like. The division into small groups is inevitable, however, for it follows the basic sociological principles that we have just reviewed. Because the addition of each person rapidly increases connections (in this case, "talk lines"), conversation becomes more difficult. The guests break into smaller groups in which they can look at each other directly and interact comfortably with one another.

FIGURE 3 The Effects of Group Size on Relationships

A Dyad — One relationship

A Triad — Three relationships

A Group of Four — Six relationships

A Group of Five — Ten relationships

A Group of Six — Fifteen relationships

A Group of Seven — Twenty-one relationships

Leadership

All of us are influenced by leaders, so it is important to understand leadership. Let's look at how people become leaders, the types of leaders there are, and their different styles of leadership. Before we do this, though, it is important to clarify that leaders don't necessarily hold formal positions in a group. **Leaders** are people who influence the behaviors, opinions, or attitudes of others. Even a group of friends has leaders.

Who Becomes a Leader? Are leaders born with characteristics that propel them to the forefront of a group? No sociologist would agree with such an idea. In general, people who become leaders are perceived by group members as strongly representing their values or as able to lead a group out of a crisis (Trice and Beyer 1991). Leaders also tend to be more talkative and to express determination and self-confidence.

These findings may not be surprising, since such traits appear to be related to leadership. Researchers, however, have also discovered traits that seem to have no bearing on the ability to lead. For example, taller people and those who are judged better looking are more likely to become leaders (Stodgill 1974; Judge and Cable 2004). Some of the factors that go into our choice of leaders are quite subtle, as social psychologists Lloyd Howells and Selwyn Becker (1962) found in a simple experiment. They had groups of five people who did not know one another sit at a rectangular table. Three, of course, sat on one side, and two on the other. After discussing a topic for a set period of time, each group chose a leader. The findings are startling: Although only 40 percent of the people sat on the two-person side, 70 percent of the leaders emerged from that side. The explanation is that we tend to interact more with people facing us than with people to the side of us.

leader someone who influences other people

345

Types of Leaders. Groups have two types of leaders (Bales 1950, 1953; Cartwright and Zander 1968). The first is easy to recognize. This person, called an **instrumental leader** (or *task-oriented leader*), tries to keep the group moving toward its goals. These leaders try to keep group members from getting sidetracked, reminding them of what they are trying to accomplish. The **expressive leader** (or *socioemotional leader*), in contrast, usually is not recognized as a leader, but he or she certainly is one. This person is likely to crack jokes, to offer sympathy, or to do other things that help to lift the group's morale. Both types of leadership are essential: the one to keep the group on track, the other to increase harmony and minimize conflicts.

It is difficult for the same person to be both an instrumental and an expressive leader, for these roles tend to contradict one another. Because instrumental leaders are task oriented, they sometimes create friction as they prod the group to get on with the job. Their actions often cost them popularity. Expressive leaders, in contrast, who stimulate personal bonds and reduce friction, are usually more popular (Olmsted and Hare 1978).

Leadership Styles. Let's suppose that the president of your college has asked you to head a task force to determine how the college can improve race relations on campus. Although this position requires you to be an instrumental leader, you can adopt a number of **leadership styles,** or ways of expressing yourself as a leader. The three basic styles are those of **authoritarian leader,** one who gives orders; **democratic leader,** one who tries to gain a consensus; and **laissez-faire leader,** one who is highly permissive. Which style should you choose?

Social psychologists Ronald Lippitt and Ralph White (1958) carried out a classic study of these leadership styles. Boys who were matched for IQ, popularity, physical energy, and leadership were assigned to "craft clubs" made up of five boys each. The experimenters trained adult men in the three leadership styles. As the researchers peered through peepholes, taking notes and making movies, each adult rotated among the clubs, playing all three styles to control possible influences of their individual personalities.

The *authoritarian* leaders assigned tasks to the boys and told them what to do. They also praised or condemned the boys' work arbitrarily, giving no explanation for why they judged it good or bad. The *democratic* leaders discussed the project with the boys, outlining the steps that would help them reach their goals. They also suggested different approaches and let the boys work at their own pace. When they evaluated the project, they gave "facts" as the bases for their decisions. The *laissez-faire* leaders were passive. They gave the boys almost total freedom to do as they wished. They offered help when asked, but made few suggestions. They did not evaluate the boys' projects, either positively or negatively.

instrumental leader an individual who tries to keep the group moving toward its goals; also known as a *task-oriented leader*

expressive leader an individual who increases harmony and minimizes conflict in a group; also known as a *socioemotional leader*

leadership styles ways in which people express their leadership

authoritarian leader an individual who leads by giving orders

democratic leader an individual who leads by trying to reach a consensus

laissez-faire leader an individual who leads by being highly permissive

Adolf Hitler, shown here in Nuremberg in 1938, was one of the most influential—and evil—persons of the twentieth century. Why did so many people follow Hitler? This question stimulated the research by Stanley Milgram.

Pictorial Press Ltd/Alamy

The results? The boys who had authoritarian leaders grew dependent on their leader and showed a high degree of internal solidarity. They also became either aggressive or apathetic, with the aggressive boys growing hostile toward their leader. In contrast, the boys who had democratic leaders were friendlier and looked to one another for mutual approval. They did less scapegoating, and when the leader left the room they continued to work at a steadier pace. The boys with laissez-faire leaders asked more questions, but they made fewer decisions. They were notable for their lack of achievement. The researchers concluded that the democratic style of leadership works best. This conclusion, however, may be biased, as the researchers favored a democratic style of leadership in the first place (Olmsted and Hare 1978). Apparently, this same bias in studies of leadership continues (Cassel 1999).

You may have noticed that only boys and men were involved in this experiment. It is interesting to speculate how the results might differ if we were to repeat the experiment with all-girl groups and with mixed groups of girls and boys—and if we used both men and women as leaders. Perhaps you will become the sociologist to study such variations of this classic experiment.

Leadership Styles in Changing Situations. Different situations require different styles of leadership. Suppose, for example, that you are leading a dozen backpackers in the mountains, and it is time to make dinner. A laissez-faire style would be appropriate if the backpackers had brought their own food, or perhaps a democratic style if everyone is expected to pitch in. Authoritarian leadership—you telling the hikers how to prepare their meals—would create resentment. This, in turn, would likely interfere with meeting the primary goal of the group, which in this case is to have a good time while enjoying nature.

Now assume the same group but a different situation: One of your party is lost, and a blizzard is on its way. This situation calls for you to exercise authority. To simply shrug your shoulders and say "You figure it out" would invite disaster—and probably a lawsuit.

The Power of Peer Pressure: The Asch Experiment

How influential are groups in our lives? To answer this, let's look first at *conformity* in the sense of going along with our peers. Our peers have no authority over us, only the influence that we allow.

Imagine again that you are taking a course in social psychology, this time with Dr. Solomon Asch. You have agreed to participate in an experiment. As you enter his laboratory, you see seven chairs, five of them already filled by other students. You are given the sixth. Soon the seventh person arrives. Dr. Asch stands at the front of the room next to a covered easel. He explains that he will first show a large card with a vertical line on it, then another card with three vertical lines. Each of you is to tell him which of the three lines matches the line on the first card (see Figure 4).

Dr. Asch then uncovers the first card with the single line and the comparison card with the three lines. The correct answer is easy, for two of the lines are obviously wrong, and one is exactly right. Each person, in order, states his or her answer aloud. You all answer correctly. The second trial is just as easy, and you begin to wonder why you are there.

Then on the third trial, something unexpected happens. Just as before, it is easy to tell which lines match. The first student, however, gives a wrong answer. The second gives the same incorrect answer. So do the third and the fourth. By now, you are wondering what is wrong. How will the person next to you answer? You can hardly believe it when he, too, gives the same wrong answer. Then it is your turn, and you give what you know is the right answer. The seventh person also gives the same wrong answer.

On the next trial, the same thing happens. You know that the choice of the other six is wrong. They are giving what to you are obviously wrong answers. You don't know what to think. Why aren't they seeing things the same way you are? Sometimes they do, but in twelve trials they don't. Something is seriously wrong, and you are no longer sure what to do.

When the eighteenth trial is finished, you heave a sigh of relief. The experiment is finally over, and you are ready to bolt for the door. Dr. Asch walks over to you with a big smile on his face and thanks you for participating in the experiment. He explains that you were the only real subject in the experiment! "The other six were stooges. I paid them to give those answers," he says. Now you feel real relief. Your eyes weren't playing tricks on you after all.

FIGURE 4 Asch's Cards

Card 1

A B C

Card 2

The cards used by Solomon Asch in his classic experiment on group conformity

Source: Asch 1952:452–453.

What were the results? Asch (1952) tested fifty people. One-third (33 percent) gave in to the group half the time, providing what they knew to be wrong answers. Another two out of five (40 percent) gave wrong answers, but not as often. One out of four (25 percent) stuck to their guns and always gave the right answer. I don't know how I would do on this test (if I knew nothing about it in advance), but I like to think that I would be part of the 25 percent. You probably feel the same way about yourself. But why should we feel that we wouldn't be like *most* people?

The results are disturbing, and researchers are still replicating Asch's experiment (Bond 2005). In our "land of individualism," the group is so powerful that most people are willing to say things that they know are not true. And this was a group of strangers! How much more conformity can we expect when our group consists of friends, people we value highly and depend on for getting along in life? Again, maybe you will become the sociologist to run that variation of Asch's experiment, perhaps using female subjects.

But do Asch's experiments apply to everyday life, where no stooges are giving wrong answers on purpose? Read the following Down-to-Earth Sociology box to find out.

Down-to-Earth Sociology

The Power of Cascades: When Error Escalates

Cascades are eerily similar to Asch's experiments. In a *cascade*, someone unintentionally gives a wrong answer, others agree with it, and eventually that agreement turns the wrong answer into "truth." You might think that such things belong to the past, but cascades powerfully influence our attitudes, beliefs, and behavior today (Sunstein and Hastie 2008).

Cascades are especially common in medicine because few doctors do research. They get their ideas from others as a consensus emerges about some medical condition. Not long ago, for example, almost every doctor knew that tonsils were bad. A little problem in a child's throat, and the scalpel came tearing into the mouth. Everybody knew this was the right thing to do.

The same was true of fat and heart disease (Taubes 2007; Tierney 2007). In the 1950s, doctors began to treat a lot more patients with heart disease. What could have been causing this new epidemic? Ancel Keys, a medical researcher, became convinced that the cause was diet, that Americans were eating too much fat. He compared the diets and heart disease rates in the United States, Japan, and four other countries. His findings matched his theory—more fat and more heart disease.

When Dr. Keys became a member of a committee of the American Heart Association, he promoted his research, convincing the AHA to recommend a lower-fat diet to Americans. His findings were considered so important that Keys was featured on the cover of *Time* magazine, and in 1980 the U.S. government incorporated his ideas into its "food pyramid," which it promoted around the country. Soon experts and non-experts, doctors and patients alike, "knew" that diets rich in fats led to heart attacks. This became such established knowledge that in 1988 the Surgeon General of the United States announced that ice cream had become a major health hazard.

There were two problems with the Keys research. First, and rather relevant, there was no new epidemic. Heart disease had become more common, certainly, but this was because people were living longer, giving them more years to come down with heart problems. Second, if Keys had analyzed all twenty-two countries for which there were data, not just four of them, he would have found no correlation between fat and heart disease.

We are taught the food pyramid in school. Does it represent fact, or is it the result of a cascade?

©Arnold Gold/New Haven Register/The Image Works

Some researchers disagreed with what "everyone" had come to know to be fact, but it was difficult for them to speak out against such almost unanimous agreement. When they published contradictory findings, they tended to be ignored as exceptions. Some medical researchers didn't express their doubts because they didn't want to disagree with "everyone"—much like the victims of Asch's experiments.

For Your Consideration

What else do we "know" that you think might be the result of cascades?

The Power of Authority: The Milgram Experiment

Let's look at the results of another experiment in the following Thinking Critically section.

ThinkingCRITICALLY

If Hitler Asked You to Execute a Stranger, Would You?
The Milgram Experiment

Imagine that you are taking a course with Dr. Stanley Milgram (1963, 1965), a former student of Dr. Asch's. Assume that you do not know about the Asch experiment and have no reason to be wary. You arrive at the laboratory to participate in a study on punishment and learning. You and a second student draw lots for the roles of "teacher" and "learner." You are to be the teacher. When you see that the learner's chair has protruding electrodes, you are glad that you are the teacher. Dr. Milgram shows you the machine you will run. You see that one side of the control panel is marked "Mild Shock, 15 volts," while the center says "Intense Shock, 350 Volts," and the far right side reads "DANGER: SEVERE SHOCK."

"As the teacher, you will read aloud a pair of words," explains Dr. Milgram. "Then you will repeat the first word, and the learner will reply with the second word. If the learner can't remember the word, you press this lever on the shock generator. The shock will serve as punishment, and we can then determine if punishment improves memory." You nod, now very relieved that you haven't been designated the learner.

"Every time the learner makes an error, increase the punishment by 15 volts," instructs Dr. Milgram. Then, seeing the look on your face, he adds, "The shocks can be very painful, but they won't cause any permanent tissue damage." He pauses, and then says, "I want you to see." You then follow him to the "electric chair," and Dr. Milgram gives you a shock of 45 volts. "There. That wasn't too bad, was it?" "No," you mumble.

The experiment begins. You hope for the learner's sake that he is bright, but unfortunately he turns out to be rather dull. He gets some answers right, but you have to keep turning up the dial. Each turn makes you more and more uncomfortable. You find yourself hoping that the learner won't miss another answer. But he does. When he received the first

In the 1960s, social psychologists did highly creative but controversial experiments. This photo, taken during Stanley Milgram's experiment, should give you an idea of how convincing the experiment was to the "teacher."

shocks, he let out some moans and groans, but now he is screaming in agony. He even protests that he suffers from a heart condition.

How far do you turn that dial?

By now, you probably have guessed that there was no electricity attached to the electrodes and that the "learner" was a stooge who only pretended to feel pain. The purpose of the experiment was to find out at what point people refuse to participate. Does anyone actually turn the lever all the way to "DANGER: SEVERE SHOCK"?

Milgram wanted the answer because millions of ordinary people did nothing to stop the Nazi slaughter of Jews, gypsies, Slavs, homosexuals, people with disabilities, and others whom the Nazis designated as "inferior." The cooperation of so many ordinary people in the face of all this killing seemed bizarre, and Milgram wanted to see how ordinary, intelligent Americans might react in an analogous situation.

Milgram was upset by what he found. Many "teachers" broke into a sweat and protested that the experiment was inhuman and should be stopped. But when the experimenter calmly replied that the experiment must go on, this assurance from an "authority" ("scientist, white coat, university laboratory") was enough for most "teachers" to continue, even though the "learner" screamed in agony. Even "teachers" who were "reduced to twitching, stuttering wrecks" continued to follow orders.

Milgram varied the experiments. He used both men and women. In some experiments, he put the "teachers" and "learners" in the same room, so the "teacher" could see the suffering. In others, he put the "learners" in an adjacent room, and had them pound and kick the wall during the first shocks and then go silent. The results varied. When there was no verbal feedback from the "learner," 65 percent of the "teachers" pushed the lever all the way to 450 volts. Of those who could see the "learner," 40 percent turned the lever all the way. When Milgram added a second "teacher," a stooge who refused to go along with the experiment, only 5 percent of the "teachers" turned the lever all the way.

Milgram's research set off a stormy discussion about research ethics. Researchers agreed that to reduce subjects to "twitching, stuttering wrecks" was unethical, and almost all deception was banned. Universities began to require that subjects be informed of the nature and purpose of social research.

Although researchers were itching to replicate Milgram's research, it took almost 50 years before they found a way to satisfy committees that approve research. The findings: People today obey the experimenter at about the same rate people did in the 1960s (Burger 2007).

For Your Consideration

Taking into account how significant Milgram's findings are, do you think that the scientific community overreacted to these experiments? Should we allow such research? Consider both the Asch and Milgram experiments, and use symbolic interactionism, functionalism, and conflict theory to explain why groups have such influence over us.

Global Consequences of Group Dynamics: Groupthink

Suppose you are a member of the U.S. president's inner circle. It is midnight, and the president has just called an emergency meeting to deal with a terrorist attack. At first, several options are presented. Eventually, these are narrowed to only a couple of choices, and at some point, everyone seems to agree on what now appears to be "the only possible course of action." To express doubts at that juncture will bring you into conflict with all the other important people in the room. To criticize the proposed solution will mark you as not being a "team player." So you keep your mouth shut, with the result that each step commits you—and them—more and more to the "only" course of action.

From the Milgram and Asch experiments, we can see the power of authority and the influence of peers. Under some circumstances, as in this example, these factors can lead to

groupthink. Sociologist Irving Janis (1972, 1982) used this term to refer to the collective tunnel vision that group members sometimes develop. As they begin to think alike, they become convinced that there is only one "right" viewpoint and a single course of action to follow. They take any suggestion of alternatives as a sign of disloyalty. With their perspective narrowed and fully convinced that they are right, they may even put aside moral judgments and disregard risk (Hart 1991; Flippen 1999).

Groupthink can bring serious consequences. Consider the *Columbia* space shuttle disaster of 2003.

> Foam broke loose during launch, and engineers were concerned that it might have damaged tiles on the nose cone. Because this would make reentry dangerous, they sent e-mails to NASA officials, warning them about the risk. One engineer even suggested that the crew do a "space walk" to examine the tiles (Vartabedian and Gold 2003). The team in charge of the Columbia shuttle, however, disregarded the warnings. Convinced that a piece of foam weighing less than two pounds could not seriously harm the shuttle, they refused to even consider the possibility (Wald and Schwartz 2003). The fiery results of their closed minds were transmitted around the globe.

The consequences of groupthink can be even greater than this. In 1941, President Franklin D. Roosevelt and his chiefs of staff had evidence that the Japanese were preparing to attack Pearl Harbor. They simply refused to believe it and decided to continue naval operations as usual. The destruction of the U.S. naval fleet ushered the United States into World War II. In the war with Vietnam, U.S. officials had evidence of the strength and determination of the North Vietnamese military. They arrogantly threw such evidence aside, refusing to believe that "little, uneducated, barefoot people in pajamas" could defeat the U.S. military.

In each of these cases, options closed as officials committed themselves to a single course of action. Questioning the decisions would have indicated disloyalty and disregard for "team playing." No longer did those in power try to objectively weigh events as they happened; instead, they interpreted everything as supporting their one "correct" decision. They plunged ahead, unable to see alternative perspectives.

Groupthink knows few bounds. Consider what I mentioned earlier, when in the aftermath of 9/11 government officials defended torture as moral, "the lesser of two evils." Thought narrowed so greatly that the U.S. Justice Department ruled that the United States was not bound by the Geneva Convention that prohibits torture. Facing protests, the Justice Department backed down (Lewis 2005).

The U.S. military involvement in Iraq appears to be similar. Top leaders, convinced that they made the right decision to go to war and that they were finding success in building a new Iraqi society, continuously interpreted even disconfirming evidence as favorable. Opinions and debate that contradicted their mind-set were written off as signs of ignorance and disloyalty. Despite mounting casualties, negative public sentiment, and political opposition to the war, it was as though the president and his advisors had been blinded by groupthink.

Preventing Groupthink. Groupthink is a danger for government leaders, who tend to surround themselves with an inner circle that closely reflects their own views. In "briefings," written summaries, and "talking points," this inner circle spoon feeds the leaders the information it has selected. The result is that top leaders, such as the president, become largely cut off from information that does not support their own opinions.

Perhaps the key to preventing the mental captivity and intellectual paralysis known as groupthink is the widest possible circulation—especially among a nation's top government officials—of research that has been conducted by social scientists independent of the government and information that media reporters have gathered freely. If this conclusion comes across as an unabashed plug for sociological research and the free exchange of ideas, it is. Giving free rein to diverse opinions can curb groupthink, which—if not prevented—can lead to the destruction of a society and, in today's world of nuclear, chemical, and biological weapons, the obliteration of Earth's inhabitants.

groupthink a narrowing of thought by a group of people, leading to the perception that there is only one correct answer, in which to even suggest alternatives becomes a sign of disloyalty

351

SUMMARY *and* REVIEW

Societies and Their Transformation

What is a group?

Sociologists use many definitions of groups, but, in general, **groups** consist of people who interact with one another and think of themselves as belonging together. **Societies** are the largest and most complex group that sociologists study.

How is technology linked to the change from one type of society to another?

On their way to postindustrial society, humans passed through four types of societies. Each emerged from a social revolution that was linked to new technology. The **domestication revolution,** which brought the pasturing of animals and the cultivation of plants, transformed **hunting and gathering societies** into **pastoral** and **horticultural societies.** Then the invention of the plow ushered in the **agricultural society,** while the **Industrial Revolution,** brought about by machines that were powered by fuels, led to **industrial society.** The computer chip ushered in a new type of society called **postindustrial** (or **information**) **society.** Another new type of society, the **biotech society,** may be emerging.

How is social inequality linked to the transformation of societies?

Social equality was greatest in hunting and gathering societies, but as societies changed social inequality grew. The root of the transition to social inequality was the accumulation of a food surplus, made possible through the domestication revolution. This surplus stimulated the division of labor, trade, the accumulation of material goods, the subordination of females by males, the emergence of leaders, and the development of the state.

Groups Within Society

How do sociologists classify groups?

Sociologists divide groups into primary groups, secondary groups, in-groups, out-groups, reference groups, and networks. The cooperative, intimate, long-term, face-to-face relationships provided by **primary groups** are fundamental to our sense of self. **Secondary groups** are larger, relatively temporary, and more anonymous, formal, and impersonal than primary groups. **In-groups** provide members with a strong sense of identity and belonging. **Out-groups** also foster identity by showing in-group members what they are *not.* **Reference groups** are groups whose standards we refer to as we evaluate ourselves. **Social networks** consist of social ties that link people together. Developments in communications technology have given birth to a new type of group, the **electronic community.**

Group Dynamics

How does a group's size affect its dynamics?

The term **group dynamics** refers to how individuals affect groups and how groups influence individuals. In a **small group,** everyone can interact directly with everyone else. As a group grows larger, its intensity decreases but its stability increases. A **dyad,** consisting of two people, is the most unstable of human groups, but it provides the most intense intimate relationships. The addition of a third person, forming a **triad,** fundamentally alters relationships. Triads are unstable, as **coalitions** (the alignment of some members of a group against others) tend to form.

What characterizes a leader?

A **leader** is someone who influences others. **Instrumental leaders** try to keep a group moving toward its goals, even though this causes friction and they lose popularity. **Expressive leaders** focus on creating harmony and raising group morale. Both types are essential to the functioning of groups.

What are three leadership styles?

Authoritarian leaders give orders, **democratic leaders** try to lead by consensus, and **laissez-faire leaders** are highly permissive. An authoritarian style appears to be more effective in emergency situations, a democratic style works best for most situations, and a laissez-faire style is usually ineffective.

How do groups encourage conformity?

The Asch experiment was cited to illustrate the power of peer pressure, the Milgram experiment to illustrate the influence of authority. Both experiments demonstrate how easily we can succumb to **groupthink,** a kind of collective tunnel vision. Preventing groupthink requires the free circulation of diverse and opposing ideas.

THINKING CRITICALLY

1. How would your orientations to life (your ideas, attitudes, values, goals) be different if you had been reared in a hunting and gathering society? In an agricultural society?

2. Identify your in-groups and your out-groups. How have your in-groups influenced the way you see the world? And what influence have your out-groups had on you?

3. Asch's experiments illustrate the power of peer pressure. How has peer pressure operated in your life? Think about something that you did not want to do but did anyway because of peer pressure.

ADDITIONAL RESOURCES

What can you find in MySocLab? mysoclab www.mysoclab.com

- Complete Ebook
- Practice Tests and Video and Audio activities
- Mapping and Data Analysis exercises

- Sociology in the News
- Classic Readings in Sociology
- Research and Writing advice

Where Can I Read More on This Topic?

Cross, Robert, and Andrew Parker. *The Hidden Power of Social Networks: Understanding How Work Really Gets Done in Organizations.* Cambridge, Mass: Harvard Business School Press, 2004. Based on their research and experience in organizations, the authors explain how understanding networks can improve communication and productivity.

Homans, George C. *The Human Group.* New Brunswick, N.J.: Transaction, 2001. First published in 1950. In this classic work, the author develops the idea that all human groups share common activities, interactions, and sentiments.

Hughes, Richard L., Robert C. Ginnett, and Gordon J. Curphy. *Leadership: Enhancing the Lessons of Experience,* 5th ed. New York: McGraw-Hill, 2006. Supplementing empirical studies with illustrative anecdotes, the authors focus on what makes effective leaders.

Janis, Irving L. *Groupthink: Psychological Studies of Policy Decisions and Fiascoes,* 2nd ed. New York: Houghton Mifflin, 1982. Janis analyzes how groups can become cut off from alternatives, interpret evidence in light of their preconceptions, and embark on courses of action that they should have seen as obviously incorrect.

Newman, Mark, Albert-Laszlo Barabasi, and Duncan J. Watts, eds. *The Structure and Dynamics of Networks,* 6th ed.

Princeton, N.J.: Princeton University Press, 2007. The authors of these papers analyze the significance of social networks for individuals and the functioning of society.

Purcell, Patrick, ed. *Networked Neighborhoods: The Connected Community in Context.* New York: Springer, 2007. The authors of these papers analyze the impact of the Internet on our social relationships, community, work patterns, and lifestyles.

Small, Mario Luis. *Unexpected Gains: Origins of Network Inequality in Everyday Life.* New York: Oxford University Press, 2009. The author's thesis is that some people have larger, more supportive, or useful networks because of the organization in which they participate: colleges, firms, gyms, day care centers, beauty salons, and churches.

Venkatesh, Sudhir. *Gang Leader for a Day: A Rogue Sociologist Takes to the Streets.* New York: Penguin Press, 2008. The adventures of a naïve graduate student in sociology as he explores a drug-dealing gang in a Chicago public housing project.

Wilson, Gerald L. *Groups in Context: Leadership and Participation in Small Groups,* 7th ed. New York: McGraw-Hill, 2005. An overview of principles and processes of interaction in small groups, with an emphasis on how to exercise leadership.

How Sociologists
Do Research

From Chapter 5 of *Sociology: A Down-to-Earth Approach*, 10/e. James M. Henslin. Copyright © 2010 by Pearson Education. Published by Allyn & Bacon. All rights reserved.

How Sociologists Do Research

South Korea

Chung Sung-Jun/Getty Images

Cindy Hudo, a 21-year-old mother of two in Charleston, South Carolina, who was charged with the murder of her husband, Buba, said:

I start in the car, and I get down the road, and I see Buba walking, and he's real mad. . . . I pull over, you know, and [I said] "I didn't know to pick you up. You know, I'm sorry." And he didn't even say nothing to me. He just started hitting on me. And that's all I wanted to do, was just get home, because I was just self-conscious. I don't want nobody to see him hitting me, because I didn't want him to look bad.

"I don't want nobody to see him hitting me, because I didn't want him to look bad."

I had to go to work in a half-hour, because I was working a double-shift. And he told me I had forty minutes to get all my furniture out of the house and get my clothes and be out or he was going to throw them out. And I was sitting there, because I could talk him down. You know, because I didn't want to leave him. I just talked to him. I said, "Buba, I don't want to leave." I said, "This is my house." And then he told me . . . (unclear) . . . "my kids." And I said, "No, you're not taking my kids from me. That's too much." And so I said, "Just let me leave. Just let me take the kids. And, you know I'll go, and you know, I won't keep the kids from you or nothing like that." And he said, "I'm going to take them, and you're getting out."

[After they went inside their trailer, Buba threatened to shoot Cindy. He loaded a shotgun, pointed it at her, and said]: "The only way you're going to get out of this is if you kill me, and I'll—I'll kill you." [Buba gave me the shotgun and] turned around and walked right down the hall, because he knew I wouldn't do nothing. And I just sat there a minute. And I don't know what happened. I just, you know, I went to the bedroom, and I seen him laying there, and I just shot him. He moved. I shot him again because I thought he was going to get up again. . . .

I loved him too much. And I just wanted to help him.

Source: Transcript, ABC Television, *20/20,* October 18, 1979.

What Is a Valid Sociological Topic?

Sociologists do research on just about every area of human behavior. On the macro level, they study such broad matters as race relations (Schaefer 2008), the military (Caforio 2006), and multinational corporations (Kristensen and Morgan 2006). On the micro level, they study such individualistic matters as pelvic examinations (Henslin and Biggs 1971/2007), how people interact on street corners (Whyte 1989, 2001), and even shyness (Scott 2006). Sociologists study priests and prostitutes, cops and criminals, as well as all kinds of people in between. In fact, no human behavior is ineligible for sociological scrutiny—whether that behavior is routine or unusual, respectable or reprehensible.

What happened to Cindy and Buba, then, is also a valid topic of sociological research. But exactly *how* would you research spouse abuse? As we look at how sociologists do research, we shall try to answer this question.

Common Sense and the Need for Sociological Research

First, why do we need sociological research? Why can't we simply depend on common sense, on "what everyone knows"? Commonsense ideas may or may not be true. Common sense, for example, tells us that spouse abuse has a significant impact on the lives of the people who are abused.

Although this particular idea is accurate, we need research to test commonsense ideas, because not all such ideas are true. After all, common sense also tells us that if a woman is abused, she will pack up and leave her husband. Research, however, shows that the reality of abuse is much more complicated than this. Some women do leave right away, some even after the first incident of abuse. For a variety of reasons, however, some women suffer abuse for years. The main reason is that they feel trapped and don't perceive any viable alternatives.

This brings us to the need for sociological research, for we may want to know why some women put up with abuse, while others don't. Or we may want to know something entirely different, such as why men are more likely to be the abusers. Or why some people abuse the people they say they love.

In order to answer a question, we need to move beyond guesswork and common sense. We want to *know* what is really going on. To find out, sociologists do research on about every aspect of social life. Let's look at how they do their research.

A Research Model

As shown in Figure 1 on the next page, scientific research follows eight basic steps. This is an ideal model, however, and in the real world of research some of these steps may run together. Some may even be omitted.

1. Selecting a Topic

The first step is to select a topic. What do you want to know more about? Many sociologists simply follow their curiosity, their drive to learn more about social life. They become interested in a particular topic and they pursue it, as I did in studying the homeless. Some sociologists choose a topic because funding is available for that topic, others because a social problem such as domestic violence is in the news and they want to help people better understand it—and perhaps to help solve it. Let's use spouse abuse as our example.

Barry Batchelor/PA Photos/Landov

Because sociologists find all human behavior to be valid research topics, their research runs from the unusual to the routines of everyday life. Their studies range from broad scale social change, such as the globalization of capitalism, to smaller scale social interaction, such as people having fun.

2. Defining the Problem

The second step is to define the problem, to specify what you want to learn about the topic. My interest in the homeless increased until I wanted to learn about homelessness across the nation. Ordinarily, sociologists' interests are much more focused than this; they examine some specific aspect of the topic, such as how homeless people survive on the streets. In the case of spouse abuse, sociologists may want to know whether violent and nonviolent husbands have different work experiences. Or they may want to learn what can be done to reduce spouse abuse.

The topics that sociologists study are far-ranging. In fact, sociologists do research on any aspect of social life that interests them. The "problem" can be as earth shattering as trying to figure out why nations would ever contemplate nuclear war, as perplexing as understanding how "good" people can torture and kill, or as simple as wanting to find out why Native Americans like Westerns.

3. Reviewing the Literature

You must read what has been published on your topic. This helps you to narrow the problem, identify areas that are already known, and learn what areas need to be researched. Reviewing the literature may also help you to pinpoint the questions that you will ask. You might even find out that the problem has been answered already. You don't want to waste your time rediscovering what is already known.

4. Formulating a Hypothesis

The fourth step is to formulate a **hypothesis,** a statement of what you expect to find according to predictions from a theory. A hypothesis predicts a relationship between or among **variables,** factors that change, or vary, from one person or situation to another. For example, the statement "Men who are more socially isolated are more likely to abuse their wives than are men who are more socially integrated" is a hypothesis.

Your hypothesis will need **operational definitions**—that is, precise ways to measure the variables. In this example, you would need operational definitions for three variables: social isolation, social integration, and spouse abuse.

5. Choosing a Research Method

You then need to decide how you are going to collect your data. Sociologists use seven basic **research methods** (or *research designs*), which are outlined in the next section. You will want to choose the research method that will best answer your particular questions.

6. Collecting the Data

When you gather your data, you have to take care to assure their **validity;** that is, your operational definitions must measure what they are intended to measure. In this case, you must be certain that you really are measuring social isolation, social integration, and spouse abuse—and not something else. Spouse abuse, for example, seems to be obvious. Yet what some people consider to be abuse is not regarded as abuse by others. Which definition will you choose? In other words, you must state your operational definitions so precisely that no one has any question about what you are measuring.

You must also be sure that your data are reliable. **Reliability** means that if other researchers use your operational definitions, their findings will be consistent with yours. If

FIGURE 1   The Research Model

① Select a topic.
② Define the problem.
③ Review the literature.
④ Formulate a hypothesis.
⑤ Choose a research method.
- Surveys
- Participant observation
- Case studies
- Secondary analysis
- Documents
- Experiments
- Unobtrusive measures
⑥ Collect the data.
⑦ Analyze the results.
⑧ Share the results.

Generates hypotheses

Stimulates more ideas for research

Source: Modification of Figure 2.2 of Schaeffer 1989.

hypothesis a statement of how variables are expected to be related to one another, often according to predictions from a theory

variable a factor thought to be significant for human behavior, which can vary (or change) from one case to another

operational definition the way in which a researcher measures a variable

research method (or research design) one of seven procedures that sociologists use to collect data: surveys, participant observation, case studies, secondary analysis, documents, experiments, and unobtrusive measures

validity the extent to which an operational definition measures what it is intended to measure

reliability the extent to which research produces consistent or dependable results

359

replication the repetition of a study in order to test its findings

survey the collection of data by having people answer a series of questions

your operational definitions are sloppy, husbands who have committed the same act of violence might be included in some research but excluded from other studies. You would end up with erratic results. If you show a 10 percent rate of spouse abuse, for example, but another researcher using the same operational definitions determines it to be 30 percent, the research is unreliable.

7. Analyzing the Results

You can choose from a variety of techniques to analyze the data you gather. If a hypothesis has been part of your research, now is when you will test it. (Some research, especially participant observation and case studies, has no hypothesis. You may know so little about the setting you are going to research that you cannot even specify the variables in advance.)

With today's software, in just seconds you can run tests on your data that used to take days or even weeks to perform. Two basic programs that sociologists and many undergraduates use are Microcase and the Statistical Package for the Social Sciences (SPSS). Some software, such as the Methodologist's Toolchest, provides advice about collecting data and even about ethical issues.

8. Sharing the Results

To wrap up your research, you will write a report to share your findings with the scientific community. You will review how you did your research, including your operational definitions. You will also show how your findings fit in with what has already been published on the topic and how they support or disagree with the theories that apply to your topic.

When research is published, usually in a scientific journal or a book, it "belongs" to the scientific community. Your findings will be available for **replication;** that is, others can repeat your study to see if they come up with similar results. As Table 1 on the next page illustrates, sociologists often summarize their findings in tables. As finding is added to finding, scientific knowledge builds.

Let's look in greater detail at the fifth step to see what research methods sociologists use.

THE FAR SIDE® BY GARY LARSON

© 1984 FarWorks, Inc. All Rights Reserved/Dist. by Creators Syndicate

"Anthropologists! Anthropologists!"

A major concern of sociologists and other social scientists is that their research methods do not influence their findings. Respondents often change their behavior when they know they are being studied.

Research Methods

As we review the seven research methods (or *research designs*) that sociologists use, we will continue our example of spouse abuse. As you will see, the method you choose will depend on the questions you want to answer. So that you can have a yardstick for comparison, you will want to know what "average" is in your study. Table 2 discusses ways to measure average.

Surveys

Let's suppose that you want to know how many wives are abused each year. Some husbands also are abused, of course, but let's assume that you are going to focus on wives. An appropriate method for this purpose would be the **survey,** in which you would ask individuals a series of questions. Before you begin your research, however, you must deal with practical matters that face all researchers. Let's look at these issues.

TABLE 1 How to Read a Table

Tables summarize information. Because sociological findings are often presented in tables, it is important to understand how to read them. Tables contain six elements: title, headnote, headings, columns, rows, and source. When you understand how these elements fit together, you know how to read a table.

1. The **title** states the topic. It is located at the top of the table. What is the title of this table? Please determine your answer before looking at the correct answer at the bottom of this page.

2. The **headnote** is not always included in a table. When it is, it is located just below the title. Its purpose is to give more detailed information about how the data were collected or how data are presented in the table. What are the first eight words of the headnote of this table?

3. The **headings** tell what kind of information is contained in the table. There are three headings in this table. What are they? In the second heading, what does *n* = 25 mean?

Comparing Violent and Nonviolent Husbands

Based on interviews with 150 husbands and wives in a Midwestern city who were getting a divorce.

Husband's Achievement and Job Satisfaction	Violent Husbands *n* = 25	Nonviolent Husbands *n* = 125
He started but failed to complete high school or college.	44%	27%
He is very dissatisfied with his job.	44%	18%
His income is a source of constant conflict.	84%	24%
He has less education than his wife.	56%	14%
His job has less prestige than his father-in-law's.	37%	28%

Source: Modification of Table 1 in O'Brien 1975.

4. The **columns** present information arranged vertically. What is the fourth number in the second column and the second number in the third column?

5. The **rows** present information arranged horizontally. In the fourth row, which husbands are more likely to have less education than their wives?

6. The **source** of a table, usually listed at the bottom, provides information on where the data in the table originated. Often, as in this instance, the information is specific enough for you to consult the original source. What is the source for this table?

Some tables are much more complicated than this one, but all follow the same basic pattern.

ANSWERS
1. Comparing Violent and Nonviolent Husbands
2. Based on interviews with 150 husbands and wives
3. Husband's Achievement and Job Satisfaction, Violent Husbands, Nonviolent Husbands. The *n* is an abbreviation for number, and *n* = 25 means that 25 violent husbands were in the sample.
4. 56%, 18%
5. Violent Husbands
6. A 1975 article by O'Brien

Selecting a Sample.   Ideally, you might want to learn about all wives in the world. Obviously, your resources will not permit such research, and you will have to narrow your **population,** the target group that you are going to study.

Let's assume that your resources (money, assistants, time) allow you to investigate spouse abuse only on your campus. Let's also assume that your college enrollment is large, so you won't be able to survey all the married women who are enrolled. Now you must

population a target group to be studied

TABLE 2 Three Ways to Measure "Average"

The Mean	The Median	The Mode
The term *average* seems clear enough. As you learned in grade school, to find the average you add a group of numbers and then divide the total by the number of cases that you added. Assume that the following numbers represent men convicted of battering their wives:	To compute the second average, the *median*, first arrange the cases in order—either from the highest to the lowest or the lowest to the highest. That arrangement will produce the following distribution.	The third measure of average, the *mode*, is simply the cases that occur the most often. In this instance the mode is 57, which is way off the mark.

The Mean — EXAMPLE

```
  321
  229
   57
  289
  136
   57
1,795
```

The Median — EXAMPLE

```
   57        1,795
   57          321
  136          289
  229    or    229
  289          136
  321           57
1,795           57
```

The Mode — EXAMPLE

```
   57
   57
  136
  229
  289
  321
1,795
```

The Mean	The Median	The Mode
The total is 2,884. Divided by 7 (the number of cases), the average is 412. Sociologists call this form of average the *mean*. The mean can be deceptive because it is strongly influenced by extreme scores, either low or high. Note that six of the seven cases are less than the mean. Two other ways to compute averages are the median and the mode.	Then look for the middle case, the one that falls halfway between the top and the bottom. That number is 229, for three numbers are lower and three numbers are higher. When there is an even number of cases, the median is the halfway mark between the two middle cases.	Because the mode is often deceptive, and only by chance comes close to either of the other two averages, sociologists seldom use it. In addition, not every distribution of cases has a mode. And if two or more numbers appear with the same frequency, you can have more than one mode.

---

sample the individuals intended to represent the population to be studied

random sample a sample in which everyone in the target population has the same chance of being included in the study

stratified random sample a sample from selected subgroups of the target population in which everyone in those subgroups has an equal chance of being included in the research

respondents people who respond to a survey, either in interviews or by self-administered questionnaires

questionnaires a list of questions to be asked of respondents

self-administered questionnaires questionnaires that respondents fill out

select a **sample,** individuals from among your target population. How you choose a sample is crucial, for your choice will affect the results of your research. For example, married women enrolled in introductory sociology and engineering courses might have quite different experiences. If so, surveying just one or the other would produce skewed results.

Because you want to generalize your findings to your entire campus, you need a sample that accurately represents the campus. How can you get a representative sample?

The best way is to use a **random sample.** This does *not* mean that you stand on some campus corner and ask questions of any woman who happens to walk by. *In a random sample, everyone in your population (the target group) has the same chance of being included in the study.* In this case, because your population is every married woman enrolled in your college, all married women—whether first-year or graduate students, full- or part-time—must have the same chance of being included in your sample.

How can you get a random sample? First, you need a list of all the married women enrolled in your college. Then you assign a number to each name on the list. Using a table of random numbers, you then determine which of these women will become part of your sample. (Tables of random numbers are available in statistics books and online, or they can be generated by a computer.)

A random sample will represent your study's population fairly—in this case, married women enrolled at your college. This means that you can generalize your findings to *all* the married women students on your campus, even if they were not included in your sample.

What if you want to know only about certain subgroups, such as freshmen and seniors? You could use a **stratified random sample.** You would need a list of the married women in the freshman and senior classes. Then, using random numbers, you would select a sample from each group. This would allow you to generalize to all the freshman and senior married women at your college, but you would not be able to draw any conclusions about the sophomores or juniors.

Asking Neutral Questions. After you have decided on your population and sample, your next task is to make certain that your questions are neutral. Your questions must allow **respondents,** the people who answer your questions, to express their own opinions. Otherwise, you will end up with biased answers—which are worthless. For example, if you were to ask, "Don't you think that men who beat their wives should go to prison?" you would be tilting the answer toward agreement with a prison sentence. The *Doonesbury* cartoon below illustrates another blatant example of biased questions. For examples of flawed research, see the Down-to-Earth Sociology box on the next page.

Questionnaires and Interviews. Even if you have a representative sample and ask neutral questions, you can still end up with biased findings. **Questionnaires,** the list of questions to be asked, can be administered in ways that are flawed. There are two basic techniques for administering questionnaires. The first is to ask the respondents to fill them out. These **self-administered questionnaires** allow a larger number of people to be sampled at a lower cost, but the researchers lose control of the data collection. They don't know the conditions under which people answered the questions. For example, others could have influenced their answers.

The second technique is the **interview.** Researchers ask people questions, often face to face, sometimes by telephone or e-mail. The advantage of this method is that the researchers can ask each question in the same way. The main disadvantage is that interviews are time-consuming, so researchers end up with fewer respondents. Interviews can also create **interviewer bias;** that is, the presence of interviewers can affect what people say. For example, instead of saying what they really feel, respondents might give "socially acceptable" answers. Although they may be willing to write their true opinions on an anonymous questionnaire, they won't tell them to another person. Some respondents even shape their answers to match what they think an interviewer wants to hear.

In some cases, **structured interviews** work best. This type of interview uses **closed-ended questions**—each question is followed by a list of possible answers. Structured interviews are faster to administer, and they make it easier to *code* (categorize) answers so

David Young-Wolff/PhotoEdit, Inc.

Sociologists usually cannot interview or observe every member of a group or participant in an event that they want to study. As explained in the text, to be able to generalize their findings, they select samples. Sociologists would have several ways to study this protest in San Francisco against U.S. foreign policy.

interview direct questioning of respondents

interviewer bias effects that interviewers have on respondents that lead to biased answers

structured interviews interviews that use closed-ended questions

closed-ended questions questions that are followed by a list of possible answers to be selected by the respondent

Improperly worded questions can steer respondents toward answers that are not their own, which produces invalid results.

Doonesbury © G. B. Trudeau. Reprinted with permission of Universal Press Syndicate. All rights reserved.

363

Down-to-Earth Sociology
Loading the Dice: How *Not* to Do Research

The methods of science lend themselves to distortion, misrepresentation, and downright fraud. Consider these findings from surveys:

Americans overwhelmingly prefer Toyotas to Chryslers.
Americans overwhelmingly prefer Chryslers to Toyotas.

Obviously, these opposite conclusions cannot both be true. In fact, both sets of findings are misrepresentations, even though the responses came from surveys conducted by so-called independent researchers. These researchers, however, are biased, not independent and objective.

It turns out that some consumer researchers load the dice. Hired by firms that have a vested interest in the outcome of the research, they deliver the results their clients are looking for (Armstrong 2007). Here are six ways to load the dice.

1. **Choose a biased sample.** If you want to "prove" that Americans prefer Chryslers over Toyotas, interview unemployed union workers who trace their job loss to Japanese imports. The answer is predictable. You'll get what you're looking for.
2. **Ask biased questions.** Even if you choose an unbiased sample, you can phrase questions in such a way that you direct people to the answer you're looking for. Suppose that you ask this question:

   We are losing millions of jobs to workers overseas who work for just a few dollars a day. After losing their jobs, some Americans are even homeless and hungry. Do you prefer a car that gives jobs to Americans, or one that forces our workers to lose their homes?

   This question is obviously designed to channel people's thinking toward a predetermined answer—quite contrary to the standards of scientific research. Look again at the Doonesbury cartoon on the previous page.
3. **List biased choices.** Another way to load the dice is to use closed-ended questions that push people into the answers you want. Consider this finding:

   U.S. college students overwhelmingly prefer Levis 501 to the jeans of any competitor.

fotoshoot/Alamy Royalty Free

Sound good? Before you rush out to buy Levis, note what these researchers did: In asking students which jeans would be the most popular in the coming year, their list of choices included no other jeans but Levis 501!

4. **Discard undesirable results.** Researchers can keep silent about results they find embarrassing, or they can continue to survey samples until they find one that matches what they are looking for. As has been stressed in this chapter, research must be objective if it is to be scientific. Obviously, none of the preceding results qualifies. The underlying problem with the research cited here—and with so many surveys bandied about in the media as fact—is that survey research has become big business. Simply put, the money offered by corporations has corrupted some researchers.

   The beginning of the corruption is subtle. Paul Light, dean at the University of Minnesota, put it this way: "A funder will never come to an academic and say, 'I want you to produce finding X, and here's a million dollars to do it.' Rather, the subtext is that if the researchers produce the right finding, more work—and funding—will come their way."

The first four sources of bias are inexcusable, intentional fraud. The next two sources of bias reflect sloppiness, which is also inexcusable in science.

5. **Misunderstand the subjects' world.** This route can lead to errors every bit as great as those just cited. Even researchers who use an adequate sample and word their questions properly can end up with skewed results. They may, for example, fail to anticipate that people may be embarrassed to express an opinion that isn't "politically correct." For example, surveys show that 80 percent of Americans are environmentalists. Most Americans, however, are probably embarrassed to tell a stranger otherwise. Today, that would be like going against the flag, motherhood, and apple pie.
6. **Analyze the data incorrectly.** Even when researchers strive for objectivity, the sample is good, the wording is neutral, and the respondents answer the questions honestly, the results can still be skewed. The researchers may make a mistake in their calculations, such as entering incorrect data into computers. This, too, of course, is inexcusable in science.

Sources: Based on Crossen 1991; Goleman 1993; Barnes 1995; Resnik 2000; Hotz 2007.

they can be fed into a computer for analysis. As you can see from Table 3, the answers listed on a questionnaire might fail to include the respondent's opinions. Consequently, some researchers prefer **unstructured interviews.** Here the interviewer asks **open-ended questions,** which allow people to answer in their own words. Open-ended questions allow you to tap the full range of people's opinions, but they make it difficult to compare answers. For example, how would you compare the following answers to the question "Why do you think men abuse their wives?"

> "They're sick."
>
> "I think they must have had problems with their mother."
>
> "We oughta string 'em up!"

TABLE 3	Closed and Open–Ended Questions
A. Closed–Ended Question	**B. Open–Ended Question**
Which of the following best fits your idea of what should be done to someone who has been convicted of spouse abuse? 1. probation 2. jail time 3. community service 4. counseling 5. divorce 6. nothing—it's a family matter	What do you think should be done to someone who has been convicted of spouse abuse?

Establishing Rapport.   Research on spouse abuse brings up another significant issue. You may have been wondering if your survey would be worth anything even if you rigorously followed scientific procedures. Will women who have been abused really give honest answers to strangers?

If your method of interviewing consisted of walking up to women on the street and asking if their husbands had ever beaten them, there would be little basis for taking your findings seriously. Researchers have to establish **rapport** ("ruh-POUR"), a feeling of trust, with their respondents, especially when it comes to sensitive topics—those that elicit feelings of embarrassment, shame, or other deep emotions.

We know that once rapport is gained (often by first asking nonsensitive questions), victims will talk about personal, sensitive issues. A good example is rape. To go beyond police statistics, each year researchers interview a random sample of 100,000 Americans. They ask them whether they have been victims of burglary, robbery, or other crimes. After establishing rapport, the researchers ask about rape. They find that rape victims will talk about their experiences. The National Crime Victimization Survey shows that the actual incidence of rape is about 40 percent higher than the number reported to the police—and that attempted rapes are *nine* times higher than the official statistics (*Statistical Abstract* 2009:Tables 303, 304).

A new technique to gather data on sensitive areas, Computer-Assisted Self-Interviewing, overcomes lingering problems of distrust. In this technique, the interviewer gives a laptop computer to the respondent, then moves aside, while the individual enters his or her own answers into the computer. In some versions of this method, the respondent listens to the questions on a headphone and answers them on the computer screen. When the respondent clicks the "Submit" button, the interviewer has no idea how the respondent answered any question (Mosher et al. 2005).

Participant Observation (Fieldwork)

In the second method, **participant observation** (or **fieldwork**), the researcher *participates* in a research setting while *observing* what is happening in that setting. But how is it possible to study spouse abuse by participant observation? Obviously, this method does not mean that you would sit around and watch someone being abused. Spouse abuse, however, is a broad topic, and many questions about abuse cannot be answered adequately by any method other than participant observation.

Let's suppose that you are interested in learning how spouse abuse affects wives. You might want to know how the abuse has changed the wives' relationship with their husbands. How has it changed their hopes and dreams? Or their ideas about men? Certainly it has affected their self-concept as well. But how? Participant observation could provide insight into such questions.

For example, if your campus has a crisis intervention center, you might be able to observe victims of spouse abuse from the time they report the attack through their participation in counseling. With good rapport, you might even be able to spend time with them in other

unstructured interviews interviews that use open-ended questions

open-ended questions questions that respondents answer in their own words

rapport (ruh-POUR) a feeling of trust between researchers and the people they are studying

participant observation (or fieldwork) research in which the researcher participates in a research setting while observing what is happening in that setting

Dinodia/The Image Works

Participant observation, participating and observing in a research setting, is usually supplemented by interviewing, asking questions to better understand why people do what they do. In this instance, the sociologist would want to know what this hair removal ceremony in Gujarat, India, means to the child's family and to the community.

settings, observing further aspects of their lives. What they say and how they interact with others might help you to understand how the abuse has affected them. This, in turn, could give you insight into how to improve college counseling services.

Participant observers face two major dilemmas. The first is **generalizability,** the extent to which their findings apply to larger populations. Most participant observation studies are exploratory, documenting in detail the experiences of people in a particular setting. Although such research suggests that other people who face similar situations react in similar ways, we don't know how far the findings apply beyond their original setting. Participant observation, however, can stimulate hypotheses and theories that can be tested in other settings, using other research techniques. A second dilemma is the extent to which the participant observers should get involved in the lives of the people they are observing. Consider this as you read the Down-to-Earth Sociology box on the next page.

Case Studies

To do a **case study,** the researcher focuses on a single event, situation, or even individual. The purpose is to understand the dynamics of relationships, power, or even the thought processes that led to some particular event. Sociologist Ken Levi (2009), for example, wanted to study hit men. He would have loved to have had a large number of hit men to interview, but he had access to only one. He interviewed this man over and over again, giving us an understanding of how someone can kill others for money. Sociologist Kai Erikson (1978), who became intrigued with the bursting of a dam in West Virginia that killed several hundred people, focused on the events that led up to and followed this disaster. For spouse abuse, a case study would focus on a single wife and husband, exploring the couple's history and relationship.

As you can see, the case study reveals a lot of detail about some particular situation, but the question always remains: How much of this detail applies to other situations? This problem of generalizability, which plagues case studies, is the primary reason that few sociologists use this method.

Secondary Analysis

In **secondary analysis,** a fourth research method, researchers analyze data that others have collected. For example, if you were to analyze the original interviews from a study of women who had been abused by their husbands, you would be doing secondary analysis. Ordinarily, researchers prefer to gather their own data, but lack of resources, especially money, may make this impossible. In addition, existing data could contain a wealth of information that wasn't pertinent to the goals of the original researchers, which you can analyze for your own purposes.

Like the other methods, secondary analysis also poses its own problems. How can a researcher who did not carry out the initial study be sure that the data were gathered systematically and recorded accurately and that biases were avoided? This problem plagues researchers who do secondary analysis, especially if the original data were gathered by a team of researchers, not all of whom were equally qualified.

Documents

The fifth method that sociologists use is the study of **documents,** recorded sources. To investigate social life, sociologists examine such diverse documents as books, newspapers, diaries, bank records, police reports, immigration files, and records kept by organizations. The term *documents* is broad, and it also includes video and audio recordings.

To study spouse abuse, you might examine police reports and court records. These could reveal what percentage of complaints result in arrest and what proportion of the men arrested are charged, convicted, or put on probation. If these were your questions, police statistics would be valuable (Kingsnorth and MacIntosh 2007).

generalizability the extent to which the findings from one group (or sample) can be generalized or applied to other groups (or populations)

case study an analysis of a single event, situation, or individual

secondary analysis the analysis of data that have been collected by other researchers

documents in its narrow sense, written sources that provide data; in its extended sense, archival material of any sort, including photographs, movies, CDs, DVDs, and so on

Down-to-Earth Sociology
Gang Leader for a Day: Adventures of a Rogue Sociologist

Next to the University of Chicago is an area of poverty so dangerous that the professors warn students to avoid it. One of the graduate students in sociology, Sudhir Venkatesh, the son of immigrants from India, who was working on a research project with William Julius Wilson, decided to ignore the warning.

With clipboard in hand, Sudhir entered "the projects." Ignoring the glares of the young men standing around, he went into the lobby of a high-rise. Seeing a gaping hole where the elevator was supposed to be, he decided to climb the stairs, where he was almost overpowered by the smell of urine. After climbing five flights, Sudhir came upon some young men shooting craps in a dark hallway. One of them jumped up, grabbed Sudhir's clipboard, and demanded to know what he was doing there.

Sudhir blurted, "I'm a student at the university, doing a survey, and I'm looking for some families to interview."

One man took out a knife and began to twirl it. Another pulled out a gun, pointed it at Sudhir's head, and said, "I'll take him."

Then came a series of rapid-fire questions that Sudhir couldn't answer. He had no idea what they meant: "You flip right or left? Five or six? You run with the Kings, right?"

Grabbing Sudhir's bag, two of the men searched it. They could find only questionnaires, pen and paper, and a few sociology books. The man with the gun then told Sudhir to go ahead and ask him a question.

Sweating despite the cold, Sudhir read the first question on his survey, "How does it feel to be black and poor?" Then he read the multiple-choice answers:"Very bad, somewhat bad, neither bad nor good, somewhat good, very good."

As you might surmise, the man's answer was too obscenity laden to be printed here.

As the men deliberated Sudhir's fate ("If he's here and he don't get back, you know they're going to come looking for him"), a powerfully built man with a few glittery gold teeth and a sizable diamond earring appeared. The man, known as J.T., who, it turned out, directed the drug trade in the building, asked what was going on. When the younger men mentioned the questionnaire, J.T. said to ask *him* a question.

Amidst an eerie silence, Sudhir asked, "How does it feel to be black and poor?"

"I'm not black," came the reply.

"Well, then, how does it feel to be African American and poor?"

"I'm not African American either. I'm a nigger."

Sudhir was left speechless. Despite his naïveté, he knew better than to ask, "How does it feel to be a nigger and poor?"

As Sudhir stood with his mouth agape, J.T. added, "Niggers are the ones who live in this building. African Americans live in the suburbs. African Americans wear ties to work. Niggers can't find no work."

Paresh Gandhi Courtesy of Sudhir Venkatesh, Columbia University

Sudhir Venkatesh, who now teaches at Columbia University, New York City.

Not exactly the best start to a research project.

But this weird and frightening beginning turned into several years of fascinating research. Over time, J.T. guided Sudhir into a world that few outsiders ever see. Not only did Sudhir get to know drug dealers, crackheads, squatters, prostitutes, and pimps, but he also was present at beatings by drug crews, drive-by shootings done by rival gangs, and armed robberies by the police.

How Sudhir got out of his predicament in the stairwell, his immersion into a threatening underworld—the daily life for many people in "the projects"—and his moral dilemma at witnessing so many crimes are part of his fascinating experience in doing participant observation of the Black Kings.

Sudhir, who was reared in a middle-class suburb in California, even took over this Chicago gang for a day. This is one reason that he calls himself a rogue sociologist—the decisions he made that day were serious violations of law, felonies that could bring years in prison. There are other reasons, too: During the research, he kicked a man in the stomach, and he was present as the gang planned drive-by shootings.

Sudhir eventually completed his Ph.D., and he now teaches at Columbia University.

Based on Venkatesh 2008.

But for other questions, those records would be useless. If you want to learn about the victims' social and emotional adjustment, for example, those records would tell you little. Other documents, however, might provide answers. For example, diaries kept by victims could yield insight into their reactions to abuse, showing how their attitudes and

The *research methods* that sociologists choose depend partially on the questions they want to answer. They might want to learn, for example, which forms of publicity are more effective in increasing awareness of spouse abuse as a social problem.

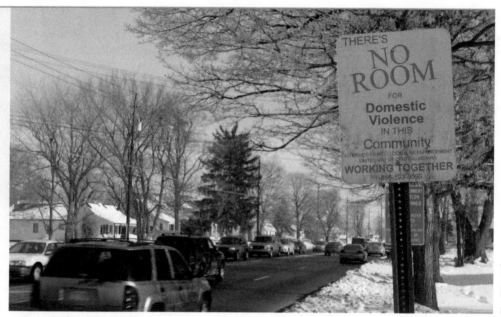

Jim West/Alamy

relationships change. If no diaries were available, you might ask victims to keep diaries. Perhaps the director of a crisis intervention center might ask clients to keep diaries for you—or get the victims' permission for you to examine records of their counseling sessions. To my knowledge, no sociologist has yet studied spouse abuse in this way.

Of course, I am presenting an ideal situation, a crisis intervention center that opens its arms to you. In actuality, the center might not cooperate at all. It might refuse to ask victims to keep diaries—or it might not even let you near its records. *Access,* then, is another problem that researchers face. Simply put, you can't study a topic unless you can gain access to it.

Experiments

experiment the use of *control* and *experimental groups* and *dependent* and *independent variables* to test causation

experimental group the group of subjects in an experiment who are exposed to the independent variable

control group the subjects in an experiment who are not exposed to the independent variable

Do you think there is a way to change a man who abuses his wife into a loving husband? No one has made this claim, but a lot of people say that abusers need therapy. Yet no one knows whether therapy really works. Because **experiments** are useful for determining cause and effect (discussed in Table 4 on the next page), let's suppose that you propose an experiment to a judge and she gives you access to men who have been arrested for spouse abuse. As in Figure 2 below, you would randomly divide the men into two groups. This helps to ensure that their individual characteristics (attitudes, number of arrests, severity of crimes, education, race–ethnicity, age, and so on) are distributed evenly between the groups. You then would arrange for the men in the **experimental group** to receive some form of therapy. The men in the **control group** would not get therapy.

FIGURE 2 The Experiment

Source: By the author.

368

TABLE 4 Cause, Effect, and Spurious Correlations

Causation means that a change in one variable is caused by another variable. Three conditions are necessary for causation: correlation, temporal priority, and no spurious correlation. Let's apply each of these conditions to spouse abuse and alcohol abuse.

(1) The first necessary condition is *correlation*.

If two variables exist together, they are said to be correlated. If batterers get drunk, battering and alcohol abuse are correlated.

Spouse Abuse + Alcohol Abuse

People sometimes assume that correlation is causation. In this instance, they conclude that alcohol abuse causes spouse abuse.

Alcohol Abuse ⟶ Spouse Abuse

But *correlation never proves causation*. *Either* variable could be the cause of the other. Perhaps battering upsets men and they then get drunk.

Spouse Abuse ⟶ Alcohol Abuse

(2) The second necessary condition is *temporal priority*.

Temporal priority means that one thing happens before something else does. For a variable to be a cause (*the independent variable*), it must *precede* that which is changed (*the dependent variable*).

Alcohol Abuse ⟶ **Spouse Abuse**
(precedes)

If the men had not drunk alcohol until after they beat their wives, obviously alcohol abuse could not be the cause of the spouse abuse. Although the necessity of temporal priority is obvious, in many studies this is not easy to determine.

(3) The third necessary condition is *no spurious correlation*.

This is the necessary condition that really makes things difficult. Even if we identify the correlation of getting drunk and spouse abuse and can determine temporal priority, we still don't know that alcohol abuse is the cause. We could have a *spurious correlation;* that is, the cause may be some underlying third variable. These are usually not easy to identify. Some sociologists think that male culture is that underlying third variable.

Male Culture ⟶ Spouse Abuse

Socialized into dominance, some men learn to view women as objects on which to take out their frustration. In fact, this underlying third variable could be a cause of both spouse abuse and alcohol abuse.

But since only some men beat their wives, while all males are exposed to male culture, other variables must also be involved. Perhaps specific subcultures that promote violence and denigrate women lead to both spouse abuse and alcohol abuse.

Male Subculture ⟶ **Spouse Abuse** / **Alcohol Abuse**

If so, this does *not* mean that it is the only causal variable, for spouse abuse probably has many causes. Unlike the movement of amoebas or the action of heat on some object, human behavior is infinitely complicated. Especially important are people's *definitions of the situation*, including their views of right and wrong. To explain spouse abuse, then, we need to add such variables as the ways that men view violence and their ideas about the relative rights of women and men. It is precisely to help unravel such complicating factors in human behavior that we need the experimental method.

MORE ON CORRELATIONS

Correlation simply means that two or more variables are present together. The more often that these variables are found together, the stronger their relationship. To indicate their strength, sociologists use a number called a *correlation coefficient*. If two variables are always related, that is, they are always present together, they have what is called a *perfect positive correlation*. The number 1.0 represents this correlation coefficient. Nature has some 1.0's, such as the lack of water and the death of trees. 1.0's also apply to the human physical state, such as the absence of nutrients and the absence of life. But social life is much more complicated than physical conditions, and there are no 1.0's in human behavior.

Two variables can also have a *perfect negative correlation*. This means that when one variable is present, the other is always absent. The number –1.0 represents this correlation coefficient.

Positive correlations of 0.1, 0.2, and 0.3 mean that one variable is associated with another only 1 time out of 10, 2 times out of 10, and 3 times out of 10. In other words, in most instances the first variable is *not* associated with the second, indicating a weak relationship. A strong relationship may indicate causation, but not necessarily. Testing the relationship between variables is the goal of some sociological research.

Your **independent variable,** something that causes a change in another variable, would be therapy. Your **dependent variable,** the variable that might change, would be the men's behavior: whether they abuse women after they get out of jail. Unfortunately, your operational definition of the men's behavior will be sloppy: either reports from the wives or records indicating which men were rearrested for abuse. This is sloppy because some of the women will not report the abuse, and some of the men who abuse their wives will not be arrested. Yet it may be the best you can do.

Let's assume that you choose rearrest as your operational definition. If you find that the men who received therapy are *less* likely to be rearrested for abuse, you can attribute the difference to the therapy. If you find *no difference* in rearrest rates, you can conclude that the therapy was ineffective. If you find that the men who received the therapy have a *higher* rearrest rate, you can conclude that the therapy backfired.

Ideally, you would test different types of therapy. Perhaps only some types work. You might even want to test self-therapy by assigning articles, books, and videos.

Unobtrusive Measures

Researchers sometimes use **unobtrusive measures,** observing the behavior of people who are not aware that they are being studied. For example, social researchers studied the level of whisky consumption in a town that was legally "dry" by counting empty bottles in trashcans (Lee 2000). Researchers have also gone high-tech in their unobtrusive measures. To trace customers' paths through stores, they attach infrared surveillance devices to shopping carts. Grocery chains use these findings to place higher-profit items in more strategic locations (McCarthy 1993). Casino operators use chips that transmit radio frequencies, allowing them to track how much their high rollers are betting at every hand of poker or blackjack (Sanders 2005; Grossman 2007). Billboards read information embedded on a chip in your car key. As you drive by, the billboard displays *your* name with a personal message (Feder 2007). The same device can *collect* information as you drive by. Cameras in sidewalk billboards scan the facial features of people who pause to look at its advertising, reporting their sex, race, and how long they looked (Clifford 2008). The billboards, which raise ethical issues of invasion of privacy, are part of marketing, not sociological research.

It would be considered unethical to use most unobtrusive measures to research spouse abuse. You could, however, analyze 911 calls. Also, if there were a public forum held by abused or abusing spouses on the Internet, you could record and analyze the online conversations. Ethics in unobtrusive research are still a matter of dispute: To secretly record the behavior of people in public settings, such as a crowd, is generally considered acceptable, but to do so in private settings is not.

Deciding Which Method to Use

How do sociologists choose among these methods? Four primary factors affect their decision. The first is *access to resources.* They may want to conduct a survey, for example, but if their finances won't permit this, they might analyze documents instead. The second is *access to subjects.* Even though they prefer face-to-face interviews, if the people who make up the sample live far away, researchers might mail them questionnaires or conduct a survey by telephone or e-mail. The third factor concerns the *purpose of the research.* Each method is better for answering certain types of questions. Participant observation, for example, is good at uncovering people's attitudes, while experiments are better at resolving questions of cause and effect. Fourth, *the researcher's background or training* comes into play. In graduate school, sociologists study many methods, but they are able to practice only some of them. After graduate school, sociologists who were trained in quantitative research methods, which emphasize measurement and statistics, are likely to use surveys. Sociologists who were trained in qualitative research methods, which emphasize observing and interpreting people's behavior, lean toward participant observation.

How Hwee Young/epa/Corbis

To prevent cheating by customers and personnel, casinos use *unobtrusive measures.* In the ceiling above this blackjack table are video cameras that record every action. Observors are also posted there.

Controversy in Sociological Research

Sociologists sometimes find themselves in the hot seat because of their research. Some poke into private areas of life, which upsets people. Others investigate political matters, and their findings threaten those who have a stake in the situation. When researchers in Palestine asked refugees if they would be willing to accept compensation and not return to Israel if there were a peace settlement, most said they would take the buyout. When the head researcher released these findings, an enraged mob beat him and trashed his office (Bennet 2003). In the following Thinking Critically section, you can see how even such a straightforward task as counting the homeless can land sociologists in the midst of controversy.

ThinkingCRITICALLY
Doing Controversial Research—Counting the Homeless

What could be less offensive than counting the homeless? As sometimes occurs, however, even basic research lands sociologists in the midst of controversy. This is what happened to sociologist Peter Rossi and his associates.

There was a dispute between advocates for the homeless and federal officials. The advocates claimed that 3 to 7 million Americans were homeless; the officials claimed that the total was about 250,000. Each side accused the other of gross distortion—the one to place pressure on Congress, the other to keep the public from knowing how bad the situation really was. But each side was only guessing.

Only an accurate count could clear up the picture. Peter Rossi and the National Opinion Research Center took on that job. They had no vested interest in supporting either side, only in answering this question honestly.

The challenge was immense. The *population* was evident—the U.S. homeless. A *survey* would be appropriate, but how do you survey a *sample* of the homeless? No one has a list of the homeless, and only some of the homeless stay at shelters. As for *validity*, to make certain that they were counting only people who were really homeless, the researchers needed a good *operational definition* of homelessness. To include people who weren't really homeless would destroy the study's *reliability*. The researchers wanted results that would be consistent if others were to *replicate*, or repeat, the study.

As an operational definition, the researchers used "literally homeless," people "who do not have access to a conventional dwelling and who would be homeless by any conceivable definition of the term." With funds limited, the researchers couldn't do a national count, but they could count the homeless in Chicago.

By using a *stratified random sample*, the researchers were able to generalize to the entire city. How could they do this since there is no list of the homeless? They did have a list of the city's shelters and a map of the city. A stratified random sample of the city's shelters gave them access to the homeless who sleep in the shelters. For the homeless who sleep in the streets, parks, and vacant buildings, they used a stratified random sample of the city's blocks.

Their findings? On an average night, 2,722 people are homeless in Chicago. Because people move in and out of homelessness, between 5,000 and 7,000 are homeless at

Research sometimes lands sociologists in the midst of controversy. As described here, the results of a study to determine how many homeless people there are in the United States displeased homeless advocates. Homelessness is currently growing at such a pace that many U.S. cities have set up "tent cities." Shown here is a tile worker in St. Petersburg, Florida, who lost his home and lives in a tent.

some point during the year. On warm nights, only two out of five sleep in the shelters, and even during Chicago's cold winters only three out of four do so. Seventy-five percent are men, 60 percent African Americans. One in four is a former mental patient, one in five a former prisoner. Projecting these findings to the United States yields a national total of about 350,000 homeless people.

This total elated government officials and stunned the homeless advocates. The advocates said that the number couldn't possibly be right, and they began to snipe at the researchers. This is one of the risks of doing research, for sociologists never know whose toes they will step on. The sniping made the researchers uncomfortable, and to let everyone know they weren't trying to minimize the problem, they stressed that these 350,000 Americans live desperate lives. They sleep in city streets, live in shelters, eat out of garbage cans, and suffer from severe health problems.

The controversy continues. With funding at stake for shelters and for treating mental problems and substance abuse, homeless advocates continue to insist that at least 2 million Americans are homeless. While the total is not in the millions, it has doubled recently to 672,000. As a sign of changing times, veterans, many of them emotionally disturbed, make up 15 percent of this total.

Sources: Based on Anderson 1986; Rossi et al. 1986; Rossi et al. 1987; Rossi 1989, 1991, 1999; Bialik 2006; Chan 2007; National Coalition for the Homeless 2008; Preston 2008.

Gender in Sociological Research

You know how significant gender is in your own life, how it affects your orientations and your attitudes. You also may be aware that gender opens and closes doors to you. Because gender is also a factor in social research, researchers must take steps to prevent it from biasing their findings. For example, sociologists Diana Scully and Joseph Marolla (1984, 2007) interviewed convicted rapists in prison. They were concerned that their gender might lead to *interviewer bias*—that the prisoners might shift their answers, sharing certain experiences or opinions with Marolla, but saying something else to Scully. To prevent gender bias, each researcher interviewed half the sample. Later in this chapter, we'll look at what they found out.

Gender certainly can be an impediment in research. In our imagined research on spouse abuse, for example, could a man even do participant observation of women who have been beaten by their husbands? Technically, the answer is yes. But because the women have been victimized by men, they might be less likely to share their experiences and feelings with men. If so, women would be better suited to conduct this research, more likely to achieve valid results. The supposition that these victims will be more open with women than with men, however, is just that—a supposition. Research alone will verify or refute this assumption.

Gender is significant in other ways, too. It is certainly a mistake to assume that what applies to one sex also applies to the other (Bird and Rieker 1999; Neuman 2006). Women's and men's lives differ significantly, and if we do research on just half of humanity, our research will be vastly incomplete. Today's huge numbers of women sociologists guarantee that women will not be ignored in social research. In the past, however, when almost all sociologists were men, women's experiences were neglected.

Gender issues can pop up in unexpected ways in sociological research. I vividly recall this incident in San Francisco.

The streets were getting dark, and I was still looking for homeless people. When I saw someone lying down, curled up in a doorway, I approached the individual. As I got close, I began my opening research line, "Hi, I'm Dr. Henslin from. . . ." The individual began to scream and started to thrash wildly. Startled by this sudden, high-pitched scream and by the rapid movements, I quickly backed away. When I later analyzed what had happened, I concluded that I had intruded into a woman's bedroom.

This incident also holds another lesson. Researchers do their best, but they make mistakes. Sometimes these mistakes are minor, and even humorous. The woman sleeping in the doorway wasn't frightened. It was only just getting dark, and there were many people on the street. She was just assertively marking her territory and letting me know in no uncertain terms that I was an intruder. If we make a mistake in research, we pick up and go on. As we do so, we take ethical considerations into account, which is the topic of our next section.

Ethics in Sociological Research

In addition to choosing an appropriate research method, we must also follow the ethics of sociology (American Sociological Association 1999). Research ethics require honesty, truth, and openness (sharing findings with the scientific community). Ethics clearly forbid the falsification of results. They also condemn plagiarism—that is, stealing someone else's work. Another ethical guideline states that research subjects should generally be informed that they are being studied and should never be harmed by the research. Ethics also require that sociologists protect the anonymity of those who provide information. Sometimes people reveal things that are intimate, potentially embarrassing, or otherwise harmful to themselves. Finally, although not all sociologists agree, it generally is considered unethical for researchers to misrepresent themselves.

Sociologists take their ethical standards seriously. To illustrate the extent to which they will go to protect their respondents, consider the research conducted by Mario Brajuha.

Protecting the Subjects: The Brajuha Research

Mario Brajuha, a graduate student at the State University of New York at Stony Brook, was doing participant observation of restaurant workers. He lost his job as a waiter when the restaurant where he was working burned down—a fire of "suspicious origin," as the police said. When detectives learned that Brajuha had taken field notes (Brajuha and Hallowell 1986), they asked to see them. Because he had promised to keep the information confidential, Brajuha refused to hand them over. When the district attorney subpoenaed the notes, Brajuha still refused. The district attorney then threatened to put Brajuha in jail. By this time, Brajuha's notes had become rather famous, and unsavory characters—perhaps those who had set the fire—also wanted to know what was in them. They, too, demanded to see them, accompanying their demands with threats of a different nature. Brajuha found himself between a rock and a hard place.

For two years, Brajuha refused to hand over his notes, even though he grew anxious and had to appear at several court hearings. Finally, the district attorney dropped the subpoena. When the two men under investigation for setting the fire died, the threats to Brajuha, his wife, and their children ended.

Misleading the Subjects: The Humphreys Research

Sociologists agree on the necessity to protect respondents, and they applaud the professional manner in which Brajuha handled himself. Although it is considered acceptable for sociologists to do covert participant observation (studying some situation without announcing that they are doing research), to deliberately misrepresent oneself is considered unethical. Let's look at the case of Laud Humphreys, whose research forced sociologists to rethink and refine their ethical stance.

Laud Humphreys, a classmate of mine at Washington University in St. Louis, was an Episcopal priest who decided to become a sociologist. For his Ph.D. dissertation, Humphreys (1971, 1975) studied social interaction in "tearooms," public restrooms where some men go for quick, anonymous oral sex with other men.

Humphreys found that some restrooms in Forest Park, just across from our campus, were tearooms. He began a participant observation study by hanging around these restrooms. He found that in addition to the two men having sex, a third man—called a "watch queen"—served as a lookout for police and other unwelcome strangers.

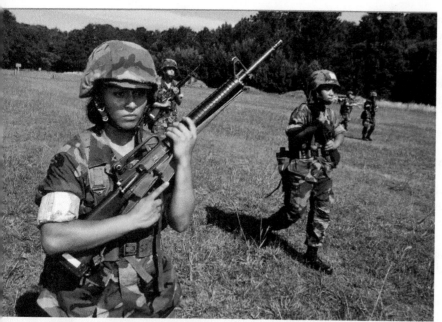

Drew Crawford/The Image Works

Ethics in social research are of vital concern to sociologists. As discussed in the text, sociologists may disagree on some of the issue's finer points, but none would approve of slipping LSD to unsuspecting subjects like these Marine recruits in basic training at Parris Island, South Carolina. This was done to U.S. soldiers in the 1960s under the guise of legitimate testing—just "to see what would happen."

Humphreys took on the role of watch queen, not only watching for strangers but also observing what the men did. He wrote field notes after the encounters.

Humphreys decided that he wanted to learn about the regular lives of these men. For example, what was the significance of the wedding rings that many of the men wore? He came up with an ingenious technique: Many of the men parked their cars near the tearooms, and Humphreys recorded their license plate numbers. A friend in the St. Louis police department gave Humphreys each man's address. About a year later, Humphreys arranged for these men to be included in a medical survey conducted by some of the sociologists on our faculty.

Disguising himself with a different hairstyle and clothing, Humphreys visited the men's homes. He interviewed the men, supposedly for the medical study. He found that they led conventional lives. They voted, mowed their lawns, and took their kids to Little League games. Many reported that their wives were not aroused sexually or were afraid of getting pregnant because their religion did not allow them to use birth control. Humphreys concluded that heterosexual men were also using the tearooms for a form of quick sex.

This study stirred controversy among sociologists and nonsociologists alike. Many sociologists criticized Humphreys, and a national columnist even wrote a scathing denunciation of "sociological snoopers" (Von Hoffman 1970). One of our professors even tried to get Humphreys' Ph.D. revoked. As the controversy heated up and a court case loomed, Humphreys feared that his list of respondents might be subpoenaed. He gave me the list to take from Missouri to Illinois, where I had begun teaching. When he called and asked me to destroy it, I burned the list in my backyard.

Was this research ethical? This question is not decided easily. Although many sociologists sided with Humphreys—and his book reporting the research won a highly acclaimed award—the criticisms continued. At first, Humphreys defended his position vigorously, but five years later, in a second edition of his book (1975), he stated that he should have identified himself as a researcher.

How Research and Theory Work Together

Research cannot stand alone. Nor can theory. As sociologist C. Wright Mills (1959) argued so forcefully, research without theory is simply a collection of unrelated "facts." But theory without research, Mills added, is abstract and empty—it can't represent the way life really is.

Research and theory, then, are both essential for sociology. Every theory must be tested, which requires research. And as sociologists do research, they often come up with surprising findings. Those findings must be explained, and for that we need theory. As sociologists study social life, then, they combine research and theory.

The Real World: When the Ideal Meets the Real

Although we can list the ideals of research, real-life situations often force sociologists to settle for something that falls short of the ideal. In the following Thinking Critically section, let's look at how two sociologists confronted the ideal and the real.

ThinkingCRITICALLY

Are Rapists Sick? A Close-Up View of Research

Two sociologists, Diana Scully and Joseph Marolla, whose research was mentioned earlier, were not satisfied with the typical explanation that rapists are "sick," psychologically disturbed, or different from other men. They developed the hypothesis that rape is like most human behavior—learned through interaction with others. That is, some men learn to think of rape as appropriate behavior.

To test this hypothesis, it would be best to interview a random sample of rapists. But this is impossible. There is no list of all rapists, so there is no way to give them all the same chance of being included in a sample. You can't even use prison populations to select a random sample, for many rapists have never been caught, some who were caught were found not guilty, and some who were found guilty were given probation. And as we know from DNA testing, some who were convicted of rape are innocent. Consequently, Scully and Marolla confronted the classic dilemma of sociologists—either to not do the research or to do it under less than ideal conditions.

They chose to do the research. When they had the opportunity to interview convicted rapists in prison, they jumped at it. They knew that whatever they learned would be more than we already knew. They sent out 3,500 letters to men serving time in seven prisons in Virginia, the state where they were teaching. About 25 percent of the prisoners agreed to be interviewed. They matched these men on the basis of age, education, race–ethnicity, severity of offense, and previous criminal record. This resulted in a sample of 98 prisoners who were convicted of rape and a control sample of 75 men convicted of other offenses.

As noted earlier, because the sex of the interviewer can bias research results, Scully and Marolla each interviewed half the sample. It took them 600 hours to gather information on the prisoners, including their psychological, criminal, and sexual history. To guard against lies, they checked what the individuals told them against their institutional records. They used twelve scales to measure the men's attitudes about women, rape, and themselves. In order to find out what circumstances the men defined as rape or when they viewed the victim as responsible, they also gave the men nine vignettes of forced sexual encounters and asked them to determine responsibility in each one.

Scully and Marolla discovered something that goes against common sense—that most rapists are not sick and that they are not overwhelmed by uncontrollable urges. The psychological histories of the rapists and the nonrapists were similar. These men rape for a variety of reasons: to "blow off steam" over problems they are having with others, to get sex, to feel powerful, and to hurt women (Monahan et al. 2005). Some rape spontaneously, while others plan their rapes. Some rape as a form of revenge, to get even with someone, not necessarily their victim. For some, rape is even a form of recreation, and they rape with friends on weekends.

Scully and Marolla also found support for what feminists had been pointing out for years, that power is a major element in rape. Here is what one man said:

> Rape gave me the power to do what I wanted to do without feeling I had to please a partner or respond to a partner. I felt in control, dominant. Rape was the ability to have sex without caring about the woman's response. I was totally dominant.

To discover that most rape is calculated behavior—that rapists are not "sick"; that a motivating force can be power, not passion; that the behavior stems from the criminal pursuit of pleasure, not from mental illness—is significant. It makes the sociological quest worthwhile.

In comparing their sample of rapists with their control group of nonrapists, Scully and Marolla also made another significant finding: The rapists are more likely to believe "rape myths." They are more likely to believe that women cause their own rape by the way they act and the clothes they wear, that a woman who charges rape has simply changed her mind after participating in consensual sex, and that most men accused of rape are innocent.

Connecting Research and Theory

Such findings go far beyond simply adding to our storehouse of "facts." As indicated in Figure 1, research stimulates both the development of theory and the need for more research. Scully and Marolla suggest that rape myths act as neutralizers, that they allow "potential rapists to turn off social prohibitions against injuring others."

This hypothesis needs to be confirmed by other research. It also pinpoints the need to determine how such myths are transmitted. Which male subcultures perpetuate them? Do the mass media contribute to these myths? Do family, religion, and education create respect for females and help keep males from learning such myths? Or do they somehow contribute to these myths? If so, how?

Sociologists have begun to build on this path-breaking research, which was done, as usual, under less than ideal conditions. The resulting theorizing and research may provide the basis for making changes that reduce the incidence of rape in our society.

Sources: Marolla and Scully 1986; Scully 1990; Scully and Marolla 1984, 2007.

Sociology needs more of this type of research—imaginative and sometimes daring investigations conducted in an imperfect world under less than ideal conditions. This is really what sociology is all about. Sociologists study what people do—whether their behaviors are conforming or deviant, whether they please others or disgust them. No matter what behavior is studied, systematic research methods and the application of social theory take us beyond common sense. They allow us to penetrate surface realities so we can better understand human behavior—and, in the ideal case, make changes to help improve social life.

SUMMARY *and* REVIEW

What Is a Valid Sociological Topic?

Any human behavior is a valid sociological topic, even disreputable behavior. Spouse abuse is an example. Sociological research is based on the sociologist's interests, access to subjects, appropriate methods, and ethical considerations.

Common Sense and the Need for Sociological Research

Why isn't common sense adequate?

Common sense doesn't provide reliable information. When subjected to scientific research, commonsense ideas often are found to be limited or false.

A Research Model

What are the eight basic steps of sociological research?

(1) Selecting a topic, (2) Defining the problem, (3) Reviewing the literature, (4) Formulating a **hypothesis**, (5) Choosing a research method, (6) Collecting the data, (7) Analyzing the results, and (8) Sharing the results.

Research Methods

How do sociologists gather data?

To collect data, sociologists use seven **research methods** (or research designs): **surveys, participant observation** (fieldwork), **case studies, secondary analysis, documents, experiments,** and **unobtrusive measures.**

How do sociologists choose a research method?

Sociologists choose their research method based on questions to be answered, their access to potential subjects, the resources available, their training, and ethical considerations.

Controversy in Sociological Research

Why is sociological research often controversial?

Some people get upset because sociologists do research on disreputable or illegal activities or on personal or intimate areas of life. Other people get upset when research findings go against their interests or biases.

Gender in Sociological Research

What is the relationship between gender and research?

There are two aspects. First, findings based on samples of men do not necessarily apply to women and findings based on samples of women do not necessarily apply to men. Second, in some kinds of research, such as studying abused spouses, rape victims, and rapists, the gender of the researcher could affect findings.

Ethics in Sociological Research

How important are ethics in sociological research?

Ethics are of fundamental concern to sociologists, who are committed to openness, honesty, truth, and protecting their subjects from harm. The Brajuha research on restau-rant workers and the Humphreys research on "tearooms" were cited to illustrate ethical issues that concern sociologists.

How Research and Theory Work Together

What is the relationship between theory and research?

Theory and research depend on one another. Theory generates questions that need to be answered by research, and sociologists use theory to interpret the data they gather. Research, in turn, helps to generate theory: Findings that don't match what is expected can indicate a need to modify theory.

THINKING CRITICALLY

1. Should sociologists be allowed to do research on disreputable or disapproved behavior? On illegal behavior? Why or why not?

2. What factors make for *bad* sociological research? How can these be avoided?

3. What ethics govern sociological research?

4. Is it right (or ethical) for sociologists to not identity themselves when they do research? To misrepresent themselves? What if identifying themselves as researchers will destroy their access to a research setting or to informants?

ADDITIONAL RESOURCES

What can you find in MySocLab? mysoclab www.mysoclab.com

- Complete Ebook
- Practice Tests and Video and Audio activities
- Mapping and Data Analysis exercises

- Sociology in the News
- Classic Readings in Sociology
- Research and Writing advice

Where Can I Read More on This Topic?

Bryman, Alan. *Social Research Methods,* 3rd ed. Oxford: Oxford University Press, 2008. An overview of the research methods used by sociologists, with an emphasis on the logic that underlies these methods.

Creswell, John W. *Research Design: Qualitative, Quantitative, and Mixed Methods Approaches,* 3rd ed. Beverly Hills, Calif.: Sage, 2008. This introduction to research methods walks you through the research experience and helps you to understand when to use a particular method.

Drew, Paul, Geoffrey Raymond, and Darin Weinberg. *Talk and Interaction in Social Research Methods.* Thousand Oaks, Calif.: Sage, 2006. The authors stress the importance of talk in a variety of social research methods.

Lee, Raymond M. *Unobtrusive Methods in Social Research.* Philadelphia: Open University Press, 2000. This overview of unobtrusive ways of doing social research summarizes many interesting studies.

Lomand, Turner C. *Social Science Research: A Cross Section of Journal Articles for Discussion and Evaluation,* 5th ed. Los Angeles: Pyrczak, 2007. This overview of the methods of research used by sociologists includes articles on current topics.

Neuman, W. Lawrence. *Social Research Methods: Qualitative and Quantitative Approaches,* 6th ed. Boston: Allyn and Bacon, 2006. This "how-to" book of sociological research describes how sociologists gather data and the logic that underlies each method.

Schuman, Howard. *Method and Meaning in Polls and Surveys.* Cambridge, Mass.: Harvard University Press, 2008. Examines how the wording of questions can change findings and how to understand the results of surveys.

Whyte, William Foote. *Creative Problem Solving in the Field: Reflections on a Career.* Lanham, Md.: AltaMira Press, 1997. Focusing on his extensive field experiences, the author provides insight into the researcher's role in participant observation.

Wysocki, Diane Kholos, ed. *Readings in Social Research Methods,* 3rd ed. Belmont, Calif.: Wadsworth, 2008. The authors of these articles provide an overview of research methods.

Writing Papers for Sociology

Booth, Wayne C., Gregory G. Colomb, and Joseph M. Williams. *The Craft of Research,* 3rd ed. Chicago: University of Chicago Press, 2008. How to plan a paper, build an argument, anticipate and respond to the reservations of readers, and create introductions and conclusions that answer the demanding question, "So what?"

Richlin-Klonsky, Judith, William G. Roy, Ellen Strenski, and Roseann Giarusso, eds. The Sociology Writing Group. *A Guide to Writing Sociology Papers,* 6th ed. New York: Worth, 2007. The guide walks students through the steps in writing a sociology paper, from choosing the initial assignment to doing the research and turning in a finished paper. Also explains how to manage time and correctly cite sources.

Index

Page references followed by "f" indicate illustrated figures or photographs; followed by "t" indicates a table.

9

9/11, 340

A

Aborigines, 331
Aborigines, of Australia, 331
abortion
   medical, 283
   rate, 125
   rates, 124
   statistics, 124-125
Abstract thinking, 77
Abuse/violence
   by women, 152-153, 246
Academic achievement, 91, 143
Acquaintance rape, 166
Acting out, 84
Adler, Peter, 91
Adolescence, 95, 150, 228
Adoption
   in China, 217
Adulthood, 94-95, 242, 331
advertising agencies, 312
Affair, 147, 259, 335
African Americans (, 157
   in sports, 155, 187
Afrikaners, 180
Agape, 27, 367
Aggravated assault, 118
Aggression, 140, 244, 311, 329
Aging
   global, 248
   study of, 250, 318
Aging society
   gender gap in, 162
   personality and, 210
Agricultural societies, 96, 254, 324, 332
Albania, 83, 260
Alcohol
   abuse, 29-30, 164, 282, 368-369
   socialization, 93, 109
Alcohol abuse, 29, 369
Alcoholics, 92, 123
Alcoholics Anonymous, 92
Alcoholics Anonymous (AA), 92
Algeria, 260
Alimony, 271
Amato, Paul R., 242
Amish, 308-309, 340
and Spanish, 255
Angola, 260
Anime, 85
Anthropology, 61, 103, 189
Anticipatory grief, 228
Anticipatory socialization, 91
anti-Semitism, 186
Applied sociology, 12, 341
Armaments, 262
Armenians, 191
Arranged marriages, 223
Aryan Nations, 183
Aryans, 176
Asch experiment, 347
Asch, Solomon, cards, 347
Ascribed status, 256, 301
Asian Americans (, 198, 288
Asian immigrants, 231
Atlanta University, 10
Authoritarian leaders, 186, 346
Authoritarian personality, 186
Avatars, 335

B

Baby boomers, 59
Back stages, 314
Background assumptions, 106, 154, 318-320
Baptists, 284
Barbie dolls, 56, 82
Bargaining, 187, 266
Battered women, 245
Batterers, 29, 369
Belarus, 260
berdache, 217
Bicyclists, 19-20
Bikers, 112
Bioengineering, 334
Biotech society, 331
Birth control, 31, 309, 374
Black Americans, 183
Black English, 202
Blended families, 234
Blended family, 234
Boards of directors, 278
body image, 317
Body language, 310, 345
Bolivia, 260
Bonded laborers, 255
Bonding, 73-74
"Boomerang children", 227
booms, 187
Boot camp, 92-93
Border Patrol, 195
Bosnia, 83, 176, 260
Botox, 59
Boy Scouts, 152
Brazilians, 179
Breaking up, 14
Bronfenbrenner, Urie, 242
Bronx Zoo, 189
Brooks, David, 126
buggies, 309
Bullfighting, 43
Bureau of Indian Affairs, 205

C

Cablinasian, 177
callbacks, 201
Cambodia, 70, 240, 261-262
Capital punishment, 106
Capitalist class, 119-120, 278-280
Caregivers and caregiving
   men as, 141, 218
Cascades, 348
Caste system, 256-257
Caucasian, 177
Causation, 28-29, 76-77, 368-369
Cause and effect, 28, 76, 368
Center for American Women and Politics, 168
Centers for Disease Control, 8, 205
Chafetz, Janet, 153
Chambliss, William, 321
Champagne, 274
Cheadle, Jacob, 242
Cheating, 120, 335, 370
Cheerleaders, 114, 154
Cherlin, Andrew, 243
chief executive officers (CEOs), 272
Chiefs, 332
Child maltreatment
   incest, 60
child pornography, 114
Child rearing, 61, 94, 226, 293
Child support, 219
Childbearing, 15, 142
Childbirth, 15, 65, 146, 185, 224
Childless couples, 232
Children
   Asian American, 192, 228
   custody of, 145, 241
   European immigrants, 204-205
   moving in with, 242
Children and childhood, 100
Chinese Exclusion Act, 203
Chronic conditions
   by gender, 140
   cancer, 152, 334
Chronological age, 72
Church of Scientology, 66
circumcision, 44, 142, 257
Citigroup, 117, 273
Civil Rights Act, 199
Civil Rights Act of 1968, 199
Class consciousness, 268
Class system, 223, 257, 298
Class systems, 292
classroom, 80-81, 115, 299-300
Clinton, Hillary, 168
Clitoris, 150
Cloning, 334
Closed-ended questions, 24-25, 363-364
Cloward, Richard A., 115
Cohabitation
   premarital, 237
Colombia, 15, 44, 260
colonialism, 188, 262
Colored Baptist Ministers', 189
Columbia, space shuttle, 351
Commitment
   what is, 20, 238
Common sense, 19, 50, 179, 358
Communication
   gender differences and, 171
Compatibility, 14
Comte, Auguste, 6
Concentration camps, 92
concessions, 17
Concrete operational stage, 77
Conflict perspective, 17-18, 119, 208, 220, 266, 306
Conflict perspective on, 248
Conflict theory, 13, 83, 107, 151, 184, 268, 307, 350
conformists, 111, 186
Congo, 189, 261-262
Conscience, 78, 111, 340
Conservation, 189
Contemporary dating
   hooking up, 325
Contempt, 56, 105, 186
Contraception, 232
Control group, 28, 72-73, 175, 368
control theory, 109
Cooley, Charles, 337
Cooley, Charles H., 337
corporate crime, 116
correlations, 29, 369
Counseling, 26, 334, 365-366
Countercultures, 53-54
Cowboys, 57, 84
Credit cards, 5, 117, 271
Crime
   conflict theory, 107, 167
   drugs and, 104, 282
   gender and, 166
   pornography, 85, 114
   power and, 119, 167
   punishment, 109
   victims of hate crimes, 128
Criminal justice
   courts, 110, 284
   death penalty, 124-127
   death row, 124-125
   sentencing, 124
criminal justice system, 119-121, 212, 284
criminology, 134
Critical sociology, 250
criticisms of, 12

Croatia, 260
Crying, 46, 129
Cuba, 49, 196-198, 260
cults, 92
Cultural goals, 115-116
Cultural lag, 63
Cultural leveling, 63-65
Cultural norms, 133
Cultural relativism, 43-44
Cultural shock, 41-42
Cultural universals, 65
Culture shock, 41-43, 103
Curriculum, 89
Custody, 145, 241

D

Darwin, Charles, 7, 61
Darwin, Charles, natural selection, 7, 61
Darwinism, 6-7
Date (acquaintance) rape, 166
Dating
    online, 219
Death penalty, 124-127
Death row, 124-125
Debt, 95, 184, 216, 255
declining significance of race, 201
Decoding, 331
Deferred gratification, 232
Degradation ceremony, 92-93, 110-111
Dehumanize, 190
Delinquents, 112, 143, 241
Democratic leaders, 346-347
Democratic party, 168, 339
Democrats, 284
Denmark, 120, 260
Denominations, 284
Department of Education, 157
Department of Homeland Security, 307
Deutscher, Irwin, 206
Developed nations
    global stratification, 257-258
Deviant paths, 115
differential association, 107
Differential association theory, 107
diffuse, 64
"Dirty work", 188, 339-340
Disabled, 302
Disorientation, 41
"Distance zones", 324
Divorce
    personal factors, 281
    same-sex, 234
    symbolic interactionism, 13-14, 247
    trends in, 235
DNA, 124, 334, 375
dolls, 56, 82, 142
Domestic partnerships, 234
Domestication revolution, 331
Domhoff, G.William
    upper class, 279
dominant groups, 180
Double standard, 237, 339
Downward social mobility, 285
Dramaturgical analysis, 314
Dramaturgy, 313-314
Drinking water, 265
Drug abuse
    history of, 250, 259
Drug use
    socialization and, 141
Drunk driving, 110, 281
Du Bois, W.E.B
    conflict theorists, 34, 187-188
    racism, 9-10, 211, 255
Duggar, Michelle, 225
Duke University, 164
Durkheim, Emile
    deviance, 112-114
Dyad, 226, 343-345
Dyads, 343
dysfunction, 16
dysfunctions, 15-16, 113, 208, 218, 266

E

Eating disorders, 317
Ecstasy, 109
Ecuador, 45, 260
Education

academic achievement, 91
    adult, 57, 89
    assets and, 278
    computers and, 195
    elementary, 91, 191
    hidden curriculum, 89
    marriage and, 121, 213-214, 285
    myths, 60, 375-376
    social structure and, 295-296
Einstein, Albert, 7
Elder care, 238
Elderly
    homosexual, 126
    never married, 248
elections, 168
Electronic communities, 342
elementary schools, 91
Embezzlement, 116
Emotional overload, 220
Endogamy, 218, 256
Engels, Frederick, 145
English language, 207
Enjoyment, 88
environmental justice, 211
Episcopalians, 284
Equal Rights Amendment, 284
equality of opportunity, 56
Estrogen, 143
ethical issues, 35, 360
Ethiopia, 139, 261
ethnic cleansing, 191
ethnic identity, 181-182
Ethnic maps, 183
Ethnic work, 181-182
Ethnocentrism, 41, 139, 186
Ethnography, 36
ethnomethodology, 318
Ethnos, 178
Exclusion Act, 203
exogamy, 218
Experimental group, 28, 73, 368
Experimental groups, 28, 368
Experiments, 20-21, 73-74, 175, 222, 348-350, 359
Expressive leaders, 346

F

Face-saving behavior, 316
Face-to-face interaction, 13, 337
False class consciousness, 268
Families
    domestic partnerships, 234
Family
    affection and, 109
    blended, 234
    blended families, 234
    child abuse, 244
    cohabitation, 235-237
    diversity in, 90, 177, 228, 286, 307
    marital satisfaction, 225
Family abuse/violence
    explanation of, 13, 82, 262
Family, changes in
    cohabiting couples, 236-237
    one-parent families, 232
Family conflict
    reactions to, 74-75, 104, 207, 367
Family development theory
    research methods and, 376
Family functions
    primary groups, 337-339
Family structure
    of Asian American families, 231
    of Latino families, 230
Family, theoretical perspectives on
    conflict perspective, 17-18, 124, 208, 220, 266, 306
Family violence, 250
fear
    of divorce, 232
Female circumcision, 44, 147, 257
Female infanticide, 147
Femininities, 138
feminism
    radical, 153
Feral children, 70
Fertility drugs, 233
Fieldwork, 26, 103, 365
Firestone tires, 116
first impressions, 311
Flexibility, 314

Food supply, 190, 331-333
Forcible rape, 166
Forests, 59, 70, 103
Formal operational stage, 77
Formal organizations, 323
Freud, Sigmund, 7, 77-78, 129
Front stages, 314
Functional analysis, 13
Functionalism
    criminal justice, 108
    drug use, 124
    environment, 187
    health care, 185
    inequality, 18
    media, 84, 187, 349
functionalist perspective, 16, 113, 208, 218, 306
Functionalist perspective on, 248
functionalists, 15-19, 113, 210, 218-220, 266-268, 298

G

Gabon, 260
gang member, 329
Gates, Bill, 270
Gay and lesbian families, 234
Gay/lesbian relationships
    parenting in, 242
    problems in, 12
Gender
    division of labor, 147, 307
    education and, 201, 291
    income and, 118
    sociological perspectives on, 171
    stereotype, 84, 188, 312-313
Gender differences, 79, 138
gender discrimination, 140
Gender equality, 158, 244
Gender gap
    in earnings, 160
Gender inequality, 144, 202
gender issues, 30, 372
Gender norms
    violating, 50, 80, 106
Gender pay gap, 161-163
gender roles
    in education, 147, 293, 306
    in politics, 147, 254
    sociobiology, 61, 106
Gender roles, learning sources of
    teachers, 17, 49, 78, 143, 256, 299
Gender segregation, 171
Gender socialization, 81-82, 158
Gender stereotypes
    in the workplace, 160, 250
Gender tracking, 158
Generalizability, 26, 342, 366
Generalization, 246
Genetic predispositions, 106
Geneva Convention, 351
genocide
    Armenian, 191
German Americans, 49
G.I. Bill, 157
Gilligan, Carol, morality of care, 79
Glenn, 231
global capitalism, 268
Global issues, 34
Global stratification
    causes of, 254
    quality of life, 293
Global superclass, 258
Global village, 5, 62
Globalization of capitalism, 32, 64, 263, 358
Gordon, J., 353
Government
    American Indian care and, 204
Grades, 11, 73, 305, 340
Greenland, 120, 260
Grey's Anatomy, 314
Group dynamics, 343
Group size, 343-345
Groupthink, 350-353
Guam, 203
guilt, 78-79, 227
Guinea, 45, 147, 188, 216, 261
Guinea-Bissau, 261
Guns, 8, 82, 117, 142, 195, 302, 348
Gynecological examinations, 320
gypsies, 176, 350

H

hair color, 114
Harlow experiments, 74
hate groups, 184, 340
Hawaii, 187, 239
Hawaiians, 192
Head Start, 227
Health care
    for Latinos, 289
    sexism in, 155
    two-tier system of, 282
Hearing, 69-70
Heart disease, 155, 348
Hell's Angels, 56
Herpes, 334
Heterosexual couples, 234
Hetherington, E. Mavis, 242
Hidden curriculum, 89
Higginbotham, Elizabeth, 285
Hirschi, Travis, 109
Hitler, Adolf, 176, 346
HIV/AIDS
    spread of, 12
Hmong, 42
Holocaust, 339
Homeland security, 307
Homicide rates, 200
Homogamy, 224
Honor killing, 170
"Honor killings", 147
Hooking up, 325
Horatio Alger myth, 290
Horticultural societies, 144, 331-332
Hottentots, 190
Hull-House, 12
Human development, 72
Human nature, 69-70, 140, 240
Human sexuality, 105
humanism, 231
Humor, 84, 125, 310
Humphreys, Laud, 31, 373
Hunger, 77, 204, 266
Hunting and gathering society, 330-331
Hussein, Saddam, 341
Hutus, 176
Hysterectomies, 156
Hysterectomy, 156

I

Iceland, 260
id, 77, 125, 161, 193, 239, 287
Ideal culture, 57-58
Iger, Robert, 273
Illegal drugs, 111
Illegitimate opportunity structure, 116
Illegitimate opportunity structures, 116
Imitation, 75
Immersion, 27, 126, 367
Immigrants and immigration
    resistance to, 205
    multiculturalism, 210
Immunity, 190
Implicit Association Test, 183
impression management, 314
imprisonment, 106
Incarceration, 133
Incest, 60, 218
Incest taboo, 60, 218
Income inequality, 272
Incompetence, 140
Indentured service, 255
Independent variables, 28, 368
Industrialized countries, 258
Industrializing Nations, 258-260
Infanticide, 147
Infertility, medical/high-tech solutions to
    fertility drugs, 233
    surrogacy, 233
Inflation, 187, 280
In-groups, 187, 339-340
Inheritance, 217-218
Initiation, 95, 329
Initiation rites, 95
In-laws, 247
Inner circle, 350-351
innovators, 115
Insider trading, 120

Instincts, 4, 61, 72
Institutionalized means, 115-116
instrumental leader, 346
Instrumental leaders, 346
Intergenerational mobility, 285
intergroup, 188
Internal colonialism, 188
internalization, 183
Internet
    pornography on, 114
Interracial marriage, 218
Interracial student organizations, 177
Interviewer bias, 363
Intimacy rape, 245-246
IPods, 56, 116
Iran, 144-145, 261
Iraq War, 64
Israel, 181, 260, 371

J

Jackson, Jesse, 200
jail time, 26, 365
James, LeBron, 271
Japanese Americans, 190
Jealousy, 227
Jeffrey, 134, 212, 313-314
Jewishness, 180
Jim Crow laws, 197
Justice system, 119-121, 212, 284

K

Kazakhstan, 260
Kenya, 39, 105, 139, 261, 332
Khmer Rouge, 70
Kim Possible, 84
Kindergarten, 85
Kohlberg, Lawrence, 78
Kosovo, 190
Kraybill, Donald B, 309
Ku Klux Klan, 66, 183-184, 340

L

Labeling, 111-113, 190
labeling theory, 111
Labor force
    inequality in, 160, 250, 272, 353
    social class in, 269-271
Laissez-faire leaders, 346-347
Languages, 11, 180, 231
Laos, 42, 261
Latent dysfunctions, 15
latent functions, 15, 89
Latinas, 232
Latvia, 260
lawyers, 140, 278, 334
Leadership styles, 346-347
Least Industrialized Nations, 94, 153, 191, 258-262
Legal divorce, 237
Legal system
    abortion and, 284
Lesbians and gay men
    abuse in, 368
    in intimate relationships, 17
Lewis, Oscar, 266
Libya, 260
Liebow, Elliot, 298
Life chances, 201
Life course, 93-97, 171, 226, 301
Listening, 7, 76, 123, 247, 336
Liver, 44, 334
Living together, 235
Locke, Harvey, 14
Longitudinal research
    on intelligence, 73
looking-glass self, 74
Lopez, Jennifer, 271
Lottery winners, 277
Love
    of love, 15, 222
Love/loving
    attraction and, 14
    demanding, 226
Lower class, 202
Lower middle class, 280
lumpenproletariat, 270
Lynching, 9-10
lynching, of African Americans, 157

M

Macrosociological perspective, 299
macrosociology, 298-299
Mafia, 108-109
Malaysia, 150, 260
Male dominance, 141
manifest functions, 89
Manslaughter, 110
maquiladoras, 263
Marginal working class, 119
Marietta College, 166
Marijuana, 123, 137
Marital history, 243
Marital rape, 244-246
Marital satisfaction, 225
Marital status, 121, 183, 302
Marriage
    age at, 99, 235
    cohabitation and, 236
    elderly, 16, 181, 231, 282
    expectations of, 84
    interracial, 177, 218
    long-term, 59, 242, 282
    religion and, 8
    sex in, 209
    studying, 222
    trial, 176
    troubled, 176
Marriage and family, 213-214
Marriage, communication in
    nagging, 226
marriage patterns, 224
Marriage, right reasons for
    permanence, 66, 236
Marriage, variables to successful
    compatibility, 14
Martineau, Harriet, 9
Marxism, 7
Masculinities, 138
Massey, Douglas, 202
Massey, Douglas S., 202
Master status, 104, 138, 181, 302-303
Matchmaking, 219
Mate selection, global view on
    arranged marriages, 223
    homogamy, 224
    traditional societies, 146, 217
Matriarchies, 141
matrilineal, 217-218
Matrilineal lines, 217
Matrilocal, 217
McIntosh, Peggy, 194
means of production, 6-7, 268-271, 300
Media
    advertisements, 317
    advertising, 84, 317
Medical research, 279
Medicalization of deviance, 128-129
Menstruation, 155
Mental health
    counseling, 36, 334
    disorders, 129
    sexism and, 171
Mentors, 163
meritocracy, 267
Merton, Robert, 15, 339
Miami Dolphins, 274
Microsociological perspective, 310
microsociology, 298
Microsoft Corporation, 279
Middle age, 96
Midwives, 147
Milgram experiments, 350
military service
    in Iraq, 351
Mills, C.Wright
    sociological imagination, 4
Modeling, 55
Monarchies, 5, 333
Monkeys, 46, 70, 189
monogamy, 56, 217
Montagu, Ashley, 178
Moore, Wilbert, 267
Moral holidays, 51-52
Moral reasoning, 79
Mormons, 56
Morocco, 39-40, 261, 319
Motorcyclists, 54

mulatto, 177, 286
Murderers, 126
Murdock, George, 60, 146

N

NAFTA, 212, 263
Nagging, 143, 226, 280
Namibia, 260
National Association for the Advancement of Colored
        People,, 12, 51
National Crime Victimization Survey, 24, 166, 365
National Guard, 305, 333
national identity, 181, 262
National Survey of Black Americans, 183
National Women's Political Caucus, 168
Native Americans (, 121, 198, 288
Native Americans, 82, 121, 198, 288
native languages, 231
natural resources, 262
Natural selection, 61
naturalization, 193
Nazis, 4, 71, 111, 176, 339-340
Near poor, 293
Negative sanctions, 50, 106
Negligence, 342
Neolocal, 217
Neo-Nazis, 183-184, 340
Net worth, 271
Neutralization, 111-112
Never married, 121, 236
New Guinea, 45, 147, 216, 261
New World Order, 34, 176
New Zealand, 258, 334
Nicaragua, 49, 261
Nonmaterial culture, 40-42
Nonverbal interaction, 19
North American Free Trade Agreement (NAFTA), 263
Nursing homes
    Asian Americans and, 198
    on Indian reservations, 57

O

Objectivity, 25, 364
Office of Immigration Statistics, 195
Oil-rich nations, 261
Old Order Amish, 309
Oneida tribe, 206
One-parent families, 232
Open-ended questions, 24, 365
Operational definitions, 21, 359-360
oppressed groups, 268
Oral sex, 31, 373
Ordnung, 309
organized crime, 134
Orphanages, 72-73, 189, 264
Outer controls, 111
Out-groups, 339-340
Overweight, 282

P

pan-Indianism, 206
Parenting
    discipline and, 216
    factors, 88, 242
    mass media and, 247
Parents/parenting
    friendships, 308, 339
    permissive, 231
Parity, 261
Parole, 284
participant observation, 20-21, 100, 108, 156, 184,
        293, 359-360
pass laws, 307
Passenger pigeon, 59
Pastoral and horticultural societies, 331-332
Pastoral societies, 331
patriarch, 83
Patriarchies, 141
Patrilineal, 217-218
Patrilocal residence, 217
Pay gap, 160-163
Pearl Harbor, 203, 351
Peer pressure, 347
Pelvic examinations, 321, 358
Penis, 138
people with disabilities, 310, 350
Pequot tribe, 206
Permanence, 66, 236

Personal distance, 313
Personal identity kit, 92
Personal space, 43, 310-311
perspectives in sociology, 13
Peru, 260
Physical attractiveness, 45, 312
Physical contact, 74
Physical disabilities, 176
Physical punishment, 87, 227
Piaget, Jean, 76
Piaget, Jean, theory of cognitive, 76
Pluralistic society, 56
Pokot, 105
Police discretion, 128-129
political force, 197
politics
    money and, 142, 196
polyandry, 216
polygamy, 217
Pornography, 12, 85, 114
Portes, Alejandro, 207
Positive sanctions, 50
positivism, 6
Postindustrial economy, 281
Postindustrial societies, 95, 305
Postponing marriage, 235
Power
    in marriage, 221
    marital power, 247
Premarital sex, 237
Preoperational stage, 76
Preschools, 227, 284
preservation of privilege, 229
Primary groups, 337-339
Primary sex characteristics, 138
Private hospitals, 282
Probation, 26, 284, 365-366
problem solving, 36, 378
Property crimes, 143
Proposition, 208, 234
Protestant ethic, 8-9
Protestantism, 7
Protestants, 7-8, 129, 193, 224
psychoanalysis, 77, 129
Psychological theories, 210
Public Health Service, 178
Public policy
    analyzing, 12
public relations, 163
Public sociology, 32-33
Pygmies, 189, 331

Q

Qatar, 256
Qualitative research, 370
Qualitative research methods, 370
Quantitative research, 370
Quantitative research methods, 370
questionnaires, 23, 57, 222, 362-363

R

race
    marriage between, 257
    minority groups, 188
race and ethnic relations, 176
race and ethnic relations in, 212
race and ethnicity
    gendered division of labor, 171, 222
    median family income, 198
    sentencing and, 124
racial profiling, 211
Racial–ethnic groups, 56, 156, 177, 229-230, 268, 336
Racial–ethnic relations, 188
Rain forests, 103
random sample, 23-24, 143, 224, 362-363
Random samples, 246
Rape, 12, 44, 106, 165-167, 191, 245, 375-377
Rapists, 19, 123, 166, 372
Rapport, 24, 365
Reagan, Ronald, 270
Real culture, 60, 105
rebels, 115
Recidivism rate, 125
Reckless, Walter, 109
religious groups, 306
Remarriage
    legal, 237
Remarried families

challenges, 286
replication, 32, 342, 360
Representative samples, 244
Republican Party, 281
Research
    methods of, 25, 364
Research designs, 21, 359-360
Research, family
    experiments, 20-21, 73-74, 222, 349-350, 359
    secondary analysis, 20-21, 359
research methods
    causation, 28-29, 77, 368-369
    independent variables, 28, 368
    objectivity, 25, 364
    quantitative, 36, 370
reservations, 36, 57, 188, 378
Reserve labor force, 187
Reskin, Barbara F., 207
Resocialization, 92
Resolution, 141
Retreatism, 115
retreatists, 115
reverse discrimination, 207
Riis, Jacob, 269
rising expectations, 199
Ritualism, 115
ritualists, 115
role conflict, 315
Role confusion, 220
Role exit, 316
Role performance, 314
role strain, 315
Role taking, 75
Roman Catholics, 8, 224
Romance, 293
Romantic love, 58, 222
Roosevelt, Franklin, 9
Roosevelt, Franklin D., 9
Rossi, Alice S., 142
Rumbaut, Rubén, 207
Rumors, 341
Rwanda, 147, 176, 261

S

Saddam Hussein, 341
Salvation Army, 323
Same-sex relationships, 234
Samples, 24-25, 143, 244, 363-364
Sampling, 245
Sanctions, 46, 106, 150
"Sandwich generation", 238
Sapir, Edward, 50
Sapir-Whorf hypothesis, 50
Satanists, 66
Scapegoating, 186, 347
school systems, 256
Schwarzenegger, Arnold, 270
Scientific method, 6, 305
Second Life, 335
Secondary analysis, 20-21, 359
Secondary sex characteristics, 138
Selective perception, 188
Self-administered questionnaires, 23, 362-363
self-concept, 74-76, 111, 190, 245, 304, 339, 365
Self-control, 87, 109
self-determination, 205
Self-fulfilling stereotypes, 312
Self-sacrifice, 290
Sensation, 189, 254
Sensorimotor stage, 76-77
Separate but equal, 140
Serbs, 176
Serial fatherhood, 242-243
Serial murder, 126
Sex
    adolescent, 317
    adulthood, 94-95
    knowledge of, 90, 311
Sex (cont.)
    purpose of, 43, 370
    ratio, 159-160
Sex ratio, 158
sexual abuse
    of children, 218-221, 334
sexual assault, 166, 246
Sexual attraction, 222
Sexual behavior, influences on
    siblings, 73, 133, 286
Sexual behavior, types of

oral sex, 31
  sexual intercourse, 74, 150, 246
Sexual desire, 150
Sexual deviance
  prostitution, 116
  rape, 106, 165-167, 245, 375-376
Sexual discrimination, 155
sexual relations, 60, 105, 142, 246
Sexuality
  influences on, 325
Sexuality and human development
  through life, 93
Shakespeare, William, 303
Shamans, 330
Shame, 78-79, 109-110, 194, 231, 289, 365
Shaming, 109-111
sharecropping, 280
Shepard, Matthew, 128
Sherif, Carolyn, 187
Shoplifting, 110-111, 201
Sierra Leone, 261
Significant others, 75-76
Single mothers, 226-227, 288
Sioux Manufacturing, 119
Sioux tribe, 205
Skywalk, 206
Small world phenomenon, 342
Smith College, 152
Snake handling, 306
social class
  lower class, 202
    marital roles and, 18
social Darwinism, 6-7
social distance, 191, 313
social inequality, 119, 147, 267, 332-333
Social issues, 284, 304
Social location, 4, 94, 128
Social mirror, 75
Social Register, 279
Social research, 10, 350, 372
Social science research, 88, 378
Social Security Act (1935)
  amendments to, 209
social skills, 88, 227
Socialization
  in gender roles, 170
Sociobiology, 61, 106-107
Sociological imagination, 4, 40
Sociological perspective, 4, 104, 293
sociologists, early, 10
sovereignty, 212
Soviet Union, 191, 258
Spanish language, 195, 230
Spencer, Herbert, 6-7
Spirit of capitalism, 9
Split labor market, 187, 266
Spouse abuse, 20-21, 244-245, 358-361
Spurious correlation, 29, 369
Spurious correlations, 29, 369
Sri Lanka, 261
Staring, 39, 103, 253
statehood, 56
statistics on, 125
Status inconsistency, 276-278, 303
Status set, 300
Status symbols, 279, 302
Steroids, 142
Strain theory, 115-116
Straus, Murray A., 244
Street crime, 116-118
Street gangs, 107
Streetcorner men, 297-298
Structural mobility, 285
Structured interviews, 363
Studied nonobservance, 316
Submission, 269
Subordinates, 165
Sudan, 44, 150, 256
suicide rates, 7-8
superego, 78
Surgery, 59, 140, 185
Surrogacy, 233
surrogate mother, 233
Surveys
  on samples, 377
Survival needs, 18, 306
Survivalists, 53
suspicions, 90
Sutherland, Edwin, 116

Swaziland, 260
Sworn virgins, 83
Sykes, Gresham M., 111
Symbolic culture, 40
Symbolic interactionist perspective, 100, 107, 208,
  220, 325
Syphilis, 175
Szasz, Thomas, 129
Szasz, Thomas S., 129

T
Taboos, 60
Taken-for-granted assumptions, 41
Taking the role of the other, 74
Tasmania, 190
Tattooing, 55
Tattoos, 66, 340
Teamwork, 316
Techniques of neutralization, 111-112
Techno Patriots, 195
Technology
  communication with, 126
  cultural lag, 63
Testosterone, 123, 143
texts, 305
Thailand, 44-45, 261
The Rich Get Richer and the, 134
The Wage Gap, 20
The White House, 151
Theoretical frameworks, 34
Thinness, 316-317
Thomas theorem, 319
Title IX, 155
Tobacco, 103-104, 137, 189, 334
Tomb Raider, 86, 335
Torah, 305
Torture, 126, 150, 259, 339-340, 359
"Torture warrants", 340
Torturing, 126
Total institutions, 92
tracking, 158
Trail of Tears, 205
Tranquilizers, 282
Transitional adulthood, 94-95
treaties, 205-206
Triad, 226, 344-345
Triads, 343
Trial marriage, 237
tribal groups, 144
Tumin, Melvin, 267
Tunisia, 137, 260
Turkmenistan, 260
Tutsis, 190
Two-parent families, 232
Two-tier system of medical care, 282

U
U. S. Department of Justice, 351
Ukraine, 260
University of Michigan, 74, 209, 223
Unobtrusive measures, 20-21, 359
Unstructured interviews, 365
Urban revolts, 199
U.S. Census Bureau
  sexual orientation, 234
U.S. Department of Justice, 351

V
Vaginal examinations, 320
Value clusters, 58
Value contradictions, 58
Veterans
  homeless, 371-372
Vick, Michael, 112
Victims of crime
  hate crimes, 128-129
Vietnam Veterans Study, 143
Violent crimes, 118
Virtual reality, 334-335
vocational schools, 115
Voting Rights Act, 199

W
Wage gap, 20
Wallerstein, Judith S., 241
Weber, Lynn, 285
Western culture, 41
Westerns, 204, 359

Westward expansion, 205
White House Conference on Aging
  in 1981, 195
White-collar crime, 116
Whorf, Benjamin, 50
Widowhood, 227
Widows and widowhood
  poverty of, 264
Williams, Robin, 56
Williams, Robin, U. S. values, 56
Winfrey, Oprah, 286
Women
  American Indian, 204
  life expectancy, 205, 281
Women, working
  sexual harassment and, 164-165
women's liberation movement, 58
women's movement, 145
women's rights, 151
"women's work", 147
Woods, Tiger, 123, 176-177
Woolworth's, 199
Work policies, family
  child care, 168, 220-222, 287
  elder care, 238
workers
  population in, 121, 292
World Factbook, 261
World Health Organization, 150
World Wars, 49
Wounded Knee, 205

X
X chromosome, 138

Y
Y chromosome, 138
Yanomamö Indians, 4
Yemen, 261
Yugoslavia, 190-191

Z
Zapotec Indians, 105